Standards, Principles, and Techniques in
Quantity Food Production
Third Edition

Standards, Principles, and Techniques in

Quantity Food Production

Third Edition

By Lendal H. Kotschevar, Ph.D.
Foodservice Consultant and
Former Professor of Restaurant Management,
School of Hotel, Restaurant, and Institutional
Management, Michigan State University

A CBI Book
Published by Van Nostrand Reinhold Company

A CBI Book
(CBI is an imprint of Van Nostrand Reinhold Company Inc.)

Copyright © 1974 by Lendal H. Kotschevar

Library of Congress Catalog Card Number

ISBN 0-8436-0583-9 (Trade edition)

Printed in the United States of America

Published by Van Nostrand Reinhold Company Inc.
115 Fifth Avenue
New York, New York 10003

Van Nostrand Reinhold Company Limited
Molly Millars Lane
Wokingham, Berkshire, RG11 2PY, England

Van Nostrand Reinhold
480 La Trobe Street
Melbourne, Victoria 3000, Australia

Macmillan of Canada
Division of Canada Publishing Corporation
164 Commander Boulevard
Agincourt, Ontario M1S 3C7, Canada

16 15 14 13 12 11 10

Library of Congress Cataloging in Publication Data

Library of Congress Catalog Card Number: 73-84173

Contents

Preface to the Third Edition

Quantity Food Production has had wide acceptance from its first publication in 1964. In this short period, however, enough changes have occurred to require a third edition. A *completely* revised work has had to be produced.

While this new text still emphasizes the basic production of food from the standpoint of techniques, standards and principles, it is set now against a backdrop of new systems and a wide variety of new foods coming onto the market. For those who wished a simpler work, technical material is now presented in chapters that can be skipped or kept as desired. New systems and new equipment are explained. Service needs have been emphasized. A chapter on nutrition has been added which, while rudimentary, gives essential information needed to observe good dietary practices in producing food. Safety and sanitation have been updated and the chapter on work simplification rewritten. Because of the increasing emphasis on new systems with new procedures for processing, handling and preparing foods, a separate chapter has been added covering some of the basic concepts needed to understand the use of heat and energy in these new systems and in the use of these new foods. Many technical tables formerly in the appendix are in this chapter. The book looks forward also to the time when we may be converting to the metric system by including information whereby quantities and measurements from our cumbersome system may be converted to this much more logical one. To give proper updating, new illustrations have been added but many of the old ones have been retained since they so vividly portray essential standards, techniques or principles. The use of many new foods as they modify food production has been mentioned. Conciseness has been sought and a shorter book with more in it has been the result. The book is not a rudimentary one but is designed to develop competency to enter the foodservice industry at a fairly high level.

The author wishes to thank the many users of this book who took the time to indicate their views and needs for a third edition. He is also thankful for the assistance of the many professional individuals and his students who made this book possible, especially Mr. and Mrs. Jack Ryan, who did so much in editing to give a happy book.

Honolulu, Hawaii   LENDAL H. KOTSCHEVAR, PH.D.
February 1973

Preface to the First and Second Editions

This book is written to state some of the standards, principles, and techniques required to produce food in quantity. It is not a recipe book but one that attempts to give the *what, why,* and *how* behind the use of recipes. It is written for managers and supervisors who must bear the responsibility for food production and for students who must learn how to bear this responsibility. It is intended as a working manual. Management will find the illustrations and explanations helpful not only to itself but also as a training guide for workers. The main emphasis of this book is on standards and how they are achieved. While the young manager close to food production will find this book helpful in his immediate problems of administration, he will find it continually useful as he rises in management responsibilities and becomes less and less involved in the actual production of food, for it should remain a constant source of reference in food production.

The operation of a quantity food kitchen cannot be learned, however, from a book. For this knowledge, the student must work with foods, see actual reactions in large quantity cooking, and learn to use food production equipment by operating it. Menu planning, scheduling of employees, ordering and storing of foods, preparation, service, and the application of management principles must be related to actual conditions. The dynamic flow of food production under the stress of meeting a meal deadline can only be learned when work situations are real and not hypothetical.

As a text, this material should be related to lectures, demonstrations, and actual work experiences. Many of the illustrations found in this book have been duplicated in color on film strips along with recordings which explain the principles and techniques illustrated on the strips. It is hoped that the visual and oral joining of textual materials, along with lectures, demonstrations, and laboratory experiences, will vastly improve learning and interest as well as allow students to study more on their own.

While many people have assisted in the production of this book, special thanks are due to Mr. Michael Palmer, Research Chef of Proctor and Gamble, and Mr. Stan Rosswurm, Field Baker for Pillsbury Company, for their assistance in making many of the illustrations in the chapters on cakes and breads.

This book is dedicated to my students who have inspired and encouraged me to write it.

Seeley Lake, Montana   LENDAL H. KOTSCHEVAR, Ph.D.
June 1963

Section I

Management in Quantity Food Production

1

Planning

Quantity Food Production*

The difference between small and quantity food production is difficult to define. Most food standards, many principles and a large number of the techniques are the same. Some define quantity production as the preparation of 25 or more orders but a single broiled steak, an order of scrambled eggs or a plate of boil-in-the-bag spaghetti can be. When we speak of quantity production we think of an organization of professional workers using special equipment producing food in large quantities for the consumption of others. The organization is quite complex and specialized knowledge is required such as menu planning, merchandising, selling, forecasting, purchasing, staffing and training, controlling, manufacturing, service, sanitation and safety. Therefore, quantity food production is perhaps more distinguished by the organization and mode of operation than by any other factor.

There are those today that say a knowledge of food production is not needed because so much food is purchased in an almost ready-to-serve state. This is not true. In the first place, most operations still prepare all or almost all of their food from scratch. And, even though a

---

* Many schools teach much of the material in this section in separate courses. For these, this section can be omitted or used as a review. It is presented for those who lack this management background which is needed to understand completely quantity food production.

large part of the food is purchased ready-to-serve, a knowledge of food production is still needed to evaluate quality, to do an adequate job of purchasing, handling and serving and to control costs in merchandising the products. Oftentimes, the problem of handling, serving and merchandising these new foods is such that more, not less, technical knowledge is required to use them adequately. What probably is meant is that the state of the art is changing and different knowledge is required. For some this may be true but as long as food is served in quantity from a kitchen in some form or other, a knowledge of basic quantity food production will be needed. Foods are temperamental, losing quality rapidly. They are highly perishable. Unless the right knowledge is used in their handling and preparation, inferior products result. Furthermore, with the increasing lack of professional knowledge among workers, someone has to know something about production, and management oftentimes finds it has the "buck passed to it." Unless management at this point has the requisite knowledge, the operation may be in trouble. While a manager need not be capable of working in a quantity kitchen—although it helps—he should understand the functions it must perform and be able to direct it along the paths he wants. Just knowing the language of the kitchen is oftentimes important.

The growing trend to produce food in central commissaries, package, store, freeze or chill, transport and then merchandise it in outlying satellites has created a need for a whole new field of knowledge in quantity food production. A central commissary is not a kitchen blown up in size. It is a factory in which processing methods, types of ingredients and other procedures are all new from those used even in the largest kitchens. Cooking a 30-portion pot of stew is a much different problem from cooking 4000 gallons of it in a large steam-jacketed kettle. Cooling it down fast enough is another one. Some say that a computer can take a 50- or 100-portion recipe and multiply it up to 1000 portions or more without making any change. This is not always true. Differences in batch weight, cooking reactions, the power of thickening agents, evaporative losses and other factors make a great difference. Recipes of the past have not been designed for products that are to be cooled, chilled or frozen, packaged, stored, transported and then rewarmed for service. The new food is now subjected to many physical stresses, subtle oxidative changes, flavor or texture loss and a host of other things. New recipes must be designed with emulsifiers, anti-oxidants, new flavorings and a host of other ingredients never used, to achieve desirable results. This change in the state of the art is creating demands for new knowledge. However, this must be built solidly on a knowledge of food production as it has existed in the past. We are not

Figure 1–1. Large commissaries such as Fairfield Farms of Marriott's are today processing millions of meals for shipment to outlying units that are largely service units. This development is drastically changing production methods in the foodservice industry. (Courtesy Dr. Lewis Minor)

attempting to get an entirely new output from an entirely new material. We are attempting to produce the same products from the same materials by a new method and therefore a lot of what we already know is still applicable. There have been some notable failures in new types of production centers because this was not realized.

Perhaps the opinion that a knowledge of quantity food production is less essential today is colored by the fact that basic management techniques are changing in the foodservice industry and we are developing better controls and information systems upon which management decisions can be made. Automatic data processing has been found to eliminate much detail in menu planning, recipe calculation and forecasting, purchasing, nutritional evaluations, inventory control, payroll and other record maintenance. New management methodologies such as linear programming, queuing theory, probability theory, PERT, Monte Carlo techniques and others which have been programmed for the computer are finding application in the industry. These new techniques are, however, based on knowledge and the practice of quantity food production as it exists, not upon some theoretical world, and the practical side must be known if these new techniques are to be most effectively applied.

There is on the other hand a danger that one will hold too long to

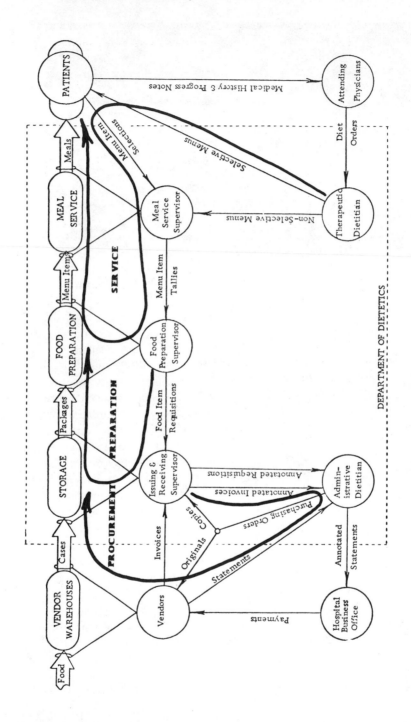

THREE-CYCLE OPERATION OF THE LOGISTICS INFORMATION AND CONTROL SYSTEM

Figure 1–2. A computer now can handle all the accounting and recording detail for a dietary department. This chart shows the entire food production program as it is handled through the computer. (Courtesy Paul Konnersman and Am. Hospital Assoc.)

old knowledge and not recognize that change has occurred or is occurring. The half-life of knowledge in all areas is rapidly decreasing and managers, chefs, dietitians and others in the industry who would seek to maintain a maximum potential for meeting new problems in a changing environment must be constantly learning new information and discarding the obsolete.

Organizations for Quantity Food Production

Food production organizations vary as the need and type vary. In view of the continued shortage of top production supervisors and management people, we can look perhaps to a trend to simplified management structures.

The location of the food department in the overall organization is most important. Experience has shown if it is too far down in the chain of command, the department functions less effectively than when placed at a higher level. The importance and complexity of the department make it advisable to have top management close to it.

Food production organizations are much the same. Management may rest with an owner, food and beverage manager, manager or dietitian. It can be responsible at times to a higher level of management such as a superintendent, manager, owner, etc. A chef, foodservice supervisor, food production manager or other individual is usually in direct charge of production. Supervisors and workers complete the staff. Figures 1-3, 1-4, 1-5 and 1-6 show some of these organizations. The classical (continental) organization is not shown because it varies so widely. In such an organization, a *chef du cuisine* (executive chef) is in charge and a *sous chef* (under chef) supervises the kitchen and the heads of various sections (*chefs des parties*) such as *chef du saucier* (head of sauces) or *chef du rotisseur* (head of roasting). Under these heads are assistant cooks and others called *commis*. An *abboyeur* (announcer) is used to call orders to the cooks as they come from the waiters. This reduces confusion in the kitchen and also sees that the right order is placed with the right section. A chief steward who purchases foods and supplies is in charge of storage spaces, laundry, china and silverware and may plan the menu or assist the *chef du cuisine* in planning it. A working chef may manage while at the same time doing food preparation and other tasks. This arrangement meets the needs of a small organization.

RESTAURANT ORGANIZATION

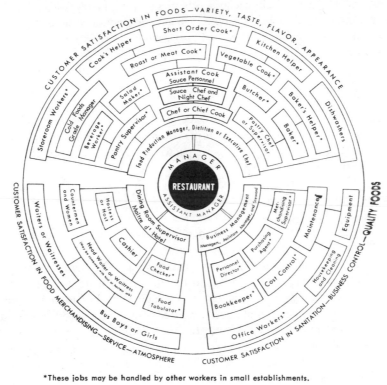

*These jobs may be handled by other workers in small establishments.

Courtesy National Restaurant Association

Figure 1–3. A different organization is required for each kind of foo
service operation. The above chart from the National Restaurant Associati
would apply to many different ones. While broad differences exist, they
basically the same organizationally and the same principles of control app
to all.

CONTROLS

Controls are essential to reach goals. They should be simple and qui
to use, giving desired results at modest cost. The most frequently need
controls in food production are cost, quantity and quality.

A good control program must have standards or benchmarks esta
lished by which achievement may be judged. Also, a good flow of
formation must be set up to compare performance with these standar

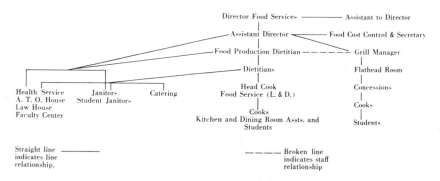

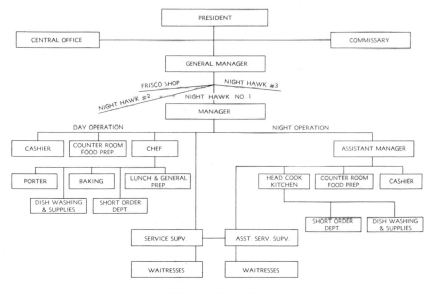

Figure 1–4.   The organization of a foodservice department in a university.

THE **NIGHT HAWK**

Figure 1–5.   The organization for the Night Hawk Restaurants of Texas. Note that this is a chain group with only the Night Hawk No. 1 being shown in detail. (Courtesy Harry Aiken)

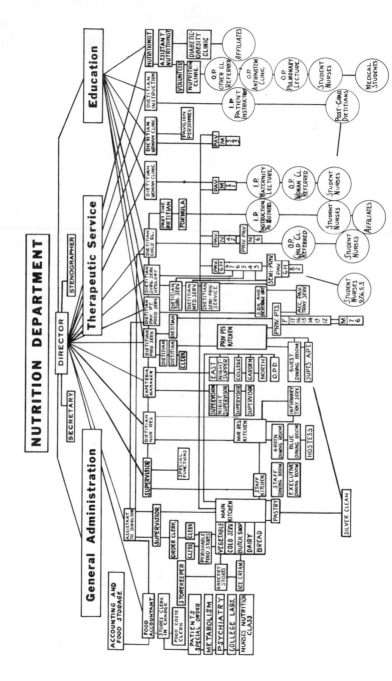

Figure 1–6. The organization of a large nutrition department in a hospital. Note the department has a general administration section where food production occurs, a therapeutic service in which most dietary matters are handled and an education section, established for instruction.

Techniques to use for correcting situations not meeting these standards must be devised. Management by objectives is built on these three factors of control.

Cost Control

A good cost control system must control *all* costs. Non-food and non-labor costs are so significant today it is impossible to neglect them. A good flow of accounting information should be established giving a total cost picture. Normally, combined food and labor costs are not over 65% of sales in commercial units with 35% for other costs and profit. Non-commercial units may have higher food and labor costs and still function efficiently. Non-commercial operations may work with dollar values allowing so much per person per day or per meal instead of working with percentages.

Budgets are control devices. A budget is a practical standard of expected costs and from time to time performance is compared to the budgeted figure to evaluate performance. Precosting is highly desirable. With the advent of data processing it is more feasible. Some computer systems give an automatic printout of food costs when a menu is planned. Normally, costs should be known the day after operation if not before.

Food Cost

Food cost may vary from 20 to 50%. The type of institution, pricing structure, other costs and other factors dictate what it should be. A very low food cost may not be desirable, indicating customers are not getting their money's worth, or poor quality food is served or an improper pricing structure exists. Or, it could indicate that it is being achieved at the expense of labor cost. A lettuce wedge even when lettuce is expensive may be lower in final cost when the labor for making a sliced orange or cole slaw salad is added to these much cheaper ingredients.

Selling high food cost items may be advisable over selling low food cost items because the dollar yield after food cost is deducted is so much more from a high cost item. For instance, a steak dinner at $5.75 with a 45% food cost ($2.59) brings in more money to cover other costs and profit (4.61) than does a $2.75 chicken pie dinner with a food cost of 25% ($ .69) leaving only $2.06 to cover other costs and profit. A high food cost may draw in business because patrons recognize they get a lot of food for their money. Low cost steak houses have a food cost of between 55 to 60% but other costs are so low and the volume so great that the net is excellent. It is usually desirable to vary food cost percentages for menu items rather than have a standard food cost markup for each item.

Food Cost Control Techniques

Recipe costing can control food costs. Calculate both total and portion cost. A food cost percentage to selling price may be helpful. If the cost of ingredients per portion is 32¢ and the selling price is 95¢, the food cost is 34% (32¢ ÷ 95¢ = 34%). If a 40% food cost is desired and the portion cost is 32¢, the selling price is 80¢ (32¢ ÷ 40% = 80¢). In recipe costing, it is recommended that ingredient costs be calculated to the nearest ½¢ and any cost less than ¼¢ be omitted. Some do not add seasoning costs but add to the ingredient cost of a recipe the percent the total year's cost of seasonings, etc., is to the total food cost for the year. For instance, if the cost for seasonings is $360 and total food cost is $18,000 for the year, seasonings are 2% of the total food cost. Now, if a recipe has an ingredient cost of $9.50 without seasonings, 2% of $9.50 or 19¢ would be added to give a total recipe cost of $9.69.

The need to recalculate recipe costs can be avoided by increasing or decreasing recipe costs by the percentage the food index moves up or down in a period. Do this about every six months, but recalculate whenever prices change drastically.

Basing selling price on food cost is not recommended. Instead, it is best based on the food and labor cost with fixed and variable costs plus profit percentages added in. For instance, if food cost is 30¢ and labor is 26¢ (total 56¢) with fixed costs of 10%, variable costs of 10% and a desired profit of 8% (total percentages 28%), the 56¢ plus 28% equals the desired selling price or 100%. Then, 56¢ equals 72% (100% — 28% = 72%) and the selling price is 78¢ (56¢ ÷ 72% = 78¢). In this example, the food cost percentage is 38.5% (30¢ ÷ 78¢ = .385) and the labor cost percentage is 33.3% (26¢ ÷ 78¢ = .333) giving a total food and labor cost percentage of approximately 72%.

Good purchase specifications and practices are another way to lower food cost. All items purchased should have a well written specification established for them. A specification states exactly what is needed in a product indicating grade or quality, amount, size and other factors required. Well written specifications lower food cost while poorly written or non-existent ones raise it. Good receiving and inspection are also needed to complete the purchasing task, assuring that the quality and quantity paid for are obtained. Also, storage areas should be properly maintained in temperature, sanitary factors and security. Rotate stocks

WORK SHEET FOR RECIPE STANDARDIZATION

RECIPE FOR (Name of Item)_____WORK ORDER NO._____

TESTED BY_____ DATE_____APPROVED BY_____DATE____ _____

COSTED BY_____DATE_____CHECKED BY_____DATE_____-

PRODUCTION RECIPE PREPARED BY_____DATE_____FIRST SERVED (date)_____ ___

FOOD INGREDIENTS USED	WEIGHT AND/OR MEASURE For (Portions) (number) (Gallons) ( ) (other)	A/P or E/P	PRO- CEDURE No. (See back of this sheet for detailed procedure)	UNIT A/P	COST PER UNIT A/P	COST OF QUANTITY OF INGREDIENT USED IN THIS RECIPE
	TOTAL COST OF FOOD USED					

FOOD PRODUCTION RECAPITULATION

YIELD: Weight and/or Measure____Lbs____oz____(Gallons) PORTIONS: No.____ Size:_____ ___
                                                                  (No.) (Unit)

PANS: No. Counter pans (size:____"x___"x___") ____Wt/pan____lbs____Oz No. Portions/pan____ ____

COST: Portion $____Selling Price/Portion $____Food Cost Percent (Cost/Portion) _____%
                                                              (Selling Price)

LABOR COST RECAPITULATION

OPERATION	TIME (min.)	EMPLOYEE (Class No.)	RATE (Hr.)	LABOR COST
ASSEMBLY OF MATERIALS AND EQUIPMENT REQUIRED				
PRE-PREPARATION OF FOODS (Washing, peeling, cutting, etc.				
FINAL PREPARATION OF FOODS (Mixing, cooking, baking, etc.				
GARNITURE AND/OR PORTIONING				
SERVICE				
DEAD TIME (Watching and waiting)				
TOTAL DIRECT TIME AND LABOR COST		XXXXXXXXXXXX		
OVERHEAD AND MANAGEMENT (%)				
TOTAL LABOR COST OF RECIPE				

LABOR COST/PORTION $_____LABOR COST: PERCENTAGE (Labor Cost/Portion)_____%
                                                        (Selling Price)

FOOD PLUS LABOR COSTS/PORTION $_____FOOD PLUS LABOR COSTS: PERCENT_____%

RECIPE REVIEW DATE_____

Figure 1-7. A form useful for recording data in recipe costing or development. (Courtesy Dr. Jack Welch)

using the FIFO principle (first-in-first-out). A good forecasting system must join purchasing so correct amounts are purchased avoiding either under- or over-purchasing.

Good menu planning can control food cost.* Check carry-over foods and storage areas before planning so foods needing to go into production do. Do not list menu items by price. Mix prices up so patrons see something they like before they find one by price. Placement on the menu or other factors can help sell items management finds more profitable. It is usually not desirable to plan menus based on food prices because this may result in a poor menu but some guidance of market prices can be helpful in reducing food cost. The U. S. Department of Agriculture publishes lists of plentiful foods in most newspapers and trade journals which indicate which foods are high in quality but low in price during a period.

Good supervision and well standardized recipes are useful cost controls. Waste or loss can result from production failures or poor recipes. Furthermore, it does little good to have well standardized recipes if they are not followed. This failure may produce a sub-standard item or raise cost. Adding a quart of whipping cream to a cream soup improves it but adds considerably to the cost. Seeing that proper yields are obtained is also important. Carelessness in prepreparation, such as in peeling vegetables, or in production, such as cooking roasts at too high a temperature, raises costs. Security is also important to food stores as is good portion control.

Equipment must be in good working order to control food costs. A poorly operating slicer can mutilate slices so that a high waste occurs. Seeing that employees develop the right techniques also helps to lower food cost by reducing chances for production failures and obtaining desirable yields.

Labor Cost

Labor can be the largest single cost category in the food production department and even exceed food cost. Its control is, therefore, important.

Many operations have a labor cost from 25 to 40% of sales. Some work with an allowance of either time or dollars to control its cost. For instance, a health facility may allow 18% of its total hours and 20% of its total dollars of the facility's payroll to be spent by the food service department. Or, an operation may attempt control by allowing so many

---

* See also the discussion later in this chapter on menu planning.

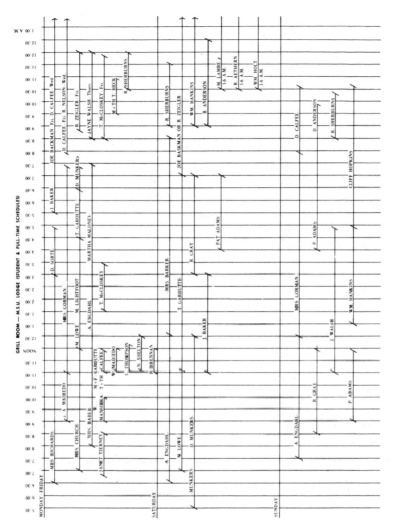

Figure 1-8. A line drawing schedule which shows at a glance coverage of hours in an operation.

hours of labor per meals produced. Thus, for 14,000 meals in a month, the department may allow 2800 hours on the payroll or five meals produced for each hour used. The following are the average meals produced per hour of labor in some institutions:

Hotels and clubs	1.75	Small hospitals and	
Restaurants	3.00	nursing homes	5.00
Schools, elementary	12.50	Large state hospitals	11.60
Schools, dormitory	11.00	Large private hospitals	3.00

Other operations may allocate labor based on the number of guests or covers or meals produced in a shift. For instance, in a day a cook might produce 100 meals, a hostess seat 300 guests and a waiter wait on 80 people. Other operations allocate labor on the basis of sales, saying it allows an hour of labor for every $5.50 in sales.

If labor needs could be forecast better, labor cost could be reduced. Oftentimes work activity is spasmodic with either lots of work or no work to do. Checking the production schedule and then allocating labor is helpful in avoiding this or setting up lists of tasks to be done when slack time exists. Some establish labor budgets allocating so many hours to various work sections. If this is done, retain enough flexibility to shift labor between sections when the need arises or work needs drop.

Three types of schedules are usually used to control labor: 1) days off, vacation time and days on the job, 2) position hours, and 3) a production schedule. The latter should indicate the meal or period covered, menu items and work to be done and by whom, amount to produce, recipe to use, portion size, time for completion, run-out time, slack time assignments, selling price and comments. Comments should cover how work is co-ordinated between sections or between other departments.

Using skilled labor to do unskilled jobs wastes labor. To control this, some compare the number of skilled hours to the number of unskilled hours used in a period. A 40-60 ratio suffices in many non-commercial operations; in others it does not. Each institution should establish its own ratio after studying the problem. In one operation it was found that skilled workers should spend 75% of their time working at skilled jobs and 25% of their time on non-skilled ones.

Good labor supervision saves. Supervisors should know approximately how long a job should take so they can evaluate performance rates. Time standards should be set for doing jobs but keep these flexible.

Many operations have high labor costs because they use inefficient production methods or fail to eliminate unnecessary work. New foods should be utilized when labor savings are greater than increased material cost provided quality is the same or improved. Good menu planning reduces labor requirements. Cycle menus make it possible to set up repetitive procedures that reduce work. Watch preparation and do as much as possible ahead. Balance work loads between busy and light days. Parties and banquets that use regular menu items, rather than special ones, take less labor. The use of an ingredient room can save much time. Keep a diary noting in scheduling or production where time can be saved. Good training reduces time requirements.

Other Costs

Non-labor and non-food costs may run as high as 25% of sales in commercial operations and in others around 15%. Information as to the nature and magnitude is important to their control. Normally, repair and maintenance costs run from 2 to 4%; heat, light and water around 4%; glassware, dishes and silverware $1\frac{1}{2}$%; and cleaning supplies, soaps and detergents 2%. Some commercial operations may have advertising, occupancy and other costs not borne by non-commercial units. Occupancy (rent) or space costs vary from 5 to 15% depending upon utilities, equipment or the services given with it. Advertising costs run less than 1% usually. Management should establish benchmarks for these costs and, when they differ from the standard, investigate the cause and take steps to control them.

Quality Control

This text attempts to establish some food standards but each individual operation must establish its own. A good quality standard should cover essential characteristics that indicate quality in a product. Not all operations can or should serve products of superior quality. A good average quality suffices. A quality control program makes it possible to serve a consistent standard. Employee evaluations, taste panel scoring, customer reactions and other means can be used to evaluate quality. One problem is a lack of objective measures and the need to depend so much upon human evaluations in measuring quality. An individual judging color or tasting a food may find the factors adequate but a colorimeter might indicate the sauce was too dark or a salimeter that the sauce was too salty. Watch plate waste and patron selections. Good recipe evaluation, testing and developments can help control quality. Also, if employees possess the requisite skill, quality is higher and more consistent.

It is important to transfer to workers a recognition of when a product meets a quality standard. This requires good communication. Frequently, pictures showing what the product should look like, or well written descriptions help. Train employees to evaluate every product they make. This text gives many factors that can be used to judge quality. Train employees to jot down quality evaluations on production schedules or on the back of recipes.

It is frequently said that a quality control program starts with the layout. This is true. Many operations cannot achieve good quality because of inadequacies in design or equipment. Good purchase specifications and finding the right product to suit the production need can do much to raise and maintain quality standards.

Quantity Control

Proper forecasting of quantities needed in production and controlling portion sizes are two essentials of good quality control. To find the quantity needed, multiply portions times the portion size. Know what losses to expect also from AP (as purchased), to EP (edible portion) to AS (as served). Casserole items lose in baking around 5% of their weight by evaporation; a 4% additional loss usually occurs in holding for service. Serving losses may run for different foods from 0 to 8%. Potatoes can lose 27% of their AP weight in paring, then increase from 2 to 5% in steaming and lose 3 to 4% in service. Roasts can shrink 10 to 35% in roasting, in slicing 5% and in serving about 5%. Baking losses in bakery goods usually runs from 4 to 16%.

Portion size varies according to the food, type of meal and patron, cost of the food, flavor and portion appearance. The food's richness or lightness is a factor in deciding how much to serve, thus a rich dessert may be dished lightly while a non-rich one is dished more heavily. A snack, a one-dish meal, a heavy breakfast, a light luncheon or a moderate supper require different portion sizes. Tradition has established some standard portions such as a pat of butter, two ounces of gravy on mashed potatoes and so forth.

Adults, teen-agers and small children consume different quantities and portion sizes vary for them. Men eat more than women; an individual doing hard work eats more than another doing sedentary tasks. Some ethnic groups traditionally eat more than others.

Giving liberal quantities of less costly foods and smaller ones of more expensive foods can be practiced. In buffets, it is customary to place bulky and less expensive goods first and more expensive ones last. Serving a soup or an appetizer first may make it possible to reduce portions of more expensive foods in the main course.

Luncheon Menu

SALAD

Crisp Lettuce Wedge, Roquefort Dressing 45
Pear, Pineapple and Cottage Cheese, Chantilly Sauce 35

SOUPS

Tomato Madrilene 25   Boston Clam Chowder 25
Davenport Onion Soup 25

ENTREES

ALL VEGETABLE HEALTH PLATE - Western Carrots,   𝍱
Green Beans, Spinach, Mexican Corn, Tiny Whole Beets. 1.40 **5**

ALASKAN SHRIMP NEWBURG - Served over Golden Baked Rice, 𝍱 𝍱
Western Carrots, Crisp Green Salad. 1.75 **10**

ROAST TOP ROUND OF CHOICE BEEF AU JUS - Mexican Red Beans, 𝍱 ///
Baby Pearl Onions with Garden Green Peas. 1.95 **8**

WESTERN SALAD BOWL - Julienne of Turkey, Avocado and Bacon - 𝍱 /
tossed with Crisp Greens and Caesar Dressing. 1.60 **6**

BUTTERED SPAGHETTI with Ripe Olives and Fresh Mushrooms Saute - 𝍱 𝍱/
topped with Grated Parmesan Cheese, Tossed Green Salad. 1.45 **11**

Coffee, Tea or Milk -- Roll and Butter

SANDWICHES

Deviled Egg . 𝍱 /	75	**6**	Tuna Fish . . 𝍱 𝍱 /	1.05	**11**
Baked Ham . . ///	1.05	**3**	Swiss Cheese . . ////	80	**4**
Chicken. . 𝍱	1.35	**5**	Beef or Pork . . . ///	1.05	**3**
American Cheese . 𝍱 / . .	75	**6**	Baked Ham & Cheese. . ////	1.20	**4**
Lettuce & Tomato. 𝍱 /// . .	80	**8**	Early Birds Club. . 𝍱	1.60	**5**
Chicken Salad . ////	1.20	**4**			

Choice of - Potato Salad, Cottage Cheese, Potato Chips or
Fruit Salad with above Sandwiches

DESSERTS

Assorted Pies 35   Chocolate or White Layer Cake 35
French Vanilla or Chocolate Ice Cream 35
Rice or Bread Pudding with Cream 35
Choice of Sherbet 30   Cup Custard 30

Executive Chef - Dean Atkinson   Friday

EARLY BIRDS

Figure 1–9.   This menu shows the sale of different items as maintained by the cashier in her spare time. Such a record is extremely helpful in indicating later information useful in menu planning.

The portion appearance is important. Appearance is affected by the size and shape of the dish, decoration and width of the rim, dish color and food arrangement. A garnish or sauce can make a portion appear larger. A thick Swiss steak may appear small but, if cut thinner, its greater surface area may make it appear larger. Tightly packed food versus food that is lightly packed will require different portion weights even though the portion size may appear the same.

Portion control should start by listing the portion size on the menu. Purchase items giving the correct size portion. Specify 10 weiners to the pound, if two are given, and frankfurters six to the pound if giving one. Do not expect cooks to serve correct portions of rib roast if the purchase specification fails to set up the right size rib. Planning fails if pears 25 count per No. 10 are served instead of 40 count. The cook who marks a pan of meat pie three by six instead of four by six may cause a last-minute frantic rush to prepare more when the supply is gone during the peak of service.

The system of forecasting amounts to prepare should be based on accurate quantities. Serving a fixed number and a non-selective menu in an institution simplifies forecasting. In other instances, patient counts in hospitals, weekend dormitory absentee predictions or other checks can be helpful. Restaurants and other establishments with a variable drop-in trade find it desirable to keep records of past experience and the effect of factors such as weather, menu offerings, season, etc. For banquets or parties, guarantees are frequently required with a 5 to 10% over or under the guarantee allowed.

State total production needs on recipes and production schedules in meaningful units: pounds, quarts, gallons or other common measures. Just under 14 pies are needed for 100 portions when cut seven per pie but when 100 portions of five-ounce cube steaks have to be obtained from a round of beef, the amount needed AP is not as easy to calculate. Use tables of quantities required in good cookbooks or use standardized recipes which give portion information. The USDA publishes useful information on amounts required to serve specific numbers; for instance, Handbook, No. 16, *Planning Food for Institutions,* is a good guide.

Batch times and batch sizes need careful prediction so a steady, even flow of fresh products goes to serving areas. Freshly cooked vegetables should reach service stations every 20 minutes. (See Vegetable Cookery.) Batch cooking, besides being an important factor in controlling quality, acts as a brake against over-production.

Servers should be informed before service on the size of portions by weight, volume or count, the dish in which they are served, the serving tool to use and other information needed to assure a correct portion size.* Establish lists of portion sizes and place these in work areas

* A No. 10 scoop gives level full 10 scoops per quart of solid product; a No. 30 scoop level full gives 30. Thus, a No. 10 scoop gives 3.2 ounces and a No. 30 about an ounce.

NEIMAN MARCUS
Food Production Schedule

DEPT. _____

	MONDAY	TUESDAY	WEDNESDAY	THURSDAY	FRIDAY	SATURDAY
ZODIAC						
LITTLE DIPPER						
PRESTON CENTER AND HASKELL						
SPECIAL ORDERS						

Form No. 908

Figure 1-10. The menu planning form used by Helen Corbitt at Neiman Marcus. Note every day of operation and various dining services are covered.

WORK SHEET

Food Quantities

BREAKFAST	Total Prepared Weight or Count	Carry Over or Run Out Time	Total Used Weight or Count	Meal Count
LUNCH				
DINNER				
Bread				
Butter				
Milk				
Cream				
Coffee				

Figure 1–11. A production schedule work sheet. Many other work sheets also indicate who is to prepare the various items, date and meal, recipe to use, time for completion, etc. Note information is also compiled so this work sheet can be filed away for use in future planning.

for quick reference. List portions obtained per pound, package, piece or other unit. Melons 45 per crate should be portioned into halves, a third cup of fruit cocktail is a portion and three ounces of crab meat is a portion for a crab salad. Give precise portioning directions such as "set slicer at No. 8." List the number of items to be placed on salads or other dishes. Show pictures, if possible. All recipes should list portion size and the number of portions obtained from the recipe. Give exact planning instructions and have pans marked with their weights so calculations of net quantities can be quickly ascertained. Establish raw deposit weights for cookies, cream puffs or other items. List the right size scoop, spoon, ladle or other tool needed for dishing specific foods. Mark stainless steel rods to measure quantities in mixers, steam-jacketed kettles or pots. Train workers to check quantities against those listed on production schedules. If 550 eight-ounce servings of hash are being served, it will take 14 pans each filled with 20 pounds of hash to serve this quantity. A cook should see that this much is in production. Use portion scales and correctly sized dishes, souffle cups and so forth to control portions. Preportion so in busy periods the correct amount is on hand. Check portioning equipment frequently to see it is in good working order and is used properly. Be practical. Specify a No. 10 scoop instead of a No. 8 one to give a four-ounce portion. It is easier and more exact when working at high serving speed to serve a rounded No. 10 scoop than a No. 8 scoop level full.

MENU PLANNING

The menu authorizes production. It is like a production order in a factory setting in motion a series of planning, procurement and manufacturing functions that culminate in a finished product. The menu sent to the production department should state what is to be produced, when, how much and the recipe to use. If used as a production schedule, it should list other pertinent information indicated under Production Scheduling.

Selecting Menu Offerings

The items on a menu will be determined by specific needs of patrons. In some institutions they must follow a meal plan which may be a 3-meal-a-day routine with specific items served at certain meals. A breakfast on such a menu may follow a pattern of having a fruit or fruit juice, cereal and milk, meat or protein substitute, bread item, butter and jam or jelly and beverage. The usual division of calories on such a meal plan for a day is breakfast 30%, dinner 40% and supper 30% or breakfast 25%, lunch 33% and dinner 42%.

For a commercial operation, an *a la carte* menu offers items separately at individual prices and classifies items usually in groups in the order eaten. Thus, soups and appetizers may come first, then salads and sandwiches, then entrees, with desserts and beverages last. A *table d'hote* menu which offers a group of foods together at an established price may allow for no selection or may have items which may be selected within categories — a cocktail, soup or other appetizer may be offered for choice in one category; several different kinds of salads may be offered in another category; and perhaps several entrees will be offered, one to be selected etc. It is becoming increasingly common to reduce offerings on *table d'hote* menus and have patrons select the omitted items from *a la carte* offerings. This might mean that no soup, appetizer or cocktail or dessert is offered. It is common to have *a la carte* items printed on a hard cardboard paper menu that folds and then attach a *table d'hote* menu inside which is changed daily. The term *du jour* means "of the day." In some cases, foods may be grouped together under a *du jour* but usually the offering is individual. "Soup du jour" is a soup being offered as a specialty item that day.

Selling meals and lodging together at one price is called the American plan; selling meals and lodging separately is called the European plan. A table setting for one person is called a *cover*.

More than one person should participate in menu planning. One of these should be experienced in food production and be a good merchandiser. Do not ignore ideas or comments from employees or patrons. Menu selectors, tallies listing popular items, lists of popular food combinations, ideas from magazines, cookbooks, advertisements, articles or even competitors' menus may be helpful. Some menus feature specialty items and there is little difficulty in their selection. Some selections are traditional for the season, holiday or locale. Keep a reminder list of these.

Some menus must meet special dietary requirements and selections will be conditioned by such requirements. A rule in menu planning usually followed is that when selection is possible, the menu should enable selection of an adequate diet, but when little or no choice is offered and the individual must obtain a large share of his food in that operation, the menu should assure adequacy.

Many factors can dictate menu selections. Health facilities may have to select items to meet dietary needs; a Type A menu for a school must use specific amounts of certain foods to qualify for federal subsidy.

Aged, ill or mentally-ill patients may need enriched foods because of a low food intake. More and more people are becoming aware of the importance of good nutrition and menu planners should recognize this and plan menus to meet these individuals' desires. Many on modified diets eat away from home and their needs must be met. (See Chapter 4 on Nutrition.)

Considerations in Planning Menus

A menu should be planned for those eating the food. The economic, social, regional, ethnic, religious and behavioral backgrounds of people affect their food habits and preferences. Teen-agers want hot dogs, hamburgers and French fries and rebel against artichokes, lobster curry and other foods with which they have little acquaintance. The Southerner wants hominy grits at breakfast and black-eyed peas for good luck on New Year's day. Sex and age affect food choices. The menu for a women's social club will differ considerably from that of a men's athletic club. After 55 the need for calories drops but not the need for other nutrients. Older people should eat less but still obtain the same amount of nutrients as they did when consuming fewer calories.

Cost restrictions are frequently a challenge. Some planners set up lists that classify selections by food or other cost. Some set up guides that allow a percentage of the total meal for specific courses. Thus, 8 to 10% is spent for the appetizer, 50 to 55% for the entree, 10 to 12% for the potato and vegetabe, 12 to 15% for dessert, and 10% for beverage, bread, and butter.

Menu prices and selections should be based on the market's ability to pay. It is easier to change prices on popular items than on less popular ones. Raising a price on an item at one time and another price on another later is sometimes a method used. Some drop an item from the menu and then later bring it back at a new price. Some offer a slightly different item at a new price. Others change prices when the menu is changed.

Variety is oftentimes not so much a matter of offering a wide number of foods as it is the manner in which foods are served. Variety and interest can be won by offering an old favorite served in a slightly different form. Combining menu offerings or using a special garnish or sauce or a slightly different form of preparation can change an old item into a new one. The use of a food out of season, and featuring it in a manner to gain maximum merchandising, can dress up a whole menu. Seek a variety in offerings but remember that some items have to appear on the menu to give satisfaction. Thus, people eat beef 50 to 60% of the time so poultry, veal, lamb and other flesh foods cannot go much over their percent of desirability and hold satisfaction. A list indicating how often foods should be served can be helpful. Use special care in planning dishes from carry-over foods; weak disguises bring customer rejection.

Planners should know what can and cannot be accomplished by workers and equipment. Knowing production capabilities of the staff and consulting lists that give the capacities of equipment and production times can assist in reducing complications in the kitchen.

The type of service may affect menu selections. Table, counter, cafeteria, buffet, drive-in, automatic or vending service need special items for service. The occasion may also dictate choices. A wedding breakfast will differ greatly from foods offered at a stag buffet. An operation seeking a rapid turnover must watch menu offerings carefully if it wishes to achieve its goal.

Menu offerings should be selected to give contrasts in form, texture, flavor, color and temperature. Form should include consideration for variation in height and food shapes. Also, on a buffet or cafeteria counter vary the height of foods to add interest. Texture contrasts such as a crisp cracker with a soft, crab cocktail help improve food acceptance. Seek flavor contrasts. Use mild bread dressings with strongly flavored meats and stronger dressings with mildly flavored meats. Broccoli and cole slaw are too closely related in flavor to be on the same meal. Tart, spicy foods such as mint jelly go with lamb, or applesauce with roast pork. They help mask the strong flavor and the sensation of fattiness in these meats. Avoid unnatural food colors; gain maximum appearance with foods possessing natural high color values. Seek temperature differences. A hot cup of bouillon might go well before a fruit salad served with sherbet while a cold cup of jellied consomme might not.

A computer can plan a menu. In addition, it will set up restraints on costs, nutrients and item repetition. It can also print out recipes giving the portions needed to fill the forecast. It will print out orders and requisitions for purchase and do additional computing tasks. As yet, menu planning by computer has been used more in hospitals and the military service than anywhere else. There is a tendency in institutions to continue to plan menus manually while adapting other production tasks to the computer.

Menu Writing

The importance of the menu as a selling medium should not be missed. It is usually the first and best bit of advertising a customer sees. Colorful language helps sales and creates positive impressions if descriptions are kept meaningful and what is promised is delivered. Terms such as "tart honey-fruit dressing," "minted green peas," "crisp hash browns" and others help picture a product. Do not use terms that embarrass or confuse patrons because they do not understand them. Menus written with a lot of foreign phrases are fast losing popularity. Use only foreign terms that are generally known.

Menu Format

A menu's format varies for different institutions. A hospital menu may be printed on different slips of paper so patients can select items within specified dietary regimes. A cafeteria may need to list items on a board near points of service. A child's menu may be in a comic book. Or, a menu may be a placemat or a sales slip.

Simplicity, rapidity in reading and clarity as to pricing (if pricing is a factor) are three goals of menu format. Of course, the main goal is to tell what is available. Avoid clutter or getting too much on the menu. About a third to a fourth of a menu should be blank space. The menu should be large enough to be easily handled but not so large as to make it difficult to hold and read. Avoid fine print. Main items should stand out, with accompanying ones listed so their relationship is evident. To give emphasis and to simplify reading and interpretation, large and small type, indentation, bold print, italics and variation in spacing can be used. Do not list items in a column in single space; this makes for difficult reading. If clip-ons are used, do not cover essential material with them. The menu paper should be stiff enough to hold firm while the patron is reading. Glazed paper soils less easily. Unglazed paper may be enclosed in transparent, stiff material.

Study the menus of others for ideas on presentation and layout. Score them for simplicity, ease of reading, clarity, attractiveness, etc. Check your own for these same values.

Menu Writing

The following rules may be helpful in writing menus.

1. Capitalize all words except articles, prepositions and descriptive material.
2. Arrange foods in the order in which they are eaten in a meal or course. Group foods logically together.
3. Consider symmetry and form; utilize space, print and other factors to give rapid comprehension.

4. Give the main course or meal items the most prominent placement (usually at the left). Accompaniments, in small print, should follow or be placed directly below, such as:

Prospector's Stew with Parsley Dumplings **$2.35**

with selection of salad, roll, butter, beverage and dessert

5. Do not list condiments, butter, cream, sugar, etc., unless special or to remind those in production or service they are to be served.
6. Use accurate descriptions and develop key words, locations or other devices to identify items. Unless patrons know the meaning of foreign words or phrases, do not use them.
7. Specialties, sandwiches or other items may be listed in a separate group on the menu.
8. Do not arrange items by order of price.

The reader may find the glossary of this text helpful in establishing menu terms. Consult also bibliographical references for help in writing menus.

THE STANDARDIZED RECIPE

The menu authorizes production while the recipe *controls* it. No factory manufactures a product until blueprints, purchase specifications, labor, equipment, materials and methods are established in detail. These are

BECHAMEL SAUCE				O. SAUCES No. 14
YIELD: 2 Gallons or 100 Portions				EACH PORTION: ¼ Cup
INGREDIENTS	WEIGHTS	MEASURES	PORTIONS	METHOD
Stock, white........... Onion, sliced........ Carrots, chopped Bay leaves.............	 2 oz............ ½ lb............	1½ gal...... ¼ cup....... 1½ cups..... 2 leaves......		1. Cook together 20 minutes. Strain. There should be 4 quarts of liquid.
Butter, melted..... Flour, sifted.........	1 lb............ 1 lb............	2 cups........ 4 cups........		2. Blend butter and flour. Stir into strained stock.
Milk, hot............. Salt..................... Pepper............. Pepper, red.........	 ½ oz..........	1 gal........ 1 tbsp........ 1 tsp.......... few grains...		3. Add hot milk, salt, and pepper. Stir and cook until thick and blended.

NOTE: 1. For a yellow sauce, stir the sauce into beaten yolks of 16 eggs.
            2. Serve with meat croquettes.

Figure 1–12.   An example of a standardized recipe following the form developed by the author of this text for use in the Navy Recipe Service.

to a factory what the recipe is to the production department. *A standardized recipe produces a known quantity of food of desired quality.* It centers production control in management and reduces human failure by standardizing production.

Three files of standardized recipes should be maintained: 1) the master file in the manager's office, 2) one in the production supervisor's office, and 3) those used in production sections in the kitchen. To reduce soiling when used, place recipes in plastic cases. A device that holds the recipe so the worker does not have to handle it to read it saves worker time.

Recipe Format

The lower the employee skill, the more information the recipe must give. A standardized recipe usually contains:

1. Name of the food item and its file code.
2. Total quantity and number of portions of a specific size obtained.
3. Ingredients by weight and measure and sometimes by count.
4. Procedures and times for combining ingredients.
5. Cooking or baking temperatures and times.
6. Panning information.
7. Cost information.
8. Standard of quality expected.
9. Total time for producing the recipe.

Recipe names should be brief, descriptive and lead to immediate recognition. Use different colored cards to assist identification: all entrees on white, all breads on green, all cakes on blue, etc. State total quantities produced in terms related to portion size; for instance, the yield noted on a recipe "26 lb. or 192 portions — scale each 18 x 26 in. pan 6½ lb. each" relates well to the portioning instructions "cut each pan 6 x 8 for 3 x 3 in. squares (2 oz. each)." Portions should be stated in quantities AS using count, size, weight, volume or portioning tool used, as "Portion: No. 12 scoop rounded."

The most successful recipe file in institutional work has used the following rules for format:

1. Use large print or space to give emphasis or for special directions. Do not crowd. Lines help to separate ingredients handled or treated together in procedures.
2. Use 5 by 8 or 6 by 8 cards.

3. Place the title at the top center and filing or index code at the top right.
4. Below the title on the right-hand side, list the portion size.
5. Opposite on the left-hand side, list total yield and portions.
6. In procedures, state work done in advance first.
7. List ingredients in order of use on the left-hand side. Procedures for handling ingredients are on the right-hand side. Between these, list weights and measures. Count may be indicated beneath or beside measure in parentheses. Do not use abbreviations in methods. Number procedures in sequence arranging them opposite ingredients used.
8. An extra column can be left for changing weights and measures.
9. List panning instructions at the recipe bottom. List pan sizes and quantity put into each. State any portioning information needed such as marking crusts, etc.
10. Follow the recipe at the bottom with notes and variations. Number these when more than one.
11. Write all abbreviations for weight and measure in the singular, such as 4 qt, 3 gal, 2½ lb, 5 oz. *except* that "cups" may be written out and pluralized if more than one cup is indicated.
12. Do not put periods after abbreviations except for inches (in.) and number (No.), capitalizing the abbreviation for number.
13. Use t and T for teaspoon and tablespoon respectively.
14. Use 8 to 10 minutes or 8 by 10 inches, not 8-10.
15. Use No. 10 can or No. 2 can instead of #10 or #2.
16. It is preferable to capitalize for emphasis rather than to underline.
17. Put all substitutions for ingredients and consequent changes in procedures in notes.
18. Capitalize AP, EP and AS for *as purchased*, *edible portion* and *as served*, respectively.
19. For shell eggs use: Eggs, whole   1 lb   1 pt
                                              (10 eggs)
20. State milk in form used and, if needed, the water required to bring this to a proper liquid state such as:

Milk, liquid, whole	8½ lb	1 gal
or		
Milk, dry, instant non-fat	1 lb	2½ qt
Water, tap	7½ lb	3½ qt
or		
Milk, evaporated	2¾ lb	5½ c
Water, tap	5¾ lb	11½ c

21. Do not continue a recipe on the back; use a new card. Use space at the bottom or on the reverse side for instructions on

garnishing, serving, holding time, storing, etc. Or, use the back for a picture of the item.

Recipe Development

Keep a file of new recipe ideas that seem practical and desirable for future development and testing. All food services need new recipes or to revise old ones. New foods, improved ingredients and new equipment are constantly appearing on the market, making it necessary to make changes in recipes. Cost requirements make it desirable to check recipes frequently for possible savings. Progress and efficiency are achieved by instituting a good recipe development program. This is as essential to success of a foodservice as is the development of a new model car for automobile manufacture.

Recipe development is a highly specialized task. Careful study of the recipe is required before testing. Certain well-defined ratios are needed in ingredients for a successful product; if necessary, adjust these. Visualize the item as it goes through production. Are procedures and their sequence correct? Can work be simplified? Consider quality factors involved. A good sense of flavor is required. Flavors can be subtle and the experienced person with taste acuity will select those that are the most pleasing and true. Combining foods so flavors are compatible is an art. One should not only be able to remember flavors during a test but should also carry them in the memory to compare with other flavors

Figure 1–13.   A panel of food tasters evaluate a product.

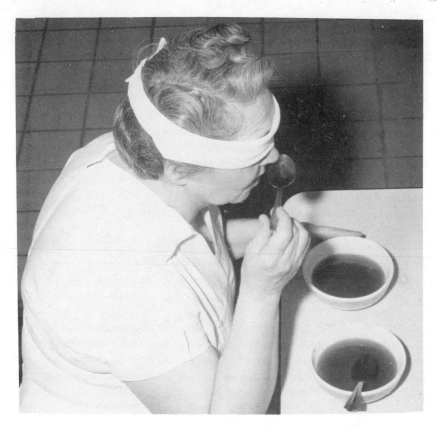

Figure 1–14. Tasters must sometimes be blindfolded to prevent them from distinguishing by sight rather than by taste products to be evaluated.

later. An accurate knowledge of what patrons are apt to like or disike is also required. Too frequently menu items are what the chef, manager or someone else in authority likes but few others do.

After careful checking of the recipe, write it up in the smallest quantity that will give a good estimate of appearance, flavor, texture, yield and portion size. Test. Evaluate the product. Be extremely critical. Slight imbalances might not seem important but in a larger quantity might be critical. Note comments and suggested changes in detail using colored ink or pencil. Retest and repeat testing until yield and quality factors meet standards.

Panel taste testing is recommended. Select panel members that possess good food standards, can taste well and know something about quantity food and its service. Non-smokers usually have more taste acuity but, if an otherwise desirable judge does not smoke for two hours before a test, he may regain taste acuity. Colds, emotional disturbances, fatigue and other factors may cause an otherwise competent judge to lose taste acuity, so all panel members may not be expert at every test. Methods for ascertaining a temporary loss of taste can be found in the literature. Allow members failing to pass the preliminary tests to taste; then, eliminate their judgments but do not inform them they failed the test and their judgments were not used. Build confidence in the judges. Use judges of different ages and sex. Elderly people may still retain good taste sense which, coupled with experience, makes them good judges. Use score sheets listing factors to be judged. In addition to quality factors, judge adequacy of portion and acceptability with patrons. Judge in a quiet room with good natural light or light that is natural for the conditions under which the food will be consumed.

Food consumed two hours before a test dulls the palate; 11:30 a.m. and 4:30 p.m. have been found to be times when individuals possess highest taste acuity. Alcohol dulls the palate. Because flavors are not as prominent in cold foods as in hot, the former must be more highly seasoned than hot ones. Flavor judgment is not only a matter of sense acuity but is also a matter of experience.

We have four tastes: salt, bitter, sweet and sour. Sweet taste buds are at the tongue's tip, salty on either side, sour at the back on the sides and bitter in the V-shaped field at the back of the tongue. Most food has some odor and sensory organs in the nose detect these. These odors combined with the four basic tastes make up what we call flavor. The ability to evaluate flavor is one of judging taste and aroma combined. Flavor evaluation can be developed and a good taster is one who can differentiate and identify between subtle flavor differences.

Salt subdues excessive sweetnesss, bitterness or tartness at the same time assisting in bringing out other delicate flavors masked by these excessive tastes. The other major tastes similarly subdue the others and bring out slight flavor differences. A small quantity of sugar added to vegetables or a meat sauce smooths out and blends flavor together better. Only true flavors are acceptable. Texture can affect acceptability. Greasy soup, rubbery pie filling, over-cooked meat or soggy griddle cakes will be unpalatable even though satisfactory in flavor.

To change a recipe yield, convert all weights to ounces. If possible, ingredients given by count or volume should also be changed to ounces. If this cannot be done, establish a factor for the change and multiply by this. Multiply also the ounce weights by the change. The following indicates how this might be done in increasing a recipe from 50 to 250 portions or increasing it five times:

UNITED FRUIT and FOOD CORP.

30 ST. JAMES AVE., — BOSTON 16, MASS.

TECHNOLOGICAL EXAMINATION

NAME_____ DATE_____ 19____

ITEM_____

COLOR									
ODOR									
FLAVOR									
TEXTURE									
APPEARANCE									
SAMPLE NUMBER	EXTREMELY POOR	VERY POOR	POOR	BELOW FAIR ABOVE POOR	FAIR	BELOW GOOD ABOVE FAIR	GOOD	VERY GOOD	EXCELLENT

REMARKS:

Figure 1–15.   A judging form that makes possible later statistical evaluation of scores. (Courtesy United Fruit Corporation)

Coconut Drop Cookies

Ingredients	Columns				
	(1)	(2)	(3)	(4)	(5)
Milk, condensed	$1\frac{1}{2}$ c	17 oz	85 oz	$7\frac{1}{2}$ c	1 gal less 1 c
Coconut, shredded	1 lb	16 oz	80 oz	5 lb	10 lb
Vanilla	1 T	$\frac{1}{2}$ oz	$2\frac{1}{2}$ oz	$\frac{1}{3}$ c	$\frac{2}{3}$ c
Nuts, chopped	8 oz	8 oz	40 oz	$2\frac{1}{2}$ lb	$7\frac{1}{2}$ lb

In the first column, the weights or measures as they appear in the recipe are listed. Column 2 shows the conversion to ounces while Column 3 gives the result of increasing the recipe by five. Reconversion is made in Column 4 to original values on the recipe card. Corrections for variations in weights or measures are made here so these are even and stated in meaningful values. If the cookies were to be scaled at one ounce in-

SCORE SHEET FOR JUDGING VEGETABLES

Type of Vegetable——————————Judge————————————

Date————————————————

	Maximum Score	Score
Exterior Appearance	20	

Regular, unbroken, even-shaped pieces
Correct size
Good color, bright, even, clear, fresh; not dull, pale
   or muddy
Proper moistness; not dry, watery, or shriveled

Interior

Texture: tender, slightly crisp, very crisp, mushy,   30
   stringy, tough, woody, hard
Good color

Palatability   45

Flavor: pleasant, true, not lacking in flavor, raw or
strong; well-seasoned, not burned
Temperature proper

Portion

Adequacy of portion   5
Attractiveness of serving   ——
       100

Figure 1–16. A score sheet form for judging vegetables.

stead of a half ounce, the recipe would have to be doubled. The quantities in Column 5 indicate such a change. Testing should also be made to check yield and product quality.

Before using a newly developed recipe in production, go over essential points with the worker making the product. If necessary, set up a work sheet to record data needed. Enlist the cooperation of the worker, telling him the aims and giving him the responsibility and credit for doing a critical task. Work through the heads of departments also. The chef, head cook or baker or food production supervisor should be close to the program and their ideas should receive careful consideration. Bake off new recipes introducing them at group meetings so employees also have a chance to judge a new product.

SERVICE

Good service can do much to enhance food acceptance. The trend in service is toward less formal types to reduce time, give faster turnover, reduce cost and simplify procedures. Table 1-1 gives some service times.

Cafeteria Service

Cafeteria service is simple, direct, fast and low in cost. The guest selects his food from a counter and a server dishes it up and hands it to him. If guests dish up their own food, service is delayed. Usually 4 to 8 are served per minute, with a good fast operation averaging six. Lines where special foods can be selected speed service and separate those wishing to eat quickly. Cafeteria counters over 50 feet in length lose efficiency in terms of service speed. A scramble system or shopping center discourages lines by moving patrons from service area to service area thus avoiding having patrons stand in line while someone ahead makes up his mind.

Buffet Service

Foods placed on counters so guests help themselves are being used frequently for lunches or dinners. Quick breakfast service may be achieved also by this method. The meal is usually served at a set price and patrons take as much as they wish. This service is largely used to reduce service personnel. It is also slightly faster than seated service.

Counter Service

In counter service, guests seat themselves and select foods from a menu.

Table 1-1. Times and Space Requirements for Service Areas

	Average Service and Eating Time			Square feet per Seat
Type Service	Breakfast	Lunch	Dinner	
Cafeteria	10–15 min.	15–20 min.	20–30 min.	15–18
Counter	12–18 min.	15–25 min.	25–35 min.	18–20
Seated service, coffee shop	20–25 min.	20–35 min.	30–40 min.	18
Seated service, deluxe dining	25–45 min.	35–60 min.	45–75 min.	18–25

Note: Waiting time for counter or seated service is usually 25 to 50% of total time; if this is reduced, so is overall service time.

(a) (b)

Figure 1–17. (a) American service setting from a student demonstration. (b) A student demonstrating wine service.

Counter service is fast and gives a rapid turnover. For this reason, some seated services may also use counters. The service person gives water and the correct silverware with a napkin when taking the order. Usually, forks are set at the guest's left and the other silver on the right but all can be at the right. Napkin dispensers may obviate the need to give a napkin. About an average of 16 patrons can be handled by a waitress at a counter.

American Seated Service

Seated service in a coffee shop usually uses American service although some very fine dining rooms can also use it. In this, foods are placed on dishes in the kitchen and are served to guests. Service is from the guest's right placing the food down with the right hand. Beverage service is from the guest's left, the waiter using his left hand. Normally, items are cleared from the right with the right hand but where items are on the guest's left, they are cleared from the left using the left hand to avoid a far reach in front of the guest. Either a tablecloth with silencer or placemat is used as the table cover. In more formal types only the table-cloth with silencer is used.

Figure 1–18. A diagram illustrating Russian service.

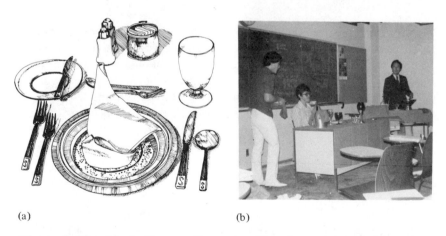

(a)   (b)

Figure 1–19. (a) A diagram illustrating French service and (b) students demonstrating it.

Deluxe Seated Service

Deluxe service can be either French or Russian; English service is rarely used. Table settings for French or Russian service are the same if the

Figure 1–20. A chef checks his buffet as foods are placed on the table for service.

meal consists of a soup or appetizer, a main course, salad and a dessert. The salad usually is served with the main course.

A more formal meal would be appetizer, soup, fish, poultry, roast and vegetable, salad, cheese, dessert and coffee. A frozen punch, ice or sherbet may be served after the roast and vegetable. Only a part of the silver and glasses may be on the table because of the number used, additional being placed on the tables as the courses proceed. No bread or butter plate, water glass or salts and peppers are on the table and bread and butter and water are not served. Second servings are not offered. The meal ends with a finger bowl service but finger bowls may be used between courses too. A service plate about 10 inches in diameter is used up to the roast and vegetable course. Then, it is removed. It is proper to return it again for the salad and cheese courses, removing it for the dessert course. The coffee spoon is placed to the right of the cup on the saucer at the time of coffee service. Menus are frequently printed with the program and placed next to the napkin. Place cards are proper.

French service uses a cart (*gueridon*) for service at the table, most foods being warmed or partially cooked there on a warmer (*rechaud*) of the open-flame type. Russian service is from a platter or dish containing food arranged on these in the kitchen. The waiter serves from the dish to the guest's plate.

In French service, the waiter (*chef du rang*) may seat guests unless this is done by a captain. (A captain usually oversees about four waiters.) The waiter does the food preparation at the cart but can be helped by the maitre d'hotel, head waiter or captain when procedures are difficult or there is a large group to serve. The waiter serves all drinks and presents the check, collecting the money. An assistant waiter (*commis du rang*) helps the waiter by getting dishes, food or utensils, taking the orders to the kitchen, placing them and then picking them up. He receives food from the waiter and serves it. He alone, or both, may clear. Service personnel frequently wear white gloves in Russian or French service.

In French service guests are served from the right with the right hand except when items have to be placed on the guest's left. If so, service is to the left with the left hand. A salad served with the main course is placed in the space above the main plate or the bread and butter plate is moved to this location and the salad is served just above the forks. In clearing, service is usually from the right, using the right hand except again items on the left are removed at the left with the left hand.

In Russian service, the waiter places the empty dishes down with his right hand from the right and serves guests from the left holding the serving dish in his left hand using the right to put food onto the guest's plate.

In extremely formal French service, the meal is made up of three different settings with separate glasses, silver, table decorations and so forth for each setting. If there are many hot foods, a *bain marie* may be set behind a screen nearby to hold them until needed. Occasionally cold foods may be placed onto the table as decorations and then removed and served. This is also done in Russian service.

Types of foods for the first course may be *hors d'oeuvres*, oysters, clams, or a large *canapé* or fruit such as melon, persimmon or mango. If small *canapés, hors d'oeuvres* or appetizers are served before a meal with a juice or cocktail, the first course is omitted at the table. Wine-type aperitifs are considered more appropriate than cocktails for a formal meal but the preference in this country is for cocktails. Russian service is frequently started with a buffet from which *hors d'oeuvres, canapés* or other appetizers are served by waiters passing them on trays to standing guests. This is sometimes called "flying tray service." A buffet Russe must feature caviar served from a glass dish or carved ice piece in the

Table 1-2. Approximate Basic Proportions in Large Quantity Food Preparation

Item	Flour*	Liquid	Fat	Eggs	Sugar	Salt	Baking Powder**	Other Ingredients
BEVERAGES								
Cocoa		1 gal milk			6 to 8 oz			4 to 6 oz (1 to 1¼ c) cocoa or 4 to 8 oz Choc.
Coffee		2 ½ gal						1 lb (1 qt) coffee
Tea		1 gal						1 oz (⅓ c)
BREADS								
Baking powder biscuits	1 lb	1⅓-1½ c	4 oz			1½ to 2 t	1 oz	
Griddle cakes	1 lb	3 to 4 c	2 to 3 oz	2	2 to 2½ oz	1 to 1½ t	¾ to 1 oz	
Muffins	1 lb	1½ to 2 c	2 to 4 oz	2	2 to 4 oz	1 to 1½ t	¾ to 1 oz	
Popover (pour batter)	1 lb	1 qt	0 to 1 oz			1 to 1½ t		
Yeast breads	1 lb (bread)	1⅓ c			¾ to 1½ oz	½ to 1 t		⅓ oz compressed yeast (varies)
CAKES								
Butter	1 lb (cake)	2 c	6 to 8 oz	2 to 4	1 to 1¼ lb	1 t	½ to ¾ oz	Flavoring
Pound	1 lb	0 to ½ c	¾ to 1 lb	1 lb	1 to 1¼ lb	1 to 1½ t		Flavoring
Angel	1 lb (cake)			1 to 1¼ lb (whites)	2 lb 9 oz	½ to 1 t		1T cream of tartar and flavoring
Sponge	1 lb (cake)	2 t		2 lb 6½ oz	1½ lb	½ to 1 t	0 to 2 t	
Cream Puffs (choux paste)	1 lb	1 qt	1 lb	1½ lb		1 t		Flavoring

*all-purpose unless stated otherwise   **double-acting

Table 1-2. (cont.) Approximate Basic Proportions in Large Quantity Food Preparation

Item	Flour	Liquid	Fat	Eggs	Sugar	Salt	Baking Powder**	Other Ingredients
Doughnuts	1 lb	1 c	1 oz	2	8 oz	1 t	¾ oz	Flavoring
Pie dough	1 lb	½ to ¾ c	11 oz			1 t		
Cereal (hot)	1 lb	1 gal				1 T		
Macaroni, spaghetti, noodles, etc.	1 lb	1 gal				1 T		
Rice	1 lb	½ gal				½ to ¾ T		½ c Oil
Custards		1 gal			1¼ lb	2 t		Flavoring and 1 lb dry milk if water used as liquid
(Eggs as thickening agents—4 to 6 whole eggs, 8 to 12 yolks, or 10 to 16 whites per qt of liquid)								
Cornstarch pudding (Blanc Mange)		1 gal		3 c	1 lb	2 t		7 oz cornstarch Flavoring and 1 lb dry milk
SAUCES OR GRAVIES								
Thin	4 oz	1 gal	4 to 8 oz			2 T		1 lb dry milk***
Medium	8 oz	1 gal	½ to 1 lb			2 T		1 lb dry milk***
Thick (heavy)	1 lb	1 gal	1 to 1½ lb			2 T		1 lb dry milk***

* all-purpose unless stated otherwise
** double-acting
*** cream sauce only

Basic flour to liquid ratios	Measure	Weight
Pour batter (popovers, etc.)	1:1	1:2
Drop batter (cakes, muffins)	2:1	1:1
Soft dough (biscuit, dumplings, yeast rolls)	3:1	1½:1
Stiff dough (pie dough, cookies)	4:1	2:1

Figure 1–21. A crew begins to set up hors d'oeuvres for a large reception and banquet. Behind this counter on the left are storage areas where food is moved into refrigerated and heated rooms for banquet service. Exits to service areas are on the right. Only part of the dishup area is shown. It is in a large U-shape and as many as 4000 people will be served for a single banquet.

center of the table. Buttered, small, thin slices of very dark rye bread are also characteristic.*

Soups for Russian or French service are dished from tureens or brought in individual containers. They are then poured into the guest's soup dish in Russian service, or poured into a bowl at the cart and served to the guest in French service. The entree of a meal can be a timbale, a creamed dish or another cooked, hot prepared food. The dessert is usually a sweet one but sometimes fruit is served. Occasionally, the fruit and cheese courses are combined at the end of the meal.

Different wines are served with different courses, sometimes one wine being served with more than one course. A wine steward may assist the host in the selection of a wine. He will secure it, show the label to the host, open it, check the quality by smelling the cork and remove the cork from the cork-puller and let the host smell it too if he wishes to

* Likewise, a Swedish *smörgaasbord* must feature pickled herring, rye bread and Primost, Myost or Gjetost cheese along with other buffet foods.

Figure 1–22. Waiters at the Biltmore Hotel, Los Angeles, report for a banquet. In the background a captain explains service requirements for the meal.

check quality. If there is doubt, the steward may pour a bit of wine into the small silver cup (*tastevin*) hanging over his chest and taste it. If satisfied, he pours a small amount into the host's glass so he too can check quality. If the host approves, the wine steward pours starting with ladies first. Wine is poured as a partial glass, usually never more than half. As pouring is ended at each glass and the bottle is lifted, the steward twists the bottle so no drop falls onto the tablecloth.

White wines are normally chilled and red ones are served room temperature (60° to 70° F). White wines are opened and served immediately. A young red wine may be opened and allowed to stand for 30 minutes "to breathe", a process in which the wine oxidizes to achieve a slightly brighter flavor. Older wines may not require as long a period to oxidize. The steward's judgment must temper this.

The glass at the far right is used first and then the additional glasses to the left are used as different wine service proceeds. No more than two or three wine glasses are on the table at one time. Aperitif wines such as dry sherry, Dubonnet or other, or cocktails may be served with appetizers. A dry or semi-dry sherry or other aperitif wine may accompany the soup. Then, a dry chilled white wine is served with the fish, the poultry and entree courses, if these are in the meal. The roast takes a rather good-bodied red wine. Normally, no wine is served with the salad. (It is very important that the salad dressing not be too tart since this interferes with wine flavors that follow). The finest wine of the meal is served usually with the cheese which is a mellow, aged one such as Stilton, Camembert or aged Cheddar. A semi-sweet or sweet wine is served with the dessert. Port, brandy or liqueurs are served after the coffee, accompanied by nuts, mints or other sweet confections.

California Service

In the early 1930's some California Bay Area operators served a chilled glass fruit plate lightly dressed with an appropriate salad dressing as a first course. This zestful, refreshing appetizer featured California fruits dominated by citrus fruit sections. Later some operators changed this to a tossed green salad with a choice of dressings serving the salad on a large plate or in a bowl. It was purposely large so both a vegetable and salad could be omitted with the main meal. Today this is a popular type of service and may be called California service after its place of origin. The remainder of the service is usually American service.

Banquet Services

American banquet service is much like regular American service. Tables are covered with banquet cloths on silencers with the cloth edge about 10 to 12 inches over each table. Water goblets are filled and butter and rolls are on a butter plate. To speed service and reduce cost, coffee cups on saucers may be on the table and be set just above the dinner knife. If an appetizer is to be served, it is placed where the napkin normally goes in the center and the napkin is on the left under the forks.

Russian banquet service is similar to regular Russian service. The appetizer may be on the table when guests are seated. After this is removed, dishes are put down and service is from platters or dishes as in regular Russian service. Each waiter may set the dishes down and serve or two may work as a team, one setting the dishes down and the other serving. Coffee is served from a side table. French service is seldom used for banquets.

Banquet service requires fast, smooth service simultaneously at a number of stations so work moves rapidly. There is a banquet captain and others supervising. Because of the need for speed, management may have to commit more labor than is usually used for regular dinner service and the price should reflect this.

New Food Production Systems

New systems involving food production are being used with increasing frequency. Some of these are changing considerably modes of operation in a food production department. Many new production units are designed to produce food for units a considerable distance from the production center. Such a satellite system requires that a transportation subsystem be designed plus a packaging and storage subsystem. Service is not immediate after production and the food may be sent either hot or cold ready for service, chilled or frozen.

Immediate Distribution Systems

If the food is served soon after it is produced in one of these new systems, it may be called an *immediate distribution system*. Distribution of the food is either hot or cold. Some items to be served warm may be cooled and transported in a chilled state and later rewarmed at the using activity (satellite). Shipment may be either bulk or in individual portion. An insulated unit is frequently used to keep this food at a proper temperature or the transporting equipment may be designed to do this. The food may either be held at the receiving unit in the shipping equipment or transferred to refrigerators, heated units or held in other spaces. Unless food to be served hot is served a short time after production, it is best cooled and then rewarmed for service, especially food that is individually portioned. The Bremerton (Washington) school food-service system has used such a method for a long time and it has been used widely elsewhere.

The problem of quality deterioration in foods that are not in some way processed to hold during the time between production and service reduces the usefulness of the immediate distribution system. Furthermore, the danger of bacterial growth is much greater in this system than in others.

A recent development in equipment has eliminated some of the problems of the system. This is a food server into which hot or cold foods can be portioned ready to be served and held up to four hours without loss of a desirable serving temperature, appearance or danger of bacterial growth. It is being used extensively in hospitals and also in airlines, schools, hotel room service and other types of feeding. The use of this server makes it possible to produce foods centrally, dish them up under the control of the producing unit and ship them for considerable distances from the production center.

The Chilled Food System

The *chilled system* is a process in which foods are prepared and quickly chilled in either bulk or portion packs and sealed into moisture-vapor-proof wraps in which they are usually also conditioned for ser-

Figure 1–23. Individual portions of food can be packaged and chilled and loaded into these wire racks for refrigerating. They can be shipped in these racks and then moved into a conveyor oven as shown for rapid reheating for service. Such a system of production and service is frequently called the Bremerton system after the place where it originated. (Courtesy Crown-X)

Figure 1–24. An insulated transport container for either hot or cold food. (Courtesy Crown-X)

vice. A good package seal must be obtained while the product is quite hot to reduce bacteria within the pack and enable holding for a considerable period of time—for some, a shelf-life of 60 days is claimed. Rapid chilling is also needed. Storage is under refrigeration. The items

Figure 1–25. A new server that allows foods to be dished up and held at a desirable serving temperature up to four hours. (Courtesy Aladdin Manufacturing Co.)

are shipped in containers to the satellites where they can be stored and withdrawn for conditioning upon demand. Conditioning is usually in a hot water bath before plating but microwave, convection oven or in a steam chamber is also possible.

One of the original chillings systems was the NACKA system developed in Sweden. The AGS system developed in this country is similar except that it utilizes the wrap used for Cryovacing meats which permits exhaustion of the air after sealing and reduces the chance for oxidation and other degenerative changes that may occur when air is present. Heating is similar to that used in NACKA. Up to this time, the use of chilled systems has been greatest in health facilities.

Figure 1–26. An automatic filling machine used for soups, sauces and other liquid products. It is adapted from milk filling machines. (Courtesy Knapps, Michigan)

Frozen Food Systems

In some respects, the use of frozen foods in these new systems simplifies many problems. There is less danger from bacterial growth and deteriorative changes are minimized. Nevertheless, oxidative and other changes can occur and the systems built around its use have not been without problems. The type of food being frozen today has been considerably extended and it is perhaps possible now with some fresh and canned foods as supplements to build a very wide variety of many kinds of menu items around frozen foods. The frozen entrees are usually packed in aluminum containers, some of them coated black for better

Figure 1–27. A vacuum packaging, pasteurizing and cooking room fully separated from initial preparation to minimize the possibility of contamination. A USDA inspector is in the back checking the procedures. These foods after being sealed are rapidly chilled and held in storage. (Courtesy AGS and Dr. Lewis Minor)

heating. The use of plastic containers that can be reheated in a water bath, steam or in a microwave unit is also common. Both bulk and individual portion packs are available. Freezing is either by contact freezing (placing food between two very low temperature plates so contact is between the top and bottom plates achieving rapid freezing), blast tunnel (putting food into a chamber into which moving air at about −60° is circulated) or using liquid nitrogen, freon or other low temperature liquids to achieve extremely low temperatures in a very short time. The more rapid the freezing the smaller the ice crystals in the product and usually the higher the quality.

The Application of New Systems

Large production centers frequently called central commissaries have been constructed by many foodservice operations to produce huge

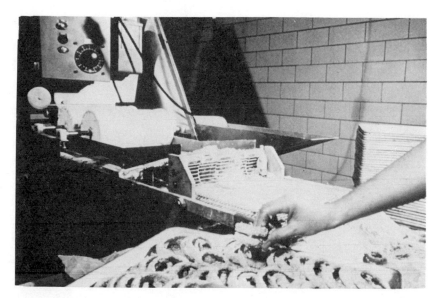

(a)

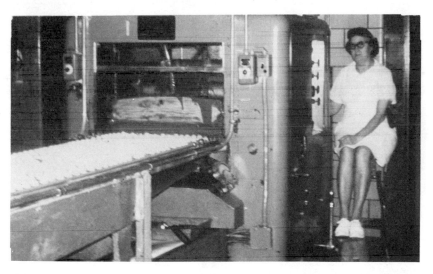

(b)

Figure 1–28.   Machines are feasible when mass quantities are produced. (a) This breading machines saves many labor hours. These onion rings will be refrigerated and sent to satellite outlets where they will be deep-fried to order in the Knapps (Michigan) units. (b) An extruder operated by the Sanders Corporation in Detroit, Michigan, that saves a tremendous number of labor hours over hand portioning. (Courtesy Dr. Lewis Minor)

(a)

(b)

Figure 1–29. (a) An assembly line from the production and blast freezing systems finally drops frozen foods down to the storage areas. (b) Selecting frozen stock for shipment in the huge frozen storeroom of Fairfield Farms. (Courtesy Marriott and Dr. Lewis Minor)

quantities of food. The State of New York for its health and mental institutions has recently constructed two extremely large units of this type and, while much production is still individual within the single unit, it is planned that more and more production will be centralized. Most items will be frozen using liquid nitrogen and shipped. The huge Fairfield Farm Kitchen plan constructed by the Marriott Corporation (Hot Shoppes) in Maryland now furnishes food for most of its operations, shipment being as far as Florida or the Twin Cities in Minnesota. In addition to producing foods for its own use this plant produces foods for others and Marriott also will produce retail products from it. Other units such as Howard Johnson's, Winn Schulers, Knapps, Ford and Horns have units that process many items for use in satellite units. Many school foodservice systems have central commissaries or are building them.

As indicated previously, the production in mass quantities of many foods is not without problems. Besides the problem of sheer weight of a batch and different reactions in cooking such large quantities, there are problems of cooling and freezing, packaging, shelf life and deterioration, shipment and reconditioning. As a result, the services of the food technologist have been sought in addition to those of the dietitian, the chef and others who have a sound working knowledge in food production. Many different types of ingredients are also being used to assist in solving some of the problems and improve quality, extend shelf life or lower cost. The whole production problem has so changed that there are those today that advocate that individuals going into food production take courses also in food technology to be able to cope with the new trends.

Centralized production has demonstrated that it can reduce considerably the labor requirements in producing food. In one study by the author it was found that one hour of labor in production in a large central commissary was the same as 10 hours in a small, individual unit but when transportation, packaging, service, cleanup and all other tasks were included, the central commissary system had a use ratio of 1:3 to the smaller system.

Some smaller units today process their own foods in a manner similar to that used by central commissaries, storing them for their own use. Most freeze and hold but some chill. Bulk or individual packs are used. Using this system, some institutions have been able to shut down production units over weekends and operate them five days a week, the stored production tiding them over for the two days. Others have lowered labor costs and extended menu offerings in using the system. The Southern Cross Hotel in Melbourne, Australia, has utilized the

(a)

(b)

Figure 1–30. (a) The control box in the foreground controls the cooking time and temperatures for these large quantity kettles. Automatic control of this kind reduces the need for labor to watch products under preparation. (b) The refrigeration equipment needed to supply cooling water for steam-jacketed kettles after cooking so foods can be cooled down in sufficient time. (Courtesy Marriott and Dr. Lewis Minor)

Figure 1–31. Huge vans loaded as shown leave the Marriott Fairfield Farm for delivery to points in Florida or Minnesota. These containers are locked and even if the delivery is made during the night when the satellite is closed, the container can be left on the loading dock to be opened later during business hours. Note that this huge van carries its own lift truck at the rear end for handling these huge containers of frozen and chilled food. (Courtesy Dr. Lewis Minor)

Ready-food System recommended by Cornell's School of Hotel Administration. It has found a number of entree and other items it can process by the method. Individual portions are frozen in plastic wraps. Freezing is in a blast tunnel and the frozen items are stored in special bins. Heating for service is in a hot water bath. The system works extremely well and is being copied by other hotels.

If a small operation sets up its own system, it must have adequate facilities to do the job. Ordinary freezers do not freeze rapidly enough and special low temperature units are required. Good food handling procedures must be established to guarantee proper sanitation. An adequate packaging, use and inventory system must be developed. Also, the items must be suitable for use by the operation and must process into good quality items. Entrees of many kinds can be processed this way but usually these should be in a sauce, gravy or liquid to retain quality. The time various foods can be held in storage varies and this must be known.

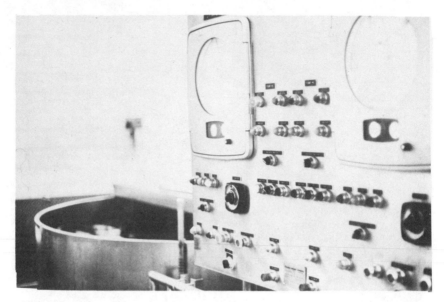

(a)

(b)

Figure 1–32. Automatic control reduces chances for error. (a) This control panel with recording thermometers regulates the cooking-cooling cycles in mass production units. (b) This unit is a liquid metering system for controlling the quantity of liquids added to foods under mass production. (Courtesy Marriott and Dr. Lewis Minor)

A number of authorities noting the growth of prepared items available on the open market are asking if going the route of the central commissary or one's own production system is the right way. These new systems take a heavy capital investment plus much technical information and it might be less expensive for an operation to purchase the foods it needs on the open market than attempt to do it itself. Many operations building these expensive sytsems may find themselves later at a competitive disadvantage because equal quality items are available at lower prices on the open market.

Suggested laboratory experiences or work assignments for Chapter 1:

1. Set up an organization for the operation of a foodservice unit.
2. Write a menu and schedule employees for its production. Give the results to other class members to critique it.
3. Standardize and cost a recipe and calculate the selling price.
4. Calculate yields required from AP, EP and AS.
5. Increase or decrease the yield of a recipe.
6. Set up and demonstrate different types of service.
7. Set up a taste panel to score a product and evaluate the recipe used to make the product.
8. Bring menus of operations into class and critique them.
9. Debate the pros and cons of producing foods from scratch versus making them in a central commissary or buying them on the open market.

BIBLIOGRAPHY

Aldrich, Pearl J., "Tailor-made Recipes for Modern Service," *Journal,* American Dietetic Association, No. 31, 9, 898–900, Chicago, 1955.

American Home Economics Association, *Handbook of Food Preparation,* revised ed., Washington, D.C., 1959.

American Hospital Association, *Hospitals,* "Systematic Management of Food Service," Special Issue, August, Chicago, Illinois, 1972.

American Hospital Association, *Hospitals,* "Electronic Data Processing in Support of Hospital Dietary Services," Vol. 43, September, October, November, Chicago, Illinois, 1969.

Callahan, James, "Recipe Expansion Made Easy," *Institutions,* 46, No. 2, Feb. 1960, Chicago, 116–118.

Cranmore, Mary K., "How to Set Up a Master Recipe File," *Food Service,* 22, No. 10, October 1960, 37–41.

Finance, Charles, *Buffet Catering,* Ahrens, New York, 1958.

Fowler, S. F.; West, B. B.; and Sugart, G, *Foods for Fifty,* 4th ed., John Wiley & Sons, Inc., New York, 1961.

Grossman, Harold J., *Grossman's Guide to Wines, Spirits and Beer,* Charles Scribners and Sons, New York, 1956.

Hoke, Ann, *Restaurant Menu Planning,* Hotel Monthly Press, Evanston, Ill., 1954.

Kotschevar, Lendal H., *Foodservice in Extended Care Facilities,* Cahners Books, Boston, 1973.

Lefler, Janet, *The Waiter and His Public,* Ahrens Publishing Co., New York, 1956.

Livingston, G. E., and Chang, C. M., "Second-Generation Reconstitution Systems," *Cornell Quarterly,* School of Hotel Administration, Cornell University, Ithaca, New York, May 1972.

Lundberg, D. and Kotschevar, L., *Understanding Cooking,* U. Bookstore, U. of Mass., Amherst, Mass., 1964.

Minor, Lewis J., "Today's Food Production Systems," *Cornell Quarterly,* School of Hotel Administration, Cornell University, Ithaca, N. Y., May 1972.

School of Hotel Administration, "Essentials of Table Service", *Cornell Quarterly,* Cornell University, Ithaca, N. Y., 1963.

Terrell, Margaret E., *Large Quantity Recipes,* J. B. Lippincott, Philadelphia, 1951.

U. S. Department of Agriculture, *Food Yields,* Agr. Handbook, No. 102, Washington, 1956.

U.S. Navy, *Navy Recipe Service* and *Form,* Washington, 1966.

University of Massachusetts, *The Cycle Menu,* Extension Department, Amherst, Mass., 1962.

Welch, John M., "Analyze Your Food Cost," Circular 723, Agr. Extension Station, University of Missouri, Columbia, Mo., 1960.

Welch, John M., "Standardizing Recipes," Paper No. 2362, Agr. Extension Station, University of Missouri, Columbia, Mo., 1961.

Wenzel, George L., *Menu Maker,* The Stech Co., Chicago, 1972.

Zaccareli, H. E., and Maggiore, J., *Nursing Home Menu Planning, Food Purchasing and Management,* Cahners Books, Boston, Mass., 1972.

2

Work Methods

The method of doing work in quantity production has much to do with the cost and quality of the food. While other industries have found ways to use machines to reduce labor requirements, foodservices have not been able to, either because too few units are produced, because products must be produced haphazardly to demand or because machines cannot duplicate worker skills. Items of the foodservice industry therefore carry a higher labor cost than do the products of other industries. Foodservices also use labor poorly; on the average, a worker in quantity work produces 47% of the time, wasting or resting the remaining 53%. Productivity should be closer to 80 to 85%. Poor work methods and planning plus inefficiently planned work areas contribute to this low worker efficiency.

Increasing worker productivity has been studied by engineers who have developed rules for organizing work, using the body and how layout, equipment, tools, materials and environmental factors improve worker productivity.

Work Methods Improvement

It has frequently been said work methods improvement tries to teach workers how to work *smarter* not *harder*. Basically, its aim is to reduce work effort so time is reduced and energy output lessened. Work methods improvement has also been called "methods engineering" or "work simplification."

Methods engineering need not be a formal program led by an engineer. An alert kitchen supervisor can watch work being done and come up with ways to improve it, especially if some of the basic principles for improving jobs are known. An informal work simplification program may do more than a formal one. It is better to think of it more as a philosophy for doing work than a science. If workers are taught to *think* work simplification many natural and spontaneous improvements will be made. Workers oftentimes know jobs better than anyone else and can do more to improve them. Indoctrinate workers with the idea there is always a better way, and small savings, while not significant in themselves, added together at the end of a day can make a substantial reduction in work effort. Jobs that are easier to do and give better quality products quickly win employee approval.

Management and Work Methods Improvement

Management should see that workers achieve a good productive rate. It not only must provide the resources needed to do the work but must provide an efficient layout or improve as much as possible present ones. It must also furnish the necessary equipment and tools to promote efficiency. Management must plan and organize the work. Advance planning of menus, purchasing and work scheduling must be done; workers need to be informed of production requirements and have materials on hand when work starts. Coordination of work with other departments is management's job. If management fails to do its part, the worker contends with this failure and loses efficiency because of it.

Work improvement starts with the selection of the worker. Job specifications should be used to indicate the type of worker needed for the job, listing what a worker needs for best performance in education, personality, ability to plan and organize, experience, manual dexterity, age and so forth. Select workers who can adequately perform the job or, if they lack this ability, see that they have the potential to learn it, and then follow through by giving them the training. Good training programs are needed to increase productivity. From the day a worker is hired he should increase in proficiency and value to the operation. If he does not, he should not have been hired. Perhaps an operation's most valuable asset is its workers; yet, many let this asset decline in value while seeking to increase the worth of other assets of less value. The needs of every worker for development should be ascertained and a program established for him to meet these. It is extremely important that workers feel management wants to develop the worker rather than just develop skills and knowledge which only help management.

Training workers for their jobs can be approached in many ways. A job description is one of management's best training devices. This tells a worker what his job is and, for this reason, quickly orients a new worker to the job so he achieves satisfactory productivity more quickly. Many training programs use the "big brother" method using an experienced worker to teach an inexperienced one. If this is used, one must be sure the instruction is that desired since older workers can frequently pass on very inefficient ways of doing work. On-the-job instruction under a planned program is very effective. Workers, supervisors and even management may teach such a course. The Culinary Federation sponsors one which covers two years. It has lessons, assignments, examinations and awards a certificate upon completion. Correspondence courses such as those sponsored by many professional associations or offered by schools are also effective and have thousands of individuals on their rolls gaining valuable knowledge. McDonald's, Holiday Inns and others have their own schools and training programs. Short courses where workers learn more about their jobs have been notably successful. Even informal discussion with workers on food standards, work methods and other factors can do much to improve job proficiency. Operations should establish standards for work performance. Workers should have to work to achieve these. Using visual aids, demonstrations and other devices help learning. Job evaluations can do much to indicate where workers can improve. Workers should know what is expected of them and how they can improve. This helps in improving job proficiency.

Management must also introduce new materials, new equipment, new systems, new work methods or new tools to improve work. Many new foods on the market can reduce labor requirements without harm to quality or cost. New equipment can do the same. New systems are becoming more and more common as ways to reduce costs. Oftentimes, a simple tool can do much to make work easier and quicker to do. New work methods or procedures should be sought. Why receive bulky vegetables, move them into refrigeration, then out again to vegetable preparation and then back to storage when from receiving they can go directly to vegetable preparation and then to storage or even, with good planning, to production? Deliveries that bypass storage save much time and promote quality by improving freshness.

The ingredient room is a big time-saver. This is a system in which the quantity of food needed for production is weighed in the storeroom or near storerooms and then delivered to the production sections. To do

(a)

(b)

Figure 2–1. (a) The ingredient room at the Ford central commissary in Dearborn, Michigan, weighs all ingredients for production. This system was first used by Horn and Hardart in New York City as early as 1948. It was then adapted for use by the U.S. Navy at some of its shore stations and later by the New York Department of Mental Health. (b) Items delivered by the ingredient room for use in a section.

this, it is desirable to have recipes duplicated in quantity on 8 x 11 inch paper. As needed, the proper recipes are taken from the file, ingredients needed for production written in and six copies sent to 1) the worker who will produce the item, 2) production supervisor, 3) head office, 4) ingredient room, 5) accounting for precosting plus 6) a file copy. Delivery at the proper time can be on mobile carts or on pallets and left at the unit until needed.

Management should try to see that as much production as possible occurs when a job is done. Every job consists of 1) a *get ready*, 2) a *do* and 3) a *put away and clean up*. *Do* adds value to the product, the other two parts do not. *Get ready* and *put away and clean up* take about the same time for any job regardless of how much is made. Therefore, the more *do* done for the other two factors, the greater the productivity. Consolidating work or jobs may help to give more *do*. If cinnamon rolls are made every day for a morning coffee break, why not do the entire week's needs at one time, freezing the excess? Then the amount needed for a day's requirement can be withdrawn in the morning, thawed in its wraps, proofed and baked. Doing just this in one activity raised productivity 280%.

Management should set up work procedures. The following shows how a plan for the production of 100 half-pear salads could be done:*

Equipment Required

100 6-inch salad plates	2 pans for catching pear juice
7 rack cart or mobile refrigerator to hold 18 x 26 inch trays	gallon container for juice
7 18 x 26 inch trays	shallow pan for crumbs
colanders for pears and lettuce	large pastry tube and No. 8 star tube

Materials Required	Portion	Storeroom Requisition
Half pears, 45 count	$\frac{1}{2}$ pear	3 No. 10's, 35 to 45 count
Leaf lettuce	2 leaves	5 lb EP, 6 lb AP
Cocoa-graham crumbs	$\frac{1}{2}$ ounce	3 lb (4 qt) or 150 crackers
Cream cheese	$\frac{1}{3}$ ounce	2 lb (1 qt)
Evaporated milk		Whatever needed from a $14\frac{1}{2}$ oz can for softening the cheese

* This plan of work is taken from a student assignment done by Andrew Castle, University of Montana, 1958.

Work Methods

Preposition the trays in front of the worker on a table. Place dishes on a tray in three rows of five, edges of plates overlapping each other. Place lettuce leaves on each plate. Roll pear halves in crumbs and place cavity side up on the leaves. The right hand should pick up the filled pastry tube and, with the left hand guiding it, make 15 rosettes in the pear cavities. Slice the completed tray onto the cart at the right and repeat the process. Pass creamy French dressing at service.

The Worker and Work Methods Improvement

"A fair day's pay for a fair day's work" has long been accepted in management-worker relations. Every worker must produce enough to make it worth while to keep him on the payroll; this is approximately $18,000 in sales per year per employee. The national average in sales per year per employee is $12,000. This is why the food service industry is not very profitable.

Planning Work

Work done according to plan is done more quickly and easily than non-planned work. All jobs have a certain motion sequence that makes them easier and quicker to do. A good worker quickly learns these. Immediately upon coming on shift, an efficient worker notes from the work schedule what must be done. He checks ahead to see materials, tools, equipment and other items needed to do the work are on hand. Ovens and other units are turned on so they are at proper temperature. He reads recipes to see he has not missed anything. Items needing longer cooking are started first. Prepreparation needed for production is done ahead. He knows production times and organizes his work so items are ready when needed. He eliminates work whenever he can. Thus, butter cake batter is made first and chocolate butter cake next so the mixer bowl does not need washing in between.

Lining Up

A phrase used often by French workers is *mise en place* which means literally "put in place" but is interpreted "keep things in order." "Lining up" means somewhat the same thing but refers also to getting things ready ahead of time. Doing this speeds production for items that must be put together at the last minute. All work that can be done with-

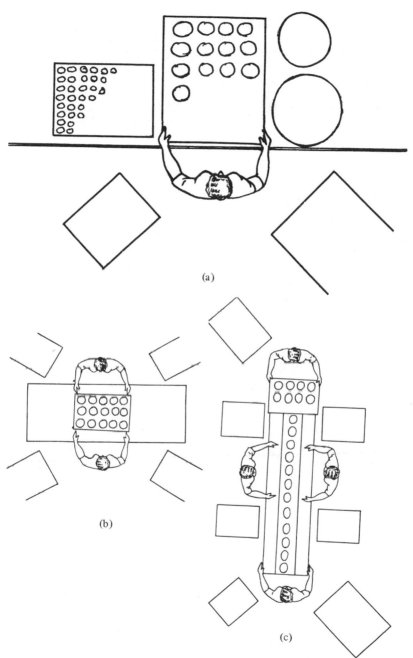

(a)

(b)

(c)

Figure 2–2. Methods that might be used (a) a single worker, (b) two workers and (c) more than two. (Taken from a student assignment by Andrew Castle, University of Montana, 1958.)

out harm to product quality must be done.-Meats should be prebreaded; all slicing, cutting or other work should be done for salads and sandwiches. In a drive-in, hamburgers, buns, onions, cheese and other grill items should be ready and placed in a convenient arrangement around the worker. *Mise en place* includes cleaning up as one works; clutter slows work down, causes confusion and lowers product quality. Workers should learn to conserve motions such as placing dirty pots and pans on a mobile cart as they accumulate so they do not have to be moved one at a time to the sink.

The Work Center

Workers should do as much work as possible within the confines of a work center. Figure 2-3 shows the horizontal and vertical maximum and normal work areas of a work center. No reach should be outside the maximum area and the most frequent ones should be in the normal work area. Where the two hands cross in the normal area, two-handed work is best done. Not only should horizontal space be used but the vertical space between 88 inches and 30 inches from the floor should be used. Motions in a work center should follow the natural job flow without criss-crossing or backtracking. Right-handed workers usually work best from left to right.

When work in one center is done, it is moved to the next center in a progressive fashion. Instead of different centers, the same one can be used for a new job by changing it. Using mobile equipment is a good way to do this. (See Figure 2-4.) Different work requires different centers. Salads usually need three: 1) a preparation center, 2) a make-up center and 3) an assembly center. If the vegetable section prepares salad items, the preparation center is eliminated. A sandwich section may use the same centers and, if volume is light, salads and sandwiches may be prepared in the same section.

Much foodservice production does not have the repetitive motions that factory production has. It is difficult to achieve this when different items are made each day and only in small quantities. Great flexibility must be put into kitchens with so much work variation and this reduces best work center utilization. Standard work centers are not possible because the work changes so much in different operations. A take-out unit has much different needs than a hotel serving regular meals, banquets and special functions.

Work Flow

If work can be done in a continuous manner or in assembly line flow the highest productivity is achieved. This may be in a straight line,

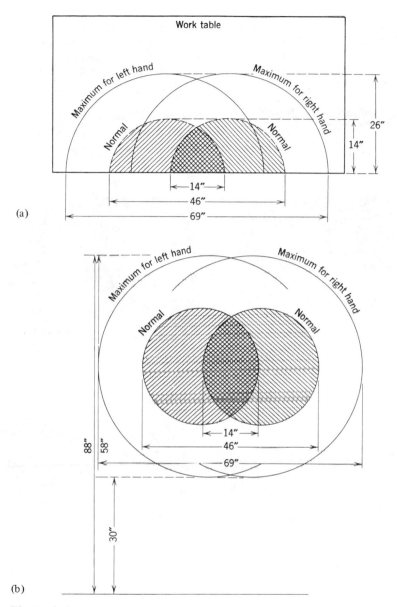

Figure 2–3. Maximum and normal work areas for a man (a) horizontal plane and (b) vertical plane (10% less for women).

U-shape, circular or any other as long as it is continuous. Many items must be made to use this type of flow efficiently and motions must be the same and repetitive. Moving belts or moving circular tables can be used. It is effective on soiled dish tables, salad, sandwich or other

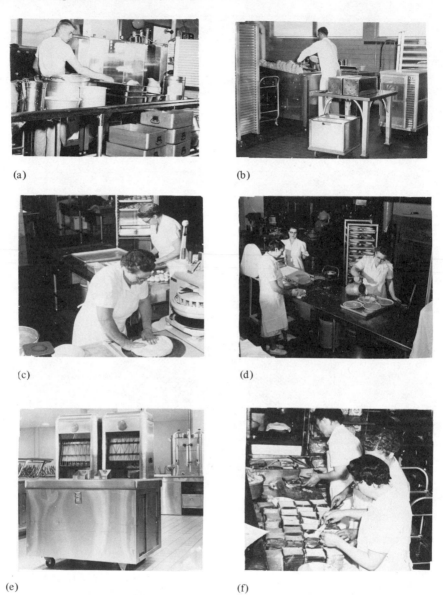

(a)

(b)

(c)

(d)

(e)

(f)

Figure 2–4. Confining work to normal and maximum work areas: (a) loading soiled items into the pot washing machine, (b) unloading dishes to carriers grouped around the worker, (c) fermented dough is cut in Dutchess cutter and then moved to panning at the next work center, (d) same area changed now to an assembly line for pie production, (e) mobile equipment such as this toaster can be moved in and out giving flexibility in arranging work centers and (f) an assembly line for sandwich making.

similar product assembly or the production of a large number of meat pies, etc.

Most work in foodservices is done by shop or unital flow where foods are processed to a certain point, then stored and then later production proceeds again. Small operations find this suited to their needs. It requires less equipment than assembly line flow but production time is usually longer. A wide number of motions is required of each worker and storage requirements are higher. Jobs such as breading meat and then storing it for future use, partially cooking and then holding sausages at breakfast time, etc., are examples of this flow. (See Figure 2-4.)

Work Motions

Productivity is promoted by combining, rearranging or eliminating work motions. A sandwich spreading spatula with a cutting edge combines spreading and cutting motions with one tool. Repeating motions without changing to others helps speed work. For instance, slice as much meat as possible and then lift all slices to a tray rather than cutting a slice and putting each individual slice down. Reducing motions to the lowest classification reduces time; the finger moves faster than the hand the hand faster than the arm and the arm faster than the body. It also improves accuracy. Using a finger to start a machine that whips a quart of cream is easier than taking a whip and whipping it using the arms.

Workers should learn to use the principles of motion economy. Most make motions as they come naturally which does not necessarily mean good efficiency. Some of the most common of these principles appear in Table 2-1.

Fatigue

As a worker tires, his productivity drops. All workers must receive rest to produce satisfactorily. There are two kinds of fatigue, physical and mental.

Physical fatigue occurs when muscular exertion uses up body energy. Avoiding body strain and heavy work reduces fatigue. Normally, men should not lift more than 50 pounds and women should not lift more than 35 pounds. Use mobile equipment to move heavy loads. Rest rebuilds energy. Sweets renew it because they are rapidly changed to body energy. Coffee helps by stimulating the liver so that it frees glycogen into the bloodstream that turns to glucose, the sugar we burn for energy. Proper work heights help reduce fatigue. The body rests on an inverted

Table 2–1. Principles and Examples of Motion Economy

Principles	Examples
Move hands in unison, starting and stopping at the same time with neither hand idle except at rest.	Worker reaches for a soup bowl with left hand while reaching for a ladle of soup with the other; hands are positioned in front when at rest.
Move arms simultaneously and in opposite and symmetrical directions for best balance in two-handed work.	The example above also shows this. Try holding an arm against the side while moving the other noting how much easier it is to move both arms.
Use the lowest movement classification to produce work with the least effort and time.	Using a finger to start a pot and pan machine is better than washing the pots in a sink.
Do work the easiest way.	Most work is easiest done with the right hand and the first and second fingers.
Use natural rhythm, continuous, curved motions that are ballistic.	Use circular rather than back-and-forth motions. Ballistic or arched movements are more accurate, easier and quicker done than straight-line movements.
Use momentum or gravity and reduce either, if possible in doing work.	Use drop delivery to deliver water from a faucet at the cook's stove. Use an arching swing in lifting a loaded pan using the momentum in the swing to help lift the pan.
Use devices, tools or equipment to free hands in doing work.	A recipe card holder keeps a recipe at eye level and a worker from frequent lifting of it to read.
Have tools, utensils, and materials within the normal and maximum work areas.	A roast cook stuffing turkey should have the dressing, turkey, seasonings, and pans conveniently located in the work center.
Avoid hunt and search.	Train workers to place tools in the same place so they know where they are.
Combine tools and equipment.	Use attachments to mixers for grinding, slicing, shredding, etc.
Promote proper motion sequence by good location of tools and materials.	Locate a knife rack close to where knives are used. Have most used spices in small bins over the baker's work table.
Provide good light.	Provide 50 to 100 foot-candles in areas where fine work is done.
Reduce equipment speed so as to promote motion rhythm.	A belt moving at 8 to 12 feet per minute does this on a dishmachine.
Arrange work heights so they are most comfortable for workers; have workers sit at work whenever possible.	A surface should be from 2 to 4 inches below a worker's elbow when small hand tools are used. When a tool serving as an extension of the worker's arm is used, such as a whip or ladle, have the surface so the worker can stand erect and place his hands easily and firmly flat on the surface.

Table 2–1. (continued)

Principles	Examples
Provide good grasps on tools.	See the discussion on this in Chapter 6.
Position all controls and levers so they manipulate easily with the least change in posture.	A good mixer has levers and controls so workers can stand and work and still easily reach them.
Minimize disturbing noise and vibration.	A noisy fan can detract from work efficiency.
Provide heat and ventilation that gives comfort.	The best temperature for work is $65°$ to $75°$ F with relative humidity not over 65%.
Allow appropriate rest periods.	The importance of rest is discussed later.
Provide good training.	This has been discussed.
Establish good personnel relations.	Workers cannot produce in an environment not conducive to trust and cordiality between workers and management.

"T" made by the spine and hips and whenever this "T" gets out of position, we use more energy and tire more quickly.

Mental fatigue may be caused by dislike of a job, boredom, noise, poor light or other poor environmental factors. A worker, not physically tired, can feel so. This is thought to be a slowing down of nerve impulses, especially at nerve endings. Figure 2-6c shows a mental fatigue curve.

Rest

Three kinds of rest must be provided workers to reduce fatigue. One is rest given muscles between work motions. The heart works continually resting between beats. If it beats too fast, an individual dies because the heart tires. Motions made too rapidly tire muscles. Rhythmic, steady motions conserve energy. The old adage "Life by the yard is apt to be hard, but life by the inch is more of a cinch" has meaning in doing work. The story of the tortoise and the hare also illustrates the benefits of a steady pace, though it need not be over-emphasized.

Workers need to set paces suited to them. Some have excess energy and like to burn some by wasting it. Let them, for restricting them from doing so creates frustrations and mental fatigue. Other workers should learn to conserve their energy so they have something left at the end of the day. Normally, a worker is tired about a fifth of his shift and most of this comes at the end of it. Teach workers to treat their energy as

(a)   (b)

(c)

Figure 2–5. (a) Violates the rule: "use both hands simultaneously in doing work" which is corrected by (b) and improved in (c).

paychecks, spending it carefully so that they are not bankrupt before the next one comes along. Plan rest periods. If workers are not given rest, they take it anyway which is only half as good as authorized rest.

The second kind of rest workers must get is a break from work. After several hours of work, a worker's energy is low and he slows down. A longer rest than just between work motions is now required.

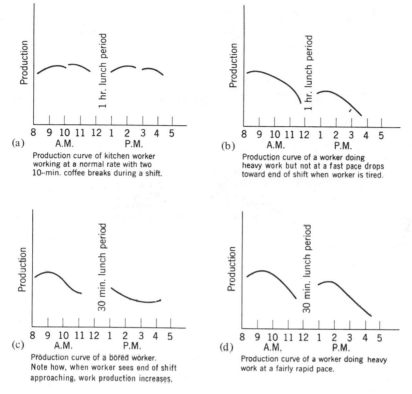

Figure 2–6. As workers tire, production drops. (a) Production is maintained by coffee breaks in the morning and afternoon. (b) Heavy work causes a significant drop in production. (c) Work curve reflecting mental rather than physical fatigue. (d) Heavy work at a rapid pace.

Short breaks of 3 to 10 minutes help reduce this fatigue. Such a break also helps to relieve mental fatigue. If a worker continues work after fatigue sets in, then giving additional rest to compensate for it is not advisable for the rest required to eliminate this fatigue increases geometrically. Getting doubly tired requires more than twice the rest—perhaps four times more.

The third type of rest needed is rest between work shifts to rebuild interest and energy. Days off or vacations are needed. Working overtime or too long without rest causes a productivity drop. During the Battle of Britain in World War II, a 60-hour work week produced less than a 48-hour one in spite of high motivation to produce. Speed-up, working the best workers longer than they should and other factors which may seem desirable may actually lower production.

Figure 2–7.   A principle of motion economy says "Use drop delivery when possible."

Storage

Use one-motion storage as much as possible. Send pots and pans to the work centers where they will be used rather than to central storage. Store items at points of first use and arrange work so the least possible distance is between work and storage. Plan temporary storage to eliminate travel to central storage. Much storage is dead storage and not an important sequence in production. Things in storage should be on the move. Use conveyors or mobile storage units to reduce handling. Plan production so storage is between two points in the processing.

Job Breakdown Techniques

There are some simple techniques engineers use to improve jobs. These can also be used by non-professionals. These are 1) time studies, 2) flow process charts, 3) travel charts, 4) simo-charts, 5) menomotion, 6) stroboscopic and 7) cyclegraph study.

The first step in making any study is to select the job to improve. One that is time consuming or causing bottlenecks or is difficult to do or workers dislike has promise. Jobs with a lot of walking or a lot of repetitive motions may be attacked with profit or one with a lot of items produced may be worth study. It is best to be sure of success on the first attempt. This builds confidence and wins over skeptics.

In breaking jobs down, productive, rest and waste components are

(a)

(b)

(c)

(d)

Figure 2–8. Mobile equipment makes work easier. (a) A scrubbing machine lowers labor costs. (b) Women should not lift loads over 35 pounds. (c) Heavy loads are easily moved in mobile equipment. (d) A good chair in which a worker can sit while working.

identified. Every component is questioned for essentiality. Questions are asked such as: *What* is done? *What* is the purpose? *What* happens? *Why* is it done? Is it necessary? Could something else be used instead? Could things be combined or rearranged to improve them? *When* should it be done? *Who* should do it? *Where* should it be done? *How* is it done? Would doing it differently improve the job and make it quicker to do? These questions are most important in getting a true insight into the job. Constantly think about different ways a job can be done. Weigh *all* alternatives. It is sometimes surprising to learn how a job is done, who is doing it, etc. Asking *what* and *why* might reveal that eggs are hard-cooked, peeled and chopped when they could be cracked into lightly-oiled pans and gently steamed until hard and then chopped to eliminate laborious shelling. Answers to *where*, *when* and *who* along with the always recurring *why* may lead to a combination, elimination or re-arrangement of work. If a product is batter-dipped rather than breaded, time is saved, for instance.

1) Time studies are not hard to do. A rough estimate is gained by checking a time, letting work proceed and then coming back to see in a given time how many units are produced. Work sampling is another method of getting a rough estimate. Casual, random observations are made in work sampling to see if workers are busy or not. By adding the percentages for times workers are busy and dividing the sum by the number of employees observed, a percentage of efficiency can be estimated; 80% or more is usually satisfactory. Or a job can be timed using a stopwatch and recording times on a sheet. Then the job is studied, revised and timed again. In establishing time standards, it is common to add 5% for personal time and 10% for additional time, making the standard 115% of that observed; some even go as high as 120%. This is done because workers usually produce better when observed.

2) A flow process chart details gross motions in doing work. Minute motions are not listed but are included in the gross motions. The

Figure 2–9.   (a) When tools such as whips or spoons are used, the work table height is correct as shown here but, when using tools such as a knife, have the work surface 2 to 4 inches below the elbow as in (b). A shallow kettle (c) makes for easier work. (d) Lift heavy loads with the strong leg muscles not the weaker back ones. (e) The worker on the right, in spite of being seated, is using more effort in working than the worker standing on the left because of poor body posture. (f) In carrying objects as shown here, workers should keep out of step and it would be better if one had his head on the other side so he could see that way.

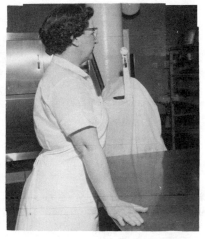

(a)

(b)

(c)

(d)

(e)

(f)

NAME	OBSERVATIONS										TOTAL	%
MARY	√	√	0	0	√	0	0	√	√	0	5	50
JOHN	0	√	0	√	0	0	√	√	0	√	5	50
SUE	0	0	√	0	√	0	√	0	√	0	4	40
TOM	√	0	√	√	0	√	0	0	√	√	6	60
ANN	√	√	√	0	√	0	√	√	0	0	6	60
KATE	0	√	0	√	0	0	√	0	0	0	4	40

Figure 2–10.   This chart shows how the sampling method is used to estimate productivity. At different times observations are made to determine who is doing productive work; a circle indicates none and a check indicates productive work is being done. The percentage of efficiency is shown on the right.

following symbols are usually used to show the different motions in doing jobs:

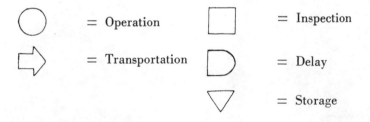

= Operation   = Inspection

= Transportation   = Delay

= Storage

3) A travel chart traces a worker's path in doing work. Usually the chart is a plan of the work place drawn $\frac{1}{4}'' = 1'$. If a brass paper fastener, pin or tack is inserted at places a worker stops, a string can trace the path as it is wound around these. This can then be unwound and, since every fourth inch equals a foot, the distance traveled easily calculated. The job is revised and the travel detailed again. A pedometer which registers the distance a worker travels in doing a job is sometimes informative.

4) Drs. Frank and Lillian Gilbreth were early pioneers in the study on how to improve jobs. To detail fine work motions they established the *therbligs* (Gilbreth backwards) as the smallest work motion that could be made. Each therblig took the same approximate time. Thus, one could add the therbligs detailed and ascertain the time needed to do a job. Usually therblig study was made using slow motion films and usually a timer or chronometer was placed so it was filmed as it ran along with the work motions. This timer has 100 equal divisions on its

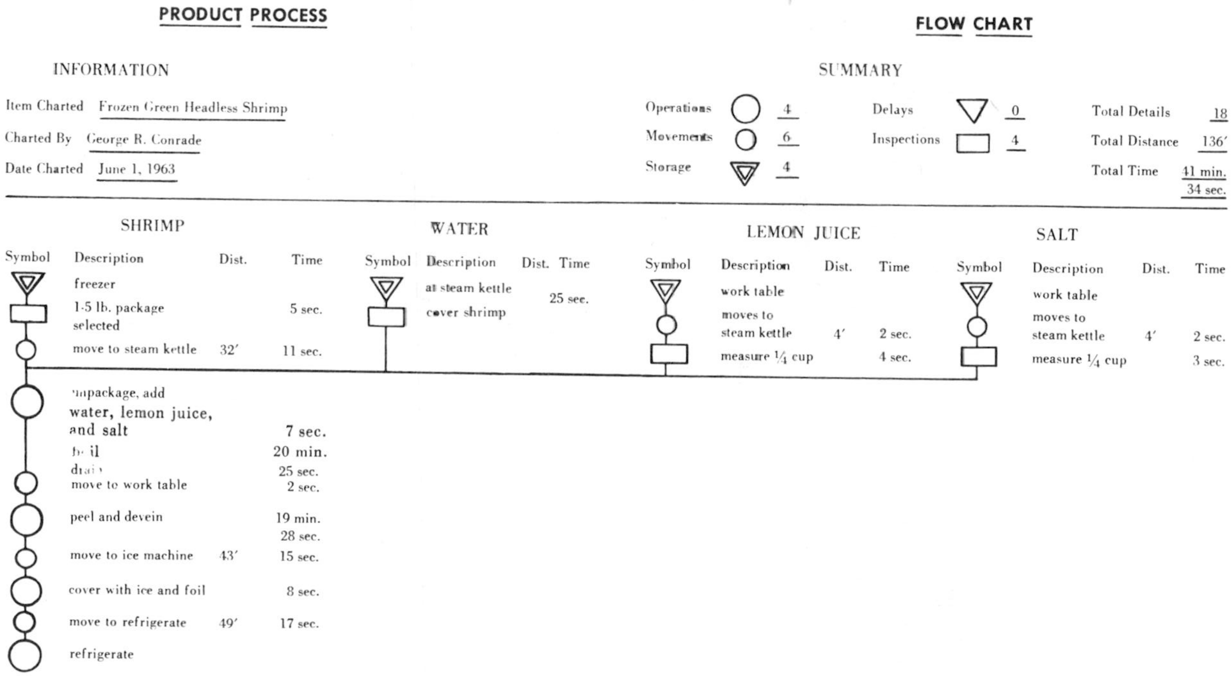

PRODUCT PROCESS

FLOW CHART

INFORMATION

Item Charted   Frozen Green Headless Shrimp

Charted By   George R. Conrade

Date Charted   June 1, 1963

SUMMARY

Operations	◯	4	Total Details	18
Movements	◯	6	Total Distance	136'
Storage	▷	4	Total Time	11 min. 34 sec.
Delays	▷	0		
Inspections	▢	4		

SHRIMP

Symbol	Description	Dist.	Time
▷	freezer		
▢	1-5 lb. package selected		5 sec.
◯	move to steam kettle	32'	11 sec.
◯	unpackage, add water, lemon juice, and salt		7 sec.
◯	boil		20 min.
◯	drain		25 sec.
◯	move to work table		2 sec.
◯	peel and devein		19 min. 28 sec.
◯	move to ice machine	43'	15 sec.
◯	cover with ice and foil		8 sec.
◯	move to refrigerate	49'	17 sec.
◯	refrigerate		

WATER

Symbol	Description	Dist.	Time
▷	at steam kettle		
▢	cover shrimp		25 sec.

LEMON JUICE

Symbol	Description	Dist.	Time
▷	work table		
◯	moves to steam kettle	4'	2 sec.
▢	measure ¼ cup		4 sec.

SALT

Symbol	Description	Dist.	Time
▷	work table		
◯	moves to steam kettle	4'	2 sec.
▢	measure ¼ cup		3 sec.

(a) Original Method

Figure 2-11.   This flow process chart summarizes flow of work in the present (a) and improved job (b). (Courtesy George Conrade)

PRODUCT PROCESS

FLOW CHART

INFORMATION

Item Charted: Freeze-Dry Shrimp
Charted By: George R. Conrade
Date Charted: June 1, 1963

SUMMARY

Operations ◯	4	Delays ▽	1	Total Details	17
Movements ◯	4	Inspection ☐	4	Total Distance	147'
Storage ▽	4			Total Time	23 min. 20 sec.

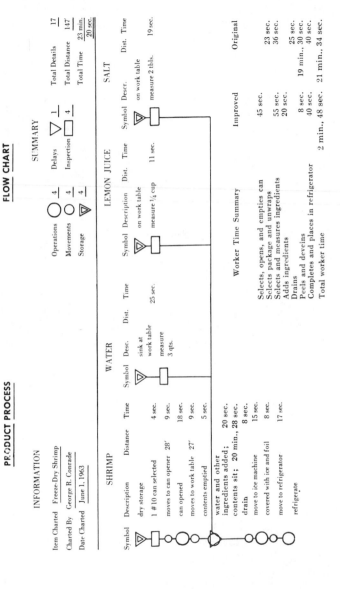

SHRIMP

Symbol	Description	Distance	Time
▽	dry storage		
☐	1 #10 can selected		4 sec.
◯	moves to can opener	28'	9 sec.
◯	can opened		18 sec.
◯	moves to work table	27'	9 sec.
◯	contents emptied		5 sec.
	water and other ingredients added; contents sit; 20 min., 28 sec.		20 sec.
	drain		8 sec.
◯	move to ice machine		15 sec.
◯	covered with ice and foil		8 sec.
◯	move to refrigerator	27'	17 sec.
◯	refrigerate		

WATER

Symbol	Desc.	Dist.	Time
▽	sink at work table		
	measure 3 qts.		25 sec.

LEMON JUICE

Symbol	Description	Dist.	Time
▽	on work table		
	measure 1/4 cup		11 sec.

SALT

Symbol	Descr.	Dist.	Time
▽	on work table		
	measure 2 tbls.		19 sec.

Worker Time Summary

	Improved	Original
Selects, opens, and empties can	45 sec.	
Selects package and unwraps	55 sec.	
Selects and measures ingredients	20 sec.	23 sec.
Adds ingredients		36 sec.
Drains	8 sec.	25 sec.
Peels and deveins		19 min., 30 sec.
Completes and places in refrigerator	40 sec.	40 sec.
Total worker time	2 min., 48 sec.	21 min., 34 sec.

(b) Improved Method

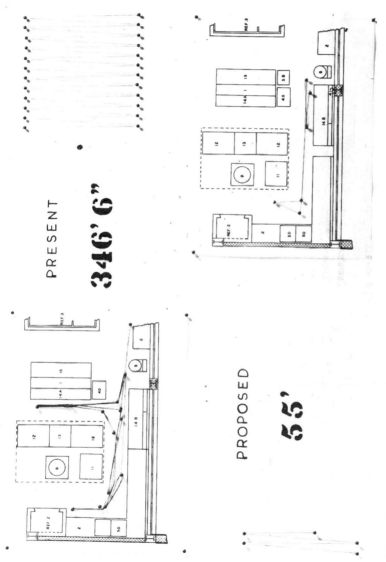

PRESENT

346' 6"

PROPOSED

55'

Figure 2–12.   This string chart shows how travel can be reduced in a bakeshop.

RECORD OF FILM ANALYSIS

Film Number 52
Date Filmed July 15, 1956
Analysis by LHK
Date July 28, 1956

Operation Trimming lettuce
Operator Hefner
Part Name _____
Part No. _____

1 Sheet of 1
Dept. H. Economics
16 frames/sec.

Therblig Symbol	Clock Reading	Subtracted Time (winks)	Left Hand Description	Right Hand Description	Therblig Symbol	Clock Reading	Subtracted Time (winks)	Body Member	Therblig Symbol	Clock Reading	Subtracted Time	Notes
TE		16	To bowl of lettuce	Holds knife	H		16					Frame 1
S		19	Selects lettuce leaf	Holds knife	H		19					not shown
TL		18	Carries lettuce leaf	Holds knife	H		18					Frame 2
P		27	Positions leaf for cutting	Holds knife	H		27					Frame 3
H		29	Holds leaf for cutting	Moves knife to cutting position	TL		29					Frame 4
H		210	Holds leaf for cutting	Trims off lettuce cups	U		210					Frames 5-12
G		17	Picks up waste lettuce	Holds knife	H		17					Frame 13
TL		21	Waste to garbage can	Holds knife	H		21					Frame 14
RL		8	Drops waste lettuce	Holds knife	H		8					Frame 15
TE		16	Returns to pick up lettuce cups to deposit in bowl on left	Holds knife	H		16					Frame 16

(a)

Figure 2-13.   A simo chart study (a) and (b).

SIMO - CHART

Method _____ Film No. _52_____

Operation _Trimming lettuce_____ Operation No. _____

_____ Part No. _____

Part Name _____ Charted by _LHK_____

Operator _Hefner_____ Date charted _July 28, 1956_

Left hand description	Symbol	Time	Total time in _sec_	Time	Symbol	Right hand description	Clock
To bowl of lettuce	TE	.50	.50	.50	H	Holds knife	
Selects lettuce leaf	S	.60	1.10	.60	H	Holds knife	
Carries lettuce leaf	TL	.60	1.70	.60	H	Holds knife	
Positions leaf for cutting	P	.90	2.60	.90	H	Holds knife	
Holds leaf for cutting	H	.90	3.50	.90	TL	Moves knife to cutting position	
Holds leaf for cutting	H	2.10	5.60	2.10	U	Trims off lettuce cups	
(continued)						(continued)	

(b)

face and the hand makes a complete circle 20 times a minute giving 2,000 divisions per minute passed by the clock's hand. One division, or 1/2,000 of a minute, is called a *wink* and the time required to complete a series of therbligs is usually recorded in winks. The record onto which the motions of the right and left hand were transferred in making this study was called a simo-chart because motions of the hands were simultaneously shown on the right and left sides. Simo-charts are used to study work motions frequently repeated because small savings can be significant in such work. (See Figure 2-13.)

5) A camera that takes a frame per second rather than the normal 16 per second is used for menomotion study. The film can then be pro-

Figure 2–14. A cyclegraph study uses lights to study the movement of a worker's hands.

jected at regular speed so eight hours of work can be shown in 30 minutes. A job can be revised and another picture taken at the same speed and again studied. It is best used to indicate travel in and out of work centers.

6) On one picture negative, a worker can be shown doing a job in different work positions. The job can be revised and another picture taken using one negative again to record the different work positions. This technique is called stroboscopic study.

7) Tiny lights operated by a battery hidden on the body of a worker can be placed on the hands and a camera used in a slightly darkened work area so that as work motions are made, the lights' paths are etched on the film. This can be studied, the job revised and another picture taken. This technique is called cyclegraphic study. (See Figure 2-14.)

Suggested laboratory or work experiences for Chapter 2:

1. Detail 10 ways in which management can promote a work simplification program.
2. Set up a work schedule for a worker preparing an item. Indicate work saving methods.
3. Design a work center and then change it to another using mobile equipment.
4. Set up an assembly line for doing work. List equipment and mate-

rials used. Describe the work following the procedures outlined in this chapter for the making of the pear salads.

5. Make string or flow process charts of a job showing the present and revised jobs.
6. List 10 ways in which an operation you know could raise worker productivity.

BIBLIOGRAPHY

Barnes, Ralph M., *Motion and Time Study,* John Wiley & Sons, Inc., New York, 1958.

Kotschevar, Lendal H., and Terrell, Margaret E., *Foodservice Planning,* 2nd edition, John Wiley & Sons, Inc., New York, 1973.

Niebel, B. W., *Motion and Time Study,* Richard D. Irwin, Homewood, Ill., 1955.

Schell, Erwin H., *Production Line Techniques,* McGraw-Hill Co., New York, 1944.

3

Sanitation and Safety

Sanitation and safety are the joint responsibility of management and the workers. Management must make it possible to have a clean and safe operation by providing good facilities, equipment and materials by which sanitation standards can be met. It must also set up programs to achieve desirable objectives and see they are carried out, plus provide the training and leadership needed to accomplish these programs. Workers must learn how to do the sanitation tasks in an efficient and proper way. They must be impressed with the need for seeing that maximum sanitation and safety are achieved and that they contribute to this in every way possible. Laws require that minimum standards in sanitation and safety are met but meeting them only because they are legally required may defeat the real benefits to an operation, since complete accomplishment in sanitation and safety brings the highest rewards to the foodservice.

SANITATION

Good food not only tastes and appears good but is also nutritious, clean and safe to eat. Clientele demand high standards of sanitation and refuse to eat in an operation not meeting adequate standards. They also demand neatness and order. The operation presenting a tidy parking lot, bright, sparkling windows, trim and neat landscaping and a clean, inviting interior wins customers.

The Food Service Sanitation Ordinance and Code of the U.S. Public Health Service usually establishes minimum standards for foodservice sanitation. Federal, state and local inspectors see that these are carried out and will assist operations to do so. Codes and standards have also been set up by the National Sanitation Foundation and our own professional associations. These groups work actively with the authorities to establish desirable practices.

Principles

Food can become unsuitable for human consumption from living organisms, chemicals or spoilage. A good sanitation program eliminates or controls these factors and makes the foods served safe to eat. Besides being safe individuals eating in a foodservice have a right to expect that the food is clean and has not been handled in any repugnant manner.

Bacteria, Viruses and Parasites

Bacteria and viruses are all about us in the air and in and on everything. Both are living things—probably plants. Some can grow in food and develop toxins or poisons which make people ill when they eat the food. Thus, it is not the food or the organism that causes illness but toxins developed in the food by their growth. Even though the organisms are destroyed by heating, the toxins remain to make one ill. Such organisms are called *intoxicants*. Another kind must be taken *into* the body where they grow and make one ill. These are called *infectants*. Both grow best at body temperature. They grow slowly below 45° F and are destroyed at temperatures above 140° F. Thus, the danger zone is between these two extremes. They must have food and moisture to grow and most like substances containing both protein and starch. That is why custard fillings, unless properly cared for, are excellent cultures for these pathogens and we must refrigerate cream puffs, eclairs, cream pies and other products containing them in warm weather. Broths are excellent cultures for them. In fact, most food substances are. Some need air to grow and others do not. One particular one, *Clostridium Botulinum*, which we will discuss later, will not grow in the presence of oxygen and so must be sealed off from air to grow. Others cannot grow unless they have oxygen present.

Bacteria multiply by a process called budding. That is, they grow larger and larger until they split in two. Now we have two and these two grow and split and make four and the four make eight and the eight make 16 and then 32 until we have huge numbers developing in a short time. Time is always a factor to consider in their development. If only a few infect a food and have a *limited* time for growth, enough do not develop to harm us. But if time is extended enough and growing conditions are good, food poisoning is bound to develop. Usually any food standing over four hours at room temperature is not safe. Because workers are such poor time keepers, we take no chances and get food under refrigeration or to a cooking temperature as rapidly as possible. Chilling or freezing arrests growth. Bacteria in frozen food gradually die but the process is slow; diphtheria germs in raw oysters lived for over three months in the frozen state.

Scarlet fever, hepatitis, tuberculosis, typhoid and so forth can be eaten in food or beverages and multiply in the body. In a few days or few weeks the host becomes ill with the disease. Some other infectious bacteria may cause only food poisoning or digestive upset. The most common infectious types are *Salmonella, Clostridium Perfringens* and *Bacillary Dysentery (Shigella).* Vomiting, cramps, a headache and perhaps diarrhea develop in a few hours. There may also be a fever.

Staphylococcus is a common intoxicant bacteria developing in food a toxin that makes one ill about 2 to 4 hours after consuming it. The symptoms are the same as those for infectious food poisoning organisms. A deadly intoxicant is *Clostridium Botulinum,* producing a toxin causing paralysis of the muscles and nerves. Antitoxin administered soon after consumption may help but over 70% die within 4 to 8 days after consuming it. It is so potent a half cup is enough to destroy all the people on earth. If acid is present, this bacteria will not grow. Also it must grow sealed from oxygen, as mentioned previously. Most deaths come from eating non-acid home-canned foods such as spinach, beets, etc. While 20 minutes of boiling will destroy this and many other toxins, one should never take the chance. Also, never taste any food suspected of spoilage. It is not worth the chance!

Other organisms that cause illness in human beings are parasites such as endamoeba *histolytica,* trichinae or tapeworm. Endamoeba is found in impure water, in the soil, on fruits or vegetables or other foods. The intestinal tract of people and animals can be infected with it and it can easily be transferred to other people through water, root vegetables, lettuce, fruit or anything else eaten uncooked. Food handlers can carry it on their hands. Trichinae are usually found in pork but also can be in bear, rabbit or other meat. They are small larvae that grow in the body, lay their eggs in the muscles and cause a disease called trichinosis characterized first by nausea, cramps and diarrhea and then aching muscles, fever and chest pain. The chance that trichinae can be in pork is the reason why we cook it well done. Eggs of the tapeworm in raw meat are usually the source of its infection in the body.

Poisons

We have many poisonous foods, such as some types of mushrooms and some fish. A small algae called the "red tide" can develop in the sea and when consumed by shellfish makes them poisonous. Whenever this algae develops, the U.S. Public Health Department stops the collection of all shellfish from the waters and forbids the sale of any seafood from the area. Many substances in food are poisonous. The green material in a potato, called solanine, is poisonous, only one has to eat about 17 pounds of it to die from it. Green rhubarb leaves are poisonous. So are raw poke salad greens and the berries of the common privet hedge. The foliage of larkspur is poisonous. Cows give a poisonous milk if they eat snake root. Ergot, a poisonous fungus, develops in moist rye or rye flour. A foodservice has no business having any of these poisonous products or any others on the premises.

Many chemicals are poisonous such as lead, antimony and cadmium. Lead is a common substance in many plumbing units, in paints and in some equipment. Antimony is sometimes used in enameled dishware and on the enameled bodies of equipment. Cadmium is also used in the manufacture or repair of food utensils. These metals usually must come in contact with an acid to develop the poison, but not necessarily lead. Acids on copper can also develop a poisonous substance. Many dangerous substances are used to poison insects or animals. These should not be allowed around foods or food spaces. A highly poisonous roach powder containing fluoride looks very much like dry milk and has been mistaken for it. Oxalic acid is an excellent bleach on wood table tops and other surfaces but it is poisonous and should never be allowed around food. Cyanides are extremely poisonous and some silver polishes contain them. As a rule, all poisonous substances are kept out of the foodservice areas and, if they are allowed, are kept separate from everything else, are plainly labeled, are kept under locked storage and are used only by those who know how to use them.

Food Deterioration

Food spoils for a number of reasons. Within the food itself are substances called enzymes that bring about spoilage changes. Fresh fruits and vegetables, cheese and meats contain many of them and if

Table 3-1. Summary of Factors Involved in Food Poisonings

	Incubation Period	Duration of Illness	Symptoms
Staphylococcus Aureus	2-4 hours.	24 to 36 hours.	Vomiting, cramps, abdominal pain, diarrhea, headache, nausea. Sometimes accompanied by fever.
Clostridium Botulinum	18-36 hours. Shortest 4 hours. As long as six days.	70% die in 4-8 days.	Nervous symptoms: diplopia. weakness and paralysis of muscles. Inhibition of body secretions, unable to swallow. Constipation.
Salmonella Typhimurium, etc.	6-12 hours. As long as 72 hours.	1-3 days.	Nausea, vomiting, cramps, diarrhea, fever, headache, prostration.
Typhoid (Eberthella typhosa)	3-28 days.	3-4 months.	Continued fever, skin (rash) eruption, diarrhea, depression, prostration, enlargement of spleen.
Bacillary Dysentery (Shigella)	2-7 days.	Self-limited. Several weeks.	Acute febrile, bloody diarrhea, nausea, prostration.
Amoebic Dysentery (Entamoeba Hystolytica)	10-14 days. Variable months.	Chronic.	Bloody diarrhea, abdominal pains, abcesses in liver, spleen and intestines.
Fluoride	15 minutes to one hour.	Several hours.	Cold sweats, nausea, vomiting, cramps, desire to sleep (Lachrymation).
Cadmium	15 minutes to ½ hour.	Several hours.	Nausea and violent vomiting.
Antimony	15 minutes to ½ hour.	Several hours.	
Cyanide			Cyanosis, mental confusion, glassy eyes.
Lead	Chronic.		Blue line on gums, cramps in stomach, bowels, and legs, constipation. Wrist drop.
Trichinosis (Trichinella Spiralis)	Primary: 24-72 hours. Secondary: 4-5 days.	As long as a year or more.	Pri: Nausea, vomiting, abdominal pain, diarrhea. Sec: Sub-orbital edema. chest pain, muscular pain, fever.
Wild mushrooms. 1. Inedible. (Boletus) 2. Poisonous. (Amanita)	Several hours. 6-14 hours.	24 hours. Muscarine 15 minutes 3-4 days. followed by death.	1.) Nausea, vomiting. cramps, diarrhea. 2.) Sudden severe abdominal pain, intense thirst, nausea. retching, vomiting, contracted pupils, convulsions, delirium. coma.
Weils Disease (Leptospira Icterohemorrhagica)	5-7 days.	Several months.	Jaundice, muscular pain, fever, spleen and liver enlargement. Constipation.

Foods Implicated	Mode of Transmission	Prevention
Under favorable conditions toxin is formed in many foods — custards, chopped or comminuted foods, chicken salad, fish salad, meat salad, etc., gravies, soups, hollandaise sauce, hash. etc.	Infections in food handlers. Droplet infection from nose or throat.	Sanitation, sterilize, and refrigerate perishable foods. Careful food handling. Healthy food handler. Heating to 190° F. (toxin is heat-resistant).
Foods kept under anaerobic conditions. Prefers protein foods but grows in all common foods. (Canned and improperly processed foods.)	Soil and dirt contaminated foods. 1.) Spores not killed in processing. 2.) Toxin easily destroyed.	Autoclave, under pressure, canned foods of pH over 4.0. Home canned foods, boil for 20 minutes after removal from can. Use of antitoxin proper type soon after attack if infected.
Salads, milk, comminuted foods. custards, soups, gravies, sauces, meats, shellfish. Under favorable conditions.	Fecal contamination of food. Bathing in polluted water. Shellfish from polluted water. Diseased animals. Carriers (Ducks).	Good personal habits of food handlers. Sufficient cooking and refrigeration of perishable foods. Controlled shellfish production.
Shellfish, salads. raw vegetables, milk and milk products, water, soft cheese, fresh cheddar.	Carriers, sewage, polluted water supplies. contact (flies and rodents) through food. Shellfish.	Sanitary water supplies. Proper sewage disposal. Control of known carriers. Shellfish sanitation.
Milk or any food or water may be vehicle.	Carriers, polluted water and milk. Contact.	Personal habits of food-handlers. Sanitary water supplies and sewage disposal. Sanitary plumbing installations.
Water or food may be vehicle, raw vegetables.	Cyst in feces of carriers, through food or polluted water supplies,	Sanitary plumbing and water supplies. Personal habits of food handlers.
Accidental contamination of any food or drink by insecticides.	Insecticides.	Careful use of insecticides.
Acid food or drinks.	Cadmium plated vessels.	Prohibit use of cadmium in manufacture or repair of food utensils.
Acid food or drinks,	Pigments. Chipped enamel lined utensils.	Discard chipped enamelled pots and pans.
Accidental in any food or drink.	Silver polishes. Fumigation.	Prohibit use of silver polishes containing cyanides. Close supervision of fumigators.
Water pipes, acid fruits in contact with lead vessels — Beer — CO^2 — water.	——————	Lead should not be used in any food plant for containers or in repairs of them, or piping or paint.
Pork and pork products.	Poorly cooked pork. Improperly processed pork products.	Eliminate uncooked garbage feeding of swine. Enforce proper processing of pork products. Cook all pork until well done.
Mushrooms picked wild.	Eating wild mushrooms, not knowing identification.	Do not pick wild mushrooms. Use cultivated commercial varieties.
Anything contaminated by the urine of rats with the disease.	By mouth or through skin.	Warfare against rats. Sanitation. Guard foods against contamination. Cooking. Protection of skin.

Taken from the *Sanitation Manual* published by the New York State Restaurant Association, Inc., from a table originally prepared by Joseph Schiftner, former Supervising Health Inspector in charge of Food Poisoning for the New York City Health Department.

we allow these items to remain too long in storage or do not take proper care of them, they spoil and cannot be consumed. Bacteria can invade food and spoil it. This happens when meat putrefies or milk sours. Molds and yeasts also spoil foods.

While some organisms spoil foods, others may be helpful to them or the same organism can at one time be harmful and at another time beneficial. Yeast can destroy food by fermenting it but it also can assist in the leavening of bread, in making wines, beers or other alcoholic beverages and in causing other desirable reactions in foods. Lactic acid bacteria can spoil some foods but are extremely helpful in making sauerkraut, soured milks and cheese. Molds are helpful in Roquefort cheese and other blue cheeses. They also are used in other foods to make desirable changes. Bacteria and other substances are useful in aging some items such as cheese. Enzymes also are helpful in this and yet both they and bacteria are commonly associated with food spoilage.

We can never live completely isolated from organisms that might harm us and we must build up immunities against them as well as do everything we possibly can to eradicate them from our presence. Some individuals are extremely sensitive to even the mildest infection or toxic dose. At times, an individual may not feel well, thinking he has a slight headache or cold when actually he is suffering from some mild infection or toxic reaction. While it is proper to stress protection from major chances for infection or intoxication, we need to avoid the lesser ones also. The economic loss and the suffering incurred through these lesser illnesses have never been calculated but if they were, the loss to society would be tremendous.

Spoilage can be controlled by using foods as fresh as possible and never letting these organisms get a chance to work. All operations should see that they buy clean food and that the purveyors from whom they purchase have clean operations and handle the food in an approved manner. Inspected and passed meats only should be used. Also, seafoods should come from beds inspected by the Public Health Service. Unpasteurized milk, unpasteurized processed eggs and many other products should be avoided. Check constantly to see that the foods purchased are not apt to be the source of contamination in the food-service operation.

Cleaning food well and keeping it and other items around it clean also reduce chance of contamination. Enzymes, molds, yeast and bacteria work well at room temperatures. Freezing or cooking stop their action. Refrigeration also retards it. Foods also can be preserved so deterioration does not set in. Canned foods are cooked so that all organisms are destroyed, and the foods are kept in a sealed container that prevents further contamination. Another method of preservation is salting. A food higher than 5% salt resists deterioration and around 8% is preserved. Food above a 50% sugar content keeps fairly well. Drying takes away the moisture the spoilage agents need to grow and so preserves a food. Pickling is another method of introducing acid and sometimes other preservatives to keep a food. An acid reaction retards bacterial growth. Mayonnaise and cooked salad dressings are not dangerous foods because their pH is such that bacteria and other spoilage agents cannot grow in them. It is only when they are mixed with other foods and the acidity is reduced that they become good bacterial cultures. We wipe down meats that are aging with a cloth moistened with vinegar to retard bacterial and mold growth on the surface of the meat. Curing is another means of preservation, creosotes from smoke and other substances retarding food deterioration. The curing salts also are effective in arresting deteriorative change.

Cleaning and Sanitation Procedures

The harmful or deteriorative organisms that spoil food can be destroyed by bactericides such as chlorine, iodine or other substances but only on equipment or other areas because they harm food. We can use soap, detergents and friction to remove dirt or substances we do not want on utensils, tools, equipment or other places. Once we remove it, we rinse or wash the soil away so it does not get back on the item we have cleaned. Soap and detergents do not destroy these organisms but they retard their growth. We use these plus friction to get rid of the soil or substances in which these organisms might grow and then, after we get rid of them, we introduce sanitizing agents that destroy any remaining organisms. Ten seconds of hot water spray or immersion in 180° F water is sufficient to destroy most pathogens or 170° F for 30 seconds does the same thing. Chlorine or iodine in the water also destroys them; 50 parts per million (ppm) of chlorine or 25 ppm of iodine in water at 75° F with a minute immersion destroys most pathogens. We usually start with 100 ppm for chlorine and 50 ppm for iodine to be sure we keep above these levels. The following amounts in 10 gallons of water give desirable levels: 4¼ tablespoons (2¼ ounces) 5½% sodium hypochlorite; 1½ tablespoons (¾ ounce) 12% sodium hypochlorite; 1½ teaspoons (¼ ounce) 70% calcium hypochlorite; ½ cup (4 ounces) iodine-type disinfectant. We may introduce in mechanical dishwashers' final rinse a wetting agent that contains chlorine. This plus hot water gives better sanitizing. We also use dips containing sanitizing agents for silverware.

A wetting agent in the final rinse also gives better run-off of water so items do not spot. More rapid drying also occurs. Air-drying is recommended to give less chance of putting undesirable organisms back onto the cleaned and sanitized items. Frequently, even stronger agents such as detergents are used to sanitize areas and to scrub floors. In hospitals, some of these may contain fairly strong bactericides. Proper use of all these compounds should be made. Workers should know that using more than the recommended amount does not do a better job but may defeat the job to be done.

One may hear the words "chelating" or "sequestering" in discussing detergents. The reference is to substances with the ability to hold onto soil and keep it away once it is removed in cleaning. "Chela" means claw as on a crab or lobster; "sequester" means to hide away. Thus, a chelating compound picks items up and holds onto them while a sequestering one hides them away figuratively. Detergents and soaps clean by getting into soil and loosening it. Some emulsify or saponify soil. They are also effective because they open the way for water to wet it. Many think that it is the detergent or soap that does the cleaning job. This is erroneous. They can do up to 30% of it and friction or "elbow grease" must do the rest.

Following good sanitation practices after sanitizing in handling and storage is desirable. Items should be under cover as much as possible. Glasses and cups should be racked inverted. Working ends and eating ends of silverware should be up in canisters.

It is often said that sanitation failures are about 5% caused by failure of equipment and materials and 95% by human failure. Good body hygiene is terribly important in reducing chances for food contamination. People are one of the chief sources of food contamination. Our bodies harbor many harmful organisms and we spread these around. *Staphylococci* are in our nasal passages and throats and when we sneeze or cough they are scattered about widely. They also grow in massive quantities in a cut, boil or anywhere there might be the development of pus. If there is any body abrasion, the Staph in it can be a source of contamination. *Salmonella* and other bacteria are in our intestinal tracts and, if we fail to wash our hands after going to the toilet, they can be the source of food poisoning. Our clothes, hair, skin, hands and fingernails should always be clean as we can keep them.

Soil should be eliminated as much as possible. Good scrubbing can clean floors and equipment. Steam is an excellent cleaner and should be used to clean and sanitize. Garbage collection should be frequent and cans and areas where it is present kept scrupulously clean. The interior of poultry is frequently contaminated with *Salmonella* which can be transferred to some other food item which, if not cooked and left to stand, develops enough bacteria to make individuals ill. Flies, insects and animals can also be sources of contamination. Keep them out of food spaces.

It is very important that training be given employees on how to clean and sanitize properly. The time taken is well worth the gain. Also, schedules for cleaning and the correct procedures should be posted and followed. Daily checks of work areas, storage spaces and other spaces should be made. Violations of good practices should be called to the attention of a worker. The National Sanitation Foundation says that cleanliness is a way of life and in a foodservice operation it is the only way.

SAFETY

Safety is freedom from danger. Foodservices are notorious for the large number of accidents that occur in them. In fact, it is said that it is safer to work in a mine than in a foodservice operation as far as the chances of an accident happening is concerned.

Work areas, equipment and other facility factors can be hazards to workers, and workers and management should see that these are eliminated as much as possible. Surprise factors are frequently one of the greatest causes of accident and a search should be made to reduce these. Equipment should bear the stamp of approval of the American Gas Association (AGA) or the Underwriters Laboratories (UL). Proper maintenance should be given and from time to time inspections made to see that equipment is in proper working order and in good repair. Schedules should be established for this so the check is periodic. Make it a good one. Be extremely critical. Look at wiring and mechanical equipment carefully. Is it in good order? Are moving gears and other parts guarded as much as possible? Are disconnect switches close by? The location of turnoffs for water, steam, electricity and other utilities should be known and easy to reach. Do not keep them locked so that quick access is not possible.

Workers should be trained to respond quickly to emergency situations and should go through drills for it. They should be taken on tours from time to time and the location and operation of emergency equipment explained and learned. It is most important that the location of a blanket be known in case an individual catches fire and the blanket is needed to extinguish the fire. First aid procedures for cuts, burns, electric shock should be known and a first aid kit easily available. Workers should learn how to protect themselves and others and should know how to move guests and others out of areas when an emergency arises.

Unless management takes the initiative to see that these things receive attention before they happen, it may regret it later.

There are three types of fire. Type A is one that results from the burning of combustible material such as paper, wood or rags. Type B is a grease, gas or petroleum fire, while Type C is one resulting from electrical malfunction. Each must be fought differently and the instructions for doing this should be given by some competent person. The use of the specific fire fighting equipment needed for each type should be demonstrated and workers taught to use it. Workers should know that fires result when 1) there is something around that can burn, 2) there is heat sufficient to cause a fire or conditions to give rise to it and 3) oxygen is present so a fire can burn. Removing any of the three eliminates the chance for a fire.

Good work habits can eliminate many accidents. Alertness and awareness of danger is an important habit to develop. Learning how to do a job is also. Some individuals are accident prone because they are careless, are not on guard or do not realize danger can be present. As individuals tire, accident rates rise. All facilities should take the time to tell workers how to handle knives, to take care of broken glass and in other ways work safely. All should be trained to immediately wipe up spills or clean an area where one can slip on something. To the experienced worker, safety is a part of working. It is a habit. The inexperienced worker must learn this and the faster he does the better it will be for him.

Suggested laboratory or classroom experiences for Chapter 3:

1. If possible, have a teacher acquainted with bacteriology let a student touch two cultures with his fingers: one before and one after washing his hands *thoroughly;* also carefully place a hair on a culture and remove it. Let someone sneeze or cough over a culture. Now, let all the cultures incubate 24 to 48 hours and show the class what has happened.
2. Show films or slides from some of the leading manufacturers of soaps and detergents.
3. Post a copy of the Food Service Inspection Report of the Public Health Service so students can see how inspections are made of foodservices. This is PHS-4006, 4-62 form of the Public Health Service.
4. Set up 10 of the most important rules that should be followed in a foodservice operation for safety.
5. Establish plans for fire drills or other safety programs.
6. Set up a simple lesson plan for teaching employees the basic facts of safety or sanitation in a foodservice.

BIBLIOGRAPHY

Economics Laboratories. *Food Equipment Sanitation Cleaning Procedures.* New York: By the Laboratories, 1965.

Hickey, W. V., "Model Food Ordinance," *Sanitarian,* Winter, 1961.

Iowa State Department of Health. *Sanitation of Food Service Establishments.* New York: Economic Laboratories, 1962.

Joiner, C. R., "Legal Requirements for Food Safety," *Cornell Quarterly,* School of Hotel Administration, Cornell University, May, 1972.

Longree, Karla, *Quantity Food Sanitation.* New York: John Wiley and Sons, 1967.

Rakosky, Joseph Jr., *Sanitation Simplified,* Chicago: By Central Soya, Chemurgy Division.

Richardson, Treva M., *Sanitation for Foodservice Workers.* Boston: By Institutions/VFM, 1969.

Texas State Department of Health. *Preventing Food-Borne Diseases,* 2nd Rev. Austin, Texas: Texas State Department, 1966.

U. S. Department of Health, Education and Welfare. *"You Can Prevent Foodborne Illness."* Washington, D.C.: Government Printing Office, 1963.

U.S. Department of Health, Education and Welfare. *Environmental Aspects of the Hospital, Vol. I, "Infection Control"* and X, *"Food Services."* Washington, D. C.: Government Printing Office, 1960.

U. S. Department of Health, Education and Welfare. *Selection and Use of Disinfectants in Health Facilities.* Washington, D. C.: Government Printing Office, 1967.

University of Massachusetts. *Bacterial Food Poisoning.* Amherst, Mass.: Food Management Leaflet No. 1, 1959.

White, James, "Bacterial Contamination of Food," *Cornell Quarterly,* School of Hotel Administration, Cornell University, Ithaca, N.Y., May, 1972.

4

Nutrition

Many foodservices must not only serve food possessing a maximum of nutrients but should be able to meet limited dietary needs of patrons as well. No operation should plan a diet if it does not have a qualified person to do so. However, even if no dietitian is available, most operations should still be able to serve some of the most common diets.

The Foods We Need

To grow and remain healthy we need food and drink. All foods and drink do not contribute the same kind and amount of nutrients. So, to grow and stay healthy, we must make a proper selection of foods, eating them in correct quantities. Figure 4-1 indicates the foods and their amounts needed for an adequate diet. Table 4-1 indicates the quantity of specific nutrients various kinds of individuals need each day.

There are five nutrients in foods: 1) carbohydrates, 2) proteins, 3) fat, 4) vitamins and 5) minerals. In addition, foods furnish 6) water and 7) bulk; both are needed for good health and growth. Alcohol is not a food but it does furnish calories and could be considered one. Some foods furnish many nutrients while others furnish only one. Thus, an apple gives carbohydrates, minerals, vitamins and a trace of protein and fat; salad oil furnishes only fat and granulated white sugar only carbohydrate.

Figure 4–1. Foodservices, while they may not be able to direct menu selections, must make possible the selection of nourishing foods which assure an adequate diet. (Courtesy American Institute of Baking)

Calories

We measure the amount of heat or energy foods give us in Calories.* For instance, a slice of bread yields 60 Calories, an apple 70 and 2½-ounces of roast beef about 150. The Calories found in a gram of the following foods are: carbohydrate 4, protein 4, fat 9 and alcohol 7. Thus, carbohydrate and protein have less than half the calories that fat has and nearly half as much as alcohol. Many times individuals think

---

* The heat needed to raise 1 kg of water (2.2 lb) 1° C is a large Calorie or kilocalorie and is oftentimes capitalized; a small calorie (gramcalorie) is the heat needed to raise 1 cc of water 1° C and is not capitalized. The small calorie, sometimes written gcal, is used in sciences such as physics and chemistry and the large Calorie, sometimes written kcal, is used in biological sciences such as physiology or biology.

Table 4-1. Food and Nutrition Board, National Academy of Sciences–National Research Council Recommended Daily Dietary Allowances,[a] Revised 1968 Designed for the Maintenance of Good Nutrition of Practically All Healthy People in the U.S.A.

Group	Age[b] (years) From Up to	Weight (kg)	Weight (lbs)	Height (cm)	Height (in.)	kcal	Protein (gm)	Fat-Soluble Vitamins — Vitamin A Activity (IU)	Vitamin D (IU)	Vitamin E Activity (IU)	Water-Soluble Vitamins — Ascorbic Acid (mg)	Folacin[c] (mg)	Niacin (mg equiv)[d]	Riboflavin (mg)	Thiamin (mg)	Vitamin B6 (mg)	Vitamin B12 (μg)	Calcium (g)	Phosphorus (g)	Minerals — Iodine (μg)	Iron (mg)	Magnesium (mg)
Infants	0–1/6	4	9	55	22	kg × 120	kg × 2.2[e]	1,500	400	5	35	0.05	5	0.4	0.2	0.2	1.0	0.4	0.2	25	6	40
	1/6–1/2	7	15	63	25	kg × 110	kg × 2.0[e]	1,500	400	5	35	0.05	7	0.5	0.4	0.3	1.5	0.5	0.4	40	10	60
	1/2–1	9	20	72	28	kg × 100	kg × 1.8[e]	1,500	400	5	35	0.1	8	0.6	0.5	0.4	2.0	0.6	0.5	45	15	70
Children	1–2	12	26	81	32	1,100	25	2,000	400	10	40	0.1	8	0.6	0.6	0.5	2.0	0.7	0.7	55	15	100
	2–3	14	31	91	36	1,250	25	2,000	400	10	40	0.2	8	0.7	0.6	0.6	2.5	0.8	0.8	60	15	150
	3–4	16	35	100	39	1,400	30	2,500	400	10	40	0.2	9	0.8	0.7	0.7	3	0.8	0.8	70	10	200
	4–6	19	42	110	43	1,600	30	2,500	400	10	40	0.2	11	0.9	0.8	0.9	4	0.8	0.8	80	10	200
	6–8	23	51	121	48	2,000	35	3,500	400	15	40	0.2	13	1.1	1.0	1.0	4	0.9	1.0	100	10	250
	8–10	28	62	131	52	2,200	40	4,500	400	15	40	0.3	15	1.2	1.1	1.2	5	1.0	1.2	110	10	250
Males	10–12	35	77	140	55	2,500	45	4,500	400	20	40	0.4	17	1.3	1.3	1.4	5	1.2	1.4	125	10	300
	12–14	43	95	151	59	2,700	50	5,000	400	20	45	0.4	18	1.4	1.4	1.6	5	1.4	1.4	135	18	350
	14–18	59	130	170	67	3,000	60	5,000	400	25	55	0.4	20	1.5	1.5	1.8	5	1.4	1.4	150	18	400
	18–22	67	147	175	69	2,800	60	5,000	400	30	60	0.4	18	1.6	1.4	2.0	5	0.8	0.8	140	10	400
	22–35	70	154	175	69	2,800	65	5,000	–	30	60	0.4	18	1.7	1.4	2.0	5	0.8	0.8	140	10	350
	35–55	70	154	173	68	2,600	65	5,000	–	30	60	0.4	17	1.7	1.3	2.0	5	0.8	0.8	125	10	350
	55–75+	70	154	171	67	2,400	65	5,000	–	30	60	0.4	14	1.7	1.2	2.0	6	0.8	0.8	110	10	350
Females	10–12	35	77	142	56	2,250	50	4,500	400	20	40	0.4	15	1.3	1.1	1.4	5	1.2	1.2	110	18	300
	12–14	44	97	154	61	2,300	55	5,000	400	20	45	0.4	15	1.4	1.2	1.6	5	1.3	1.3	115	18	350
	14–16	52	114	157	62	2,400	55	5,000	400	25	50	0.4	16	1.4	1.2	1.8	5	1.3	1.3	120	18	350
	16–18	54	119	160	63	2,300	55	5,000	400	25	50	0.4	15	1.5	1.2	2.0	5	1.3	1.3	115	18	350
	18–22	58	128	163	64	2,000	55	5,000	400	25	55	0.4	13	1.5	1.0	2.0	5	0.8	0.8	100	18	350
	22–35	58	128	163	64	2,000	55	5,000	–	25	55	0.4	13	1.5	1.0	2.0	5	0.8	0.8	100	18	300
	35–55	58	128	160	63	1,850	55	5,000	–	25	55	0.4	13	1.5	1.0	2.0	6	0.8	0.8	90	18	300
	55–75+	58	128	157	62	1,700	55	5,000	–	25	55	0.4	13	1.5	1.0	2.0	6	0.8	0.8	80	10	300
Pregnancy						+200	65	6,000	400	30	60	0.8	15	1.8	+0.1	2.5	8	+0.4	+0.4	125	18	450
Lactation						+1,000	75	8,000	400	30	60	0.5	20	2.0	+0.5	2.5	6	+0.5	+0.5	150	18	450

a. The allowance levels are intended to cover individual variations among most normal persons as they live in the United States under usual environmental stresses. The recommended allowances can be attained with a variety of common foods, providing other nutrients for which human requirements have been less well defined. See text for more-detailed discussion of allowances and of nutrients not tabulated.

b. Entries on lines for age range 22-35 years represent the reference man and woman at age 22. All other entries represent allowances for the midpoint of the specified age range.

c. The folacin allowances refer to dietary sources as determined by *Lactobacillus casei* assay. Pure forms of folacin may be effective in doses less than 1/4 of the RDA.

d. Niacin equivalents include dietary sources of the vitamin itself plus 1 mg equivalent for each 60 mg of dietary tryptophan.

e. Assumes protein equivalent to human milk. For proteins not 100 percent utilized factors should be increased proportionately.

carbohydrate (starchy) foods are fattening and avoid them turning to foods that actually contain more calories than the starchy foods do.

Not everyone needs the same amount of calories and this is evident if we check Table 4-1 where we see a wide variation depending upon weight, sex and age. Activity, climate and individual temperament also affect caloric needs. More energy is used in playing tennis than sitting at a desk and more heat is needed at the North Pole than in Hawaii. Nervous individuals usually require more calories than placid ones. A tall, thin individual, because of a greater body surface area, will lose more body heat than a compact, shorter one. He therefore needs more calories.

Carbohydrates

Carbohydrates are the body's main source of heat and energy. Rice, wheat and other cereals, sugars, dried legumes and potatoes are examples of foods high in carbohydrates. About 50 to 60% of our calories should come from carbohydrates. If this much is not consumed, the body takes protein or fat and converts them into energy and heat. Using proteins instead of carbohydrates not only raises the cost of the diet but may not be desirable for some individuals. If the body uses fat for heat and energy without having carbohydrate to burn with it, the fat is only partially metabolized and undesirable products called ketones build up in the body. If too much develops, an individual becomes ill from ketosis, goes into a coma and dies. Individuals under heavy reducing diets should always consume some carbohydrate each day to avoid running the danger of ketosis.

Complex carbohydrates such as starches and dextrins found in pasta, bread, potatoes, legumes and so forth are preferable in a normal diet to sugars and sweets. Many individuals, especially the aged, chronically ill and mentally disturbed, seem to handle complex carbohydrates better than the simple ones. Furthermore, we have evidence that a diet high in sugar may be harmful to some having high blood pressure, heart or other arterial malfunctions.

The Diabetic

Diabetes is a disease caused by a lack of insulin, a hormone manufactured in the pancreas. Insulin is needed in the body to metabolize carbohydrates. If insulin is taken as a medication, many diabetics can eat a normal diet.

In a diabetic diet, the amount of carbohydrate allowed is controlled and five meals rather than three a day may be given to spread the food intake over a longer period. Protein and fat are increased and these are utilized for heat and energy in place of carbohydrate. Severe diabetics are always in danger of running out of energy, fainting and then going into a coma which can end in death. If in a travel status, such as in an airplane, a diabetic should indicate to the stewardess his condition and also be sure to consume some food during long periods of travel. Even a carbonated beverage containing some sugar may be helpful in tiding one over.

Protein

Protein is needed to support growth and promote important body functions. Proteins contain substances called amino acids about 8 to 10 of which are needed to sustain life and promote growth. Animal substances such as meat, fish, poultry, cheese, milk and eggs contain these essential amino acids. Cereals, nuts and dried legumes contain good quantities of amino acids but not all the essential ones. Fresh fruits and vegetables may lack them both in quantity or quality.* A blend at the same meal of non-animal-source foods may give an adequate amount of essential amino acids. For instance, a meal of Boston brown bread and baked beans would give them, the bread containing enough of the essential amino acids the beans lack and the beans containing what the bread lacks. The people of India have done well for centuries on a diet of wheat which they eat as chapata (bread) along with a legume called dali.

From 10 to 15% of our total calories should come from protein; 40% of this protein should come from animal-source foods. A normal individual should have about 2½ ounces of protein per day. A pint of milk along with several servings of eggs, meat, fish, poultry or cheese combined with normal amounts of breads or cereals, vegetables and fruits easily give this. Table 4-1 indicates that different individuals may require different amounts of protein. Doing hard work does not increase our need for protein.

Fat

Salad oil, lard and hydrogenated fats are 100% fat; butter and margarine are 81%; some meats may be 20% or more fat and some other foods such as corn, nuts and avocados can be fairly high in fat. Since fats are high in calories, individuals wishing to reduce or not gain weight

* Soy beans contain a liberal supply of all essential amino acids.

should consume limited amounts. About 20% of the total calories in the diets should come from fats, but in this country the average is over 40%.

Fat is needed in the body to act as padding around the organs and to protect other parts of the body. It is also essential to some body functions. Linoleic acid, a fatty acid, is essential to growth and good body functioning. Some fats are also carriers of vitamins, cod liver oil being high in vitamins A and D.

The Cholesterol Problem

Some fats and oils, called saturated, may be restricted in the diet of some individuals because they contain cholesterol, a waxy substance that is frequently found clogging the arterial system of individuals having heart problems, high blood pressure or arteriosclerosis. Unsaturated fats and oils such as corn, safflower or peanut or fish oils may be allowed because they do not build up cholesterol. Fat beef, lamb or pork may be limited in the diet; poultry having a less saturated fat may be allowed in greater quantity and most fish will be allowed because its fat is usually unsaturated. Other items limited will be egg yolk, butter, some margarines and shellfish.*

Not everyone agrees that cholesterol alone is the problem. Some indicate that a substance made up of phosphorus and fats, called phospholipids, plus cholesterol, may be out of balance and thus cause the basic problem. Others doubt that diet can be effective in controlling cholesterol levels since the body can manufacture its own cholesterol. Nevertheless, the American Medical Association has recommended the restriction of saturated fats in diets of individuals having coronary or other related problems.

Vitamins

Vitamins are compounds that help carry on essential body functions. They are required in extremely small amounts but, if not present, life cannot be sustained or will function very poorly.

Vitamin A

We started to name our vitamins as we discovered them by alphabetical order and, thus, vitamin A was the first discovered. It is a fat-

---

* An unsaturated fat contains the same amount of calories per gram as a saturated one; thus, in a diet that must limit calories as well as saturated fats, the allowance of unsaturated fats may also have to be restricted.

soluble vitamin needed to promote good body tissue health, to ward off infections especially in the mucous membrane tracts and to aid in building teeth and bones. It also prevents the formation of a rough, hard skin. Individuals who lack vitamin A develop night blindness. Xerophthalmia, a dryness of the eye that can end in blindness, is caused by a lack of vitamin A.

Vitamin A is plentiful in fish liver oils, liver, cream, egg yolk and butter. It is added to margarine and some milk products. Yellow or orange fruits and vegetables and green vegetables contain a pigment called carotene. This can be changed in the body to vitamin A. Too much vitamin A can be absorbed in the body and so overdoses of it should be avoided. A good source of vitamin A should be consumed every other day. Investigations have shown that vitamin A is a nutrient that is commonly lacking in many diets.

The B-vitamin Complex

The first vitamin B discovered was not sufficiently refined to indicate that it was a blend of vitamins. Later when this was known, the various parts were sublabeled B_1, B_2, etc. In this B-group we have thiamine, riboflavin, niacin, pyridoxine, folic acid, pantothenic acid, biotin, choline and vitamin B_{12}. All are water soluble so they can be lost easily from the body in excreted body fluids. They should be consumed daily in adequate amounts to keep up a desirable supply. Being water soluble they are easily leached out in soaking or cooking water. In most kitchens we recommend that the cooking water of vegetables be used in making gravies, soups or added to stock pots where stock is being made. Similarly, the liquor of canned vegetables should be retained and used.

Thiamin (B_1) is needed for the metabolism of carbohydrates. It is also concerned with the proper maintenance of the body's nervous system. Beriberi, a disease of the nervous system, is caused by a lack of thiamine. Good sources are whole grain or enriched cereals, meats (especially liver and pork), legumes, nuts, milk and yeast. Thiamine is easily destroyed by heat especially in an alkaline medium. This is why we avoid adding soda to speed the cooking of legumes and to keep green vegetables green.

Riboflavin (B_2) is needed to utilize other nutrients in the body cells. A lack of the vitamin is indicated by skin lesions or a redness and soreness around the corners of the eyes and mouth and around the eyelids. Riboflavin is water soluble and easily leached from foods. The drip of frozen meat contains a high amount of this plus other water-soluble B vitamins. Riboflavin is easily destroyed by sunlight. It is found in enriched or whole grain cereals, milk and meats. Thiamine and riboflavin are two nutrients often lacking in diets.

Niacin is important to many metabolic functions of the body. It is plentiful in meat, nuts, cereals and yeast. Tryptophan is an amino acid the body converts to niacin and so foods rich in this substance such as milk and dairy products can be good sources of niacin. Since niacin is rather widely distributed among foods, it is usually not lacking in most diets. The diet of southern people in the United States, consisting largely of cornbread, boiled turnip greens and side pork, may be giving rise to a disease called pellagra which is an evidence of the lack of niacin. Niacin is a fairly stable vitamin but is water soluble.

Most of the other B vitamins are common in plants and animal foods and so are usually sufficiently plentiful in most diets. Pyridoxine (B_6) is important in promoting good protein utilization in the body and is needed to convert tryptophan to niacin. It also appears to be important in the metabolization of some fats. Folic acid is plentiful in leafy or green vegetables as well as legumes. It helps to make blood in the body. A lack of it can cause anemia which is a lack of red corpuscles in the blood. Pantothenic acid is important in cell functioning and the operation of some of the body enzyme systems. Choline is essential but the part it plays in the body is not completely understood.

Vitamin C (Ascorbic Acid)

Scurvy is a disease caused by the lack of vitamin C. Scurvy is evidenced by the swelling of muscles, inflamed gums, loose teeth and the poor healing of wounds. Tiny lesions can also appear under the skin because the capillary structures are weakened. Vitamin C is also important in the formation of bone material, the functioning of the adrenal glands and in the utilization of some of the amino acids in the body. Many individuals lack vitamin C in their diets. The vitamin is plentiful in citrus fruits, tomatoes, berries, cabbage and potatoes. It is also found in fair amounts in most fresh fruits and vegetables. It is water soluble and easily oxidized. Therefore, a significant amount would be lost if the vegetable or fruit were chopped and allowed to stand where air could strike the cut surface or if placed in water where it could be leached out. It is destroyed when it comes in contact with an alkaline substance especially in the presence of heat. This is another reason why we never use soda to keep green vegetables from losing their color when we cook them. We should have one serving of a good source of ascorbic acid a day. Six ounces of orange, grapefruit or tomato juice or one serving of tomatoes, cabbage or two of potatoes per day plus other fruits and vegetables will meet the requirement.

Fat-Soluble Vitamins

Vitamin D assists in metabolizing calcium and phosphorus in the body and therefore is important for the formation of bones and teeth and their maintenance. Children lacking the vitamin develop rickets which is sometimes indicated by bowed legs and malformed bones. Sunlight striking fat just below the skin manufactures vitamin D or, if fat is exposed to ultraviolet rays, the vitamin will be made. Black or dark people manufacture less from the sun's rays than white. Vitamin D is plentiful in eggs, dairy products, organ meats, cod liver oil and fat fish. We may add it to milk, margarine and other foods. The quantity required for the ordinary person is small but women during pregnancy and lactation and rapidly growing children require somewhat larger amounts than others. Some authorities think vitamin D is more a hormone than a vitamin. Vitamins E and K are two fat-soluble vitamins we use. Vitamin E is thought to have something to do with body functions and may be involved in arterial functions but we are not sure of this. It is an antioxidant and may be important in the body for this reason. It is important to the fertility of rats. Vitamin E is found in cereal oils, vegetable oils and fruits. Vitamin K is important in blood clotting and can probably be manufactured by human beings in the intestinal tract.

Minerals

Many minerals are water soluble and can be easily lost by soaking or cooking foods in water. Some minerals are rendered ineffective in an acid or alkaline medium; some other compounds are antagonistic to minerals, making them unavailable for absorption. For instance, it is doubtful if the calcium is spinach is utilized because other compounds in spinach interfere with its availability. Minerals are in all plant and animal foods. They may be concentrated in certain areas in fruits and vegetables. Deep paring of potatoes loses much of their iron and vitamin C since they are concentrated under the skin. An apple's magnesium is largely around the core.

Calcium and Phosphorus

Teeth and bones require calcium and phosphorus. These minerals are also needed to maintain a proper acid-alkaline balance in the body.

Both may be needed for good muscle and cell functioning. Phosphorus may be important in nerve-cell functioning. Both are plentiful in milk; two cups a day usually meets the adult requirement for them. Phosphorus is also plentiful in cereals. Most diets do not lack this element. Calcium is found in many fruits and vegetables but if milk is not in the diet it is difficult to get enough to satisfy the body's calcium needs.

Iron and Copper

The red corpuscles of the blood need iron and copper for their formation. Meats, eggs, brans, whole-grain cereals, leafy green vegetables, legumes and dried fruits are good sources of iron and some contain some copper. Copper is found in many foods, so the 2-mg per day requirement is not hard to get. Most individuals need from 10 to 15 mg of iron a day but the body probably absorbs less. Growing children and menstruating or pregnant women need more than others. Anyone having an operation or a loss of blood should get additional iron. Iron is a nutrient commonly lacking in many diets.

Iodine and Fluorine

The thyroid gland needs iodine to produce the body hormone, thyroxine, which regulates the release of energy in the body. It is also needed for normal growth. Individuals lacking iodine may have an enlarged thyroid gland called a goiter. The water in the northern states from Ohio to the Pacific lacks iodine needed to prevent goiter. For this reason the region is called the "goiter belt." Shellfish and seafish contain plentiful amounts of iodine. If iodized salt is used, individuals also secure enough. In areas where iodine is plentiful in the soil, plants will contain enough for the normal individual's needs.

Potassium and Sodium

Sodium is important in body cell and fluid functions as is potassium which is also used in muscle contraction and enzyme operation. Both are important in maintaining a proper acid-base balance in the body. Some people with high blood pressure, edema, kidney or other problems may have to limit sodium in their diet. Since table salt contains sodium, it is usually limited. In strict sodium-free diets some foods high in sodium such as carrots, beets and other root vegetables may be taboo. An individual on a 2500-mg per day sodium diet can have lightly salted foods but no additional salt. Potato chips, olives, sauerkraut, cured meat, catsup, chili sauce and other salty foods are avoided. Similarly, medications such as alkalizers, sweeteners with sodium, the seasoning monosodium glutamate and others are not allowed. Hard water, high in sodium, may be restricted. Some may take drugs that are diuretics. In the moisture loss that occurs from these, an excessive amount of potassium may be lost from the body. For this reason, individuals on diuretics may have to consume larger amounts of orange juice, meats, bananas and other foods high in the element.

Trace Minerals

Chlorine, magnesium, sulfur, cobalt, zinc, managanese, molybdenum, selenium, chromium and some other minerals are found in trace amounts in the body. We have evidence that some of these are there for a purpose but for others we are not sure. Insulin contains zinc, cobalt is in vitamin B_{12} and sulfur is in thiamine, in the muscle cells and in some essential amino acids. Chlorine is found in many body substances.

Alcohol

The calories in an ounce of 86-proof spirits is about equal to its proof. Thus, an ounce of 100-proof spirits contains about 100 calories. Proof is always twice the percent of alcohol. A 100-proof spirit is 50% alcohol. An ounce is 28 grams, so there are 14 grams of alcohol in a 100-proof ounce. This 14 multiplied by seven, the Calories in pure alcohol, gives 98 Calories. In a 4-ounce portion of 12% dry dinner wine, the calories per ounce would be calculated: $4 \times 28 \times .12 \times 7 =$ 94.08 which with the other calories in it would probably bring it close to 100 Calories per ounce. Sweet, fortified wines such as sherry or port are about 20% alcohol and have a fairly large amount of sugar. They have twice the Calories of dry wines. A 12-ounce portion of beer or ale has around 175 Calories.

Water

About 6 to 8 glasses of ꜒ater are required by an individual a day since this is needed to carry on essential body functions. Many chemical reactions in the body occur in the fluids. The body manufactures water when it burns carbohydrates and uses it. It also reuses water. Water is lost in exhaled air, sweat and evaporation from the body, urine and in the feces. In some areas, calcium and other minerals in the water are used by the body. Distilled water may have to be used by some individuals on low-sodium diets if they live in a hard water area.

Bulk or Residue

Bulk is needed in food to promote digestion and assist in eliminating the feces. It is largely cellulose, an undigestible carbohydrate for humans but utilizable for ruminants such as cows, deer, rabbits, etc. Cellulose is the fiber in fruits and vegetables. The bran of cereals is largely cellulose. If we lack bulk in our digestive system, the food is too concentrated and absorption is hampered. Movement of the food through the digestive tract is also retarded. Some with colitis, an irritation of the lower intestine, or other digestive problems may have to reduce bulk in the diet and consume more refined foods.

The Acid-Base Balance

Some foods have an acid reaction in the body and others an alkaline one. To maintain an almost perfect neutrality, the body uses either alkaline or acid reserves to counteract the acidity or alkalinity of foods. Also, certain body reactions promote acid or alkaline residues and the body uses its alkaline or acid reserves to neutralize them. Proteins, quinic acid in cranberries, phosphorus, chlorine or other acid-associated minerals are acid in the body. Carbon dioxide, produced in burning carbohydrates, is absorbed by water in the body becoming a mild acid called carbonic acid (H_2CO_3). Likewise, other acid substances are formed such as uric acid, urea, etc. Oddly, lemon juice and many other fruit acids become alkaline in the body. Calcium, sodium and other base-associated minerals give an alkaline reaction in the body. The body stores acid and alkaline substances as reserves so when needed it uses them to keep a neutral balance. The body also uses buffers to neutralize acids and alkalies. Proteins and some chemical substances such as phosphates or carbonates can absorb either alkaline or acid substances preventing them from displaying their chemical characteristics.

Individuals with ketosis or uremic poisoning from kidney malfunctioning may have to avoid some foods but most normal individuals will find their bodies perfectly capable of maintaining a perfect acid-base balance. Attempting to influence the body's acid or base balance should be done *only upon medical recommendation.*

Empty Calories and Food Fads

An individual can be poorly nourished even though he eats a lot of food and gains weight. Such a diet is often called an "empty calorie" diet because, while many calories are consumed, few other nutrients are. Teenagers eating a lot of potato chips, hamburgers or hot dogs, sweets and carbonated beverages, omitting milk, eggs, fruits, vegetables and other protective foods, are on just such a diet. Others who eat too rich foods or consume too many calories in alcohol do the same thing. And, while such individuals may not immediately show the effects of their diet, in the long run they will. Individuals eating such a diet lack stamina and vigor and are more susceptible to attack from disease. Their physiques and appearance are also adversely affected. Older individuals will age more quickly and begin to have a number of illnesses.

Many millions of dollars are wasted each year by individuals who purchase vitamin pills or diet foods. The body absorbs only so many nutrients and an excess is usually eliminated. Therefore, any more nutrients than a well balanced diet offers do little good. Harm can be done by an excess of some nutrients; individuals have died from massive doses of Vitamin A. A great deal of harm and misinformation comes from individuals who claim to be authorities in nutrition but are not. Before an individual's advice on diet is taken, the competency of that individual to give such advice should be known.

Undoubtedly, some food additives and sprays, fertilizers or drugs that encourage rapid growth in animals or plants or protect them from disease are harmful to humans. A more aggressive program to prevent contamination of our foods should be sought by the foodservice industry so that our food supply, the best in the world, remains that way. The trend today toward "organic" foods is perhaps based on the fact that some of our foods are contaminated and lack the nutrients they should. With many individuals, however, the eating of organic foods is a fad and is allowing others to profit by their ignorance. As far as we know, the iron absorbed by a plant from a commercial fertilizer is as nutritious as the iron a plant absorbs from natural organic fertilizers. As far as we know, whole ground cereals contribute no more nutrients than enriched refined ones. Raw sugar does contribute some iron and other nutrients that refined sugar does not but, as far as we know, there is no other difference in them. Very frequently items for sale in a natural food store come from the very same stock as those on a supermarket shelves. Many times these items are higher in price. Others are lower in quality and of doubtful sanitary value, especially bulk packs. And, while the trend toward natural foods may in some respects be desirable, the excesses to which some are going are a waste of money, doing little good and, in some instances, doing harm.

Suggested laboratory experiences or work assignments for Chapter 4:

1. Using Table 4-1 plan a menu for a day that includes all the foods you need. How many calories do you get?

2. Study the menu of a commercial operation to see if an individual could select a balanced breakfast, lunch and dinner from it. Could a diabetic get a meal low in carbohydrates?
3. Plan a vegetarian menu considered balanced, using milk and eggs for the required calcium and animal-source protein.
4. Plan a talk to give to the employees of a foodservice on procedures to use in quantity production to reduce nutrient losses in the handling, preparation and serving of food.

BIBLIOGRAPHY

Cooper, L. F., et al., *Nutrition in Health and Disease,* Lippincott, Philadelphia, Pa., 1963.
Proudfit, F. T. and Robinson, C. H., *Normal and Therapeutic Nutrition,* The Macmillan Co., New York City, 10011, 1961.
Turner, D., *Handbook of Diet Therapy,* 4th ed., American Dietetic Association, 610 N. Michigan, Chicago, 1965.

5

Cooking and Heat

Cooking changes food, making it more acceptable. Cooking is performed in different ways such as boiling, steaming, broiling, frying, barbecueing or roasting. Cooking softens or firms food, changing its texture, color, form and flavor. It also sanitizes it. It can make food more or less digestible. To apply the science and art of cooking, we must know a lot about heat and how it affects food. We must also learn to use and control it.

Heat

Heat is developed by 1) friction, or 2) chemical or 3) physical change. The friction from contacting particles of matter develops heat. A fire can start from rubbing two sticks of wood together. Molecules of gas forced together in compression bump into each other so much before they come to equilibrium that heat is formed. Slowing the flow of electrons in an electrical element develops a great amount of friction and thereby heat. Dielectric heat results when electricity is directed into food which resists the flow of electricity just as an electrical element does forming heat.

When carbon and hydrogen combine chemically with oxygen, they give off heat. This is seen in burning wood. Steel combining with oxygen rusts but, if we ignite steel wool with a match, so much heat is developed that the steel wool flames. Combustion is a process in which heat develops so rapidly a flame results. The temperature at which something takes fire is called the "ignition" or "flash" point. Cooking oils and fats are almost pure hydrogen and carbon having a flash point around 600° F.

Physical change in matter causes heat. The sun is a seething mass of matter undergoing physical change. This generates terrific electro-magnetic energy, a part of which is heat. So much energy is developed that what the sun sends the earth in 45 hours is more than we have in all our reserves of gas, coal or oil. Much of the sun's energy is in the form of infra-red waves which are closely related to light waves. Infra-red also moves with the speed of light, 186,000 miles per second. It takes only a few seconds for the heat of the sun to reach the earth. Infra-red waves pass easily through glass and quartz but are stopped by metals. We have been able to concentrate the sun's heat here on earth to develop temperatures as high as 6300° F. Some authorities predict that by 2060 the sun's rays will be delivering 40% of our required energy with the atom delivering much of the balance.

Heating and Cooking

Heat does many things in cooking. It swells starch in the presence of moisture causing thickening. This gelatinization or swelling starts in cornstarch around 150° F and ends around 203° F. Proteins denaturate (lose moisture) around 140° F and coagulate around 160° F. Coag-ulation is a process in which the protein becomes firmer. A color change may occur as happens when an egg coagulates. Heat plus moisture changes collagen, the white connective tissue in meat, into water and gelatin. Heat plus acid breaks down a thickened starch mixture making it thin. Baking powder or soda when moistened and heated develops carbon dioxide gas which leavens bakery items. Cellulose, pectins and other fibrous products in fruits and vegetables are softened by heat and moisture.

Heat must be controlled to achieve desired results in cooking. Too much heat burns or scorches food while too little leaves it raw and underdone. An eclair results only if we use a lot of heat at the start to get rapid expansion from steam, then lower the temperature to achieve complete baking. Heat must be adjusted in bakery goods to get the proper gelatinization of starch and the coagulation of protein at the same time that we get maximum expansion from the leavening agent. A sugar solution must be cooked to a certain temperature if one wishes it to crystallize after cooling.

How Much Heat?

Temperature is an indicator of the level or intensity of heat. It does not tell us how much heat there is. In cooking we use the Fahrenheit scale where water freezes at 32° F and boils at 212° F. Many countries and scientists use the Centigrade scale where water freezes at 0° C and boils at 100° C. Thus, there are 180° from freezing to boiling in Fahrenheit and 100° for Centigrade. Therefore, a degree of Centigrade equals 9/5 (180/100) of a Fahrenheit degree and a Fahrenheit degree is 5/9 (100/180) of a Centigrade degree. To change Fahrenheit to Centigrade, subtract 32° from the Fahrenheit temperature and multiply by 5/9. To change Centigrade to Fahrenheit multiply the Centigrade temperature by 9/5 and add 32°. For instance, to change 182° F to Centigrade: 182 − 32 = 150 × 5/9 = 83.5° C and to change 75° C to Fahrenheit: 75 × 9/5 = 135 + 32 = 167° F.

Table 5-1. Equivalent Fahrenheit and Centigrade Degrees

Fahrenheit	Centigrade	Fahrenheit	Centigrade	Fahrenheit	Centigrade
0	-17.8	60	15.6	120	48.9
10	-12.2	65	18.3	150	65.6
15	-9.4	70	21.1	200	93.3
20	-6.7	75	23.9	212	100.0
32	0	80	26.7	250	121.1
35	1.7	85	29.4	300	148.9
40	4.4	90	32.2	350	176.7
45	7.2	95	35.0	400	204.4
50	10.0	100	37.8	450	232.2
55	12.8	110	43.3	500	260.0

Rule: Fahrenheit to Centigrade: Subtract 32 from Fahrenheit degrees and multiply the remainder by 5/9; product is centigrade degrees.
Centigrade to Fahrenheit: Multiply centigrade degrees by 9/5 and add 32; product is Fahrenheit degrees.

Heat and Expansion

Many things expand when heated. Fill a pot full of cold water and heat it; it runs over because the water expands on heating. Alcohol and mercury expand also when heated. Put a small quantity of colored alcohol or mercury into a glass thermometer and, as the temperature rises, the liquid rises and, as the temperature drops, the liquid falls. Dividing the spaces on this thermometer from freezing to boiling water into 180 or 100 even units gives either a Fahrenheit or Centigrade thermometer. Metals also expand or contract as temperatures change and different metals expand at different rates. For instance, aluminum expands more than brass. If we cement aluminum and brass tightly together, they will bend when the temperature varies because one expands more than the other. This phenomena is used to make a thermostat. Figure 5-1 shows how a thermostat makes or breaks an electrical contact. A dial thermometer used in cooking or on a refrigerator is made by putting a coil of two bound metals with different expansion rates into a metal tube. The coil, attached at right angles to a small pointer, moves the dial as the coil twists from expansion or contraction.

Heat Transfer

Heat is transferred by conduction, convection or radiation. Conducted heat moves from one particle of matter to another. It moves faster in solids than liquids and most slowly in gas. We capture air, a gas, in plastic foam to make an insulated hot cup or use cork, urethane or fiber glass which holds a lot of air to insulate ovens or refrigerators. The best heat conductor is copper, then aluminum, iron, silver and chromium in that order. Stainless steel is a very poor heat conductor and we put copper on the bottom of a stainless steel pan to get heat evenly through it. We also can put a thin layer of iron between two sheets of stainless steel so the iron core spreads heat out evenly. If we cook in a stainless steel pan, "hot spots" develop and the food sticks there and scorches. Stainless steel's inability to transfer heat makes it buckle and discolor when a high amount of heat is applied to it. Glass is a poor conductor of heat. It shatters when a great deal of heat strikes it, because the part near the heat expands faster than the other parts. We can help glass conduct heat by blending metals into it. Sodium-aluminum-borosilicate is contained in glass dishes used for cooking.

Convection occurs by physically moving heated matter from one place to another. A fan in a convection oven blows hot air around the

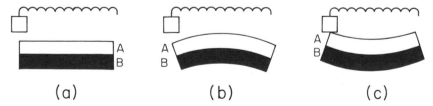

Figure 5–1. Metal A expands more than B as heat varies. B pulls A downward in (b) because A expands more than B when both are warm. A contracts more than B when they are cool bending them upward to make contact with the electrical point as shown in (c). When the temperature rises sufficiently B pulls A downward breaking the contact. At (a) both metals are at equilibrium.

Table 5-2.   Approximate conversions from customary to metric and vice versa

	When you know	You can find:	If you multiply by:
Length	inches	millimeters	25
	feet	centimeters	30
	yards	meters	0.9
	miles	kilometers	1.6
	millimeters	inches	0.04
	centimeters	inches	0.4
	meters	yards	1.1
	kilometers	miles	0.6
Area	square inches	square centimeters	6.5
	square feet	square meters	0.09
	square yards	square meters	0.8
	square miles	square kilometers	2.6
	acres	square hectometers (hectares)	0.4
	square centimeters	square inches	0.16
	square meters	square yards	1.2
	square kilometers	square miles	0.4
	square hectometers (hectares)	acres	2.5
Mass	ounces	grams	28
	pounds	kilograms	0.45
	short tons	megagrams (metric tons)	0.9
	grams	ounces	0.035
	kilograms	pounds	2.2
	megagrams (metric tons)	short tons	1.1
Liquid volume	ounces	milliliters	30
	pints	liters	0.47
	quarts	liters	0.95
	gallons	liters	3.8
	milliliters	ounces	0.034
	liters	pints	2.1
	liters	quarts	1.06
	liters	gallons	0.26
Temperature	degrees Fahrenheit	degrees Celsius	5/9 (after subtracting 32)
	degrees Celsius	degrees Fahrenheit	9/5 (then add 32)

U.S. Dept. of Commerce

interior. Warm air will rise and cool air fall. This natural convection occurs in regular ovens and other cooking units. Heated gases rise by convection and escape on their own in a chimney.

Radiated heat as used in conventional cooking is largely infrared waves coming from glowing heat such as charcoal, an electrical element or gas flame. It is used for toasting or broiling. All hot substances will radiate some heat even though they do not glow. Heat radiates best from a dark, rough-textured surface and next best from a lighter, rough-textured surface until we get to an all-white one. A smooth surface radiates less heat than a rough one; authorities say that texture seems to be more important than color in radiating heat. A bright shiny surface radiates heat poorly; bright aluminum foil turned outward helps keep heat inside. Heat is absorbed better on a dark surface than a light one. Lampblack absorbs about 97% of the heat striking it. Bright pans reflect heat away more than dark ones do. For this reason, frozen food to be heated in its pan now comes in aluminum pans with darkened outsides.

Microwaves are radiated energy. They have longer wave lengths than infrared waves and are manufactured usually in a cathode tube. These waves penetrate food disturbing the molecular structure, causing friction sometimes called a kinetic action, developing heat that cooks food.

Color and Heat

Heat has different colors at different temperatures. A flame will be almost red at 900° to 1100°F, dark red 1100° to 1500°F, bright red 1500°F to 1800° F, yellowish red 1800° to 2200° F and white over 2200° F. The sun and stars reflect a white heat; the surface of the sun is presumed to be around 6000° C but much hotter inside. A yellow gas flame is wasting fuel and may be sooting up equipment because some carbon is not being burned. It should be a bluish white. Some new char-broilers have special ceramic units that heat up to an almost white heat intensity.

Quantitative Heat Measurement

Temperature indicates the *quality* of heat. The *quantity* is indicated by British thermal units (Btu's) or calories. A Btu is the heat needed to raise a pound of water 1° F and a calorie is the amount of heat needed to raise 1 cc of water 1° C. A pound of the following fuels gives these Btu's when they burn: fuel oil 19,000, kilowatt hour (kwh) of electricity 3416, coal 14,000 and a cubic foot of natural gas 1000 or of propane gas 3200. If all the heat in a kwh went into 12 gallons of water (100 pounds), the water would rise 34.16° F or, if all the heat in a cubic foot of gas went into this water, it would cause a rise of 10° F. It is estimated it takes 1150 Btu's of heat to cook an average meal.

Not all the heat in fuel is captured in cooking. A lot is lost from the equipment, exhausting fumes or from the food itself. About 50% is usually estimated to cook food while the rest is lost. Gas, coal and fuel oil lose more heat than electricity in cooking because about 40% is lost in exhausting fumes. It takes 1.6 times more gas Btu's to equal those of electricity in cooking. Thus, to equal a kwh we need 5466 Btu's of gas (3416 × 1.6 = 5466). Since a cubic foot of gas yields 1000 Btu's, 5.5 cubic feet of natural gas equals 1 kwh of electricity. If electricity sells for 2¢ per kwh, gas to be competitive would have to sell for about 0.364¢ per cubic foot (2¢ ÷ 5.5 = 0.364¢) or $3.64 per 100 cu ft of gas, the way gas is sold.

Specific Heat

The quantity of heat an object can hold is called *specific heat*. The amount of heat water holds is given a value of one and this is a standard for measuring heat in all other things. Thus, fresh peas have a specific heat of 0.79, frozen peas 0.42, fat 0.5, copper 0.092, aluminum 0.22, tin 0.054 and iron 0.11. Using the same quantity of heat for both, 100 grams of iron becomes nine times hotter than 100 grams of water (1.00 ÷ 0.11 = 9). An aluminum steam-jacketed kettle weighing 200 pounds and filled with 30 gallons of stock (total 450 pounds) would take 45,158 Btu's to heat both from 55° to 212° F.* Without considering heat loss, about 13.35 kwh of electricity is needed for this. If it costs 2¢ per kwh and only 50% is lost in cooking, the final cost would be about 53.4¢. If gas were used, we would need 45.1 cu ft of gas to raise the 440 pounds to 212° F and if only 50% of this were used to cook the food, the cost would be about the same as with electricity: 45.6 × 0.364¢ × 1.6 = 26.56¢ × 2 = 52.5¢, a negligible difference.

Heat and the Change of State

At absolute zero which is no heat at all (−460° F) all molecular motion stops. As heat increases, molecular motion does. Solids turn to liquids when molecules move so fast they break from their bonds and move freely about. Some bonding remains but not nearly as much. This bonding or pull that holds liquids together at the surface is called *surface tension*. An inner pull occurs at the surface creating a slight "skin". This is why a drop of water stays a sphere on glass. Oil and vinegar do not mix because both have too much pull to allow blending. A detergent reduces surface tension so water wets dirt and aids in cleaning. An emulsifier breaks the antagonism of vinegar and oil and allows us to make a permanent emulsion.

A solid, to become a liquid, must absorb heat, while liquid, to be-

---

* 212° − 55° = 157°; 200 lb × .22 × 157° = 6908 plus 250 × 1 × 157° = 39,250; 6908 + 39,250 = 45,158.

come a solid, gives off heat. A gram of water at 32° F gives off 80 calories in freezing. When a gram of ice melts, it needs 80 calories to do it. We call this *heat of fusion.* A fondant sirup slightly thins and becomes shiny just before crystallizing. This heat given off in turning to a solid is sufficient to cause a slight thinning and shininess. Different liquids change to solids at different temperatures. Alcohol freezes at −114.6° F and olive oil becomes a solid at around 40° F. We can change the temperature at which a liquid or solid makes a change of state. Ice and salt melt at −4° F (−20° C). An ice cream mix containing sugar and other substances freezes at 24° F and not at 32° F. Potatoes and other foods freeze at slightly below 32° F because they contain substances that lower the freezing point. A potato stored below 50° F develops sugar which lowers its freezing point. (This sugar makes it a poor cooking potato.) A parsnip is left in the ground until after a sharp frost, as it is sweeter because the chilling makes it develop some of its starch into sugar. Dry onions are sweeter if refrigerated. Adding substances to liquids raises their boiling points. If vigorously boiling water has salt added to it, it stops boiling. Adding sugar to water increases its boiling point as we note in cooking sugar products.

Liquids change to a gas when heat makes their molecules vibrate so fast they spin out of the liquid. We call this boiling if it happens at a rapid rate. Boiling takes place only when the internal energy equals the external energy pressing on the liquid. This external energy is called *atmospheric pressure.* Reducing the external pressure lowers the boiling point; water boils at 180° F on Pike's Peak, Colorado, which is 14,000 feet above sea level and the atmospheric pressure is 7 psi. It takes longer to boil potatoes and other foods at this level and so we usually have to cook them in pressure steamers to get them done. Water boils at 100° F under 1 psi and ice at 32° F will sublimate* if it is at 0.1 psi which is a vacuum. Conversely, increasing pressure raises the boiling point. At 18 psi (18 pounds above normal atmospheric pressure) water boils at about 254° F. Today we have a method of asceptically canning foods at 18 psi which eliminates cooking the food in steam pressure retorts. Sometimes this method is called "Flash-18."

Air becomes liquid at −141° C under 37 atmospheres (37 × 14.7) of pressure and oxygen becomes a liquid at −119° C and 50 atmospheres. Nitrogen liquifies at −147° C at 33 atmospheres. Liquid nitrogen is so cold it freezes foods almost instantly. A fresh tomato frozen by liquid nitrogen can be thawed and sliced because the freezing is so fast the ice crystals do not expand and rupture the tomato's cellular

---

* Sublimation is the changing of a solid to a gas without ever becoming a liquid.

structure. The gas refrigerants, sulfur dioxide and ammonia, can be made into liquids respectively at 14° and −28.3° F. In a refrigerator compressor this is done at even higher temperatures.

It takes heat to change a liquid to a gas. This is called the heat of *vaporization*. At sea level, water at 212° F must absorb 972 Btu's per pound (572 calories/gram) to change to steam at 212° F. A gas condensing to a liquid gives off heat, therefore steam in condensing on food gives off this extra heat of vaporization plus the heat it holds as a hot liquid. When we put steam under pressure, it absorbs more heat. Steam under pressure cooks more quickly because it has this extra heat plus the heat of vaporization and the heat needed to raise it to a boiling temperature.

Refrigeration

The following calories are needed per gram to expand from a liquid to a gas: freon 44, carbon dioxide 75, sulfur dioxide 100 and ammonia 325. These gases in a refrigerator take this heat from the refrigerator, the air or the food. The gas is then carried to a compressor outside the refrigerator where a pump compresses it back to a liquid. This compression develops heat which is removed in the compressor coils by water or by air circulated by a fan. The liquid is then returned to the refrigerator where it can expand and absorb more heat.

Evaporation

Evaporation is the slow vaporization of a liquid. Molecules move very rapidly even in cold liquids and from time to time leap from the surface where air picks them up and moves them away. It takes some heat to do this. A gram of water takes 80 calories to evaporate, the same as required for water to become steam. Sweat as it evaporates from our bodies takes body heat to change to a vapor and thus cools us down. Alcohol rubbed on the arm is cooling because it evaporates fast taking heat from the arm to do this.

If the rate of return of a vapor to a liquid is as great as its escape, an item will not dry out. Thus, a moisture-vapor proof wrap which will not let moisture escape sets up a state of equilibrium around the item so moisture returns to the product as fast as it leaps out.

Distillation is a method of creating vapor by boiling, then cooling so condensate can be collected. Alcohol boils at a lower temperature than water and so we can separate them. In a fermented liquid we boil the alcohol away before the water boils separating them in the process.

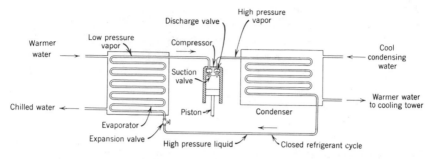

Figure 5–2. The diagram for a refrigerating system that cools water. A refrigerant liquid in the condenser moves as a high pressure liquid through the expansion valve into the evaporater where it turns into a gas. To do this it needs heat which it takes from the water flowing around the condenser coils. (Note where warm water flows in and chilled water flows out.) This low pressure gas now moves to the compressor where a piston puts pressure on it forcing it into a liquid again. The hot liquid now flows as a high pressure vapor into the condenser where cool condensing water flows around coils extracting the heat in the liquid caused by compressing it from a gas in the compressor. The warm water flows out and up to a cooling tower where air carries away the heat. This water is then returned to the condenser to cool again. In the meantime, the cooled liquid moves into the closed refrigerant cycle to start the cooling process all over again.

Some esters and other aromatic substances are volatile at the same temperature as alcohol and so come off with the distillate, giving it a special flavor. This is why some brandies and other distilled items have distinctive flavors.

Solids can evaporate by a process called *sublimation*, a condition of a solid turning to a vapor without forming a liquid in between. Freeze-drying is a process of sublimation in which ice crystals boil in a frozen food until most of the moisture is extracted. To make the ice boil, food is frozen, put into a chamber and a vacuum is pulled until the vapor pressure is less than 0.1 psi. Enough heat must be provided to change the ice to a vapor (heat of fusion and vaporization). It is necessary to remove the vapor as fast as it is formed so that a state of equilibrium does not form.

Sometimes frozen foods in moisture-vapor wraps build up ice crystals inside the wrap. This occurs because temperatures fluctuate. When temperatures are up, vapor forms inside the wrap, and when they drop, this vapor condenses and freezes forming ice. This harms food quality. When this happens, frozen meats and some other foods develop "freezer burn," a dry, white, pulpy condition on the surface of food that even after cooking does not return the food to an acceptable condition. A fluctuating temperature on other crystalline substances also is harmful because it changes fine crystals to coarse ones. This can happen in ice cream, fondants and frostings. Holding frozen foods at $-10°$ F and not allowing the temperatures to fluctuate delays coarse crystal growth.

Humidity

Air can hold a certain quantity of moisture. If it contains too much, it rains. This occurs at *absolute humidity* which is the maximum amount of moisture that air can hold at that temperature. Cold air holds less moisture than warm air. Warm air picking up moisture can lose it when it rises into cold regions and rain or snow occurs. A cold front meeting warm moist air brings thunder showers or snow. Moisture in air condensing on the cool sides of a glass can form beads of water on the sides. *Relative humidity* means the quantity of moisture air has in it at a specific temperature compared to its total ability to hold moisture at that temperature (absolute humidity). If we say "50% relative humidity," it means that 50% of the moisture the air *could* hold is in it. When we cook sugar solutions, we must correct for the amount of moisture in the air if the relative humidity is high.

pH

Slight differences in alkalinity or acidity in food or the cooking medium can cause major differences in cooking results. For instance, many color pigments in vegetables are changed by a slight difference between alkalinity to acidity or vice versa. Myoglobin, the color pigment in meat, changes at a lower temperature to hematin, the color of cooked meat if the meat is slightly acid. Legumes cook much more quickly in an alkaline medium than in an acid one. A pH of 3.1 to 3.6 is needed to make a good jelly, under 3.1 making a tough jel and over 3.6 making too soft a one.

Alkalinity or acidity is indicated frequently by the symbol *pH*. A number indicates whether the item is alkaline or acid and the degree of either. Neutral is 7 and the strongest alkali is indicated by 14 and the strongest acid by 0. There is a ten-fold increase in acidity from pH 7 to pH 6 and a 10,000,000-fold increase from pH 7 to pH 0. A change of pH 4 to pH 6 is 100 times less acid and to pH 7 1000 times less. Some pH's of substances found in the kitchen are:

Mild hand soap	9.0	Tomato juice	4.3
Strong soap	11.0 — 13.0	Bananas, beets	4.8
Deteriorated egg	7.5	Some vinegars	3.0
Soda cracker	7.8	Lemon or lime juice	2.0
Ripe olives	7.6	Good bread	5.0 — 5.4
Egg white	7.2	Destroys rope	4.6
Meat	6.9 — 7.0	Some fruit cakes	6.4
Distilled water	7.0	Fresh milk	6.8

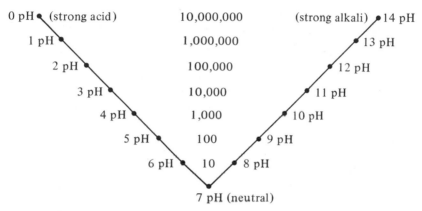

Figure 5–3. A diagram showing variations in pH: 7 is neutral and anything less is acid and anything more is alkaline. The figures in the center indicate gradations from neutral which is zero.

Suggested laboratory experiments or working experiences for Chapter 5:

1. a) Rub two pieces of wood together vigorously and feel the heat developed by friction; b) let air from a tire or balloon strike the back of the hand as it escapes and note the cooling action of an expanding gas; c) burn paper or wood in a container and then seal the air from it and note how the fire dies out without oxygen to combine with the hydrogen and carbon of the paper or wood; d) use a reading glass to concentrate the sun's rays on a piece of paper until it smokes or catches fire. Indicate the reactions seen.
2. Show the effect of heat upon starch in the presence of moisture, on egg yolk, on the fibers of celery in the presence of moisture and in caramelizing sugar.
3. Light a match under 100 grams of water in a glass container and do the same under 100 grams of iron and feel the temperature difference.

4. Secure a thermostat and open it up showing how the heat from a lighted match near it causes it to react.

5. a) Heat the end of a metal wire and feel the heat travel along the length by conduction and b) hold the hand above a lighted match and feel the warm air travel upward by convection. Then, hold the hand to the side of the match. If any heat is felt, it is perhaps not by conduction and not likely convection but by radiation.

6. Using a bunsen burner, show when a gas flame is adjusted correctly to give the most heat. The hollow spot inside the blue flame is gas; oxygen cannot get to it at this spot to ignite it.

7. Place ice and salt in a glass and note the temperature after 10 minutes. Let the glass stand and note how condensation occurs on the cold glass.

8. Rub water and then alcohol on the arm and feel the difference in in the sensible temperatures because of a difference in evaporation rates.

9. Put 10 pounds of potatoes into boiling water and bring them to a boil. When they start to boil, put another 10 pounds into a pressure cooker and start them to cooking. When the potatoes are done in the pressure cooker, test the doneness of the boiling potatoes. The steam under pressure being hotter should have cooked the second lot of potatoes faster.

10. Take a piece of dry ice and watch it smoke as it sublimates. Set a piece of ice in a dish and watch it turn to a liquid. Discuss the difference in the physical phenomena occurring between the two solids.

11. Put a thermometer under a black piece of cloth and another under a white piece of cloth. Let both be under the sun's rays. After a time note temperature differences.

BIBLIOGRAPHY

American Gas Association, *Commercial Kitchens,* New York City, 1962.

Adler, Irving, *Hot and Cold,* John Day Co., New York City, 1959.

Allen, Herbert S. and Maxwell, R. S., *Textbook of Heat,* Macmillan Company, London, 1939.

Becker, Richard, *Theory of Heat,* 2nd ed., Springer-Verlag, New York City, 1967.

Cork, James M., *Heat,* Chapman and Hall, London, 1942.

Efron, Alexander, *Exploring Heat,* Hayden Book Co., New York City, 1969.

6

Quantity Food Equipment

The proper use of equipment in quantity production can do much to reduce labor, facilitate work and improve food. Some equipment is so simple to use that a description here is unnecessary. Others are so difficult and complex to operate that one cannot learn to use it by reading but must learn by on-the-job instruction. Actual use is the best teacher anyway for the operation, maintenance and care of equipment. Thus the information that follows should be considered more an introduction to the use of equipment than instructions on how to use it. Additional information is to be found in the respective chapters on how some equipment is used in quantity production.

To assist those unacquainted with equipment and its operation, written instructions for operation should be posted in work centers or on equipment. Operating manuals should also be available on how to use and maintain major pieces. Acquaint novices with a preventative maintenance schedule and let them see when, how and by whom it is done. It is essential that those who work in foodservices know what equipment can do, how to use it and how it is maintained. Unless this is known, adequate performance in food production cannot occur.

HAND TOOLS AND SMALL UTENSILS

Hand Tools

The grasps of hand tools should be big enough to permit holding without cramping the fingers but not so large that a good grasp cannot be maintained. Indentations giving a more secure grip reduce fatigue and facilitate use. Hardwood handles of rosewood or cherry are preferred to plastic. Balance in hand tools is important. An offset spatula that tips back every time it is used is undesirable. Metal should be firmly joined to the grasps. All hand tools should be sturdy and strong, easily cleaned and maintained.

Knives

Knife blades and some other hand tools should be high carbon steel or vanadium steel for extra hardness. Use stainless steel for fruit knives. Finger guards should be on knife grasps where the hand can slip down onto the blade. Store knives in racks to protect blades. Magnetic racks set with two magnets two inches apart are preferred to slotted ones. Many workers have their own knives and hand tools and keep these wrapped in a soft towel and in a locker when off duty.

A French knife about 10 to 12 inches long is used to slice, dice or otherwise cut food. Usually, the point of the knife is set onto the cutting surface, the handle grasped firmly and, as the food is pushed under the knife, it is rocked up and down on its tip cutting through the food. The fingers of the hand holding the food should be kept curled to almost a clenched position so that the knife side rides against the second joints of these fingers. Do not extend the fingers on this hand. For greater control, the thumb of the hand using the knife can be on the left and the first finger on the right side of the blade. To cut long strips, lay the food flat upon the cutting surface, holding it firmly with the thumb and first finger of the other hand. Then move the tip of the knife down along the length of the food in a sweeping motion, cutting a strip the desired width. To cut a round, hard food, slice a thin strip first on one side making a flat surface. Rest the food on this flat spot and place the blade at the place for cutting, and using good pressure, press down. If this is not enough, take the palm of the other hand and press with this on the top of the blade, forcing the knife through the item. Hold the knife firmly. An uneven cut results if the knife twists.

The blade of a slicer knife is thinner and more flexible than that of a French knife. Many slicers are used, such as a roast beef slicer 12 to 14 inches long, ham slicer 12 inches and chef's slicer 10 inches. The latter is designed to slice roasts such as legs of veal, lamb, etc. To slice, insert a fork firmly into the item—sometimes the exposed hock bone may be grasped firmly in the hand instead. Hold the slicer firmly and cut through with a drawing motion, putting even and good pressure onto the blade. Use as much of the blade as possible using a long stroke. Hold the knife straight to get even slices. Cut through the meat or to the bone. If to the bone, do not detach slices until a number are cut. Then

roast beef slicer

ham slicer

chef's slicer

french cook knife

cimeter steak knife

boning knife

butcher knife

bowl spatula

offset spatula

frosting spatula

Figure 6–1.   Examples of good grasps and riveting on small tools. Note the finger guard on the boning knife.

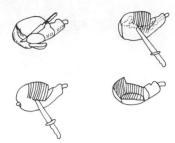

Figure 6–2. The method of cutting through the thick muscle of a roast. Note how the smaller leg muscle slices differ.

turn the knife at right angles to the slice and cut along the bone starting at the hock end. Frequently novices can slice faster and get more and more even slices using a mechanical slicer.

For bread, cake or other items a serrated or scalloped-edge slicer is used. Use a sawing motion with a light pressure, cutting through the item. Hold the knife straight so an even slice is obtained.

Figure 6–3. Carving a boned and rolled roast. Note that the cut is made across the grain.

A boning knife has a sturdy blade from 5 to 6 inches long. It is used for cutting around bones where the tip is used more than the cutting edge. A finger guard should be on the handle. The knife is grasped in the hand with the thumb up and the little finger closest to the blade. The blade is rotated around bones by turning and twisting the wrist. For scalping (cutting to free a bone without cutting through the meat) the cutting hand's position may be reversed and the cutting edge used more than the point.

Pare fruits and other round items starting at the stem or flower end, rotating the item with the other hand as the blade makes a thin, continuous peel. Pare all items before doing other manipulations unless the quantity is so great it cannot be stored or the items may tarnish if left stand. Then complete the remainder of the paring tasks. Slotted or swivel parers can be used. The slotted parer is also a corer. Frequently the skins of peaches, tomatoes, apricots, etc., can be removed more easily after scalding. Some items may be dipped into an anti-oxidant solution such as ascorbic acid, citrus juice or pineapple juice to prevent tarnishing. A salt solution or water is not as effective. Stainless steel blades reduce tarnishing.

Butcher or cimeter knives are used for slicing and dicing meats or other general cutting. Cleavers are used to chop through bones, split chickens and do other heavy work. Light, sharp cleavers may be used for some cutting. A bench knife or dough scraper is used in the bakeshop as a scraper and to cut items such as doughs into desired sizes.

Many experienced workers will sharpen their own knives and cutting tools but even they frequently will send them to be sharpened by the maintenance department or to one special person who does this in the facility. Most workers use a steel to maintain a good edge on a sharp tool. To use a steel, hold the knife blade at about a 20° angle and, working with the wrist, bring the blade against the tip of the steel and sweep the blade down running it from the tip to base of the steel. Keep an even, light pressure. Use care not to sweep onto the fingers. With the other side of the blade at the same angle, sweep it down similarly on the other side of the steel. Quickly reversing the action in this manner on either side of the steel and with a twisting, turning of the wrist complete sharpening the tool. Lighten pressure on the last strokes to get a finer edge.

Cutters

Many different cutting tools are used for miscellaneous work, some of which may need some simple directions for use. Place a ball cutter's cutting edge at about a 45° angle on the product and with a twisting motion, turn the cutter down into the product coming out with a round ball on the other side. A failure to push outward during the start, down during the middle of the cut and inward at the end produces a misshapen ball.

An egg slicer does the job quicker and usually better than slicing with a knife. A firm, even downward stroke is needed to get good slices. An egg boiled rather than simmered is tougher and better for slicing. Biscuit, doughnut, cookie and other cutters used in the bakeshop should be sharp and well maintained to give desirably shaped products. Dip cutters into flour and then cut down with an even straight motion; twisting as they go through a dough gives a misshapen product. Cut a large number before stopping. Then, complete other manipulations. Roller type cutters may be manually or mechanically operated. Their use is specialized and professional workers should give instructions for it.

Cutting Boards

In place of hard maple, laminated cutting boards, hard rubber or plastic ones from an inch to four inches thick are being used more. They are more sanitary, are not damaged by water but last a shorter time. Use a cutting board on metal or non-wooden working surfaces.

Spatulas, Servers, Scoops, Etc.

Spatulas and servers should be made of high carbon stainless steel or chrome-vanadium steel. Grasps should be similar to those on knives. If used to scrape around mixing bowls or spreading frosting, use extra flexible ones. For sandwich spreading or removing items from baking sheets use flexible ones and for regular work use firm ones. Larger, offset spatulas are used for grill work and other cooking jobs. The offset keeps the hand away from a hot surface. Its sides should be beveled so that the edge moves easily under a product. It can be used for turning and also as a scraper to remove grease and other materials into grease troughs. Plastic or rubber spatulas are used in the bakeshop or elsewhere where good flexibility is desired and strength is not important. A rubber or plastic spatula can be used also for folding in foams but normally a whip is used. A wide number of servers, turners, spreaders or cake and pie spatulas are used for specific needs.

Forks of higher carbon stainless or good forged steel are used for lifting and turning roasts and other items or for holding items while they are sliced. They should have a good hardwood grasp and be sturdy and strong to take the heavy work they do.

Ladles and dippers are used for portioning food or moving it from one place to another. Various sizes are available for portioning. While they will be sturdy with handles firmly welded or riveted to strong seamless bowls, care must be taken not to bang them too hard against the edge of pots or other equipment. Large scoops and dippers will be used mostly for movement of items but if a worker knows how much they contain, amounts produced can be calculated by counting the number of such units moved.

Ice cream scoops are used not only for dishing frozen desserts but for portioning puddings and other desserts, mashed potatoes, etc. A round type and a cone-shaped type have releases inside worked by the thumb. A rounded hooked type that rolls frozen desserts into a ball instead of scooping gives highest yields because it packs less. To work well, scoops should have a sharp cutting edge, be dipped into cold water and then drained before each use. Scoop, dipper and ladle sizes are found in Table 6-1. In some portioning of thick foods it is easier and quicker to portion with a smaller rounded tool than to try to achieve a level full measure with an exact measure.

A perforated skimmer is used to remove scum or other items from the top of stocks, gravies and other liquids. A regular skimmer is used to remove grease and other items but oftentimes a ladle placed into the liquid so the product can flow into it is preferable. A slotted spoon

Table 6-1. Cup, Scoop and Ladle Sizes

Cup Size	Ounces	Scoop Size	Measure	Ounces
$1/4$	2	No. 6	$2/3$ c	5
$1/2$	4	No. 8	$1/2$ c	4
$1/3$	2.7	No. 10	$3/8$ c	$3^1/4$
$2/3$	5.3	No. 12	$1/3$ c	$2^3/4$
$3/4$	6	No. 16	$1/4$ c	2
1	8	No. 20	$3^1/5$ T	$1^1/2$
		No. 24	$2^2/3$ T	$1^1/3$
		No. 30	$2^1/5$ T	1
		No. 40	$1^3/5$ T	0.8
		No. 60	1 T	0.5

Ladle Size	Measure	Bowl Diameter	Handle Length
1 oz	2 T	$1^3/4$ in.	10 in.
2 oz	$1/4$ c	$2^3/8$ in.	$9^3/8$ in.
4 oz	$1/2$ c	$3^3/8$ in.	$12^5/8$ in.
6 oz	$3/4$ c	$3^1/2$ in.	$12^3/8$ in.
8 oz	1 c	4 in.	$12^5/8$ in.
12 oz	$1^1/2$ c	$5^1/4$ in.	$12^1/8$ in.
16 oz	2 c (pt)	$4^3/8$ in.	14 in.
24 oz	3 c	6 in.	$18^1/8$ in.
32 oz	4 c (qt)	$8^1/8$ in.	17 in.

is frequently used to dish vegetables and other items that are in liquid but must be served drained. Regular spoons are used for basting, stirring, serving and general work. Both serve about three ounces when rounded. Care should be taken not to bang them too hard against the edge of pots and other utensils.

Extra strong, durable grocer's scoops with handles integral to seamless bowls are used for dipping sugar, flour and other dry items. Workers should learn the approximate amounts these hold so, in dipping items to be weighed, a quick, approximate amount can be scooped onto the scales.

Colanders, Sieves and China Caps

A colander is used to drain food from liquid. Special ones are used such as one for draining spaghetti. Allow food to drain several minutes and then give a good shake or two to free any liquid in the food. Heavy duty, rust proof strainers with their screen mesh sized from 14 to 20 per square inch are used for finer straining. These are somewhat fragile and should be handled carefully. It is wise to wash immediately after use because dry food is hard to remove and creates extra wear on the mesh. A heavy duty China cap is conical in shape. Besides being used for straining liquids from solid products, it is used to puree items. To force foods through, a roller is rotated around the edges or a ladle can be inserted into the center of the material in the cap and then pulled up and down to create a suction on the upstroke and pressure on the downstroke.

Whips and Stirrers

Small, fine wire whips about 8 to 10 inches long are helpful in working into corners and mixing foods such as hollandaise sauce and a flour and water slurry. Larger ones with coarse, stronger, stiffer wires are used to work with large batches of sauces or thicker items. For fast mixing, a whip can be grasped by the handle with the little finger toward the wires and the thumb up and worked with a quick forward and backward motion of the wrist. Reversing the hand allows the arm muscle to exert more powerful strokes for stirring larger or thicker batches.

Whips are used to fold foams into other ingredients. They can whip small quantities of eggs, cream or other items but more frequently this is done by a mixer or electric beater. Do not attempt to mix too thick products with a wire whip. Use a mixer and a paddle. Occasionally, when quantities are small, hand rotary beaters are used in quantity work. Both wire and rotary whips are harmed by rough handling. Do not bang them around and keep wires and blades straight and true. Cleaning may become a problem because of the many areas where food can adhere. Washing soon after using helps in cleaning because food cannot dry on the unit.

A stirring paddle or whip may be used to mix food in steam-jacketed kettles and stock pots. The handle should have at least a $1\frac{1}{2}$ inch outside diameter to give a good grip. If a scratch or mark is put on them to indicate how much product is in standard containers, workers can quickly calculate how much product is being made. Since aluminum paddles are lighter, they may be preferred over stainless ones but they are not as durable. Stainless steel can scratch aluminum kettles. The electrolytic action (flow of electrical particles) between stainless steel and aluminum can cause pitting in aluminum and so we avoid using these metals too much together.

Pots and Pans

Good heat conduction is needed in pots and pans. Aluminum and black cast iron are good conductors. Very few stainless steel copper bottom pans are used in quantity work. Copper is the best heat conductor and is often preferred for this reason but it must be tinned inside where food touches the surface. Copper has great beauty when polished but it is also expensive. Copper can destroy ascorbic acid and may form harmful food substances with strong acids. Nevertheless, with good care, copper pans are excellent for cooking.

All pots and pans should be heavy duty, seamless, with double strength bottoms and tops or with a strong bead at the top. Thick bottoms give good heat spread and prevent sticking. Strong edges take the wear and withstand the heavy rap of spoons and other utensils on them. Even, flat bottoms give good contact with heating units and capture heat effectively. Rounded corners make for ease in cleaning. Loop handles should be firmly brazed or strongly riveted and welded to the pot. Sauce pan handles should also be strongly welded or riveted to bowls and long enough to give good handling and to extend from the hot surface over which the pan is used. Some large pots will be equipped with sanitary bibb or dairy type faucets and strainers. These will be used for draining stocks and other liquids. Special pots are used for the making of gravies, soups and sauces. Special sauce pots are shallower than stock pots so that work can be done more easily in them. Braisers are special pots in which items are sauteed and then covered and braised. A covered pot comes to a boil more quickly than an uncovered one and needs less heat

Figure 6–4.   Strong handles and good heat conduction are needed for pans. The sloped sides enable a worker to work into the pan more easily.

to continue to cook. The working capacity of pots and pans is less than the total capacity. Food closer than three inches from the top is apt to spill in stirring, mixing or boiling.

Heavy duty sauce pans are used for making sauces, gravies, fillings and other items in general kitchen work. Shallow types are used when considerable work must be done on the product or a good evaporative loss is desired. Deeper ones are used when the product is cooked for a long time.

Double-boilers are used when foods must not receive too much heat such as a stirred custard. A lower container holds water which transfers heat into an upper container holding the food to be cooked. A rounded bottom in the top part favors reaching all areas with a whip or spoon.

Frying or sauté pans are much like sauce pans except they are shallower and have slanted sides so that work can be done in them easily with a spatula or other hand tool. Fit the pan to the quantity fried. Otherwise spots not covered will burn and char. A straight-sided pan should be used for sautéing and braising or where there is danger of foaming up.

When a large quantity must be sautéed, a large ¼-inch thick heavy duty griddle with two integral handles may be used. After frying, foods

Figure 6–5. A roast pan with trivet on the bottom and a strong cover. Note rounded corners for easy cleaning. Also note strong riveting of handles. The cover, if of slightly heavier material, could be used also as a griddle.

can be removed, put into deeper pans, covered and braised. Sometimes quite heavy tops for roasters can be used. Frying or sauté pans may be conditioned for use, a process described later under griddles.

Heavy duty roasting pans equipped with tight-fitting covers are needed. They should have two strong handles and sometimes four, if very large. To reduce weight, they can be made of strong aluminum alloy, hardened to be dent resistant. Black japanned-steel or hotel steel strap-pans are also satisfactory. Various sizes are needed since the size of the pan should be suited to the quantity roasted in it. Most of the bottom should be covered with product to prevent charring of juices. A trivet or rack, perforated to allow juices to drain through, is needed to raise meat from the pan bottom. This trivet should be equipped with long handles which permit lifting the rack and meat from the pan.

Lighter weight pans of many types are used for storage, transport or as tote boxes. They should have strong beads at the top. Extra strength is gained by strapping. Stainless steel pans are suitable for storage or use in serving food at steam tables but not for cooking. Many of these miscellaneous pans can be plastic if heat is not applied.

Many 18 x 26 inch baking sheets are used. These are usually dent resistant aluminum. Some are textured with a pebbly bottom to assist in removing items such as cookies, etc. Pie, cake, loaf or other smaller pans are usually aluminum, black japanned steel or hotel steel which must be conditioned. For this, wipe the new pans clean, place them in a 400° F oven and allow them to remain until tinged with a bluish-black color. Remove, grease lightly with oil or a plastic fat and return to the oven for 3 to 4 minutes. Allow them to cool and wipe clean. Aluminum pans do not need conditioning. All baking pans should be of heavy enough material to take care of the heavy wear. They should have strongly beaded edges. Handle with care, not banging around or dropping them so they lose shape. Avoid heat warping. Use cake pans only for cake production. Glass pans are fragile and do not brown items well on the bottom.

Some muffin, popover and other pans may be conditioned by putting them into a hot oven after liberally greasing them. They are removed while hot, and salt on a soft cloth is rubbed vigorously into the hot surface. This may be repeated several times. After such treatment the pans are not washed but may be lightly greased for the product and the product baked and dumped. The pan is thoroughly cleaned with a clean, soft absorbent cloth and stored. Washing destroys the surface and makes the pan stick. Paper liners can also be used to prevent sticking.

Weighing and Portioning Equipment

Weighing rather than measuring is preferred in quantity work because of its greater accuracy but occasionally measuring is done for speed or where accuracy is not a critical factor. Pour, do not dip, thick fluids into a measure and scrape well to empty it with a rubber or plastic spatula. Use a glass measure for liquids and see that the liquid reaches the measure mark at the edge, not the center.

Overfill a measure with dry ingredients, tap gently and level off. Some items must be sifted before measuring but dry milk, presifted flour, leavening agents and sugar are not sifted. Remove lumps from brown sugar by rolling it or heating it gently in an oven. Pack brown sugar lightly until it holds its shape when dumped from the measure. Stir before measuring items that pack such as baking powder, graham flour and dry milk. To measure by spoon or small measure, dip out a heaping measure and level off with a spatula. Use full measures to obtain fractions. Thus, a half teaspoon measure should be used to get a half teaspoon instead of attempting to divide a full teaspoon into half. A pinch is about 1/16 teaspoon. To speed work and give accuracy know equivalents between weights and measures. (See the tables in the appendix for many of these.) Use time-saving methods such as cutting a pound of butter in half to obtain a cup or eight ounces.

A set of measuring spoons usually contains a tablespoon, teaspoon and a half and quarter teaspoon. Cup measures are cup, fourth, half, three-fourths, one-third and two-thirds. Large measures may be a pint, quart, half-gallon and gallon.

A portion scale is frequently used to obtain accurate portions. This is a beam-type scale on which one can set the ounce portion desired on the beam. An indicator shows when the amount weighed is over, under or exactly right.

Table 6-2. Conversion of Water From Measure to Weight

Cups	Pints	Quarts	Ounces*	Pounds and Ounces*	
½	¼	⅛	4.15	0	4
1	½	¼	8.31	0	8¼
1½	¾	⅜	12.46	0	12½
2	1	½	16.62	1	½
2½	1¼	⅝	20.77	1	4¾
3	1½	¾	24.93	1	9
3½	1¾	⅞	29.08	1	13
4	2	1	33.24	2	1¼
4½	2¼	1⅛	37.39	2	5¼
5	2½	1¼	41.55	2	9½
5½	2¾	1⅜	45.70	2	13¾
6	3	1½	49.86	3	1¾
6½	3¼	1⅝	54.01	3	6
7	3½	1¾	58.17	3	10¼
7½	3¾	1⅞	62.32	3	14¼
8	4	2	66.48	4	2½
8½	4¼	2⅛	70.63	4	6½
9	4½	2¼	74.80	4	10¾
9½	4¾	2⅜	78.94	4	15
10	5	2½	83.10	5	3¼
10½	5¼	2⅝	87.25	5	7¼
11	5½	2¾	91.40	5	11½
11½	5¾	2⅞	95.56	5	15½
12	6	3	99.72	6	3¾
12½	6¼	3⅛	103.87	6	8
13	6½	3¼	108.03	6	12
13½	6¾	3⅜	112.18	7	¼
14	7	3½	116.34	7	4¼
14½	7¼	3⅝	120.49	7	8¼
15	7½	3¾	124.65	7	12½
15½	7¾	3⅞	128.80	8	1
16	8	4	133.00	8	5

*For whole milk equivalents multiply by 1.032, and for light sirups (20° Brix) multiply by 1.373.

Table 6-3. Weights, Measures, and Their Abbreviations

Measure	Abbreviation	Equivalent
Teaspoon	t	3 t or 1 T
Tablespoon	T	16 T or 1 c
Cup	c	2 c or 1 pt
Pint	pt	2 pt or 1 qt
Quart	qt	4 qt or 1 gal
Gram	gm	
Ounce	oz	28.35 gm or 1 oz
Pound	lb	16 oz or 1 lb
Gallon	gal	

Note: 2 T of liquid or solid matter usually equals 1 oz; 5⅓ T equals ⅓ c, 4 T equals ¼ c, a pinch equals about 1/16 t and a dash less than ⅛ t.

Table 6-4. Dry and Liquid Measure Equivalents

Dry

2 pt	1 qt	1.101 liters
8 qt	1 peck	8.808 liters
4 pecks	1 bu	35.24 liters

Liquid

4 gills	1 pt	473.25 cubic centimeters
2 pt	1 qt	0.9465 liters
4 qt	1 gal	3.786 liters
31½ gal	1 barrel	
2 barrels	1 hogshead	

Table 6-5. Liquid Measure Conversion Table

	United States measure				Imperial measure (British)				Metric measure		Weight of indicated volume of water	
	Gallon	Quart	Pint	Gill	Gallon	Quart	Pint	Gill	Liter	Cubic centimeter	Pound (avoirdupois)	Kilogram
United States measure												
1 gallon..........	1	4	8	32	0.833	3.33	6.66	26.66	3.785	3,785.4	8.33	3.785
1 quart..........	.25	1	2	8	.208	.833	1.666	6.67	.946	946.4	2.08	.946
1 pint..........	.125	.5	1	4	.104	.417	.833	3.33	.473	473.2	1.04	.473
1 gill..........	.031	.125	.25	1	.026	.104	.208	.833	.118	118.3	.26	.118
Imperial measure (British)												
1 gallon..........	1.2	4.8	9.6	38.4	1	4	8	32	4.543	4,543.5	10	4.543
1 quart..........	.3	1.2	2.4	9.6	.25	1	2	8	1.136	1,135.9	2.5	1.136
1 pint..........	.15	.6	1.2	4.8	.125	.5	1	4	.568	567.9	1.25	.568
1 gill..........	.038	.15	.3	1.2	.031	.125	.25	1	.142	142.0	.312	.142
Metric measure												
1 liter..........	.264	1.057	2.11	8.45	.220	.880	1.761	7.044	1	1,000	2.20	1.
1 cubic centimeter.	.0003	.001	.002	.008	.0002	.0009	.002	.077	.001	1	.002	.001

See also Table 6-8

Table 6-6. Conversion Table: Grams, Ounces, Pounds

Grams	Ounces	Pounds	Grams	Ounces	Pounds	Grams	Ounces	Pounds
28.35	1	.06	198.45	7	.44	340.20	12	.75
56.70	2	.13	226.80	8	.50	368.55	13	.81
85.05	3	.19	255.15	9	.56	396.90	14	.88
113.40	4	.25	283.50	10	.63	425.25	15	.94
141.75	5	.31	311.85	11	.69	453.60	16	1.00
170.10	6	.38						

Table 6-7. Volume Conversion Table (*Fluid Ounces to Milliliters*)

Fluid Ounces to Milliliters

Fl. Oz.	Ml.	Fl. Oz.	Ml.
1	29.6	17	502.8
2	59.1	18	532.3
3	88.7	19	561.9
4	118.3	20	591.7
5	147.9	21	621.0
6	177.4	22	650.6
7	207.0	23	680.2
8	236.6	24	709.8
9	266.2	25	739.3
10	295.7	26	768.9
11	325.3	27	798.5
12	354.9	28	828.1
13	384.5	29	857.7
14	414.0	30	887.2
15	443.6	31	916.8
16 (1 pint)	473.2	32 (1 quart)	946.4

Table 6-8. Equivalents of Household Food Measures

Quarts	Pints	Standard Cups	Fluid Ounces	Table-spoonfuls	Tea-spoonfuls	Milli-liters
1.0	2.0	4.0	32.0	64.0	192.0	946.4
0.5	1.0	2.0	16.0	32.0	96.0	473.2
0.25	0.5	1.0	8.0	16.0	48.0	236.6
0.125	0.25	0.5	4.0	8.0	24.0	118.3
....	0.125	0.25	2.0	4.0	12.0	59.2
....	....	1.125	1.0	2.0	6.0	29.6
....	....	....	0.5	1.0	3.0	14.8
....	....	....	......	0.33	1.0	4.9
....	....	....	......	......	0.2	1.0

A baker's scale is a balance beam scale. Quarter ounce graduations up to 16 ounces can be set on the beam. Additional weights over this are placed on the right side with ounces and partial ounces put onto the beam. The ingredients are placed on the left side. A container on the left platform is used for dry ingredients and a standard tare weight is used on the right to make up for its weight. Frequently an empty pan identical to the one being filled on the left is placed on the right to tare out its weight. Scale small quantities first and then heavier ones. For highest accuracy, scale items singly. A scale is inaccurate if it is not level. Avoid jarring the scale, which can lead to inaccuracy. Spring scales can be used for speed where complete accuracy is not important, such as where quantities of entree items or other cooked foods are placed into pans for baking. A good supermarket scale is useful for some work but a heavy duty one with a large dial is better. A heavy duty scale should be used for receiving heavy items. Receiving scales that print the weight and date are desirable and they should be equipped with a beam scale for taring container weights. Scales are good only if they are accurate. Therefore, care should be taken to see that they are properly cleaned and handled in order that soil does not interfere with their action. Lift scales from the bottom. Check accuracy frequently and do not leave objects on them when not in use.

HEAVY EQUIPMENT

Heating Equipment

Heat is brought to food in cooking by air, metals, water, steam, ether or fat. Various equipment units help to do this.

Range Tops

The work horse of the kitchen is frequently a range top. If specialized equipment such as deep-fryers, steamers, steam-jacketed kettles and griddles are not available their work is done on the range top. However, in some kitchens range tops are not used, steam equipment, ovens and others doing their jobs. Tops will be heated usually by gas or electricity but some few may be heated with oil or even coal or wood. Thermostat control is used for some tops while others may be manually controlled by workers manipulating the controls. Most modern units are capable of coming to a desirable cooking temperature in a short time and so units may be turned on and off as needed and not left on as in the past when tops were left on full so as to be ready at all times. This practice resulted in rapid deterioration or buckling plus heavy fuel waste. See that tops are covered as much as possible with items needing cooking. Using more than one plate makes it possible to have variable temperatures so that one can shift items from fast to slower cooking or vice versa. A baker's stove is a small open plate or solid range top used to make sugar solutions, pie fillings, sauces, puddings, etc. It is low so work can be done more easily when tall pots are used.

It is important to keep ranges clean. Check gas burners frequently to see that they are not clogged and give a blue flame with a white tip. Adjust air flow until flame appears as indicated.

Griddles*

Griddles cook foods directly on their surface by sautéing or frying, a process of cooking in shallow fat. They should be heavy duty and be equipped with splash backs, grease troughs and rounded corners for easy cleaning. Remove drip pans and grease catchers daily and clean them well. Polish the griddle surface with a soapstone, pumice brick or griddle cloth at the end of every day's use. Do not salt foods over a griddle since this builds up gummy deposits making it more difficult to clean the griddle. Have available a grease mop, oil can, shakers of seasonings, forks, tongs and spatulas in addition to cleaning materials. Keep the griddle wiped off with a soft, clean cloth.

To condition a griddle or sauté pan, cover the surface with some high quality oil or fat, sprinkle salt lightly on this and heat the griddle until the fat almost smokes. Then, using a soapstone, pumice brick or griddle cloth, polish the surface until it shines. Wipe clean with a dry cloth or soft paper. Repeat until a smooth, non-sticking surface is obtained. Water destroys this finish, so every time the griddle or pan has water on it, it must be reconditioned to prevent sticking.

A tilting braising pan, operated with either gas or electricity sautés, deep-fries, braises, griddles, simmers or boils items. It has great flexibility and is extremely convenient to use since so many different things can be done in it. It can also be tilted to deliver items. Gas models must come equipped with an attachment to give flexibility for tilting. These units can be adapted for small units if a production program is worked out around the pan, just as can be done frequently for using a vertical-cutter.

Broilers

New heavy duty broilers take from 15 to 30 minutes to heat to a broiling temperature. Charcoal takes about 45 minutes to come to 350° F at the grid level while older types of gas and electric broilers take about the same time. These usually have a gas or electrical unit

---

* Unlike the French, we use the term *griddle* to mean frying or sautéing. The French use it to mean broiling or cooking by radiant heat.

Figure 6–6. (a) Conditioning a pan using hot oil and salt and a pumice stone. (b) Conditioning a grill top with pumice brick.

Figure 6–7. A heavy duty broiler. The oven overheat can be used for finishing items. Storage can be underneath.

over a grid but some of the newer types have heating units underneath. Some of the newer broilers heat ceramic tiles to obtain more radiant heat. Temperatures as high as 2000° F are claimed for them. Foods can be broiled in a vertical position. If charcoal is used for this, it is held in place by putting it in a grid. Large broilers such as the one in the convention center in Detroit, Michigan, have infrared lamps face to face in a narrow chamber where steaks, hung on a moving chain at various levels, pass through them. Some of the newer broilers can be thermostatically controlled. Temperature control is also achieved by raising or lowering the broiler grid. To estimate temperatures, hold the hand at the cooking level. If it can be held only two seconds, it is a fast fire (350° to 400° F); three seconds, a medium fire (300° to 350° F); and four seconds, a slow fire (275° to 300° F). A salamander is a small overhead broiler designed to brown au gratin and other dishes, but it can also be used for the preparation of some broiled items.

A charcoal fire is started with hardwood kindling or some pieces of charcoal soaked for several hours in a can of lighter fluid or wood alcohol. Fit the can with a good lid and keep it away from fire. Or a half cup of wood alcohol or lighter fluid may be poured onto some charcoal and, after standing two minutes, lit. An excess may cause a fire. Kerosene or other fuel oils give off undesirable flavors, and therefore, special gas or electric lighters may be used. After the charcoal is well lighted, spread it out, add additional charcoal until a bed 2 to 3 inches deep is obtained and let it burn until the charcoal is covered with a light white ash and glows. Have the bed slightly larger than the grid and a bit deeper at the edges than in the center because of the cooling that occurs there. Some cooks adjust the depth of the charcoal to control temperature but most vary the level of the grid above the charcoal for this. A container of cold water containing chipped ice or a syringe of cold water should be kept nearby to control flames or heat. Hardwood rather than softwood charcoal should be used as softwood gives a resinous flavor to broiled items. Some authorities claim the tars from softwood charcoal may be carcinogenic the same as tars and smoke from cigarettes may be.

Keep broilers very clean. Remove all traces of grease and empty drain cans daily. A broiler can easily start a dangerous grease fire. A self-closing vent should be above to close in case of fire.

Deep-fryers*

New deep-fryers are heated with gas or electricity and are thermostatically controlled. Keep these units scrupulously clean. Filter fat after every heavy use, and after filtering, wipe the empty kettle free of fat removing gummy substances. Removable kettles and equipment should be taken to a sink and thoroughly scrubbed with hot soapy water. Fill nonremovable kettles with a good detergent or deep-fryer cleaner and boil well. Drain, rinse with clean water and repeat if need be. Dry thoroughly

* For additional information consult Chapter 12 on deep-fat frying.

Figure 6–8. Deep-fat fryers in the foreground in a dormitory. Note on the right the small trunnion tilt kettles and the steam-jacketed kettles in back of the fryers.

before adding fat. Check the accuracy of temperature controls frequently.

Pressure fryers are on the market which develop from 9 to 14 psi of steam while deep-frying foods at around 325° F. Some have water injectors which add water for the steam while others utilize moisture in the food for this. Advantages claimed for these pressure fryers are increased flavor and tenderness of product while reducing cooking time to half or less of conventional time.

Ovens

One or several single ovens under range tops may suffice for oven needs in a small operation, while a large revolving oven holding as many as 80 large baking sheets or a huge moving belt unit over 100 feet long may be required in large operations. Gas, electricity, infra-red waves or microwaves may be the heat source.

A revolving oven has shelves between wheels that rotate. Mechanisms stabilize shelves, keeping them always in a horizontal position. An indicator outside shows shelf location so an operator can stop any shelf at the door for loading or unloading. Good maintenance is required because jarring, uneven heat or unlevel shelves can cause problems. The oven is cleaned inside usually by allowing it to cool, then lowering a man into the oven on a shelf so he can clean the inside. Mechanical parts can usually be oiled from a small door on the oven side.

Ovens under range tops hold two 18″ x 26″ baking pans on two shelves but because of heat variation frequently only one shelf is used, or an item such as a tall turkey permits the use of only one shelf.

Long ovens moving items on a moving belt are used for heavy production as in bakeries. It is possible to vary heat in different areas to suit baking needs of products and also to change belt speed.

Stack ovens have baking shelves one on top of the other, those for baking being eight inches high and for roasting 12 inches high. Each shelf may be individually controlled. Often an old-fashioned stack gas oven can give different shelf temperatures with the hottest being at the bottom where the heat source is and cooler shelves progressively toward the top.

Deep brick-lined or hearth ovens are used for baking hard-crusted breads and other bakery items. They also perform well in roasting. Because of their mass and size, they take a long time to warm up and may be left on low heat overnight to reduce the heating time the next day. Hard-crusted breads are baked directly on the hearth. A long peel or flat paddle is used for loading or unloading. These ovens have steam inlets in them to build up moisture during baking to assist in keeping the crusts soft during baking and to allow the bread to expand fully. This steam is turned off later and a good hard crust is then formed. Other ovens may also have steam brought into them for this purpose. Workers should learn when oven vents should be open or closed.

A convection oven is usually about as large as the oven under a range top but some larger ones are also used. The regular size can take from 6 to 11 large baking sheets. A fan at the back moves heat around making it possible to have shelves quite close together and still obtain adequate heat between them. When fully loaded, some convection ovens bake unevenly and workers must learn how much of different products can be loaded. These ovens are often used to warm up large quantities of precooked foods, toast sandwiches or to bake pastries. The fan must be off for some baking. For instance, ripples form on cakes from the strong air currents if fans are on when they are baked.

Microwaves have cathode tubes that generate waves which penetrate the food, disturbing the molecular structure (developing kinetic action) that causes the development of heat. These waves bounce around the

Figure 6–9. A convection oven loaded from a mobile cart. Such an oven is excellent for warming a large number of units as shown here. If these units were chilled and to be warmed for service, it would be patterned on what is frequently called the Bremerton system of foodservice. (Courtesy of Market Forge)

metal chamber which they cannot penetrate but they can penetrate paper, plastics or ceramics. Items cannot be cooked in metal containers in them. If a metal pan comes in contact with the metal of the oven, arcing occurs which can badly damage the expensive cathode tube. Microwave energy is very intense and cooks foods much more quickly than conventional heat. It can easily overcook. For instance, thick foods can become overcooked quickly at the edges before the interior is done. This can be avoided by taping metal around the edge of a casserole or plate to prevent microwaves from going through at this point *but this metal should never be allowed to touch any other metal surface in the oven.* Some items may have to be covered to reduce dehydration. Items leavened by chemical agents or foams cook almost too rapidly to be quality products. Meats have a higher shrinkage when cooked by microwave. In large meats circular rings develop in the muscle portions. However, continued investigation is solving some of these problems.

Microwave is efficient for warming frozen or other precooked foods for service. The depth and type of foods cooked together must be properly adjusted, for some foods can be overcooked before others are done. Cooking speed is indirectly related to the quantity of food. Small quantities are processed very fast but, as the mass increases, cooking time increases. It is possible to overload a microwave oven to the point where cooking time may be longer than in a conventional oven.

The use made of a microwave unit should receive study before one is purchased and a program of utilization established for it. Employees unacquainted with its operation will tend to follow traditional patterns and avoid using it. They must be taught to use it and be shown how helpful it can be in doing many small, rapid heating tasks.

(a)

(b)

Figure 6–10. (a) A microwave oven. Note easy-to-use timer system and controls. Foods are placed in this oven and the door closed where it heats in a very short time. (Courtesy Hobart) (b) A new oven that heats the foods in the container in which they are served. The resistance element is in the dish itself. (Courtesy of Minnesota Mining Co.)

Many different ovens have been developed for warming foods for service in new systems. The Foster Recon holds foods under refrigeration until a timer starts the heating cycle. Heat input cycles on and off which is said to prevent overcooking outer areas and give more even heat build-up throughout products. Ovens using quartz tubes or quartz plates generate infrared waves that give a steady, even heat bringing a large quantity of food to a serving temperature. A unit has appeared on the market equipped with electrical contacts in slides so that dishes loaded into the unit resting on the slides make electrical contact. A heating element is inside the ceramic material of the dish holding the food and resting on the slide and the food is thus warmed.

In addition to these, microwave, convection and conventional ovens plus steam equipment are used to warm foods for service. One of the most efficient methods for preparing bulk food for service is to place covered containers of food into steam units and bring them almost to a serving temperature. They are then removed, uncovered and brought to final temperature in a conventional oven. Covering in steam prevents condensation from thinning or watering the foods down. Special water bath equipment, bain maries, steam tables or even deep-fryers filled with water are used to reheat foods either in bulk or individual packs.

One of the greatest enemies of quality in quantity cookery is holding food at high temperatures for long periods of time. Procedures should be worked out so that foods are freshly prepared. And, if not that, then the foods should be heated as closely as possible to the time of service so as to be as fresh as possible. Some of this new equipment does this.

Leaving ovens on at high heat burns out linings or warps and buckles shelving. Thermostats also burn out and become defective. Every oven has its own idiosyncrasies which must be learned to get the best performance from it. Most new ovens heat to a desirable temperature in 15 to 20 minutes so it is no longer necessary to leave them on at full temperature to have them ready for use. For adequate performance, do not overload ovens, nor allow pans to touch each other nor the sides of the oven. Heavily moistened cloths or water should not be used on interiors, especially electrical ovens. Oven vents must be left open at the start of heating so moisture can escape. Unvented ovens may have the doors left open for this. Moisture can short out an electrical oven or cause rusting or other deterioration. Operating, maintenance and cleaning instructions for ovens vary. Follow manufacturer's instructions for this. Some new ovens may be self-cleaning.

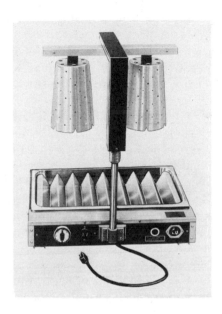

Figure 6–11. Food warmer with underneath heater and overhead infrared heating lamps. Base holds 12 × 20 inch standard pan. (Courtesy Crescent Metal Products)

Food Handling Equipment

Food can be kept warm in standard equipment such as ovens and steamers or left on heating units such as range tops where the food sits in a container of hot water to prevent further cooking.

A bain marie keeps food hot in a shallow vat of water that is heated either by steam, gas or electricity. The food sits on a large perforated shelf set into the hot water. Dry heat or waterless bain maries are also used and the containers rest on the bottom. A steam-table is similar to a bain marie but holds food more in service than in operating areas. It is covered with a top so that 12 x 20 serving pans or their multiples can be set into it. Meat pans have tent-like covers for roasts and other foods. A bain marie or steam-table can be used to cook some foods such as hollandaise sauce, scrambled eggs, poached eggs, eggs cooked in the shell or sauces, but foods can overcook in bain maries and steam-tables unless temperatures are carefully controlled. Rare roasts cook to a medium or well done, eggs turn dark and strong in flavor, vegetables lose flavor, texture and color in them. To keep foods fresh for service, only a small amount should be held and fresh batches sent periodically from production. This gives best quality to eggs, vegetables and other items that lose it quickly. Steam-tables may operate with water heated by steam, gas or electricity. Units of dry heat, thermostatically controlled, are also used.

Special food handling chambers may be built into walls or set in work areas to hold hot food until needed for service. Some may be pass-throughs into which food is placed so that it is ready for service on the other side. Banquet service often needs a lot of food ready at one time and a special heated room or unit may be designed into which carts of food can be rolled to await service. These are usually located behind service areas and near the banquet or service areas. (See Figure 1-21).

Some food systems are built around holding and transport equipment just as they are around some types of production equipment. Hot food carts holding bulk food, much the same as dry heat steam-tables, are used for this purpose, while other carts may hold and transport individual portions or dished meals. Some units are preheated by plugging them into electrical outlets, and after transport, again plugging in to keep the foods warm. Refrigerated units can be used the same way. Trucks may also be designed to hold and transport foods, dispensing meals from the truck. Hot food may be put into insulated containers and held. Insulation is urethane, fiber glass, cork or other materials and holding may be possible up to several hours. Large containers for bulk or portioned food or meals may have to be handled by fork-lift trucks. Others may be easily handled by a single worker and may be disposable foam-types. The Aladdin server into which foods can be portioned as a meal for service (mentioned in Chapter 1) will hold foods up to four hours either hot or cold, and hot or cold food can be dished separately next to each other in compartments in these servers.

Special devices may be used to hold hot food. Infra-red lamps can diffuse a steady, dry heat so that when placed over foods, the foods retain temperature. They are especially good for holding deep-fried foods, the dry heat retaining crispness. A rare baron or rib of beef can be under this for a long period without further cooking. Other similar warmers on the market use chromalux or other types of heating units.

Heated metal pellets can be put under foods to hold their temperature. This unit is then put onto a tray with the cold foods and transported to a service area. Hospitals have made much use of the pellet system.

Steam-Cooking Equipment

Free-vented steamers are little used in quantity work, most steam cooking being done with pressure units, many operating on steam sent from a central boiler. If pressures are too high, pressure reducers can

Table 6-9. Holding and Serving Temperatures

Type Food	Holding (°F)	At Service (°F)
Soups, tea, coffee, thin gravies, sauces, etc.	180	160
Entrees, medium and well done meat, thick sauces, etc.	160	140
Rare meats	140	135
Chilled foods such as salads, cocktails, juices, etc.	35–40	45–50
Frozen foods	8–15	24

lower them for the equipment. Self-contained units develop their own steam. Some of these automatically fill from the regular water supply while others have to be manually filled with water for steam. Manufacturer's directions should be followed for operation. All units have protective devices on them to release excess steam or disconnect if heating devices become too hot. Never tamper with safety pressure valves or other protective devices. Check operation frequently to see that all is in order. Some safety devices can be released manually as well as automatically. Most steamers cannot be filled with steam until doors are properly sealed and these cannot be opened also until all pressure inside is gone. Many steamers will automatically release air and water in the equipment through a discharge valve before building steam pressure. Some steam-jacketed kettles have a bleeder valve to release condensed steam if it builds up in the kettle's jacket during operation.

STEAMERS

High pressure steamers rapidly process foods at pressures around 15 psi. Their speed facilitates batch cooking and so quantities cooked need not be large. If two are used, it is possible to keep up an almost continuous supply of foods to service outlets. Some of these have browning equipment in them. Large compartment steamers capable of holding a bushel (60 lb) per chamber cook at 5 to 8 psi. These may be equipped with timers and pull-out shelves. Some vegetables may be put into perforated pans to facilitate steam getting to them while others must be put into pans of water. If water must be used, it is a signal that boiling in a steam-jacketed kettle or stock pot is a better procedure. Most frozen items cooked in steam are best thawed before cooking to prevent the outsides cooking before complete thawing has occurred. Food cooked in steam should be separated so that steam can get around

Table 6-10. Steam Pressures and Temperatures

Pounds Pressure	°F	Pounds Pressure	°F	Pounds Pressure	°F
0	212	8	235	25	267
2	218	10	240	30	274
4	224	15	250	40	287
6	230	20	259	50	298

it. If food packs such as peas, spinach or rice, cooking may be uneven unless placed in a lot of water. Since foods cook quickly, especially at high pressures, the use of timers to indicate the end of cooking time is recommended. Food flavors can build up in the water used for steam in self-contained units, so therefore it is important that old, used water be flushed out frequently and new water added to steam-generating tanks. Steam pressures should be released slowly from equipment. Too rapid a release may cause liquids in a steamer to leap out of pans, peas jump out of their skins or some other products disintegrate.

STEAM-JACKETED KETTLES

Shallow steam kettles are easier to work into than deep types. Some of the deep units are so tall that special platforms or ladders have to be used so that workers can work into them. Both types are used for the making of stocks, soups, braising meats, making entrees, cooking beans and other legumes, boiling vegetables and any other production work in which stock pots on top of the range were used. Kettles may be sized from 2 to 4000 gallons and operate usually on from 5 to 8 psi.

Most non-tilt kettles have spigots and drains on the bottom through which liquids can be drained. Large kettles may have electrical stirrers so that paddles can be lowered into mixtures and mechanically agitated. These should be capable of variable speeds and the agitator should tip out. Another feature is that some may be cooled with cool tap water inside the jacket after steam has been turned off. For larger kettles refrigerated water or glycol is used to obtain a more rapid cooling rate. Pumps for emptying large steam-jacketed kettles are also used.

Tilting steam kettles are used for cooking vegetables, pie fillings, puddings, salad dressings, entree mixtures, etc. Small units for cooking small quantities or batches are usually on a table with a drain in front. Tilting is by lever. Larger units are tilted by a wheel moving the gears. Both tilting and stationary kettles may be self-contained or operated by steam from a central boiler.

Most foods cooked in steam-jacketed kettles are cooked in liquids.

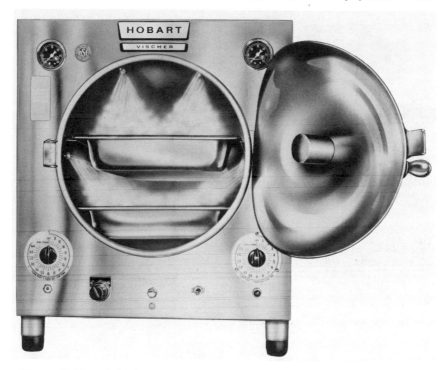

Figure 6–12. A high speed steamer. Note NSF approval stamp upper left. (Courtesy Hobart)

Browning of meat is possible by leaving the meat without liquid and frequently turning. Some foods are first washed and the water run off. Closing the lid saves heat and reduces evaporative loss. Hard boiling water is no hotter than gentle boiling water. Water boils hard because it is getting rid of excess energy being put into it. Besides costing more to heat, the excess heat loss makes work areas uncomfortable and increases cost in pumping it out. Hard boiling breaks up some foods and can toughen meats.

Perforated containers may be used to hold vegetables cooked in a steam kettle, thereby simplifying removal. With mild-flavored vegetables, the cooking water can be used several times before new water must be used. About $\frac{2}{3}$ to $\frac{3}{4}$ of the total capacity of a kettle is used, as room must be left for boiling action or for work to be done in the kettle.

Clean kettles immediately after use or fill them with cold water to soak so that food does not dry in them. Use warm water with a good detergent and a stiff brush on the interior. Disassemble the spigot and clean. Clean the drain with a long-handled bottle brush, run off the

Figure 6–13. A shelf-contained battery of (from left to right) tilting brais-ing pan, standard steamer, tilting steam-jacketed kettle and convection oven. (Courtesy Market Forge)

water and fill the kettle for rinsing. When completed, wipe dry and leave the top open. Wipe down outside areas and clean away soil with soapy water, brushes, cloths and scrapers. Rinse and dry.

Beverage-Making Equipment

An ideal coffee maker is one "which provides essentially fresh brew in each cup and meets the general requirements of the establishment in which it is used with respect to cost, size, rates of dispensing and ap-pearance."*

Urns are sized from $2\frac{1}{2}$ to over 100 gallons. In each, brewing $\frac{3}{4}$ or more of the urn capacity should be made. Two $2\frac{1}{2}$-gallon urns are more flexible than one 5-gallon urn since a batch of brew is on hand while the other is being cleaned and readied. If service is slow, it is better to have smaller batches on hand. Some metals are attacked by brew compounds and others give a metallic flavor and off-color to a brew. The best to least desirable metals for coffee equipment are stainless steel, silver, nickel or chrome, copper, aluminum and tin plate. Glass, porcelain and other ceramics are excellent but they are fragile.

Urns operate by water dripping through coffee grounds in a bag or basket. The latest types refill automatically and have timers to adjust

* Niven, W., Jr., and B. C. Shaw, "Critical Conditions for Quantity Coffee Brew-ing," *Coffee and Tea Industries,* 80:44; 75–76, April, 1957.

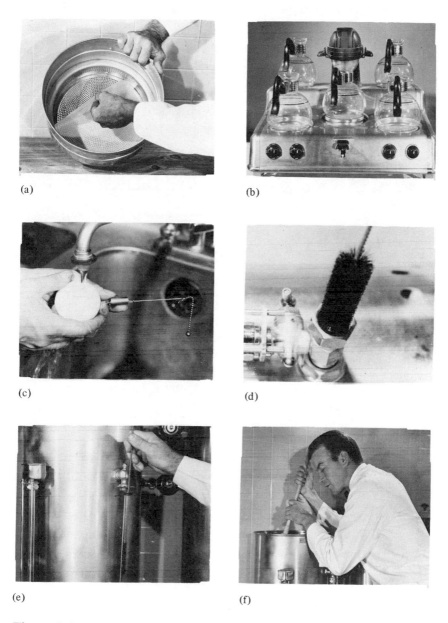

(a)

(b)

(c)

(d)

(e)

(f)

Figure 6–14. (a) A paper filter in a container such as this is one of the best units for an urn. (b) A drip coffee maker. The cup holding the ground coffee is in the unit shown in the center. Water is heated in an instant heater in this unit and flows through the grounds into the center pot. (c) Wash thoroughly all cloth filters before using them, preferably in hot water but at least with cool water as shown here. (d) Use a brush to get into tubes and gauges as shown in (e). (f) Scrub thoroughly with a good brush to remove all coffee sediment and oils. (Courtesy Coffee Brewing Institute)

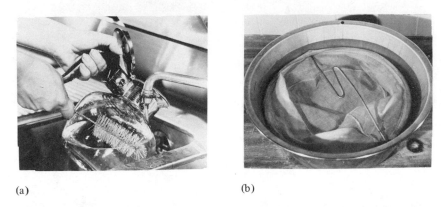

(a)   (b)

Figure 6–15. (a) Soak cloth bags in cold water when not in use. (b) Scrub these pots until all traces of coffee are removed. Rinsing is not enough. (Courtesy Coffee Brewing Institute)

to the amount of brew made. Swivel-arm sprays are also convenient. A clear brew is desirable and the bag or basket is a critical factor in achieving it. Some metal filters with perforated plates or metal discs with holes clean easily and do not clog as readily as screen filters, but may allow sediment to go into the brew. Metal baskets using paper filters are usually efficient as are cloth bags with a good tight weave. An urn bag sagging into a brew gives over-extraction making a dark brew with a strong, bitter flavor, therefore a riser that holds the bag up and makes it possible to get a more even extraction should be used. Fine coffee grounds act as a filter. It is not correct to repour coffee through grounds to clarify it. Water should pass through only once. Filters should be easily cleanable; some woven-wire screen filters catch fine grounds and these give off-flavors to a brew. Filters should also control the flow of water so that a proper contact time is achieved. Clear, bright brew holds quality longer than a cloudy one. Coffee urns should make the water the right temperature. Interiors and parts should be stainless steel so that they clean easily and give good brew quality. Ceramic liners are acceptable but, if they craze, they can hold coffee oils and sediment in the cracks and harm the brew. Bags and filters should be sized for the equipment and give proper contact time. A system that discards filter papers each time a brew is made is good. New urn bags or cloth filters should be washed thoroughly in 140° F water to remove starch or sizing and other foreign material because hot water swells the starch which is retained in the cloth fibers. After washing, they should be rinsed well in cold water.

Vacuum equipment has a top and bottom. The bottom holds the

Figure 6–16. A riser such as shown here gives more even extraction from the grounds over a bag that hangs down and allows all the water to flow out from the center. (Courtesy Coffee Brewing Institute)

brewing water which when boiled develops steam, forcing the hot water up through a spout onto grounds in the top. When the unit is removed from the heat, the steam condenses, forming a vacuum in the bottom which sucks the brew down into the bottom leaving the grounds in the top on a filter. (See Figure 6-17.)

Much coffee today is made in drip units of 8 to 12 cup capacity. These operate much the same as an urn with hot water passing through grounds filtering down into a bowl from which the coffee is served. Most are automatic, delivering the correct amount of water at a proper temperature. "Instant heaters" are used which have a very high heat input so that a $\frac{1}{4}$-inch flow of cold water is instantly heated as it flows through. Preportioned drip coffee packs are usually used. These are placed into

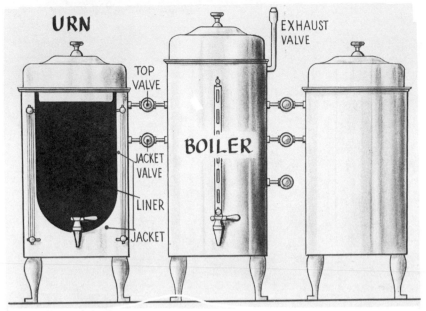

(a)

(b)

Figure 6–17. (a) The working units of an urn battery. (b) The principle on which the vacuum maker works. Steam pressure forces the hot water up into the grounds and when this steam condenses a vacuum is formed that pulls the brew down into the bottom bowl, leaving the grounds in the top.

filter cups. Some operations grind fresh coffee beans for each new pot of brew. The grinder automatically delivers the correct amount of coffee into the cup. Brewing cups should be easily cleaned and maintained.

Coffee makers for instant coffee will make from 300 to 500 cups per hour. Most have instant heaters for heating the water. Some agitation and a 2-minute rest favor flavor development. The maker may have at its top roasted coffee beans in a glass container to remove the psychological stigma that some attach to instant coffee.

CLEANING

Coffee deposits and oils easily oxidize and give rancid flavors. They spread as a thin film on equipment. Some are transparent and cannot be seen. Coffee equipment should be designed to reduce surfaces where coffee substances remain. It should be very easy to clean. This includes faucets, gages, bags, filters, bowls and other equipment parts. Special instructions should be given workers for cleaning and maintaining the equipment and the right cleaning tools and compounds should be supplied.

Clean urns with hot water and a stiff urn brush after each use. Scrub the sides and use a small, long-wired bottle brush to clean gages, faucets and outlet pipes. Clean-out caps usually facilitate this operation. Clean thoroughly, running the cleaning water off and filling with fresh water. Rinse well and run this water off. The water should run clear. Rinse off the inside of the lid and dry leaving it ajar on top of the urn. Fill the urn with several gallons of water and before using the urn, drain this water and rinse several times. Wash cloth bags and filters thoroughly using no soap, detergent or bleach. If cloths become sour, stained or retain the odor of coffee, discard. Place cloths into clean, fresh cool water to reduce the opportunity for oxidation of coffee oils or sediment remaining.

Vacuum or other drip equipment should similarly be cleaned after each use. Use a special brush that reaches into all areas of the bowls. Clean filter equipment thoroughly. Rinse everything well in clean water. Do the same for automatic equipment.

Once a week fill an urn nearly full of water. Add cleaning compound following manufacturer's directions and turn on the heat. Allow the urn to stand several hours. If left overnight, do not leave the heat on. Then clean well as described above, and rinse and scrub again. Rinse several times until all traces of the cleaning solution are gone. Fill the urn with several gallons of water and leave the lid ajar. Empty before using. Most urns have an outer jacket of water surrounding the brew container. It is important that this jacket be sufficiently filled at all times.

Check urns for this frequently, even those with automatic devices for filling them.

Clean coffee-making equipment for other units in the same manner once a week, soaking at least 30 minutes in hot water containing good cleaning compounds. Scrub well, cleaning all areas. Rinse sufficiently to free the equipment of all traces of cleaning compound.

Miscellaneous Cooking Equipment

Electric or gas toasters with a belt that moves around a heating element are used for producing quantities of toast but for toasting bread, rolls or other items at location, pop-up toasters are used. Items can also be toasted under salamanders, broilers, griddles or even infrared lamps.

Waffle irons should be conditioned by heating a well-greased grid until it nearly smokes, then holding this temperature 5 to 10 minutes, wiping very clean with a soft cloth and repeating the procedure. Service personnel may operate these units just as they frequently do toasters for their own toast orders.

Roll warmers heat breads and other foods at temperatures around 180° to 200° F. Some of the drawers are vented to prevent products from becoming soggy from moisture build-up. Pies, puddings, sauces and other products needing to be warm for service can also be held in them.

Mechanical Equipment

Some mechanical equipment can do much to facilitate work in quantity production. Time can be reduced and quality of performance improved. Equipment can also help minimize work strain and thus reduce fatigue.

Cutting Equipment

Food choppers (grinders) are used to chop or grind meat, nuts, vegetables crumbs and other foods. A variation in the particle size is possible by using plates of different size holes. The food is fed into a hopper and forced down with a wooden or plastic mallet into a screw that pushes the food through the plate. A rotating blade usually assists in cutting the food. Some juice may develop and this drip should be caught. The hands should never be used to push food down the hopper. Choppers should be cleaned or soaked immediately after use because food that dries on parts is difficult to remove. Choppers may be separate pieces of equipment or attachments on other power equipment.

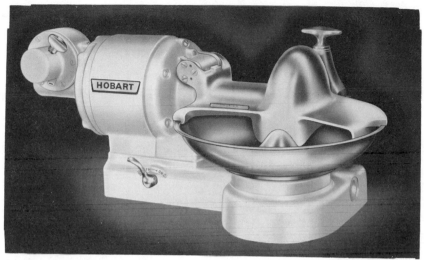

(a)

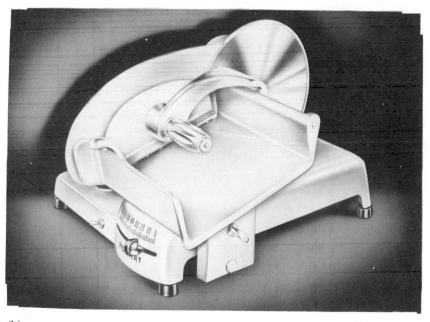

(b)

Figure 6–18. (a) Two knives rotate at extremely rapid speed under the raised portion of the hood on this cutter while the bowl rotates moving food under these knives. (b) A slicer. End weight is shown in the back. Note also the gauge settings for giving different slice thickness. (Courtesy Hobart)

Figure 6–19. A vertical cutter. The baffle is shown on the open lid. The knives are on the vertical axle in the center of the lower bowl.

A different food cutter has two knives that spin on a very rapidly rotating axle under a cover. The bowl turns automatically so that all areas pass under the knives. Food can be fed into the knives with a mallet. Careless operation, especially pushing food into the knives with the hands, can cause a serious accident. It is important that the knives be true and well sharpened to cut rather than bruise food. The bowl can be filled to a $\frac{1}{3}$ to $\frac{1}{2}$ capacity. Food can be finely minced or coarsely chopped by regulating time. Nuts, hard-frozen meat, whole grain cereals and hard-crusted breads can dull the knives. The chopper can be a separate piece of equipment or be an attachment to other mechanical equipment.

Slicers, graters or cubers for vegetables that are attachments to food choppers or mixers find good use in quantity work. The slicer forces down food into a rotating blade which can be varied to give different slice thickness. It is especially effective for slicing cabbage for slaw, slicing salad vegetables, potatoes, etc. The grater operates in a similar manner to the slicer and different size blades make it possible to get different size gratings. A special feeding device and cutters are required for the cuber.

The Qualheim cutter slices from 1/64 to $\frac{1}{4}$ inch thick, dices food into various sizes, cuts strips from julienne to French fry size and does other preparation tasks. The machine has several different openings and uses different cutters for each task. Food is fed into the machine with a metal mallet. The time for assembly, disassembly and cleaning is practical only when a large quantity of food can be processed through it.

A vertical cutter and mixer has two knives on a vertical axle that spins in an enclosed bowl at high speed, operating much on the same principle as a small blender. It can process a large quantity of food in a short time. For instance, it processes 20 pounds of lettuce for salad in $1\frac{1}{2}$ seconds. It can be used to make fine emulsions such as mayonnaise. Some foods must be chopped with water in the bowl to reduce bruising. It is possible to vary the position of the blades to obtain different cutting results. If half or less of the bowl capacity is used, the blades should be at the bottom. A failure to keep blades sharp and true can lead to poor results. Hard-frozen meat, nuts, crusts and whole-grain products can dull the knives quickly. The machine cannot be opened when in operation nor operated when the lid is up. Capacities are 15 to 80 quarts. On the 15-qt and 25-qt models a mixing baffle which moves food into the rotating knives is operated by hand. On the larger models this baffle is operated mechanically. The baffle moves counterclockwise and opposite to that of the knives. A short jerk during turning helps to free food that might be caught on the baffle and moves it into the blades. The manufacturer's instructions for operation and maintenance should be closely followed. Unless a program for use is well worked out, this machine can stand idle much of the time. With planning, however, this machine can do many tasks now done by other machines.

A slicer is used to give uniform slices of cheese, meat, vegetables or some bakery goods. A gauge can be set to give different thicknesses. It is easier to get good slices from one having a slanted blade than one having a vertical one since slices tend to fold on the latter. To use, set the gauge and place the food on the carrier, placing the food so that it is cut across the grain and the best shape and size is obtained. If necessary, pretrim and preshape. Place an end weight on the back of the food to give a steady pressure, forcing the food down into the rapidly rotating blade. Pressure from the hands gives uneven slices and creates a potential safety hazard. Turn the machine on when the gauge is set and the food in position. Some machines have a carriage that operates automatically, going back and forth to obtain slices, while others operate the blade only mechanically and the worker moves the carriage back and forth manually to obtain slices. Holding the hand in a plastic wrap carefully under large slices or tender products and lowering them onto a container reduces breaking. Some of the newer automatic machines have devices to catch and lower the slice. Follow the manufacturer's instructions for maintaining and operating the unit. It is important that the blade be kept very sharp and true. A special sharpening stone is used, held against the blade at the proper angle as the motor turns the blade.

Mixers

A mixer is used to mash potatoes and to mix foods. The pantry uses it for dressings, to mix foods and ship items. The bake shop uses it extensively to mix batters and doughs, make frostings, whip foams and do other jobs. In a large bakeshop a horizontal mixer is used for mixing large batches of bread, cookies or other stiff doughs. Upright mixers are sized from 5-qt to 140-qt. Adapter rings and different size agitaters to fit the same machine make it possible to use mixing bowls of different sizes and thus vary the batch size for different mixers. Normally, in a large bakeshop an 80-qt and 20-qt mixer will be used with adapters for each. The cooks need a large mixer that can be adapted from 80-qt to 60-qt, 40-qt and 30-qt size. The pantry needs a 20-qt that adapts to 12-qt and 10-qt. Bowl dollies and trucks are used for large mixers and some have motors that raise and lower the bowls.

Different types of agitators are needed. Dough hooks are used for bread doughs and a special scalloped one is used for making richer sweet doughs. It gives good mixing action but pulls the dough less. A pastry cutter has a wire or cutter on the front side that moves through the flour and shortening, blending the two. This should be removed and a dough hook or paddle used to finish making dough after water is added. Flat beaters are used to make cookie doughs or cakes, giving good creaming and blending action. Wire whips of different kinds are used for jobs where air is incorporated into egg foams, whipping cream, etc. A wing whip with projecting wire wings does a good job of creaming and whipping at the same time. Agitators may be interchanged during production of the same product. For instance, an egg foam may be prepared for an angel cake with the whip and then the wing whip used to mix in the flour, sugar and other ingredients. Agitators should reach to about 1/16 inch of all bowl parts. To scrape down, the machine should be stopped, and with a flexible spatula sufficiently long to reach the bowl bottom and flexible enough to bend around the bowl contour, the bowl should be completely scraped down, with a twisting-turning motion of the wrist to remove all material on the sides and bring it into the center. Scraping down must be frequent in some work. Many mixers

Figure 6–20. A vertical mixer. The bowl is raised by the lever on the right and speed settings and starting and stopping mechanism are shown on the right face. In front is an opening into which grinders, slicers, choppers, graters and other auxiliary units can be attached and driven by the motor. (Courtesy Hobart)

Figure 6–21. A bench model mixer. (Courtesy Hobart)

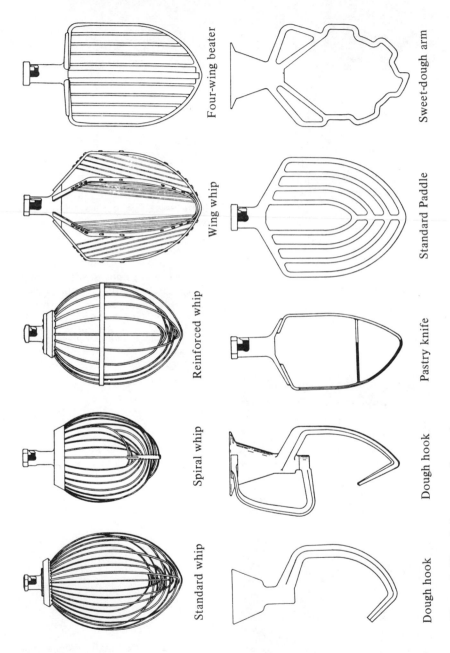

Four-wing beater

Sweet-dough arm

Wing whip

Standard Paddle

Reinforced whip

Pastry knife

Spiral whip

Dough hook

Standard whip

Dough hook

Figure 6–22.   Agitators used on mixers.

are designed to use attachments such as choppers, slicers, cutters, dicers and other devices.

Refrigeration and Freezers

Large refrigerated walk-ins are used to hold foods at sufficiently low temperatures to hold quality and safeguard against bacterial growth. Different units are used to hold different foods, as some foods cannot be mixed. For instance, eggs and dairy products easily absorb other food flavors and must be kept separate. Walk-in refrigeration is used to store garbage and other waste in warm climates. If mobile equipment can be moved in and out of walk-ins use is increased. Walk-ins are mostly used to store foods awaiting production but often they also hold foods under production that cannot be conveniently stored in reach-in refrigerators. All foods in freezers and refrigerators should be covered or protected from air and dust. Moisture-vapor-proof wraps or tight-fitting covers on containers reduce evaporation losses. Warm foods cool to nearly room temperature outside refrigerators almost as fast as they do under refrigeration, and therefore, they should be cooled outside until nearly room temperature, then put under refrigeration. Stirring liquids or setting foods in running water baths will promote faster cooling, as will placing food in front of a fan or an open window or in a good draft. If a knife or other instrument is placed underneath a container, the cooling is faster. Thick foods such as puddings, gravies, dressings, etc., should not be put into refrigerators in large masses but spread out into shallow lots so they cool quickly.

Walk-in freezers are used more for storage than immediate production, and mobile equipment should be able to be moved in and out of them. Because low temperature storage dehydrates foods, the use of moisture-vapor-proof wraps or closed containers is necessary. Frequently, when slack time is available, workers may prepare parfaits and other party items, as well as bakery goods or frozen meals, for storage.

Reach-in refrigerators are largely located in work centers. They are usually used for on-going production and not food storage although foods used frequently in production needing refrigeration are stored there. Some may have shelving that can be changed to suit storage needs. All foods should be covered and frequently checked to see that no foods needing discarding are kept. It is important in storing foods not to pack them in too tightly since they need good air circulation around them. In refrigerators that depend upon natural convection, the bottom area is usually coldest. If a fan operates inside, all areas should be about equal

Figure 6–23. On the left a mobile hot cabinet, on the right a mobile refrigerator. (Courtesy Crescent Metal Products)

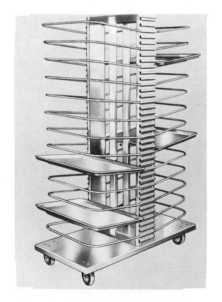

Figure 6–24. A spider used in the bakeshop to hold production awaiting delivery or for loading or unloading into ovens. (Courtesy Crescent Metal Products)

Figure 6–25.   A refrigerated unit that holds a mobile cart. (Courtesy Market Forge)

temperature and work planned to open doors as little as possible. This helps keep a lower and more even temperature.

Mobile refrigerators are used for storing foods and then distributing them to service areas, for banquet service or other areas where refrigeration units are lacking. Also, chilled foods can be placed into well insulated carts and held until needed.

Pass-through refrigerators hold foods from production to service units. They are usually sized to hold pans 18 x 26 inches, 14 x 18 inches and 12 x 20 inches and some are designed so roll-in equipment can be moved into them.

Freezers in work areas are not frequently used except for holding frozen desserts and some other frozen items. However, with the increasing use of frozen prepared foods the use of on-location freezers is increasing.

Special Butchershop Equipment

Small operations seldom do much butchering and the small amount done can occur at the cook's unit where a cutting board, meat saw and knives can be stored for the work. In large units a band saw is used. It is especially useful for cutting through frozen meats. A saw on a circular band rotates rapidly and novices should not be allowed to use it. A butchershop uses also meat grinders, meat cubers, tenderizers and special chopping equipment. Poultry singers, tendon pullers and other specialized equipment may also be used. Because the work in this section is so highly specialized and is somewhat hazardous and so few individuals now work at it, detailed discussion of the equipment is perhaps not needed.

Special Bakery Equipment

A dough divider and rounder is used to cut bread doughs into desired sizes and then roll them into rounded shapes. It can be used this way for pan rolls or flattened for hamburger buns, elongated for weiner buns, or folded for Parker House rolls, etc. Small operations usually use a manually operated divider but larger ones use mechanical ones. In large operations dough dividers and rounders are separate units connected to other production units in assembly line fashion. Fermented dough will be automatically moved through these two units and then into an overhead proofer and panned. Dough rollers or sheeters are used for rolling out pie, bread or other doughs. Bench-type rollers are used on tables. Rollers are also part of pie machines for rolling top and bottom crusts. Sheeters are similar to rollers but handle larger masses of dough. Special settings are required on these units for Danish pastry, puff paste and other rolled-in doughs. Yeast products must be properly rested to be relaxed enough to go through a sheeter and other doughs such as cookie and pie must be refrigerated to be stiff enough to go through the machine. A proofing cabinet is used to condition yeast doughs after panning and before baking. It must maintain temperatures around 90° F and a relative humidity of 80 to 85%. Some are automatically controlled so temperatures and humidity hold within narrow ranges, while others may require manual operation of heating units and a pan of water may be placed on the bottom over the heating unit to give proper humidity.

These proofers can be mobile but usually are stationary and carts are rolled in and out of them.

A bakeshop uses much specialized equipment depending upon what is produced there. For instance, if pulled-sugar work is done, a heating unit to keep batches of pulled sugar warm will be needed. This equipment is so highly specialized and varies so much that its description, use and what it will do is best learned on the job.

Suggested laboratory experiments or work assignments for Chapter 6:

1. Take students to a quantity kitchen pointing out the different equipment, explaining operation, use and what it can do.
2. Assign students the task of studying a special piece of equipment and reporting to the class on maintenance, care, use and operation.
3. Assign students the task of demonstrating a show-and-tell lesson on the maintenance, care, use and operation of equipment, the learner being inexperienced and unacquainted with the equipment.
4. Assign a group of students the task of setting up a preventative maintenance schedule for a selected group of equipment.
5. Have students submit short reports on equipment used when doing quantity production assignments.
6. Have students read the current literature and report on new equipment or new food systems.
7. Have students prepare a list of dangerous equipment and some of the major safety regulations to follow in using this equipment.
8. Have students disassemble, clean and assemble a major piece of equipment. Have others demonstrate how to sharpen and maintain kitchen cutting tools.

BIBLIOGRAPHY

Blaker, Gertrude and Longree, Karla, *Quantity Food Equipment,* John Wiley and Sons, Inc., New York City, 1970.

Folsom, LeRoi A., *How to Master the Tools of Your Trade,* Dimensions Press, Guilford, Conn., 1965.

Kotschevar, L. and Terrell, M., *Food Service Planning,* John Wiley and Sons, Inc., New York City, 1961.

Terrell, M. E., *Professional Food Preparation,* John Wiley and Sons, Inc., New York City, 1971.

(Also consult brochures of various equipment manufacturers.)

Section II

Kitchen Production

7

Pantry Production

The pantry makes salads, appetizers, sandwiches, other cold items and may prepare breakfasts. In the continental kitchen, the pantry is usually separated from the *garde manger* section that prepares cold meat and fish but the *garde manger chef* may be in charge of both. Some pantries make beverages, fountain items and dish desserts.

Pantry work is characterized by the production of many small units requiring considerable hand labor and much dexterity and speed. Wide variety in the types of foods made and the need to have last-minute assembly to preserve freshness and temperature make it necessary to use work simplification as much as possible. While the technical knowledge required may not be as great as for cooking or baking, perhaps a better sense of artistry and proportion in food is needed. Workers should have the ability to organize well, keep work areas clean and withstand pressure. Good space utilization will be needed because of the quantity of items to be carried in the section and the number of items that must be preprepared awaiting demand.

Workers should know how to set up good work centers and have proper work flow between them. In making a number of similar items, one set of motions should be repeated for a group and another set until the work is done. Thus in making a large number of cocktails, all glasses should be placed on a tray at one time, filled with cocktail product, covered with sauce, garnished with parsley and all lemon slices added.

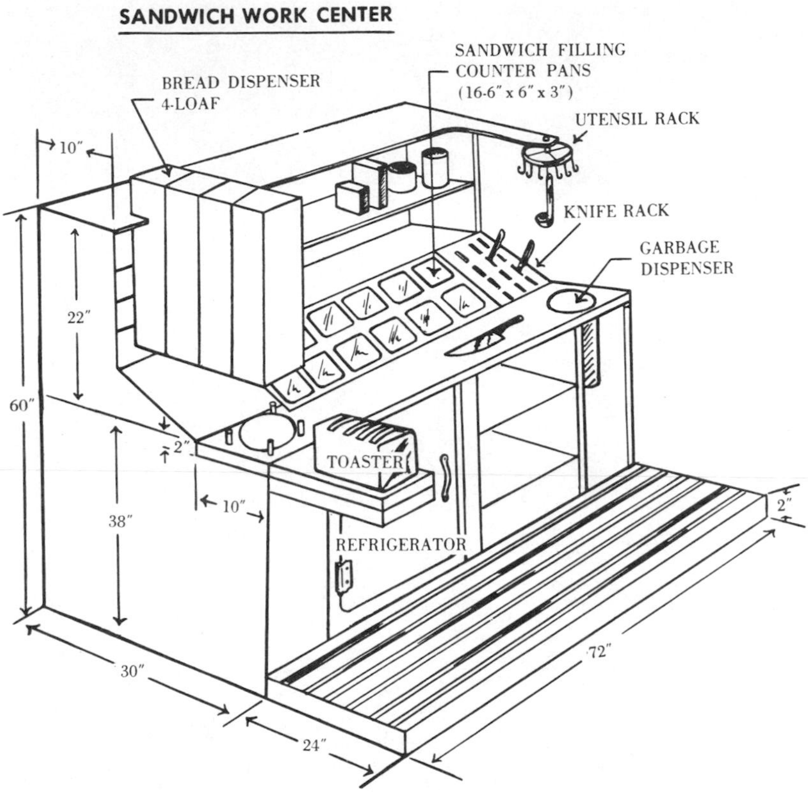

SANDWICH WORK CENTER

Figure 7–1. A rough drawing of a work center that might achieve high production with minimum utilization of space and worker effort. (Courtesy Z. Eppel)

The cocktail product and sauce could be added in alternate motions using two hands and the parsley and lemon slice added last using two hands. Groups of two or more workers facing each other across a table sharing work to limit motions can do more in the same time than individuals working separately. Moving belts or moving circular tables may be used moving at a speed of from eight to 12 feet per minute. Highest production is achieved when the pace in work is steady and even; excessive speed can destroy this rhythm. Some attention must be given to resupply of the pantry because a considerable quantity of a number of bulky items must be transported to it. (See Chapter 2.)

High standards of sanitation must be practiced. The fact that pantry foods are not cooked and are good culture for bacteria makes it necessary to use caution and assure that all foods are fresh. Refrigerated

Figure 7–2. See that tools are arranged conveniently for work use, especially in areas where speed is important.

units should provide 40° F constant temperatures under heavy production use. Only the food needed for a day's production should be made up at one time if it is perishable and only that needed for a meal should be removed from the batch. Provide covers for food when not in use. No materials should be allowed to stand at room temperature for a total time of over four hours. Handle goods as little as possible. Keep all utensils, and storage and work spaces scrupulously clean. Watch carry-over foods for these may quickly spoil and cause trouble. Where production occurs before patrons, have workers use tongs, forks and other tools to handle foods. Plastic gloves are recommended.

Evaluate preparation requiring large amounts of labor, such as fancy sandwiches, complex fillings, elaborate garnishes and dishes requiring a great deal of arrangement. Attractiveness is essential but cannot be achieved at a high labor cost. Simplicity may create more eye appeal than elaborate design or garnish. A sprig of mint may do more for a fruit salad than an elaborately stuffed date. Fluting a cucumber or peeled banana with a fork before slicing may create more interest than cutting into fancy shapes. An unpeeled red apple slice not only adds color but saves time over peeling. Bite-sized pieces in a myriad of form and color can achieve a desirable artistic effect in a salad. Overworking foods gives them a fatigued appearance. Even though a food may be low in cost, the time required for its preparation such as stuffed eggs, Waldorf salad, sliced orange salad, etc., may make it a costly item.

Attractiveness can be gained by using good arrangement and food combinations in distinctive dishes. A balanced arrangement of sandwich pieces with a cup of hot soup or an arranged fruit salad on a chilled glass plate may be more appealing than elaborately decorated food. Cutting a sandwich into varied shapes may add more than an elaborate garnish. A coquille shell filled with seafood salad or fruit salad served in half a cantaloupe may create much appeal. A large sherbet glass can be used for a chilled fruit salad. Different shaped dishes can add interest and give form and variety to a buffet.

Figure 7–3. A pantry worker assembles fruit cups for a large banquet. Note how he completes a total set of motions before moving to another set. This makes for higher productivity. (Courtesy Biltmore Hotel, Los Angeles)

Figure 7–4. This baked bean and tomato salad is well merchandised because of its fresh and attractive appearance. (Courtesy H. J. Heinz Co.)

SANDWICHES

Sandwiches are good sellers and satisfy many food needs. Most are used for a light meal or snack but they may also be used for desserts or even for breakfast in such forms as a scrambled egg and bacon sandwich or a toasted marmalade rolled sandwich. A hot sandwich with a vegetable salad can be a meal.

A sandwich is bread filled with some type of food. A typical sandwich consists of a filling inside two slices of bread but this is varied widely. Sandwiches might be classified as follows:

Hot Sandwiches	*Cold Sandwiches*
regular	regular
broiled	open-face
grilled	decker types (dagwood)
deep-fried	rolled or pinwheel
baked	finger, layered or checker-board

A regular hot meat sandwich is meat, bread and gravy either closed or open-face; gravy can be omitted. Toasted bread can be used for either hot or cold sandwiches. Open-face sandwiches may be large, fancy small or canapés.

Old favorites should be offered frequently but good merchandising is offering new ideas with these. Unusual fillings, variety bread, service on attractive dishes or unusual presentation may be used to create sales. If attention is given to the presentation of sandwiches in plastic wraps, sales can be increased. They should be wrapped so that the cut side identifies fillings and garnishes.

Standard

Bread, fillings and garnishes for sandwiches should be absolutely fresh. Fillings should be pleasantly flavored, tender in texture, easily eaten and rich enough to give an appetite-satisfying sandwich. Excess flavor such as sweetness or tartness or harsh or bland flavors should be avoided.

Figure 7–5.   The worker is reaching too far in the making of these baked cranberry and cheese sandwiches. Confine distances of reach to 14 inches, if possible, and never more than 26 inches. (Courtesy American Baking Institute)

Chopped fillings should be distinct and not messy. Soft fillings should contain some crisp material such as chopped celery, green pepper, lettuce, thinly sliced cucumber. About a third to half of the total sandwich weight should be filling. The filling should not hang over the edge. Bread should be fresh, firm with a close, smooth crumb of good flavor and moistness. It should be capable of being picked up without bending or losing filling. Bread containing an excess of softeners does not make good sandwiches. Sandwiches cut raggedly or unevenly or barely holding together are unattractive. Cold sandwiches should be cold and hot sandwiches hot. Grilled or toasted sandwiches should have a crisp, outer crust. Interesting color and design should be sought and garnishes should be edible and suitable to the sandwich. Plates or containers should suit the size and type of sandwich.

Sandwich Ingredients

Bread

Fresh bread should be firm and not have a pasty texture. It should be stored for immediate use from 75° to 85° F in a dry place. Store soft-crusted breads in original wraps, but hard-crusted ones without wraps in a place where there is free air movement. A mobile rack or simple drawer is adequate for storage. Hard-crusted breads have a relatively short storage life. Bread can easily absorb odors and even cigarette odor on a worker's hands can flavor it. Storage areas should be cleaned daily with a soft, dry brush or with an industrial vacuum cleaner and scrubbed and dried once a week. Old and new supplies should be separated each day, old bread to be used for toasting, grilling or French toast. Supplies should be planned to have only enough for a day's production. Refrigerating bread stales it faster than holding at room temperature while freezing retards staling best of all. Frozen bread should be thawed in its wraps and may be spread, filled and then wrapped.

Spreads

Flavor, richness or moistness may be reasons for selecting a spread. Margarine or butter are most commonly used but mayonnaise, salad dressing, cheese mixtures, peanut butter, jelly or others may be used. The danger of soaking is increased when butter or margarine are melted and used or when they are softened with added milk or other moist products. Flavored butter or margarine spreads may eliminate fillings but the spread should be soft and plastic with no air incorporated in softening.

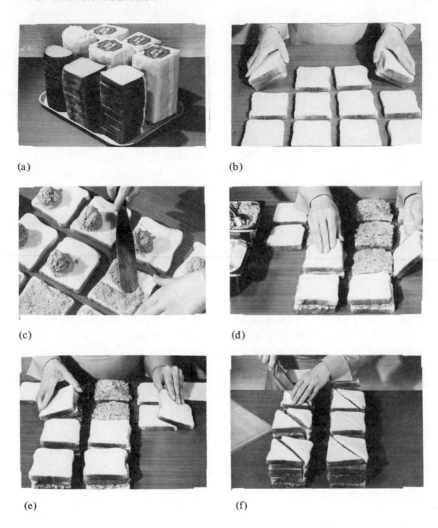

(a)

(b)

(c)

(d)

(e)

(f)

Figure 7–6. A one-worker method for making sandwiches in quantity. (a) Slit through wrappers in the center and place each half on its open side down on a tray. Remove wrappers as bread is used. (b) Pick up four slices of bread in each hand and start from center out to line slices to form four rows on working surface as shown. (c) An efficient spreading technique. Spread filling with spatula in one motion. With tip of spatula, press filling lightly, moving from upper right to upper left corner. Complete "S" motion to lower right and then left portion of slice. (A left-handed person would reverse this procedure.) (d) Using both hands, cap. (e) An alternate method is shown with the worker topping completed sandwiches and adding another row of fresh bread, spreading and filling as shown in (c). This may be repeated and the tier of three sandwiches may be cut at one time as shown in (f). (Courtesy American Baking Institute)

Table 7-1. Bread Slices in Standard Loaves

Loaf	Size Loaf (lb)	Slice Thick-ness (in.)	No. Slices (no ends)	Loaf	Size Loaf (lb)	Slice Thick-ness (in.)	No. Slices (no ends)
Regular, white	1¼	⅝	19	Rye, regular	1	⅜	23
Regular, white	1½	⅝	24	Rye, regular	2	⅜	33
Regular, whole wheat	1	⅝	16	Quick bread	1¾	⅜	20
Regular, whole wheat	2	½	28				
Regular, whole wheat	3	½	44				
Regular, whole wheat	3	⅜	56				
Sandwich, white*	2	½	28				
Sandwich, white*	2	⅜	36				
Sandwich, white*	3	½	44				
Sandwich, white*	3	⅜	56				

*4½ inches square

Table 7-2. Yields of Some Common Sandwich Materials

Item	Portion*	Quantity for 100 Sandwiches
Butter or margarine	2 to 3 t	2 to 3 lb
Jelly or jam	2T	3 qt (1 No. 10 can)
Spread-type filling	2½ T	1 gal
Peanut butter	1½ T	2½ qt
Mayonnaise	2 to 3 t	1 to 1½ qt
Lettuce	1 leaf	5 medium heads or 5 to 7½ lb
American cheese	1 to 1¼ oz	6¼ to 8 lb
Meat	1½ to 2 oz	9½ to 12½ lb

*Two slices of bread per portion; rough textured bread will require more spread than smooth textured bread.

Fillings

The filling gives a sandwich much of its character. Sliced meats or cheese are most common but salad mixtures are also popular. A standard ratio for a salad filling would be one part chopped vegetable and one of pickles to four of meat or other product. Mixtures such as banana, bacon and peanut butter or combinations with jellies, jams or other sweet items are popular and give variety. Many vegetable combinations are used, including the always popular lettuce and tomato sandwich. Fruit fillings such as date and nut can be used for special needs with variety breads. Many convenience fillings are available also on the market.

Filling mixtures should spread easily and be of good consistency for eating, neither too dry nor too moist, and messy fillings should be avoided. Mixed fillings with a fresh and distinct appearance increase acceptability. Limp or greasy bacon or limp, wilted lettuce can ruin an otherwise good sandwich. Meat or cheese slices should fit the bread and be sliced evenly.

Figure 7–7.   Bags may be used for wrapping sandwiches and then flip sealed. (Courtesy American Baking Institute)

Fillings should be prepared ahead and chilled well. Carry-over foods may find good use in sandwich materials but those of inferior quality should be discarded.

Garnishes

The garnish should suit the sandwich in texture, form, color and flavor. It may be substantial in quantity and it may be questioned whether a cup of broth, a small coleslaw salad or a spiced peach half are garnishes or food accompaniments. Lettuce, parsley, romaine, radishes, potato chips, shoestring potatoes, nuts, cheese, catsup, chili sauce or others can be garnishes.

Work Methods

Sandwich work centers will differ depending upon whether sandwiches are made in batches or to order and whether one or more workers make them. Normally, it takes as much time to line up for sandwich production as it does to make them. *Mise en place* is important for clutter can cause confusion, poor quality products and time loss. Tool and material location should follow the sequence of flow, arrangements being kept always the same to prevent workers from having to search. Vertical space reduces reach. A foot lever may be used to drop bread onto the work board or moving belt. Most operations will want rapid production. In one study 44 sandwiches per minute were made by using a wooden board slightly longer than five slices of bread, making five sandwiches. When two high, they were cut in half, the board then being placed on a moving belt for transfer to a mechanical wrapper and another board replacing it. Assembly lines speed production. The American Baking Institute, 400 East Ontario Street, Chicago, can be of assistance in working out methods to give good quality products with low labor cost.

Fancy Sandwiches

Fancy sandwiches are often used for teas or receptions. They are served assorted and attractively arranged on plates or trays covered with doilies and may accompany other foods. They are usually considered finger foods. Forms may be closed, open-face, pinwheel, rolled or other. Occasionally they may be hot. For variety, different breads may be used, such as date and nut, banana, fruit bread with interesting combinations

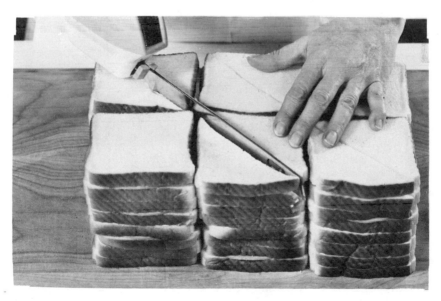

Figure 7–8.   An electric knife speeds work and saves tearing the sandwiches. (Courtesy American Baking Institute)

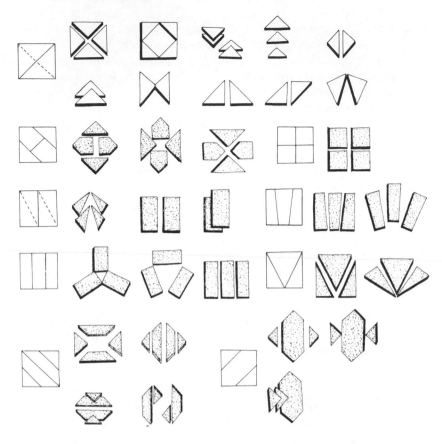

Figure 7–9. Cut and arrange sandwiches as shown here to achieve variety and interest. (Courtesy American Baking Institute)

using cream cheese, fruit, vegetable or meat salad. Day-old bread may be best for rolled or shaped sandwiches which should be made as close to service as possible. If they must be stored, they should be covered with a moisture-vapor-proof cover and frozen. A moist cloth may be used over a layer of wax paper for temporary storage. Oblong shapes about $1\frac{1}{2}$ by $3\frac{1}{4}$ inches, round ones not over 2 inches in diameter and oval ones about $2\frac{1}{2}$ inches long and about $1\frac{3}{4}$ wide are most effective.

Hot Sandwiches

About two ounces of sliced meat plus two $\frac{1}{4}$-inch to $\frac{1}{2}$-inch thick slices of bread makes a good regular hot sandwich. Spread may be omitted and the meat and bread covered with about 2 to 3 ounces of very hot gravy. If the meat is hot, this makes a warmer product to be served with mashed potatoes and a vegetable or salad for a meal.

Grilled sandwiches are best made of one-day or two-day-old bread, fairly dry and firm, buttered on top and bottom outsides and placed on a grill. A light weight on top gives more rapid and even browning. Fillings of sliced meats, cheese, ham and some salad mixtures are most suitable for this type of sandwich.

A toasted sandwich is made of toasted slices of bread. Two slices are toasted and then used the same as bread in making a regular sandwich.

Deep-fried sandwiches are egg-coated and deep-fried. They may be prepared ahead of service and cut into desired sizes. Upon order, they are dipped into egg and fried to order. The egg should not be thinned with milk or other liquid. Fillings should adhere rather tightly to the bread to hold shape while frying. Sometimes these sandwiches are grilled or baked in a very hot oven on greased pans.

Cold Sandwich Handling

Wrapping

Depending upon need, sandwiches may be sent to service wrapped or unwrapped. Vended sandwiches or those held a long time need wrapping. Wrapping procedures should be worked out so that they are accomplished with a minimum of effort and time. Uncut wrapped sandwiches should be clearly labeled, preferably with freezer marking pens which write easily on wax paper and plastic wraps. Cut sandwiches may be easily identified if the wrapped cut side is displayed but some identification helps speed selection. Only moisture-vapor-proof wraps should be used for sandwiches held a long time and heat sealing is recommended. Sandwich bags save labor. If sandwiches are to be heated or frozen in their wraps, the wrap should be suitable for the particular type of treatment.

Storing

Store sandwiches with perishable fillings under refrigeration, which may encourage bread staling but removes the danger of deterioration of the filling. Protect unwrapped sandwiches from drying out or absorbing odors. Do not cover with moist cloths unless some protecting medium is placed between the cloth and sandwiches. Place trays or wire baskets of prepared sandwiches in large moisture-vapor-proof wraps allowing

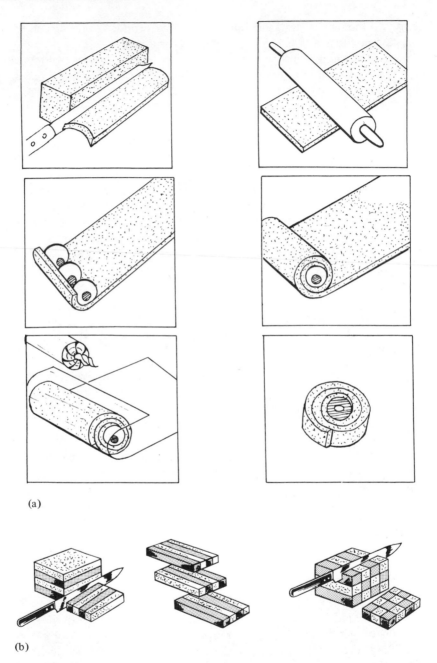

(a)

(b)

Figure 7–10. Techniques for making fancy sandwiches: (a) pinwheel, (b) finger or checkerboard, (c) mosaics, (d) envelopes, (e) cornucopias and (f) roll-ups.

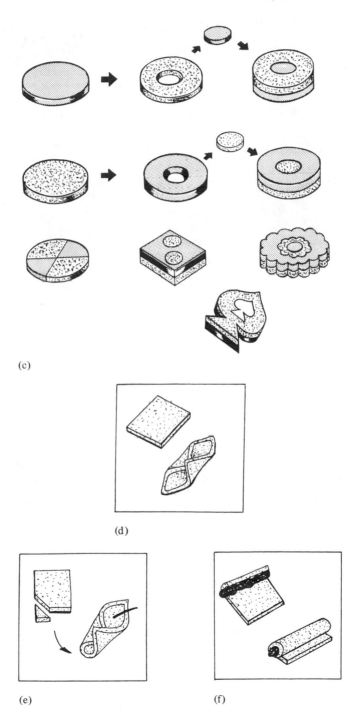

(c)

(d)

(e)   (f)

Figure 7–11. Fancy sandwiches arranged for a tea. (Courtesy American Baking Institute)

(a)   (b)

Figure 7–12. A breaded fried sandwich gives variety. (a) Dip the sandwich quickly into an egg-milk mixture (six eggs to one pint of milk gives best results, but more eggs to milk may be used). (b) Cover completely in crumbs after draining off excess egg-milk mixture. Use bread crumbs or other crumbs

Figure 7–13. Sandwiches can be desserts. Here a caramel-pecan-covered sandwich after toasting under a broiler is covered with a scoop of vanilla ice cream. (Courtesy American Baking Institute)

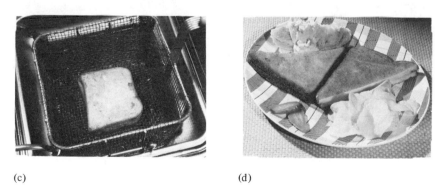

(c) (d)

that brown rapidly. (c) Place covered sandwich in frying basket, weight down lightly by covering with another basket or a metal screen, and fry one minute at 375° F. (d) The sandwich is sliced and served.

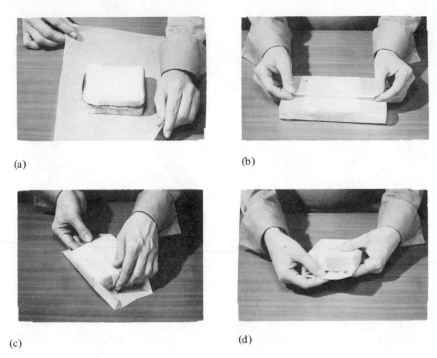

(a)

(b)

(c)

(d)

Figure 7–14. A method of wrapping uncut sandwiches. (a) Place an oblong piece of wrapping paper with the short sides parallel to the counter top. The sandwich is centered so the top and bottom crusts are parallel to the long side of the paper. (b) Bring ends of paper together in a pharmacist's fold. A neat, stay-in edge is formed that keeps air out. (c) Seal by tucking in ends of the paper, folding the top side in first. (d) Fold in the bottom side to form a neat, secure package. (Courtesy American Baking Institute)

good air space between containers in refrigerators. These containers may be on mobile racks and wheeled into walk-in refrigerators. Maximum storage time is 12 hours at 40° F. Freezing holds for longer periods but not all fillings can be frozen. Do not stack wrapped sandwiches more than three high nor unwrapped ones more than two high. Sandwiches with moist fillings soak easily when stacked.

Quantities to Use

Slices per pound of bread vary according to the size of the loaf, width of the slice and density of the bread. Thinly sliced bread is $\frac{1}{4}$-ich thick while $\frac{5}{8}$-inch slices are considered thick slices. A $\frac{1}{2}$-inch or $\frac{3}{8}$-inch slice is the usual thickness for sandwiches. Quick loaf bread is usually sliced

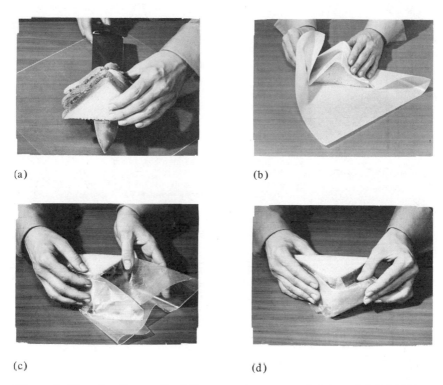

(a) (b)

(c) (d)

Figure 7–15. Another method for wrapping cut sandwiches. (a) Wrapping paper should be precut to proper size. Place the paper on the working surface so a corner points toward the worker. (b) Transfer the sandwich, cut side down, to the center and turn in the paper on both sides. (c) Lay the sandwich over on its side and fold the paper against the crust edges. (d) Tuck in the excess securely at the upper edge. Note all wrapping movements are away from the worker. (Courtesy American Baking Institute)

¼-inch. If a No. 20 scoop (1½ oz) is used, a quart of filling is sufficient for 20 sandwiches. One quart of jelly or jam will spread about 30 sandwiches with two tablespoons each and a quart of peanut butter will spread about twice that number a tablespoon each. A pound of soft butter or margarine or a pint of mayonnaise or salad dressing spreads about 100 sandwiches a teaspoon per slice. A 4-inch square cheese slice is usually an ounce and about 1½ to 2 ounces of meat serves for a sandwich, but hot meat sandwiches may have over two ounces of meat. Wieners run 10 per pound and hamburger patties are from 1½ to 5 ounces. A deluxe, open-face steak sandwich may use an 8 to 10 oz steak. Needs should be carefully calculated ahead since stopping to prepare additional food when busy hampers efficiency.

Table 7–3. Amounts Obtained Per Pound of Sandwich Material Used

Ingredient	Quantity per Pound or Other
Bacon, sliced	18 to 25 slices; 2½ c cooked and chopped
Butter or margarine	2 c
Cheese, Swiss or cheddar	16 slices about 4 by 4 inch 3/32 inch thick; 1 qt ground
Cheese, cream or cottage	1 pt
Date and nut filling	1 pt (scant)
Eggs, hard-cooked	10 large eggs, chopped equals 3 c
Fish, flaked	2½ c; each portion about 1½ oz or 2 T
Jelly, jam or preserve	1¾ c
Lettuce	1 medium head yields 16 leaves about ¾ oz each, leaving about 3 to 4 oz of heart
Meat	chicken, sliced 12 to 16 portions, 1½ to 1 oz each; ham, beef, or other 8 to 12 portions 2 to 1½ oz each; ground, cooked meat, 3 c
Olives, drained, chopped	3 c
Peanut butter	1⅞ c
Tomatoes, fresh	18 to 32 slices, 6 to 8 slices per tomato, 3/16 inch thick; a large tomato 5 by 5 size, about 2 to 2½ to the lb will give about the right size slice for a regular sandwich
Vegetables, chopped or diced	Celery, onions, carrots, peppers, etc. 2½ to 3 c

Table 7–4. Sandwich Filling Ingredients and Freezing

These Freeze Well	These Freeze Poorly
Cooked egg yolk	Cooked egg white
Peanut butter	Cream cheese or cottage cheese
Chopped or sliced cooked meats, poultry or fish	Process cheese
Lemon juice or orange juice	Chopped cooked bacon
Butter or margarine	Tomatoes, celery, lettuce, cucumbers, green peppers, radishes, carrots, watercress, onion, cabbage, apples
Dried beef	Jelly, jam, or preserves
Bread and buns	Mayonnaise or salad dressing
Baked beans	Sliced cheese
Crushed pineapple or chopped pineapple	Cheese spreads
Roquefort or bleu cheese	Nuts, whole or chopped
Milk	Chili sauce or tomato catsup
Sour cream	Whole frankfurters
Applesauce	Honey
Horseradish	Swiss or cheddar cheese
	Liverwurst
	Olives, sliced or chopped
	Pickles, dill or sweet
	Pimiento
	Prepared mustard
	Sweet relish

Note: Freezing adds nothing to sandwich quality. Thaw under refrigeration 24 hours prior to use; once thawed, sandwiches should be eaten, for palatability is lost on standing. Keep refrigerated until used.

SALADS

It is difficult to define and classify salads; they can be classified as hot or cold and according to ingredients or use. A salad is usually made of crisp, leafy greens for an underliner, a body, dressing and a garnish. All but the body can be omitted. Perhaps a salad can best be defined as a combination of ingredients served with a dressing, one of the ingredients being a crisp green. Salads may accompany meals, may be a complete meal or a snack. A fruit salad is proper served at a wedding breakfast, for instance.

Figure 7–16. An array of salads.

Standard

Salads must be light and refreshing and balanced in flavor, texture and color with the other foods it accompanies. Color and artistry are achieved either through a set pattern, through uniformity and symmetry of design or by careful carelessness of no set pattern. Light heaping of different greens or fruits and vegetables may do this. A fatigued or overworked appearance must be avoided. Ingredients should be distinct and not messy and usually of bite size. Neat cutting without raggedness is needed. Bright, clear, fresh colors contribute to bloom and freshness. Selection at proper maturity helps give these qualities. Good proportion should be observed. A salad should be a picture with about a half inch of the rim of the plate as the frame. Form and height should vary as should soft with crisp foods. Cooked fruits and vegetables should not be overly soft. Flavors should be piquant and zestful, not harsh or bland. The body should be complemented with a dressing that is more tart and flavorful than the body. Blending of flavors is desirable. A touch of chervil, mustard greens, or a crushed sprig of peppergrass, dill, mint, anise or basil adds

Figure 7–17. A good standard is shown here for a molded salad. (Courtesy General Foods)

subtle flavor. Nasturtium leaves or its tender seeds, capers and many other herbs give contrasting flavors which add interest.

Ingredients

Underliner

Leafy greens are used as underliners but it is not unusual to use attractive bowls or dishes with no underliner. Iceberg, bibb, leaf, cos (romaine), escarole, curly endive, chicory, Whitloof endive, dandelion, watercress, spinach or other crisp, tender greens make good underliners. Chopped, pulled or sliced greens are also used. The cost and labor in lettuce cups is avoided by using leaf lettuce.

Body

The main part of a salad is the body which can be almost any crisp mixture with a piquant or zestful quality. Good quality products should be used. Meat should be well flavored and tender and fish is best cooked in court bouillon before flaking from the bones. Macaroni products should be of semolina, cooked to have some slight bite left in them. The fresher, crisper and more tender the green used, the better the salad; heavy ribbing, coarse stems, large leaves and evidence of seeding indicate age. Wilted greens may not recrisp.

Salad greens should be washed carefully to remove dirt and insects, and imperfections trimmed away. The cores of headed greens should be given a sharp rap against a firm surface and then finished with a sharp twist, breaking it from the head. A forceful spray of water can be run into the open heart to loosen tightly wrapped leaves. If no separation of leaves is needed, the heads should be placed open end down to drain. Washed greens can be placed into terry towel sacks and whirled to centrifuge water from them and then stored. Moisture must be present for crisping as completely dry leaves do not crisp well.

Crisping occurs by a process called osmosis. A plant cell contains moisture plus some minerals. This solution pulls water through the cell membranes to swell the cell. When many cells swell, they crowd each other and make the product crisp. Air helps assist in the process so greens should not be too tightly packed. Chilling also helps. Soaking can crisp but not as well as slight moistening and air. Sometimes there is not enough air in water and the product "drowns" rather than crisps. Wilting occurs because moisture is pulled from the cells either by evaporation or osmotic pull by salt, vinegar, salad dressing or something else

Figure 7–18. For a change, offer a make-your-own vegetable salad on a platter as shown here. (Courtesy H. J. Heinz Co.)

outside the cell. This is why these items are not added to salads until service.

Greens should be stored in moistened cloth bags, or baskets or colanders covered with damp cloth. Light packing into polyethelene bags is good for short-time storage and closed, mobile bins work well. Fine cutting is done after crisping, using extremely sharp tools to avoid bruising. Pulling or tearing to proper size also avoids bruising. Cabbage, turnips, carrots or other vegetables can be grated without loss of texture or quality.

Mise en place is very important in salad making. Doing jobs during the peak of service that should have been done before is the mark of an amateur or inefficient worker. Molded and frozen salads should be prepared 24 hours in advance. All work should be carried toward service as far as possible. Arranging tools and materials in good work center arrangement and where work is repeated sets up standard procedures. Workers are assisted in producing good products by the use of pictures, patterns or designs. Tallies of the number of pieces to use on various salads are helpful.

Figure 7–19. Fruit and vegetables combine well to make an attractive salad. Note the pleasing affect achieved by the variety and distinctness of shape of lightly tossed ingredients. (Courtesy Fruit Dispatch Co.)

Garnish

Salad garnishes should contribute form, color and texture. The garnish should be suited to the salad and, of course, should be edible. It may be made of one of the ingredients used in the body or be a complementing food. Garnishes should be kept simple but different enough to make them distinctive such as using a few caraway seeds over coleslaw or chopped cranberries on a Waldorf salad, flakes of green burnet with its subtle flavor of cucumber, a pineapple slice edged with chopped mint, a crisp food such as crackers, toast or cheese straws or a brightly colored gelatin cut into fancy shapes.

Dressings

Salad dressings are used to add flavor and tartness to salads. There are three kinds: French, mayonnaise and boiled or cooked dressing. Each has many variations made by adding different ingredients to them.

Ingredient quality is important. Fresh corn, cottonseed, peanut,

Figure 7–20.   An attractive fruit salad. Note how distinctness of ingredients adds to this salad. (Courtesy Fruit Dispatch Co.)

soy or other vegetable oils are good for mayonnaise. These or olive oil of sublime or virgin quality are used for French dressing. Bacon fat, animal fats, butter or margarine are used for cooked salad dressings. Mineral oil is not considered an edible oil and cannot be used. Good, clear, double-strength vinegar and good quality fruit juices are preferable. Eggs should be of highest quality. Spices and seasonings should be sterilized and fresh. Clean utensils and good sanitary practices are required since dressings can spoil. They should be stored in ceramic, glass or stainless steel containers at from 40° to 50° F. Oil is highly perishable and an opened container should be stored in a cool place and used within 10 days. Taste for rancidity. A thin film of oil oxidizes (gets rancid) quickly therefore an oil held for some time should never be mixed with fresh oil since the entire lot can then become quickly rancid. Oil containers must be cleaned thoroughly before adding new oil. For dressings that are chilled, winterized oil, treated so that it will not solidify in a refrigerator, should be used. (See also Chapter 12.)

Salad dressings are emulsions which are commonly used in food production. Gravy is an emulsion composed of fat globules surrounded

Figure 7–21. Fluting a cucumber to give a simple yet attractive garnish. (Courtesy General Foods)

by a starch paste. Meringues are emulsions of egg white and sugar surrounding air. The finer the emulsion of shortening in a cake batter, the finer the final texture of the cake. Salad dressings are oil-in-water emulsions, the water forming a continuous network around tiny globules of oil. These emulsions have two parts or phases, water being a continuous phase around oil which is a broken phase. Oil and liquids form unstable or temporary emulsions. When the oil remains in a constant broken phase, a stable or permanent emulsion is formed. French dressing is usually a temporary or unstable emulsion unless emulsifiers are added to it, and mayonnaise and boiled dressings are permanent or stable emulsions. Emulsifiers such as whole egg, egg yolk, starch, agar-agar, tragacanth, hydrophylic colloids, gelatin, casein, gum arabic, pectins, Irish moss or condensed milk are used in making dressings. The Food and Drug Administration regulates the emulsifiers that can be used in foods.

Mayonnaise should be semi-solid and non-flowing (hold its shape), with a good, clear sheen and a yellowish cream color. The texture should be smooth and the flavor sweet, with no trace of rancidity or off-flavor. There should be a distinct tartness. A power mixer makes a finer and more stable emulsion than hand-whipping. Commercial manufacturers use powerful homogenizers that make such a stable emulsion that freezing does not break it down. Undermixing or air beaten into an emulsion makes it unstable. Most mayonnaise is unstable if it has less than 20% eggs. Over 15% vinegar makes it unstable because of excess liquid. Good commercial mayonnaise is 50 to 80% oil, 6 to 20% egg yolk and 12% vinegar while a kitchen-made one will usually be 65% oil, 20% yolk and 12% vinegar. Starch pastes can be added but only a small quantity. Federal standards state that mayonnaise may not contain less than 50% edible oil and the sum of the percentages of oil and egg must not be less than 78%. Ingredients at 60° to 70° F favor the formation of a stable emulsion. Freezing can destroy an emulsion as can heat, as seen sometimes when gravies or sauces develop oil on their surfaces. Salt can draw out moisture which breaks the emulsion, so the salt should be combined with the vinegar and an excess avoided. A broken emulsion may be reformed by mixing well. If this fails, a bit of liquid or emulsifier may be added to a bowl and then the broken emulsion gradually poured in, meanwhile beating it vigorously to reform it. Mayonnaise is made usually by beating oil slowly into eggs. The bowl should be small enough so that the agitators can pick up the emulsifier to mix it with the oil. Too much surface can make an unstable emulsion. When a good emulsion is formed, oil can be added at a more rapid rate. Some blend the eggs, vinegar and seasonings in the bowl at the start and then add oil. Others advise no liquid until a good emulsion is formed with the emulsifying agent, then seasonings are added dissolved in the vinegar. Others report that if salt and seasonings only are blended with the egg before

Figure 7–22. A broken and a reformed mayonnaise. The broken emulsion is reformed by adding it slowly with good agitation to some liquid such as vinegar, water or egg yolks.

adding oil, they withdraw moisture from the egg, giving it better emulsi-fying properties.

French dressing is made with two parts oil to one part liquid. The liquid is usually vinegar or lemon juice. Wide variety is achieved by adding ingredients such as honey, chives, Roquefort cheese, capers or poppy seeds.

A cooked or boiled dressing is a mixture of liquids and seasonings thickened with starch and perhaps eggs. The liquids may be water, milk, vinegar, lemon or fruit juices; seasonings may be salt, sugar and spices; the starch thickeners may be cornstarch, flour, arrowroot or other starches. It is a semi-solid paste much like mayonnaise but it may be slightly thicker. It is often used with other liquids which thin it. These dressings may contains about 5% oil or fat but some commercial and other boiled dressings may be 35% fat to give them the consistency and flavor of mayonnaise. Boiled dressings are excellent for potato salads, coleslaw and many meat and fish salads.

There are many variations for mayonnaise and boiled dressings. A sour cream dressing is made from boiled dressing by adding sour cream, vinegar and seasonings. Russian dressing, tartar sauce, Thousand Island and many others are variations of either mayonnaise or boiled dressing.

A marinade is not a typical dressing but a flavorful product much like French dressing, although some may not have oil in them but be only vinegar, seasoned vinegar or a thin boiled dressing, sour cream dressing or other liquid containing seasonings. They are used to build flavor into foods which are placed to soak in them. Vegetables or fruits which do not wilt easily such as cooked fruits or vegetables, firm structured fresh fruits and vegetables such as cauliflower, carrots, cucumbers and toma-toes are marinated. Tender, succulent greens cannot be marinated but can be dipped quickly into a marinade and served at once. Cooked or uncooked marinades can be used for meat, usually game, soaking it for several hours or even days. A sauerbraten (sour roast) is a German dish made from meat that is marinated.

Types of Salads

Molded Salads

Molded salads are made from either plain gelatin or a gelatin des-sert. High quality gelatins that have bright sparkle, clean color, good setting ability and a true, pleasing flavor should be used. Gelatin desserts are plain gelatin, sugar, flavoring and coloring. Plain gelatin comes in sheets or granular form.

Figure 7–23. The procedure for unmolding salads is shown. The cup is set into hot water to just free the gelatin and then unmolded and set on the leaf as shown. (Courtesy General Foods)

Gelatins vary in setting strength but normally a 2% solution gives a satisfactory gel. Proportions are a pound of gelatin to 7 gallons of liquid or 2¼ oz (½ c) per gallon, and for gelatin 1½ pounds per gallon or 4 oz (½ c) to a pint of liquid. Sugar increases the firmness of a gel, while acids decrease it. Gelatin foams may require more gelatin than a plain, solid mass. Milk gives a stronger set than water. Chopped ingredients weaken a gelatin structure. Gelatin sets at from 48° to 57° F. Cooling slowly to 100° F and then refrigerating until the mixture is 40° F takes from 1½ to 2 hours but gives a firmer mass than rapid setting. For rapid set, a fourth or half the liquid is sufficient to dissolve the gelatin product, with the addition of crushed ice to a measure filled with water to give the additional liquid needed. The ice is stirred until melted. Plain gelatin must be soaked in cold liquid for about 5 minutes before dissolving it. Gelatin goes into solution at 100° F slowly but normally 170° F or higher will obtain more rapid solution. Uncooked pineapple, figs, papaya and some other fruits contain enzymes that digest gelatin, so they must be cooked before being used with gelatin mixtures.

If a gelatin mixture sets partially before ingredients are added, they

Figure 7–24. Folding fruit and gelatin into a mixture of mayonnaise and whipped cream to make a mousse-like mixture. This may be frozen and served as a frozen salad. Note the garnish to add appearance. (Courtesy General Foods)

will not float to the top. A gelatin should be whipped when it becomes sirupy; set it in a bed of crushed ice. Items may be folded into foams after whipping.

Molded salads are colorful and can be made into attractive designs. Layering of colors can give striking contrasts. Part solid and part foam mixtures can give interest and using different molds or cutting into different shapes can vary the design. For instance, a molded salad square composed of a bottom of chopped apples in apple gelatin, a center of chopped cranberries and orange peel in cherry gelatin and a top layer of cottage cheese in lime gelatin wins attention. Designs can be put on the bottom of molds and a thin layer of gelatin at the sirupy stage poured carefully over it. After setting, additional gelatin can be added.

Tossed Salads

Greens for tossed salads should be broken into small pieces and as materials accumulate, drop-delivered into a large container. A baker's mixing bowl is excellent since it facilitates light, deft mixing. This bowl can be covered with a damp cloth or other good cover to prevent ingredients drying out. It can then be placed on a mobile stand for storage and rolled into a walk-in refrigerator.

Tossed salads should usually be flavored with herbs, one being always a member of the onion family, and one or more chapons (pieces of dry bread rubbed heavily with garlic) added. A ravigote of chopped herbs may be added also. Dressings, salt, pepper and other seasonings that destroy texture should be added just before service or by the customer. Chopped egg, sliced salami or Parmesan cheese placed lightly over the dished salad make decorative garnishes.

Service may be at the table. For this, set-ups should be arranged in the pantry so that all materials needed are available, possibly using a mobile cart. Salad greens should be dry in order to hold the dressing. Excess moisture dilutes the dressing. It is preferable to add the oil first and toss and then the vinegar or acid ingredient but, if coddled egg is added, this should be done before adding the oil. (Add the egg, toss well, add the oil, toss again and add the acid ingredient and herbs last). Coddled egg is used in Caesar salad.

Fruit Salads

Most fruit salads are fragile and are not tossed. To make such a salad with greens, broken greens are placed on the bottom of a bowl, then well-drained fruit, sized as desired, over them. More greens are added, then more fruit, until the salad is prepared. Salad dressing should be drizzled over the layers as they are made if service is immediate, but if not, at service. The dressing is usually slightly sweet and may be flavored with fruit juices. Time to produce arranged fruit salads can be reduced by pictures or diagrams showing fruit placement. If fruit salads are sent to buffets on platters or bowls for dish-up, the salad should be prepared with this dishing in mind.

Figure 7–25. Convenience foods save many manipulations. Note the difference in ingredients for the same salad dressing. Lower labor cost results in using the prepared item. (Courtesy General Foods)

Frozen Salads

Frozen salads are usually made of fruit but vegetables can be used. To the fruit, nuts and some chopped crisp vegetables can be added for texture. Ingredients should be selected for color and flavor, bearing in mind that not all fruits freeze well. A frozen salad base is usually whipped cream, cream cheese or cottage cheese into which fruit and mayonnaise are lightly folded. A contrasting tartness to the sweetness lends interest.

Complete Meal Salads

The body of a salad used for a complete meal or a large portion of it will be quite substantial. Meat, egg, fish or cheese may be combined with vegetables, legumes, potatoes, macaroni products, rice, etc. The dressing can also be substantial and it is usually mixed in with the ingredients.

Hot Salads

Some hot salads must have immediate service. A wilted lettuce or dandelion salad loses quality rapidly and is best made in small batches. Other hot salads such as celery root, German potato, slaw and cauliflower hold well and can be made in quantity in pans, either on top of the range or in ovens. If too much is made, such a salad can become messy in appearance. Marinate ingredients that can receive such treatment for hot salads.

A hot salad is made by putting oil or fat from fried bacon, salt pork or ham into a pan and adding vinegar or acid liquid in a ratio of two to one. Seasonings and a bit of sugar may be added. Sometimes a small bit of starch can be added to give a bit of thickening to the dressing. The dressing is heated and the ingredients added and tossed quickly, each particle being coated with dressing. Skill is required to preserve shape and texture, and the salad must be served at once with a crisp garnish such as croutons, diced radishes, celery, cucumber, or cabbage. Often crisply fried bacon, bacon soyettes, ham or other small pieces of meat are added for flavor. Individual skillets, attractive in design and appearance may be provided and the salad served directly in them at the table.

Quantities Required

Bulk in relation to weight varies for different salads. From 4 to 6 gallons of tossed salad are required for 100 portions with portions measuring from $\frac{3}{4}$ to a cup; and weight is around 2 to $2\frac{1}{2}$ ounces. It takes 17 pounds of greens AP or 13 pounds EP to give this; but if trimming loss is high the quantity AP may have to be closer to 20 pounds. Pounds needed may be increased if heavy materials such as celery, cucumbers or tomatoes are used. If the garnish makes the salad appear larger, less may be required. A No. 12 scoop (3 oz level, 4 oz rounded) is frequently used to dish solid salads such as fruit or potato, about 10 to 12 portions being obtained per quart. About a third to half cup of molded or frozen salad makes a portion; if cut from pans, this is a piece about an inch deep by two inches square; slightly over three gallons give 100 portions. When a complete meal salad is served, the portion is usually doubled or more. Additional information on quantities will be found in the tables of this chapter or in the appendix.

APPETIZERS

An appetizer is a small food used to whet the appetite. It may be an hors d'oeuvre, a relish, a canapé or a cocktail. It may be served as a

Table 7-5. Yields of Some Common Salad Materials

Item	Normal Portion	Yields
Apples, raw, sliced	½ c, 2 oz	2 salads per apple, 113 size (3 to lb AP) 1½ lb AP equals 1 qt sliced
Apples, raw, diced	1/3 c, 2 oz	1 lb unpared yields 4½ c
Apricots, pitted	4 halves	1 22 lb lug yields about 100 salads
Artichoke, globe	one, medium size	Order 60's to 72's per container
Asparagus	3 to 4 stalks	12 to 15 medium stalks per lb
Avocados	½ medium or 3 to 5 slices	16 slices per avocado, medium size (Calavo)
Bananas	¾ banana, split or 1/3 c slices	25 lb AP gives 100 salads
Cabbage, shredded	1/3 c	7 lb EP yields 50 salads
Carrot, grated	3 oz, ½ c	lb AP equals 3⅓ c
Celery, diced	2 oz, ½ c	3 c diced per lb AP
Cheese, sliced	1 oz, 1 slice	6¼ lb for 100
Cherries, pitted	3 oz, ½ c (12 cherries)	20 lb AP for 100 salads
Chicken, diced	2 oz, 1/3 c	12½ lb EP for 100 salads; 30 lb AP ready-to-cook; 40 lb AP dressed
Crab meat	2 oz, 1/3 c	
Cucumbers, sliced	5 slices	6 inch cucumber yields 30 slices
Endive, curly, underliners	1/20 head	
Endive, curly, chopped	⅛ head	
Endive, French (Whitloof)	1½ to 2 oz	Usually one endive split makes a salad
Escarole	1/12 head	
Figs	2 to 3 medium split	6 6-lb boxes, 48 per box, yields 100 salads
Fish, flaked	2 oz, 1/3 c	16 lb cans salmon or 15 18-oz cans tuna for 100 salads
Grapes	½ c	14 lb AP for 100 salads
Grapefruit	5 sections	12 sections per grapefruit; 42 grapefruit for 100
Lettuce, Boston, underliner	⅛ head	
Lettuce, Boston, chopped	¼ head	
Lettuce, iceberg, underliner	1/15 head	Trimmed head usually weighs lb
Lettuce, iceberg, wedge	1/6 head	
Lettuce, leaf, underliner	2 leaves	12 to 15 leaves per bunch
Lettuce, leaf, chopped	¼ bunch	
Lettuce, Romaine, underliner	1/10 head	
Lettuce, Romaine, chopped	⅛ head	
Lobster meat	2 oz, 1/3 c	
Onions, sliced	2 oz, 4 slices	Purchase Bermudas or sweet Spanish; 1 lb AP diced yields about 2½ c
Onions, green, diced		1 lb AP yields 2½ to 3 c
Oranges, sliced	½ orange, 3 slices	6 to 8 slices or 8 to 9 sections per orange
Oranges, diced	3 oz, ½ c	8 to 9 doz medium size will yield 100 salads
Pears	½ pear	120 per box
Persimmon	1 whole	8 wedges may also be obtained per persimmon
Pineapple, sliced	2 half slices	100 salads per case of 24 size pineapple (fresh)
Potatoes, new diced	3 oz, ½ c	2 lb AP yields 1 qt diced

(continued)

Table 7–5 (cont.)   Yields of Some Common Salad Materials

Item	Normal Portion	Yields
Meat, ground	1¾ oz, 1/3 c	
Meat, diced	2 oz, 1/3 c	
Meat, sliced	3 to 4 oz, 2 slices	
Melon, cantaloupe, ring	1 ring	8 rings per melon, 36 to 45 size
Melon, cantaloupe, balls	8 balls	30 to 35 balls per cantaloupe, 36 to 45 size
Salmon (See fish, flaked above)		
Shrimp, small or Pacific	2 oz, 1/3 c	
Shrimp, large, diced	2 oz, 1/3 c	Serve four 25 to 33 per lb shrimp per salad
Tangerine	5 sections	10 sections per tangerine
Tuna (See fish, flaked above)		
Turkey meat	2 oz, 1/3 c	12½ lb net, 25 lb AP dressed, 20 lb AP ready-to-cook
Tomato, slices	3 slices ⅜ in.	about 6 slices per tomato; for 100 salads purchase 17 lb AP
Tomatoes, diced	1¾ oz, 1/3 c	
Watercress	¼ bunch	15 bunches per basket; 1 basket is about 3 lb

first course to guests before or after seating or as a snack at social gatherings and receptions. When used for the latter purpose, wide variety is characteristic and they may be passed or guests may obtain them at buffets.

Hors d'oeuvres

Originally, an hors d'oeuvre was a hot or cold food such as a timbale, creamed dish or bits of seafood or other food in aspic served immediately after the soup at a formal meal. The Russians changed them to a food passed to guests before a meal or at receptions. They called them "flying dishes" because they were passed by hurrying servants. Today a more common name for them is "finger foods." Any small piece of piquant, appetizing food served as an appetizer is today called an hors d'oeuvre. This can be a relish which is either a crisp fresh vegetable or a pickled

Table 7–6.   Quantities of Salad Dressing Required

Item	Portion	Yield
Cheese, bleu	1½ T	Use 5 oz bleu cheese per quart dressing
French	1½ T	Use 2¼ qt per 100
Mayonnaise or salad dressing	1½ T	Use 2¼ qt per 100

Figure 7–26. A student fills small cream puff shells with a tangy filling for hot canapés for a cocktail buffet.

item. The term "relish" may also be properly used to indicate pickles, conserves or sweetened vegetables or fruits served with a meal.

Chilled relishes may be celery sticks or hearts, raw cauliflower buds, partially cooked vegetables marinated in spicy vinegar or red or white cabbage sliced thinly and allowed to make a brine for four days in a refrigerator and then brought to a boil in spiced sweet vinegar, drained and chilled. Tidbits of cheese, smoked oysters or clams, canteloupe or watermelon pickles, pickled walnuts or mushrooms as well as the more commonly pickled items may be used. Smoked meats, fish, sausages, thinly sliced meat, cheese, cheese straws or pieces of green pepper, carrots, etc., dipped in tangy dips are hors d'oeuvres. Hot ones can be filled choux pastes, fritters, tiny patties, rissoles, oysters broiled in bacon, tiny croquettes, timbales or mousselines, rolled tiny pancakes filled with mixtures, deep-fried clams, fried frog legs, mussels, shrimps or other shellfish, snails bordelaise, hot casseroles of golden duck, oyster or clam poulette, deviled lobster or other dishes. Picks or forks are often used to pick up foods that do not lend themselves to eating with the fingers.

Canapés

Canapés are small pieces of bread, toast, wafer, pastry, etc., covered with piquant food. They are used as appetizers before a meal but may also be served at receptions or parties as finger foods. A canapé served as a first course may be large enough to serve on a plate and be eaten with a fork; for instance, a crab in aspic canapé may be served on a 5-inch plate on a doily. It could consist of a thin slice of rounded toast covered with a mold of aspic, capers and crab decorated with mayonnaise, green pepper and pimento strips. Frequently, pastes or other finely minced foods are incorporated into basic butter and spread onto the bread for canapés before other foods are added. Canapés are usually decorated but high decoration should be avoided. Blending some decorated items with more simply decorated ones often gives a pleasing effect. All should be neat and trim. Good flavor, form, color and texture and bright freshness are essential. Overworked form and dried edges or a wilted appearance should be avoided. Good arrangement on the trays or platters do much to make canapés presentable.

Canapés are usually made from day-old, unsliced pullman loaves, sliced longitudinally about 3/16-inch thick, rolled lightly with a rolling pin to firm the bread, spread with basic butter and a filling or paste put over this. Both should be worked to the outer edges as in making sandwiches, then cut into desired shapes. Decoration is usually added after cutting. Tangy pastes, mushrooms, truffles, anchovies, slices of stuffed olives, caviar, cheese and other piquant foods may be used for decoration. Some canapés are spread with tangy fillings, then toasted, broiled or sautéed and served hot. Seasonings in a hot canapé will be stronger than in a cold one, and less decoration is needed. Small choux pastes filled with tangy items, cheese straws and other prepared items may reduce labor, plus the use of tiny pastry shells, toasted forms, wafers and melba toast. Teaching the making of canapés involves setting up dia-

Figure 7–27. Different types of garnishes simply made to add to the attractiveness of salads or cocktails.

grams, listing tools and ingredients and proceeding as in Work Methods for making salads.

Cocktails

Cocktails are either alcoholic or non-alcoholic. The former are usually consumed before guests seat themselves. Hors d'oeuvres or canapés may be served and the first course omitted. Alcohol in any quantity blunts the appetite. Aperitifs or wines having flavor qualities to stimulate the appetite are recommended, such as vermouth, dry sherry, Madeira, Byrrh or Dubonnet. A fruit punch with or without alcoholic spirits is sometimes used. Cocktails should be served in their proper glass but it is becoming more common to use a roly-poly glass or 4-ounce glass for all drinks. There is also a trend to have cocktails "over the rocks" which makes such a glass highly desirable because a 2-ounce cocktail over the rocks in a typical cocktail glass causes the drink to overflow.

Some common measures used in bar work are:

Dash	3 drops
Pony	fluid ounce or 2 T
Jigger	1½ oz or 2 fluid oz (3 to 4 T), usually 2 fluid oz
Part	more or less than a jigger, depending upon taste
Split	1 c or ½ pt

A silver, chrome, stainless steel or glass shaker or large container is used for mixing cocktails. A glass rod or silver spoon is used to stir those containing wine as an important ingredient, while others are shaken. Cocktails should never be left in ice, but the ice removed after chilling. Metals other than those mentioned may flavor cocktails. Service bars can be set up so that work proceeds rapidly. Fruit or vegetable juices may be passed with alcoholic drinks for those who desire them.

Juice cocktails may be fruit or vegetable. Colors should be natural, bright and clear. Carbonized water or sweetened carbonated drinks may be added to fruit juices and served in frosted glasses. A coarse frappe, sherbet or ice may be put into a glass of fruit juice at the last minute.

Raw oysters or clams on the half shell, a slice of melon or mango with a wedge of lemon or lime can be a first course. Others may be a juice, a fruit or vegetable cup or a flaked fish or seafood cocktail. Canapés or hors d'oeuvres are also proper. Italian antipastos, hot foods in tangy sauce, fruit cups or other foods can be served to whet the appetite.

Fruit or vegetable cups should possess attractive colors and be fresh appearing. Colors should contrast pleasantly, be bright, clear and of contrasting shape and size. Sameness of texture should be avoided. Fresh fruits in season served in their own juice or in sweetened juice, canned or cooked dried fruits combined with fresh fruit are interesting possibilities. Fruit cups should not be too sweet, the natural sweetness and acid being sufficient to stimulate the appetite. Contrasts in flavors should be sought if they blend happily. Fruits that tarnish can be dipped into citrus or pineapple juice to keep colors bright, but usually the cocktail liquid is sufficiently acid to do this.

Flaked crab or other seafood or fish served with a tangy sauce is popular. The delicate flavor of the basic ingredients should not be destroyed by the sauce. Too much seasoning or too tart a sauce lowers eating pleasure. Some chopped vegetables such as celery, cucumber or other crisp food may be combined to give texture but should not extend the cocktail too much. Pieces should be bite size and distinct in form. Color contrasts and interesting combinations create interest. Blend flavors to be pleasing.

Quantities Required

The quantity of finger food needed may be difficult to determine. The variety and popularity may govern this as well as the type of function, its length. etc. Usually 2 to 8 pieces of food per person are sufficient and. while the range is wide. factors specific to the function indicate quantities needed within it. Bowls of dips and crisp foods. easy to replenish. may give flexibility. Some operations plan a run-out time and toward the end of serving have only a few foods remaining.

About $1\frac{1}{4}$ to $1\frac{1}{2}$ ounces of base material plus half to an ounce (1 to 2 T) makes a fish or seafood cocktail, if a standard cocktail glass of 3 ounces is used. From 8 to 10 pounds of crab, lobster or other flaked fish are needed for 100 cocktails. The use of large cocktail glasses with a heavy underline of lettuce or a lot of chopped celery in the fish or seafood to give the impression of a larger portion is not recommended. Liquid or solid foods such as fruit cup require nearly a full 3-ounce portion ($\frac{1}{3}$ c) or about 2 to $2\frac{1}{4}$ gallons (16 to 18 pounds) per 100 portions.

Garnishes

Garniture is probably used more extensively in the pantry and *garde manger* sections than any other. The *garde manger* section may do much decoration on cold meats and buffet items. Wide variety may be obtained from a few basic sauces or soups by using only different garnitures.

Elaborate garnishes once popular in continental cooking are losing favor and simplicity is now more in fashion. Some garnishes may be traditional and be more accompaniments than garnishes, such as Yorkshire pudding with roast beef, sautéed mushroom caps on steak or chopped parsley on new potatoes. Mushrooms, truffles, diced poultry breast, meat salipiçons, chicken livers, pâté de fois gras, julienne or

Table 7-7. Yields and Portions for Some First Course Accompaniments

Item	Portion	Quantity per Pound
Cheese Straws	1 or 2	32
Saltines	1 or 2	130 to 140
Soda, 2 inch square	1 or 2	100
Soda, large	1	50
Toast, Melba	1 or 2	30
Potato chips or shoestring potatoes (See Table 7–9 on garnish yields)		

Table 7-8. Appetizer Yields

Item	Portion	Yield
Carrot strips	2 to 3⅛ in. julienne, 3 in. long	90 strips per lb EP
Carrot curls	2 curls	8 per carrot, 6 to 8 carrots per lb EP
Celery curls	1 curl	3½ lb EP or 4½ lb AP yields 100 curls
Clams, Cherrystone	4 clams in shell	300 per bushel
Crab meat	1¼ to 2 oz	8 to 12 cocktails per lb EP
Crab legs	2 to 3 legs	about 18 to 22 dungeness crab legs to the lb
Fruit cocktail	3 oz, 1/3 c	2 1/3 gal for 100 cocktails
Melon cup, balls	9 balls	30 balls per cantaloupe, 36 per crate; 54 per honeydew melon, 8 per crate
Melon cup, diced	3 oz	12 oz per cantaloupe, 36 per crate; 30 oz per honeydew, 8 per crate
Melon, slice		¼ cantaloupe, 45's, 1/6 Persian, 1/8 casaba and 1/6 honeydew
Onions, green	3 whole	Purchase 5 lb AP for 100
Orange cup	1 orange	8 to 9 sections per orange
Orange juice	4 oz	3 32-oz cans frozen concentrated; 11 qts juice from Florida oranges and 9 qts from California per 4/5 bu carton
Oysters, Bluepoint, unshucked	4 oysters	300 cocktails per bushel; serve in shell cocktails
Oysters, Olympia, shucked	1¼ oz	100/per gal
Oysters, small, shucked	2 oz, ¼ c	4 to 5 oysters, 60 per qt
Pineapple cup	3 oz, ½ c	20 oz diced, 24 size pineapple per crate
Punch	3 oz	1 punch cup
Shrimp, small Pacific	1½ oz, 1/3 c	9 lb EP for 100 cocktails
Shrimp, jumbo or large	4 to 5 shrimp	25 to 33 per lb green headless

macedoine of cooked vegetables, finely chopped or stuffed vegetables, parsley, chopped fine herbs, tiny deep-fried calves' brains or sweetbread pieces, purees of vegetables, small fritters or filled choux pastes, cooked cereals such as barley, glazes such as cranberry or brown sugar for ham, milt or roe of fish, tiny sausages or sliced sausages, olives, pickles, cheese, fresh fruits and many others are used as garnishes. Tiny pieces of poached forcemeats or royales are used—if white meat and egg whites are used, it is a mousseline shaped into quenelle form. A godiveau is forcemeat made from kidney and suet instead of meat. Timbales are molded forcemeat larger than a quenelle. (See Glossary.)

Standard

All garnishes should be edible and complement the flavor, color and texture of the foods they garnish. They may be hot or cold. Excessive pattern, color or form should be avoided but some contrast is

Table 7-9. Garnish Yields

Item	Portion	Yield
Apples, sliced	2 thin wedges	12 wedges per 113 size apple
Apples, ring	1 ring	5 rings per 113 size apple
Apricots	½ or 1	20 halves or 40 wedges per pound
Avocado	1 slice	30 slices per avocado, 24 per crate size
Banana, split, 1 inch slice	1 or 3 round slices	12 bananas or 2½ c slices per lb AP; 1 banana (3 to lb AP) yields 30 1 inch slices split
Blackberries	3 berries	1 qt yields 100 berries
Blueberries	3 to 5	1 qt (1½ lb) 360 to 800 berries
Cantaloupe	3 balls or small wedges	30 balls or 45 wedges per 45 size per crate
Capers	1 t	10 to 15 capers per t
Carrots (See Table 4-8)		
Celery (See Table 4-8)		
Cheese, shredded, moist	1 T (½ oz)	
Cheese, shredded, dry	1 T (¼ oz)	
Cheese, cream	2 T (1 oz)	for stuffing celery
Cheese, cottage	1 No. 20 scoop,	1½ oz
Cherries, maraschino	½ or 1	640 per gal
Cherries, sweet, fresh	1	40 per lb
Chocolate tidbits	1 T	40 portions per lb
Coconut, long shred	1 T rounded	1 lb equals 6½ c or 60 portions
Currants	3 currants	1 lb equals 150 currants
Dates	1 date	60 dates per lb
Decorettes	1 t	160 portions per lb
Endive, curly	1 leaf	45 per head
Figs	1 fig	48 per box, 6 lb
Grapes	3 grapes	50 grapes per lb, medium size
Grapefruit	1 to 2 sections	12 sections per grapefruit
Kumquats	1 kumquat	1 lb equals 24 kumquats
Lemons, wedge	1/6 to 1/8 lemon	1 doz lemons yield 144 rind twists
Limes, wedge	¼ to 1/6 lime	1 doz limes yield 62 twists or rind
Mint	2 to 3 leaves	300 leaves per bunch
Mushrooms, cap	1 cap	15 to 20 caps per lb AP
Nuts, chopped	1 T	1 lb chopped is 4 c
Nuts, salted for tea	1 T	1 lb nuts is about 4 c; use 3 lb for 100 people
Walnuts, whole	½ walnut	8 oz is 2 c or about 150 halves
Oranges, sections	3	8 to 9 sections per 82 size orange; 1 doz orange rinds yields 164 rind twists
Olives, green	1 or 2	1 qt (1¼ lb) equals 100 extra large
Olives, stuffed, sliced	1 or 2	1 medium size olive yields 6 slices
Olives, ripe	1 or 2	1 qt small size yields 120 olives
Parsley, curly	1 sprig	80 sprigs per bunch
Peach	1 wedge	8 wedges per medium peach
Pear	1 wedge or slice	12 wedges per 5 oz pear
Pepper, ring	1	10 rings per medium size pepper
Pickles, sweet, medium (3 in.)*	½ pickle	24 pickles per qt
Pineapple	1 wedge or 2 to 3 diced pieces	60 wedges or 150 diced pieces per 18 size pineapple
Plums, Santa Rosa	1 medium	70 per till (5 x 5 size)
Pomegranate	5 seeds	25 garnishes per pomegranate
Potato chips or shoestring potatoes	¾ oz	1 c; eight ounces is about 2½ qt
Prunes, dried	1	30 to 40 per lb AP

(continued)

Table 7–9 (cont.) Garnish Yields

Item	Portion	Yield
Radishes	1 or 2	15 to 20 per bunch; 1 bunch 10 oz; 1½ c topped and tailed equals 8 oz or about 25 radishes
Raspberries	5	1 qt yields 300 berries
Rhubarb	1 or 2 curls	1 lb yields 100 curls
Sardines	1 3 in. long	1 lb yields 48 sardines
Strawberries	1	1 qt yields 60 medium size berries
Tangerines	3 to 4 sections	10 sections per tangerine
Tomatoes	1 wedge	8 wedges per medium tomato
Watercress	1 sprig	30 sprigs per bunch

*Pickles sized per gallon are frequently used: Gherkins 200, pickle rings or slices 400, small sweets (3 in.) 80 to 100, large dills (4½ in.) 25.

desirable, as are natural colors and simple design. A high degree of garnish may be proper on a wedding cake, *chaud-froid* piece or something emphasizing an occasion. At most times a red strawberry, a few sugar-glazed grapes or a few pomegranate seeds will suffice for a fruit salad while a few capers, a sprig of chervil or cheese wedge can do much for a cold plate. A grilled ripe tomato slice, a lemon wedge, a broiler-browned spiced pear filled with currant jelly or a sprinkle of spring vegetables will increase interest by goodness as much as color or design. Cream of corn soup may be given extra appeal when garnished with a few croutons of popped corn. Labor should be considered in garniture. Freshness of appearance, good taste in color and form or texture are the essentials of good garnish. The appearance of overworked food, dried brown edges and a wilted condition destroys appeal in spite of high design and color. Garnish size should be related to the size of the food it garnishes.

Elaborate garnish with *chaud-froid* (sho-frwa) may be desirable. A *chaud-froid* is a cooked food, chilled and then covered with a gelatin glaze, the glaze being usually decorated with pieces of food in it. Two types of glaze are used: an aspic or clear gelatin seasoned with beef, chicken or fish stock or a *chaud-froid* glaze made by adding gelatin to a cream sauce or mayonnaise, mayonnaise being especially desirable for fish. Designs made from pieces of pimiento, beets, ripe olives, truffles, cucumbers, green pepper, chives, leeks, lemon peel, carrots or other fruits and vegetables are used. The glaze, when ready to set but still sirupy, is poured over the food until it is covered. It is then chilled in a refrigerator. After the glaze is set, another layer is applied until a complete covering is obtained. This may be five to eight layers. The design is set into the glaze on the last coating. A light wash of clear aspic is then used to cover the design set into the glaze.

Suggested exercises or laboratory experiences for Chapter 7:

1. Set up a complete production schedule for the making of items for a pantry indicating quantities required, work methods, etc.
2. Set up various work centers for different work done in the pantry.
3. Prepare a gelatin mixture and divide it into six equal parts. To one add fresh figs, pineapple or papaya. To another, add some granulated sugar and dissolve it. Mix in a considerable amount of chopped vegetables in another. Add some vinegar to another. Beat another to a foam after chilling to a sirupy texture. Allow the last to remain as a control. Chill. Check textures.
4. Prepare a number of fancy sandwiches and canapés. Use the best possible labor saving methods.
5. Cut a large lettuce leaf in half. Sprinkle half liberally with salt. Moisten another with water, shake off the excess and put into a damp cloth. Chill both samples. Explain why one is crisp and the salted one is not after chilling.
6. Prepare mayonnaise, French dressing and a cooked salad dressing. Make from these different variations. Add some gum tragacanth or other emulsifier to the French dressing and shake it, noting how a permanent emulsion is formed. Reform a broken emulsion.

BIBLIOGRAPHY

American Baking Institute, Consumer Service Department, *Modern Sandwich Methods*, Chicago, 1952.

American Baking Institute, Consumer Service Department, *Turn to Sandwiches*, Chicago, 1957.

DeGouy, Louis P., *Sandwich Manual for Professionals*, Dahl Publishing Co., Stamford, Conn., 1939.

Duffy, Patrick G., *The Standard Bartender's Guide*, Revised, Permabooks, New York, 1962.

Elliott, Janet, "A Sandwich Symposium," reprint from *Vend Magazine*, Chicago, 1962.

Fruit Dispatch Co., Home Economics Department, *Banana Salad Bazaar*, New York, 1941.

General Foods, Inc., *Album of Jellied Salads and Aspics*, White Plains, New York, 1955.

Good Housekeeping's Sandwich Manual, Hearst Corporation, New York, 1961.

Knox Gelatine Company, *Knox Gelatin Book*, Johnstown, New York, 1958.

National Restaurant Association, *NRA News*, Vol. 1, No. 5, June 1958.

National Restaurant Association, *Sandwich Maker's Album*, Chicago, 1956.

National Restaurant Association, *Sandwich Meals Are Profitable*, Technical
  Bulletin 122, Chicago, 1956.
National Restaurant Association, "Sandwich Time," *NRA Ad Builder*, Chi-
  cago, 1957.
Pierre, J. Berard, *Pierre's 60 Profitable Sandwiches*, No. 14, Dahl Publishing
  Co., Stamford, Conn., n. d.
Shircliffe, Arnold, *The Edgewater Beach Hotel Salad Book*, Hotel Monthly
  Press, Evanston, Ill., 1930.
Sunkist Growers, Inc., *Fresh Citrus Quantity Handbook*, Los Angeles, 1959.
Swift & Company, *Helpful Hints on Salad Dressing Preparation*, Chicago,
  January 1955.
U. S. Department of Health, Education, and Welfare, Food and Drug Ad-
  ministration, *Dressings for Foods*, Washington, June 1957.

8

Stocks, Soups, Sauces and Gravies

Soups, sauces and gravies are related foods in that they are made from a stock which can be the same for any of them. Their differences frequently are matters of consistency, a few ingredients or seasonings.

STOCKS

The quality of many foods is directly related to the quality of the stock used in their preparation. Stocks are not made but are built by a careful blending of ingredients until a rich, flavorful liquid is obtained.

A stock is a thin liquid flavored by soluble substances of meat, poultry, fish, vegetables and seasonings. *Stock, broth* and *bouillon* are not synonymous terms. A broth is a simple stock served as a soup with perhaps a few added ingredients. A bouillon is a clarified broth of definite beefy flavor. Stocks are widely used for many foods other than soups, sauces and gravies.

Reducing a stock a fourth in volume makes it a *glaze* and to half its volume, a *demi-glaze*. These are used to enrich soups, sauces and gravies. Prepared food bases have replaced glazes in most kitchens and are rapidly replacing stocks, sauces and gravies in many others. A demi-glaze from meat is called *glacé de viande,* from fish *glacé de poisson* and from chicken *glacé de poulet.* Fish and game are frequently sim-

Figure 8–1. Good stocks result when fresh, high-quality ingredients receive proper preparation. In (a) and (b) stocks are shown simmering on the range.

mered in or steamed over a concentrated stock called a *fumet* or *essence.** A rich fish stock used similarly is called a *court bouillon.*

Ingredients

Not all products contributing to the flavor of meat have been identified. Meat and bones, which are largely protein substances, non-protein nitrogenous fractions and fat, give stock its primary flavor. Aromatic substances from fat carry much flavor and contribute richness. Flesh from different animals and even parts of the same animal differ in flavor and we blend them in stocks for their flavor contribution. Pork is acid, turkey or lamb are distinctively astringent and pungent, and chicken gives a mild, sweet flavor to a stock.

Meat flavors are more soluble in salted than in unsalted water. Good stock must possess body which comes largely from gelatin dissolved from the meat and bones. Stock gels if it contains about two ounces of gelatin per gallon and gelatin can be added to do this. Stock flavor is modified by vegetables and spices. Its color is also governed by its ingredients and sometimes by the browning of meat, bones and vegetables.

The bones for stock are usually well trimmed of meat, cut into 3-inch to 4-inch lengths and split. Knuckle, shank and neck bones are

---

* The terms *fumet* and *essence* are also used to indicate the use of concentrated flavors or flavoring items such as "essence of mushrooms" or "fumet de concombre."

(a)

(b)

(c)

(d)

Figure 8–2. (a) Ingredients for making a good stock. (b) A *mirepoix.* (c) Washing bones for a stock. (d) Steam-jacketed kettles are excellent for making stocks.

preferred for stock in that order. (If bones are put into a stock pot or steam-jacketed kettle equipped with a spigot, washing with cold water is facilitated.) Young animals' bones are high in gelatin. Bones showing rich red centers and a good marrow give a good flavored stock. Bones, trimmings and skin from cured, smoked pork may be used for specific flavor, and uncured pork bones are used to give richness to some stocks.

Meat for stock is usually not washed. The tougher cuts from older animals give a richer flavor and darker color. Lean meat is preferred and may be diced into inch cubes but if used for other dishes, leaving it in larger chunks may make it easier to remove when it is done.

For a gallon of stock, five quarts of water are used to cover four pounds of meat and bones plus a pound of mixed vegetables which are called a *mirepoix*. For extra-rich stocks the quantity of meat and bones are doubled. Many good stocks result as by-products from steaming or boiling meat or poultry.

Because stocks may be reduced in volume in cooking, seasonings should be light. *Bouquet garni* or *sachet* bags (mixed spices in a cloth bag) should be removed when the seasoning is correct. Some prefer leeks to onions because of their milder flavor. Vegetables and seasonings are often added midway in the cooking to prevent them from giving harsh or bitter flavors to the stock. The small round nubs on the tops of whole cloves are often removed, as these can give a bitter clove flavor to a stock.

Procedures

Steam-jacketed kettles are best for stock building but stock kettles are also used on top of the range. Both should have a spigot to use in withdrawing the stock so as not to disturb it.

Beef bones and meat should be simmered 6 to 10 hours.* Meat and bones from young animals and chickens are cooked a shorter time and fish is usually simmered no longer than $1\frac{1}{2}$ hours. Flavor in cooking meat develops up to about three to four hours and then declines. The smooth, mellow flavor of a stock does not develop until gelatin and other compounds are extracted. Stocks should be simmered at 185° F, not boiled as extended cooking may cause them to cloud and hard boiling increases this tendency. Starting in cold water extracts slightly more flavor but it is doubtful if there is any increase in nutrients.** Most

---

* Ecoffier says "at least 10 to 12 hours of cooking" should occur before the materials "can yield all their soluble properties."
** The nutrient value of stocks is small but meat flavors in stocks whet the appetite and start the flow of gastric juices.

Figure 8–3. A stock should be simmered, not boiled. The stock on the right has been boiled for a long time. The one on the left has simmered slowly for two hours.

meat substances, soluble in cold water, coagulate in cooking and this coagulated substance is usually skimmed away. A hot water start gives a clearer stock. To achieve a milder flavored stock, some cooks recommend bringing bones and meat, especially chicken, quickly to a boil from a cold water start, running this off and then starting again with cold water, a bit of salt, vegetables and seasonings; then simmering. Stock is strained at the completion of simmering through several thicknesses of cheese cloth into another pot. Cooling should be rapid and the pot should be covered. Meat on the bones may be trimmed and used for prepared dishes.

Many kitchens keep a stock pot simmering continually. For this, fresh bones are added to lightly salted water and as clean, edible foods accumulate, such as vegetable trimmings, vegetables from the steam table at the end of service, liquor from cooked and canned vegetables, bones from roasts and poultry and other products, they are added to the pot. Stock is withdrawn as needed, being replaced from time to time with fresh water. Once started, such a stock can be kept going for four or five days. After this, the stock becomes too weak for use and also may cloud. The materials are discarded and another stock pot is started with fresh bones.

Figure 8–4.   Cool a stock, covering it after placing it into a sink. Allow cold water to fill the sink slowly going out through the overflow. Insert a small object under the pot so that colds water flows under the bottom.

Stock Care

Stock, an excellent culture for bacteria, can sour quickly. A pot of cooking stock should be kept simmering even overnight. If heat is not continued it should be placed in a running water bath or in a cool, well-ventilated area. Finished stock should be cooled covered, at room temperature until 110° to 120° F. A running water bath induces more rapid cooling, with something inserted under the bottom to allow water circulation there. Stirring speeds cooling and giving maximum surface area also helps. After cooling, place under refrigeration at 35° to 40° F. Fat may be left on top to congeal and form a protective seal. If stocks remain over four hours from 50° to 140° F they should be reboiled for use and chilled. Maximum storage is 7 to 10 days at 40° F. Quality is lowered if a stock is reheated, recooled and returned to refrigeration.

Clarification

Stock may be clarified in two ways: cooling and decanting or clarifying with egg white. To decant, it should be chilled for 24 hours; if a stock

will gel, it can be chilled until sirupy and then decanted leaving flocculent material on the bottom. A better method of clarification is to
blend two raw egg whites into a cup of cold water and mix with 1½
pounds of lean, ground beef, adding this to five quarts of cool, rich
stock. Seasonings and chopped vegetables may be added at this time.
This is brought to a slow, rolling simmer. After the egg whites and meat
begin to cook, *the stock must not be disturbed.* The coagulated mixture,

(a)

(b)

(c)

(d)

Figure 8–5. (a) Strain stock through several thicknesses of cheesecloth. Be
careful in taking the last bit not to allow flocculent materials to come off with
the stock. (b) One method of clarifying is to decant after chilling. A stock
about to gel is decanted away from flocculent materials on the bottom. (c)
Ingredients used for clarifying a stock. The well browned onions are added to
increase color and flavor. (d) To allow the raft to act as a filter, break away
a small piece and allow the stock to bubble up and over the raft in a slow roll.

called the *raft* or *crust*, rises to the top with the vegetables and seasonings carrying with it most of the flocculent material. A small piece of the raft is broken carefully at the edge so the stock can bubble up at this point and be filtered through the raft. After several hours the clarified stock is carefully drawn through a spigot and strained through several thickness of cloth. Clouding materials on the bottom or from the raft must not be allowed to run off with the clear stock. This remaining liquid and raft are added to a new stock. The yield from five quarts of stock is a gallon of clarified stock.

Types of Stock

There are two stocks: brown and white. A brown stock is made from well-browned meat, bones and vegetables and a white stock is made from these same materials, unbrowned. Fish stocks are usually white. Beef or veal make a brown stock, with a *mirepoix* of vegetables and a *sachet* of spices. A bit of fat aids in browning the meat and vegetables faster. To add flavor and color, thick onion slices can be browned evenly on a hot griddle or range top. All materials are covered with water and brought to a simmer. Since salt delays browning, it should be added with the water, using a minimum quantity since the stock may be reduced later. Tomatoes, tomato puree and tomato trimmings may be added. The finest white stocks are made from chicken or veal. To give the most delicate and lightest white stock, a light colored *mirepoix* is used. Some chefs even avoid carrots while others are not so particular. A fish stock is made from white, lean deep-sea fish such as cod, haddock, whiting or flounder; bones, heads, skins and trimmings may be used. Fat fish such as salmon, black cod and mackerel give a dark, heavily-flavored stock. Seasonings may be slightly more pungent for fish stock and simmering time shorter to avoid clouding. Tables 8-1 and 8-2 indicate how stocks are used in the kitchen to form the base for a wide range of soups and sauces. These tables are simplified and are not all-inclusive.

SOUPS

Soups at one time were used for a complete meal only. Carême, one of the early great chefs, first introduced soup as a first course, feeling that light soups, many of which he originated, stimulated the appetite. Escoffier, many years later, agreed, quoting the great gastronomist, Grimod de la Reynière, as saying: "Soup is to a dinner what the porch

Figure 8–6. Browning bones, meat and vegetables to make a brown stock.

or gateway is to a building. . . it is devised to convey some idea of the whole to which it belongs, or, after the manner of an overture to a light opera, it should divulge what is to be the dominant phrase of the melody throughout." Today light soups are often used as a first course but heavier soups are still used as complete or nearly complete meals.

Standard

A soup is a liquid food. Unlike a sauce, it does not complement another food. Standards vary according to the type of soup. Hot soups should be served at above 170° F and cold soups at from 40° to 50° F. Portions vary according to use. A portion for a first course is around six ounces ($\frac{3}{4}$ c), while a more substantial portion is a cup (8 oz). Where soup is a substantial part of a meal, 10 ounces ($1\frac{1}{4}$ c) is served.

The thickness of the soup may vary according to its type and ingredients. Clear soups should resemble thin broth but they must possess body and not be too thin or watery. A cream soup, bisque or light puree should delicately coat a spoon, while heavy, thick country-style (*paysanne*) soups can build a mound of ingredients when placed into a bowl. Some soups may be almost as thick as stews or ragoûts. Whether a

Figure 8–7.   Ingredients for a consommé. Note that clarification in cooking occurs in the making of this type of soup.

bouillabaisse or a gumbo is a stew or soup has been argued. The form of soup ingredients should be distinct and clear, not mushy or broken, unless the soup is a puree, where no evidence of form is desirable. Thickened soups should be free of lumps.

Flavors should be distinct, mild, pleasant and characteristic for the soup. Seasonings should be delicate, not predominant, and colors can vary according to ingredients but should be natural and pleasing. Contrasting colors are desirable as in a chicken gumbo where the red of tomato, green of okra and white of rice gives a pleasing variety of colors.

A clear soup, such as consommé or bouillon, may show a sheen of minute globules of fat, but only a trace. Heavier soups that have more fat bound in them can have fat globules only slightly larger than this on the surface. Fat should never be in pools or large, round globules. Clear soups should have bright, sparkling clarity. A puree or cream soup should be smooth in texture. All particles should be bite size except in special soups which have whole slices of meat, chunks of fish, shellfish in shells or other products in them. A puree should remain in suspension. Cold soups should be seasoned more highly than hot soups, for chilling reduces the flavor. Cream soups should not be flat or dead-white

(a)   (b)

Figure 8–8. (a) The first step in preparing a cream soup is to make a velouté base. Here we see a stock being added to a mixture of roux and vegetables for the velouté. (b) Next, after thorough cooking of the velouté mixture, the velouté is blended with good agitation into hot rich milk.

but have a rich, cream color unless modified by other ingredients as in cream of tomato soup. There should be no curdling.

Types of Soups

It is difficult to classify soups. Classification by consistency is perhaps as good as any other, for this determines how they will be used: very thin, medium or lightly thickened, and heavy or thick.

Thin Soups

Most thin soups are clear, being largely rich stock. Bouillon is made from brown stock, usually beef flavored, and is clarified. Consommé comes from the word "consummate" which means "to bring to completion or perfection." Its delicate flavor is built on a stock made from two or more kinds of bones, one of which is usually veal or chicken. It is highly clarified. Broths are rich stocks frequently containing a few vegetables, rice, etc. Some milk soups are thin such as oyster stew, bisques, cream soups and *vichysoisse*. Light oxtail soup, light purees and turtle soup are other examples of thin soups. A thin soup is frequently used as a first course. Menu planners often use the dictum, "A light soup, a heavy dessert."

Curdling is often a problem in making a cream soup. For best stability, a moderately heavy velouté may be made, adding the vegetable puree which will give the main flavor (a pint per gallon of soup). Hot rich milk or thin cream is used for thinning the velouté mixture. The velouté is added to the milk or cream—*not the other way around*—and should be stirred well in this blending. The milk or cream is lightly thickened for soups that curdle easily. Only the amount required for a 20- to 30-minute serving period should be added; never mix a new and an old batch together. Excess salting or heating may encourage curdling. Some cream soups may be finished with a liaison which is a mixture of one part egg yolk well blended into three parts cream, cooked only to thicken eggs, never boiled. A fairly stable cream soup is made by using bechamel sauce, blending in the flavoring puree (a pint to a gallon of soup) and then thinning to desired consistency with hot milk or cream, pouring the bechamel mixture *into* the milk or cream.

Figure 8–9.   Another method to prepare a cream soup is to add a thickened vegetable puree to a thin, hot bechamel or white sauce.

Another method is to prepare a white sauce, blend in the puree and thin with milk or cream if the sauce is too thick. This last method is the least stable of the three. (Consult Chapter 10 for the cooking of milk products.) A good cream soup should have the consistency of a moderately heavy cream. A bisque is a cream soup with shellfish as its main flavoring ingredient.

(a)

(b)   (c)

Figure 8–10. (a) The ingredients for a liaison. (b) To use a liaison, blend some of the hot soup mixture into it. (c) Next, add this liaison mixture to the soup, using good agitation. After the liaison is added, do not heat above 190° F.

Lightly-Thickened or Medium Soups

Thickness in soup may come from ingredients such as rice, maca-roni, dumplings or vegetables, or thickening agents such as flour, starch, eggs or panadas. Most of these are not as clear, thin or delicate as thin soups. They can be the first course of a light meal or part of a luncheon served with a soup and salad. Purees gain their thickness in two ways: by using pulp of starchy vegetables such as beans, lentils, peas or pota-toes, or by using the pulp of succulent vegetables such as carrots, aspar-agus, turnips, celery or green peas and some starch. For a medium con-sistency about two pounds of legumes or a quart of pureed product is needed per gallon of soup. Doubling the quantity gives a heavy soup. In some purees starch can be used to hold items in suspension.

Figure 8–11.   Forcing split peas through a china cap with an up and down motion of the ladle to make a puree.

Heavy Soups

Thick or heavy soups such as potages, heavy purees, gumbos, chowders or French onion usually gain their thickness from ingredients rather than a starch thickener. Their base may be broths or milk. Most chowders contain chopped onions and other vegetables such as diced potatoes sautéed lightly in ham or bacon fat or mixed with diced bacon or salt pork. A main ingredient giving the chowder its identity such as clams, corn, mussels, lima beans or mushrooms is added. Fish stock plus tomatoes is the base for Coney Island (Manhattan or Philadelphia) chowder. If milk is a base, tomatoes and fish stock are not used and the chowder is called Boston or New England chowder.

Cold Soups

There are a number of cold soups such as *vichysoisse,* cold borsch, jellied consommé or bouillon. The Scandinavian people are fond of a cold, slightly sweetened soup which has dried fruits in it. Such soups can be used to give variety and interest to a meal.

Figure 8–12. The main ingredients for a brown sauce: brown stock, *mirepoix*, sachet and roux.

Garnishes

Table 8-1 shows that just a change in garnish changes the soup. If garnishes are used, they are usually cooked separately and added at service. Starchy products must be blanched thoroughly after cooking so they will not cloud the soup.

SAUCES AND GRAVIES

A sauce or gravy is usually a richly flavored stock or liquid that gives moistness, richness or flavor or otherwise complements another food. It may or may not be thickened. Some give color and form to foods and should contrast in flavor with the food they accompany. A sauce may act as a garnish. The sauce or gravy should never mask or disguise the flavor of the food it accompanies but should rather heighten it. A standard portion of a sauce or gravy is two ounces but this may be varied according to the need.

The Standard

Sauces or gravies should have a soft sheen imparted by tiny pinpoint globules of emulsified fat while some should be so rich that they have the sheen of varnish. The texture should be smooth and velvety with no lumps. No flavor should predominate in a sauce but gravies should possess the flavor of the meat from which they are derived. There should be no evidence of uncooked starch either in taste or texture. The color of a brown sauce should be a rich mahogany modified by added ingredients. A white velouté should be a clear, creamy white color. A bechamel, white or cream sauce may have a slightly opaque quality and a creamy color. A dead, pasty, white and a lack of sheen indicate poor quality.

The sauce consistency may vary but pasty, excessively thick ones are undesirable. Thin sauces are served over or with foods needing flavor complement but do not have the body of a heavy sauce. Sauces should at times be fairly thick to give cling, such as hollandaise which must hold to broccoli. Pan gravy, *au jus* or meat essences are almost as thin as broth. The clarity of a sauce may vary according to the ingredients but no sauce should be murky or cloudy. Many sauces should have brilliance.

Neutral sauces are made without meat stock. They vary widely in characteristics. Some, like mayonnaise and hollandaise, have a high oil content and possess a high sheen. Their color should be delicate yellow

Table 8-1. Soups and their Derivation

Meat Base

BROWN STOCK

Bouillon (beef base)
  French Onion (onions)
  Tomato Bouillon with Rice (tomato ragout and cooked rice)
  Windsor Bouillon (spaetzels of egg, flour, and cream)
  Jellied Bouillon
    Avocado Jellied Bouillon (puree of avocado, sour cream garnish)
    Beet Bouillon, Polonaise (minced beets, beet juice, sherry, lemon juice, sour cream garnish)
Consommé
  Argenteuil Consommé (asparagus tip (garnish)
  Vaudoise Consommé (leeks, white turnips, and parsnips julienne)
  Vert-Pré Consommé (tapioca, green peas, string beans, asparagus tips, spinach puree)
Broth
  Beef Broth (rice or macaroni products are usually added)
  Scotch Broth (lamb or mutton stock, pearl barley, diced vegetables)
  Vermicelli Broth (vermicelli)

WHITE STOCK[2]

Consommé
  Printanier (spring vegetables)
  Florentine (chopped spinach, almonds)
  Princess (princess royal garnish)
Broths
  Chicken Noodle Soup (noodles)
  Mulligatawny Soup (apples, curry, eggplant, cream)
  Chicken Creole (onion, okra, rice, tomatoes, celery)
Veloutés (creams)
  Creme of Cressionère (watercress, liason)
  Cream of Chicken (diced chicken, rice pulp thickening, liason)
  Creme d' Amandine (almond paste, almonds, liason)
  Cream of Mushroom (mushroom essence, liason)

Meat Base

WHITE STOCK[2]

Veloutés. fish (bisques)[1]
  Clam Bisque (chopped clams, clam juice, cream finish)
  Lobster Bisque (lobster essence, brandy, cream finish)
  Shrimp Bisque (shrimp essence, cream, sherry, diced shrimp meat)
Chowders[2]
  Manhattan Clam Chowder (potatoes, salt pork, clams, tomatoes, onions, celery, green peppers)
  Washington Chowder (salt pork, onions, potatoes, corn, celery, green peppers, tomatoes, milk)
  Okra Chowder (tomatoes, okra, onion, parsley, peppers, celery, potatoes)
Purees (cured meat stock may be included)
  Split Pea (split peas)
  Navy Bean (navy beans)
  Potato and Leek (leeks, potatoes)
  Puree of Artichoke (artichoke heart puree, starch thickened)

Neutral*

TOMATO
  Cream of Tomato Soup (blend tomato velouté with hot milk or cream)
  Moute Rouge Soup (carrots, potatoes, marjoram, tarragon)
  Mongole Soup (equal parts puree of split pea and tomato ragout)
  Madreilene Soup (consommé in equal parts to tomato and beet juice)

MILK
Cream Soups[1]
  Cream of Asparagus (white sauce, asparagus, liason)
  Cream of Broccoli Soup (white sauce, broccoli. liason)
  Cream of Spinach Soup (white sauce, spinach, liason)
Bisques[1]
  Oyster Bisque (crushed and mashed poached oysters in cream sauce, hot milk)
  Scallop Bisque (pulp of cooked scallops in cream sauce, hot milk)

[1]A cream or white sauce, a velouté sauce thinned with rich milk or cream, or a bechamel may be used interchangeably in making the numerous cream soups.

[2]The stock used may vary. Chicken, beef, or fish stock may be used for the various types of soups, sometimes interchangeably, and so exact definition is difficult. A beef bouillon, for instance, may be used for an oxtail, vegetable. or barley soup, and so forth, but a white stock from chickens might do almost as well. Usually fish stocks are used for fish-base soups, such as chowders.

*Neutral means that meat stock is not used.

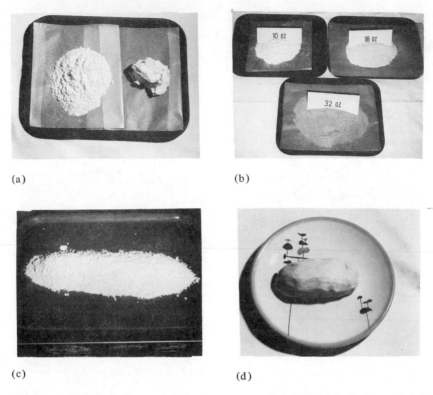

Figure 8–13. (a) Fat and flour for a roux. (b) Unbrowned flour, lightly browned flour and heavily browned flour in quantities required to give equal thickening to a gallon of stock. (c) A dry roux. (d) A *beurre manie* is a kneaded mixture of equal parts of flour and butter used to give final correct thickness to a sauce or soup.

for hollandaise and a yellowish cream for mayonnaise. The consistency and texture of fruit sauces, such as applesauce or cranberry sauce, should be sufficiently firm to hold a mound and leave little or no liquid seepage on standing.

Ingredients

The stock for sauces should be top quality. Some stocks are reduced in volume before they are used. Wines also may be added and reduced. Frequently shallots rather than onions are used because of their milder flavor.

Sauces may be finished with a final addition of cream, butter, a liaison or wine. After adding, the sauce is not boiled but only brought to a correct serving temperature. To prevent scum formation, a sauce may be tightly covered while warm, melted butter may be brushed over the surface or oiled paper laid on the surface. If the sauce is to stand for a short time, the surface may be brushed lightly with a liquid such as milk, cream, wine or water.

Thickening agents for sauces are usually flour or cornstarch but other starches can be used. A mixture called a *roux,* half fat and half flour by weight, is most often used. The fat is melted, flour added and the mixture cooked about 10 minutes until it is quite frothy and leaves the pan bottom easily. A roux when properly cooked has a light hazelnut odor and a slightly gritty texture. Chicken fat is highly prized for roux for bechamel, velouté or white sauce. Brown, pale (blond) or white (light) roux are made respectively from well browned, lightly browned or unbrowned flour. Browning destroys some of the thickening power, a heavily browned flour having about a third the thickening power of unbrowned flour. A dry roux is made by heating flour in an oven without fat until it is slightly gritty. It is desirable when a regular roux would give an overly rich product and perhaps a broken emulsion.

Some starches or flour are blended with liquid to make a slurry for thickening called "whitewash." It gives a less smooth flavor and is more apt to lump. A *beurre manie* is made of equal parts of butter and flour kneaded together and used for giving final consistency to a sauce or soup.

Roux can be stirred into a moderately hot liquid or the liquid can be stirred into the roux. Some chefs use a cold roux with a hot liquid and a hot roux with a cool liquid. Good agitation should be employed when the two are blended. The mixture should cook for at least 10 minutes to complete gelatinizing the starch. Flour, cornstarch and most other starches start to thicken at around 144° to 162° F and complete final thickening at around 203° F. A failure to cook such starches completely may give graininess and a raw starch flavor. Waxy maize starch thickens at around 155° to 167° F and no second thickening occurs. If this starch is heated above 195° F a slight thinning occurs.

The type of starch should be suited to the production need. Waxy maize or modified starches are desirable for fruit pie fillings or sauces and gravies that are to be frozen. Instant starches are available to thicken in the cold stage. They are little used in sauce cookery, however.

Acid breaks down starch. For this reason acid ingredients may not be added until cooking is completed. Meat stock and drippings are slightly acid and sauces containing these or wines will require more starch. More starch per gallon is required to thicken large batches than small ones, because large batches may not rise to as high a temperature as small batches.

(a)

(b)

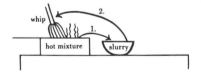

Step 1.   After making a smooth thin paste of
          the starch thickener and liquid, add
          some of the hot mixture to the
          slurry and blend well.

Step 2.   Then add all the warmed slurry to
          the hot mixture, giving good agita-
          tion as it is poured in slowly.

Figure 8–14. (a) Roux may be added to a stock in the manner shown or (b) stock may be added to a roux in thickening a sauce or soup. (c) To use a flour or starch slurry, add some of the hot mixture to the slurry and blend well. Then, with good agitation add this mixture to the hot mixture. This method is also used in adding a liaison to a soup.

Figure 8–15. Acid destroys the thickening power of starch. The sample on the left had equal starch added as the one on the right but vinegar was used as the liquid rather than water.

The process of starch gelatinization or swelling is not completely known. There are about 770 billion starch granules in a pound of cornstarch. These are insoluble in cold water but in hot water they swell. When enough are in solution, the swelled particles crowd one another and cause the liquid to thicken. Lumping occurs if the starch is not separated before swelling occurs. Separation by fat in a roux or by liquid in a slurry are two ways of dividing the starch. It can also be blended with sugar and poured directly without moistening into hot liquids. In any addition, good agitation is needed.

Starches differ in thickening power, viscosity and clarity. See Figure 8-16 for thickening power differences of some starches. Flours differ in their clarity and thickening powers because of differences in gluten and starch content. Pastry and cake flours have more starch and less gluten than bread flour and so thicken better, but give a more opaque and stringy paste because gluten is the substance giving opaqueness and stringiness while starch gives clarity. Cornstarch gives a fairly clear paste because it is largely starch. Waxy maize and modified starches give a very clear paste which is as thick when hot as it is when cold. Fruit pies and other products needing a paste of high clarity and soft texture are best made from these. Cornstarch gives a paste that breaks rather sharply when cool rather than clings and is desirable for cream pies, *blanc manges* and other products. Tapioca, sago, rice, potatoes, rice or potato flour, bread crumbs, egg yolks and other ingredients are also used for thickening.

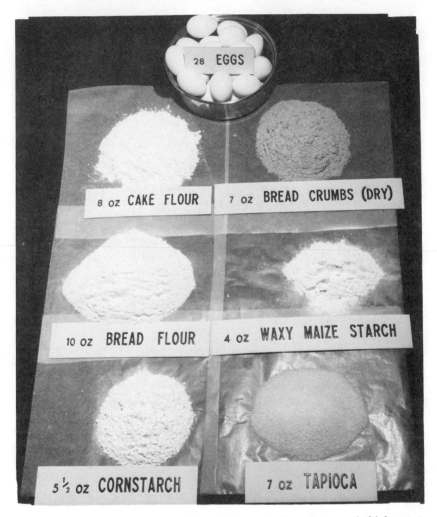

Figure 8–16. The amount of thickening required to give equal thickness to a gallon of stock of medium thickness.

Types of Sauces

Many sauces are made from only a few basic ones called *foundation* or *mother* sauces. The derived sauces are called *secondary* or *small* sauces.

The three basic sauces having meat stock as a base are brown (espagnole), velouté and bechamel. A fourth, tomato, may or may not have meat stock in it but usually does. (See Table 8-2)

Brown stock thickened with a brown roux and seasoned with a

Table 8–2. Sauces and Their Derivation

Meat

BROWN STOCK

Brown Sauce (Espagnole)
Bordelaise Sauce (red wine, shallots, beef marrow)
Chateau Sauce (white wine, shallots, butter)
Chasseur Sauce (tomato ragoût, fine herbs, mushrooms, white wine)
Madeira Sauce (Madeira wine)
Mushroom Sauce (mushrooms, red wine)
Poivrade Sauce (tarragon vinegar, red wine, tabasco, tomato ragoût)
Grand Veneur Sauce (game essence, truffles)
Sauce Diane (whipped cream, truffles, hard-cooked egg)
Moscovite Sauce (juniper berries, malaga grapes, almonds, raisins)
Provencale Sauce (tomato ragoût, garlic)
Robert Sauce (mustard, red wine, shallots, tomato ragout)
Salmis (currant jelly, mushrooms, port wine)
Fruit Sauces[2] (sweetened brown sauce)
Bigarade Sauce (orange juice and peel, lemon juice, brandy)
Cumberland Sauce (orange and lemon peel and juice, ginger, cayenne, port wine, mustard)
Brandy Peach Sauce (peach preserves, brandy)
Pineapple Sauce (pineapple)
Raisin Sauce (vinegar, raisins)

WHITE STOCK

Velouté Sauce
Allemande Sauce (egg yolks)
Poulette Sauce (cream)
Soubise Sauce (onion puree)
Supreme Sauce (cream)
Princes Sauce (mushroom essence, glace de poulet)
Reine Sauce (almond butter, truffles)
Vin Blanc Sauce (Fish Velouté)
Cardinal Sauce (cream, chopped shrimp or lobster meat)

Flamande Sauce (mussel essence, parsley, mustard, lemon juice)
Normandy Sauce or Nantua (egg yolks, cream)
Nantaise Sauce (chopped crayfish, or chopped lobster or chopped shrimp)

Neutral

TOMATO

Tomato Ragoût Sauce[1]
Creole Sauce (onions, garlic, tomatoes, green peppers)
Spanish Sauce (onions, celery, okra, mushrooms, garlic, tomatoes, green peppers, stuffed green olives)

MILK (White Sauce)
Cheese Sauce (cheddar cheese)
Cream Sauce (cream finish)
Curry Sauce (curry, apples, onions)
Egg Sauce (hard-cooked eggs)
Mornay Sauce (Parmesan cheese)
Mustard Sauce (prepared mustard)
Newburg Sauce (sherry wine)

EGG YOLK, VINEGAR AND OIL EMULSIONS

Hollandaise Sauce
Bernaise Sauce (tarragon vinegar)
Figaro Sauce (tomato puree, celery)
Glace Royale Sauce (mousseline sauce, mornay sauce, or cream sauce)
Grimod Sauce (saffron)
Maltaise Sauce (orange juice and grated peel)
Mousseline Sauce (whipped cream)
Mayonnaise
Chaud-froid Sauce or Mayonnaise Collée (gelatin)
Imperial Sauce (onion, mushrooms, mustard, pickles, pimiento, cream sauce)
Ravigote Sauce (shallots, chives, capers, chopped eggs)
Remoulade Sauce (dill pickles, anchovy, capers, mustard)
Russian Sauce (chili sauce, chopped pimientos, chives)
Chiffonade Sauce (chopped eggs, beets)
Tartar Sauce (dill pickles, onions, parsley)

BUTTERS

Compounded Butters
Anchovy Butter (anchovy paste)
Caper Butter (capers)
Garlic Butter (garlic juice or crushed garlic)
Lobster (lobster pulp)
Melted Butters
Clarified Butter (pour melted butter from its curd)
Noisette Butter (Brown Butter) (brown to hazelnut color)
Maitre d'hotel Butter (lemon juice, cayenne, parsley)

(continued)

Table 8–2 (cont.)   Sauces and Their Derivation

Meat

Bechamel Sauce (chicken or veal stock)[3]
  A la King Sauce (green peppers, mushrooms, pimientos)
  Bretonne Sauce (fish stock, leeks, onions, mushrooms, celery)
  Caper Sauce (capers))
  Dill Sauce (fresh dill)
  Newburg Sauce (sherry wine)

TOMATO

Tomato Ragoût Sauce[1]
  Barbecue Sauce (onions, garlic, sugar, mustard, vinegar, lemon or lime juice, worcestershire, barbecue spice)
  Italian or Spaghetti Sauce (garlic, onions, celery, green peppers, basil, oregano, bay leaf, olive oil)
  Milanaise Sauce (mushrooms, ham, tongue)

Neutral

Caper Butter (capers)
Irish Butter (tomato catsup, nutmeg)
Mustard Butter (dry mustard)
Polonaise Sauce (fine bread crumbs)
Meunière Butter (brown maitre d'hotel butter)
  Amandine Butter (sliced almonds, onion juice)
Lemon Butter (lemon juice)
Noir (black) Butter (brown until very dark)

BREAD SAUCE

Gooseberry Bread Sauce (gooseberry preserves)
Horseradish Bread Sauce (horseradish, cream)
Mustard Bread Sauce (dry mustard)
Onion Bread Sauce (minced onions or onion puree)

SOUR CREAM SAUCES

Horseradish Sauce (horseradish)
Smitane (onions, white wine, lemon juice)

FRENCH DRESSING SAUCES

Avocado Sauce (avocado, hard-cooked egg yolk, tarragon)
Cambridge Sauce (hard-cooked egg yolk, anchovy, capers, fine herbs, mustard)
Chiffonade Sauce (fine herbs, hard-cooked egg, beets)
Vinaigrette Sauce (capers, pickles, pimiento, mustard, hard-cooked eggs, chervil, tarragon, parsley)

WINE STOCK SAUCES

Spadoise Sauce (red dry and port wine, bread crumbs, currants, nutmeg)
Raisin Sauce (Burgundy wine, raisins, currants, mustard, sugar, cloves, nutmeg, cinnamon)
Port Wine Sauce (Port wine, orange and lemon juice, orange rind, thyme, velouté sauce)

[1]Tomato ragoût sauce may be made from tomato puree which is combined with a meat stock as well as from a stock brought up from the start with tomatoes in it; sauces made with a neutral or meat tomato ragoût are used interchangeably.

[2]Melt several teaspoons of sugar over low heat until it is caramelized; add brown stock and a bit of vinegar and then proceed with the derived sauce.

[3]Variations found in bechamel sauce are applicable also to secondary sauces made from cream sauces; likewise, some sauces made from bechamel or from cream sauce may also be derived from allemande or supreme sauces. A *bechamel maigre* is made from fish stock and can be used for some sauces that otherwise would be made from a fish velouté sauce base.

mirepoix, bouquet garni and perhaps red wine and tomatoes makes a brown sauce or espagnole. It is widely used as a base for red meat and game. Velouté is made from white roux, white stock and seasonings, while a fish velouté, oftentimes called *sauce vin blanc* or white wine sauce is made from fish stock and dry white. A fricassee gravy is a velouté. Escoffier made bechamel sauce by first cooking veal flesh in milk and thickening it with a roux of butter and flour. Today it is made by thickening rich chicken or veal stock with white roux and thinning it with rich milk or cream. Heating milk with a *mirepoix* and *bouquet garni*, salt and seasonings, then straining and thickening with a white roux is white sauce and, if cream is added, it becomes cream sauce. Because of terminology confusion on types of white sauces, the following may be helpful:

White sauce	Sauce made from milk and thickened with white roux.
Cream sauce	White sauce with cream added.
Bechamel	Rich veal or chicken stock, thickened with white roux and thinned with rich milk or cream.
Velouté	White stock thickened with white roux.

Thickened tomato puree or tomato puree or brown stock flavored with vegetables and seasonings may be called tomato sauce or tomato ragoût. Tomato should predominate in color and flavor and seasonings should be fairly pungent.

Gravies are meat drippings thinned with stock or other liquid and then thickened. A pan gravy or an *au jus* is an unthickened gravy. A pan gravy, sometimes used in Southern cooking, may or may not be thickened, such as the "red-eye" gravy obtained from ham drippings. Some pan gravies contain milk.

Brown meat drippings left after sautéing are called *fond brun*. These are extracted by a process called "swishing and swirling," essentially one in which liquid is added to the pan and the drippings brought into solution using a fork or spoon to lift them from the pan bottom. This sauce is frequently poured over the items that were sautéed in the pan.

Bread can be used to thicken a sauce served with vegetables and meats, and many sauces can be derived from this one. American bread sauce is made by sautéing minced shallots or onions in butter, adding hot milk, soft bread crumbs and seasonings and stirring over low heat, finishing it with cream. The English make the same sauce seasoning it

(a)

(b)

(c)

Figure 8–17. A process called "swishing and swirling" is used to extract encrusted materials from sauté pans. (a) A stock is added and the encrusted materials are brought into solution. This is then reduced and poured over the sautéed item as a gravy. (b) Some of the fat and drippings may be left in the pan and a roux made as shown here. (c) Stock is then added and the mixture cooked about 10 minutes to give a thickened gravy.

Table 8-3. Approximate Equivalent Thickening Power of Thickeners

Ingredient	Ounces	Cups	Ingredient	Ounces	Cups
Pastry flour	4	1	Tapioca	$3^1/_2$	$^2/_3$
Bread flour	5	$1^1/_4$	Bread crumbs, dry	$3^1/_2$	$^3/_4$
Cornstarch	$2^3/_4$	$^3/_4$	Whole eggs	22	$2^3/_4$ *
Waxy maize starch	2	$^3/_8$	Egg yolks	20	$2^1/_2$ **

*approximately 14 large eggs.

** approximately 28 large yolks.

Table 8-4. Proportions of Roux for Soups and Sauces per Gallon of Liquid*

Product	Fat		Flour		Use and Consistency
	oz	cups	oz	cups	
Soups:					
Thin	6	¾	4	1	For light cream soups or other thin soups
Medium	8	1	6	1½	For succulent purees, light chowders, medium creams
Thick	12	1½	10	2½	For heavy, thick soups
Sauces:					
Very thin	6	¾	4	1	Escalloped potatoes; thin, creamy sauces
Thin	8	1	8	2	Thick enough to coat a spoon
Medium	12	1½	12	3	Creamed dishes, newburg or mornay sauce, escalloped dishes and gravies
Heavy	16	2	16	4	Soufflé bases, heavy sauces thinned by the addition of other liquids
Very heavy	20	2½	20	5	For croquettes, cutlets and so forth

*If pale roux, double flour. If brown roux, increase three times; fat may be increased in proportion. If cornstarch, potato starch, or arrowroot is substituted for plain flour, reduce to about three-fourths of flour given here.

with onion juice instead of shallots and onions. The French use no milk or cream and use a rich velouté and wine.

Basic butter or butter sauce is made from butter or margarine, a bit of strained lemon juice and a few grains of cayenne. Compounded butter is basic butter plus a minced or pulped item such as anchovy paste, garlic or mushrooms and is used as spreads for canapés. A *maitre d'hotel* is melted unbrowned butter; *meunière* butter is lightly browned basic butter—it may be called hazelnut or *noisette* butter from its color and flavor—and adding slivered almonds to it makes Sauce Almandine. Black butter (*beurre noir*) is quite darkly browned basic butter. *Maitre d'hotel* and *meunière* butters are served over steaks, chops or fish. Black butter is good served over scrambled eggs or calves' brains.

Suggested laboratory experiences or work experiences for Chapter 8:

1. Evaluate various soup bases against meat or poultry stocks. Compare costs.

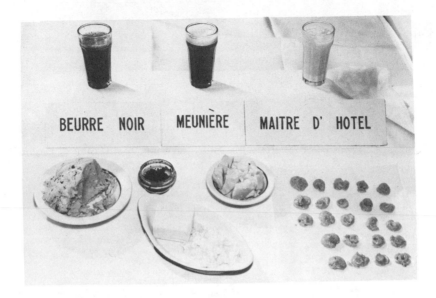

Figure 8–18. Three of the basic butters used in food preparation are shown on the top. Some basic butters and their ingredients are shown on the bottom. These are frequently used as spreads for sandwiches or canapés.

Figure 8–19. Reducing a wine previous to using it as a liquid for a sauce.

2. Boil fish bones hard for about four hours and note clouding. Simmer beef bones for four hours and note color and flavor. Simmer six more hours and then note color and flavor.
3. Make three cream soups: a velouté, bechamel and white sauce base. Evaluate.
4. Prepare a white roux, dry white roux and a *beurre manie* and use each to thicken a stock. Evaluate their use.
5. Thicken a stock with flour, cornstarch and waxy maize using equal quantities of thickener with equal quantities of stock. Compare the resulting paste and degree of thickening from each.
6. Prepare a *maitre d'hotel*, a *meunière* and a black butter.
7. Using one of the basic sauces, prepare a table indicating how at least six secondary sauces can be derived from it.

BIBLIOGRAPHY

Breland, John, H., *Chef's Guide to Quantity Cookery*, Harper and Bros., New York, 1947.

Culinary Institute, *Professional Quantity Cooking, Basic Courses*, Dahl Publishing Co., Stamford, Conn., 1958.

Culinary Institute, *Professional Chef*, rev. ed., Institutions, Chicago, 1963.

Escoffier, A., *The Escoffier Cook Book*, Crown Publishers, New York, 1959.

Kotschevar, L., and McWilliams, M., *Understanding Food*, John Wiley & Sons, Inc., New York, 1969.

Lundberg, D., and Kotschevar, L., *Understanding Cooking*, University Bookstore, U. Mass., Amherst, Mass., 1965.

Montague, Prosper, *Larousse Gastronomique*, Crown Publishing, New York, 1965.

Ranhofer, Charles, *Epicurean*, The Hotel Monthly Press, John Wiley, Inc., Evanston, Ill., 1920.

Terrell, Margaret E., *Professional Food Preparation*, John Wiley & Sons, Inc., New York, 1971.

9

Beverages

Beverages are often an important accompaniment to a meal or snack. They are delicate substances and require exacting care in their making. Frequently, patrons judge operations on the quality of the beverages served.

COFFEE

Consumers differ on what makes quality in coffee. In one study 62% said flavor, 24% strength and 13% aroma. Consumer preferences may vary. Young people may prefer a milder coffee than older ones and some foreign groups want coffee more heavily flavored, bodied and colored than others. A breakfast cup may be milder than an after-dinner one and the demitasse may be milder than a cup of espresso.

Standard

Coffee should be evaluated on the basis of flavor (taste and aroma), clarity, color and body, and should be judged fresh when not over 30 minutes old. No cream or sugar should be added, although coffee cream may be added last to test body.

In tasting coffee, the brew should be swished into the mouth in a spray so that the aroma rises into the nostrils as the mouth identifies various tastes. The taste and aroma should be balanced and sufficiently strong to give a pleasing flavor. Weak coffee is called green or undeveloped. Some coffees such as Turkish, espresso or after-dinner should be quite strong and heavy. Many mistakenly judge coffee strength by noting color.

Coffee taste should be pleasing and properly balanced between bitterness (astringency), acidity and sweetness with no off-flavors. The aroma should be fragrant, mellow, heavy and rich with coffee bouquet, not acrid, burnt, rancid or oily. No excessive bouquet or fruitiness associated with aldehydes or other compounds may be present. There should be no trace of oiliness.

Clarity is directly related to the quantity of insoluble solids in a brew. Types of grind and handling of the brew can affect clarity. Coffee should be bright, clear and so sparkling that a silver spoon lowered nearly to the cup bottom can be seen. There should be no evidence of floating grounds, flocculent material, cloudiness, dullness or muddiness.

Brew color should be rich, deep brown. Lightness or paleness of color or a heavy dark brown of almost blackish cast lowers quality.

Body refers to a brew's density, which is directly related to the quantity of coffee solubles and which can be measured by a hydrometer. Body is denoted by a sensation of something more than water in the mouth. Espresso or demitasse possesses a heavy body and may give a feeling of thickness or sirupiness. Body should not come from fine or pulverized grounds in the brew. If 18% cream is added, it should not immediately blend as it would with hot water but should feather or layer out. Stirring is necessary to blend it. Heavier creams feather more than lighter ones, so use coffee cream (18% fat).

Principles

The coffee itself is an important factor in quality. It should come from a full plump bean grown under good weather conditions at elevations from 2,000 to 5,000 feet above sea level. The coffee we like comes from a blend of beans from Brazil, Colombia, Venezuela and perhaps Mexico. The beans should come from the last harvest and have good care in storage and shipping. Roasting develops coffee flavor and color, both increasing as the degree of roasting increases. Dark or heavy roasts are used for demitasse, espresso and Turkish coffees but for most operations a medium (mild) roast is preferred. After roasting, coffee is ground. The right grind size must be used to give proper water contact time with the coffee, as an improper grind that extends or decreases this time can give poor coffee. The terms *steel-cut, cornmeal, drip, urn* and others for grind are interpreted differently by manufacturers and grinder settings such as urn at a 4 to 6 setting or drip 3 to 5 or vacuum 1 to 3 are also unreliable because grinders vary. Testing the grind in the equipment is recommended.

Coffee flavors are highly volatile and easily deteriorate by becoming rancid or stale. Coffee should be stored in a dry cool place because flavor loss and deterioration increase with time and temperature. Refrigerating coffee retards loss, holding at -4° F almost stops it. A ground coffee after 5 to 8 days at room temperature, because of volatile and staling loss, grades from fair to poor quality. At room temperature ground coffee in three days loses 20% of its aroma and at the end of 20 days it will have lost 50%. Coffee in the bean remains fresh for a much longer time than ground coffee. Coffee easily absorbs odors. Deliveries should be planned and stocks rotated so that fresh coffee is always on hand. Some grind on the premises just a day's supply to assure freshness. Quality of beans is indicated by an even roast, full plump beans with little or no foreign material in them. Ground coffee can be judged by the brew it makes.

Vacuum-packed coffee is freshly ground and packed under vacuum to reduce flavor loss. After a year flavor loss is stabilized. Ground coffee releases carbon dioxide and this may swell cans. Many manufacturers of institution coffee pack it in plastic bags, which also assist in retarding flavor loss. Purchasing coffee in the proper size container to fit the equipment is recommended.

Water

Moderately hard or soft water produces a good brew but an extremely soft or hard (alkaline) water will not; permanently hard waters are not usually harmful to quality. Chlorine, sulfur, ammonia and other compounds must be in tap waters in greater concentration than normal to give off-flavors. Detergents on utensils or cups can give off-flavors. Waters with over four ppm (parts per million) of iron give a brew a greenish color when cream is used. Normally, regular water is not this heavily contaminated unless it comes from rusted pipes or from some other source where iron is present.

Sodium bicarbonate combines with coffee grounds to make a gel that slows the flow of water through the grounds, giving a bitter and harsh brew. Polyphosphate softeners can correct this problem; however, water softened by a sodium process may turn carbonates into sodium bicarbonate.

Procedures

Correct brewing procedures must be established and coffee and water measured accurately. The coffee should be fresh, of good quality and of the proper grind, the water of the proper condition and temperature, the right equipment clean and free from coffee soil and the holding and serving procedures adequate.

Coffee is made by hot water extracting soluble flavors from coffee. The particle size of the grind and the time the water is in contact with it govern how much flavor is extracted. The aromatic and milder flavors are extracted first and the bitter or more pungent flavors last. A long contact time gives over-extraction and too short an extraction time a weak, pale brew. The size of the grind governs contact time: fine, automatic drip or vacuum needs 2 to 4 minutes, drip or urn 4 to 6 minutes and regular or percolator 6 to 8 minutes. Extraction is increased as water increases in temperature. Agitation of the grounds reduces the amount of contact time required. From 18 to 22% or $2\frac{3}{4}$ to $3\frac{1}{2}$ ounces of solids per pound of the grounds should be extracted. For this, a pound of coffee to $1\frac{3}{4}$ to $2\frac{1}{2}$ gallons of freshly boiled water should be used. Do not use water that has been heated a long time or left too long to heat in equipment. The best extraction occurs between 195° to 203° F. If water is of the right condition and if the temperature, contact time and grind are correct, a brew with from 1.15 to 1.35% total coffee solids will result. Two gallons of water give approximately $1\frac{3}{4}$ gallons of brew or 40 $5\frac{1}{4}$-ounce cups. The grounds absorb about a quart of water. If brew is made using three gallons of water to a pound, an extraction of 24% must occur to give a 1.15 to 1.35% solid content but the brew may be bitter because of an excessive extraction. Poor coffee may result even if the coffee-water ratio is correct (see Figure 9-1), for excessive contact time, too hot water, too much agitation or other factors may also be the reasons. Weak coffee results if these factors are varied inversely. Strong, bitter coffee may result even if more than the correct quantity is used, as shown in the upper right-hand corner of Figure 9-1. In addition, too fine a grind, the wrong coffee blend, bicarbonates or other factors may be a cause. A weak, bitter coffee can be produced with similar incorrect coffee-water ratios if the opposite conditions are true, as shown in the lower right-hand corner of Figure 9-1.

It is preferable, if coffee *must* be stretched, to use a ratio of from $1\frac{3}{4}$ to 2 gallons of water to a pound of coffee, give proper contact time and, after removing grounds, dilute to the desired volume with hot water. While the brew will not be of proper strength, body or color, it will at least be in somewhat proper balance and not over-extracted, as would be the case if the entire quantity of water came in contact with the grounds.

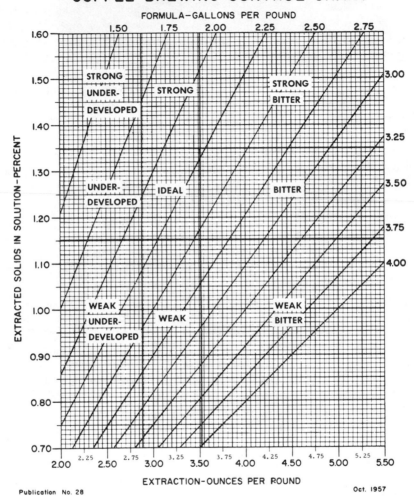

THE COFFEE BREWING INSTITUTE INC.
120 Wall Street, New York 5, N. Y.

COFFEE BREWING CONTROL CHART

FORMULA-GALLONS PER POUND

Publication No. 28   Oct. 1957

Figure 9–1. The above chart shows the effect of under-developing or over-developing a brew. (Courtesy Coffee Brewing Institute, Inc.)

Coffee-Making

Measure coffee accurately, either by securing it in preweighed units in exact quantity for a batch or by weighing. If measured, use a standard, level measure. Measure water accurately also, using standardized measures. Check to see that equipment which gives an automatic measure of water is correct.

Table 9–1. Proportions for Making Coffee in Quantity

Number of People	Number of Portions ($5\frac{1}{2}$ oz each)	Coffee Required (lb)	Water Required (gal)
25	40	1	2
50	80	2	4
75	120	3	6
100	160	4	8
125	200	5	10
150	240	6	12

URN COFFEE

For urn coffee, spread grounds evenly in 1 to 2 inches deep in a well rinsed bag or basket, then spray or pour the water over the grounds in a slow, circular motion, wetting all grounds. If the water is boiling, the temperature on the grounds will usually be correct unless the elevation is so high that water is boiling at a temperature around 200° F. See that proper contact time occurs and then remove the grounds. Draw about a gallon of the brew and dump it back to give a good mixing action, mixing fractions of different density which come off at different times in the brewing. Do not pour brewed coffee over grounds. Keep the cover on as much as possible to prevent heat loss during brewing.

AUTOMATIC DRIP COFFEE

The newer machines give the proper amount of water at the proper temperature in the proper contact time if they are working properly. Check occasionally. Merely add the proper amount of coffee in the container, set it into place and push a button. Remove the coffee grounds and clean the filtering unit as soon as the brew is made.

VACUUM COFFEE

Fill the lower bowl with fresh water to the proper level and place it on heat, leaving an inch at the top free for water expansion. Adjust the filter into the upper bowl and add the right amount of coffee. When the water boils briskly, set the upper bowl firmly into the lower bowl, twisting slightly to make a tight seal. The steam pressure in the lower bowl will force the boiling water up. Turn down the heat to prevent violent boiling. Stir the water for about 30 seconds; at the end of 2 to 4 minutes, allow the brew to filter into the lower bowl. (Some bottom bowls have a steam vent on the tube above the water line so that the top can be attached to the lower bowl at the start and this vent left open; it is closed when boiling starts.)

(a)

(b)

(c)

(d)

(e)

(f)

(g)

(h)

(i)

(j)

Figure 9–2. Steps in making coffee. (a) See that the urn is filled with fresh water. (b) Turn on the heater to heat the water. (c) When the water boils, the urn is ready. (d) Rinse out the urn well with fresh, hot water. (e) Add the proper amount of coffee (f) spreading it out evenly in the basket so that water from the overheat spray reaches all areas. (g) Turn on the water so that it begins to flow from the overhead spray onto the grounds. (h) Or, if an overhead spray is not used, draw out the proper amount of boiling water and (i) pour it over the grounds seeing that it is distributed evenly. (j) Remove the grounds as soon as the water has left them.

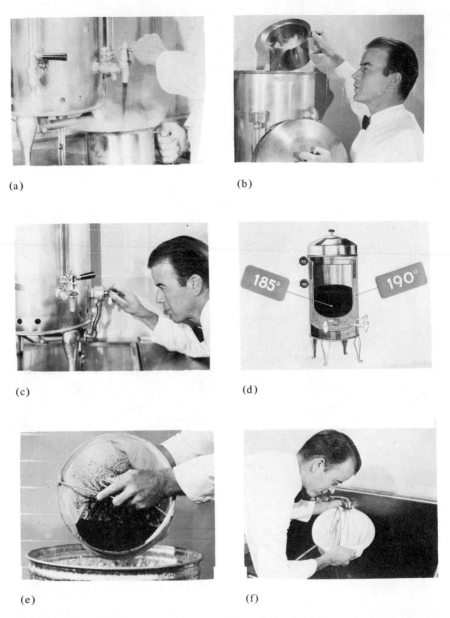

(a)　　　　　　　　　　　　(b)

(c)　　　　　　　　　　　　(d)

(e)　　　　　　　　　　　　(f)

Figure 9–3.　(a) Remove about a gallon of the fresh brew and (b) pour it into the urn obtaining a good mixing action to spread out the brew to be the same all over the urn. (c) Check to see that the temperature for holding is correct; (d) the water in the outer jacket should be 190° F and the brew 185° F. (c) Dump the grounds and (f) rinse the bag thoroughly and soak in cold water.

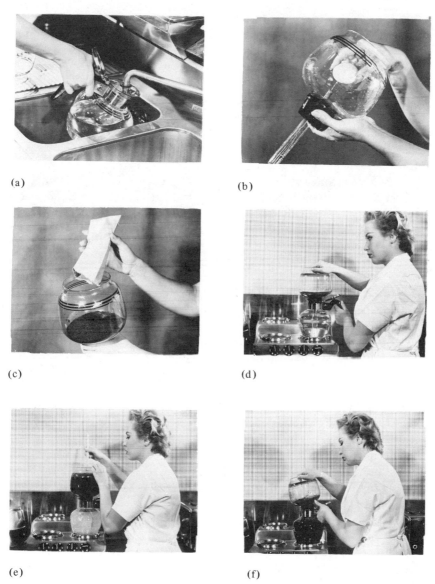

(a)

(b)

(c)

(d)

(e)

(f)

Figure 9–4. To make vacuum coffee (a) fill a pot to the proper measure and put on heat. (b) Place the filter into the top after moistening the cloth. (c) Fill the top with the proper amount of coffee, usually in a premeasured amount. (d) When the water in the lower bowl is boiling, place the top part into it. (e) Allow the steam to push the water into the upper bowl and stir. Remove the pot and allow the vacuum to pull the fresh brew down into the lower bowl. (f) Remove the top and wash it thoroughly, especially the filter. Put the filter cloth to soak in cold water.

MISCELLANEOUS COFFEE-MAKING PROCEDURES

Coffee may be made in a drip pot, old-fashioned pot or in a kettle on the range, etc. In using these, never boil the coffee for this causes a loss of aroma and an over-extraction. Use 2 level tablespoons or ⅜ ounce of coffee per 5½-ounce cup.

A drip pot has a container holding drip grind coffee over which boiling water can be poured to filter through the grounds into a lower pot. It makes good coffee. Some of these use filter papers. Correct contact time is 4 to 6 minutes. Stir the brew to mix strata of different density brew.

To make coffee in a kettle or steam-jacketed kettle, measure the correct amount of fresh cold water into the kettle and turn the heat on high. Select a clean cloth sack and half-fill with dry coffee, which allows for coffee expansion and circulation of water over the grounds during brewing. Rinse in warm and then cold water and squeeze out the excess. Measure coffee and tie the sack so that no grounds can escape. Fasten with a cord to the kettle handle and submerge in boiling water. Reduce heat to below boiling and push the sack up and down frequently to get proper extraction. Allow contact time of 8 to 10 minutes. Remove sack, drain well. Serve as soon as possible.

Boiled coffee can be made in the old-fashioned coffee pot. For this, measure the right quantity of fresh, cold water into a clean pot, and place on high heat. When the water comes to a boil, lower the heat to just below boiling, add the correct quantity of coffee and stir. Steep 6 to 8 minutes. If the grounds have not settled, add a bit of cold water using not more than a cup per pound of coffee. Strain to remove the brew from its grounds.

Iced coffee can be made by making extra-strength coffee using two-thirds the usual amount of water and pouring this over ice cubes. Regular strength coffee may be brewed and frozen into cubes in a non-metallic container freezing quickly to prevent coffee solids from separating from the brew. These are used with regular coffee. Or instant coffee can be mixed with a small amount of cold water and ice cubes and water added to give the proper strength. Stir well. For individual service, add the correct amount of coffee and water and ice cubes to a glass and serve after stirring.

Holding Coffee After Brewing

Coffee holds best at from 185° to 200° F. and for 1½ hours maximum time but preferably under 60 minutes. Excessive grounds or flocculent material in the brew reduces holding time. A fluctuating temperature may cause solids to precipitate and make the coffee turbid. Do not cool coffee and then reheat it. Patrons should receive coffee at 160° F or higher.

Variety Coffee

Demitasse coffee is made using 1½ to 1⅔ gallons of water to a pound of coffee using standard equipment. Use a dark roast. Serve in demitasse cups. Sugar, lemon peel and liquors may be offered with it. A mixed spice of equal parts of cardamon seed, whole cloves and broken cinnamon stick can be offered, or just cardamon seed alone. This mixture may also be served with Italian coffee. Sugar is proper but cream is usually not.

Coffee espresso (*caffe espresso*) or Italian coffee is made with either a drip pot, a macchinetta or an espresso maker. The macchinetta is a drip pot of two units, one of which has a spout. The non-spouted cylinder has a container for coffee at the top with top and bottom sieves. The water is measured into the non-spouted cylinder, the sieved container containing coffee fitted into this and the spouted cylinder is fitted over both, spout down. When the water is at full boil, stop the heat and turn the macchinetta upside down, allowing the water to drip through the grounds into the spouted unit. An espresso maker uses steam pressure to force water up and through grounds much as is done in making vacuum coffee. The roast is quite dark and the grind is fine. About double the coffee is used as for regular coffee. Service should be in small 4-ounce cup or glass with a twist of lemon. Sugar, brandy or other liquors may be offered but no cream.

Caffe cappuccino is Italian coffee blended with an equal quantity of hot milk. Both are poured simultaneously from two pots into a cup, a bit of cinnamon or nutmeg sprinkled over the top, or whipped cream added. A touch of grated orange may also be added. The cups used are tall.

About twice as much coffee to water as for regular coffee is used for Turkish coffee. The roast is dark and the grind almost pulverized. The brew is made in a pan with high sides, called an *ibrik*. Sugar is added at the start and the mixture is brought to a boil and allowed to froth up three times. This froth is called *face*. After removal from the heat, a few drops of cold water are added to settle the grounds, the face or foam is spooned into tiny, egg-shaped cups and the brew is poured in. The key to good Turkish coffee is not to "lose face". The flavor is strong.

Viennese coffee is about the strength of demitasse coffee. It may

Figure 9–5. *Café diable* (coffee made with flaming brandy) can be used to end a fine dinner. Student Andrew Castle demonstrates the technique of making it.

be thinned with hot milk or served plain but it is always topped with whipped cream (*mit schlag*). It may be sweetened. French coffee or *café au lait* is equal quantities of regular-strength or slightly stronger coffee and hot milk poured from two different pots into a cup at the same time. It is usually served at breakfast but may be served at other times.

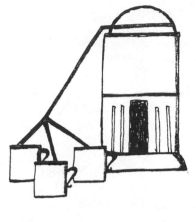

Figure 9–6. Espresso coffee-makers use steam pressure to brew true Italian Espresso coffee. Small electric Espresso machines are available for home use.

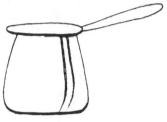

The ibrik is commonly used in Egypt, Syria, and Turkey. Only the coffee of the Middle East and Near East countries requires boiling.

The two-tiered macchinetta is the Italian version of our drip coffee-maker. It makes excellent demitasse or Italian coffee.

TEA

The quality of tea brew is governed partially by leaf size. Normally, the standard pluck is two leaves and a bud from the tip of a branch. Higher grade teas have fewer leaves than this, lower grades more. As the leaves progress down the branch, tea quality drops. Tea grown and picked late in the season is lower in quality than early or mid-season tea. The area of growth, soil, elevation and processing also affect the tea quality.

All tea, after plucking, is withered, rolled and fired and some teas may be fermented after rolling. Black tea is fully fermented, oolong is partially fermented and green tea is not fermented. Green tea may be steamed to prevent it from fermenting. Fermentation causes oxidation of tea tannins which make them less soluble. It is done by spreading tea on trays and allowing it to stand in a humid atmosphere for a few hours. Some essential oils and flavor substances also change, giving fermented teas their characteristic aroma, taste, heavier body and darker color. Firing stops fermentation and dries the tea so that it keeps. Black tea when dry is almost black. The brew from green tea is somewhat green and pale in color. Since quality depends upon rapid extraction, tea may be broken up and placed into individual bags. A good tea may be a blend of as many as 30 different teas.

Standard

Judge tea by its flavor, strength, clarity and color. Unlike coffee, body is not considered. Tea tannins give a slightly bitter taste, green tea having the most, oolong next and black tea the least. Some sweetness and acid may be present. The aroma should be fruity and fragrant although an excess lowers quality. Like coffee, tea should be swished into the mouth to blend taste and aroma at the same time. A tea lacking flavor is called thin or weathery. If balanced in flavor, the description is "brisk" indicating a zestful, stimulating quality. There should be no apparent oiliness. Clarity is essential. No tea leaves or silt should be in the brew. Typical brew colors are, for green, a pale greenish-yellow; oolong, light yellow-green with a shade of tan; black, amber, reddish-copper. Both oolong and green tea show some green from chlorophyll.

Principles

Tea's soluble substances are the alkaloid theine (caffeine), tannins and other astringent compounds, acids, sugars, carbohydrates, some essential oils and coloring matter. As the water temperature increases, tannin becomes more soluble. The best contact time for water and tea is three minutes in water around 200° F. The cooling effect of equipment should be considered in judging water temperatures. Over-contact gives excess tannin extraction plus other undesirable compounds. The essential oils or aromas of tea are highly volatile, especially in brewing, and may be rapidly dissipated in boiling. Because of this, tea should be made and served and not held. Tea infuses more rapidly in soft or mildly hard waters than in hard, alkaline waters. Clouding (tannins precipitating) may be evident with hard water, which produces a dark, dull tea, sometimes indicated by a thin film over the brew. Flavor may be affected by hard-water salts. A bit of acid, such as lemon juice, changes the pH sufficiently to dissolve tannates, lighten color and give a brisker flavor. At times, however, these acids have no effect, as in an acid punch, where clouding may occur if iron tannates form. Rapid cooling can induce clouding if the tea is high in tannins. Tea stored in a refrigerator may cloud. Hold strong infusions for iced tea at room temperature and discard at the end of the day. Metals such as aluminum, brass or iron, as with coffee, give a metallic taste; glass, earthenware, vitrified china, enameled ware or stainless steel should be the materials used in tea equipment.

Procedures

A teaspoon of tea per cup gives strong tea or two cups of milder tea. A tea bag holds this amount: there are 18 teaspoons per ounce of tea. Between 5 and 8 ounces are required to serve 100 people, as this produces 4 to 7 gallons or from 100 to 150 cups. Tea bags holding an ounce can make a gallon of quite strong tea. For making tea in quantity from leaf tea, tie the tea loosely in a cloth bag and steep in hot water. A level cup of tea (16 T) or about an ounce makes about 50 cups or a little over two gallons.

Rinse the tea container with very hot water, add the tea and pour boiling water in the correct amount over it. This is called wet service. It is incorrect to pour water into the container and then add the tea or to serve a tea bag on the side of a cup or pot of hot water. Tea in quantity can be made by bringing water to a boil in a kettle on the range or in a steam-jacketed kettle. Stop boiling, add the tea and stir to blend, then steep for three minutes. Decant and serve immediately. Use the right kind of water, freshly boiled, as water boiled or kept hot for any length of time is flat.

Tea is frequently served with lemon. Some individuals also use sugar. Cream masks the delicate flavor of tea while milk allows its subtle flavor to be smoothed out but not lost. A clove may be served with a cup of tea.

Iced tea should be made from a slightly greater proportion of tea to water since dilution by ice occurs. Make the tea as for regular tea, using care in steeping; too much extraction of tannins gives a tea that easily clouds. Green tea is highly susceptible to clouding but is not often served iced, oolong is next and black tea is the least susceptible. Certain black teas from India cloud easily. Hold infusions in glass or crockery containers equipped with a spigot. A tall glass can be filled with ice and the brew run over this. Quite strong fresh hot tea may also be poured over ice in a glass, the ice in melting giving a tea of proper concentration. Instant tea is often used for iced tea. Mint or lemon may be served with it. The Tea Council recommends the 1-2-3 method for making iced tea: for a gallon of iced tea pour

> 1 quart of boiling water over
> 2 ounces of tea; steep 6 minutes, stir, remove tea and pour into
> 3 quarts of cold tap water.

For larger quantities, multiply the 1 qt., 2 oz. and 3 qt. by the number of gallons of iced tea desired. The boiling water should completely cover the tea. Finished iced tea can be held for four hours without loss of flavor.

Teas may be blended with fruit juices and other liquids for special occasions. Russian tea is sweetened tea with orange, lemon and pineapple juice, seasoned with cinnamon. Spiced tea is seasoned by steeping with orange and lemon rind, whole cloves, cinnamon sticks and sugar.

COCOA

Where the service of cocoa is infrequent, it is best to use individually packaged mixes, of which there are many of adequate quality. Where service is regular or large, cocoa can be made from dry cocoa, sugar and either liquid or dry milk.

Standard

The color of cocoa or chocolate should be a pleasing, rich brown color. A pale weak color or a gray or muddy one indicates poor quality. There should be no scum on the surface or mixed in the cocoa. Foam may be present on the batch from which the cocoa is dispensed but none should be on the cup unless whipped cream or marshmallows have been added. The flavor should be delicately sweet with the rich, aromatic, mellow flavor of the cacao bean evident. There should be richness, especially in chocolate, which will also have a richer color. Flatness or lack of flavor or a scorched or raw flavor is undesirable. Lowered quality is indicated by poor blending, a large quantity of sediment, definite wateriness or a sirupy quality. Cocoa has more body than hot milk. Starch in cocoa and chocolate cause some thickening but this should be evident as body only in a minor way. Adding starch to give this body is not recommended.

Principles

Cocoa comes from the same bean as chocolate, but it has had some cocoa butter removed. Chocolate has about 50% cocoa butter while breakfast cocoa has 22%. Low-fat cocoas contain less than 10% cocoa butter and medium-fat ones 10 to 22%. If cocoas contain too much cocoa butter, they will not remain pulverized but will solidify. If the richness or fat content of cocoa is not adequate, butter or margarine may be added and beaten into the mixture or cream may be added to give richness.

Suggested laboratory and work experiences for Chapter 9:

1. Vary the making of coffee so that the brew of one is under-developed, another correctly developed and another over-developed. (Use Figure 9-1 to assist in this.)
2. Take a good sample of instant coffee and instant tea and compare them with freshly made coffee and freshly made tea.
3. Make coffee from a freshly ground sample and one from one that has been allowed to stand open at room temperature for over 21 days.
4. Make a strong infusion of black tea and refrigerate half for over 8 hours and allow the other to stand at room temperature for this time. Make a chilled glass of tea from each and see which one clouds.
5. Make a cup of cocoa using a good prepared mix, another cup from a good Dutch-process cocoa, a breakfast cocoa and one from chocolate. Evaluate these.

BIBLIOGRAPHY

Campbell, C. L.; Dawes, R. K.; Deolalkar, S.; and Merritt, M. C., *Effects of Certain Chemicals in Water On the Flavor of Brewed Coffee,* The Coffee Brewing Institute, Inc., Publication No. 38, New York, March 1958.

Clements, Robert L., and Deatherage, F. F., *Chemical Study of Coffee Flavor,* The Coffee Brewing Institute, Inc., Publication No. 26, New York, October 1957.

Gardner, D. G., *Water Composition and Coffee Brewing,* The Coffee Brewing Institute, Inc., Publication No. 31, New York, March 1958.

Lentner, C., and Deatherage, F. F., *Organic Acids in Coffee in Relation to The Degree of Roasting,* The Coffee Brewing Institute, Inc., Publication No. 45, New York, 1958.

Little, Angela C.; Chichester, C. O.; and Mckinney, G., *On The Color of Coffee, II,* The Coffee Brewing Institute, Inc., Publication No. 37, New York, November 1958.

Little, Angela C.; Chichester, C. O.; and Mackinney, G., *On the Color of Coffee, III, Effect of Roasting Conditions on Flavor Development for a Given Color. Role of Initial Moisture Level on Roasting Characteristics of Green Coffee Beans,* The Coffee Brewing Institute, Inc., Publication No. 48, New York, May 1959.

Lockhart, Ernest E., *Characteristics of Coffee Relation to Beverage Quality,* The Coffee Brewing Institute, Inc., Publication No. 40, New York, May 1959.

Lockhart, Ernest E., *Chemistry of Coffee,* The Coffee Brewing Institute, Inc., Publication No. 25, New York, September 1957.

Lockhart, Ernest E., *Coffee Grinds, II, Classification and Analysis,* The Coffee Brewing Institute, Inc., Publication No. 39, New York, 1959.

Lockhart, Ernest E., *Coffee Solubles and Beverage Acceptance,* The Coffee Brewing Institute, Inc., Publication No. 27, New York, November 1957.

Lockhart, Ernest E., *Storage Properties of Vacuum Packed Coffee,* The Coffee Brewing Institute, Inc., Publication No. 30, New York, February 1958.

Lockhart, Ernest E., *The Coffee Hydrometer,* The Coffee Brewing Institute, Inc., Publication No. 43, New York, February 1958.

Lockhart, Ernest E., *The Strength of Coffee,* The Coffee Brewing Institute, Inc., Publication No. 44, New York, October 1959.

Lockhart, Ernest E.; Tucker, C. L.; and Merritt, M. C., *Water Impurities and Brewed Coffee Flavor,* The Coffee Brewing Institute, Inc., Publication No. 6, New York, February 1956.

Merritt, M. C., and Proctor, Bernard E., *Effect of Temperature During The Roasting Cycle on Selected Components of Different Types of Whole Bean Coffee,* The Coffee Brewing Institute, Inc., Publication No. 46, New York, November 1958.

Merritt, M. C., and Proctor, Bernard E., *Extraction Rates For Selected Components in Coffee Brew,* The Coffee Brewing Institute, Inc., Publication No. 47, New York, November 1958.

Niven, W. W., Jr., and Shaw, B. C., *Critical Conditions for Quantity Coffee Brewing,* The Coffee Brewing Institute, Inc., Publication No. 19, New York, April 1957.

Nejelski & Company, Inc., *Survey of Beverage Coffee,* The Coffee Brewing Institute, Inc., Publication No. 5, New York, January 1956.

Ruffley, J., *About Good Coffee,* Research Department Bulletin, No. 21, National Restaurant Association, Chicago, Ill., 1958.

Rhoades, John W., *Coffee Aroma Analysis by Gas Chromatography,* The Coffee Brewing Institute, Inc., Publication No. 34, New York, July 1958.

Segall, Stanley, and Proctor, Bernard E., *The Influence of High Temperature*

Holding Upon the Components of Coffee Brew, The Coffee Brewing Institute, Inc., Publication No. 41, New York, January 1960.

Segall, Stanley, and Proctor, Bernard E., *The Influence of High Temperature Holding Upon the Components of Coffee Brew, II, Volatile Reducing Substances,* The Coffee Brewing Institute, Inc., Publication No. 42, New York, August 1959.

10

Eggs and Dairy Products

Eggs and milk products are often studied together because many of the principles for cooking them are closely related.

EGGS

Egg cookery is not simple. Much must be known and good techniques must be practiced to obtain good products. Some techniques required are the most exacting and difficult in cooking. Eggs are used as entrees, appetizers or salads, for thickening or binding agents in custards, pie fillings or puddings, meat loaves or for covering French toast or breaded or batter-fried items. They incorporate air into cakes, soufflés, etc., and are excellent emulsifiers, especially the yolks. Their ability to coagulate and give cell strength gives them utility in baking. Consommés or bouillons can be clarified with them. Eggs as an ingredient give stability to frozen desserts and candies. They add color, richness and flavor to food and are complete proteins, easily digested, contributing significant amounts of vitamin A, thiamin, riboflavin, niacin, vitamin D, fat, minerals and calories.

Egg Quality

High egg quality is important to final product quality, especially in breakfast eggs. The quality of frozen, freeze-dry or dried eggs depends

Figure 10–1. The dried eggs shown in the scoop were used to make the angel cake shown on the right. Prepared cake mixes also make equally good products.

upon the fresh egg quality from which they came and subsequent care given them in processing and storage.

A good egg has a well-centered yolk with a firm membrane surrounding it. The white should be firm, thick and viscous and the air sac small. A good egg broken onto a flat surface has a white that forms a rounded mass close to the yolk with only a small quantity of thin, watery white and a yolk that stands high. A fresh egg is slightly acid but as it ages and losses quality, it becomes more alkaline. The white becomes thin and the yolk loses its central position. The yolk breaks easily when the egg is shelled because the membrane is weak. Eggs lose quality rapidly at room temperature. Older eggs have a strong flavor or may easily develop it in cooking. Some off-flavors bake out in old eggs used in baking goods unless caused by bacteria, yeasts or molds. Only high quality eggs should be used for breakfast. Lower quality can be used for baking.

Egg Standards

A soft-cooked egg should have a partially coagulated white with a half to three-fourths of the white firm, depending upon doneness. The yolk should be warm throughout but liquid. A medium-cooked egg has a white cooked only to the yolk with the yolk still liquid. A hard-cooked

(a)

(b)

(c)

(d)

Figure 10–2. (a) Eggs country-style show high quality with a good sheen, high yolks and soft-cooked edges. (b) A high quality egg on the left and a poor one on the right. (c) Well scrambled eggs; note the soft texture and good sheen, indicators of quality. (d) A hard-cooked, medium-cooked and soft-cooked egg, all of good standard.

egg has a firm, glossy white and a solid, mealy yolk with a bright yellow or orange-yellow color. The yolk should be uniformly coagulated and not dark on the outside. Eggs cooked in the shell should have a pleasing egg flavor and appear bright and fresh. Colors should be natural and clear. There should be no toughness, rubberiness, crumbliness, stickiness or other undesirable texture. Boiled eggs are firmer than those cooked at lower temperatures and boiling may be done purposely to produce eggs firm enough to slice or stuff. Eggs processed by dipping in oil may leave a film of oil on the surface of the cooking water, which in no way indicates an egg of poor quality.

A fried egg should have a bright, glossy appearance and be compact much like a poached egg but not quite as bunched. A "sunny-side up" egg should have a bright yellow or orange-yellow, well-rounded yolk. If cooked country style ("over-easy" or hard-cooked), the yolk is covered with a thin film of coagulated white and the yolk, depending upon the degree of cooking, is firmer than when cooked sunny-side up. A fried egg should appear shiny, not dull, wrinkled, porous or watery and be soft underneath with no hard edges. The coagulated areas should be firm, yet tender, not tough or rubbery.

Poached eggs should have a bright appearance with some shiny white adhering closely to bright yolks. They should not be spread out or porous. Raggedness, wrinkling, dullness or other undesirable qualities are an indication of either poor cooking or poor eggs.

A shirred egg's standard is about the same as for a fried egg cooked country-style. It should be bright and not over-cooked or dry on the surface or edge nor have a dark ring around the yolk. It should be tender.

Scrambled eggs should be bright and clear with a soft sheen, a uniform, pale color and have no evidence of browning. The egg segments should be small but not fine. The cooked mass should be tender, moist and delicate in texture, not hard, dry, powdery or watery. Heavy, compact, completely coagulated eggs are not desirable but the eggs should not be runny. Avoid a hard layer on the bottom or foaminess on top. A strong flavor, a dark, green color and rubberiness indicate overcooking or poor quality eggs.

A plain (French) omelet should have many of the qualities of scrambled eggs except that the outside may be browned to a delicate light tan. The omelet also may be firmer and have a more continuous mass than scrambled eggs. No moist, large segments should be seen. Moistness, tenderness and delicacy of flavor should be evident. The folded or rolled shape should be even and represent a uniform, well rounded unit neither ragged, uneven nor separated. A foamy omelet may be served unfolded but it is usually folded in half or rolled. It should be well puffed, of good volume and well rounded, not fallen or collapsed. It should have a uniform, delicate tan top and a delicate brown bottom. Uneven or pale color or excessive browning is undesirable. The texture and consistency should be uniform, well blended, tender, firm and moist, not tough or dry. There should be no raw eggs in the center. No unmixed egg white should be apparent nor foaminess on top nor toughness caused by solidified material on the bottom. The flavor should be delicate, not pasty, flat, raw or burned. A foamy omelet depends for its quality upon the light, airy leavening of beaten whites and yolks, and this texture delicacy should weigh heavily in evaluating it.

A soufflé should have many texture qualities of a foamy omelet. The top should be slightly rounded, well puffed and only slightly cracked with a surface that is smooth, shiny and unsunken. Its color should be an even, delicate brown. No unmixed egg white should be apparent.

Baked custard mixtures should be clear, creamy and shiny and have a delicate flavor. An eggy, flat or tasteless flavor is undesirable. The texture should be smooth, not stiff, tough, rubbery, curdled or uneven. No wateriness or porosity should be evident. The top should be shiny and clear, lightly touched with a delicate tan. Stirred custards should be creamy and smooth with a delicate, light flavor.

Principles

Coagulation

When subjected to heat above certain temperatures, eggs coagulate or become firm. Coagulation is not instantaneous but occurs somewhere around 156° F for whole eggs, 144° to 158° F for yolks and 140° to 149° F for whites. Mixing eggs with liquids, sugar or other substances raises the coagulation temperature—a custard coagulates around 175° to 185° F. Raising the temperature slowly causes coagulation to occur at a slightly lower temperature. Coagulation can also be caused by

Figure 10–3. A country-style egg (left), over-easy (center) and sunny-side up (right).

beating or by chemical actions such as reactions with strong acids or alcohol. Low or moderate temperatures are best for cooking eggs. High temperatures toughen them and develop unpleasant flavors. Mild acids make eggs more tender, retard undesirable flavor development, increase thickening power and lower their temperature of coagulation.

Egg protein holds its moisture loosely when raw but, when it coagulates, the water is bound in tightly to the protein developing a firmness. If egg protein is diluted with moisture, high temperatures break the moisture away producing an open, curdled texture called *syneresis*. The protein fractions are now bunched together separately from the moisture. Additional heat toughens and hardens this curd. Milk also is subject to syneresis or curdling. Syneresis is seen in overcooked custards, grainy rarebits or curdled soft custards and in milk that is sour.

Coagulation is an endothermic reaction; that is, heat is absorbed in the process. A thickening custard does not rise in temperature but, when coagulation is complete, the temperature rises again. This second rise indicates coagulation is complete and the custard should be removed from the heat. Curdling soon follows if cooking continues. Custards usually develop syneresis around 190° F. Stirring a custard gives a smooth, slightly thickened liquid, and baking without disturbing gives a smooth, solid mass.

Eggs, especially whites, contain sulfur which may give off-flavors or off-colors to eggs, especially in an alkaline medium. If this sulfur joins with the iron in the yolk, iron sulfide which has a strong flavor and a dark greenish color is formed. Overcooking can produce both. Sulfides form at around 155° F but this is not rapid until 185° F or above. Sulfide development is slowed by 1) cooking at lower temperatures, 2) using fresh eggs, 3) using some acid or 4) shortening cooking time. Fast cooling of cooked eggs or a cooked egg mass helps to reduce sulfide formation.

Foams

Age, temperature, egg quality and pH are factors that affect foaming ability and foam stability. Fresh eggs may lack good foaming ability. Aging tenderizes egg proteins and makes them more extensible and, for this reason, old shell, storage shell, dried or frozen eggs may foam more satisfactorily than fresh eggs. Yolk and whites separate best when the egg is above 60° F.

Each egg protein has different foaming abilities. Ovalbumin makes the strongest foam, developing structures that support many times their own weight of other ingredients. Eggs form a good foam at 50° F but it

(a)   (b)

Figure 10–4. (a) This cheese soufflé shows a high standard and good stability. (b) A foamy omelet is made very much the same as a soufflé but cooked differently.

is deficient in stability. The best volume and stability is obtained at over 115° F but in quantity production, eggs are whipped usually between 75° F and 110° F. Thawed frozen or reliquefied dried eggs should be around 110° F and handled similarly to fresh shell eggs. Frozen or dried eggs can be overbeaten the same as fresh eggs.

Egg pH is important to foaming. Some fractions such as ovalbumin foam best at a pH of 3.7 to 4.0, while others such as albumen develop a better foam when slightly acid or somewhat alkaline (6.5 to 9.5 pH). In quantity preparation, eggs perform best in cooking and in foam development with a pH of around 6.5 or lower. About two-thirds tablespoon (¼ ounce) of cream of tartar to each pound of eggs (2 c) is normally used for this, although lemon juice or other acids are also good. Acid tenderizes egg protein so that it extends more easily, and it also lightens the pigments. The addition of salt seems to encourage foaming. Sugar gives foam stability and aids in creating foam because its rough edges draw in air in beating. The acid and salt are usually added at the start of beating and sugar later when the eggs become foamy or nearly whipped. The early addition of sugar helps to buffer the eggs, especially whites, against overbeating. An egg white will not foam if fat is present. Even the smallest quantity such as that in egg yolk will destroy foaming ability. Utensils used for beating whites should be scrupulously clean and free of fat. The color of eggs lightens as foam increases. The most common fault in beating yolks is underbeating.

Processed dried whites used for meringues or angel cakes can be

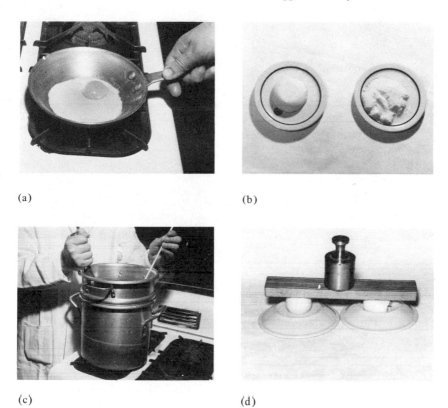

(a)

(b)

(c)

(d)

Figure 10–5. This egg is coagulating, a process specific to proteins. (b) Overcooking an egg causes the protein to lose some of the moisture, developing syneresis. (c) Using a thermometer is a good way to tell when a stirred custard is done. Since coagulation is an endothermic action, the temperature does not rise when coagulation is occurring but the custard immediately starts to show a rise when coagulation is complete. At this time, remove the custard from the heat. (d) An egg hard cooked at low temperature on the right while one hard-cooked by boiling is shown on the left. The one on the left will slice or cut in half for filling much better than the one on the right.

beaten to a stiffer, dryer foam without overbeating than can regular egg whites because they contain substances that stabilize them and give a more durable and elastic foam. Phosphoric acid salts, bile salts or triethyl citrate may be added to increase stability and volume. Dried eggs, especially whites, have a longer shelf life if the small amount of glucose is removed in processing—usually by fermentation. If dried egg products are acidified and packed in gas, shelf life is extended. Storage under refrigeration also increases shelf life and stability.

(a)

(b)

Figure 10–6. (a) Cook shirred eggs gently under broilers so as not to toughen them. (b) If hard-cooked eggs are to be chopped, prepare as shown.

Recipes should state the stage to which eggs are to be beaten, even indicating at times whether this is the top or lower range of the stage. The four stages to which eggs are beaten to foam are:

	First Stage	*Second Stage*	*Third Stage*	*Fourth Stage*
Appearance	Liquid but well blended; foam is in large bubbles.	Medium size air cells throughout mass; foam is shiny, moist and fluid; tips fold over into rounded peaks, and liquid separates out in standing.	Stiff foam; small air cells; no longer fluid, especially whites; still moist, smooth, and glossy; points stand when peaked.	Dry, dull, brittle foam; flakes off and can be cut into rigid parts; curds may appear, indicating coagulation; it is difficult to beat whole eggs or yolks to this stage.
Use	Clarifying soups, French toast, coating foods, and for blending into mixtures as liquid.	Sponge or angel cakes, soufflés, foamy omelets.	Cooked frostings, divinity, soft or hard meringues, tortes, sponge cakes.	Has no use in food work; eggs are so overextended that they will not extend further in baking, causing a failure in the product.

(a)   (b)

Figure 10–7. (a) Second stage of whites, yolks and whole eggs. (b) Third stage of these same eggs.

Techniques of Cooking

Cooking eggs to order should be done whenever practical. The high perishability of quality in breakfast eggs makes it difficult to prepare them in large quantity and hold them. Fried, shirred or scrambled eggs can be cooked in quantity to almost done and finished for service in an oven.

Cooking in Water

BOILING

Have eggs at room temperature or warm them slightly in lukewarm water before adding them to hot water; if the eggs are cold, they may crack. Times for cooking shell eggs are:

	212° F*	190° to 195° F*	Steam Pressure, 7 psi
Soft-cooked	3 min	6 min	1 min 25 sec
Medium-cooked	4 min	8 min	
Hard-cooked	12 to 15 min	20 to 25 min	3 min 10 sec

*These times vary at elevations above 3,000 feet.

Egg boilers operated by service personnel hold about four eggs at a time. To cook shell eggs in quantity, place the eggs in a perforated insert and set this into tepid water in a steam-jacketed kettle or a pot that can be quickly brought to boiling. The water should cover the eggs about an inch deep. For breakfast eggs, bring the water to 190° to 195° F. After cooking plunge the eggs immediately into cold water and send to service. Eggs for slicing or stuffing should be cooked at higher temperatures and cooled in cold water 5 to 10 minutes. Peel immediately, cracking the shell well and rolling to give good shell break-up. Start at the large end and peel down, using running water, if necessary, to help loosen the shell from the egg. If hard-cooked eggs are to be chopped, crack them into lightly greased pans not over an inch deep, steam or bake and then chop. If eggs are steamed in the shell, times must be based on the same size egg at the same temperature in the same batch. Steam pressures must also be the same. Because of this, it is frequently difficult to steam eggs to any condition other than hard-cooked and get exactly the doneness desired.

CODDLED EGGS

Have eggs for coddling at room temperature and add boiling water in the ratio of a pint of water to each egg; cover tightly and allow to stand without heat until the desired doneness is obtained.

POACHED EGGS

For poaching have the water from 2 to $2\frac{1}{2}$ inches deep in a 4-inch flat pan with a tablespoon of salt and two tablespoons of vinegar per gallon of water. The salt and vinegar cause the egg protein to bunch together, retarding spread. Bring to a gentle boil. About 8 to 16 eggs may be poached per gallon. The water can be used for 3 to 4 batches before discarding. Crack eggs onto platters and slide them in toward the pan side, not in the center. This helps to keep the yolks in the center of the

(a)   (b)

Figure 10–8.   (a) To peel a hard-cooked egg, crack it well and start at the broad end using water to assist in loosening the shell. (b) To poach eggs, gently let them slide into the hot water, striking the side of the pan to cushion their entry and allow them to bunch up.

white and retards spread. Cook from 3 to 5 minutes depending upon desired doneness. Remove with a perforated ladle or slotted spoon to give good drainage. They may be sent to service slightly undercooked in hot lightly salted water. Eggs poached at low temperatures may be too tender to handle well in quantity service. Eggs may be poached in the steam table, starting a few at a time so service is constant. Eggs may be steam poached in greased cups. These poachers may be set into a special unit in the steam table.

Cooking with Dry Heat

Fried Eggs

Eggs are frequently fried to order even when a large quantity is needed. Single egg pans should be four inches in diameter at the bottom and double egg pans from 6 to 8 inches. The pans should be conditioned and used solely for this purpose. (See how to condition pans in Chapter 6.)

To fry eggs, add fat or butter (preferably the latter) about ⅛-inch deep in the pan. Have the fat hot and slide the eggs into it, immediately reducing the heat to avoid forming a hard surface under the egg or at the edges. The hot fat retards spread by starting coagulation. Covering the pan tightly cooks the egg country-style, a process in which steam from the egg or steam from a bit of added water coats the top of the egg with coagulated white. Basting with hot fat can also coat the egg. Turning the egg over and cooking it slightly is called "over easy." Use plenty of butter or fat on a clean and conditioned grill set at 300° to 325° F. Grilled eggs are not as attractive as those fried in individual pans but production is faster. Place eggs on the grill in the same rotation so that they can be removed in the same order. Eggs may be prebroken into a device with many cups so that they can be placed on the grill at one time. For cafeteria service cook eggs until just set, place in a well buttered steam table pan, cover and send to finish cooking as they are held for service in the steam table.

To fry in mass quantity, break the eggs onto platters and slide into 2 to 2½ inch deep fat at 265° to 280° F in 4-inch deep flat pans. Drain well before sending to service. Some grease 18 x 26 -inch hamburger bun pans, place the eggs in the indented spaces and then ovenize them in an oven.

Shirred Eggs

Shir or bake eggs by cooking under a broiler or by baking in an oven. Place the eggs first in well buttered cassolettes or shallow baking dishes and season. Place the dish over low heat for several minutes

(a)

(b)   (c)

(d)

Figure 10–9.   (a) A fried egg should have no brown or crisp part on the bottom. (b) Scramble eggs by stirring constantly, removing from the fire when about this consistency. (c) Have the hash hot if eggs are to be shirred in it. Place in a hot oven and cook until the white is almost cooked.   The heat in the hash will finish cooking the eggs. (d) A spinach timbale is shown on the left while a cheese custard is being prepared on the right.

until the eggs show slight coagulation. Then place under a broiler or in an oven and cook the eggs to near doneness since cooking will continue after removal from the heat. High heat toughens the eggs. Cream, milk, cheese, bacon, chicken livers or other foods may be added before cooking or sauces may be added during the last stage or at the end of cooking.

Scrambled Eggs

Scrambled eggs are easily prepared in quantity. Usually four ounces of cream, milk or some other liquid is added per pound of whole eggs. Cooking may be in a large greased pan in the oven, under a broiler, in a steam-jacketed kettle, in a *bain marie,* in a steam table, in individual skillets or in a steamer or double boiler. The heat at the start should be fairly high, then should be lowered rapidly as the eggs coagulate. Lift the eggs carefully from the bottom, allowing the uncooked portions to flow to the bottom and cook. The eggs should be left in about ¼-inch segments. Excess stirring gives too fine pieces. Remove the eggs while still soft and send to service so that they will be just about the right consistency. Too much heat or extended heat toughens them and develops off-colors and off-flavors. Whole eggs are sometimes combined with a medium white sauce and cooked until just set. These hold well at 200° F for 30 minutes, longer than eggs prepared without the sauce.

Omelets

Foamy omelets are seldom prepared because of their delicate nature and the skill required to make them. Plain and foamy omelets are usually cooked to order. Plain omelets can also be baked in large pans, steamed in pans or cooked in a double boiler, a *bain marie* or a steam-jacketed kettle. Oven temperatures are about 325° F and time is about 25 to 30 minutes.

One egg makes a small omelet, two a medium one and three a large one. They should not be frothy. The addition of liquid is not recommended. Use a well conditioned pan covered about ⅛-inch deep with clarified butter, margarine, oil or fat. Bring to a fairly high temperature so that the eggs bubble as they are poured in. Tilt the pan in all directions to spread the eggs quickly to the outer edges. Then drop the heat and cook at a moderate temperature. Lift cooked portions up carefully to allow uncooked liquid to flow underneath but do not break or allow to bunch or form a mass in the center of the pan. While the surface is still moist, increase the heat to brown the bottom. To fold or roll, tip the pan to about 60° angle and shape with a spatula. Before folding, fill with creamed items, chicken livers, chopped bacon or ham, cheese, jelly, preserves or marmalade. Press the still moist edges lightly to seal them and

(a)   (b)

(c)   (d)

Figure 10–10.   (a) To make a French omelet, have the fat fairly hot and pour the whole eggs (stage one) into the pan. (b) Lift until the entire mass is well coagulated. Then, fill and fold as shown. (c) Shape, if desired. (d) If the filling is sweet, dust with powdered sugar and burn with a poker as shown.

turn and cook for a short time. Turn onto a plate, shape with a clean cloth and serve. Omelets with sweetened centers are frequently "burned" which is a process in which the omelet is sprinkled liberally with powdered sugar and a hot metal instrument is used to burn a design onto the omelet top.

Foamy omelets are made by whipping the yolks and whites separately and folding them together. They are baked in an oven or cooked covered over heat. As with plain omelets, they can be filled, folded and scored.

SOUFFLÉS

For a soufflés blend stage-one yolks (see table on p. 278) into a thick starch base and carefully fold the whites at stage two, upper level, into this mixture. Chopped meat, cheese or other foods can be added. Sweetened soufflés are used for desserts. Tapioca-thickened soufflés perform well in quantity service. Bake soufflés at around 300° F to obtain a dry and stable product. Baking for a shorter time at 375° F in a pan of water gives a good product. To guard against sudden collapse, after baking leave the soufflé at the oven entrance with the door open so that it will stabilize. As it cools, the volume decreases, although a well-made soufflé shrinks only slightly.

FONDUES AND TIMBALES

There are many fondues; one is made of cheese, white wine, starch and kirsch, another by deep-frying small pieces of meat and serving these with tangy sauces; still another is a custard-like dish with bread or bread crumbs for lightness. It is somewhat like a soufflé. Chopped chicken, cheese or other items may be added. A timbale uses a strong custard to bind in chopped items such as vegetables or meats, and is baked.

Processed Eggs

All processed eggs must now be pasteurized by heating them for 3 to $3\frac{1}{2}$ minutes at 140° to 143° F, temperatures below their coagulation point. Many new prepared egg products are on the market. We can obtain today many dried egg mixtures which with the addition of water will make custards, scrambled eggs, omelets and other egg dishes. Frozen omelets and other egg products are on the market. A recent market addition is a long tube of cooked white surrounding cooked yolk, and when thawed and sliced, looks exactly like the center slice of a hard-cooked egg. The elimination of waste plus the saving of labor makes this a product of interest in quantity work. Operations should be testing these new items on the market and using them whenever they are found to have quality and possess other desirable features, including cost.

Frozen or dried eggs are used extensively for cooking or baking. All processed eggs must be pasteurized so that they can be used in uncooked items, as only high quality products should be used in uncooked foods. Only products that have been federally inspected and passed should be accepted.

Frozen whole eggs, frozen yolks, frozen whites, a sugared yolk with approximately 10% sugar and whole eggs containing added yolks (proprietary eggs) are available. A high quality frozen whole egg mixture is available for omelets, scrambled eggs, French toast or other breakfast items. For the most part, dried and frozen eggs come from eggs lacking quality and these should not be used for breakfast purposes. Store frozen eggs at 0° F or less. Thaw frozen eggs under refrigeration. A 30-pound can takes two or more days to thaw at 40° F and should be mixed well before using to distribute egg solids.

A case (30 dozen) of large eggs weighs net 45 or more pounds and yields about 40 pounds of shelled egg or 20 to 22 pounds of whites and 16 to 18 pounds of yolks. A 30-pound can contains about 300 large eggs, or 670 yolks or 540 whites. If whites and yolks are to be blended to make whole eggs, a 55:45 ratio should be used. This is not the proportion in the shell but corrects for the fact that in separating eggs, some white is always left with the yolk. Frequently to obtain a pound (pint) of whole egg, 1¼ cups of whites to ⅞ cup of yolks is mixed. Eggs by count in recipes are calculated as large eggs (24 ounces per dozen in the shell); if medium or extra large eggs are used, decrease or increase respectively 10%.

Eggs are dried by the spray or tray (pan) drying method. The ratio of water to dry whole eggs in reconstituting may be 2:1 by weight, whites 3:1 and yolks 1:1¼ but, as much as possible, we try to mix the dry eggs with dry ingredients adding the water with the liquid ingredients. It should be noted that equivalents in Tables 10-2 and 10-3 for yolks are not the same, bakers preferring to use more yolks. Manufacturer's directions should always be checked for ratios to be sure. Dried eggs are available as whole eggs, whites, yolks and special blends as fortified eggs (70% whole, 30% yolks) or baker's special with 20 to 30% sucrose to improve foaming ability. Dried eggs should be vacuum-packed in nitrogen gas. If acidified, they are more stable in use and have a longer shelf life and should be stored at 0° F or lower. After opening, store at 32° to 40° F in a tightly sealed container to reduce lumping. If measured, stir lightly with a fork before measuring, but it is preferable to weigh. To reconstitute, spread evenly over lukewarm water, stirring constantly with a wire whip or use a mixer. Let stand for 5 to 10 minutes; stir again and use.

Table 10-1.   Frozen and Fresh Egg Equivalents

Type Egg	Weight (lb)	Volume (pt)	Fresh EP Equivalent (large eggs)* (24 oz per dozen)
Whole eggs	1	1	9 to 11 whole eggs
Whites	1	1	17 to 19 whites
Yolks	1	1	20 to 24 yolks

*If medium eggs, increase count about 10%; for a lb (pt) of whole eggs use 9 oz whites to 7 oz yolks.

Table 10-2.   Miscellaneous Equivalents of Processed and Fresh Eggs

Processed Product	Egg to Water	Fresh Equivalent EP (large eggs)
No. 10 can (3 lb) dried whole		100 whole eggs
1 lbs dry whole eggs and 2½ pt water	1:2½	3½ lb whole eggs
1 lb dry yolks and 1½ pt water	1:1½	2½ lb yolks
6 oz dry whole and 1⅞ c water	3:7	dozen whole eggs
1 lb dried whole and 2½ pt water	1:2½	3 doz whole eggs (3½ lb)
1 lb dried whites and 5 pt water	1:5	100 whites (6 lb)
1 lb dried yolks and 1¾ c water	8:7	47 yolks

Table 10-3. Quantities of Dried Eggs Required to Make a Pound Fresh EP Equivalent

Type Egg and Number to Give 1 lb	Quantity for 1 lb Equivalent			
	Dried Egg		Water	
	Ounces	Measure	Ounces	Measure
Whole egg, 9	$4^1/_2$	1 c 2 T	$11^1/_4$	1 c 7 T
White, 17 to 19	$2^1/_4$	$^1/_2$ c	$13^3/_4$	$1^3/_4$ c
Yolk*, 20 to 24	$7^1/_4$	1 c	$8^3/_4$	1 c 1 T
Yolk**, 25 to 27	$7^1/_2$	1 c	$8^1/_2$	1 c 1 T
Yolk***, 16 to 20	$6^1/_2$	1 c	8	1 c

*43% solids

**45% solids

***Add 1.6 oz of sugar to give yolks with 10% sugar as used in the bakeshop for frozen sugared yolks.

DAIRY PRODUCTS

Milk is a common fluid in which many foods are suspended or dissolved in cooking. It contributes flavor, color and richness plus valuable minerals and vitamins. Cream gives moistness, richness and smoothness of flavor. Butter and cheese contribute flavor and nutrients. Dry milk is low in cost, easy to handle and low in perishability and its products are equal in quality to regular milk.

Standard

The standard for foods containing dairy products should be identified with the standard for the particular food rather than for the product because the identity of the dairy product is lost. Foods high in milk are significantly modified, however, by milk properties. These foods should be smooth and non-curdled in texture, colored considerably by the white color of milk, the yellow color of cheese or the delicate cream of butter. The flavor should be mild, sweet and pleasant as well as rich. Cooking plus the addition of other ingredients may modify dairy flavors and this should be considered in evaluating products. Margarines are considered dairy products.

Types

Table 10-4 indicates the approximate composition of different milks. Coffee cream has 18% milk fat, light whipping cream 30 to 35% and heavy whipping cream 36 to 40%, while half-and-half (not a cream) is

Figure 10–11. The top is curd set with rennet which can be used to make a cheese as shown on the right. The curd on the bottom is set with souring from bacterial action and could be used to make cottage cheese.

about 12% milk fat. Sour cream must be 18% or more milk fat and have about 0.2% lactic acid.

Buttermilk was originally a liquid left after making butter, but today it is made from pasteurized non-fat milk soured by special bacteria and contains 8½% or more non-fat solids. Some buttermilks may contain small particles of butter giving a product somewhat like old-fashioned buttermilk. Cultures of *bacterium bulgaricum* are used to sour some buttermilks which are claimed to have therapeutic value.

Sour milk is pasteurized and then soured with lactic-acid-producing bacteria. Pasteurized milk is difficult to sour because the souring bacteria have been destroyed. It can be soured by adding ¼ cup of vinegar per quart, as can cream. Yogurt is a fine, smooth, semi-solid clabbered milk containing 20% milk solids.

Butter is churned from cream and is 80% milk fat. Clarified butter is melted butter poured from the liquid that forms underneath it. Margarine is made from vegetable or animal fats and is flavored with dairy products to give it a butter flavor. It is 80% fat, the remainder being largely dairy products. Margarine with lecithin foams and browns. Some

Table 10–4. Approximate Composition of Milks Used in Cooking

Type Milk	Fat	Non-fat solids	Water	Sucrose
Fresh whole milk	3.5	8.5	88	
Fresh non-fat milk	trace	9	91	
Evaporated whole milk	8	18	74	
Evaporated non-fat milk	trace	20 to 30	80 to 70	
Sweetened condensed whole milk	8	20	30	42
Dry whole milk	27	70	3	
Non-fat dry milk	trace	96	4	

of the vegetable margarines contain unsaturated fats and are used for special diets. The fat in butter and other dairy products is saturated.

Cheese is a food high in milk fat and milk proteins. Most cheese comes from the curd of milk but some may be partially from whey.

Principles

Curdling

Fresh milk has a pH of 6.5 to 6.6. The casein, the major milk protein, is held in stable colloidal suspension at this pH but at 4.6, the casein becomes unstable and curdles or precipitates out. This is why acids such as lemon juice with a pH of 2 curdle milk so easily. Evaporated milk is most stable, fresh milk next and dry milk the least stable. Curdling is a process in which casein separates into curds from the whey. Clabber is a soft, shiny, smooth solid mass like custard. When a clabber is broken, curdling results. Agitation or heat may break up a clabber. Compounds such as salts, tannins or strong food acids curdle milk without producing a clabber, while mild acids, bacteria or rennet clabber milk. The acidity of milks increases in a number of ways. There is a loss of carbon dioxide in standing which increases acidity, or acid may be introduced in cooking ingredients or bacteria may sour it. Tannins act as a denaturing agent, drawing moisture from the protein, causing curdling. Cooking salt, curing salts and salts in foods such as calcium chloride encourage curdling as does heat.

Some milk proteins are coagulated by heat. The scum on top of heated milk or the precipitate deposited in utensils in which it is heated are the coagulated portion. Scum can be avoided by covering tightly during heating, whipping to create a foam on top or allowing melted fat to cover the surface.

Figure 10–12. (Right) Fresh milk curdled by vinegar. (Center) Dry milk curdled by the same amount of vinegar. (Left) Evaporated milk curdled by vinegar. It took twice the amount of vinegar to get curdling from this product since it is the most stable of the three. Its curd is also softest and tenderest.

Cream may curdle in coffee, especially if the brew is quite hot or high in acids and tannins and the cream somewhat unstable. Adding cream Boston style by pouring it into a cup before adding coffee may reduce the tendency to curdle. Very hard water can also cause cream to curdle. If this is a problem, water softeners should be installed.

Scorching

Milk scorches easily and should be heated over water, in a steam-jacketed kettle or in a steamer. Prolonged heating below scorching temperatures may darken milk and give it a somewhat caramelized flavor, or cause it to become flat and less flavorful, probably because of the loss of gas or air.

Homogenization

The fat in milk is held in suspension by a protein emulsifier adsorbed on the fat surface. The binding power of the emulsifier declines as milk cools and thus cream comes slowly to the top being lighter than the milk. Milk fat can be separated from milk by centrifuging. Dividing the fat globules very finely by a process called *homogenization* gives a greater amount of surface area and a small globule with less upward pull so that the emulsifier can hold the fat globules down in suspension. Homogenized cream does not whip well as the globules are too finely divided to bunch together well, a factor needed to have cream whip forming a fine network of cream around air bubbles.

Figure 10–13. On the left a slightly thickened white sauce is being poured over parboiled potatoes for escalloping. On the right is another method in which dry milk, flour and seasonings are blended together with raw potatoes and then water added before baking. In either method, chances for curdling can be reduced.

Pasteurization

Most milk products are pasteurized by holding at high temperatures for a specific time, milk for 30 minutes at 143° F or 15 seconds at 160° F. Pasteurization destroys harmful bacteria but also enzymes and lactic-acid producing bacteria. Milk is heated to make bread to destroy therophilic bacteria and enzymes not destroyed by pasteurization. Pasteurization changes the coagulation properties of milk so it has a more tender clabber or custard and a softer, finer curd.

Techniques

Curdling

The tendency of milk to curdle can be reduced. Low salting helps. Also, adding the acid or tannin-containing food slowly into milk using good agitation, or thickening both the milk and the acid or tannin-containing food, reduces the potential for curdling. The gelatinized starch in slightly thickened milk binds in the casein so that it separates out with more difficulty. Some recommend adding milk in several portions during the cooking of items such as baking cured ham in milk. Having both the milk and curdling agent at the same temperature may help. Adding bicarbonate of soda or other compounds to reduce the acidity of a food to be combined with milk is not recommended because of the adverse effect of soda on flavor, color and vitamin content. Shortening cooking time or reducing the temperature helps. (See also Figure 10-13 for some other specific suggestions. The methods for making cream soups in Chapter 8 should also be reviewed.) If proper techniques are used and service is fairly soon after preparation, tart foods can be combined with milk. For instance, if horseradish is added to warm heavy velouté sauce and then combined with good agitation with hot evaporated or rich milk, a fairly stable horseradish sauce to serve with roast beef can be made. Sometimes the acids in molasses or brown sugar curdle puddings or pie fillings, but if the sweetener is blended with the thickening agent or added after thickening occurs, curdling will be retarded.

Because of dry milk's lesser stability, it should not be boiled long in sauces, soups or other products made from it. Make dry milk solutions thicker than required and thin to proper consistency just before service, adding salt at the last minute also. If dry milk is made a day before use, it is more stable; even making it 20 minutes ahead of use helps. Make dry milk solutions with less water than needed and thin just before service with the proper quantity of water. Custards made with dry milk are unstable and even dishing them up when hot can cause syneresis. A strong custard of 2 to $2\frac{1}{2}$ pounds of eggs per gallon of milk must be made when dry milk is used and this is so much more costly that it is perhaps better to use evaporated or fresh milk.

Use of Dry Milk

Table 10-5 gives the proportions to use in making sauces from dry milk. These proportions differ slightly from those given for sauces made from milk in Chapter 8. About 13 ounces of non-fat dry milk per gallon of water gives the equivalent of fresh non-fat milk although normally a pound is used. Adding five ounces of butter, margarine or fat makes an equivalent of about a gallon of fresh milk in fat and calorie content. Increasing milk solids in some bakery products and frozen desserts can

Table 10–5. White Sauce Proportions Using Non-fat Dry Milk (per 1 gal sauce)

Type Sauce	Water	Non-fat Dry Milk	Butter, Margarine or Fat	Flour*
Thin	$3\frac{1}{2}$ qt	1 lb 6 oz	$6\frac{1}{2}$ oz	4 to 8 oz
Medium	$3\frac{1}{2}$ qt	1 lb 6 oz	$8\frac{1}{4}$ oz	8 to 12 oz
Thick	$3\frac{1}{2}$ qt	1 lb 5 oz	10 oz	1 lb
Very thick	$3\frac{1}{2}$ qt	1 lb 5 oz	$12\frac{1}{2}$ oz	$1\frac{1}{4}$ lb

*Quantity of flour used will depend upon type of flour and thickness desired.

Figure 10–14. Many processed dairy products are used today in quantity food preparation. Here a dairy whip is shown used on three products. (Courtesy General Foods)

improve quality. In some instances, recipes must be adjusted if additional milk solids are used. Normally a pound of dry milk is four cups but 5¾ cups of instant milk is a pound. Instant dry milk goes into solution more easily than regular dry milk. Whenever possible, dry milk is added with sifted dry ingredients and the required liquid added with the other liquid in the recipe. Dry milk may be blended into water by sifting it over the top, using good agitation to bring it into solution. Dry milk should be weighed rather than measured.

Dairy Product Foams

Air can be beaten into milk or cream to make a stable foam. Cream of less than 30% milkfat content does not whip unless special methods or ingredients are used. Recipes usually state whipped cream in unwhipped measure, the volume increase usually being 2 to 3 times. It should be used soon after whipping as drainage can be evident an hour after whipping. To whip whipping cream (30 to 40% milkfat) use pasteurized,

Table 10–6.   Equivalents for 1 Gal Liquid Milk

For 1 gal whole liquid milk use:
  18 oz dry whole milk
  $7^1/_2$ lb or $3^3/_4$ qt water
        or
  13 oz non-fat dry milk
  5 oz melted fat
  $7^1/_2$ lb or $3^3/_4$ qt water
        or
  $4^1/_4$ lb evaporated whole milk
  $4^1/_2$ lb or $2^1/_4$ qt water
        or
  4 lb condensed whole milk
  $6^1/_4$ lb or $3^1/_4$ qt water*

For 1 gal non-fat liquid milk use:
  13 oz dry non-fat milk
  $7^3/_4$ or 3 qt $2^1/_2$ c water
        or
  $4^1/_2$ lb non-fat evaporated milk
  $4^1/_4$ lb or 2 qt $^1/_2$ c water
        or
  3 lb condensed non-fat milk
  7 lb or $3^1/_2$ qt water**

*Will also contain 1 lb 10 oz sugar.
**Will also contain 1 lb 5 oz sugar.

unhomogenized cream that has been aged at least 48 hours to give improved stability and volume. (Pasteurization slightly decreases volume and stability of a whipped cream foam.) To improve stability add 1½ ounces of non-fat dry milk per quart of cream, preferably before it is aged or use 1½ tablespoons of 10% suspension of lime per quart. Using powdered sugar as a sweetener instead of granulated sugar seems to improve stability. Have the utensils cold and the cream below 40°F. The bowl should be deep enough to give good agitation. Do not overbeat since this can produce butter by bunching the fat globules together. After whipping, add sugar and flavorings and store in a cold place. Cream as low as 18% milkfat can be whipped using a 10% suspension of lime but it is not as stable nor does it give the same volume.

To whip evaporated milk, scald the milk or place the cans into boiling water from 5 to 10 minutes. Soaking ½ teaspoon of gelatin in two tablespoons of cold water and adding this to a pint of hot milk improves stability. Chill to 40° F and use chilled equipment and a deep enough bowl. When almost to the desired foam add three tablespoons of lemon juice per pint of evaporated milk. Add the sugar and flavoring and finish whipping. Hold chilled below 50° F.

Either whole or non-fat dry milk may be whipped. The increase in volume is about four times but the foam is not stable over several hours. Poor-quality milks will not develop good foams. Use ¾ quart of regular dry milk or a quart of instant to a quart of ice water and beat to a soft peak. Add a cup of lemon juice and beat until stiff. Add two cups of sugar and flavoring and complete beating. Hold chilled below 50° F.

Imitation products are on the market that can be whipped to make products similar to dairy foams. They are widely used and besides giving

Figure 10–15. To whip evaporated milk, add a bit of dehydrated gelatin to the scalded milk and then chill. Whip in a bowl of ice. Many omit the gelatin but a slightly more stable product is obtained if it is used.

fairly good products are lower in cost than whipping cream. Aerosol-type containers are also used for dispensing these and the regular dairy foams.

Cream

Patrons add coffee cream to coffee until they see it is at a desired color. The more fat in the cream, the more color whiteness is reflected in the combination of cream and coffee. About a tablespoon or $\frac{1}{2}$ ounce of 18% cream is sufficient for a portion. Portioning loss in pouring into individual containers is around 6%. Homogenized cream gives a smoother flavor to coffee than non-homogenized cream. There is a trend for individuals to drink their beverages without cream or use a lighter product. Half-and-half is frequently offered in place of cream. There

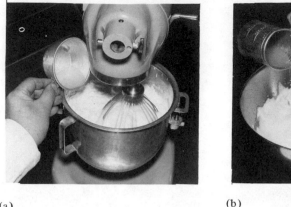
(a)

(b)

Figure 10–16. (a) Evaporated milk also forms a more stable foam if some lemon juice is added after a good foam develops. (b) Similarly dry milk is also improved in foam stability if some lemon juice is added during the beating.

are a number of successful liquid products on the market now that are also offered in place of cream for beverages.

Cream or sour cream are used as finishing agents for sauces and other products, and are blended into the product just before service and never boiled after adding to the item. This finishing is done to smooth out flavors and to increase richness.

Cheese

Like eggs and milk, cheese should be cooked at low heat. Ripened cheese blends more easily into sauces or other foods than medium or current cheese, and cheese blends into sauces better around 125° F than at higher temperatures. A hard, dry cheese blends better if it is grated and moistened with warm milk a short time before it is added to the product. In adding cheese to a thickened starch mixture that also requires eggs, the eggs should be added first and then the cheese, since this seems to aid in blending the cheese. If this is used to make a firm structure in baking, as for a cheese soufflé, it cannot be done. Processed cheese has emulsifiers added to it which makes it easier to blend into foods than regular cheese. It is also more stable in products.

Suggested exercises or laboratory experiences for Chapter 10:

1. Cook an egg correctly and incorrectly by boiling, poaching, frying and shirring.

2. Add a bit of cream of tartar or lemon juice to an egg and scramble it. Omit either the cream of tartar or lemon juice and scramble another egg. Place both over steam and allow to stand. Note the difference in texture, flavor and color between the two samples.
3. Prepare a purchased angel cake mix and prepare one from scratch of the same type. Evaluate from the standpoint of quality, cost and time.
4. Whip whole eggs, yolks and whites to the different foams.
5. Add vinegar or lemon juice to prepared dry milk, fresh milk and evaporated milk and note the difference in stability in the three.
6. Sour some dry milk or fresh milk with acid or bacteria. Warm it slightly and then drain the curd from the whey. Salt the curd. Taste it. This is the curd used for cottage cheese and many other cheeses.
7. Blend a very young grated cheese into a *hot* white sauce and then one at around 140° F. Blend some aged cheese similarly into two batches of sauce at these temperatures. Do the same using processed cheese. Note the variation of each in going into solution.

BIBLIOGRAPHY

Aldrich, Pearl J. and Miller, Grace A., *A New Milky Way for Your Own Favorite Quantity Recipes,* Circular Bulletin 225, Agr. Experimental Station, Michigan State University, E. Lansing, April, 1958.

Aldrich, Pearl J. and Miller, Grace A., *Whole and Nonfat Dry Milk in Quantity Food Preparation,* Circular Bulletin 223, Agr. Experimental Station, Michigan State University, E. Lansing, October 1956.

American Dry Milk Institute, *Quantity Recipes,* Bulletin, 503, Chicago, 1954.

National Dairy Council, *Newer Knowledge of Cheese,* revised ed., and *Newer Knowledge of Milk,* Chicago, 1954.

Poultry and Egg Board, *Eggs,* n. d. and *Ways with Eggs,* n. d., Chicago.

U. S. Department of Agriculture, *Cooking with Dried Egg,* Bulletin No. 50, Washington, D. C., 1956.

11

Vegetable Cookery

An operation can serve good vegetables if it buys good ones and prepares them correctly. Quality depends much upon factors easily destroyed by improper preparation or cooking. To cook vegetables well takes skill and knowledge. There is a wide variety and many must be handled differently. Differences in processing also change cooking requirements. Vegetable cooking usually includes some items not vegetables but served in place of them, such as dressings, rice, macaroni pastes, cooked cereals, etc.

STANDARDS

Cooked vegetables are judged on the basis of texture, flavor and appearance, the latter including form and color. Temperature at service affects quality. A vegetable is usually not the dominant item of a meal so it must be judged in relation to the other foods with which it is served. Vegetable flavors should be neither bland nor strong but natural, sweet and pleasant, without a trace of rawness, if cooked. Seasonings or sauces which mask natural flavors should be avoided in favor of those giving mild contrasts which blend happily as a light, delicate complement to

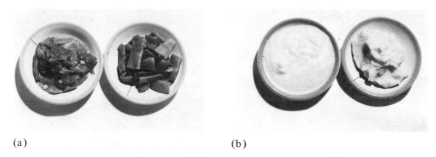

(a)   (b)

Figure 11–1. Which vegetable would you select? The portions of the paired vegetables on the left lack the form, texture or color required for best acceptability.

the vegetable. Texture requirements vary according to the vegetable. Some firmness is good in high moisture vegetables such as carrots, string beans and cabbage. For this, cooking to a slight under-doneness, especially if some cooking occurs in holding, is recommended. An overly soft, sloughy or overly hard texture is undesirable. Starchy root vegetables, legumes and cereal should be completely soft while fried vegetables may be crisp outside and soft inside. Potatoes can be mealy but other vegetables are objectionable this way. Excessive wateriness, dryness, softness, crispness, hardness, woodiness, stringiness or other poor texture qualities should be absent.

Form should be distinct, not messy or broken. Uniformity is often desirable. Vegetable firmness should show as a soft sheen. When dished, vegetables should be rounded, not flat or runny. Colors should be bright, lively, attractive, clear and natural not dull, pale, muddy, intensified or false. Poor quality is frequently indicated by a color loss.

PRINCIPLES

Cellulose and pectins form most of a vegetable's skeletal or fiber structure. Cooking softens them. The amount of cellulose varies with variety, age or growing conditions. For instance, spinach has less than carrots, old vegetables more than young ones and vegetables grown under good conditions are more tender than those grown under sparse ones. One part of a vegetable can be tougher than another and must be cooked more to reach the same tenderness. The stems of broccoli or asparagus can be set into boiling water, then the entire vegetable can be tipped into the water and cooked to give a uniformly-cooked product. Splitting the stems also speeds tenderization as does peeling away some of the fibrous

Figure 11–2. These Brussels sprouts show a good standard in form and texture. (Courtesy Brussels Sprout Marketing Program)

skin on stems. Cutting string beans on the bias (slant) or lengthwise cuts through more fibrous cellulose to make the beans more tender.

Sugar or calcium chloride strengthens cellulose. The latter gives firmness to pickles and canned vegetables. Alkalis soften cellulose. Where water is hard (alkaline), boiled vegetables can easily become too soft. A bit of cream of tartar, vinegar, lemon juice or other acid reduces this alkalinity.

Acid may bring about undesirable reactions, so care must be taken in its use. An alkaline reaction softens dry beans or other legumes in cooking while an acid reaction retards softening. Adding tomatoes or other acid foods to them before they are completely tender extends cooking time.

Cooking changes vegetable flavors; some people like a vegetable cooked but not raw or vice versa. Vegetables carry salt, sweet, bitter and acid compounds but their characteristic flavor comes mainly from aromatic esters or essential oils which are volatile—that is, they escape easily on cooking. To avoid their loss, cooking time must be shortened. Fats or oils absorb these esters and sometimes about a tablespoon of salad oil per gallon of water is used to hold these flavors in the cooking water. Some flavor loss may be desirable in strongly flavored vegetables so they may be uncovered to allow flavors to escape. Most vegetable acids are also volatile. Acid can destroy some vegetable colors or develop strong flavors during cooking. The mustardy, pungent flavor of the cabbage and turnip families comes largely from a glucoside called

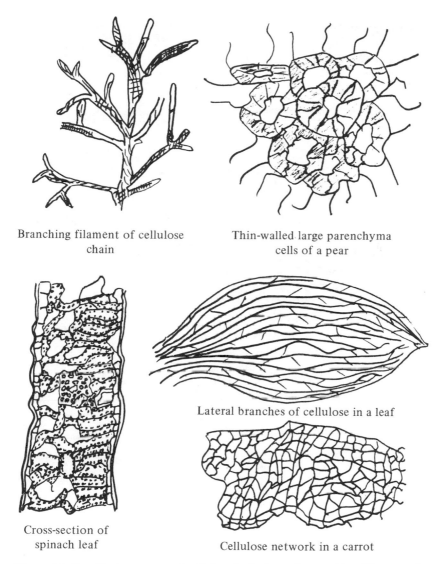

Branching filament of cellulose chain

Thin-walled large parenchyma cells of a pear

Lateral branches of cellulose in a leaf

Cross-section of spinach leaf

Cellulose network in a carrot

Figure 11–3. Various types of cellulose in fruits and vegetables. The quantity and types vary and this variation is important in deciding toughness or tenderness.

sinigrin. Heat favors its separation and acids speed it. The sharp flavor of the onion family comes from a sulfur substance called allyl sulfide. Cooking breaks it down so that its flavor is less pungent.

Vegetable freshness is an important quality factor. Sugars change rapidly to starch above 50° F in corn, green peas and other vegetables.

Freshness may also be associated with glutamic acid. Corn loses 30% of its glutamic acid 24 hours after harvest and fresh peas 25%. Refrigeration reduces glutamic acid and sugar loss. Dehydration, oxidation and poor handling are other causes of a loss of freshness, nutrients or quality.

Care is necessary in preparing and cooking vegetables. Poor preparation techniques can result in messy, poorly shaped vegetables that not only lack appearance but cook poorly. Hard boiling, excessive manipulation or stirring or overcooking can produce a very unattractive product. Cooking by other than boiling may reduce movement and retain form.

Vegetable color pigments are *anthocyanins* or *lycopenes* in red vegetables, *carotenes* in yellow or orange ones, *chlorophyll* in green and *flavones* in white ones.

Acids keep anthocyanins bright red while an alkaline medium turns them into a dirty blue or purple. If red cabbage turns green, it is from a combined reaction in which red pigments turn blue and white ones yellow. Iron combines easily with anthocyanins. Red cabbage or beets may darken for this reason when cut with a steel knife and an iron pot can cause beets to become brownish red or muddy. This color reaction can also occur in red punch. For instance, iron salts in canned pineapple juice can combine with anthocyanins in raspberry juice. Anthocyanins also can join with tannins to form a cloudy precipitate. Tea has tannins in it and, if used in a red fruit punch, can bring about clouding. Acid retards these reactions of anthocyanins with tannins and iron. Anthocyanins are water soluble and can be leached out into water leaving a pale vegetable.

Carotenes and lycopenes are closely related substances chemically. Both are stable to heat, acids and alkalis. Lycopenes are red pigments found in tomatoes. Carotenes are changed in the body to vitamin A. Oxidation can destroy carotenes. They are not water soluble.

Chlorophyll in green vegetables is easily destroyed by heat or acid but an alkaline medium tends to preserve it. Chlorophyll is not water soluble.

The white pigments, flavones, are white in an acid medium and yellow in an alkaline one. Thus, onions can turn a deep yellow if cooked in hard water. Other white vegetables may darken. A bit of acid such as cream of tartar or lemon juice can quickly correct the color. Flavones are water soluble and unaffected by heat.

We depend a great deal on vegetables for many of our vitamins and minerals. Therefore, proper cooking for highest nutrient retention should be emphasized, especially in quantity preparation where losses

3   2   1

Figure 11–4.   The effects of alkaline, acid and neutral cooking mediums on vegetables: (1) acid, (2) alkaline and (3) neutral.

are usually high. Prepreparation procedures, cooking stress and long holding can take a heavy toll of nutrients. Vegetable preparation and cooking should be scheduled in sufficient time to give smooth progress of work but not so far as to unnecessarily lose nutrients. If fresh, young vegetables are purchased at peak condition and given proper handling, storage and cooking, and if time and conditions are established to retain quality and nutrients, good quality vegetables of maximum nutrient value will be served.

Many nutrients are concentrated under the skin of a vegetable or fruit and deep paring causes a large loss. To reduce leaching loss, pared items should be cooked a minimum time. Anti-oxidants into which the items are dipped can reduce leaching loss and also protect against oxidation loss of nutrients. Cooking by steaming, baking or other methods that use little or no water reduces leaching loss, as does reducing cooking times and temperatures.

Ascorbic acid and thiamin are destroyed easily by heat. Soda or hard-water salts in small quantities are not harmful to these nutrients but as their concentration increases destruction is more rapid. Salt reduces ascorbic acid loss some. Copper is harmful to ascorbic acid.

The use of the best cooking method to preserve nutrients is not always possible. Steaming under pressure reduces leaching but its higher cooking temperature increases the loss of heat-labile nutrients. Using lots of water gives a milder flavored rutabaga but increases loss by leaching. The best method is the one giving the most flavorful and attractive product because this is also the one that is most nutritious. Little is gained if a vegetable is cooked well but not eaten because people "don't like them cooked that way." This is winning a battle but losing a war. It is important that vegetables be eaten so if there is some small loss but the vegetables are eaten, cook them that way. It's better than having them go into the garbage can!

As indicated, quality vegetables result when one secures the right product and prepares them properly. Fresh tender vegetables given proper care and quickly used give a maximum chance for having good vegetables. Corn-on-the-cob consumed a few hours after picking is far superior to corn 24 hours old. Fresh, tender spinach loses much quality if stored. Cauliflower, artichokes and broccoli are blossoms and should be tight buds to be of good quality. An old fibrous beet, carrot or other root vegetable is tough and unflavorful. Potatoes high in starch and low in sugar are good for baking, mashing or French frying while those lower in starch and perhaps higher in sugar will be moist and waxy, qualities making them desirable for salads, hash browns or creamed, boiled or steamed potatoes. High starch potatoes have a specific gravity of 1.08 or more (17% or more starch) while those of 1.07 or less (13% or less starch) are moist or waxy. Mature potatoes are higher in starch than new ones. Potatoes high in sugar may streak or darken in frying. Frozen potatoes show dark streaks when deep-fried. Storing potatoes below 50° F develops sugar and 3 weeks above 50° F is needed to condition them properly if such storage occurs. Sprouting potatoes are high in sugar.

Some fruits and vegetables tarnish easily because tannins oxidize. This is stopped by holding under water, such as soaking potatoes or using anti-oxidant dips, such as those containing ascorbic acid, to stop this discoloraton. Dipping fruits or vegetables into citrus, pineapple or other fruit juices avoids tarnishing. Adding salt to water may help some but not much. Stainless steel or plastic tools can be used to cut items that tarnish easily since these do not leave iron salts that combine with tannins to give dark substances.

Many vegetables contain starch. Corn, green peas and some others have a considerable quantity while potatoes, rice, macaroni pastes, dry beans and others have much more. In these, cooking must swell or gelatinize the starch to give a soft, tender product. Because starch imbibes water, some products high in starch may have to be cooked in a considerable quantity of water.

PROCEDURES

Prepreparation

For the recommended procedures for preparing fresh vegetables see Table 11-1. Proper prepreparation starts with receiving. The items should be handled with care to prevent damage and moved quickly to proper storage, then used as soon as possible.

Fresh vegetables are living plants and continue to live after harvesting. Firm, fresh vegetables lose quality rapidly from the action of bacteria, molds, yeasts, enzymes or from chemical changes, surface dehydration, odor absorption or aging. Refrigeration delays many of these undesirable changes. Clean vegetables and fruits deteriorate less, so, if not clean, they should be cleaned upon receipt. Soaking, especially in water containing a tablespoon of salt per gallon, helps to loosen soil. Soaking cauliflower, broccoli, cabbage, brussels sprouts, etc., for a half hour in cold, salted water encourages mites to leave the vegetable. Cleaned items should be drained well and stored in covered units.

Much edible food can be lost in vegetable preparation. Crisping or

Table 11-1.

Vegetable	Preparation Procedures
Asparagus	Cut or break off tough or woody portion at or approximately ½ inch above white portion. Scrub well; remove lower scales, as dirt or grit may be under them. The lower portions may be scraped. Clean and rinse thoroughly. Tips may be cut from ends. Toughest ends may be set aside for pureeing for soup.
Beans, snap	Use only young, tender beans which snap readily when bent to a 45° angle. Cut into 1 inch sections or French by cutting lengthwise into strips. Rinse thoroughly. Beans cook more readily if cut lengthwise or at an angle instead of crosswise.
Beans, lima	Purchase fresh shelled beans or frozen beans. Cook frozen beans and fresh beans thoroughly and drain.
Beets	Leave uncut 1 inch of stem and all of root. Trim and wash, scrubbing if necessary to remove soil. Boil or steam. Beets may be machine-peeled and cooked, but a heavy loss of red pigment occurs when this is done.
Broccoli	Wash well and cut off tough ends of the stalks. Remove tough outer leaves. Clean and rinse thoroughly. Split ends of thick stalks, or cut ends from tops. Cut into 2 inch by ½ inch wide strips and cook, adding tops after 5 minutes of boiling.
Brussels sprouts	Trim yellowed or coarse outer leaves. Soak in salted water ½ hour, clean, and rinse.
Cabbage	Strip off wilted outer leaves, remove core, rinse thoroughly, and cut into sections or shred. For sectioning, coring is often omitted.
Carrots	Remove tops if present. Pare in peeler. Less flavor loss occurs in cooking if carrots are sliced lengthwise, since this avoids cutting across the fibrovascular structure (juice-retaining fibers.) Very young carrots may be cooked by first scrubbing and then cooking, removing skins after cooking. Cool by plunging into cold water and remove skins while warm and wet.
Corn-on-the-cob	Strip the husks and remove silk. Trim any inedible portions. Keep cold.
Onions, dry	Trim. Peel outer skins with paring knife. Rinse. Chop, slice, or prepare as required.
Parsnips	Peel. Trim and rinse. Slice lengthwise to avoid cutting fibrovascular bundles and increased flavor loss in cooking.
Peas, green	Shell. Rinse in colander in cold water. Purchase and cook frozen.
Potatoes, Irish	Scrub well for baking, pare for others. Steam for mashing, hash browns, etc. Cooking in skins and then paring gives a darker potato and higher labor costs.
Potatoes, sweet	Best cooked in skins and then pared, but may be machine-pared if uniform in size and not long and thin. Machine-paring loss may be high with some shapes. Wash before cooking in skins.
Rutabaga or Turnip	Pare in peeler. Trim and rinse thoroughly. Slice into slices ½ inch thick or dice into ½ inch cubes.
Spinach	Remove tough stems, wilted leaves, and roots. Wash in large quantity of water, lifting spinach up and down to loosen dirt. Lift spinach from water and drain well. Continue washing until no evidence of soil or grit shows. The water clinging to the leaves of fresh spinach may be sufficient to cook it in a steam-jacketed kettle.
Squash, summer	Trim ends. Rinse. Cut into slices approximately ¼ inch thick or into bite-size pieces.
Squash, winter	Cut into pieces of convenient size. Remove seeds and fiber. Steam. Remove peel. Complete by mashing or baking or as required. For baking, squash may be portioned before steaming.

Note: Vegetables that must be held for long periods before cooking should be, after prepreparation, placed into containers or polyethylene bags and held under refrigeration.

freshening in cold water can reduce waste by reducing wilt or producing a more firm product that handles better in preparation. Limp root vegetables pare poorly but, if given some presoaking in cold water to firm them up, they pare and cut more easily. Bruised parts of young leaves should be trimmed away and the remainder used in stocks or soups or for seasonings for roasts. Edible vegetable parts that cannot be used otherwise may be handled the same way. Woody stalks or stems or other parts not otherwise usable can be cooked and pulped for use in cream soups, purees or other dishes. Using proper tools and observing proper peeling times reduce loss from waste. Even sizing gives more uniformly cooked products. Select for evenness of size for machine paring. The labor cost is repaid if potatoes are separated into small, medium and large sizes. Large potatoes can be used for baking or making into deep-frying potato strips. Paring wastes are higher when different sizes or crooked or knobby items are used. After paring all peel and blemishes are removed. Mold spots show as dark spots on deep-fried potatoes. Pare only long enough to remove peels; some remaining and other portions needing trimming can be processed after paring.

Potato strips for deep-frying are about 3 to 4 inches long and $\frac{3}{8}$ to $\frac{1}{2}$-inch thick, while shoestrings are about $\frac{1}{4}$ to $\frac{1}{8}$-inch thick and juliennes are closer to a $\frac{1}{4}$-inch thick. The length of both should be around 2 to $2\frac{1}{2}$ inches. That soaking reduces the tendency of potatoes to stick together in frying has not been verified but soaking may be required to give potato chips an even color. Soft, flabby strips do not fry well, so they may be crisped by dropping into cold water and refrigerating. Wafered or waffle potatoes are made by a device that cuts across the width of the whole potato giving a round slice with tiny waffled holes in it. Parisienne ball potatoes are cut from raw, pared potatoes with a round melon-ball cutter. Soufflé potatoes are made by cutting crisp, high quality, mature potatoes into slices about $2\frac{1}{2}$ inches long, $1\frac{1}{4}$ inches wide and 1/8 to 3/16 inch thick. All pieces should be even and of the same size and crisped in ice water 30 minutes. Browned or rissolé potatoes are usually selected a potato to a portion, about five ounces pared, and rounding accomplished in a potato peeler. After cutting potatoes for deep-frying, dip into a bleach solution, drain, place into pans, containers or polyethylene bags and store at 32° to 40° F until needed. Prepare only the quantity required for a 24-hour operating period. Many facilities today purchase their potato and other vegetable products prepared ready for cooking.

Most dried, dehydrated or freeze-dried vegetables require some soaking before cooking. Use lukewarm or cool water salted 3 tablespoons to the gallon. Do not use hot water unless the manufacturer recommends it. Soaking is usually 20 to 30 minutes but the yield is

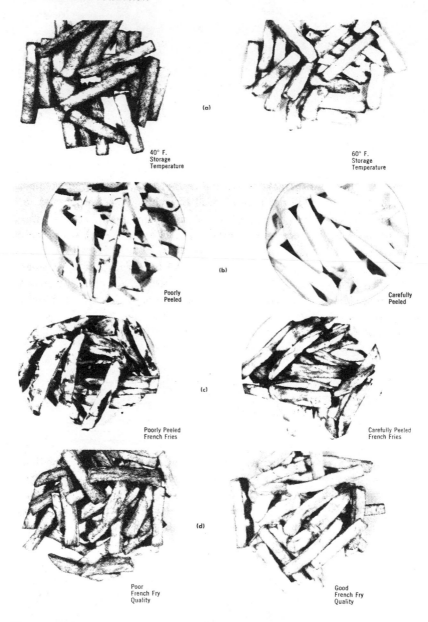

40° F.
Storage
Temperature

60° F.
Storage
Temperature

(a)

Poorly
Peeled

Carefully
Peeled

(b)

Poorly Peeled
French Fries

Carefully Peeled
French Fries

(c)

Poor
French Fry
Quality

Good
French Fry
Quality

(d)

Figure 11–5. Select a potato that has received the right kind of treatment for French frying. (a) The potatoes stored at 40° F have too high a sugar content for good frying. Hold at least three weeks above 50° F to condition them. (b) Prepare potatoes properly. (c) After frying the potatoes shown in (b), note how preparation affects quality. (d) For best quality, select a good quality potato.

higher if soaking occurs overnight. Weigh rather than measure. High-moisture dried vegetables require about two gallons of water per pound and starchy vegetables, such as potatoes, rutabagas and turnips a gallon per pound. Few dried vegetables swell to their original size in soaking. Cooking assists in rehydration. Manufacturers' recommendations should be checked and followed in using dried vegetables. Dry beans, split peas, and other legumes cook quicker if pre-soaked. Sort, wash, drain and cover these with water; soak 2 to 6 hours. Washing, soaking and cooking in a steam-jacketed kettle may save labor.

Blanching vegetables or fruits to remove skins facilitates the work. Have the water boiling. Drop the items into the water turning them so all areas are blanched. Do not leave too long. Drop into cold water and remove skins. Treat those items immediately that tarnish easily.

COOKING

Planning

The fragile quality of many vegetables makes it desirable to set up con-tinuous batch-cooking procedures to have quality vegetables during the entire service period. With proper planning, labor requirements need not be increased by batch cooking. Regular steamers, steam-jacketed kettles or pots on the range top can be used but work is facilitated if high-pressure steamers or tilt steam-jacketed kettles, a quart to 4 quart size, are used. These can be directly behind service areas to shorten transport. Perforated, stainless-steel inserts that can be set into the kettle facilitate addition and removal of the product. A timer on steam-ers, set to operate automatically, will exhaust steam and guard against overcooking. Vegetables may remain a few minutes in the open steam chamber without loss of quality.

Production schedules should list the meal, the vegetable, the batch quantity, the total amount needed, the time required and the service area to which the vegetable will be sent, if several exist. Time is needed for loading, cooking, removing and sending the vegetables to service. Most vegetables should be served 20 to 30 minutes after cooking. Serve all of a batch before another is used unless the vegetable being used is not acceptable. Do not mix batches. Experience will guide proper timing of batch starts and the cook in charge should be respon-sible for this. Some use the rule that a new batch is started when half of the preceding batch is served. Cook only to tenderness with some bite in the center, because such vegetables are brighter in color, have

Table 11-2. Cooking Times and Quantities Required in Vegetable Preparation

Vegetable	Boiling*	Steaming** Free Vent	Steaming** 15 lb psi	Steaming** 5 lb psi	Baking	Approx. Min. Prep. Time 100 Portions	Quantity per 100 3 oz Portions AP (lb)	Quantity per 100 3 oz Portions EP (lb)
Artichoke, French, whole, fresh	30 to 45		10 to 12	20 to 25		30	56	8⅓ doz
Artichoke, Jerusalem, whole	25 to 35	35			30 to 60	40	25	18
Asparagus, whole or butts, fresh	9 to 15	10 to 16	1 to 1½	8 to 10		85	38	25
Asparagus, tips, fresh***	7 to 9	8 to 12	½ to 1½	6 to 8			20	20
Beans, lima, green, fresh	15 to 25	20 to 30	1 to 2	10 to 15		120	48	20
Beans, lima, green, frozen	6 to 12	8 to 15	1 to 1½	8 to 12			20	20
Beans, lima, dry	60 to 150	60 to 150	15 to 25	20 to 30			6	6
Beans, snap, cut, fresh	15 to 25	20 to 30	2 to 3½	20 to 30		60	21	20
Beans, snap, Frenched, fresh	10 to 20	15 to 25	1 to 2½	18 to 25		75	24	20
Beans, snap, frozen, cut	8 to 10		2 to 3½	15 to 20			20	20
Beans, snap, frozen, Frenched	5 to 10		1 to 2	12 to 18			20	20
Beans, dry, navy or kidney	60 to 150	60 to 150	20 to 35	25 to 35			5½ to 6	5½ to 6
Beets, new, whole, medium, fresh	30 to 45	40 to 60	5 to 10	40 to 50	40 to 60	15	25***	20
Beets, old, whole, medium, fresh	45 to 90	50 to 90	10 to 18	60 to 75	50 to 75	15	26****	20
Broccoli, cut or split, fresh	7 to 12	12 to 18	1 to 3	7 to 10			35	22
Broccoli, cut or split, frozen	5 to 8	10 to 15	1 to 2	4 to 6			20	20
Brussels sprouts, whole, fresh	10 to 15	10 to 20	1½ to 3	10 to 12		30	24	20
Brussels sprouts, whole, frozen	4 to 9	8 to 15	1 to 3	8 to 10			20	20
Cabbage, shredded, fresh	6 to 10	6 to 10	½ to 1½	5 to 10			25	20
Cabbage, quartered, fresh	8 to 15	15	1½ to 3	8 to 12			25 to	20
Carrots, whole, fresh	15 to 25	20 to 30	2 to 5	15 to 20	35 to 45	30	26****	20
Carrots, sliced, fresh	10 to 20	15 to 25	1½ to 4	12 to 15	30 to 40		26****	20
Carrots, sliced, frozen	10 to 20	15 to 25	1½ to 4	10 to 12				20
Cauliflower, whole, fresh	8 to 12	8 to 12	10	15			50 to 60	26
Cauliflower, broken up	4 to 8	6 to 10	2 to 3	8 to 10			50 to 60	26
Cauliflower, frozen	6 to 15	8 to 20	1½ to 2½	6 to 8			20	20
Celery, cut up, fresh	5 to 15	10 to 15	2 to 3	10 to 12			27	20
Corn-on-the-cob*, fresh	5 to 8	8 to 12	3 to 4	8 to 10	30(in husks)		50 to 75	8⅓ doz
Corn-on-the-cob, frozen	2 to 3		2 to 3	6 to 8			8⅓ doz	8⅓ doz
Corn, kernel, frozen			2 to 3	2 to 3			20	20
Eggplant, sliced	10 to 18	10 to 20	½ to 1	2 to 3			26	20

(Greens in quantity are difficult to steam because of packing.)

Vegetable								6¼ gal soup
Greens								
Beets, greens only, fresh	3 to 10						33	20
Beets, frozen	3 to 10						20	20
Chard, fresh	8 to 15						27	20
Dandelion, fresh	10 to 20						35	20
Kale, fresh	10 to 20						27	20
Mustard, fresh	20 to 30						32	20
Mustard, frozen	8 to 15						20	20
Turnip, fresh	10 to 30						27	20
Kohlrabi, sliced	15 to 20	25	4 to 5	15 to 25			35	21
Mixed vegetables, frozen	10 to 20	15 to 25	1 to 2	8 to 15			20	20
Okra, sliced, fresh	10 to 20	20	2 to 4	10 to 18			23	18
Onions, small, whole or cut	15 to 25	25 to 35	3 to 5	15 to 20			25	22
Onions, large, whole	30 to 35	35 to 40	5 to 8	25 to 30			25	22
Parsnips, whole, fresh	20 to 40	30 to 45	8 to 10	15 to 20		50 to 60	24	21
Parsnips, quartered, fresh	15 to 30	25 to 40	4 to 8	12 to 18		30 to 45	24	20
Peas, green, fresh	6 to 8	10	1	4 to 5			53	20
Peas, green, frozen	4 to 7	8	1	3 to 4			20	20
Peas, dry, split	90 to 120				100		5	
Potatoes, Irish, whole, fresh	25 to 40	30 to 45	9 to 15	20 to 25		45 to 60	39	28
Potatoes, Irish, quartered, fresh	20 to 25	30 to 40	4 to 12	18 to 22			39	28
Potatles, Irish, diced, fresh	10 to 15	30 to 35	5	10			39	28
Potatoes, sweet, whole, fresh	25 to 35	30 to 35	5 to 8	20 to 25		30 to 45	35	26
Potatoes, sweet, quartered, fresh	15 to 25	25 to 30	6				35	26
Rutabagas, diced ½ in, fresh	20 to 30	25 to 35	5 to 8	15 to 25			32	28
Rutabagas, sliced ½ in, fresh	15 to 25	25 to 35	4 to 7	15 to 20			32	28
Spinach, fresh	3 to 10	5 to 12					31	26
Spinach, frozen	1 to 4	2 to 6			20		20	20
Squash, hubbard, pieces	20 to 30	25 to 40	6 to 12	15 to 20		40 to 60	46	32
Squash, summer, sliced	10 to 15	15 to 20	1½ to 3	8 to 12		30	24	20
Tomatoes, fresh	7 to 15		1½ to 3	5		15 to 20	23	22
Turnips, whole, fresh	20 to 30	20 to 25	8 to 10	10 to 15			25****	22
Turnips, fresh, sliced or diced	15 to 20		1½ to 2	10			25****	22

*Time is calculated from time water comes to boil after vegetable has been added; corn on the cob is sometimes placed into cold water and brought to a boil and then sent to service.

**Increase free vent times at higher altitudes. Steam time will depend upon type of pan; fill solid pans less full; solid pans increase steaming time over perforated pans; thaw frozen corn on the cob before cooking it.

***Reduce times slightly for frozen tips.

****topped

more flavor and are more nutritious. Test for doneness of large vegetables such as beets, potatoes or parsnips by piercing them with the tip of a sharp paring knife or a long, thin-tined fork. Smaller vegetables may be pressed between the thumb and forefinger or pressed against the container side with a spoon.

This text gives the usual recommended proportions of salt but many facilities prefer to undersalt. Where salt-free diets must be prepared, salt will be omitted. Since frozen and canned vegetables contain some salt, these should be salted less than the others. Use a ½ cup of butter or margarine per five pounds EP of vegetable and one to 1½ quarts of sauce for this quantity. Fats seasoned by cooking lightly with spices, etc., give a more subtle and smooth flavor than when added separately.

Processed Vegetables

Cooking methods depend frequently on how the vegetable is processed.

Canned Vegetables

Careless preparation of canned vegetables has undoubtedly caused much of the criticism directed at institutionally prepared vegetables. Just warming a canned vegetable does little to increases its acceptability. String beans delicately seasoned with crisp brown bacon bits, canned peas lightly flavored with mint leaves, succulent kernel corn bright in contrast with bits of sautéed pimiento and green pepper, sauerkraut simmered with juniper berries, caraway seed or a sprinkling of crisp bacon cracklings, or soy bacon bits over succotash are some things that improve acceptability. Use a light hand with seasonings. Canned vegetables are already cooked and require only seasoning and heating in about half their own liquor for service. Heat as close to service as possible. Botulinum toxin is destroyed in most canned vegetables if heated above 190° F for 10 or more minutes but beets, spinach and other non-acid foods are frequently heated 20 to 30 minutes. This poisoning is now so rare in commercially canned vegetables that one wonders if such precautions need be observed. Perhaps they should because of the deadliness of the poison and the chance that a large number of individuals could otherwise be endangered.

The drained weight of many canned vegetables will be 60 to 65% of total can contents. A No. 10 can gives 20 to 25 3-ounce portions of drained vegetables such as peas or string beans but 35 3-ounce portions of vegetables not drained such as cream-style corn, tomatoes or succotash.

Frozen Vegetables

To cook frozen vegetables, simply break into chunks and drop frozen into boiling salted water. Use 1 to 2 tablespoons of salt per gallon of water. Corn-on-the-cob and some leafy greens perform better if thawed, especially if steamed. Cooking time is shorter than for fresh vegetables, for blanching before freezing partially cooks them. Dehydro-

Figure 11–6. Break mild-flavored, high-moisture frozen vegetables into chunks and drop into boiling salted water. Bring to a boil and cook rapidly until tender. Cook in quantities of about five pounds per batch.

frozen vegetables have about 50% of their moisture removed. This water must be replaced in cooking so the quantity of water used will be more than normally recommended. Follow manufacturers' instructions for cooking these and other frozen vegetables.

Dried Vegetables

After soaking, succulent dried vegetables should be cooked similarly to fresh ones. Simmer to encourage plumping. Cooking time is often slightly less than for the same item fresh. Bring dry legumes to a boil, then drop to simmering. Cook covered to preserve heat. Use from 2 to 3 tablespoons of salt per gallon of water for all dried vegetables.

Cooking Methods

Vegetables are cooked by boiling, steaming, baking, ovenizing, deep-frying, sautéing or broiling. The method should be based on what is desired in the final product plus whether the product is mild-flavored or strong-flavored, high or low in moisture or high or low in starch. For the most part, the discussion that follows is directed at the cooking of fresh vegetables but these methods also apply in many ways to other types.

Kinds of Vegetables

Vegetables are usually separated into four classes for cooking. These are:

1) High moisture with mild flavor: celery, spinach, green peas, string beans, carrots, summer squash, etc.
2) High moisture with strong flavor: members of the cabbage or turnip families and the onion family
3) Moist starchy vegetables: Irish or sweet potatoes, parsnips, etc.
4) Dry, starchy vegetables: a diversified group including dry legumes, macaroni products, rice, cereals and other high-starch items.

Boiling

MILD-FLAVORED, HIGH-MOISTURE VEGETABLES

Boil mild-flavored, high moisture vegetables by dropping them into boiling water, covering and bringing back to a boil as fast as possible, removing the cover *immediately after boiling starts again*, using ¾ gallon

Figure 11-7. Mild-flavored, high moisture vegetables may be steamed if they are not packed too deeply into pans.

of water, 3 tablespoons of salt and 2 tablespoons of salad oil per 5 pounds EP (25 3-ounce portions). Add about a ¼ to ½ cup of sugar, if desired. After the cover is off for 3 to 5 minutes, put it back, if desired, and cook at a slow boil until done. Send immediately to service. It is common to use only enough water to boil and some items such as carrots can be cooked covered in a very heavy pot without any water. This method is used to reduce nutrient losses by leaching. However, it has been demonstrated that using a large quantity of boiling salted water, adding the vegetables and covering until boiling starts again shortens cooking time and therefore nutrient and other losses are about the same as when vegetables are cooked in only a small quantity of water.

In quantity preparation, vegetables *may have* to be cooked in advance. If this *must* be done, boil to barely doneness, drain and save some of the cooking water to use in reheating the vegetables. Plunge the vegetables immediately into cold water stopping all cooking. Then drain well, place into a covered container and store under refrigeration. If the vegetables are leafy greens, after blanching, press out the excess water and place them in about pound mounds in a pan. Cover and store. To

(a)

(b)

(c)

Figure 11–8. (a) Add rice to rapidly boiling salted water. (b) When tender, blanch in cold water. (c) The beginning of the method used by Oriental cooks to prepare rice. In the background, cold, salted water is being poured over well-washed rice previous to its being cooked in this manner.

serve any vegetable handled this way, reheat some of the vegetable's cooking water and add the vegetable, season, heat as quickly as possible and serve. Heat only that quantity that can be used within a short period of time. This method retains nutrients and quality better than holding a large batch hot for service.

STRONG-FLAVORED, HIGH-MOISTURE VEGETABLES

The cabbage and turnip families and the onion family are best boiled to reduce flavor. Cooking in batches or, if they must be cooked ahead, boiling and then blanching, as described above, is recommended. Avoid holding the cabbage or turnip families at high heat. Use 1¼ gallons of water, three tablespoons of salt per five pounds EP of vegetable; this yields 25 3-ounce portions. Add to rapidly boiling water and cover until boiling starts again. Removing the cover during cooking allows the escape of volatile acids which help develop strong flavors in the cabbage and turnip families. Old vegetables or those stored a long time are stronger in flavor than young or those not stored long. Cutting into small pieces to give greater surface area to permit the strong flavors to be more easily dissolved into the cooking water is sometimes practiced. Fine division also shortens cooking time which is desirable for the cabbage and turnip families. The members of the onion family should be cooked longer to dissipate the pungent flavors from allyl sulfides. Fine division can be recommended for these vegetables also because this gives a greater chance to break down the pungent flavors. Sautéing or some other form of pre-cooking is often done to give these a milder flavor in sauces, dressings, etc. We may also add these vegetables early to stews, soups, etc., so that they cook longer and lose some of their pungent flavors.

Moist Starchy Vegetables

Potatoes and other moist starchy vegetables are best steamed. If boiled, drop into boiling salted water using about three tablespoons of salt to the gallon. Cover and gently boil until tender. Drain well and serve as soon as possible. Holding under water may give a soggy product.

Dry Starchy Vegetables

Beans and other legumes are presoaked in water (three tablespoons of salt per gallon) using 1½ gallons for every five pounds of legumes; 11 pounds serves about 100 6-ounce portions. After soaking, bring to a boil, cover and cook gently until tender when pressed with a spoon on the side of the kettle or between the fingers. Breaking of the skin indicates doneness or perhaps overdoneness. Add no acid until done. Cooking time varies from 1 to 3 hours, although lima beans and split peas may cook in less than an hour.

Drop macaroni products and rice into boiling salted water, stirring while adding. Use a gallon of water and two tablespoons of salt per pound of product. Cover until boiling begins. Stir, recover and cook until tender. (A small quantity of salad oil mixed into rice before moistening helps to prevent it from sticking together. For added flavor, rice can be lightly sautéed in oil and then boiled.) Test doneness by pressing with a fork or spoon against the kettle side or between the fingers. If it breaks cleanly and easily, it is done. Do not over-cook. Blanch immediately in cold water and drain. Macaroni products should be cooked until they have some chew or resistance left to the bite, called by cooks "al dente" (to the tooth). Rice should be tender but not too soft.

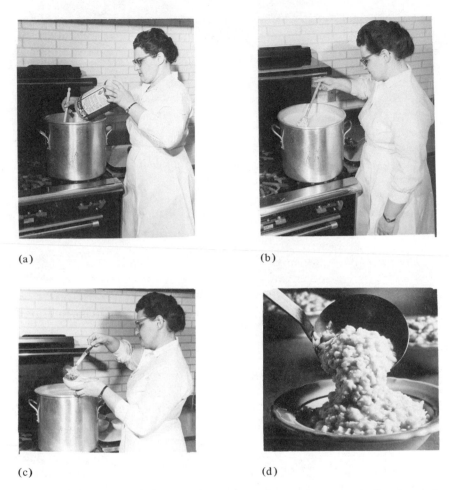

(a)

(b)

(c)

(d)

Figure 11–9. To cook dry cereals, measure the proper amount of water and salt and bring to a boil. (a) Add cereal, giving good agitation as it is stirred into the water. (b) Stir until some thickening is apparent. Then, reduce the heat to a simmer and cook covered until the cereal reaches the desired consistency and the raw starch taste has disappeared. (c) Then serve. (d) A well cooked product such as this breakfast cereal brings highest customer satisfaction. (Courtesy Quaker Oats Company)

Another method for cooking dry starchy items is to use three quarts of water and two tablespoons of salt per pound of product. Have the water boiling and stir slowly while adding. Cover. Remove from direct heat or, if a steam-jacketed kettle is used, turn off the heat. Let stand 10 minutes or until the product is tender. Drain and blanch in cold water. Heavy thick-walled macaroni products cannot be cooked by this method but thin-walled ones or rice can.

Figure 11–10. On a pressure steamer such as this, the steam lever that allows steam to enter into the chamber cannot be pulled forward until the door is closed and locked into position. Note the safety valve also to the left of the gauge.

Rice is cooked successfully by first being given several thorough washings in fresh water to remove excess starch. Then add 2 tablespoons of oil, 1¾ quarts of water and 2 tablespoons of salt per pound of rice. Cover tightly and bring to a boil. Stir only once after boiling starts. Set on low heat, covered, for about 30 minutes. During the last 10 minutes uncover so that the rice steams dry leaving the grains light and separate. If the rice absorbs all the water but is still dry and hard, add more water. Too much water gives an over-cooked rice. A steam-jacketed kettle or heavy pot can be used for this method.

For 100 5-ounce portions, use 8 pounds of rice or noodles and 10 of macaroni or spaghetti. Normally, the cooked yields are:

1 lb rice	3 to 4 lb (1½ to 1¾ qt)
1 lb macaroni, spaghetti, etc.	4 lb (2¼ to 2½ qt)
1 lb noodles	3 lb (2 qt)

Add breakfast cereals to boiling salted water. Stir well during the

Figure 11–11. Small high-pressure steamers can cook many vegetables in a few minutes. Using one or several, vegetables can be sent rapidly to service.

addition, continuing to stir until some thickening is apparent. Then reduce heat to simmering and cook covered until the cereal is thick enough and no raw taste of starch is evident. The more a cereal is stirred during thickening, the more slick and pasty it will be. Therefore, avoid stirring once thickening starts. Fine cereals that might lump can be mixed with a part of the cooking water and added as a slurry. Coarser cereals may be added slowly. For 100 5-ounce portions use 4 gallons of water and $\frac{1}{4}$ to $\frac{1}{3}$ cup of salt and 4 pounds of fine grained cereal such as cornmeal, grits or farina, or 5 pounds of coarser cereal such as oatmeal or cracked wheat. For best quality cook as close to service as possible because holding can harm quality.

Steaming

Many vegetables steam well although some few do not. Normally, if the cooking directions indicate that the vegetable should be in water in a pan for steaming, it does not respond well to steaming and should be boiled. Small high-pressure units are often used for batch cooking but compartment steamers are commonly used for large quantities. Most vegetables are cooked in perforated pans to allow steam to circulate freely around them. Vegetables that separate themselves with some space between them steam much better than those that do not. Fresh peas or spinach, for instance, will cook on the outside but not in the interior because they pack too closely to allow the steam to get to the inside areas. The moist, starchy vegetables steam well. Use care in cooking with steam because the higher temperatures can quickly cause overcooking. Table 11-3 summarizes procedures for steaming most vegetables.

Table 11-3. Recommended Steaming Practices for Quantity Vegetable Cookery

Vegetable	Recommended Procedure at 6 psi
Asparagus	Lay flat in counter pans, 2 inches deep; add small quantity of warm salted water.* Steam until stalks are tender. If desired, cut off tips, sizing end pieces to equal length of tips. Steam ends 1 minute, add tips, and steam until tips and ends are soft and done.
Beans, dry	Soak 2 to 6 hours. Cover with salted water in solid basket and steam until skins just crack.
Beans, lima, fresh	Place in solid basket to a depth of not more than 3 inches. Add small quantity of salted water.* Steam until tender.
Beans, snap	Place in flat, perforated basket up to 2½ inches deep. Steam until tender. For large quantities, place in tall, narrow, solid basket half full with small quantity of salted water.* Avoid overcrowding. Steam until tender.
Beets	Top only. Steam in perforated basket. Cool and remove skins after steaming.
Broccoli	Lay flat in counter pans with enough warm salted water* to cover stalks. Steam only until tender. Split heavy or thick stalks. Avoid overcooking because of loss of color.
Brussels sprouts	Place in counter pan about 1 inch or single layer deep. To shorten cooking time, stem ends may be split slightly.
Cabbage	Place in flat, solid basket half filled with small quantity of warm salted water.*
Carrots	Steam in perforated basket half full.
Cauliflower	Steam in flat, perforated basket, one-fourth full. Should be tender when cooked, with stems having waxy appearance, but should possess firm texture, maintaining original form characteristics.
Cereals	For each 4 pounds of the flaked or coarse type, use 4 gallons water and ¼ cup salt. Bring water to boil and add cereal. Stir to blend thoroughly. Use 5 pounds of fine granular cereal to 4 gallons water and ⅓ cup salt. Steam until done.
Corn-on-the-cob	Thaw frozen corn-on-the-cob before steaming. Place about 25 ears per perforated basket. Steam. Doneness is indicated when kernels are pierced with fork and no milk comes out.
Corn, kernel	Place in counter pan with small quantity of warm salted water.*
Dumplings	Drop on greased baking pans separated sufficiently to allow for expansion. Steam for 15 minutes.
Macaroni products	Bring salted water* to boil in solid basket. Add macaroni product, 1 pound to each gallon of water, stirring to separate for 2 minutes. Steam for 12 to 15 minutes.

*Where salted water is required, use 2½ to 2 T salt per gallon of water.

(continued)

Table 11–3. (cont.)

Vegetable	Recommended Procedure at 6psi
Onion, dry	Steam mild onions in perforated basket, third full. Strong, old onions should be steamed in solid basket with small quantity of warm salted water.*
Parsnips	Place in perforated basket, one-fourth full; steam only until tender.
Peas, green	Place in counter pans without water to a depth of not over 2 inches. If necessary, midway through cooking, pressure may be released and peas stirred.
Potatoes, Irish	Steam in perforated basket, three-fourths full. May be partially steamed in skins and baked. Steaming French fries to a partially done stage is also satisfactory.
Potatoes, sweet	Steam in perforated basket, three-fourths full, with skins on. Cool and peel. May also be partially steamed and then baked.
Rice	Wash rice well. Use approximately 2 quarts salted water* to every quart of washed rice. Bring this water to boil in solid basket. Add rice, stirring to separate, for 2 minutes. Cook until tender. Rinse with hot water and steam without water until grains are tender and separated.
Rutabaga	Steam in perforated basket, half full. Old rutabagas should be steamed in solid basket covered with warm salted water.*
Spinach	Steam in small quantity until almost cooked in solid basket containing some warm salted water.* Remove and stir. Complete cooking. Heat in spinach just before doneness may be used to complete cooking without further heat.
Squash, summer	Steam in perforated basket until soft. Do not place more than 2 inches deep.
Squash, winter	Place in perforated basket, half full, and steam.
Turnips	Place in perforated basket, half full, packed loosely. Place old turnips in solid basket with some salted water* and steam.

*Where salted water is required, use 2½ to 2 T salt per gallon of water.

Baking

Baking is usually considered roasting in an oven with dry heat. The moist starchy vegetables such as Irish or sweet potatoes, winter squash or parsnips bake well. A few high-moisture vegetables such as tomatoes may be baked. Baking is often a process in which vegetables are parboiled or steamed and then are finished in an oven. This reduces baking time and is excellent for winter squash, sweet potatoes and parsnips but Irish potatoes usually are best when baked without such precooking. Combination dishes with vegetables may be baked such as turnip soufflé, spinach timbale or corn pudding. Baked beans, *au gratin* potatoes, zucchini in tomato sauce, glazed onions or carrots are baked by braising in an oven or covering with some moisture. At times, vegetables are baked with meat such as a roast. They are added near the end of the roasting period.

(a)   (b)

Figure 11–12. (a) To bake potatoes, arrange washed potatoes as shown and brush lightly with a fat. (b) When the potatoes are done, serve at once. Open the potato immediately, pushing in the ends to give a free release of steam which otherwise would make the potato soggy.

Deep-frying*

Deep-frying imparts a nutty flavor and crisp outer texture to vegetables. Potatoes and some other vegetables deep-fry well. Some may be breaded or dipped into batter. Partial cooking by boiling or steaming and then finishing in deep fat is done. Different types of vegetable fritters are popular. Table 11-4 summarizes procedures for deep-frying vegetables.

POTATOES

Dry potato strips before deep-frying. If orders are spasmodic and demand light, use the one-operation method that cooks half-inch potato strips at 375° F in about seven minutes. If volume is high and a large amount is produced, the two-operation method is used. Blanche the potatoes at 375° F until tender but not colored. Then for service, fry for about two minutes at 350° to 380° F. The potatoes, after being blanched, can be held refrigerated up to two days, and longer if frozen. Potatoes at room temperature or slightly warmed in an oven cook more quickly. Or preblanch until partially done in steam and then fry. Commercially blanched frozen strips are commonly used in foodservices and

* See Chapter 12 for a specialized discussion of sautéing and deep-frying.

Figure 11–13.   Many vegetables deep-fry well. At the lower right are the traditional onion rings. Breaded cauliflower is just above them, while to the left are breaded eggplant sticks. Note how the operator used care in dropping the items. The basket is kept above the fat until filled and then carefully lowered into the fat.

now they outrank frozen peas in quantity sold on the institution market. Potatoes smaller than a half inch thick are fried at 360° to 380° F from 4 to 6 minutes to give a crisp product with a soft center. If complete crispness is desired, as in shoestrings, fry 6 to 9 minutes in 335° to 340° F fat until golden brown. If not crisp, drain and raise the tempera-

Table 11-4. Deep-Fat Frying of Vegetables

Vegetable	Quantity per 100 Portions (lb EP)	Temperature of Fat (°F)	Frying Time (min)	Procedure
Asparagus	24	360	1 to 3	Boil almost done; cool; dip into batter and fry until golden brown.
Carrots or Parsnips	24	360	3 to 5	Boil or steam almost done; cut lengthwise into quarters; batter or bread and fry.
Cauliflower	20	360	1 to 3	Partially steam or boil. Bread or batter and fry.
Corn-on-the-cob	100 ears	350	3 to 5	Husk ears and remove silk; fry in fat, turning frequently. If frozen corn is used, be sure it is thawed before use; frozen corn is not as satisfactory as fresh.
Cucumbers	35	360	3 to 5	Wash only. Cut into quarters and cut these quarters lengthwise into halves. Batter or bread.
Dill pickles	50 pickles	350	3 to 5	Split pickles in half lengthwise. Batter or bread. (Excellent with boiled beef, corned beef, ham, or pastrami.)
Eggplant	16	370	5 to 8	Do not pare. Cut into slices ½ inch thick or cut into ½ inch strips. Soak in salted water, ¼ cup salt per gallon for 1 hour. Batter or bread and fry.
Onions	16	375	2 to 3	Cut peeled onions into rings ½ inch thick. Separate into individual rings. Dip into evaporated milk and then into flour and continue until well coated, or dip into batter.
Potatoes, Irish (*rissolé*)	24	360	5 to 8	Steam or boil until almost done, if desired. Brown in fat. Finish baking in oven. If not partially cooked before browning, extend baking time.
Potatoes, Irish (French fried)	24			See discussion on next page and Table 12-1.
Potatoes, sweet	24	360	5 to 8	Parboil or steam ¼ inch sticks or slices. Then deep-fry.
Squash, winter	24	360	5 to 8	Parboil or steam pieces ½ inch thick. Then deep-fry.
Tomatoes	20	360	2 to 4	Slice ½ inch thick and dip into batter or bread.
Zucchini	16	360	3 to 5	Dip into batter or bread.

See also Table 12-2.

(a)

(b)

(c)

Figure 11–14. Hash brown potatoes can be (a) grilled or (b) ovenized or (c) the frozen, partially cooked product can be either grilled or ovenized. The frozen product has eliminated so much work that few facilities today use anything else.

ture to 375° F and crisp in a few seconds. These potatoes keep for a week if not salted and if held in a cool place in an airtight container.

Soak potatoes for soufflé potatoes at least 30 minutes in ice water. Dry well and cook 4 to 5 minutes in 275° F fat. Keep them separate when frying. Drain well and chill at least five minutes. Raise the fat temperature to 400° to 425° F — this requires good fat — place a few of the potatoes in the basket and lower into the fat. The potatoes will puff, become crisp and have a golden-brown color. Remove, drain and serve at once. Sweet potatoes and some other starchy vegetables are also sometimes souffléd.

Sautéing

Sautéing (grilling or pan-frying) of cooked or raw vegetables is common, especially for short orders. Hash browns, lyonnaise and many other potato dishes are sautéed. Mushrooms, string beans and bacon, breaded tomato slices, onions, parsnips, squash, shredded cabbage and other vegetables may be prepared this way. Pan-braising may be done in a pan, steam-jacketed kettle or oven. Shredded, diced or thinly sliced vegetables high in moisture are placed into a skillet with a tablespoon of oil, butter or margarine, a teaspoon of salt and two tablespoons of water per quart of vegetables. The container is covered tightly and allowed to steam or braise with occasional stirring of the vegetables. Small quantities only should be prepared.

Oven Roasting (Ovenizing)

Oven roasting or ovenizing produces results very similar to sautéing but different equipment is used. Vegetables are placed onto well greased pans, put into a hot oven where they fry and are stirred frequently. Some vegetables can be parboiled or steamed and then finished by baking in a well greased roasting pan in the oven, a method previously described as baking. Rissolé potatoes are frequently parboiled or steamed, browned in deep fat and then browned well in an oven.

Broiling

Raw tomato slices broil well if cut about an inch thick, brushed with oil and broiled about four inches from the heat. They should be turned only once. Unpeeled eggplant may be sliced a half to an inch thick, soaked in salt water for an hour, parboiled and then spread with mayonnaise on top and broiled. Other items may be partially parboiled or steamed and broiled such as mushrooms, zucchini, onion slices, carrots or parsnips. Some almost cooked vegetables are glazed under a broiler, while some broiled vegetables may be braised in an oven and given only a last-minute finish under the broiler.

STUFFINGS OR DRESSINGS

Bread dressings are frequently served in place of a moist starchy vegetable or cereal and so perhaps their inclusion with vegetables in cooking is logical. A dressing (*panada*) should blend with the main dish or meat, complementing its flavor. Strong meats should have mild dressings

(a)

(b)

(c)

(d)

(e)

Figure 11–15. (a) For a moistened dressing, wet the bread and then press out the excess with the palms of the hands. (b) A dry dressing is made with firm, fresh bread as shown here. (c) To either types of bread, add sautéed vegetables, salt and seasonings. Mix well. (d) Spread into a baking pan. Plastic gloves avert the chance for the hands contaminating the dressing with food poisoning bacteria. (e) Never let dressings stand at room temperature. Cover and refrigerate.

and rich meats lean dressings. Dry dressings may be desirable when a moist, rich sauce or gravy is served with the meal and a moist one is best if the meat is dry. With a 2- to 3-ounce portion of meat, four ounces of dressing are adequate and about two ounces are enough to stuff a pork chop or serve with a heavier meat portion. Use 3, 4 or 5 pounds of stuffing respectively for a 10-, 15- or over-15-pound bird, ready-to-cook weight, or 10 ounces (1¼ c) of dressing for each pound of ready-to-cook bird.

Bread dressing is the most popular but rice and other cereals can be used. Cornbread dressing is popular with some poultry. Almonds, chestnuts, apples, cranberries, crabmeat, shrimp, oysters, giblets or sausage may be added. For each 12 pounds of dressing use three cups of chopped or sliced almonds or chestnuts, a quart of chopped apples, a quart of ground cranberries with a fourth cup of sugar (omitting onion and poultry seasonings), a pound of either crab, shrimp or oysters with two eggs, a quart of cooked chopped giblets or two pounds of sausage. Refrigerate dressings immediately after preparing unless they are baked at once. *At no time, before or after baking,* allow dressings to stand between 40° and 125° F for over 4 hours. Place only *chilled* dressings into *chilled* birds. Bake at once. Remove dressings from cooked birds before refrigerating. It is best to bake the birds separately and dish the dressing with the meat or poultry at service. Bake in pans with the dressing about 2 inches deep. Hot dressings should be spread in shallow pans to cool before being stored under refrigeration. After cooling, cover. Reheat under steam pressure or in an oven until well above 180° F.

Dumplings, hot biscuits or pastry are also used as meat accompaniments. Their making is discussed under Section III of this book.

Table 11–5. Bread Stuffing Guide

	Poultry Weight (ready-to-cook)				
Stuffing Ingredients	4 lbs	6 lbs	10 lbs	12 lbs	20 lbs
Shortening	¼ cup	⅓ cup	½ cup	⅔ cup	1 cup
Chopped onion	½ cup	⅔ cup	1 cup	1⅓ cups	2 cups
Chopped celery	½ cup	⅔ cup	1 cup	1⅓ cups	2 cups
Fresh enriched bread: ½ inch cubes	6 cups	9 cups	15 cups	1⅛ gal	1⅞ gal
or	or	or	or	or	or
number of ⅝ inch slices	6	9	15	18	30
Salt	⅔ t	1 t	1½ t	2 t	1 T
Pepper	dash	⅛ t	¼ t	¼ t	½ t
Poultry seasoning	1⅓ t	2 t	1 T	1⅓ T	2 T
Water	⅓ cup	⅔ cup	1 cup	1⅓ cups	2 cups
Average number cups of stuffing	4	6	10	12	20

(Courtesy American Institute of Baking)

Suggested laboratory experiences or work assignments for Chapter 11:

1. Cook some soaked navy beans in neutral water, an acid medium and an alkaline one and notice the difference between the three samples. Do the same for a green vegetable.
2. Cook onions in an alkaline and acid medium. Do the same for red cabbage or beets. Cook carrots similarly. Record the changes. Which color pigments are water soluble and which are not?
3. Cook a tomato and note that the water does not turn red as with beets and other red vegetables and fruits. Explain what lycopene, the red coloring in tomatoes, is and how it differs from anthocyanins in red beets.
4. Put a potato in water, dip another piece into some anti-oxidant dip, lemon or pineapple juice. Allow another piece to stand in the air without treatment. Why does the one standing in the air tarnish and the others do not?
5. Cook some carrots in an alkaline medium, some in neutral water and others in a fairly heavy sugar sirup. Why are the latter so hard and firm?
6. Explain the osmotic action that occurs when a leaf of lettuce crisps and becomes firm. Explain what happens when we add a salad dressing and it wilts. What pulls the water from the lettuce?
7. Boil onions for a long time and do the same for cabbage. Add a bit of acid to the latter to speed the formation of an off-color and flavor. Explain the difference between the pungent flavors in the two.

BIBLIOGRAPHY

MacFarlane, Alberta M., *Cooking the Modern Way,* Groen Mfg. Co., Chicago, 1953.

National Restaurant Association, *White Potatoes,* Technical Bul. 101, Chicago, 1953.

Olsen, Grace E., "Fresh versus Pre-processed Vegetables," *Journal,* American Dietetic Association 30, No. 8, Aug., 1954, pp 762-768.

Terrell, Margaret E., *Professional Cooking,* John Wiley and Sons, New York, 1970.

U. S. Department of Agriculture, Human Nutrition Research Division, *Potatoes in Popular Ways,* Bulletin 55, Washington, 1957.

U. S. Department of Agriculture, Economic Research Division, *Use of Frozen Foods by Restaurants,* Marketing Research Report No. 144, AMS, Washington, 1956.

12

Deep-Frying and Sautéing

The simple procedure of cooking foods in fat belies the amount of technical knowledge needed to do a good job of frying. Fat is a delicate product that under high temperatures or hard use can easily break down. Knowing something about fats, how they break down and the right procedures, equipment and fat to use can do much to assure a good frying job. Poor frying occurs when one or more of these are done incorrectly. What is fat?

Fat and oil are the same thing except that a fat is solid and an oil is liquid; it can be either one depending upon temperature. Fat is a triglyceride formed when three fatty acids combine with glycerol as follows;

```
    H  H H H H H    H H H H H
H-C—C-C-C-C-C-C=C-C-C-C-C-O-O-H (saturated fatty acid)
  |  H H H H H H H H H H HH H
  |  H HH H H H H H H H H H H H H H H H
H-C—C-C-C-C-C-C-C-C-C-C-C-C-C-C-C-C-C-C-O-O-H (saturated fatty acid)
  |  H H H H H H H H H H H H H H H H H H H H
  |  H H H H         H H H H H H H
H-C—C-C-C-C-C=C=C-C-C-C-C-C-C-C-O-O-H (polysaturated fatty acid)
  H  H H H H H H H H H H H H H H
```

(glycerol radical)

In the first and last fatty acids above, the carbons (C's) join in four

different places as —$\overset{|}{\underset{|}{C}}$—, but one carbon in the first and two in the last

chains above are joined —$\overset{|}{C}$=. The C's joined with four bonds at

different places (—$\overset{|}{\underset{|}{C}}$—) are called saturated. The last fatty acid above

with two unsaturated carbons is called polyunsaturated because it has

331

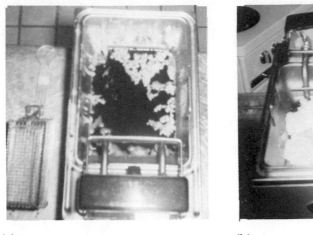 

(a)   (b)

Figure 12–1. (a) Sediment and materials left in the fat break it down. (b) Set the thermostat at 200° F until the fat is liquid around the element.

two or more unsaturated carbons. The first carbon chain is called unsaturated because it has one unsaturated carbon. The double bond in a carbon chain is a weak chemical link. The chain is apt to break apart here more easily or join with other substances, both of which reactions can be undesirable. Animal fats tend to be more saturated than vegetable, poultry or fish fats. Some fish and vegetable oils are polyunsaturated. Frozen beef or mutton can be stored for longer periods than poultry or fish because unsaturated fats break down more easily than saturated ones.

Fat Breakdown

In frying we try to keep the fat in top condition. If it changes, undesirable flavors are apt to be produced in the food or a poorly fried product is made. Fats do not boil away as does water. Instead, at certain temperatures or when subjected to certain conditions they break down. Normally, a good frying fat can be heated to nearly 450° F without breaking down — it bursts into flame around 600° F — but we can do things to a good fat to make it break down at lower temperatures. Breakdown from heat is indicated by a white smoke called acrolein, curling up from the surface. Acrolein is a sharp, acrid product irritating to the eyes, nose and throat.

Unsaturated fats have a lower smoking temperature than saturated ones, so saturated fats are preferred for frying. We can make an unsaturated fat into a saturated one by hydrogenation, a process in which

$$\text{H} \qquad \text{H}$$

hydrogen is added at the unsaturated bond changing $-C=$ to $-C-$. If

$$\text{H}$$

it is an oil, it is now apt to be solid, or if it is a fat, it probably becomes more solid.

Fats containing a lot of free fatty acids — not attached to a glycerol — have a low smoking temperature. Butter, olive oil and fish, animal or poultry fats are high in free fatty acids, while many vegetable oils contain less. For this reason vegetable oils are used frequently for frying. Manufacturers may remove free fatty acids from fats to improve their frying performance. Fats receiving poor treatment in frying may break down, putting a lot of free fatty acids into the fat. Or a lot of free fatty acids can be added to the fat when foods high in free fatty acids such as mackerel, pork or poultry are fried. Some low-priced pre-blanched potato strips are fried by manufacturers in fat high in free fatty acids, and these potatoes contaminate good fat when fried in it.

Metals encourage fat breakdown. Copper or brass are about 20 times worse than iron, while nickel, chrome or stainless steel are not harmful. Watch for exposed iron on frying baskets or other equipment. Keep iron tools out of the fat, if possible. Do not use steel wool or other abrasives on the thermostat which exposes the copper. Curing salts or cooking salt break down fat, therefore do not salt foods over a fryer or griddle. Water encourages break down, so foods should be as dry as possible when put into fat. Sediment in the fat or unclean equipment can also break it down. When fat spreads into a thin film, it breaks down more easily. For instance, a fat at the same temperature smokes much more easily on a griddle than in a larger mass in a fry kettle.

Chemical Change

A good frying fat can change chemically and cause problems, as when a fat adds oxygen, developing rancidity. An unsaturated bond joins easily with oxygen. A film of oil oxidizes more quickly than a larger mass. Failing to wash well a container that contained oil may cause new oil put into it to become rancid because once rancidity starts, it develops more quickly. Mixtures of fat grow rancid more quickly than individual fats. High storage temperatures or exposure to air or light favor rancidity development. Store in a cool, dry, dark place. Use as soon as possible after opening and store covered in a cool place. Enzymes called *lipases* can cause fats to change. Molds, especially where moisture is present, can encourage change. Some fats develop off-flavors by losing oxygen, a process called *reversion*, first detected as a beany flavor, then as a metallic one and finally as a fishy flavor. Potato chips with a fishy flavor may not have been fried in fish oil but in soybean oil which reverts easily unless treated. Salting also favors reversion. Polymers are resins, gums, and waxes formed when fats or free fatty acids join together. They are found as gummy substances on griddles, deep-fryers and broilers, and give off-flavors to food.

In addition to removing fatty acids and hydrogenating fats, manufacturers add antioxidants to help stabilize fat. They also add silicon or other substances to assist stabilization. While these help, care in using the fat is also required.

When fat contains a high amount of free fatty acids or polymers and is rancid, it develops a soft, yellowish foam and should be discarded. A good fat should have white bubbles that break sharply, and if handled correctly, should seldom have to be discarded. If from 15 to 20% of the fat is used each day or time the fryer is used, enough fresh fat is added to keep it in good condition. Replacing fat as it is used this way is called *turnover*. A fry kettle holding 15 pounds of fat should use $2\frac{1}{4}$ to 3 pounds of new fat to have proper turnover. A dozen doughnuts absorb three ounces of fat in frying, 10 pounds of potatoes absorb one pound 10 ounces and 10 pounds of batter-covered or breaded food absorb 18 ounces of fat. If a 15-pound fryer fries 25 pounds of potatoes, or 20 pounds of batter-covered or breaded items or 12 dozen doughnuts, the turnover requirement should be met. Fats should be strained as frequently as sediment or other products accumulate in it. If it is not strained and the equipment is not kept clean, even with proper turnover a good fat cannot be maintained.

Deep-frying

Good results in deep-frying occur when the right fat and technique are used and the fat and equipment given proper care. The fat selected should be flavorless, have a smoking temperature when fresh of not less than 425° F and contain anti-oxidants and stabilizers to protect it from the rigorous treatment it gets in frying. Packing solid fat around the elements and setting the temperature at 200° F until melted fat surrounds the elements prevents charring the fat while melting. Do not under- or over-fill. Refill as the level falls. If large or many small batches are fried or if volume varies, several fryers should be installed rather than a large one so that during periods of low demand, only one is operated. Since the crumbs and flour on breaded food harm fat, a kettle is often reserved just for these foods. Materials should be skimmed off as they collect on fat.

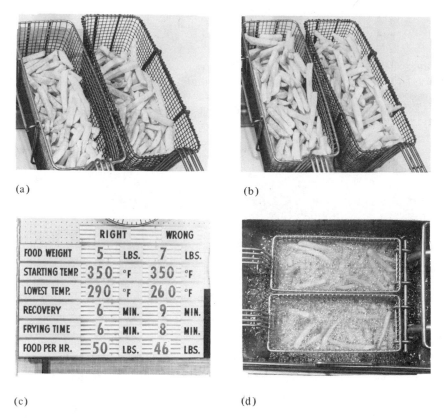

(a)

(b)

	RIGHT	WRONG
FOOD WEIGHT	5 LBS.	7 LBS.
STARTING TEMP.	350 °F	350 °F
LOWEST TEMP.	290 °F	260 °F
RECOVERY	6 MIN.	9 MIN.
FRYING TIME	6 MIN.	8 MIN.
FOOD PER HR.	50 LBS.	46 LBS.

(c)

(d)

Figure 12–2. (a) A properly filled basket. (b) An overfilled basket. (c) The results of the overload are shown. Note that the time and the cooking temperature were lower on the overfilled baskets. Product quality was poorer also as well as there being less fried per hour. (d) The properly filled potatoes being fried in a good fat. Note the sharp white bubbles. (Courtesy Procter and Gamble)

The accuracy of thermostats on a deep-fryer should be checked by using a thermometer to see if the fat temperature is what is set on the dial. An inch cube of soft bread becomes a delicate brown in 1 minute 15 seconds in fat at 350° to 360° F, 1 minute at 360° to 370° F, 40 seconds at 375° to 385° F and 20 seconds at 385° to 400° F. Escoffier says fat "is moderately hot when, after a sprig of parsley or a crust of bread is thrown into it, it begins to bubble immediately. It is hot if it crackles when a slightly moist object is dropped into it and very hot when it gives off a thin white smoke perceptible to the smell."

To deep-fry, the temperature must be raised to the *correct* level. Cold fat colors food poorly and gives a greasy, soggy product, while too hot fat burns the food without properly cooking the inside. Food pieces of the same size and kind should be used to obtain uniform cooking and browning, and only the correct amount of food to fat. About 1½ to 2 times the fat weight can be fried in food per hour. The food-fat ratio in a good fryer can be 1:5 to 1:8 and for potatoes 1:6. In an old-fashioned fryer it is 1:10. Overloading drops the temperature so low that excessive fat absorption occurs and a poorly cooked product results. This also increases fat consumption and cost. Many frying fats are designed to have sharp melting points so when they solidify they lose their greasiness. Other factors increasing fat absorption are 1) cold food, 2) cold fat, 3) a rich batter or dough, 4) large surface area, 5) excessive leavening in a batter or dough, 6) poor shape, 7) rough surfaces, 8) poor fat or 9) poor handling of the fat.

Lower the basket carefully to avoid spillover. Shake it occasionally during frying to prevent foods from sticking together. The fat should cover the food. Fry until golden brown, then lift the basket and drain. Spill into a pan or place on absorbent paper. Serve the foods hot. Keep in a dry, warm place or under an infra-red lamp. Salt just before serving since salting destroys crispness.

Fat is highly combustible and a grease fire can be very dangerous. Never overheat fats or allow them to come in contact with open flames or substances above 600° F. Never leave grease over heat unattended. Keep handles of utensils containing hot fat inward when not in use. Lower wet foods into fat carefully. Fat can give terrible burns and care should be used in handling it. Strain the fat frequently to remove sediment. Handle at below 200° F and use several thicknesses of cheesecloth, a special filter bag or a filtering machine. If sediment does not

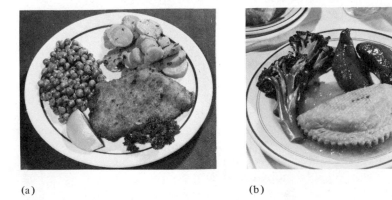

(a)   (b)

Figure 12–3.   (a) A well fried breaded veal cutlet. (b) A deep-fried turnover.

Table 12-1. Deep-Frying Temperatures and Times[1]

Type of Food	Frying Temperature ° F	Frying Time (minutes)
Potatoes:		
One operation, ½ in. cut	350	7
One operation, ⅜ in. cut	350	6
One operation, ¼ in. cut	350	5
One operation, ⅛ in. cut	360	4
One operation, ⅛ in. cut completely crisp	330	6 to 9
Two operation, ½ in. cut to ⅜ in. cut		
Blanch	350	4
Brown	350	3
Two operation, ¼ in. cut		
Blanch	350	2½
Brown	350	2½
Two operation, ⅛ in. cut		
Blanch	360	2½
Brown	360	2½
Frozen, blanched, ⅜ in. cut	350	2
Seafoods:		
Frozen breaded shrimp	350	4
Fresh breaded shrimp	350	3
Frozen fish fillets	350	4
Fresh fish fillets	350	3
Breaded clams	350	1
Breaded oysters	350	3 to 5
Fresh breaded scallops	350	4
Frozen fish sticks	350	4
Abalone, breaded	375	2 to 3
Sliced fish, breaded	350	6 to 8
Chicken: (1½ to 2 lb, sectioned)		
Raw	325	12 to 15
Steamed 20 min, then breaded	350	3 to 4
Miscellaneous:		
Breaded veal cutlets	350	3 to 4
Breaded onion rings	350	3
Croquettes, meat	350	3 to 4
Precooked cauliflower, breaded	350	3
Eggplant, breaded, raw	350	3
Tamale sticks, breaded	350	3
French-toasted sandwiches	350	1 to 2
Yeast-raised doughnuts	350	1 to 3
Hand-cut cake doughnuts	350	1 to 3
Glazed cinnamon apple rings	300	3 to 5
Corn-on-the-cob	300	3
Fritters	350	3
Turnovers, meat	350	5 to 7

(Adapted from Procter and Gamble, *Deep Frying Pointers*)

Note: The potato ratio should be 1:6 in the new type of fast-recovery kettles and 1:8 in the old type of kettles. If smaller loads of potatoes are used, use slightly lower temperatures.

[1] See also Table 11-4 for deep-frying of vegetables.

Table 12-2. Problems, Causes, and Correction in Deep-Frying

Problem	Causes	Corrections
Objectional smoke	1. Temperature too high. 2. Failure to strain fat frequently. 3. Old fat.	Use lower temperature; strain fat and store in cool place after use. Set up filtering schedule; check fat turnover.
Fat bubbles over	1. Too much fat in kettle. 2. Too much food in kettle. 3. Excessive moisture in food.	Check fill of deep kettle; add smaller quantities to be fried in basket; drain batter-dipped or egg-and-crumbed foods; dry potatoes thoroughly.
Foods not crisp	1. Frying temperature too low.	Use high temperature for frying; use frying thermometer or check temperature with bread cube.
Strong flavor and color	1. Old fat or deteriorated fat. 2. Wrong fat for frying.	Keep used fat in cool place; select proper type of frying fat; strain after use; if too many strongly flavored foods must be fried in fat, discard after use.
Excessive foaming	1. Failure to strain fat. 2. Deteriorated fat. 3. Extremely cold foods added to hot fat. 4. Too much egg and crumb or batter. 5. Frying temperature too low.	Strain fat before storing in cool place; do not take foods direct from refrigerator to kettle; drain batter-dipped or egg-and-crumbed foods; use correct temperature for frying; use thermometer or check temperature with bread cube; discard deteriorated fat.

(Adapted from Procter and Gamble, *Proper Frying*)

settle, cool below 200° F and sprinkle lightly with water so that the fine particles fall with the water to the bottom. Pour or siphon the fat from this water sludge. If a solid fat is used, allow it to solidify and pour off the sludge. Also, cut undesirable portions away from a solid chunk.

The old-fashioned frying kettle is seldom used in quantity work, but if it is, select one with straight or almost straight sides to minimize boiling over and have it large enough to permit fat to bubble up after adding the food. Fill with fat to about half full. Fit the basket to the kettle. Use heavy-gauge kettles with good flat bottoms and of good heat-conducting material. The fat ratio to surface area should be large. If used over gas, do not allow flames to rise around the sides and set fire to the fat. Cool before removing the kettle from the stove.

Sautéing

Cooking food in a thin layer of fat to about ¼-inch deep is sautéing or frying and a frying or sauté pan or griddle is used. To pan-fry, select a

Table 12–3. Recommended Quantities of Fat for Sautéing

Pan Size (diameter in inches)	Uncovered Foods	Breaded or Batter-Covered Foods
8	3 T	⅓ c
9	¼ c	⅓ c
10	⅓ c	½ c
12	½ c	⅔ c

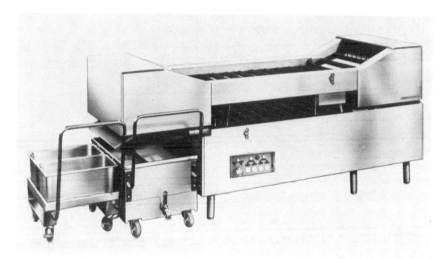

Figure 12–4. In quantity food preparation a larger deep-fryer such as this automatically moves items through the hot fat in the proper amount of time, dumping the cooked items into the carts shown on the left. (Courtesy Crescent Metal Products, Inc.)

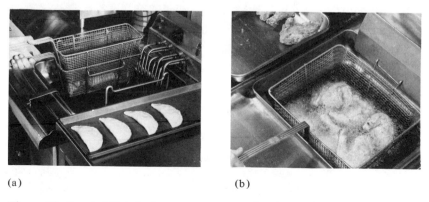

(a)   (b)

Figure 12–5. (a) Fried pies are a most popular dessert but good deep-frying techniques must be used to get a good product. (b) Deep-frying chicken. Note again the sharp, white bubbles of fat.

Figure 12–6. The liver floured in Figure 12–11(a) was sautéed in a thin layer of fat on a griddle.

low-edged heavy skillet or frying pan of good heat-conducting metal. Use a straight-edged pan either with or without a handle when foaming is a problem or when foods must be sautéed, covered and cooked, and use a slanted pan with a handle when foods must be manipulated with a spatula or other tools. Fit the pan to the quantity fried. Some pans for batch frying may be 12 to 14 inches or even larger in diameter. Small or thin items should be sautéed quickly to prevent drying them out. Put the food into hot fat, sliding it easily into the fat to prevent splashing. Cook to about half-done and turn. Add fat as required.

Thick foods may be sautéed or grilled, then finished in an oven or covered in a pan and cooked over low heat to complete cooking. Some added moisture may be needed. When large quantities of foods must be sautéed, prepare in this manner. Recrisp just before service by uncovering and drying out in a hot oven. If breaded or batter-covered foods or eggs are grilled, allow 3 to 4 ounces of oil per square foot of griddle. If the foods are not covered with batter or breading, use 2 to 3 ounces. Spread the oil lightly over the surface. Drizzle oil with an oil mop around the edges during frying on a griddle. Oil gives rapid heat conduction from the griddle to the food. Supply oil according to the fat content of the product. Bacon, unbreaded pork chops and other fatty foods will not require as much oil as leaner products.

Table 12-4.   Temperatures Recommended for Sautéing and Grilling

Item	Temperature °F	Approximate Cooking Time (min)
Hamburger, thin	340–350	5 to 8
Griddle cakes	350–360	3 to 4
Eggs, fried	300–325	3 to 4
Bacon, ham or sausages	325	4 to 5 (if thin)
Steak, $1/2$ in. thick	350	10 to 15 (well done)
Steak, 1 in. thick	340	10 to 15 (medium)
Steak, over 1 in. thick	330	10 to 15 (rare)
Pork or veal cutlets	325	6 to 8
Small fish or fillets	350	10 to 15
Small steaks or chops	340–350	10 to 15
Potatoes, hash brown or American fries	350–360	8 to 10
Toasted sandwiches	350	4 to 5
French toast	325–330	3 to 4

Table 12-5.   Problem, Causes, and Corrections in Pan and Griddle Sautéing

Problem	Cause	Correction
Food sticks	1. Not enough fat	Use more fat or oil
	2. Food too cold	Thaw or warm food slightly
	3. Surface needs conditioning	Condition with fat as directed above
	4. Surface too hot or cold	Adjust temperature
Food burns	1. Surface too hot	Adjust heat.
Food doesn't brown	1. Surface too cold	Adjust heat.
Spattering	1. Moist foods added to too hot fat	Drain moist foods thoroughly; reduce cooking temperature.
Foods not crisp	1. Food too cold	Warm food
	2. Insufficient fat	Add more fat
	3. Too low cooking temperature	Adjust heat

(Adapted from Procter and Gamble, *Proper Frying*)

Figure 12–7.   Lightly sautéing fish in butter gives a well browned, delicate product.

Figure 12–8. Sautéing cube steaks previous to braising them covered in an oven.

Preparation for Frying

Breading, batter-dipping or wrapping in dough may be preliminary treatments before frying. Excessive cover to extend a product is not condoned. Heavy covers can be tough and dark and separate easily from a product. Small items, such as shrimp, fishsticks and oysters should have a ratio of cover to product of not more than 1:2 while larger products such as veal cutlets and croquettes usually have a ratio of not more than 1:3 or 1:4. On the average, 100 pounds of batter or crumbs cover 200 to 400 pounds of food. Chicken and other similarly lightly breaded items should not increase in weight more than 10 to 15%. Dough-wrapped items should have a dough-product ratio of 1:1 or $1\frac{1}{2}$:1. High-moisture foods require a heavier and tighter cover than drier ones. Firmness is a factor, firmer foods requiring less cover. Plan good work centers and production centers for covering foods.

Breading usually has three steps: 1) flouring, 2) moistening and 3) crumbing. Paprika for color and seasonings for flavor may be added to the flour. Flour absorbs the moistening agent, setting up a good base for the adherence of the crumbs in the last step. Moisteners forming the strongest to least strong covers are eggs, eggs and liquid, evaporated milk, milk and other liquids. Moisteners containing milk give a less crisp crust than those made from water or eggs. The crumbs may be cracker, bread, other cereals or prepared mixes, and particle size should be even. Sift, if necessary to give uniformity. The finer the crumbs, the firmer will be the coating. Place products on a rack to dry at least 15 minutes before frying. If placed into pans, sprinkle a few crumbs on the bottom first to avoid bottom soaking. Prepared breadings contain monosodium glutamate and other seasonings plus substances to improve adherence. Operations making their own breadings can add these to their own. Consult a good food technologist on the substances to use.

Modify breadings to suit the food. Veal cutlets, oysters, tomatoes, eggplant, croquettes, partially cooked cauliflower and other products

Figure 12–9. Chicken dipped into batter and then sautéed in a liberal quantity of fat to give a product much like deep-fried chicken.

having some firmness may be breaded in a standard manner but some vegetables and other foods high in moisture may be best dipped in flour in the third step and not into crumbs. This gives less grease absorption but a product resembling a batter-dipped one. Some meat and fish may be covered only with flour, a process called *flouring*, and the method for frying is usually sautéing rather than deep-frying. If frozen breaded items are deep-fried, allow them to stand a short time at room temperature to thaw partially and then deep-fry as for any other breaded product.

The batter for batter-dipped items should be thick enough to adhere and give an adequate coating. Dipping the item into the batter and then holding it over the batter allows the excess to drop off. It then should be dropped easily into the hot fat without splashing. Dough-wrapped products should be tightly sealed in the dough so that the fat does not get into the product but cooks only the outside. In breaded, batter-dipped and dough-wrapped products, it is desirable to obtain a rapid coagulation of the outside surface so that fat does not penetrate.

Figure 12–10. Sautéing floured meat cubes in a steam-jacketed kettle previous to braising it.

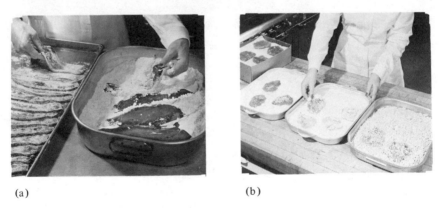

(a)   (b)

Figure 12–11. (a) Flouring liver previous to sautéing it. (b) The proper flow for breading is shown. The partially thawed veal cutlets are covered with flour and then dipped into the egg and milk and then into crumbs.

This is also true of egg-dipped items such as Monte Cristo sandwiches. The coating should cover all areas so that the coating cooks and protects the interior. Dough-wrapped products should be sealed in doughs less rich than pie dough but more so than biscuit dough. Since some fat enters into the product, about the desired richness is secured, as is also true for fried pies.

Dough-wrapped and breaded products can be placed into baskets and lowered into the fat but batter-dipped ones and pastes or batters such as crullers, fritters, etc., that are soft enough to stick to the basket should be dropped carefully into the hot fat after the basket has been lowered. The basket can then be raised later to remove the products when they are cooked. Sometimes, items must be turned in the hot fat. Placing a screen or another basket over these items so as to submerge them in the fat may make such turning unnecessary. Items should not be crowded in a basket, as while they may not stick together, crowding gives uneven and poor cooking results.

Suggested exercises or laboratory experiences for Chapter 12:

1. Heat some butter or olive oil until it smokes and take the temperature. Do the same for some good quality salad oil. Which would be preferable for deep-fat frying?
2. Sift flour into a small quantity of good quality salad oil and heat it. Take the temperature at which it smokes. Compare this temperature with the same quantity of salad oil without flour added to it.
3. Deep-fry and sauté various items to learn the proper technique for each.
4. Set up an assembly line for breading chicken, for flouring Swiss steaks.
5. Draw a carbon chain for a saturated fat, for an unsaturated fat and for a polyunsaturated fat. Indicate where the fat chain is weakest.

BIBLIOGRAPHY

Culinary Institute, *Professional Chef,* Cahners Books, Boston, 1964.

Lundberg, D. and Kotschevar, L., *Understanding Cooking,* Bookstore, U. of Mass., 1965.

Kotschevar, L. and McWilliams, M., *Understanding Food,* John Wiley & Sons, Inc., New York City, 1969.

Patrick, George, "The Fabulous Fry Kettle," *Food Service Magazine,* No. 10, October, 1957.

Proctor & Gamble Research Kitchens, *The Art of Preparing French Fried Potatoes,* 1950; *Deep Frying Pointers,* 1958; *Proper Frying,* n. d., Cincinnati, Ohio.

Ruffley, J. J., "How to Use Deep Fat Frying Effectively," *National Restaurant News,* August 1957.

13

Meat, Fish and Poultry

Meat is usually the main meal item and its selection dictates frequently the other foods in the meal. It is also the most costly item of the meal.

Acceptable meat is served if good meat is purchased and proper procedures followed. Escoffier thought a good meat cook could be trained with "application, observation, care and a little aptitude," evidently not agreeing with Brillat-Savarin who said, "Good roast cooks are born, not made."

Whether we develop meat cooks or depend upon the fortunes of birth may be an academic question because we are rapidly being introduced to a wide variety of meats that need not be cooked but only reheated for service. Under developing technology there are few meats cooked to doneness in a sauce that cannot be frozen and later reheated for service, and we are rapidly extending this knowledge to include meats cooked to almost any stage of doneness. As early as 1948 in submarine experiments, many precooked frozen meats such as chicken fricassee, beef stew, seafood Newburg, veal birds and rare sirloin roast were successfully used. Today this list has been widely extended. Items frozen in liquid have been more successful because oxidative and other deteriorative changes are less than those not in liquid. This is why many frozen vegetables are now offered in a sauce. We can obtain cooked roasts that need only thawing, slicing, warming in a stock or water seasoned with a gravy base to be an acceptable item. Today strip and

Figure 13–1.   Turkey Tetrazzini prepared from a precooked frozen item and served in attractive dishes is little different from a conventionally prepared item. (Courtesy Armour & Co.)

other steaks are seared in a broiler giving them the desired grid marks and then are blast frozen. These are placed frozen into baking pans, put into hot ovens, warmed and served as rare steaks. There is also an ever widening list of precooked meat-extender dishes and an increasing list of brown'n' serve items. Many find that precooked bacon is less costly and far easier to use than raw bacon strips.

In view of the pace of change, it might seem that a chapter on meat cookery should deal only with the reconditioning of meats received in a ready-to-serve condition, but this could not be done as too many still cook all or most of their meats from scratch. Also, to purchase or use these new meats, one must know the basic cooking principles for regular meats. Therefore, this chapter deals mostly with these basic requirements and little with the handling of new meat products, because these are usually well covered by manufacturer's directions and little would be gained by repeating all these instructions.

The flesh of animals, poultry and fish is very much alike and the principles dealing with their cooking are quite similar. Therefore, this chapter in the first part treats the flesh of these three as one. Only in the latter part is the cooking of each discussed separately.

PRINCIPLES

Composition

Meat is about 25% solids and 75% moisture. Of the solids, a fifth is fat, fat-like compounds, ash and other substances, and the rest is protein. Meat contains some sugar, glucose, which though small in quantity is quite important to color and flavor development in browning. Most of the protein, moisture, ash, vitamins and other compounds is found in the flesh.

While some meat proteins are soluble in cold water, heat coagulates most, making them insoluble. Fat is found 1) emulsified in fiber liquids, 2) as marbling and 3) as finish. As animals fatten, fat as finish forms first around the vital organs and then over the interior and exterior surfaces. As fat increases, finish spreads over the body and the quantity of flesh marbling and emulsified fat in the juices increases. Young and old animals have less fat than middle-aged ones. Body fat contains from 15 to 50% moisture, which keeps meat from drying out in cooking. Roasts are cooked fat side up and poultry with its fat back up so that the fat and its moisture run down and keep the meat moist. Meat is larded or pieces of fatty tissue are laid over it (barded) to give moisture in cooking. Marbling contributes to tenderness by separating meat tissues. Fatty tissue is more tender when hot.

Structure

Lean meat is made up of tube-like rods or fibers tapered on both ends. They measure in diameter from 1/200 to 1/1100 inch and may be up to two inches long. These can be seen as strings or shreds when well done chicken breast, boiled short ribs or beef or other meat is pulled apart. A fiber is actually a cell with many nuclei. The cell is filled with a liquid containing proteins, emulsified fat, fat-like substances, minerals, vitamins and other compounds.

The fibers are bound together by connective tissue in bundles like straws in a broom and this spreads like a network around the fibers, holding them in place. Tendrils of connective tissue even enter into the fibers. A heavier mass of connective tissue surrounds each bundle of fibers, binding bundles together to make a muscle. At the end of each muscle, long ends of the connective tissue join to form a tendonous mass attached to a bone.

The muscle fiber size has much to do with the grain or texture of the meat. Fine fibers indicate a fine, smooth texture and a tender meat. Buyers look for the velvety, smooth, soft surface indicating fine grain. The surface should also have a soft, moist sheen and show marbling.

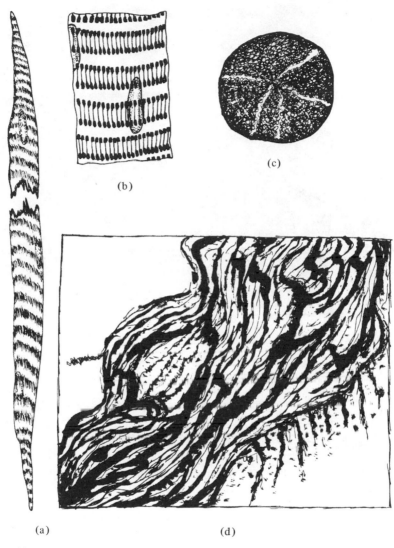

Figure 13–2. Meat fibers. (a) Long, tapered, tube-like muscle fiber. (b) Close-up of section. (c) Cross-section of fiber. (d) Dark areas show connective tissue in meat tissue.

Young animals, males castrated when young and females have finer-grained flesh than mature males or stags. The outer sheath or membrane strength of fibers also affects tenderness. Exercised muscles develop stronger sheaths and more connective tissue than those receiving less exercise. Feed, care and breed also affect tenderness but it varies much among animals of the same kind and breed.

The type and quantities of connective tissue in meat also affect

Figure 13–3. Fine quality is indicated in this roast beef. The moist, shiny surface, glittering fat and fine texture indicate fine eating quality. (Courtesy Armour & Co.)

tenderness. There are two kinds of connective tissue: white (collagen) and yellow (elastin). Collagen is changed into gelatin and water by moist heat. The cooking time, amount and thickness of collagen affect the speed and amount of breakdown. Acids speed the change but normally food acids are not strong enough to make much difference. Marinating meat in an acid solution tenderizes and adds moisture. Elastin is not changed by cooking. To make it tender, it is broken up by mechanical treatment such as grinding, pounding or cubing.

Flesh toughens as an animal ages. Some increase in the connective tissue may cause this, but it is more probable that the type of the connective tissue changes with age. Usually muscles exercised a lot contain higher quantities of connective tissue, especially elastin, than those exercised less.

Meat is tenderized by solutions containing enzymes, usually papain, which digests connective tissue. Injection of a tenderizer just before slaughter provides wide distribution throughout the capillary system, giving better tenderization over coating or spraying the meat with tenderizer after slaughter.

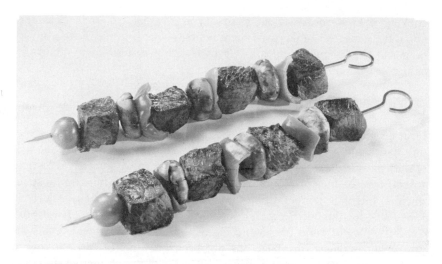

Figure 13–4. Small items like this shish-kabob should be broiled at a higher temperature than larger items by placing them closer to the heat. (Courtesy Armour & Co.)

Ripening

Rigor mortis is a muscle stiffening appearing after death. Cooking meat while rigor is present gives a tough meat. Such meat is called "green." Rigor disappears after 3 or 4 days and the meat is more tender. Since most meat takes about seven days to go through marketing channels, few are troubled with green meat. Pork develops little rigor, while chickens develop and lose it quickly.

Ripening or aging is holding meat at temperatures between 35° and 40° F under controlled humidity. This is called dry aging. Beef, lamb and mutton are aged but pork and veal seldom are. Aging increases the flavor, tenderness and moistness. After 21 days meat ages little. Molds and bacteria in aging grow with some difficulty in fat but more easily in flesh and so a good fat coverage is required to dry age meat. This protects it from mold, bacteria, surface darkening and drying out. Aging, because of a loss in weight, cost of storage and refrigeration, tie-up of money and trim, increases cost. Game is frequently aged and this may proceed almost to the point of putrefaction as in game birds. Cryovac aging, a process in which meat is placed into a moisture-vapor-proof wrap, air exhausted and the pack held under refrigeration, is more common today than dry aging. Cryovac-aged meat need not have the finish it must for dry aging because there is little or no mold or bacterial growth. It may be quite moist from juices exuded during curing but in cooking it loses more weight than dry-aged meat, so final yields are about the same. When Cryovac meat is first opened, it may have a musty odor but this soon disappears. Cryovac aging is less costly than dry aging.

Cooking

Heat coagulates meat proteins at from 160° to 175° F, changing color and flavor and giving firmness. Just before coagulation, denaturation or loss of moisture occurs around 140° F. Shrinkage loss varies according to cut, type of meat, amount of fat and other factors but the most influential factor is temperature. Minimum cooking shrinkage is beef rib rare 10%, medium 15%, well done 25%; baked ham 15%; fresh pork loin 40%; leg of lamb 25%, and leg of veal 30%. That heat "seals the pores" and reduces shrinkage has not been proven. Rather, cooking at high temperatures increases shrinkage. Searing at a high temperature and cooking at a low temperature increases shrinkage over cooking at a constant low temperature, but it may be done anyway to develop a caramelized outer surface and improve aroma. A constant low cooking temperature saves labor and fuel and reduces spattering and burning. Salt delays browning and since its penetration is small — from half to quarter inch — it is frequently omitted until just before serving. Excess cooking can dry meat out and toughen it.

Color

Meat's red color is from myoglobin pigments and some red blood corpuscles. Intensity of redness is governed by the quantity of myoglobin. Milk–fed hogs, calves or chickens have a light-colored flesh lacking myoglobin. Fish flesh has little myoglobin. Acid darkens the pigment, so ripened meat because of increased acidity is darker than fresh. Oxygen forms oxymyoglobin, a bright red pigment. Heat turns myoglobin to hematin, a gray or grayish-brown substance. Cured meats are red after cooking because the myoglobin combines with the nitrogen of the curing salts to form nitrosomyoglobin, a heat stable pigment. Meat can pick up traces of curing salts from meat blocks or cutting equipment which may cause them to be red after cooking. Onions dehydrated in nitrogen gas give a red, uncooked appearance to cooked meat loaf. Sometimes ground·meat patties, presalted and frozen, are a red color after cooking. The reason for this is not known but meat processors advise that the patties should not be salted if they are to be frozen.

Flavor

At one time, nitrogenous, non-nitrogenous extractives and waste metabolic products were thought to be the primary flavor factors in meat. While a part is contributed by these and by sweet, salt, acid and bitter components, much flavor comes from the fat. Cooking also develops flavor, amino acids breaking down into flavorful products, free fatty acids and carbonyl fractions increasing and causing the rich aroma of cooking meat. Flavor develops in cooking up to three hours and then declines.

The diet of the animal affects meat's flavor. A milk-mash diet for chickens gives a milder flavored flesh than that of barnyard fowl. Cattle fattened on distiller's mash have a sharply acid, fermented-flavored meat. Good care and environment give mild-flavored flesh, while animals that must withstand the rigors of climate and are poorly fed and housed have a strongly flavored flesh. The marine diet and iodine content of fishes' surroundings make them "fishy." Breed, sex and age affect flavor. The meat of males, unless castrated when young, is stronger than that of females and the flesh of young animals is milder than that of older ones. Meat after cooking has a characteristic sulfurous flavor which varies in intensity according to kind, diet, degree of cooking and other factors. Muscles of the same animal may differ in flavor as between the leg and breast of a chicken. Poultry is especially acid and astringent, turkey having an almost pungent flavor. Pork is sweeter but more acid and sulfurous than beef. Lamb and mutton are more alkaline than beef or pork and have a strong flavor associated with caproic, caprylic and pelagonic compounds. Meat flavor may be heightened by the use of hydrolyzed proteins such as monosodium glutamate (MSG) or related compounds. When MSG is used alone, the flavor is not that of meat but when combined with meat flavors, the meat flavor is heightened.

Doneness

Meat is cooked to make it more palatable and perhaps more digestible. When tenderness must be developed moist heat is used. Dry heat seldom tenderizes meat and overcooking with dry heat toughens flesh. High temperatures toughen more than low temperatures. Extended cooking also toughens meat and many shellfish toughen with extended cooking even with moisture. Cooked to the same internal temperature, simmered (195° F) fowl is tenderer than fowl cooked under 15 psi of steam (250° F). Doneness can be judged by outside and inside appearance.

The surest way is by thermometer, although it is difficult to use a thermometer in small pieces of meat, such as chops or steaks. There are six stages of doneness:

Very rare	The meat has only a thin portion of cooked meat. around the edge; red, almost bloody juices exude. Under finger pressure, the meat is soft and jelly-like inside.
Rare	The raw, red portion is smaller and the meat around it is pink; there is a good brown outer surface. There is a full, plump appearance and still some give to pressure. The juices are red but not bloody.
Medium rare	The interior is a rich pink. The meat is still plump; the juices are pink. Firmness to touch is more apparent; the amount of gray outer surface has increased.
Medium	The interior color is a modified rose. Pink juices are apparent but less. The exterior is well browned. The surface does not appear as plump or full. When pressed, there is definite resistance.
Medium well	The pink color has all disappeared. Juiciness is still evident but the juices are clear or gray, not pink. There is no plumpness; the meat is firm to touch.
Well	The meat is completely gray inside. Little or no juice appears. The meat has a hard, flinty touch and a shrunken appearance. The surface is brown and dry.

Temperatures indicating doneness are:

Beef	*Rare 140° F, medium 160° F, and well 170° F*
Lamb	*Medium 165° F, well 175° F*
Pork, fresh	*Well 165° to 175° F (always cook pork well; note that temperatures recommended for doneness in pork have been lowered)*
Pork, cured	*Well 155° F*
Poultry	*Well 180° F, medium 165° F*
Veal	*Well 170° F*

Aged beef at 140° F may appear medium rather than rare because the increase in acid causes myoglobin to change to hematin at a lower temperature. Large meat pieces increase internal temperature after cooking and items such as rib roasts to be rare or medium should be cooked from 15 to 25° F lower than needed at service. Time of cooking varies for doneness. Meat at room temperature cooks more rapidly than chilled meat. Cooking times for frozen meat are 2 to 3 times those of refrigerated meat. As cooking temperature increases, time is decreased but high temperatures increase shrinkage and reduce appearance, juiciness, tenderness and flavor. Usually the larger the cut, the longer the cooking time but a flat roast or meat with a large surface area cooks in less time than a more compact one of equal weight. Boned meats take longer to cook than unboned ones. Fat can act as an insulator against heat penetration and so meat with a fat cover may take longer to cook. Using aluminum foil increases shrinkage and cooking time and there is also a loss of flavor. To cook meat by the pound, calculate time by the piece and not the entire pan contents; e. g., a roast pan containing six 7-pound roasts should be timed for seven pounds not 42 pounds.

STANDARDS

It is difficult to give one standard for cooked meat because of the wide variety of meats and the many ways of cooking them. Standards for poultry, fish and shellfish will differ somewhat from those given here but not too much.

All meat should be of good flavor and pleasing appearance and drippings should be rich and of good color. The texture should be moist, not dry or crumbly with firmness consistent with doneness. It should be tender and not pulpy, stringy or excessively soft, greasy or oily. The color should be natural to the meat, cooking and degree of doneness, with no burned portions nor any burned taste. Roasts should be well browned. Veal roasts should have a reddish brown and roast pork a uniformly rich brown surface. The skin of roasted poultry and the outer surface of lamb and pork roasts should be crisp, not dry or tough. Sliced meat should be firm, juicy and tender and hold its shape. Broiled exteriors should be evenly browned, juicy and glossy in appearance. Bacon should be crisp but not brittle. Browned meats should have a rich brown color with a well-developed flavor and aroma. Braised meat should be tender and juicy, not stringy, and should hold its shape and not fall apart. A rich gloss should appear on the meat surface. Pieces should be uniform, even, symmetrical and attractive. Unbrowned meat

Table 13-1. Cuts of Meat and Recommended Methods of Cooking

BEEF	LAMB	FRESH PORK	SMOKED	VEAL	VARIETY MEATS
ROASTING					
Rib Sirloin butt Loin strip Tenderloin Rump butt* Round* Inside (top) round* Outside (bottom) round* Knuckle (tip)* Inside chuck* Shoulder clod* Loaf (ground beef)	Leg Loin Rack Rolled shoulder Cushion shoulder Loaf (ground lamb)	Ham (leg) Loin Boston butt Picnic Rolled shoulder Cushion shoulder Spareribs	Ham Picnic Shoulder butt Canadian-style bacon Loaf (ground ham)	Leg (round) Loin Rib Rolled shoulder Loaf (ground veal)	Liver
BROILING, GRIDDLE-BROILING, OR PAN-BROILING					
Rib steak Club steak T-bone steak Porterhouse steak Sirloin steak (cut from loin strip) Butt steak Tip steak (knuckle) Inside chuck steak* Top round steak* Beef patties (hamburger) Flank*	Shoulder chops Rib chops Loin chops Leg steaks Lamb patties (ground lamb)	Fresh pork is not broiled or griddle-broiled.	Sliced ham Sliced bacon Sliced Canadian-style bacon Shoulder butt	Veal is not broiled unless it is fairly mature and well-fatted, and then only loin chops or steaks.	Sliced veal or lamb liver Lamb kidneys Brains Sweetbreads

*Usually only prime to choice quality in these should be cooked in this manner.

BRAISING

Chuck (all cuts)	Chops	Breast	Breast	Heart, all kinds
Brisket	Loin	Neck	Chops	Liver
Plate	Rib	Shank	Loin	Beef
Flank	Shoulder	Shoulder	Rib	Pork
Neck	Feet		Shoulder	Kidneys
Outside (bottom) round	Hocks		Cutlets (leg)	Tripe
Heel of round	Spareribs		Neck	
Rump butt	Fresh ham steaks		Shoulder	
Shank	Tenderloin		Shank	
Short ribs				
Skirt steak				
Ox tails (joints)				

SIMMERING

Fresh	Spareribs	Neck	Neck	Kidney
Chuck (all cuts)	Backbones	Breast	Shank	Heart
Rump butt	Pigs feet	Flank	Breast	Tongue
Shank	Hocks	Shanks	Flank	For pre-cooking:
Heel of round		(Large cuts of	(Large cuts of veal	Brains
Brisket	Ham	lamb are usually	are usually not	Sweetbreads
Plate	Shoulder	not cooked in	cooked in water.)	
Flank	Picnic	water)		
Short ribs	Shoulder butt			
Corned	Hocks			
Brisket				
Rump				
Plate				
Round				

(Adapted from *Cooking Meat in Quantity*, National Livestock and Meat Board)

lacks the color and characteristic flavor developed by browning but otherwise it has similar qualities.

COOKING TECHNIQUES

Meat's tenderness largely dictates how it should be cooked. Tender cuts are usually cooked by dry heat and tough cuts by moist heat. Some tough cuts may be treated mechanically or with tenderizers to make them tender and then be cooked by dry-heat methods.

Dry heat methods are:
1. Broiling, pan broiling or griddle broiling.
2. Roasting or baking.
3. Barbecueing
4. Sautéing, pan-frying or grilling.
5. Deep-frying.
6. Ovenizing.

Moist heat methods are:
1. Braising (pot-roasting, fricasseeing, casseroling, swissing or stewing.)
2. Simmering (poaching and stewing; few meats, if any, are boiled.)
3. Steaming.
4. Blanching.

Work areas for cooking meats must be well planned. Broiling, sautéing and deep-frying require fast production. Equipment should be adapted to needs and flow of work with proper working space and landing areas provided. Small tools and materials, such as tongs, forks, knives, salt, pepper, oil, oil mop and cloths, should be located within easy reach and work motions observed. Refrigerated storage should be provided for perishable foods in the work area.

Broiling

Cooking by radiant heat is called *broiling*. *Grilling* at one time meant broiling but the term is now used to indicate sautéing or frying. Broiling temperatures are slightly higher than those used for roasting. Temperature is governed by the cut, type of meat and size of piece. Meat of low fat content or small pieces are cooked at higher temperatures to shorten cooking time and reduce chances for drying out. Thin pork chops or

Figure 13–5.   A tenderloin butt broiled and then planked. After being placed under the broiler, it is sent to service.

steaks, bacon or other thin units are cooked within 2 to 3 inches of the heat, while thick turkey breasts, chateaubriands and other pieces may be cooked 8 inches or more from it. Some larger pieces may be scored to aid heat penetration and putting metal skewers into meat speeds cooking in broiling and roasting. High temperatures develop a hard, dry crust which slows heat penetration, giving a charred outside and an undercooked inside. Very thick pieces may be broiled 5 to 8 minutes to a side and then completed in a 350° oven.

Broiled meat, poultry or fish may be planked. The item is broiled to almost doneness and placed in the center of a heated oak plank about two inches thick. A border of duchess potatoes is piped around the edge; the open spaces are filled with various hot cooked vegetables and the whole is garnished with broiled mushrooms or other items. The plank is put into a hot oven or under a broiler to warm and brown and sent to service after being drizzled liberally with melted butter. (See Figure 13-5).

Meat to be broiled can be dipped into vegetable oil, held over the oil pan a moment to drain and then placed onto the grid. Press gently onto the grid to give good contact and cook to half-doneness (100° F for rare to medium and 135° F for medium to well done). Turn and

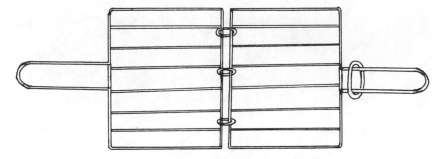

Figure 13–6. A double grid used to hold fish and other items under the broiler, a device which makes it possible to turn these items without breaking them.

season with salt—salting earlier retards browning. For large pieces, four turns may be needed and seasoning is done on the third and fourth turns. Items turned once show single grid marks (////) while those turned twice show crisscross grid marks (✕✕✕✕), achieved by making a 90° turn on successive turns. Press meat gently onto the grid each time it is turned. Edges of some foods may have to be scored (cut) to prevent curling. Meats, poultry and fish of low fat content are difficult to broil satisfactorily but if dipped in flour and then in oil and placed in a double grid to hold them firmly in place, they can be slow-broiled, basted with oil to assist in retaining moistness and give a better product.

Do not allow drippings to flame. The sooty smoke and off-flavors can ruin the meat. Grease fires may also start. Have at hand a bottle of cold water with a perforated top, a syringe of cold water or a small container of cold water containing chipped ice. Rotating horizontal spits should revolve up and over toward the worker to keep drip as much as possible over the meat.

Small pieces of meat, extremely tender flesh such as fish, or breaded foods which might stick to a grid or break in turning may be placed into a well-oiled double grid that folds like an old-fashioned toaster. (See Figure 13-6)

When many items are broiled at one time, such as for a banquet, have the broiler at the correct temperature but the grid closer to the meat. Broil only to proper color; remove, placing the items into pans. Just before service finish in a 350° to 400° F oven. To prepare lobsters in this manner, broil to a desired color, set into pans and place a weight on the tails to prevent them from turning up and charring in the oven during reheating.

(a)   (b)

Figure 13–7. (a) Dip items to be broiled into oil before placing on the grid. (b) Grid markings on these steaks indicate that they have been turned only once. (Courtesy Armour & Co.)

Table 13-2. Timetable for Broiling

Cut	Approximate Thickness	Approximate Rare	Cooking Time (minutes) Medium	Well-done
Broiler (Charcoal, Gas or Electric)*				
Rib, club, T-bone, porterhouse,	1 in	15	20	30
tenderloin or individual serv-	1½ in	25	35	
ings of sirloin beef steak	2 in	35	50	
Sirloin beef steak (whole steak)	1 in	20 to 30	30 to 40	
	1½ in	30 to 40	40 to 50	
	2 in	40 to 55	50 to 65	
Ground beef patties	1 in (4 oz)	15	20	
Shoulder, rib, loin and sirloin	1 in		12 to 15	16 to 18
lamb chops or steaks	1½ in		17 to 20	
	2 in		20 to 25	25 to 30
Ground lamb patties	1 in (4 oz)		16 to 18	
Smoked ham slice	½ in			10 to 12
	1 in			16 to 20
Bacon, Griddle or Pan Broiling				4 to 5
Individual servings of beef steaks	¾ in	4	8	12
	1 in	6	10	15
	1½ in	10 to 12	15 to 18	20
Ground beef patties	¾ in	4 to 5	8 to 10	12
	1 in (4 oz)	6 to 8	10 to 12	15
Lamb chops	1 in		10	15
	1½ in		15	20 to 25
Ground lamb patties	¾ in		10	12 to 15
	1 in (4 oz)		10 to 15	15 to 20
Smoked ham slice	½ in			6 to 10
Bacon				2 to 3

*There are automatic speed broilers which cook both sides of the meat at once and may, therefore, decrease the time to half or even a third of that given for broilers heating only from one side.

Courtesy, National Livestock and Meat Board.

Pan-broiling or Griddle-broiling

Pan-broil in fairly heavy skillets or, if there must be heavy production, on griddles. Select pans suited to the quality so that drippings do not burn. Rub the pan bottom lightly with fat. Preheat. Cook the meat on one side and then on the other turning as often as necessary to insure even cooking. Pour off the fat as it gathers. Do not cover or add water. Pan-broil only meats high in fat. To griddle-broil, place the item onto a 325° F griddle and cook without the addition of fat. Pan-broiled or griddle-broiled foods resemble sautéed foods rather than broiled ones.

Roasting

Meat for roasting should cover the pan and not leave space for drippings to burn. Sometimes a trivet or perforated underliner is put on the bottom to keep the meat from resting in its own juices and fat. The trivet is omitted for some meats such as leg of veal or where it is desirable to turn the meat in its own juices as it roasts. Some chefs add roughly chopped vegetables at the start of roasting. Salt is not added until browning is completed. Never pierce lean flesh in turning a roast or broiled item but insert the fork into fatty tissues or merely roll with a fork. Use no liquid and do not cover except for fish and a few other items requiring it. Place meat fat side up and poultry breast down. Meat lacking fatty tissue may have to be basted, larded or barded. To minimize drying out, roast small pieces at higher temperatures. In roasting

(a)   (b)

Figure 13–8.   (a) Barding is a way in which fat can be used to keep meat moist. These lean tenderloins are being treated in this manner. Larding is similar to barding except that strips of fat are pulled through the meat. (b) Set the thermometer in the center of the muscle as shown for recording the roasting temperature.

 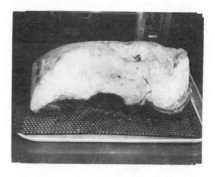

(a)   (b)

Figure 13–9. (a) The wrong way to roast a piece of meat since the fatty side does not get a chance to drip over the meat and keep it moist. (b) The right way.

batches, select the smallest piece in the lot and insert a thermometer in the center of the largest muscle. When the proper internal temperature is reached, remove the thermometer and meat. Insert the thermometer now into the next smallest piece until it is done. Continue until all pieces are done. To roast meat, place it into a pre-heated 300° F oven. Maintain this temperature throughout or preheat to 475° F and sear until well browned, then drop the temperature to 300° F to complete roasting. Gentle roasting gives more flavorful, tender meat.

En papillote means to wrap in paper and roast; this is most frequently done with fish or chicken. Cured meats may require soaking or parboiling before roasting. Follow manufacturers' directions. Do not sear cured ham.

If thermometers are not available, test doneness with the thumb or forefinger. Experience is required for this and even experts are some times fooled. Allow roasts to stand from 30 minutes to an hour before carving. Remember internal temperatures go 15° to 25° F higher as a roast stands. Hold rare or medium roasts at gentle heat to avoid further cooking. To carve, cut against the grain in thin slices. Serve at once. Machine-slicing gives, on the average, more portions per pound than hand-slicing.

Delayed service cookery is a method of roasting meat and poultry so that it can be prepared ahead and held for later service. The items are roasted in a regular 325° F oven until about 125° F (poultry about 140° F) and the product is removed and put into a holding oven that does not vary + or − more than 5° F from 140° F. Items can be held in such an oven for 48 hours or more without a quality loss. Shrinkage

Table 13–3.   Time and Temperatures for Roasting Meats

Cut	Approx. Wt. of Single Roast	No. of Roasts in Oven	Approx. Total Wt. of Roasts in Oven	Oven Temperature (F)	Interior Temperature of Roast When Removed from Oven (F)	Minutes per lb Based on One Roast	Minutes per lb Based on Total Wt. of Roasts in Oven	Approx. Total Time Roasting
	lb		lb					
BEEF								
Standing rib (7-rib)	20 to 25	1		250°	125° (rare) / 140° (medium) / 150° (well)	13 / 15 / 17		4½ hr / 5 hr / 6 hr
Standing rib (7-rib)	23	1		300°	125° (rare) / 140° (medium) / 150° (well)	11 / 12 / 13		4 hr / 4½ hr / 5 hr
Rolled rib (7-rib)	16 to 18	1		250°	150° (well)	26		7 to 8 hr
Rolled rib (7-rib)	17	1		300°	150° (well)	24		6 hr
Standing rib (7-rib)		2	56	300°	140° (medium) / 160° (well)		6 / 7 to 8	6 hr / 7 hr
Chuck rib	5 to 8	1		300°	150° to 170°	25 to 30		2½ to 4 hr
Rump	5 to 7	1		300°	150° to 170°	25 to 30		2½ to 3½ hr
Round (rump and shank off)	50	1		250°	140° (medium) / 154° (well)	12 / 14		10 hr / 11 to 12 hr
LAMB								
Leg	6 to 7	2	16	300°	180°		15	4 hr
Cushion shoulder (with stuffing)	4½ to 5½	1		300°	180°	30 to 35		2 to 3 hr

Cut	Weight, lb			Oven temp.	Interior temp.	Min. per lb.		Time
Rolled shoulder	3 to 4	1		300°	180°	40 to 45		2½ to 3 hr
Rolled shoulder		5	29	300°	180°		10	5 hr
Square cut shoulder		8	40	300°	180°		7	4 to 5 hr
FRESH PORK								
Loin (bone in)	12 to 15	1		300°	185°	16		3 to 4 hr
Loin (bone in)	11 to 15	1		350°	185°	15 to 18		3 to 3½ hr
Rolled loin (two halves tied together)		3	21	300°	185°		14	5 hr
Rolled loin (two halves tied together)		3	23	350°	185°		11	4 hr
Half loin (bone in)		6	33	300°	185°		11	6 hr
Half loin (bone in)		6	33	350°	185°		8	4½ hr
Center cut loin	3 to 4	1		350°	185°	35 to 40		2 to 2½ hr
End cut loin	3 to 4	1		350°	185°	45 to 50		2½ to 3 hr
Shoulder	12 to 14	1		350°	185°	30 to 35		6½ hr
Cushion shoulder (with stuffing)	4 to 6	1		350°	185°	35 to 40		3 to 3½ hr
Cushion shoulder (with stuffing)		3	30	350°	185°		9	4½ to 5 hr
Rolled shoulder	4 to 6	1		350°	185°	35 to 40		3 to 3½ hr
Boston Butt	4 to 6	1		350°	185°	45 to 50		3½ to 4½ hr
Ham (leg)	15	1		300°	185°	30		8 hr
Ham (leg)	10 to 12	1		350°	185°	30 to 35		6 hr
Ham (leg)		3	34	300°	185°		10 to 12	6 to 7 hr
Ham (leg)		3	38	350°	185°		10	6 to 6½ hr
Ham (leg) boned, split, and tied in two rolls	10 to 12	1		350°	185°	30 to 35		5 to 7 hr

(continued)

Table 13-3. (continued)

Cut	Approx. Wt. of Single Roast	No. of Roasts in Oven	Approx. Total Wt. of Roasts in Oven	Oven Temperature (F)	Interior Temperature of Roast When Removed from Oven (F)	Minutes per lb Based on One Roast	Minutes per lb Based on Total Wt. of Roasts in Oven	Approx. Total Time Roasting
Ham (leg) boned, split, and tied in two rolls	10	1		350°	185°	20 to 25		4 to 5 hr
SMOKED PORK								
Whole ham	10 to 14	1		300°	160°	15 to 18		3 to 3½ hr
Half ham	6 to 10	1		300°	160°	20		2 to 3½ hr
Ham, sweet pickled	16	1		350°	170°	15		4 hr
Shoulder butt	2 to 4	1		300°	170°	30 to 35		1 to 2 hr
Picnic	3 to 10	1		300°	170°	30 to 35		2 to 5 hr
Canadian-style bacon (casing on)	7	1		350°	160°	10 to 12		1 to 1½ hr
Canadian-style bacon (casing on)		3	19	300°	160°		5	1½ to 2 hr
VEAL								
Leg	7 to 8	1		300°	170°	25		3 to 3½ hr
Leg	16	1		300°	170°	22		6 hr
Leg	23	1		300°	170°	18 to 20		7 to 7½ hr
Loin	4½ to 5	1		300°	170°	30 to 35		2½ to 3 hr
Rack (4 to 6 ribs)	2½ to 3	1		300°	170°	30 to 35		1½ hr
Shoulder	7	1		300°	170°	25		3 hr
Shoulder	12 to 13	1		300°	170°	25		5 to 5½ hr

Cushion shoulder (with stuffing)	9 to 10	1		300°	170°	30 to 35		5 to 5½ hr
Cushion shoulder (with stuffing)		3	24	300°	170°		10 to 12	4 to 5 hr
Rolled shoulder	5	1		300°	170°	40 to 45		3½ to 4 hr
Rolled shoulder		3	20	300°	170°		14	5 hr
Rolled shoulder	9 to 10	1		300°	170°	35 to 40		6 to 7 hr
Round (rump and shank off)	20	1		300°	170°	20		6½ hr

(Adapted from National Livestock & Meat Board)

is minimized and flavor, tenderness, juiciness and evenness of cooking is increased. If desired, the meat can be browned in a hotter oven and the temperature dropped. Ground meats should not be handled in such an oven since the temperature is not high enough to destroy all bacteria. If the product is wrapped in aluminum foil, bright side out, it holds better. (See Figure 13-12).

Barbecueing

Broiled or roasted meat basted with a tangy sauce and meats cooked on a spit or rotisserie before an open fire or cooked in a covered pit are called barbecued. All are served with a tangy barbecue sauce.

Frying

Cooking meat in a thin layer of fat is sautéing or grilling. Cooking meat immersed in deep fat is called deep-fat frying. Both may be called frying. These two procedures are highly specialized and are applied to not only meats, fish and poultry but other foods, and therefore have been discussed in Chapter 12.

Ovenizing

The term *ovenizing* was coined to describe a process in which meats are baked by being placed onto well greased baking sheets or pans and then put into an oven so that they fry or sauté. Breaded foods require a high amount of fat when cooked in this manner and usually have fat drizzled over them in addition to the pan greasing. In total, the quantity of fat required is less with this method than with sautéing. Temperatures from 325° to 425° F are applied. Smaller foods are ovenized at higher temperatures than larger ones. Ovenizing is used to process greater quantities than can be prepared by sautéing.

Braising

Meat cooked in its own juices or in a bit of added moisture is braised. Stewing, pot roasting, fricasseeing and Swissing are forms of braising. Stewing or simmering differs from braising in that a larger quantity of moisture is used. Braisers or casseroles with straight sides about 6 to 8 inches high are used for small quantities but when large quantities are prepared, roasting pans, large pots or steam-jacketed kettles are used. Marinating may occur before braising such as the several-day marinade

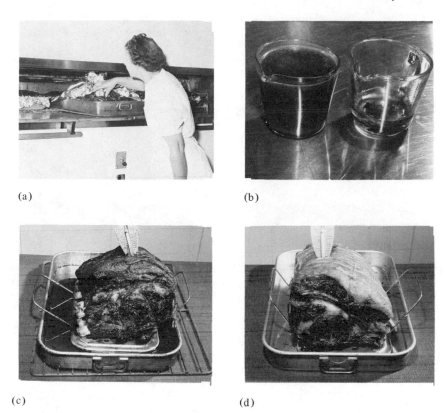

(a)   (b)

(c)   (d)

Figure 13–10. (a) Meats being braised under cover with a thermometer used to record doneness. (b) The drip obtained respectively from roasts (c) and (d) below. (c) A prime rib cooked at 400° F and (d) one cooked at 325° F.

used for *sauerbraten.* Lean meat may be blended with some fat to give moistness or it may be larded. If meat is unbrowned, the item is called "blond" or "white" such as a blond stew or white fricassee. Braised meats are usually served with vegetables, and if served without them in an earthenware casserole, they are *en casserole,* if with vegetables *en cocotte. Jugged* means braised, as in "jugged hare" To *poëler* means to brown well and then braise in juices while basting with butter. Poëlering temperatures are high; the process is partly roasting, partly sautéing and partly braising and is good for tender, young meats.

The size of braised meat may be for pot roasts, Swiss steak, inch cubes or hamburger. Poultry is portioned to be served as cooked. Often before braising, the meat is floured especially if browning is to follow.

(a)

(b)

(c)

(d)

Figure 13–11. (a) Barbecue pits ready to receive the wood for the fire. The cover is later returned and covered with gravel to seal in the heat. (b) The pits blazing at night previous to the next day's barbecue. The meat wrapped in foil is shown set beside each pit. (c) Throwing a layer of pea-sized gravel over the hot coals previous to adding the meat. (d) Dropping a layer of meat on the gravel.

Fill the pan or container well with meat so it builds moisture around it. Browning can be done over direct heat, in an oven or in a steam-jacketed kettle. Add fat to cover the pan bottom about ⅛-inch or more deep, bring to about 350° F and add the meat. Turn until the meat is richly browned. Add moisture such as water, stock, milk, tomato juice, wine or sour cream, or cover tightly and allow the meat to build up its own moisture. Diced or minced vegetables may be added for flavoring during browning. After browning, simmer the meat until tender. If vegetables are in the dish, they are usually added later in cooking to avoid overcooking. They may be cooked separately in stock and added with the meat at service. When the meat is tender, the cover may be removed and the liquid reduced until the sauce is at the desired

Table 13–4. Timetable for Braising

Cut	Average Weight or Thicknes	Approximate Cooking Time
Pot roast	3 to 5 lb	3 to 4 hr
Pot roast	5 to 15 lb	3 to 5 hr
Swiss steak	1 to 2½ in.	2 to 3 hr
Round steak or flank steak	½ in. (pounded)	45 min to 1 hr
Stuffed steak	½ to ¾ in	1½ hr
Short ribs	Pieces 2 x 2 x 2 in.	1½ to 2 hr
Fricassee	1 to 2 in. pieces	2 to 3 hr
Beef birds	½ x 2 x 4 in.	1½ to 2 hr
Stuffed lamb breast	2 to 3 lb	1½ to 2 hr
Rolled lamb breast	1½ to 2 lb	1½ to 2 hr
Lamb shanks	½ lb each	1 to 1½ hr
Lamb neck slices	½ to ¾ in.	1 to 1½ hr
Lamb riblets	¾ x 2½ x 3 in.	2 to 2½ hr
Pork chops or steaks	¾ to 1 in.	45 min to 1 hr
Spareribs	2 to 3 lb	1½ hr
Stuffed veal breast	3 to 4 lb	1½ to 2 hr
Rolled veal breast	2 to 3 lb	2 to 3 hr
Veal cutlets	½ x 3 x 5½ in.	45 min to 1 hr
Veal steaks or chops	½ to ¾ in.	45 min to 1 hr
Veal birds	½ x 2 x 4 in.	45 min to 1 hr

(Courtesy National Livestock and Meat Board)

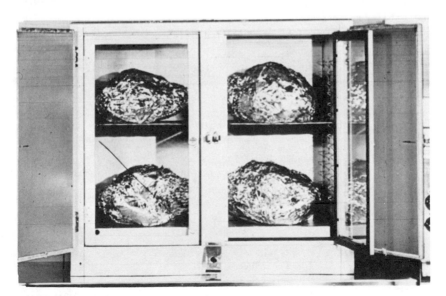

Figure 13–12. Meat after being roasted to a rare stage being held in a 140° F constant-degree oven in delayed service cookery.

consistency. If necessary, remove the meat, thicken the sauce and return the meat to the gravy.

Meats and poultry in quantity are best braised in a shallow steam-jacketed kettle. Heat the kettle, cover down with steam on full, add some melted fat and drop in even-sized pieces of meat. Pot roasts should be evenly sized between 5 to 10 pounds. Turn the meat every 15 to 25 minutes until all sides are well browned. Do not cover and keep the steam on full while browning. After browning, add a small quantity of liquid, cover, reduce heat and simmer. When done, remove the meat and make a gravy with a liquid and return the meat to it. Further discussion on the braising of poultry and fish appears later in this chapter.

Simmering

Cooking meats in a large quantity of water or other liquid may be called poaching, boiling, stewing or simmering. Few flesh foods are boiled. To simmer, bring the water to a boil, add the product and hold the temperature from 185° to 205° F. For added flavor, use stocks or rich broths instead of water. Poultry should be simmered around 190° F. Meats may be marinated, prebrowned in fat and then simmered. Avoid heavy seasoning, since the stock may be reduced later for other use. To test tenderness, insert a fork a half inch and twist. Small pieces of tender meat will break under pressure. Do not overcook causing dry, shreddy meat. Skim as necessary.

Vegetables are often boiled separately in stock and served with meat. Time cooking so they are done when required. If cooked with the meat, add them about 30 minutes before serving. Cabbage and some other vegetables which cook more quickly are added later than this

Table 13-5. Simmering Large Cuts and Stews

Cut	Average Size or Average Weight	Approximate Cooking Time	
		Min per lb	Total hr
Fresh beef	4 to 8 lb	40 to 50	3 to 4
Corned beef	6 to 8 lb	40 to 50	4 to 6
Fresh pork	Weight desired	30	
Smoked whole ham	12 to 16 lb	18 to 20	4 to 5
Smoked half ham	6 to 8 lb	25	2½ to 3½
Smoked picnic	4 to 8 lb	35 to 45	3 to 4½
Stew, lamb or veal	1 to 2 in. cubes		1½ to 2
Stew, beef	1 to 2 in. cubes		2 to 3

(Courtesy National Livestock and Meat Board)

and members of the onion family earlier. Meat may be sliced ahead of service and kept warm in stock. Meat, fish and poultry to be used later should be cooled in their own stock or in cold water, removed and then refrigerated.

Steaming

Meats, fish or poultry may be steamed over rich stock, a process called free-venting or cooking under pressure, which reduces cooking time. It is easy to overcook meats in steam pressure. Many meats may be given preliminary treatment such as prebrowning and then finished in a steam chamber. Fish is steamed over a flavored stock called *court bouillon*.

(a)

(b)

(c)

Figure 13–13. (a) Ovenizing chicken and the final result (b). (c) Ovenized stuffed pork chops filled with an apple-raisin dressing. (Courtesy Processed Apples Institute)

Table 13-6. Refrigerator Storage Time Chart

Refrigerator Temperature 36° to 40° F

MEAT (loosely covered)	Limit of Days for Maximum Quality
BEEF	
Standing Rib Roast	5 to 8 days
Steaks	3 to 5 days
Pot Roasts	5 to 6 days
Stew Meat	2 days
Ground Beef	2 days
Liver (sliced)	2 days
Heart	2 days
PORK	
Roasts	5 to 6 days
Chops	3 days
Spareribs	3 days
Pork Sausage	2 to 3 days
CURED AND SMOKED MEATS	
Hams, Picnics—	
whole or half	7 days
slices	3 days
Bacon	5 to 7 days
Dried Beef	10 to 12 days
Corned Beef	5 to 7 days
Tongue	6 to 7 days
LAMB	
Roasts	5 days
Chops	3 days
Heart	2 days
Liver (sliced)	2 days
VEAL	
Roasts	5 to 6 days
Chops	4 days
Liver (sliced)	2 days
Sweetbreads (cooked)	2 days
COOKED MEATS	
Home-cooked Meats	4 days
Hams, Picnics	7 days
Franks	4 to 5 days
Meat Loaves (sliced)	3 to 4 days
Luncheon Meats (sliced)	3 days
Bologna Loaves (unsliced)	4 to 6 days
Dry and Semi-dry Sausage (uncut)	2 to 3 weeks
Liver Sausage (sliced)	2 to 3 days
Liver Sausage (uncut)	4 to 6 days
POULTRY	
Chickens (drawn, whole)	2 days
Chickens (cut-up)	2 days
Turkeys (drawn)	2 days
Ducklings (drawn, whole)	2 days
Cooked Poultry	3 to 4 days

(Courtesy Swift & Co.)

Blanching

Dropping meat momentarily into boiling water or simmering to partially cook is called blanching. It is more a preparation treatment than cooking. Some presoaking in cold salted water may be a preliminary treatment before blanching, which is done to remove undesirable parts or to firm meats. After blanching, the item is dipped into cold water. Sweet-

Figure 13–14. Adding chopped vegetables (*mirepoix*) to a pan of precooked meat previous to cooking it in moisture in an oven. (Courtesy Armour & Co.)

breads or brains are blanched in slightly acidulated water to whiten them and facilitate removing membranes. Cooking is then by some other method.

Frozen Meat Cookery

The ability to freeze meat rapidly and avoid heavy rupture of cellular structure plus improved packaging, storing and transporting has improved frozen meats to a point where many operations now use them. Frozen meats are cooked by the same methods used for non-frozen meats. Better flavor and higher nutrient values result if meat is cooked from the frozen or partially frozen state rather than thawed state. The drip that exudes from frozen flesh is high in nutrient and flavor substances. Cooking before such loss occurs reduces drip loss. Because of time in equipment, it may not be possible to cook meat from the hard-frozen state, but partial thawing reduces time. For best results, it is recommended this be done rather than attempt complete thawing. If thawed, procedures and times are the same as for regular meats. Meats needing shaping, grinding or breading are thawed and then prepared.

Figure 13–15. Braising veal stew in a steam-jacketed kettle. The product browns as well as in an oven. (Courtesy Armour & Co.)

Hard-frozen meats take about three times as long to roast as refrigerated meats. Prepare frozen meats for roasting as if unfrozen. Place fat side up into a pan and then into a 325° F oven. Cook until thawed at which time a thermometer may be inserted. Then, roast at 300° F to 350° F.

Thin frozen steaks need only slightly longer cooking time than regular ones but thicker steaks require 2 to 3 times as much time. To broil, place thin or medium frozen steaks four inches and larger steaks 8 to 12 inches from the heat. Reduce heat and thaw, then cook as for regular items. To pan-broil, cook covered until thawed and then remove the cover and cook similarly to normal steaks. Dropping thick items into 325° F fat speeds thawing while not giving an overcooked outside. Sautéing may be preferred to pan-broiling because thawing is more rapid. Sauté or grill frozen meats at lower temperatures than normally used. Covering until thawed speeds thawing. To sauté or grill frozen breaded items, partially thaw. Braising small pieces takes only slightly longer than for unfrozen, but larger pieces take much longer. Brown while frozen. If frozen pieces can be separated, they may be dredged with flour first or they may have to be thawed first. The procedure is then the same as for regular meat. Simmering frozen meat in water differs little from handling unfrozen meat this way.

Figure 13–16. A simmered piece of corned beef and cabbage is cut for a typical corned beef and cabbage dinner. (Courtesy Armour & Co.)

Table 13-7. Broiled Steaks, Frozen

Thickness (inches)	Doneness	Average Cooking Time (Minutes) (Electric Broiler)	(Seconds)	Heat Control Setting	Distance from Heat (inches)
½	Rare	4	0	High	4
½	Medium	6	30	High	4
¾	Rare	6	30	High	5
¾	Medium	8	0	Medium	5
1	Rare	12	0	Medium	5
1	Medium	13	30	Medium	5
1¼	Rare	22	30	Medium	6
1¼	Medium	24	30	Medium	6
		(Gas Broiler)			
½	Rare	3	10	High	2
½	Medium	4	10	High	2
¾	Rare	5	30	High	3
¾	Medium	6	30	High	4
1	Rare	10	30	High	5½
1	Medium	11	30	High	5½
1¼	Rare	14	30	High	7¼
1¼	Medium	17	0	High	7¼

Note: Steaks 1½ inches thick or more should be partially thawed or thawed before broiling. (Adapted from tables of Swift & Co.)

(a)   (b)

Figure 13–17.   (a) Simmer a brisket in seasoned water as shown here. Lift carefully after moist heat has changed enough of the collagen to water and gelatin making the brisket 'tender. (b) Cook variety meats such as tongue and heart by simmering them with vegetables. (Courtesy Armour & Co.)

To thaw meat, leave it wrapped under refrigeration which takes $1\frac{1}{2}$ hours per pound in a piece. Thawing at room temperature takes about an hour per pound. Placing in front of an electric fan reduces time. Meat in waterproof wraps can be thawed in cold water or under running, cold water, but not unwrapped meat. Thawing time in water is approximately an hour per pound.

Breakfast Meats

Breakfast needs fast service and so some precooking of meats is advised for this meal. Corned beef hash, steamed salt mackerel, finnan haddie, sausages, ham and bacon need some precooking. Hash is shaped ahead and browned so that it needs only heating. The mackerel and finnan haddie are partially poached and left in hot water for quick cooking. Thin ham grills rapidly to order but thick slices may be grilled and placed in a steam table in a small amount of stock or water. Bacon may be partially baked in 18 x 26 inch baking sheets or on wire racks, the grease poured off and the bacon stacked in a shallow pan. It then takes only a few minutes on the grill to crisp it. Some place a weight on the bacon in grilling to hold its shape. Sausages or sausage patties may be parboiled or steamed. Parboil is usually from a cold-water start. Remove and hold and then, as orders arrive, brown on the griddle. Some fry sausages and then hold a small quantity in the steam table. If necessary, they can be given a quick sauté before serving. Brown'n' serve sausages

Figure 13–18. Slightly thaw sliced liver as shown and then flour and braise, sauté or ovenize. (Courtesy Armour & Co.)

require 3 to 4 minutes browning under a broiler or on top of a griddle. About two minutes in a deep fat cooks sausages but the contamination of fat from the sausage's free fatty acids is so great that this method is not recommended.

COOKING POULTRY

The methods for cooking poultry are much the same as for meat. Raw or cooked poultry or its stock is very perishable. Freshness in raw poultry is essential to quality. Fresh poultry should be received chilled. Holding at 34° F to 40° F is too high; do not store over four days. Cool stock and cooked birds to 100° F and then refrigerate. Use within 24 hours. Cover to prevent drying out. Hold frozen poultry at 0° F or lower; at 10° F, poultry holds quality for 8 months, while at 20° F for only 2 to 4 months. To thaw, place in a 40° F area. Chickens thaw in this in 1 to 2 days and larger birds in 2 to 4 days. Poultry can remain in moisture-vapor-proof wraps and defrost in cold or under cold, running water taking 1 to 2 hours for chickens and 2 to 6 hours for turkeys. Placing before a fan reduces thawing time. To speed thawing, as soon as

Figure 13–19. Ovenizing bacon is a method for preparing a large quantity simply. (Courtesy Armour & Co.)

the legs are pliable, remove giblets and neck and spread the legs and wings. Cut-up poultry can be separated as soon as crinkly. Wash thawed poultry in cold water, drain and then prepare for cooking. Never refreeze.

Poultry is cooked by the same methods as meat. Low-temperature (250° F) roasting gives less shrinkage and a moister, better appearing product. Cook old birds in moist heat and young ones in dry heat. Most poultry is cooked well done except some few such as duck. Small birds such as pigeon, squab, quail, and game birds are best cooked at tempera-

Table 13–8.   Timetable for Roasting Poultry in a 325° F Oven

Ready-to-Cook Weight in lb	Approximate Minutes per lb	Total (hr)	Ready-to-Cook Weight in lb	Approximate Minutes per lb	Total (hr)
1⅓ to 2½	30 to 40	1 to 1¾	6 to 8	30 to 40	3½ to 4
2½ to 3½	30 to 40	1½ to 2½	8 to 10*	25 to 30	3 to 3½
3½ to 4¾	30 to 40	2 to 3	10 to 14*	18 to 20	3½ to 4
4¾ to 6	30 to 40	3 to 3½	14 to 18*	15 to 18	4 to 4½
			20 to 30*	12 to 15	5 to 6

*unstuffed

Figure 13–20. Small poultry items should be roasted quickly and served at once. Here we see hot *sous cloche* bells being placed over small squabs prior to service.

tures around 400° F to speed cooking and reduce chances for drying out. Rabbit is cooked the same as poultry.

The larger the bird, the greater the net yield of meat. Turkeys over 18 pounds have about 9% skeletal structure to total dressed weight, regardless of size. The abdominal cavities of 20 to 30 pound birds are about the same size. A 3½-pound duckling cuts nicely into four portions and is served with bone and skin, cut into quarters. A 2½-pound chicken,

Table 13-9. Portions from Various Size Turkeys

Dressed Weight (lb)	Loss to Ready-to-Cook	Ready-to-Cook Weight (lb)	Sliceable Meat Cooked (lb)	Number of Portions 2 oz	3 oz	4 oz
12 to 14	15%	10 to 12	4½	36	22	12
14 to 16	15%	12 to 14	4½	42	26	15
16 to 18	15%	14 to 16	6	48	30	18
18 to 20	15%	16 to 17	6⅔	54	32	20
20 to 22	15%	17 to 18	7⅓	59	37	23
22 to 24	15%	18 to 20	8	64	40	25
30 to 35	13%	26 to 30	13½	108	67	40

no neck or giblets, gives four cooked portions of 6 to 7 ounces. Use in poultry about ¾-pound ready-to-cook weight per portion. Use less for turkey and increase to at least a pound for geese. When a portion such as boned breast of chicken is served, use about 5 ounces and about 7 ounces for an unboned item. Size poultry as carefully as steaks, chops or other meats.

Roasting Poultry

Truss the legs and wings of small but not of large birds for roasting. Brush both with fat and season inside and out. Add paprika to aid in browning. Have pans full but do not allow birds to touch. Large birds should be breast down on perforated trivets. Small birds may be breast up if basted frequently or covered with bacon, salt pork or other fatty tissues or covered with an oil-soaked cloth. Fat birds, such as geese and

(a)   (b)

Figure 13-21.   (a) Simmered chicken and dumplings served with a fricassee gravy. (b) Precooked deep-fried chicken that has been frozen can be quickly rewarmed and served to obtain an excellent product. (Courtesy Armour & Co.)

(a)   (b)

Figure 13–22. (a) Do not roast chickens, turkeys and other lean birds breast side up since the fat on the back fails to run down and keep the product moist, as noted in (b).

ducks, may be left breast side up and need no basting, but the fat is poured off as it accumulates. Sometimes ducks and geese are pre-steamed and then finished by roasting to reduce the fattiness of the flesh.

Place small birds in a preheated 325° and large ones in a 250° F oven. When almost done, turn large birds breast side up and complete roasting, basting if necessary. At this point, breaking the legs away from the side gives a more rapid heat penetration into the thigh area. Large birds may be split lengthwise in half and roasted or the breasts, legs and wings may be roasted separately and bony parts used for stock. Simmer giblets $1\frac{1}{2}$ to $2\frac{1}{2}$ hours for proper doneness. If turkey can be roasted in heavy duty ovens overnight, use a 225° F temperature or slightly lower.

Doneness is indicated by a 180° F temperature in the thigh or breast center, when the meat on the thigh or breast feels soft or the leg gives readily, or a fork inserted into the shoulder muscle of the wing twists out easily. Some cooks roast large, tender birds slightly under-done, cool and slice. Then, for service, they warm the slices in stock. Birds for banquets can be roasted slightly under-done, cooled and sliced. The slices are then placed over mounds of dressing, dark meat first, and covered with broad slices of white meat. Cover with a moist cloth and refrigerate. For service warm in an oven or steam chest. Serve a mound per plate and cover with *very hot* gravy. Yield is always greater if poultry is chilled and then carved.

Poach-roasting of poultry is done in many operations. It usually results in a plumper, more flavorful, tender and juicy product. Poach-roast by placing poultry parts into pans skin-side up and filling with water or stock until the poultry is about two-thirds covered. Bones are usually left in the meat. Season lightly and roast in a 325° F oven until

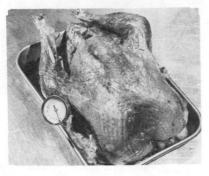

(a)   (b)

Figure 13–23. (a) Put the thermometer into the deepest part of the thigh to test for the temperature for doneness, which should be around 185° F for immediate serving or 160° F if service will be later after slicing and holding. (b) A test for doneness of broiled chicken. Note that the worker does not pierce the meat in checking for movement of the joint which indicates doneness.

tender. Let the poultry cool covered in its stock. The tops of such poultry will be a delicate brown.

Poaching Poultry

Poaching increases yield, moistness, flavor and tenderness over roasting, especially in large birds. It takes about half the time of roasting and less cooking space is required. More attractive and uniform portions are also obtained. Much of the meat can, if poached boned, be cut on a slicer. Section large birds and bone or leave the bone in large sections. Use bony parts for stock. Pick cooked meat from these and use in made-up dishes, salads, etc. Place parts for poaching, arranged skin side up in a stock pot, roasting pan or steam-jacketed kettle. Cover with hot, salted water or stock, using a tablespoon of salt and a teaspoon of white pepper for every six pounds of bird. Simmer at low heat about 2 to 2½ hours or until fork-tender. Cool covered in the stock or plunge into cold water. After reaching room temperature place in a 40° F area and chill. Then slice. Use meat and stock within three days.

Simmering

Whole or parts of birds are simmered in stock kettles or steam-jacketed kettles covered with a gallon of stock or water seasoned with a table-

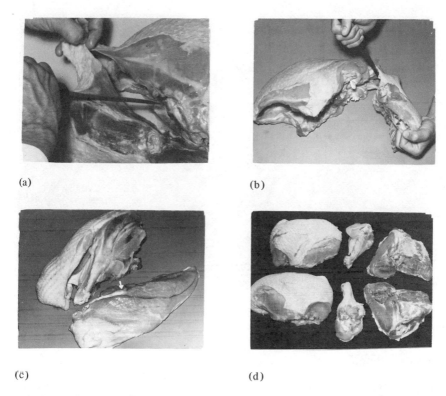

(a)   (b)

(c)   (d)

Figure 13–24.   (a) To prepare a turkey for poach-roasting, remove the legs and wings and then remove the back as shown in (b). (c) Separate the breast from the breast bone. (d) Use the back, wings and other body parts for broth and picked meat, leaving the bony parts of the wing, legs, thighs and breast for poaching.

spoon of salt for every five pounds of poultry. Vegetables and seasonings may be added. Bring to a boil, reduce to a simmer, cover, skim and cook until tender. Add water as required. Cool in the stock or in cold water.

Steaming Poultry

Older birds may be cooked by steam pressure giving a light-colored meat that can be used as picked cooked meat. It takes about half as long as simmering. Place into a pan, add a small quantity of water and steam. Watch times since cooking is rapid and overcooking occurs easily. Steam pressure cooking may toughen the flesh more than simmering.

Figure 13–25.   Poach-roasted turkey.

Braising Poultry

Poultry may be braised in the same manner as meat. Fricasséed or stewed poultry is braised poultry. This is used frequently for tougher birds but some tender ones can also be prepared by this method.

COOKING FISH

If good fish is used and it is properly prepared, it can vie in quality with the finest meat or poultry. Fish flesh is similar to meat and poultry except that it contains little connective tissue and no flesh pigment that changes color in cooking. Almost any method cooks it to desired tenderness. Fish should be cooked done except for a few items such as mollusks which may even be eaten raw. One of the most common mistakes in fish cookery is overcooking. When cooked to proper doneness, fish should flake easily and be moist. Overcooked fish breaks up easily and the meat is dry, pulpy and tough.

Both raw and cooked fish are highly perishable and extreme caution should be observed in handling it. When not required for preparation, it should be under 35° F refrigeration. See that fresh fish is used quickly and take care that cooked items are well covered, lightly packed

Figure 13–26. Good merchandising of seafoods is an excellent means of raising check averages and of pleasing patrons. (Courtesy Institutions Magazine)

in shallow layers and also used quickly. Discard items that are under suspicion.

As in poultry and meats, it is important that fish be sized to obtain desirable portions. If there is not too much bone, about five ounces of raw fish makes a portion, and four ounces of filet may be sufficient. Many fish purchased unportioned may have a high preparation waste. Whole fish may lose half its weight in removing the head, scales, fins and entrails. Whole fish is scaled and drawn for baking or steaming. Leave the head on only if the fish is for display. Wash well. An 8- to 12-pound baked or steamed fish portions well. A 12-pound fish cuts into desirable steaks if the fish is long and tapering. Fileting aids portioning. See Figures 13-27 through 13-32 for further procedures to use in preparing fish and shellfish.

Fish, if of good quality and correctly cooked, should not have a strong fishy flavor. While the flavor of cod, mackerel, herring and others may be abundant, it should never be objectionable. Fish with more abundant flavor may be cooked in ways to lose or modify some flavor.

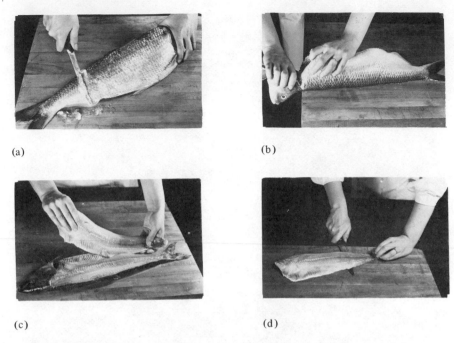

(a)   (b)

(c)   (d)

Figure 13–27. Preparing fish fillets. (a) Whole or round fish are scaled, except for trout and those that may be skinned, such as bullfish. (b) The head may be cut or broken off as shown, or left on to assist in holding in boning. Cut the fish open next on the under side and remove entrails. Wash well. (c) Lay the fish flat on a cutting board and take hold of the tail. Then cut about a half inch from the tail, slanting down to the bone, and then set the flattened knife forward, obtaining a strip as shown here. (d) Remove the skin by using the knife as shown. (Courtesy U.S. Department of Interior)

The fat content of fish flesh is from 1 to 20%. Marbling and finish are not in fish as in meats, the fat being spread as an oil throughout. The fat in fish dictates its cooking. Fat fish such as salmon, mackerel, shad or trout bake, broil or simmer or poach well. The flesh is usually moist if not overcooked. Lean fish such as flounder, halibut and cod have dry meat when cooked. Sautéing, poaching or simmering helps give some moistness. We also use more sauces with it. Both lean and fat fish deep-fry well but as a rule, lean fish makes a better deep-fried product. Lean fish is frequently breaded or batter-dipped for deep-frying, and may be baked if basted or covered with fatty tissues (barded). Baking quickly keeps lean fish more moist. Most fish, fat or lean, is accompanied by tart sauces such as hollandaise, lemon butter or Bercy sauce.

Fish, especially lean, is baked covered. It should be cooked only until done and served as soon as possible. Use moderate roasting tem-

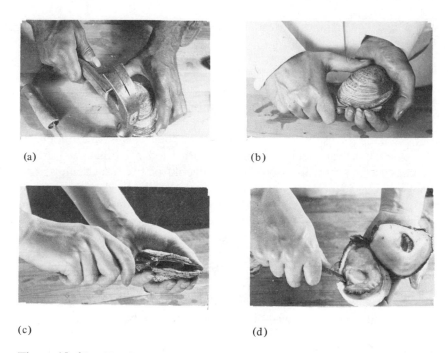

(a)

(b)

(c)

(d)

Figure 13–28. To shuck an oyster or clam: (a) Break the shell with a sharp rap of a hammer. This is called "billing." Bill at the thin shell area. (b) Hold the oyster or clam with the hinge part of the shell at the palm, as shown, or flat on a cutting board, and insert tip of knife where the shell was broken. (c) After insertion of the knife, twist it slightly to open the shell and then run the knife in and up close to the top, cutting through the adductor muscle that joins the clam or oyster to the shell. (d) Cut the adductor muscle attached to the lower shell. The clam or oyster is now ready to be served on the half shell or removed from the shell for other preparation. (Courtesy U.S. Department of Interior)

peratures. To serve, lift skin and portion in as complete a piece as possible.

Fat fish broils well but lean fish gives a dry, pulpy product lacking color and flavor. It is apt to curl under the broiler. If dipped into flour, put into a double grid and basted with butter, lean fish *can be* broiled. Broiling procedures for fish follow those given for meat.

Fish is sautéed in slightly more fat than meats and poultry, especially lean fish, which is often floured lightly, breaded or batter-dipped. Because such coverings can char quickly, care must be taken to see that adequate cooking occurs inside while giving a desirable outer appearance. Serve sautéed fish as soon as possible since a part of its quality depends upon a crisp outer layer and a fresh, moist inside. Fish can be marinated five minutes in lemon juice, Worcestershire sauce, salt and pepper and then sautéed. Many cooks believe that sautéed fish improves if salted and allowed to stand 5 to 10 minutes before cooking. Sautéed fish may be called pan-fried or à la meunière. If the latter, meunière butter is poured over the fish just before service.

To steam, simmer or poach fish, barely cover with liquid and cook gently. For large fish, cook in a cloth so that it can be raised easily without breaking, or use a lightly greased trivet that rests on the bottom of the pan. The trivet should be equipped with handles so that the fish can be raised easily. If a fish is to be served cold or decorated, allow it to cool in its own stock. Do not allow pieces to touch. A whole fish should fit freely in the pan. Use a good fish stock, salted water, court bouillon, wine or other liquid. Mild-flavored fish may be cooked in a liquid of a fourth milk and the rest water. Large pieces of fish are best started in cold liquid as a hot liquid encourages breaking up. If the fish is large score deeply to aid in cooking quickly. Strong flavored fish are best started in cold liquid. If small pieces are poached or simmered, put these into boiling liquid and immediately reduce the heat to simmering. Cook 8 to 10 minutes. Some white-fleshed fish may be baked in milk in an oven. Fish cooked in non-milk liquids are often served with a bit of rich court bouillon poured over them. Live trout may be killed, dressed and immediately poached. They take on a blue color when chilled, called *au bleu*. Fish steamed, simmered or poached is good served cold, especially if it is a fat fish such as trout or salmon.

Only firm-fleshed fish are braised. A straight-sided braising pan is used. Live, firm, fleshed fish may be stunned, scored (crimped), dressed and then soaked for a short time in cold water. This toughens the flesh so that braising is possible.* Fat fish should be used, as lean fish gives a dry product. Fish is usually skinned and left in fairly large pieces for braising. Liquids for braising may be court bouillon or white wine. If the fish is browned and a brown roux is used, red wine may be used. With white-fleshed fish or unbrowned fish, white wine is common. Because of the short cooking time, the cover may be off or loosely fitted so that evaporation occurs giving a stock of proper flavor and body. A *matelote* is fish braised with vegetables and lightly thickened. *Bouillabaisse* and *chioppino* are fish stews often served with the stock and the fish in separate bowls. The former is French from around Marseilles and the other Italian.

---

*Belle Lowe in *Experimental Cookery* mentions that meat cut soon after slaughter is tougher than that allowed to hang until rigor has left the meat. This crimping of fish to make it more firm may be related to this phenomenon. Note also that "green" meat is tougher than that left to hang for a time.

(a)   (b)

Figure 13–29. (a) Seafoods unless cooked only to doneness lose quality. One of the main faults in cooking these items is overcooking. (b) For instance, steam clams *only* until they begin to open and then remove from the heat and serve.

Shellfish, if cooked at too high a temperature or too long, becomes tough and rubbery. Simmering at 190° F is preferred to boiling. Live shellfish, placed in 140° F water are stunned and expire rapidly. Simmer shellfish in 190° F salted water (lobsters 205° F) to get a flavorful and tender item.

Green (uncooked) shrimp may be purchased fresh or frozen with heads on or headless, and cooked shrimp may be purchased in the same forms. To peel a raw shrimp, make a shallow cut along the back and peel, remove the sand vein and wash. Peeled raw shrimp may be butter-flied by splitting through to the tail. Cooked shrimp in the shell may also be peeled, deveined and washed. To cook shrimp, use a half cup of salt to a gallon of water and five pounds of raw, headless shrimp.

Figure 13–30. Fish cookery differs according to whether the fish is fat or lean. The top filets are haddock which would be cooked by deep-frying, poaching, sautéing, or cooked and served in a sauce. The whitefish filets below would be broiled, baked or served much as meat best suited to dry heat cooking methods.

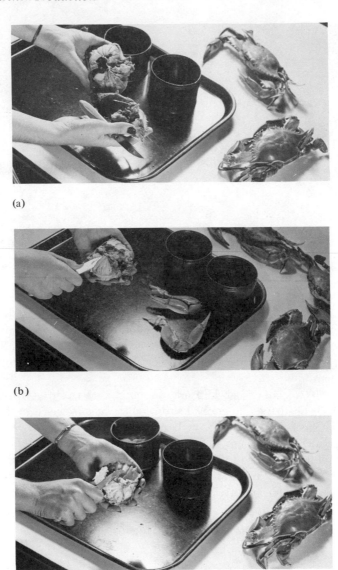

(a)

(b)

(c)

Figure 13–31. To obtain crab meat from cooked crabs: (a) Break off the large claws, pull off the top shell, and break off legs. (b) Remove gills and internal material by scraping and washing. (c) Slice the top right side of the inner skeleton by starting at the top. Remove the meat and repeat slice on left side, removing meat. Crack claws and remove meat. (Courtesy U.S. Department of Interior)

(a)

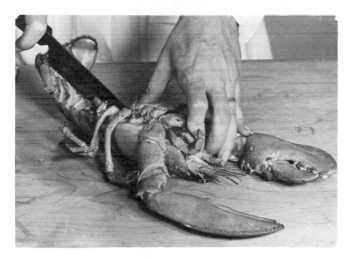

(b)

Figure 13–32. (a) To cook a live lobster, plunge it head first into water at about 150° F. Bring to a simmering temperature of about 205° F and cook about 20 to 25 minutes. (b) To split, lay lobster on its back and cut through to shell. Remove stomach back of the head and the intestinal vein which runs from the stomach to the end of the tail, but do not discard the green liver or coral roe. Many people like them. Claws may be cracked before it is sent from the kitchen.

Yield after cooking, peeling and deveining is 50%. Raw headless shrimp, shelled and deveined are available as are peeled, deveined and quick-cooked (called PDQ). Either type can be obtained fresh or frozen on some markets. Cooked yield of raw, deveined and peeled shrimp is 55%.

Wash clams or oysters in the shell thoroughly before steaming or using. To rid clams of sand, add a third cup of salt per gallon of water. Soak for 15 to 20 minutes. Wash. Repeat until the clams are sand-free. Salt water must be used, for clams will not disgorge sand in fresh water. Some cooks put the clams into salted water, add cornmeal and leave them overnight in a refrigerator. The clams eat the cornmeal and disgorge the sand.

To steam, use 6 to 8 clams ($\frac{3}{4}$ pound) per portion. Place into a container with a perforated bottom containing a cup of water per pound of clams. Steam 5 to 10 minutes or until partially opened. Serve on a plate or dish with clam nectar in a cup and a side dish of melted butter. Clams or oysters may be roasted by placing them in a baking pan and roasting 15 minutes at 450° F or until they are open. Oysters and clams may be baked or barbecued in the half shell. Where a large quantity of clams or oysters are to be shucked mechanical shuckers are used. (See Figure 13-28)

Lobster tails should be poached about five minutes and then split for broiling for a more tender and moist product than given by broiling alone. The time for broiling, using this method, is about 5 to 6 minutes. To reduce curling of the tail, thaw and split, or remove the thin undershell and bend back firmly to break the connective tissue that causes the curling.

Suggested exercises or laboratory experiences for Chapter 13:

1. Add 10 1-inch cubes of rather tough meat to a quart of water and simmer, removing a piece after one hour and another after each elapsing 15 minutes. When the 10th one is removed, cool and check for tenderness. What has the moist heat done to the collagen?
2. Grind a bit of ham fat and add it to some hamburger. Cook it as a patty. Cook a bit of hamburger without ham fat. Note the color difference.
3. Broil, roast, sauté, deep-fry, braise and steam meat to learn what procedure should be followed.
4. Bone a turkey and poach-roast it.
5. Broil, bake, sauté and poach fish to learn what procedure should be followed.

6. Steam clams or oysters for just a few minutes to cook only to doneness. Leave others to cook for a long time. Note the difference in texture.

BIBLIOGRAPHY

National Livestock and Meat Board, *Cooking Meat in Quantity*, 2nd ed., Chicago, n. d.

National Livestock and Meat Board, *Meat Manual*, 4th ed., Chicago, 1950.

National Livestock and Meat Board, *Ten Lessons on Meat*, 7th ed., Chicago, n. d.

Poultry and Egg National Board, *Golden Treasury of Turkey Cookery*, Chicago, 1953.

U. S. Department of Interior, Washington, D. C., 25.

Burtis, Jean and Kerr, Rose G., *How to Cook Crabs*, Bulletin No. 10, 1956.

Burtis, Jean and Kerr, Rose G., *How to Cook Shrimp,* **Bulletin No. 7, 1958.**

Kerr, Rose G., *Fish Cookery for 100*, No. 1, 1957.

Kerr, Rose G., *Basic Fish Cookery*, No. 2, 1957.

Kerr, Rose G., and Burtis, Jean, *How to Cook Oysters*, No. 3, 1957.

Osterhaug, Kathryn L. and Kerr, Rose G., *How to Cook Salmon*, No. 4, 1957.

Osterhaug, Kathryn L. and Kerr, Rose G., *How to Cook Clams*, No. 8, 1958.

Osterhaug, Kathryn L. and Kerry, Rose G., *How to Cook Halibut*, No. 9, 1957.

Section III

Bakeshop Production

14

Bakery Ingredients

Perhaps no other task in food production requires as much technical knowledge and skill as baking. Most bakery products are made of very similar ingredients but slight variation in proportion, preparation or baking can produce entirely different products. Success or failure may be a matter of slight detail and a knowledge of the properties ingredients exhibit in baking is essential to produce successful items. A brief discussion of these properties is therefore appropriate.

FLOUR

Flour has been defined as finely ground cereal, but some flours are not made from cereals such as flour from potatoes, almonds or soybeans. Some ground cereals are also not flours but meals such as cornmeal or oatmeal. Perhaps, for baking purposes, we can define flour as a ground starch-like product used to give structure and body to bakery products.

Wheat Flour

Different kinds of wheat flour are needed to satisfy the many different baking needs of the bakeshop. Different wheats may be blended to give these. The average wheat flour contains 63 to 73% starch, 7 to 15%

Figure 14–1. The water and bread flour slurry shown on the right has more stringy qualities than a slurry made from cake flour, the higher gluten content of the bread flour causing this stringiness while the lower gluten and higher starch content of the cake flour are responsible for the shortness displayed.

protein, 1 to 2% fat, 0.4% ash (minerals), 1 to 2% sugar and 11 to 13% moisture. Variations in these make a great difference in the flour's baking properties.

Soft flour made from soft or winter wheat is used for pastry, many quick breads, cakes and cookies. It has a clear, white color and a soft, velvety mixture. Its ratio of starch to protein is high. Spring or hard wheat is used for yeast breads and some pastry goods needing strong structures. It has a higher protein and lower starch ratio than soft flour. The color is slightly creamy and the texture is rough when rubbed between the fingers. Soft flour squeezed in the hand remains together but hard flour crumbles.

The quality as well as quantity of protein influences flour's structure-building properties. Yeast breads, puff paste and eclairs are examples of items needing strong protein while cakes, cookies and muffins need weaker protein. Hard flour is called "strong" because it produces strong structures. Soft flour is called "weak" because it produces tenderer, more delicate structures. "Strong" applied to soft flour means it has the strength in a batter to carry high ratios of sugar, fats and other ingredients.

The best wheat flours are *patents* and the poorest *clears* with *middlings* in between in quality. Patents come from the wheat kernel first in milling, middlings next and clears last. A *straight* flour is a mixture of the entire kernel except the bran. Whole wheat or graham flour is straight flour with some bran. Rye, straight flour, flour high in clears or containing bran may have to be mixed with good patents to improve its structure-building properties.

Six proteins are found in flour; the most important and by far the greatest in quantity are gliadin and glutenin, which together form the protein gluten. Gluten absorbs about 200% of its weight in moisture. When completely hydrated, it forms a tenuous, elastic, viscous, pliable mass extending as a thin, structural network throughout a batter or dough. Gluten gets its elasticity from its spring-like coiled shape. When moistened, this coiled structure can be pulled in and out. Salt and milk strengthen gluten while sugar peptizes or tenderizes it. Alkalis weaken it and acids make it more pliable and extensible. Fat, sugar and starch interfere with gluten formation. Fat surrounds gluten particles preventing them from joining together, thus giving a more tender product. Too much liquid causes gluten to become over-extended and unable to form a strong network. To perform properly, gluten must form a sufficiently strong mass to retain leavening gases and hold other ingredients in suspension. This is why even delicate cake flours need some gluten.

Moisture is needed to make gluten sticky. Then manipulation brings the gluten particles together to form a network. This is why mixing or kneading is done for some items and avoided in others. When gluten is cold or not completely hydrated it sticks together less easily but, when warm and given moisture, it develops readily, especially when the product is manipulated. Keeping muffin batter cold retards gluten formation. Limiting water in a pie dough reduces the chance for gluten to form.

Gluten development can be demonstrated by mixing hard-wheat flour into a stiff dough and kneading it for about 10 minutes. After resting approximately 20 to 30 minutes — called conditioning — the dough is carefully washed to remove its starch. A yellowish, viscous and elastic mass remains which is crude gluten. If this is formed into a ball and baked in a 375° to 400° F oven, steam develops inside, swelling it into a large honeycombed sphere.

A flour, unless aged at least 3 to 6 weeks, is apt to be "green" and be bucky or rigid and inflexible in baking. Products made from it are tough. It can give bread odd humps on the top or may break or tear it

(a)

(b)

Figure 14–2.   (a) Three gluten balls showing approximate gluten content of (left to right) cake, pastry and bread flours. (Courtesy Wheat Flour Institute) (b) Gluten development is shown in these baking powder biscuits. Note the tiny strands and the layering of the dough from gluten development. As gas pressures pushed the dough up in baking, these strands and layering of the dough were produced. (Courtesy General Foods)

because its gluten lacks proper elasticity. Overaged flour lacks extensibility and gives poor volume. Rye flours should not be aged.

Moisture absorption is an indicator of flour quality. A flour able to bind a large amount of water gives a moist product which performs well in mixing and baking and has good keeping qualities. A good hard or soft flour absorbs from 60 to 65% of its own weight in moisture and still makes a firm, pliable dough. Soft flours usually absorb slightly less moisture than hard ones. A weak gluten is indicated when a flour fails to absorb enough water, showing a poor ability in a soft flour to produce a stable batter. Sugar and acid increase gluten's moisture absorption. A yeast bread is sticky in mixing but fermenting increases acidity and this, plus additional time to hydrate, produces a soft, pliable dough. Salt reduces moisture absorption and raises the coagulation temperature of gluten.

Heat coagulates gluten and gelatinizes (swells) starch producing a firm product. Coagulation occurs around 165° F and starch starts to swell at 144° F and ends around 203° F. Other ingredients, such as eggs, may coagulate and help make a firm product. Firmness also comes from an 8 to 16% moisture loss in baking. Proper expansion or leavening must occur before an item firms. A highly complex balance must occur between the action of leavening agents, moisture, structure-forming ingredients and the introduction of heat.

Many things affect flour's performance. If ash is above 0.5%, flour does not perform properly, especially in yeast goods. The size and uniformity of the grind is also important. Too large flour granules do not absorb the quantity of liquid needed nor give the flour the capacity to carry the required sugar, shortening or other ingredients. A loaf of bread from too coarsely ground flour is heavy and shapes up with difficulty. Too fine a grind gives a pasty, tight-grained product which bakers say "has not been allowed to breathe." Too fine a hard-wheat flour gives overly rapid fermentation and excessive starch swell in baking. Unevenness of grind gives large particles with slow moisture absorption and low stabilizing ability, while small granules absorb too much moisture and have excessive stabilizing power. Good milling produces properly ground flours. Proper granule size gives products with uniform cell structure, good oven spring, maximum volume and good texture.

Store flour in a well-ventilated, dry place at about 70° F. Flour is usually purchased by the barrel or 196 pounds (2 98-lb or 4 49-lb bags). Some cake flours come in 100-lb bags. Do not stack flour over 8 bags high.

Bread or Hard-Wheat Flour

Strong hard wheat is selected to make bread flour. Its gluten is capable of development and retains strength from kneading, fermenting and baking. It should contain 65 to 70% starch, 1 to 2% fat, 12 to 16% protein of high quality, 1 to 2% sugar, 0.4% ash and 11 to 13%

moisture and be enriched with iron, thiamin, niacin, calcium and vitamin D. It should have good moisture absorption and form a pliable,
elastic, soft dough with sufficient viscosity and tenacity after mixing to
give good spring in rising and holding gas pressures. Too much viscosity
gives a bucky, unyielding dough that breaks or humps in baking. Good
flour does not become slack in fermentation. Over-elastic dough is hard
to handle. Regular and some hard-crusted breads need a flour with a
protein content of 12.5 to 12.8%. Most hard-crusted and hearth breads
need one with about 13% protein, while a 15½% protein flour is best for
blending with rye or other flours lacking good quality gluten.

Soft-Wheat or Pastry Flour

The best pastry and cake flours come from the first patents of good
soft wheat. Cake flour contains approximately 7 to 8½% protein. With
less, batters are pasty and the final product lacks volume and quality.
The flour should produce a stable batter and carry high quantities of
liquid, fat, sugar and eggs. Cake flours low in moisture absorption cannot
support the quantity of liquid and richness required to give a good
product.

Pastry flour contains more and stronger gluten than cake flour. It
normally contains 8 to 10% protein but, if more gluten is present, it
will lack some strength to make up for the greater quantity. It is used
for quick breads, pie dough and other products requiring limited structure strength. It is used also for general cooking since it is low in cost.

If *necessary*, strong flour can be used for cake or pastry by using
for each pound of cake flour 2½ ounces of cornstarch and 14 ounces of
bread flour. The amount of shortening is also increased to weaken the
flour's strong gluten. All-purpose flour is suitable for making cakes,
cookies, pastry or bread but is not adapted to specific baking needs and
so has limited use in quantity production.

SHORTENINGS

At one time the shortenings used for baking were limited. Butter was
used for cakes, cookies and other pastries and washed for puff pastes
and rolled-in doughs; lard was used for pastries, pies and breads and
oleo for crackers and bread. Chicken fat was prized for making cream
sauces and goose grease blended with other fats made mealy, tender pie
crusts. Today we can manufacture almost any shortening we want. In
fact, we can change fats so many ways, the chemist says, "You name
it, we'll make it."

Figure 14–3. A special fat for deep frying containing a product called "metasil" which stabilizes the fat against frying rigors. (Courtesy Procter and Gamble)

Hydrogenation was a big step in shortening development since it made vegetable oils solid. But, hydrogenation was used for solid fats; for instance, as much as 12% of lard is hydrogenated to improve plasticity, waxiness or to raise its melting point. Centrifuging can separate light or heavy fat fractions as well as increase or decrease a fat's firmness or melting point by removing one or the other. *Winterized* oil has its heavy molecules removed so that it does not solidify as in a salad oil when it is refrigerated. Chemists bleach, deodorize, decolor or deflavor oils and fats. Lard, for instance, can be made flavorless. Or, they create flavor as in margarines by adding milk solids and diacetyl which has a butter flavor. They make fats brown like butter by adding lecithin and add antioxidants such as butylated-hydroxy-anisole or citric acid to reduce off-flavor development from rancidity.

Fats give "slip" to a batter or dough and this slippage is important in getting correct leavening and movement in baking. A product lacking slip may not develop correctly and have a poor shape and crumb.

Shortenings tenderize (shorten) by surrounding flour particles and other ingredients, lubricating them so that they cannot stick together. Free fatty acids increase shortness and chemists vary these in fats to produce more or less shortening power.

Shortening must vary in plasticity. For a flaky pie crust or rolled-in dough, a waxy, tough, extensible, plastic, firm fat is needed so that when the dough is rolled out, layers of fat remain between the dough. For icings, a flavorless, plastic fat that creams (aerates) well, has no greasiness and carries a high amount of sugar is necessary. For some cakes, plasticity and waxiness in the fat are needed so that air is incorporated, increasing volume and creating batter lightness. Pound cakes that are leavened by such creaming must be made from such shortenings. Or, tiny air bubbles are put throughout a shortening to eliminate having to cream it in using for cakes, cookies, etc. A chemical process called inter-esterification arranges molecular structure, improving a shortening's creaming ability and plasticity. Temperature, of course, is important in controlling plasticity and softness, so therefore bakers condition shortening at the proper temperature for at least 24 hours before they use it.

Plasticity and shortness are related. A fat lacking plasticity may not spread well and thus not shorten. Tallow and oleo are too firm and brittle to spread well and therefore are poor for many uses in baking. Others are too soft and shorten too much. A chicken fat is so soft that it spreads completely throughout a batter or dough and may shorten too much. Some products such as cookies must be so short they almost crumble while others such as cakes and quick breads must be sufficiently tender to have a delicate texture but enough structure to be handled.

Emulsifiers such as monoglycerides or diglycerides help to spread a plastic shortening in fine globules in batter or dough producing more stable batters and finer grained products. We used to have a rule in cake making that "the weight of the sugar *should not* exceed the weight of the flour," but with better shortenings and flour we now say, "the weight of the sugar should exceed the weight of the flour," giving us sweeter and tenderer cakes. Emulsifiers increase shortening power without a loss in plasticity. They also increase volume, give a smoother, finer texture to the crumb and thinner cell walls. They make possible simplified mixing methods and give batters and doughs that handle better in processing. Batters are more stable, smoother and resist curdling better. Emulsified shortenings, by spreading more completely around items, retard moisture loss and thus contribute to an increase in moistness and freshness in products. But, as we learned about shortenings in deep-fat frying, emulsified shortenings have lower smoking temperatures and thus should not be used for that nor for general cooking use. They are usually quite high in cost compared to other shortenings.

SUGARS

Sugar is used in baking to give sweetness, tenderness, color, food value, good crumb texture, crust color and to furnish food for yeast. There are many different kinds of sugars. Sanding sugars are used to coat items such as doughnuts, crullers, cake tops, coffee cakes, etc. The coarsest, *confectioner's coarse AA*, is about a tenth-inch cube. *Sanding coarse* is about half this size and is widely used. *Fine granulated — bottler's*

Figure 14–4. The chocolate on the left was filled with a fondant center containing an enzyme which inverted the sugars, turning them into a sirup. The chocolate on the right was filled at the same time with a fondant center having no enzyme added. Note that it remained firm.

sugar because it is also used for carbonated beverages — is also used as a sanding sugar. *Regular granulated* is used for table sugar and *extra fine standard* may also be used for this purpose. *Fruit* sugar is slightly finer and is used for breakfast cereal and fruit. *Baker's Special, extra fine*, is used for cakes and cookies because it goes into solution rapidly and gives a uniform cell structure and good volume. If such a sugar is not available, a baker may roll regular sugar heavily under a rolling pin to create a finer sugar. *Standard powdered* sugar (6X) is used for toppings for sweet doughs, etc. *Extra fine powdered* (10X) gives a creamy icing and is also used for dusting. *Icing* sugar is the finest of powdered sugar and gives a creamy appearance and texture. Icings made from it set up fast, developing a thin, soft crust quickly with a high gloss. It has good spreadability.

Dehydrated fondant, a dried fondant, not a powdered sugar, is used for icings; some trade names are *Drivert* or *Dri-Fond.* The bakeshop also uses many sirups such as honey, sorghum or corn. These contain about 25% moisture so some moisture must be reduced in a recipe when they replace sugars. Glucose or other sugars may also be used to replace sucrose. Brown sugars, light yellow to dark brown, contain 1 to 5% invert sirup. The darker varieties have a stronger flavor than lighter ones. Molasses is also light to dark and flavored from mild to strong.

Starch, dextrin and sugar belong to the family of carbohydrates. Sugars may be complex or simple, the more common complex being sucrose, maltose, and lactose, the simple ones fructose and glucose. Granulated sugar is almost 100% sucrose and is made from cane or beets. Molasses and brown sugar contain large quantities of sucrose but also acid, minerals and other sugars making them react differently from regular granulated sugar. Maltose comes from sprouted barley and is an excellent yeast food. It may be used in foods as a sweetener and also because of its flavor. Lactose, the sugar in milk, has low solubility and has restricted use in food preparation; yeast cannot utilize it. Many natural plant or fruit sugars are either glucose (dextrose) or fructose (levulose). Honey is about 50-50 glucose and fructose. Sucrose breaks down into equal parts of fructose and glucose; maltose into two parts glucose and lactose into equal parts of glucose and galactose. (See Figure 14-5). Starches and dextrins break down into complex sugars and then into simple sugars. For instance, starch changes to dextrin, then to maltose and then to glucose.

Changing starch to complex sugars, or complex ones to simple ones, may be desirable or undesirable in food preparation. It is desirable when we use enzymes to make corn sirup from cornstarch, or use an acid to invert some of the sucrose when we cook a fondant, but un-

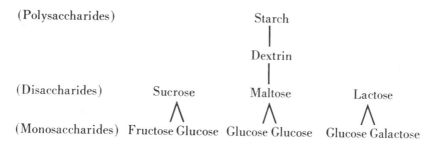

(Polysaccharides)   Starch
                                              |
                                            Dextrin
                                              |
(Disaccharides)   Sucrose   Maltose   Lactose
                        /\   /\   /\
(Monosaccharides) Fructose Glucose Glucose Glucose Glucose Galactose

Figure 14–5.   The relationship of some of the saccharides is shown. Note that starch and dextrin are complex substances that can break down into the disaccharide sugar maltose. Sucrose and lactose are two other complex sugars like maltose. All break down into monosaccharides or simple sugars.

ALKALINE | NEUTRAL

Figure 14–6.   The effect of a strong alkali on a glucose solution.

desirable when an acid breaks down a starch paste, as in a lemon pie filling. If to 5 pounds of sugar and a quart of water are added 2 ounces (¼c) of cream of tartar, an acid, and this is cooked to 240° F, about 40% of the sucrose is inverted. This will not crystallize because the invert sugars interfere with crystallization, but if a fourth to half ounce of cream of tartar is used, we get a 16 to 23% inversion producing a soft, plastic, moldable crystalline mass. If too little acid is used giving, for instance, a 7 to 12% inversion, a hard fondant mixture results. Normally, if 5 pounds of sugar, a quart of water and a fourth ounce of cream of tartar or a half cup of lemon juice are cooked to 280° F, a mixture suitable for fondants but slightly too stiff for frostings is obtained. We need not add acid to obtain inverted sugars. For instance, a half to three-fourths pound of corn sirup with 5 pounds of sugar gives about 15 to 18% invert sugar, and a pound of corn sirup to this amount of sugar gives a 20% invert content. The acid in molasses, vinegar, brown

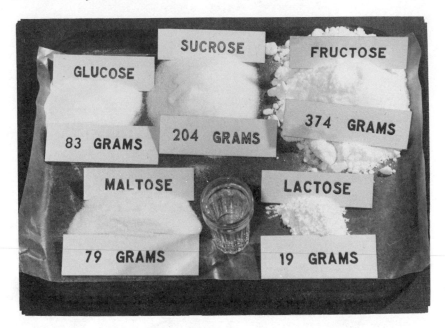

Figure 14–7. The relative solubility of the sugars found in foods. The amounts of these various sugars shown here are soluble at room temperature in the 100 cubic centimeters of water shown in the glass in the center.

sugar, honey or other foods can react with carbohydrates in cooking or baking and cause undesirable or desirable reactions.

Some sugars are hydroscopic; that is, they draw moisture to them, especially fructose. Such sugars may be used in soft but not crisp cookies. A fruit cake containing invert sugar slowly draws moisture to it making it easier to cut and more waxy. Pulled sugar work or hard candies may draw moisture on humid days and may have to be stored in airtight chambers. Some sugar products are stored in cabinets along with a drawer filled with calcium chloride. The calcium chloride has a very strong affinity for moisture and removes whatever is in the air in the cabinet. This calcium chloride can be regenerated by heating it in an oven when it finally becomes too moist for use. If a hydroscopic sugar is used in a cooked sugar solution, it may have to be cooked to a slightly higher temperature to correct for the moisture it may later attract into the product. The acid in sugar-coated candied fruit may invert the sugar coating, making the candy sticky.

Soda and other weak alkalis decompose sugars. Sucrose is more resistant to alkalis than maltose, lactose, glucose or fructose. Breakdown from alkali is shown by the development of a deep cream or light yellow color but glucose turns to a dirty gray. Cooking a sugar solution for a long time in an alkali produces a caramelization and an off-flavor. Adding a bit of acid, such as cream of tartar changes the alkalinity of water to acid preventing such an undesirable breakdown. (See Figure 14-6)

The sweetest to least sweet sugars are fructose, sucrose, glucose, maltose, and lactose. This is the same order as their solubility. The sweetness of a 50-50 fructose-glucose solution is slightly under that of a sucrose solution. Acids in molasses, honey and sorghum lessen their sweetness.

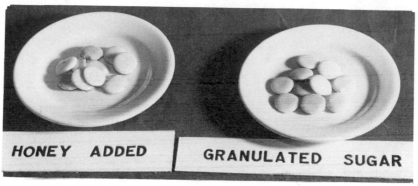

(a)

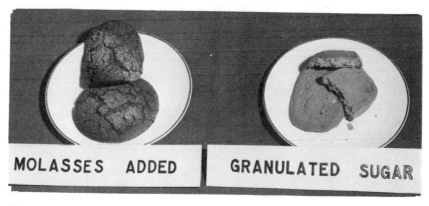

(b)

Figure 14–8. (a) Honey added to fondant made into mints contains enough fructose to draw moisture into the mints on the left, while the same recipe using granulated sugar but with cream of tartar made mints that were not hydroscopic. (b) The cookies containing molasses bend easily because molasses draws moisture, while the cookies made with granulated sugar only remain quite crisp and break when bent.

Figure 14-9 shows the solubility of some sugars. Lactose crystallizes easily as is evidenced in the graininess sometimes found in evaporated milk. Mixing dry milk a day ahead of use permits lactose to go into solution and gives a more stable, flavorful product. Glucose crystallizes easily as shown in crystallized jams, jellies and honey. The uncrystallized portion of crystallized honey is fructose whch crystallizes with difficulty. Solubility is in the following order from greatest to least: fructose, sucrose, glucose, maltose and lactose.

Warm water dissoves more sugar than cold. At 195° F water dissolves twice as much sucrose as at room temperature. While fine sugar dissolves more rapidly, no more eventually dissolves than coarse sugar. Salt, acid or invert sugar increases the solubility of crystallized sugar.

A solution completely filled with sugar is called saturated while one holding more sugar than it can is called supersaturated. Any disturbance of a supersaturated solution causes it to crystallize. A simple sirup in excess of two pounds of sugar to a pound of water may crystallize soon because, as seen in Figure 14-7, sucrose's solubility is about 2:1 to water. Moisture is lost in boiling and so the concentration of sugar in a solution increases as it boils. A solution of five pounds of sugar to a quart of water boiled to 240° F is saturated but, when cooled to 104° F, is supersaturated. Crystallization is more rapid in a warm than a cold supersaturated solution and, if stirred when warm, a supersaturated solution forms larger and fewer crystals than if stirred when cool.

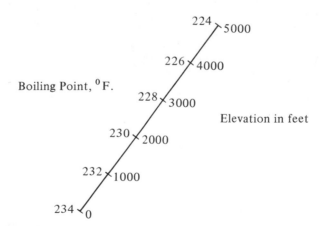

Figure 14–9. Elevation affects the boiling point of sugar solutions. If a sugar solution boils at 234° F at sea level (4 sugar to 1 water), then at various levels shown on the right of the line, the solution boils at the temperature indicated on the left side.

The greater the amount of sugar in a solution, the higher the boiling point. A 10% sucrose solution boils at 213° F, a 50% solution at 216° F and an 80% solution at 234° F. When no more moisture can be lost, sugar burns. Granulated sugar melts at 320° to 356° F and begins to burn at 410° F.

The boiling point of sugar solutions drops as altitude increases, about a 1° F drop occurring for every increase of 500 feet. A correction for altitude in sugar cooking is applied above 1000 ft. (See Figure 14-9)

When relative humidity (RH) is above 50% sirups are cooked 1° F higher for every 25% or partial 25% increase in relative humidity over 50%. Bakers cook sugar solutions 2° higher in the summer than in the winter because the humidity of the air in a kitchen in summer is higher than in winter. A slight excess in humidity may be overcome by extra mixing after crystallization starts. All temperatures in this text are for sea level with a relative humidity below 50%.

The viscosity or thickness of a sirup increases as its temperature drops. Some products, such as caramels, peanut brittle and cooked frostings, may be liquid at higher temperatures, plastic at lower ones and hard at still lower ones. Cold fondants may be warmed to work well but heating above 100° F causes them to become dull and grainy. Caramels and taffy should be warmed slightly before cutting. Sugar work is done before a batch warmer to keep the mixture workable. Moisture, invert sugars, butter and other ingredients can increase creaminess and plasticity of a crystalline mass. If the weight of butter or fat is 7% or more than that of the sugar, for every 3% increase over 7%, the cooking temperature is raised $\frac{1}{2}$° F to counteract the extra softness caused by the fat. Glycerine also increases plasticity. About $\frac{1}{2}$% of glycerine to sugar by weight gives good softness. Starch or dextrin make crystalline mixtures firmer and, when in a mixture, allowances may have to be made for it. For every 3% of cocoa or chocolate over 10% of the sugar, the final temperature may be lowered $\frac{1}{2}$° F. For instance, if $6\frac{1}{2}$ ounces of cocoa to 40 ounces of sugar are used, the temperature is dropped 1° F because 6.5/40 = 16% or two 3%'s over 10%. Sometimes chocolate may have a slightly lower correction because of its higher fat content.

The size and quantity of crystals affect the creaminess of a crystalline mass. Tiny crystals are wanted in fondants, etc., but coarser ones may be desirable on items such as sugar-coated fruits. Amorphous mixtures — crystallized sugar without form — are desirable in caramels, brittles, taffy, etc.

Stirring a supersaturated solution encourages crystal development. Smaller and more crystals are formed if the solution is cool and if stir-

Figure 14–10. The viscosity or thickness of sugar solutions changes with the temperature. The melted caramel mixture on the right is the same as that in the firm caramels on the left. The temperature difference of the two has made the change.

ring is continuous and vigorous. If few crystals are formed, they are large, while if many are formed, they are small. Agitation such as stirring or kneading encourages small crystal development. The first crystal formed influences the size of all others. To promote tiny crystal size, some fine fondant from a previous batch may be added — a process called seeding — to a new batch just before it crystallizes. To prevent seeding from coarse sugar, the sides of pans are moistened during cooking to wash down and dissolve the undissolved sugar crystals on the sides, or a pan may be covered during boiling for steam to dissolve them. Seeding can also occur from dust or other particles, so cooked solutions should be covered when they stand. Crystals can grow in size in storage. Butter, acid or other ingredients are added to discourage this growth. To give the least agitation while warm, fondant solutions are poured from their cooking pans onto a cold, flat, smooth surface such as a greased marble slab, baking sheet, stainless steel table or platter. The pan is not scraped but all the sirup possible is allowed to run from the pan. Scraping or disturbing while hot causes large crystals to form

(a)

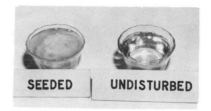

(b)

(c)

Figure 14–11. The stirring (a), seeding (b) or disturbing (c) of a supersaturated sugar solution when warm causes rapid crystallization. Note how in each case the sample that was untouched remained in an uncrystallized form.

and seed the rest of the mixture. Rough spots on the surface where fondant is poured to cool can start crystalline growth, as does putting a thermometer into the mass after boiling ceases. Putting the thermometer down onto the slab and then pouring the hot fondant over it avoids this problem.

When a liquid changes to a solid, heat is released — an exothermic action. When a sirup crystallizes, the exothermic heat causes the mixture to thin slightly and a loss of sheen is noticeable. Many use these factors as a signal to begin spreading, dropping or performing other required manipulations before the mixture becomes too firm to handle.

Doneness in a sugar solution may be indicated variously but, unless the worker is experienced, the most satisfactory way is by thermometer. A Brix or Baume scale reading may be used to indicate doneness. A Brix of 14° to 16° F is a light sirup, 16° to 19° F medium, 19° to 21° F heavy and 21° F or over extra heavy. Some objective tests in judging doneness are:

Water test: Drop sirup into 50° water; firmness indicates doneness; time in the water is a factor of firmness obtained.

Finger test: Dip the finger into cold water, then quickly into hot syrup; the doneness is indicated by the thread or ball formed.

Figure 14–12. Barley sugar (left), caramel (center) and burned sugar (right) achieved by heating granulated sugar to the temperatures indicated.

Spin test: Judge doneness by the length of the thread formed or the manner in which the sirup flows from a spoon or through a perforated ladle.

Bite test: Place a bit of sirup into the mouth. The bite or crack of the sirup will indicate doneness; a sirup that breaks between the teeth without adhering to them is at the crack stage, about 310° F.

Appearance test: Color and appearance are good indicators; the size, type, and viscosity of the bubbles formed in cooking caramels, fudge, penuche, fondant, and other mixtures may be used to tell doneness; when a sirup begins to turn slightly brown, it is at the caramel stage; because thermometers are difficult to use in the burning sugar, sight is a more reliable method to use in indicating doneness of sugars cooked above the caramel stage.

Sound test: When a sirup cracks loudly twice as it is dropped into cold water, the moderately hard crack stage of 310° to 315° F has been reached. When a sugar thread cracks very hard three times as it is wrapped around the finger, the temperature is between 316° F and 320° F. Sugar may discolor slightly at this higher temperature.

It is emphasized again that thermometers are the only reliable guide for non-experts. Even the experts use them.

LEAVENING AGENTS

Leavening is the aeration of a product during fermentation, mixing or baking to develop shape, volume and texture. Leavening agents may also do other beneficial things such as increase spread or reduce the

Table 14-1.   Production Data for Use in Sugar Cookery

Temperature °F of Sirup	Physical Characteristic at this Temperature	Cooking Term Used to Indicate This Doneness	Use of the Product
215 to 217 (30° Baume)	Faint thread forms between thumb and finger when they are separated.	Small thread (*lisse or petite fillet*)	Light sirups (1 sugar to 3 water).
217 to 220 (31° Baume)	Longer thread formed between thumb and finger when they are separated.	Large thread (*grande lisse*)	Heavy sirup (1 sugar to 1 water).
221 to 222 (32° Baume)	Thread breaks between thumb and finger.	Little pearl (*petit perle*)	Extra heavy sirups; can crystalize (2 sugar to 1 water).
222 to 223 (33° Baume)	Holds as thread from thumb to finger.	Large pearl (*grande perle*)	Working almond paste, flowing fondants.
223 to 225	Strong thread from thumb to finger.	Thread	Large crystals for crystallizing fruits.
230 to 232	Use spin test; dip perforated ladle into hot sirup; tap lightly on side of container; blow through holes and make bubbles fly out.	The blow (*au souffle or glue*)	Soft, pliable fondant mass; used to glaze fruits and nuts; dip singly and dry; adding a bit of lemon juice retards sugaring.
236 to 239	Soft ball in 50° F water; in finger test, small ball can be rolled between fingers.	Small ball (*petit boule*)	Fondant for flowing icing on petit fours; thin fudge or penuche.
239 to 243	Medium ball in 50° F water; in finger test ball has more firmness than soft ball above.	Medium ball	Firm fondant for dipping bon bons, fruits, and mints; knead when too firm to stir.
245 to 252	Firm ball in 50° F water; in finger test ball is firm.	Large or firm ball (*grande boule*)	Soft caramels at lower temperatures; higher temperatures for taffies.
250 to 258	Quite firm ball but still pliable in 50° F water.		Frostings at lower temperatures; divinity sirup, etc. at higher.
258 to 266	Hard ball in 50° F water; in finger test sirup detaches as hard material when finger is placed into cold water.	Small crack (*petit casse*)	Fondants where fruit juice is added last and temperature brought down to 242° F; nougats, hard taffies, popcorn ball mixtures.
270 to 290	Sirup spins thread; thread snaps between the teeth above 285° F.	Crack (*casse*)	Butterscotch and hard candies; taffies.
290 to 295	Cracks between teeth; crack is quite sharp.	Hard crack, lower range	Hard nougats, ribbon, English and rock candy.
295 to 310	Very sharp crack between the teeth.	Hard crack, middle range	Coating fruit and nuts; some sugar work.
310 to 316	Very brittle and hard between the teeth.	Hard crack, upper range	Pulled sugar work.
316 to 318	Hard to bite; may shatter.	Hard crack, top range	Flowers in pulled sugar work.
318 to 320	Hard to bite; may shatter.	Hard crack, upper limit	Baskets and woven items in sugar work.
338	Light caramelization noticed.	Caramel sugar	Caramel flavored sugar.
400	Almost black.	Burned sugar	Coloring material.

viscosity of a batter or dough, darken pigments and tenderize or toughen proteins.

Air, steam, chemicals or yeast are used as leavening agents. Leavening is seldom the result of one of these working alone but is a combination of two or more working together. The amount of leavening contributed by each varies. A cake made by the conventionel creaming method is leavened equally by steam, air and baking powder. Popovers are leavened mostly by steam.

The type and quantity of leavening required varies with the product, the amount and method of creaming, mixing or beating, the type and quality of ingredients, the sequence of ingredient addition, the altitude and the technique of the operator. To leaven properly, leavening gases must be retained until the structure is set by heat. Structural firmness after cooking should be sufficient to hold shape and retain desirable eating qualities. Excess shrinkage after removal from the oven is frequently caused by a lack of structural strength to support the volume obtained. Over-development of gluten in mixing may restrict movement

Figure 14–13.   Acidified water has been poured into baking soda in the glass on the left and neutral water has been poured into soda in the glass on the right. Pouring boiling water and cold water into these same types of samples brought about similar reactions.

of leavening gas and produce misshapen items with poor texture and volume. Tunnels develop in products because a batter or dough is so strong that gases cannot spread throughout but gather and force their way upward, making typical up-and-down vents called tunnels.

While only a small quantity of leavening may be used in proportion to other ingredients, its influence on quality is so great that exact measurement is necessary. Insufficient leavening yields poor volume and color, a heavy, close grain and a coarse crust. Excess leavening gives a rough, loose, uneven grain and a crumbly, hard, dry texture which lacks smoothness and flavor; over-expansion of cellular walls may produce cell development that cannot be supported and the product falls. The quantity of leavening must be related to the loss of gas occurring in mixing, benching and baking. A quite fluid or soft batter has more gas leakage than a stiffer one and will require more leavening.

Cell or grain size from leavening may be important. A large cell is desirable in a cream puff or popover, while fine cells are wanted in most cakes or similar products. Structural strength must be related to the cell wall size. A cream puff or popover must have a strong outside structure to support the large cells developed. A tender structure will support the fine texture occurring in a cake. Too fine a cell gives a compact, heavy item.

Leavening speed must be controlled. Usually the more rapid the development in baking, the more quickly the structural walls must be set. Most leavening action from chemicals should be obtained during baking and only a small amount during mixing or benching. Baking

Figure 14–14. Reaction rates of baking powders to cold water: (left) tartrate or single acting, (center) sodium acid pyrophosphate (double acting) and (right) sodium acid phosphate and monocalcium phosphate baking powder (double acting).

temperatures and times should permit free batter movement until maximum leavening volume is obtained, then the structure should set and no leavening occur after this. A cake with an overly dark crust and a cracked high center indicates that the outside has set before completion of leavening in the interior. A pie crust or cracker baked at too low a temperature sets before steam can develop between layers of the dough, losing lightness and flakiness. Products such as popovers and eclair pastes should have only the outside portion lightly set at the time steam develops in the interior. If more than this is set, the product will not rise.

Air

Creaming fats, eggs and sugar incorporates air which can leaven a baked item. If this air is retained in baking, a porous texture is obtained. Pound cakes or cookies are leavened almost completely by creaming. The air in the foam of eggs leavens products such as angel and sponge cakes, meringues, etc. Air can be incorporated in other ways such as sifting flour, beating a batter or manipulating a dough. Once air is incorporated, care must be taken to see that it is retained. Air expands about a third in volume in baking. The quantity of leavening contributed by air depends upon the quantity incorporated, the subsequent treatment of the product and the kind and amount of leavening contributed by other ingredients.

Steam

When water changes to steam, it increases in volume 1600 times. This makes steam an effective leavening agent. Popovers, cream puffs, crackers and pie crust depend almost solely upon steam for their leavening. A quart of liquid in a batter or dough is usually considered sufficient to produce enough steam to leaven a pound of flour in a product.

Chemical Leavening Agents

Soda, baking powder and baking ammonia are chemical leavening agents. Baking ammonia has limited use. To give equal leavening, $\frac{1}{4}$ ounce of soda, an ounce of double-acting baking powder and two ounces of single-acting baking powder are required to leaven a pound of flour. Chemical leaveners should be finely divided to go into solution rapidly. They also should be mixed thoroughly into a product in order to reach all areas. Coarsely ground leavening agents give grainy, open products. The finer the grind, the smaller the quantity of leavener required. Many old-fashioned recipes call for soda to be added to a liquid and then

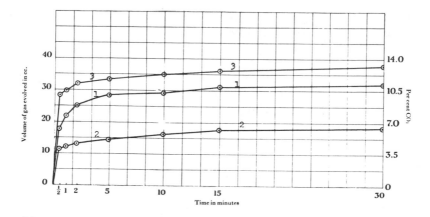

(a)

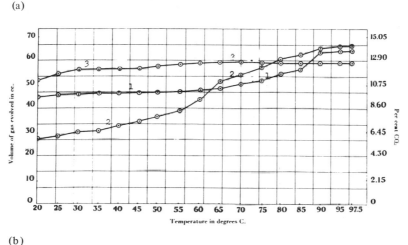

(b)

Figure 14–15. This drawing indicates the reaction rates occurring in batters containing baking powder (a) in the cold stage and (b) in the hot stage. Baking powders are (1) pyrophosphate (double acting), (2) calcium-acid-phosphate (SAS or semi-double acting) and (3) tartrate or single acting.

added to the mixture. This is because a long time ago, soda was not so fine as it is today and this method was used to get a more thorough incorporation of this leavener. Today, however, because soda is quite finely ground, this is not necessary. Such old recipes should be revised.

Soda

Sodium bicarbonate or soda produces carbon dioxide gas that leavens foods. Moisture is needed for this and heat speeds the reaction. If an acid is present such as sour milk, molasses, etc., the reaction can be quite complete and rapid in the cold stage. Without an acid, soda reacts slowly in the cold stage when moistened. When acid is not present to balance the soda or when soda is in excess of the acid, the leavened product will have an alkaline reaction which may or may not be desirable. Color pigments of cocoa or chocolate are reddened and molasses, spices, fruits, nuts, vegetables and some other foods darken when the reaction is alkaline. Longer standing of chocolate cakes before baking gives a higher development of red color if they are alkaline in reaction. The flavone pigments in flour and other items turn yellow in an alkaline medium and anthocyanin pigments turn blue or purple.

Acids in many products are used to neutralize soda completely and, if additional leavening is required, baking powder is used. An alkaline reaction softens gluten and toughens eggs. Gingerbread may sink in the middle because the soda softens the gluten too much. This can be counteracted somewhat by increasing the mixing action. After reacting alone, soda leaves sodium carbonate, a soapy, bitter-flavored residue which may be objectionable. Some acid reactors with soda leave a tasteless residue. Sour milk with soda leaves a tasteless sodium lactate.

Frequently, the quantity of soda required in recipes is guided more by the quantity of acid reactor present than the quantity of flour to be leavened. Cream of tartar is often used as an acid with soda, although slightly acid foods such as honey, fruits, cocoa or chocolate, and spices as well as more acid ones will be used for acid reactors, at least in part. Table 14-2 gives the approximate quantity of acid food needed to react with soda. It is difficult to establish proportions exactly since the acidity in these foods may vary.

Baking Powder

The most widely used leavener is baking powder which is bicarbonate of soda blended with an acid reactor to give a product which the

Table 14-2. Approximate Balanced Reactions Between Liquids and Soda in Food Preparation

Liquid	Weight	Measure	Soda Required for Complete Reaction	
			Weight	Measure
Sour milk or buttermilk	8.3 lb	1 gal	¼ oz	2⅔ T
Molasses	11.5 lb	1 gal	1¾ oz	3 to 4 T
Sorghum	11.3 lb	1 gal	1 oz	2¼ T
Honey	11.3 lb	1 gal	½ to 1 oz	1 to 2¼ T
Vinegar, 40 to 50 grain	3 oz	⅓ c	1¼ oz	2⅔ T
Orange juice	4 oz	½ c	1¼ oz	2⅔ T
Cream of tartar	5 oz	1 c	2 oz	4½ T

federal government states "yields not less than 12% available carbon dioxide," although baking powders used in quantity cooking yield 17%. The acid reactor may be tartaric acid or its salt, compounds of aluminum or acid salts of phosphoric acid or any combination in substantial proportion of these. Starch is used as a diluent to give the standard 12% yield and to act as a drying agent to reduce caking. Calcium lactate may be added to help control the reaction rate.

Certain baking powders evolve gas immediately when moistened. These are called single-acting baking powders because complete reaction can occur in the cold stage. Double-acting baking powder evolves from a fifth to a third of its gas in the cold stage but heat is required to produce the remainder. A double-acting powder may have one reactor that reacts cold and another that reacts hot.

Baking powders made of tartaric acid ($H_2C_4H_4O_6$), monocalcium phosphate [$CaH_4(PO_4)_2 \cdot H_2O$] or monosodium phosphate (NaH_2PO_4) are single acting. Tartaric acid (cream of tartar) and soda, when placed in water, react completely in two minutes. Monosodium phosphate and soda react almost as rapidly but monocalcium phosphate takes a bit longer. A baking powder containing sodium acid pyrophosphate ($NaH_2P_2O_7$) releases gas slowly in the cold stage but more rapidly when heat is applied. Sodium aluminum sulfate (SAS) [$Na_2SO_4 \cdot Al_2(SO_4)_3$] baking powder, another baking powder popular in quantity work, reacts even more slowly than a sodium acid pyrophosphate one. While sodium acid pyrophosphate and SAS baking powders are called double-acting, they are actually single-acting with the action slow when cold and fast when hot, giving a type of double action. A true double-acting baking powder used in quantity work contains calcium acid phosphate which reacts cold and sodium pyrophosphate or sodium aluminum phosphate which react hot. Sodium acid phosphate and monocalcium phosphate are used in another popular baking powder used in quantity food production.

High loss of gas before baking can occur with a single-acting baking powder. For this reason mixing procedures may call for its addition during the later stages of mixing. From 1 to 2 ounces of single-acting powder is usually used per pound of flour, compared with a half to an ounce for double-acting powder. While a small amount of gas is wanted in mixing, panning and on the bench, the amount should be limited to that required. Because an excess of some baking powders may give an undesirable flavor, only the minimum quantity required to give proper leavening should be used. Tartaric acid baking powders leave no aftertaste but, because of their single action, they are not used much in quantity work. Double-acting baking powders that react either slowly or in two distinct stages are best suited to quantity work. Good tolerance in mixing and benching is needed for bakeshop baking powders, for times and conditions may not always be optimum there.

Baking Ammonia

Ammonium carbonate [$(NH_4) HCO_3·NH_4NH_2CO_2$] (baking ammonia) is sometimes used as a leavening agent. With moisture and heat it changes to carbon dioxide, ammonia gas and water. If the reaction is complete, there is little or no aftertaste. When used in thick products, aftertaste may result, so it is used usually only in thin products such as cookies, choux pastes and the like. It gives a rapid expansion which is desirable for spread in cookies and a rapid rise in choux pastes. Since baking ammonia leaves no flavor as soda does, it should be used for spread in cookies. Machine-deposit cookie recipes usually call for a part of the leavening agent to be baking ammonia. If a recipe using only soda or baking powder is changed to ammonia to give spread, approximately half the soda or baking powder should be omitted and 40% of the omitted weight replaced with baking ammonia for baking powder, and 80% of the omitted weight with baking ammonia for soda. Thus, if a recipe called for 2½ ounces of baking powder or 1½ ounces of soda, the substitution would be respectively 1¼ ounces of baking powder and a half ounce of baking ammonia or ¾ ounce of soda and 0.6 ounce of baking ammonia.

Yeast

Special cultured yeast is used for bread. Yeast is a single-celled plant which grows by feeding upon carbohydrates. Wild yeasts in the air can be allowed to culture a potato water or other moist product containing sugar or starch, but bread made from such a leavener usually lacks quality. An old bread dough may be added to a new one to give a yeast culture. This makes sour dough bread. Compressed or active dry yeasts are the most commonly used yeasts in quantity work. A pound of active dry yeast equals 2¼ pounds of compressed yeast in fermenting action.

Yeast grows best between 78 and 90° F. Growth is slowed above 98° F and yeast is destroyed above 140° F. Moisture must be present for good growth. Salt or other chlorides retard yeast activity while sulfates and phosphates promote it. Phosphates are essential for yeast nutrition. The amount of yeast used in warm weather is less than that used in cold weather. Compressed yeast should be kept in storage at 45° F. Freezing may affect some of its activity but, even so, if not frozen for over 30 days, if thawed at 40° F and slightly more is used,

Figure 14–16. The three types of yeast. Top, compressed. Right, dry active granule. Left, old-fashioned cake which is now seldom used.

good results will be obtained. Compressed yeast is approximately 70% moisture. Active dry yeast is shaped into small pellets, dried and packed in sealed cans. It contains 8% moisture and freezing does not harm it. Crumble compressed or sprinkle dry active yeast into water. Allow it to stand for 3 to 4 minutes and then stir. The water is a part of the total

Table 14–3. Ratios for Using Compressed and Dry Yeasts

Compressed Yeast	Active Dry Yeast	Water* Weight**	Approximate Measure
1 oz	½ oz	2 oz	¼ c
2 oz	¾ oz	3 oz	½ c
4 oz	1½ oz	6 oz	1 c
8 oz	3¼ oz	13 oz	1 pt
12 oz	4¾ oz	1 lb 3 oz	1¼ pt
1 lb	6½ oz	1 lb 10 oz	1¾ pt
2 lb	12¾ oz	3 lb 3 oz	1 qt 1¼ pt
3 lb	1 lb 3¼ oz	4 lb 14 oz	2 qt 1 pt
4 lb	1 lb 9½ oz	6 lb 6 oz	3 qt 1 c
5 lb	2 lb	8 lb	4 qt

*Water temperatures should be 90° to 100° F for compressed yeast and 5° to 10° F higher for dry active yeast.
**Corrected to nearest ¼ oz.

(a)

(b)

Figure 14–17. (a) Condition dry active yeast in water at about 110° F — no higher — and condition compressed yeast in water around 100° F. (b) The effect of too warm a temperature, salt and 100° F water with a bit of sugar is shown on yeast growth.

water used. Weigh, do not measure yeast. Table 15-1 gives the amounts of yeast to use to water.

Yeast feeds on glucose, changing it in the process into heat, alcohol, water and carbon dioxide which becomes the leavener. Flour starches and dextrins are changed by enzymes in yeast into maltose; maltose is further changed to glucose. Yeast growth can be assisted by using a malt sirup which may also have in it a diastatic enzyme to help break the maltose into two units of glucose. Yeast has an enzyme in it called invertase which changes sucrose into glucose and fructose. An over-rapid growth of yeast can develop acid as well as the other products.

EGGS

Eggs are used in baking to give tenderness, structure, nutritional value, flavor, color and moisture. They also aid in binding ingredients together and in leavening, emulsifying fats and, when they coagulate, they develop a firmer structure in the product. In many recipes, eggs are counted as moisture with egg whites counted as contributing about two-thirds of their weight as liquid and yolks half. Eggs and their properties have been discussed extensively in Chapter 10 and this information should be reviewed to understand completely the properties of eggs in baking.

FLAVORINGS AND SPICES

Cocoa and Chocolate

Cocoa and chocolate are used in bakery goods to give flavor, richness and color. Chocolate is pure chocolate liquor from the roasted cacao bean with not less than 50% nor more than 58% cocoa butter and not more than 7% crude fiber. Unsweetened chocolate is 8 to 16% starch, about 30% total carbohydrate, 14% protein and around 52% cocoa butter. Cocoa is ground chocolate after about half or more of the cocoa butter has been removed. Breakfast cocoa must contain not less than 22%. High fat cocoa is over 22% cocoa butter, medium 10 to 22% and low below 10%. Cocoa contains approximately 38% total carbohydrate, 20% protein and 10 to 20% starch. The starch in cocoa and chocolate thickens in cooking and sometimes must be considered a part of the flour in a recipe. There is little difference between the richness contributed by shortening or cocoa butter and, if a cocoa is low in it, the difference can be made up with shortening. Cocoa or chocolate turn red in an alkaline reaction. Dutch chocolate or cocoa has been treated with an alkali which makes it darker, increases solubility and gives a smoother flavor. This treatment also swells some of the cellulose and partly gelatinizes the starch.

Spices

Many different spices will be used in the bakeshop. They should be of the highest quality since a small amount at little expense can make such a big difference in flavor. Limited supplies of spices should be kept on hand to assure freshness and excellent flavor, which can be lost or deteriorate. Store spices in tight containers away from heat or moisture. Always weigh; do not measure unless the amount used is so small that weighing is not possible. Some of the more important spices used in the bakeshop are:

Allspice, an evergreen's pea-sized fruit, is grown in Guatemala, Mexico or Jamaica, the latter producing the best. The flavor is a blend of cinnamon, nutmeg and cloves with cloves predominating; 14 t equal an ounce.

Anise is the seed of a parsley family plant growing in Spain, Mexico or Turkey with a flavor reminiscent of liquorice; star anise from China is a slightly different spice with a slight clove flavor touched with liquorice.

Caraway is the seed of a parsley family plant. The best comes from Poland. A black or chocolate caraway used to top some European and Russian breads is different from the regular caraway; $9\frac{1}{2}$ t equal an ounce.

Cardamon is the dried fruit of a ginger plant grown in India, Guatemala or Ceylon. Decorticated cardamon — seeds free of chaff and pods — should be used. Guatemalan and Indian cardamon are best; $14\frac{1}{4}$ t egual an ounce.

Cinnamon is the bark of the evergreen (cassia) tree growing in Ceylon, South Vietnam (Saigon), Batavia (Padang) and Korintji. The first two countries produce the best, a light, grayish brown powder. The lower quality product is reddish brown. Some of the lower quality cinnamons are hard to mix into batters and may be mixed with water to a paste first to simplify addition; $17\frac{1}{2}$ t equal an ounce.

Cloves are the unopened buds of an evergreen tree growing in Molucca, Zanzibar and Madag, all three of which produce good cloves; $14\frac{1}{4}$ t equal an ounce.

Ginger is the root of a rhizome grown in Jamaica, India and Africa. Jamaica's is lighter in color and lighter and smoother in flavor. The Indian cochin ginger is excellent for baking. African ginger is harsh in flavor and is used only in such items as ginger snaps; 14 t equal an ounce.

Nutmeg is the inner part of a peach-like seed grown in the West Indies and Indonesia; $12\frac{3}{4}$ t equal an ounce. Mace is the outer net-like structure around this seed and is slightly more pungent in flavor; 14 t equal an ounce.

Paprika comes from both Spain and Hungary; the bright red Spanish is usually preferred to the darker Hungarian product.

Poppy seed is grown in many areas. The blue poppy seed is preferred for bakery use because of its color and flavor; $11\frac{1}{4}$ t equal an ounce.

Saffron is the pistil of a small crocus grown in Spain. It is extremely expensive but a small amount is sufficient to flavor a large quantity. It is used to season breads and other items.

Flavorings

Flavoring or seasoning should be of the highest quality, as with spices, since the flavor contribution is considerable even though a small quantity is used. Some flavors bake out and these may be purchased locked to glucose or some other product to prevent this. Manufacturers and bakery supply houses can assist in suggesting good products. Freshness is essential.

Flavorings for the bakeshop are extracts made from natural esters or essential oils or imitation products dissolved in alcohol or water or other solvents. Others may be emulsions which are essential oils held in solution by gums or other emulsifiers. In many, the natural oil gives the finest and truest flavor, but for others, the chemist has been able to create an imitation which is better than the true flavor.

Suggested exercises or laboratory experiences for Chapter 14:

1. Make a gluten ball from soft, all-purpose, pastry and hard flour. Bake. When cool, cut to show the network of gluten strands inside. Compare the size of each.
2. Using a cup of water for each, cook a paste using two tablespoons of pastry flour, a tablespoon of cornstarch, two tablespoons of bread flour and one tablespoon of waxy maize. Note the thickness when hot and cold. Compare the opaque quality of each paste.
3. Note the ingredients listed for different types of baking powders.
4. Place a teaspoon each in different cups of soda, tartrate baking powder, double-acting baking powder, and a fourth teaspoon of soda plus a half teaspoon of cream of tartar, mixing the latter well. Now add to each a half cup of cold water. Note the reaction of each. Add a . tablespoon or two of vinegar to the soda and note the reaction.
5. Cook a cup of sugar with $\frac{1}{4}$-cup of water to 250° F. Cool without disturbing to 104° F and then mix until crystals form. Do the same but add 1 t cream of tartar to give a 40% inversion. Repeat, but now add a $\frac{1}{2}$ t of cream of tartar. Compare the resulting fondants.
6. In mixing these fondants in (5) note just before the fondant crystal-

lizes how it thins slightly and turns shiny indicating some heat being given off in the exothermic action of crystallization.

BIBLIOGRAPHY

Amendola, Joseph, *Baker's Manual,* 2nd ed., Ahrens Publishing Co., New York City, 1962.

Fitch, N. K., and Francis, C. A., *Foods and Principles of Cookery,* Prentice-Hall, New York City, 1948.

Kotschevar, Lendal and McWilliams, Margaret, *Understanding Food,* John Wiley & Sons, Inc., New York City, 1969.

Lowe, Belle, *Experimental Cookery,* 7th ed., John Wiley & Sons, Inc., New York, 1955.

Lundberg, D. and Kotschevar, Lendal, *Understanding Cooking,* U. of Mass. Bookstore, Amherst, Mass., 1964.

Sweetman, Marion D., *Food Selection and Preparation,* 3rd ed., John Wiley & Sons.

West, B. B., and Wood, Levelle, *Food Service in Institutions,* 3rd ed., John Wiley & Sons, 1955.

Williams, Matthieu, *Chemistry of Cooking,* Appleton & Co., New York, 1906.

15

Breads

Most food operations purchase their loaf breads but to have top quality products many make their own rolls and hot breads. Many prepared mixes are now on the market which makes it easy to produce a wide variety of both quick and yeast type products. The quality of many mixes has been found to be good and the cost, in comparison to conventional products, equitable.

YEAST BREADS

Standards

Quality factors for evaluating yeast bread are volume, crust color, symmetry of form, evenness of bake, crust character, break or shred, grain, crumb, color, texture and flavor. Since breads differ in their characteristics, these factors must be varied in judging each type.

Size to weight is used for judging volume — regular bread occupies 125 to 155 cubic inches per pound. Too brown a crust, spotting or unevenness of color detracts from the score. An even, rich golden brown or bloom is sought. Evenness of shape, good proportion and the absence of deformities are desirable. Even baking gives uniformly browned sides, ends and bottoms with no excessive browning. The crust should be

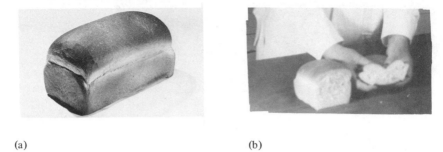

(a)   (b)

Figure 15–1.   High quality is evidenced by the loaf of bread (a) with straight sides and good color and shape. (b) Good bread should spring back to almost its original shape when squeezed.

tender, moderately thick and uniform. Hard-crusted bread may have thick and crisp crusts. Break or shred is judged by the condition of the areas between the top and side where a last minute rise inside the bread creates a break that is open and evenly shredded. A ragged, gaping break is undesirable. Small rolls do not have this break.

The character of the grain (internal appearance) is judged on the basis of size, shape, evenness of distribution and cell porosity. Even sized and evenly spaced cells should be present. A slice of bread or cut roll held at a 45° angle toward the floor in good light should have a creamy white interior with a soft sheen. A gray or uneven color is undesirable. Texture is determined by rubbing the tips of the fingers or the side of the cheek against the cut surface. A judge may also roll a bit into a ball between his fingers to test texture. Velvetiness, softness, moistness and elasticity are desirable. Any harshness or graininess detracts from the score. Overly soft, doughy, crumbly or lumpy bread with a hard, flinty texture is undesirable. Texture can be evaluated also by taste. Bread after cooling, when squeezed, should spring back to nearly its original shape as seen in Figure 15-1b. Flavor is judged by aroma and taste; the odor should be fresh and sweet with no trace of sourness or off-odor. The flavor should be sweet, wheaty and not too salty.

Types of Bread

White bread is made from high gluten, white wheat flour. It should not have over 3% other type of flour. Procedures discussed in this text are normally for white bread and, where they must be varied for other types, this is indicated.

Whole wheat (graham) bread is made from 40 to 60% whole wheat flour and 60 to 40% white flour. The dough is handled much the same

Figure 15–2. A line of flow with the baker on the left scaling the dough, putting it into duchess cutter on the right and giving the cut rolls to the other baker for panning. After filling the pans, the other baker turns and places the rolls into the proofer on the right. If the scaling center were next to the cutter, travel would be eliminated.

as for white bread except for less mixing. It also may be taken to the bench before it has reached a full rise, frequently referred to as "taking it to the bench young." The grain is slightly heavier and volume is less than that of white bread.

About 20% rye flour to 80% strong white flour is used for regular rye bread but some contain as much as 50% or more of rye flour. Rye flour lacks good gluten, usually resulting in heavy grain. When mixing, less liquid is used and less mixing done. Overmixing gives a loss of volume, holes in the crumb and split sides. A loaf can burst in baking from overextension of weak rye gluten. Some increase yeast 1% and give a shorter fermentation, with shortening and sugar kept at minimal levels. Proofing time is reduced to 30 to 35 minutes. *Docking* is common. This is a process in which about ¼-inch deep slashes are made across the top before baking or at makeup. Steam is used in the oven for the first 10 minutes of baking. Gas pressures may cause the bread to burst if docking and steam are not used. If steam is not available, cold water may be brushed over the bread as it goes into the oven and again when the bread has completely risen in the oven. Some bakers use a wash for this made by boiling 2 to 2½ ounces of cornstarch to a quart of water.

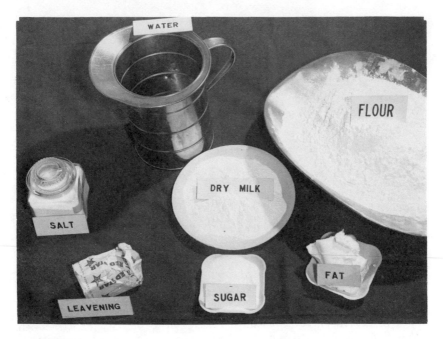

Figure 15–3. Ingredients for a lean bread. The sugar and fat could be omitted. For a rich bread, more sugar and fat and eggs would be used.

Hard, French, Italian or hearth breads require a crisp crust. A lean formula is used containing very little sugar and sometimes no shortening. These breads are frequently docked, except for braided ones. Steam is used to delay crust formation. Baking is usual on hearths or hot bricks but simulated conditions are used such as sprinkling cornmeal on pans to prevent sticking. Hard breads should not touch in baking.

Sweet doughs are used for rich dinner rolls, baba rums, breakfast breads and coffee cakes. Some sweet doughs are as rich as cakes but a less sweet dough may be used for dinner rolls. Rich doughs retard or freeze better than non-rich ones. A rolled-in sweet dough or Danish pastry has shortening rolled in as is done for puff paste. Usually a rolled-in dough is taken to the bench young for rolling in, while a Danish pastry is given a short rest after benching to loosen up a bit. Shortening is then rolled in and the dough allowed to rest about 45 minutes before makeup. Margarine or special shortening is used for rolling in, using from 2 to 4 ounces per pound of dough.

Soy flour may be added to some breads to increase protein. When used, the bread has a deep creamy, almost yellow color. Corn flour, potato flour, raisins, nuts and so forth are used for variety breads.

Ingredients

Yeast dough is made from flour, fat, liquid, yeast and salt; richer ones contain sugar, eggs and flavoring. There are two basic doughs 1) bread or lean and 2) sweet or rich. Each has many variations. Ingredient proportions are usually given in percents related to flour as 100%. Normally, ingredients for each type of dough vary within the following ranges:

	Lean	*Rich*
Flour, bread	100%	65 to 100%
Flour, cake		0 to 35%
Sugar, granulated	2 to 3%	6 to 25%
Shortening	1 to 12%	8 to 40% *
Eggs, whole		10 to 45%
Yeast, compressed	2 to 3%	2 to 8%
Liquid	58 to 60%	40 to 60%
Milk, non-fat, dry	0 to 6%	3 to 8%
Salt	1 to 2½ %	1½ to 2½ %
Spices		¼ to ½ %
Flavoring		¼ to ½ %
Conditioner	¼ to ½ %	¼ to ½ %

*Use additional shortening 20% to 50% of the flour for rolling in.

Yeast bread requires a high quality enriched hard wheat flour or the bread on mixing should be enriched with a special pellet containing the nutrients.

Salt contributes flavor, assists in developing a fine cellular structure, strengthens gluten, retards moisture absorption by the flour and gives whiteness to the crumb. Graham or rye bread doughs or those high in milk and shortening need more salt. Salt controls yeast growth, especially wild yeast. For rapid fermentation, use ½ to 1% salt as more slows fermentation down. Salt can help to control the fermentation rate where temperatures are high and cannot be controlled. Salt should never be mixed directly with yeast. Add salt in sponges in the second mixing. Low-sodium bread is made with calcium salt.

Liquids assist in controlling fermentation. A slack dough ferments faster than a firm one. Liquid is also used to obtain the correct dough temperature for fermentation. To obtain the correct temperature:

1. Add the flour temperature and room temperature plus a 10° to 15° F expected rise from mixing friction; if these are respectively 65°, 70°, and 10° F, the total is 145° F.
2. Multiply by three the desired dough temperature and subtract the result from the sum obtained in 1 above. The remainder is the proper liquid temperature. For instance, if the dough should be 75° F, the calculation is $3 \times 75° = 225° - 145° = 80°$ F.

Table 15-1. Ratios for Using Compressed and Dry Yeasts

Compressed Yeast	Active Dry Yeast	Water*	
		Weight**	Approximate Measure
1 oz	½ oz	2 oz	¼ c
2 oz	¾ oz	3 oz	½ c
4 oz	1½ oz	6 oz	1 c
8 oz	3¼ oz	13 oz	1 pt
12 oz	4¾ oz	1 lb 3 oz	1¼ pt
1 lb	6½ oz	1 lb 10 oz	1¾ pt
2 lb	12¾ oz	3 lb 3 oz	1 qt 1¼ pt
3 lb	1 lb 3¼ oz	4 lb 14 oz	2 qt 1 pt
4 lb	1 lb 9½ oz	6 lb 6 oz	3 qt 1 c
5 lb	2 lb	8 lb	4 qt

*Water temperatures should be 90° to 100° F for compressed yeast and 5° to 10° F higher for dry active yeast.
**Corrected to nearest ¼ oz.

Occasionally, chipped ice or ice water may have to be used to obtain a sufficiently low dough temperature for good fermentation.

Hard water minerals may help strengthen gluten but an excess can toughen the gluten so that it does not ripen properly in fermentation. Strong alkalis weaken gluten. Some hard water salts retard enzymatic action and cause a weak fermentation. If the water is acid, fermentation may be too rapid.

Conditioners or mineral yeast foods condition water to promote best yeast growth. Conditioners reduce fermentation time and losses and give a softer, drier dough with stronger gluten needed in machine production. Greater volume, better uniformity and improved keeping qualities, better oven spring, color, grain and smoothness of crumb result when conditioners are used. Because diastatic and maltase activity is favored with a conditioner, crust bloom is improved. Conditioners depress wild yeast action. Conditioners are added with liquids in straight doughs and with the second flour in sponges.

Product quality is affected by moisture. A lack of liquid fails to develop proper elasticity, tenacity and viscosity of the dough. The dough also does not handle well in mixing, kneading and shaping. Straight doughs take more liquid than sponges. If the absorption rate of the flour is not known, flour should be added to the liquid, stopping when the dough has proper consistency.

In quantity work, non-fat dry milk and water are used. Added shortening can replace the missing milk fat in the amount of 4½ ounces of fat per gallon of milk. Milk improves flavor, nutrient value, keeping quality and crust color. It softens cellular structure and depresses bread volume but strengthens flour proteins. Fermentation is retarded and stabilized by the buffering action of milk. Crumb color is more creamy.

Usually milk is not used for hard-crusted breads since it tends to give a soft crust. Up to 6% milk solids are used in lean doughs, while rich doughs may contain up to 8%. Excess milk solids may give a sticky dough during mixing which usually disappears in fermentation. Flour and dry milk can be sifted together in mixing.

Sugar gives flavor and improves crust color. Yeast can feed on most sugars. Lean doughs contain from 2 to 10% sugar and rich ones up to 25%; since sugar above 10% slows yeast growth, more yeast is used in sweet doughs to counteract this. Milk sugar, lactose, cannot be used by yeast but browns well and gives the crust a good color.

Emulsifying agents may be added to increase shortening's tenderizing action. These may be lecithin, monoglycerides or diglycerides. Also, the emulsifier retains softness by retarding staling and reduces moisture loss. An excess is harmful to bread quality.

Yeast is the leavener used in yeast breads. It has been discussed previously under leavening agents, Chapter 14.

Mold inhibitors are often added to dough to reduce mold growths and keep bread moist and soft. Poor sanitation or improper cooling favors mold contamination. Mold develops rapidly above 80° F and refrigeration or freezing may be needed to inhibit it. Proper handling of bread, thorough baking and the use of a mold inhibitor such as sodium propionate reduces the danger of mold or rope. Rope is caused by *bacillus mesentericus* bacteria which digests the crumb of the bread into a sticky, dark colored yellowish pasty mass with an odor similar to an over-ripe cantaloupe. When the crumb is pressed together and pulled apart, it stretches into silky threads. Rope grows best at temperatures between 90° and 95° F. It is inhibited by good sanitation, some acid in the dough or a mold inhibitor. Once infected, all bakeshop floors and equipment must be thoroughly cleaned using steam and rinsing with a mild solution of vinegar. Good bread has a pH of 5.5 to 5. A pH of 4.6 kills rope. A pint of vinegar, 40 to 45 grain, for every 100 pounds of flour in a dough or $2\frac{1}{2}$ to $3\frac{1}{2}$ to 100 pounds of white flour or 4 to 5 ounces to 100 pounds of dark flour usually controls rope.

While the use of conditioners and mold inhibitors has made possible a bread that stays soft and fresh longer, it has also given a poorer product in some ways. Bakers today use these products not only to control molds and bacteria but also to increase the amount of moisture in the product. This gives a bread which has so much moisture that it soaks easily when used with moist sandwich fillings. This bread also makes poor French toast or regular toast because the center of the slice is soft and pasty rather than possessing chew. When used for a hot beef sandwich or other moist item it also becomes soggy, pasty and slippery, developing

(a)   (b)

(c)   (d)

Figure 15–4.   (a) Crumple yeast into warmed liquid and allow to stand. (b) Then, for a rich dough add eggs and then melted or liquid fat and (c) sugar. (d) Add flour and mix until the dough is smooth and leaves the sides of the bowl as shown in Figure 15–5a.

an undesirable texture. Because of these problems some operations may make their own bread. Few bakeries will make special bread unless the order is very large.

Mixes

Prepared bread or roll mixes containing all ingredients except water and yeast are on the market. Once mixed, they are handled the same as regular breads. The number of rolls made from varying quantities of mix are:

	Yield from Pounds of Mix					
Size roll	4 lb	6 lb	8 lb	10 lb	12 lb	16 lb
1 oz rolls	75	115	150	190	225	300
1¼ oz rolls	65	100	130	160	200	250

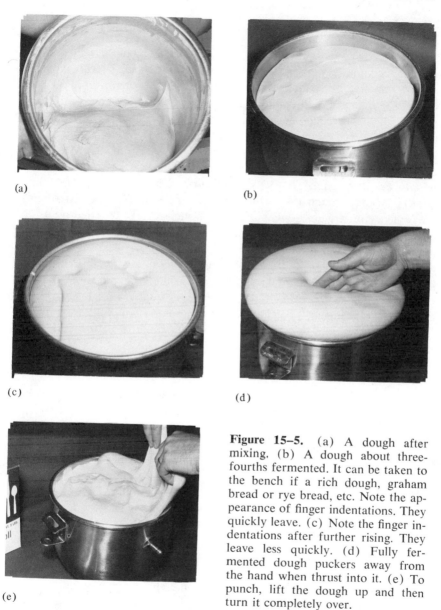

(a)

(b)

(c)

(d)

(e)

Figure 15–5. (a) A dough after mixing. (b) A dough about three-fourths fermented. It can be taken to the bench if a rich dough, graham bread or rye bread, etc. Note the appearance of finger indentations. They quickly leave. (c) Note the finger indentations after further rising. They leave less quickly. (d) Fully fermented dough puckers away from the hand when thrust into it. (e) To punch, lift the dough up and then turn it completely over.

At one time $1\frac{1}{2}$ rolls were calculated as a portion for a meal but this is now nearer to one because people are eating less bread.

Bread Production Procedures

Three types of doughs are made in institutions: 1) straight, 2) sponge and 3) no-time. Sponges are used in large bakeshops making great quantities of bread. Horizontal high-speed mixers are used. About 60% of the flour and all of the liquid and yeast are mixed together making a thick batter. This is fermented at 77° to 80° F until the dough doubles in bulk becoming wavy and ripply. At a slight touch it will collapse. After a punch, the remaining flour, the salt, sugar, shortening, milk solids, nutrient enricheners and conditioners are added and a second fermentation begun. The second fermentation time is usually at the rate of a minute for every percent of the total flour added. If 40% is added, the fermentation time will be around 40 minutes. Usually from 70 to 80% of the total fermentation time occurs in the first fermentation. Such doughs are often called 70–30 or 80–20 doughs.

A no-time dough is used when time must be reduced. Mixing is the same as for straight doughs. No-time doughs can be avoided by using retarded doughs or doughs frozen after make-up. In no-time doughs maximum levels of conditioner, sugar and yeast are used. The dough comes from the mixer at about 90° F and is fermented at this temperature. No-time doughs are taken to the bench young or about three-fourths fermented. Proofing is also shortened. Product quality of no-time dough items are not as high as straight dough products.

Most operations use the straight dough method in the following steps and with following time requirements:

1. Weighing and mixing   12 min.
2. Fermentation   45 to 60 min.
3. Punching   3 min.
4. Benching and resting   10 to 15 min.
5. Make-up   20 min.
6. Proofing   15 to 30 min.
7. Baking   rolls: 20 min.
                          loaf: 60 min.

8. Cooling
9. Storing

The total time for producing a loaf of bread or batch of rolls may be from 2 to 4 hours although work time by hand methods is about 45 minutes for 100 portions or 11 pounds of dough.

Weighing and Mixing

Use standardized recipes and weigh accurately. Assemble all ingredients before mixing. Most small operations will use an upright mixer, but if the quantity is large, a high-speed horizontal mixer is usually used. Quite small batches may be made by hand. With a vertical mixer use a dough hook.

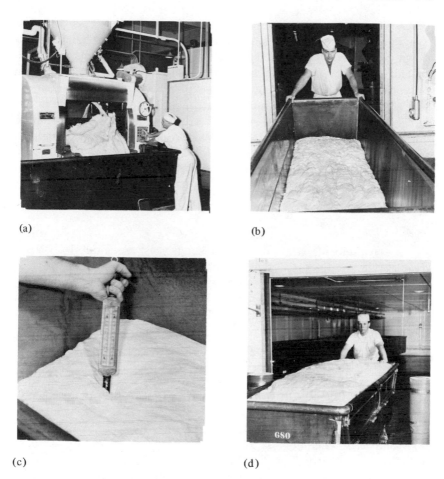

(a)

(b)

(c)

(d)

Figure 15–6. The making of a sponge dough. The sponge method is often-times used when a large quantity of bread is made. (a) Dough coming from the mixer and being dumped into a dough trough. (b) Moving the sponge in a dough trough to the fermentation room. Notice the rough quality of the dough. (c) The temperature and humidity of the fermentation room must be carefully controlled. (d) The sponge after the first fermentation being moved back to the mixer. Note the smoother quality of the dough at this stage. (Courtesy American Baking Institute)

The procedure for straight doughs is: 1) rehydrate the yeast in a small quantity of the liquid, 2) add it to the remaining liquid and fat and 3) mix in the dry ingredients, continuing mixing until a firm, solid paste is formed which leaves the sides of the bowl. During mixing, lumpiness disappears, the dough becomes firm as the flour absorbs mois-ture and the dough relaxes and becomes elastic. Do not undermix if strong flour is used. When properly mixed, the dough should stretch out in the two hands into a sheet as thin as cellophane. This sheet has a uniform consistency with no dense areas. Also, a flat hand pushed down on the dough should leave an impression and points of dough pulled up by the hand quickly subside. After five minutes of rest, a properly mixed dough may show a few bubbles on its surface about the size of a silver dollar. Too many small bubbles indicate an over-mixed dough. Vary mixing times to suit flour strength. Weak flours should be under-mixed. Slightly less water is used producing a firmer dough. A sweet dough should not be developed into as strong a dough as lean ones. Doughs should come from the mixer at 74° to 84° F. They then are allowed to ferment.

Fermentation

Carbon dioxide gas is developed when yeast feeds on glucose. As described in Chapter 14, diastase converts starches and dextrins to maltose and other enzymes change it to glucose. Invertase, an enzyme carried by the yeast, helps to convert sugar to glucose. Too strong a diastatic action gives a slack and sticky dough. Millers usually control the amount of diastase in making flour. Finely milled flour speeds fermentation because starch is more available for diastatic change. Diastase malt or special sirups may be added to give a ready supply of food for the yeast. Protein enzymes may be active in fermentation and their action can be harmful to strong gluten formation. Fresh or dried milk used for bread may be scalded to destroy them. Usually dry milks are treated to reduce their quantity. Protease activity is reduced in aged flour and when conditioners are used. Some protease activity is beneficial because it tenderizes the gluten.

In fermentation the dough ripens. The gluten completely hydrates and becomes pliable, elastic and is less tenacious having a soft, smooth almost silky quality. Extended or too rapid fermentation or too high a temperature develops excessive acidity and a sour dough. Proper times and temperatures must be observed. Fermenting rooms are used to control the temperature and humidity. A humidity of 75% is desirable. If the humidity is low, the dough should be covered or the top brushed with oil or shortening to avoid crust formation. Fermentation times vary. The end of fermentation is indicated when the dough is about double in volume or when the fingers, inserted about three inches into the dough, meet little resistance and the dough recedes or puckers away from the fingers. (See Figure 15-7d.) Doughs made from a flour lacking good gluten, graham or rye flour, no-time or sweet doughs or doughs requiring considerable handling in makeup should be taken to the bench

Figure 15–7. Final steps in making bread, The baker on the near right checks the final temperature of the dough and feeds it into the divider. The next checks the dough as it goes through the divider. The third places the rounded pieces in an intermediate proofer. (Courtesy Standard Brands)

young. After fermenting, the dough is punched. There is about a 2% loss in weight during fermenting.

Punch and Rest

Knocking or pushing a dough down is not punching. Punching is folding a dough over from its sides into the middle until most of the gas is expelled. The dough is then flipped upside down in its fermenting container. Good punching remixes ingredients to give the yeast new food. The gluten is also relaxed. If a bucky, weak or pastry flour is used, the punch may be omitted and the dough brought directly to the bench to rest. Some straight doughs may be fermented again after punching. After the punch, the dough is returned to the work bench and rested about 10 to 15 minutes to relax and become pliable for makeup. This rest time for rich doughs may be less.

(a)   (b)

Figure 15–8.   (a) A baker checks the dough as it leaves the divider to go to the rounder. (b) He checks again as it comes from the molder and places it into greased pans. (Courtesy Standard Brands)

Makeup

Makeup is a process in which items are shaped for baking. Bread is divided into proper sizes, rounded (molded) and usually given an intermediate proof, after which it is panned. Baking loss is about 12%, so for every pound of finished bread, 18 ounces is scaled. Dinner rolls should be scaled a pound per dozen and breakfast rolls, two per portion, a strong ounce each and, if a roll is a portion, slightly over two ounces each.

To roll in shortening, roll the dough to three-fourths to an inch thick in a rectangle about three times longer than wide. Then dot margarine, butter or special roll-in shortening over two-thirds of the surface. Fold the uncovered third over half the covered part and the remaining covered third over the top, giving three layers of dough and two layers of shortening. Rest under refrigeration for 35 to 45 minutes for Danish and 10 to 15 minutes for sweet doughs. Then, roll out and fold three times again. Rest again. The dough is then ready for makeup. (See Figure 15–10).

Rounding, a part of the makeup process, shapes the divided pieces of dough into smooth, round shapes. The dough should be soft and elastic and, as it is rounded and gas escapes, it may "squeak like a mouse." The rounded surface should be smooth when done. A rough surface allows gas to escape in proofing. After rounding, an intermediate proof is given of 8 to 12 minutes to allow the item to recover from the effects of makeup. If this rest is not given, the dough is tight and bucky

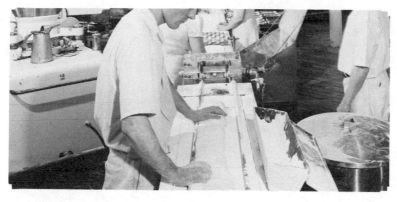

(a)

(b)

Figure 15–9. (a) In an assembly production line a baker shapes the dough as it moves into the cutter. (b) After leaving the cutter, workers place the rolls into pans.

(a)

(b)

(c)

(d)

Figure 15–10.   (a) For a rolled-in dough, the dough is rolled to about three-fourths inch thick and then two-thirds is dotted with a plastic shortening as shown. (b) The uncovered third is folded over half of the covered dough and the remaining third is folded over as shown. (c) It is rested, then turned setting the length of the roll parallel to the worker and rolled into about three-fourths inch thick. (d) It is placed into a pan to rest in the refrigerator. Two fingers pressed into the dough indicate that this dough is at its second turn or rolling.

and shapes up poorly in the pan. Adept, rapid motion is desirable in makeup procedures.

For retarded or frozen doughs, sugar and yeast are increased slightly. Richer doughs lend themselves to this handling. Take such doughs to the bench young, make up and then retard or freeze. The dough may be divided into 10-pound pieces, flattened on baking sheets, covered and retarded or frozen. A retarding temperature of 40° F and a relative humidity of 85% or more will hold a dough up to 72 hours. Retarded or frozen doughs should be covered in storage.

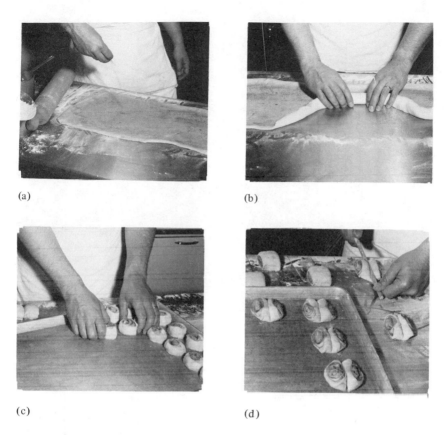

(a)

(b)

(c)

(d)

Figure 15–11. Making a sweet dough into cinnamon rolls. (a) The dough is rolled into a long rectangular strip which is liberally buttered. It is then spread with cinnamon and sugar (10 sugar to 1 cinnamon). (b) The dough is then rolled lengthwise. (c) Cut and pan on a greased baking sheet as shown. (d) To give variety, cut thicker than cinnamon rolls and crease.

Proof

Proofing gives dough its final conditioning. The gluten becomes quite tender and extended and the outer surface smooth and light in appearance. During proofing the products about double in volume from makeup size. Proofing temperatures should be between 90° and 100° F and relative humidity 80 to 85%; time varies from 15 to 45 minutes with 30 to 45 minutes a standard for loaves. No-time doughs have a shorter proofing period and are usually put into the oven slightly under-proofed.

Table 15-2.   Handling and Flow of Sweet Dough

Mix From Mixer at 74°-84° F

Normal Fermentation			Retarding*			
Sweet Dough	Rolled-in Dough	Danish	Danish	Sweet Dough		Rolled-in Dough
Give ¾ to one full rise.	Give ¾ to one full rise.	Let loosen; roll in 2 to 4 oz of butter, margarine, or shortening per pound of dough.	Let loosen; roll in 2 to 4 oz of butter, margarine, or shortening per pound of dough.	Flatten 10 to fit sheet pan; refrigerate.*	Give ¾ normal fermentation.	Give ¾ normal fermentation.
Make-up.	Roll in 2 to 4 oz. of butter, margarine, or shortening per pound of dough. Let dough loosen; make up.	Rest 45 minutes; make up.	Make up.	Bring to room temperature.	Make up.	Roll in 2 to 4 oz of butter, margarine, or shortening per pound of dough. Make up.
			Refrigerate.*	Make-up.	Refrigerate.*	Bring to room temperature.
			Bring to room temperature.		Bring to room temperature.	
Proof. Bake.			Proof. Bake.			

*Use retarding method only for richer sweet doughs; refrigerate from 35° to 40° F with relative humidity at 85%; do not retard over 72 hours.

(a)

(b)

(c)

(d)

Figure 15–12. (a) To make pan rolls, cut dough as shown on the right and roll with both hands. (b) Place a round roll into a muffin pan and divide with a wooden cutter dipped into butter as shown. (c) A quick and easy way to make clover leaf rolls. (d) To make fan tans or butter rolls, roll the dough and then fold, seeing that between folds the dough is liberally spread with butter. Cut and place into pans as shown.

Over-proofing gives an open grain, a gray color to crumb and a loss of flavor and lower volume.

Baking

Baking firms the items preserving texture and shape. The dough is fragile and therefore oven loading should proceed carefully. An over-loaded oven may not regain baking temperatures rapidly enough with the result that the bread does not rise correctly. Preheating the oven to

(a)

(b)

(c)

(d)

Figure 15–13. The make-up of (a) Parker House rolls, (b) hamburger buns and (c) finger or wiener buns. (d) Bowknots and rosettes ready for proofing.

a slightly higher temperature than needed, loading, and then setting the temperature at the desired level help avoid this.

A pound loaf should be baked at 425° F for 15 minutes and then 375° F for 45 minutes. If slightly under-proofed, it should bake an hour from 375° to 400° F. Larger loaves may require slightly lower temperatures and longer baking. Rolls spaced apart require 15 to 30 minutes at 425° F, while pan rolls and others that touch must be baked nearly as long as loaf breads. Bake rich doughs at slightly lower temperatures than lean ones. Oven dampers may need to be open or closed depending upon the type of bread and the size of the product.

During the early part of baking, the rise is quite rapid. Not only does the carbon dioxide gas expand, but yeast activity proceeds at a very rapid rate until the bread reaches 140° F, at which time the yeast is destroyed. This rapid rise is called oven spring. When heat completely swells the starch and coagulates the protein, the structure becomes firm.

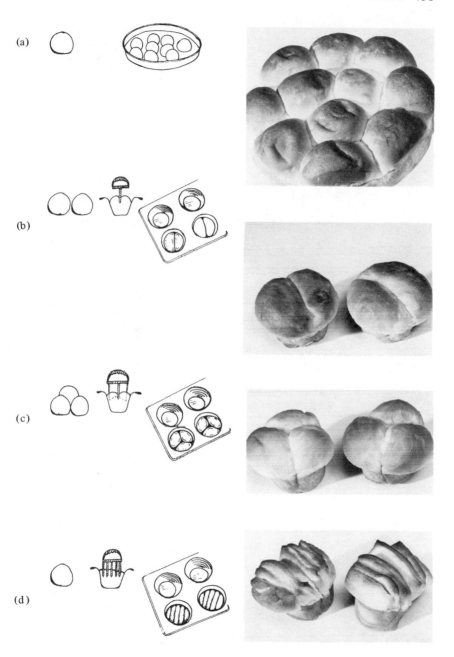

Figure 15–14. Some techniques used to make rolls are shown on the left: (a) pan rolls, (b) twin rolls, (c) cloverleaf rolls and (d) fan tans or butter rolls.

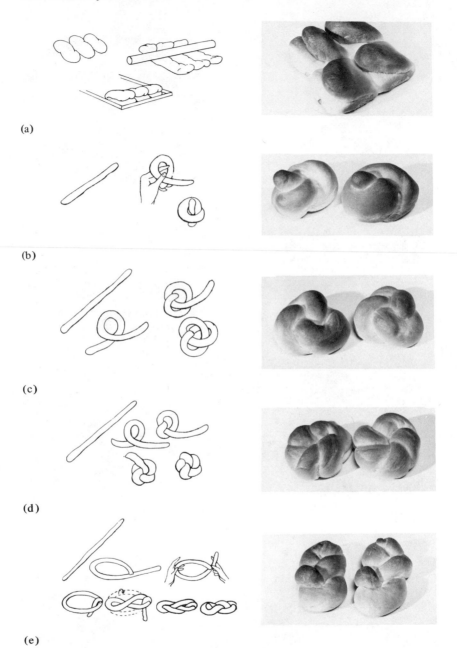

Figure 15–15.   (a) Parker House rolls, (b) single or bowknot rolls, (c) double or rosette rolls, (d) kaiser knot rolls and (e) triple or braided rolls. (Courtesy Wheat Flour Institute)

A shred or break on the side of the loaf occurs because the rise continues after the exterior is set by heat. Small products bake uniformly and do not show this shred. Docking must be used for some products to allow for this final expansion and prevent bursting. Color or bloom is now developed on the outside through a caramelization of sugars and dextrins. Low baking temperatures develop a pale, rubbery crust, poor oven spring and a poor texture. Excessive heat or sugar develops an over-brown crust. Steam is used to retard crust formation and develop thick, crisp crusts. A well baked bread gives a hollow sound when tapped.

Cooling

After baking, loaves, large rolls and rolls that touch in the pan are dumped from their pans onto cooling racks. This allows steam and alcohol to escape. Drafts or too cool air may cause breads to crack. Rolls served soon after baking should be completely baked, but rolls that are cooled and then reheated may be slightly underbaked. Brush breads with shortening to prevent the crust from becoming dry in cooling.

Storage

After cooling, wrap or place bread in moisture-vapor-proof bags for storage over 8 to 10 hours. Otherwise, store on racks. Breads need protection; store in dry, clean containers in a cool place. Use hard, crisp breads as soon as possible. Bake these daily and store in open boxes or paper bags.

The staling of bread is a deterioration characterized by a loss of aroma, increase in firmness and crumbliness and the development of a harsh crumb texture. Breads may be held for extended periods if frozen in good wraps. Best quality results with blast freezing ($-10°$ to $-20°$ F) with air moving at 500 feet per minute. Storage should be at $0°$ F or lower. To use, unwrap and thaw preferably at $115°$ F or at room temperature. Frozen rolls may be heated uncovered at $375°$ to $400°$ F for 5 to 10 minutes and served immediately. Freezing will not restore the freshness of stale or partially stale bread. Slightly stale bread may be used for French toast, toast or grilled sandwiches without noticeable loss of quality. Overly stale bread can be used for dressings or crumbs. Breads stale more rapidly under refrigeration than they do at room temperature. Freezing holds bread best.

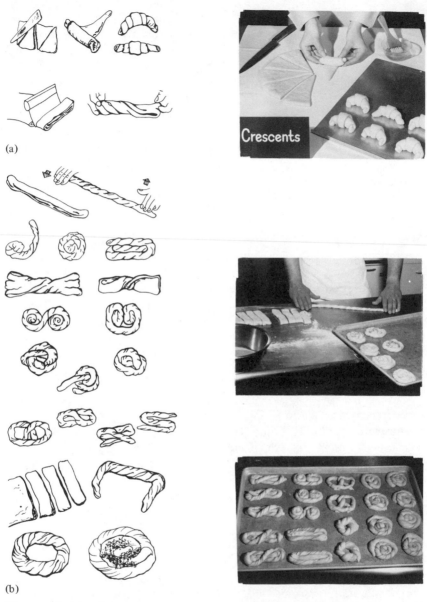

(a)

(b)

Figure 15–16. (a) Crescents may be made by several methods, as shown here. When the roll is not made into a crescent shape, it is called a napkin roll. (Courtesy Wheat Flour Institute) (b) To make twists, proceed as for cinnamon rolls, but fold the dough over after covering only half with sugar, cinnamon, and butter. Twist as shown, using a reverse roll between the left and right hands. Many different products which can be made in make-up from the twist-type product are shown at the bottom.

Figure 15–17. Rolls of dough such as those used for cinnamon rolls may be varied in size and made into a wide variety of shapes. By varying filling and cutting, an almost endless variety of products can be offered on any menu.

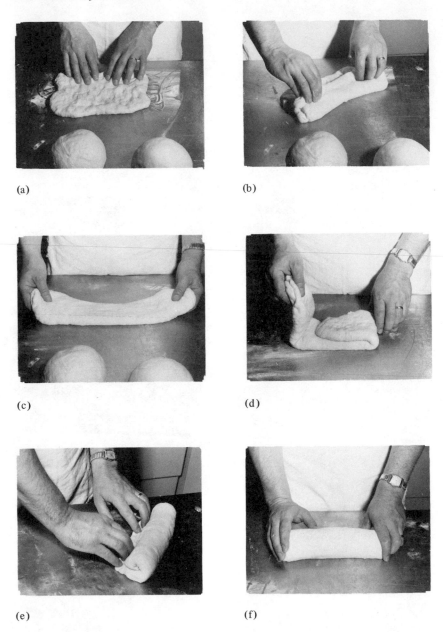

Figure 15–18. To make a loaf of bread, divide the dough and allow it to rest. (a) Shape the loaf. (b) Make a three fold and fold. (c) Stretch into a length double the pan size. (d) Fold again into three. (e) Pat the dough out and fold, sealing the edge as shown. (f) The finished loaf should be panned with the seam side down, as shown.

Table 15–3. Trouble-Shooting Bread Failures

Fault	Possible Causes	Possible Remedies
Excessive volume.	Too much yeast.	Reduce yeast to 2 to 3%; check weighing procedures.
	Too little salt.	Maintain from 2 to 2½%; check weighing procedures.
	Excess dough.	Reduce scaling weights.
	Overproofed.	Reduce proofing time; keep between 70-30 or 80-20 fermentation time for sponges.
	Too cool oven.	Increase temperature.
Poor volume.	Weak flour.	Blend strong flour into flour or use a stronger flour; give less mixing, shorter fermentation, and less proofing time.
	Flour too old or too new.	Use aged flour; check age of flour.
	Water too soft or too alkaline.	Use a conditioner; additional salt improves too soft a water.
	Lack of leavening.	Use good yeast and handle it properly; have dough at proper temperature; reduce quantity of salt.
	Undermixing.	Increase mixing times until gluten in dough is properly developed; proper volume of dough to mixer is also a factor to check.
	Overfermented dough.	Reduce fermentation time.
	Overmixing.	Reduce mixing.
	Improper proofing.	Proof between 90° and 100° F and 80 to 85% relative humidity; watch proofing time and maintain proper ratio between fermentation and proofing procedures.
	Too much or too little steam in oven.	Open or close oven dampers; if steam is introduced into oven, establish better controls.
	Too hot oven.	Reduce temperature.
Too dark crust.	Excess sugar or milk.	Reduce; check diastatic action of flour; it may be breaking down too much starch into sugars.
	Overmixing.	Reduce mixing.
	Dough too young.	Increase fermentation and proof periods.
	Too hot oven.	Correct oven temperatures.
	Too long baking.	Reduce baking time.
	Too dry oven.	Close oven damper during part of baking, or use steam.
Too pale or dull color on crust.	Wrong proportion or lack of right ingredients.	Check ratios of sugar, salt, or milk, and diastatic action of flour; increase ingredients to proper ratios; add diastase sirup.
	Soft water.	Increase salt or add conditioner.
	Overfermentation.	Reduce temperature or time of fermentation.
	Excessive dusting flour.	Cover bench only with bare minimum.
	Too high proof temperature.	Reduce temperature.
	Cool oven.	Increase temperature.
	Improper use of steam.	Avoid excessive steam; open dampers to increase oven moisture.
Spotted crust.	Improper mixing.	Follow correct mixing procedures and sequence of adding ingredients.
	Excess dusting flour.	Reduce dusting flour.
	Excess humidity in proofing.	Reduce relative humidity to between 80 and 85%.
	Water in oven or excessive moisture in steam.	Check steam pipes and ovens; open dampers.

Table 15–3 (cont.)   Trouble-Shooting Bread Failures

Fault	Possible Causes	Possible Remedies
Hard crust or blisters.	Lack of sugar or diastatic action.	Increase sugars or check diastatic action of flour; check weighing of ingredients.
	Slack dough.	Reduce liquid; check mixing.
	Improper mixing.	Check mixing procedures and sequence of ingredient addition.
	Old or young dough.	Correct the fermentation time.
	Improper molding or make-up.	Correct procedures.
	Cool oven or too much top heat.	Check damper handling procedures and oven temperatures; check heating elements and heat source to see if functioning properly; check oven circulation.
	Cooling too rapidly.	Cool more slowly; keep out of drafts.
	Too much fat on product.	Reduce brushing of fat after make-up.
Poor shape.	Improper make-up or panning.	Correct procedures.
	Overproofing.	Reduce.
Flat top or sharp corners.	New flour.	Age flour six to eight months under proper conditions.
	Low salt.	Increase; check weighing procedures.
	Slack dough.	Reduce liquid; check mixing.
	Young dough.	Increase fermentation time.
	Excessive humidity in proofing.	Reduce humidity.
Excessive break on side.	Overmixing.	Reduce mixing.
	Improper molding.	Check molding, especially seam folds; place seam folds down on bottom of pan.
	Young dough.	Correct; check proofing time.
	Hot oven.	Reduce temperatures.
Thick crust.	Low shortening, sugar, or milk.	Increase; check scaling procedures.
	Low diastase.	Check diastatic action of flour; add malt sirup or diastase compound.
	Mixing improper.	Correct mixing procedures.
	Improper proofing.	Correct temperature, relative humidity, or time of proofing; check for wet crusts after proofing.
	Old dough.	Correct fermentation and/or proofing time.
	Improper baking.	Correct temperatures and times; reduce steam and check for excessive or insufficient moisture in ovens.
Tough crust.	Old or young dough.	Check fermentation times.
	Improper mixing.	Correct.
	Excess proof or wrong proof conditions.	Correct.
	Oven cold or excess steam.	Correct.
Lack of break or shred.	Excess diastase.	Decrease amount; use non-diastatic malt: check diastatic action of flour.
	Soft water.	Increase salt or use conditioner.
	Slack dough.	Reduce water substantially; check mixing.
	Improper fermentation or proof time.	Correct.
	Too hot or too dry an oven.	Correct temperatures by damper control; introduce steam.

(continued)

Table 15-3 (cont.) Trouble-Shooting Bread Failures

Fault	Possible Causes	Possible Remedies
Ragged scaling or shelling on top.	Green or overly old flour.	Use flour properly aged.
	Old or young dough.	Check fermentation or proof times and conditions.
	Stiff dough.	Reduce flour or increase liquid.
	Crusting during proofing.	Increase relative humidity; brush lightly with shortening.
	Excess salt.	Reduce.
	Underproofing.	Increase proofing time.
	Excessive top heat in oven.	Check heat circulation and heat source in oven; check damper control.
	Cold dough.	Add warmer liquid; check mixing, fermentation, and proofing temperatures.
	Excessive dough in pan.	Check scaling.
	Lack of salt or milk.	Check recipe and weighing procedures.
Too close grain.	Low yeast.	Increase; check weighing procedures.
	Underproofing.	Correct.
	Excess dough in pan.	Check scaling procedures.
Too coarse or open grain.	Hard or alkaline water.	Add vinegar or conditioner.
	Old dough.	Excess yeast; reduce fermentation time.
	Slack dough.	Reduce liquid; check mixing times.
	Improper molding.	Correct.
	Overproofing.	Reduce time or check temperatures.
	Improper pan size.	Check.
	Cold oven.	Increase oven temperature.
	Excessive greasing.	Check oiling or greasing of dough.
Gray crumb.	High diastatic action.	Reduce.
	High dough temperature or over fermentation.	Check mixing, fermentation, and proof temperatures and times.
	Cold oven.	Check temperatures and conditions of baking.
	Pans greasy.	Check greasing.
Streaked crumb.	Improper mixing.	Check ingredient sequence of adding in mixing.
	Too slack or stiff dough.	Check liquid or flour quantities; check to see if proper mixing times given.
	Excessive oil or grease, or dusting flour used.	Correct.
	High relative humidity.	Reduce relative humidity in fermentation or proofing.
	Crusting of dough in fermentation.	Increase relative humidity or brush with fat; cover to prevent moisture loss.
Poor texture.	Alkaline or very hard water.	Use conditioner or vinegar.
	Too slack or too stiff dough.	Reduce or increase ingredients to correct ratios; check mixing.
	High sugar or excess yeast.	Check ingredient ratios; check diastase, and decrease or increase as required.
	Lack of shortening.	Increase.
	High dough temperature.	Reduce liquid temperature or temperatures during fermentation or proofing.
	Overfermentation or proofing.	Reduce.

Table 15–3 (cont.)   Trouble-Shooting Bread Failures

Fault	Possible Causes	Possible Remedies
Poor texture (cont.)	Excessive dusting of flour.	Reduce.
	Low oven temperature.	Increase.
Off- and/or cheesy flavor.	Inferior milk, rancid shortening; paint, gasoline, etc.	Check ingredients used; check flour, other ingredients for off-flavors; check storage areas where ingredients are held; check pans and other equipment for rancidity; check sanitation.
	Improper mixing or method.	Check procedures.
Flat flavor.	Low salt.	Increase salt.

QUICK BREADS

Quick breads belong to the batter and dough family. Leavening is usually by chemical leavener but steam, air or yeast can be used. Many quick breads are closely related doughs or batters. Slight variation in the quantity of ingredients or techniques used in mixing, panning or baking result in products that differ much more than one would expect. Table 15-4 indicates how the most commonly used quick breads vary in ingredient proportions.

Mixes are on the market which need only liquid and perhaps egg to produce high quality products. These save labor and require less skill. Many, with slight variation, are capable of producing a wide variety of items. They have good tolerance in handling and lend themselves well to quantity work and can be held up to six months. Operations can also prepare their own mixes. Recipes for making these can be obtained from bakery supply firms. Frozen batters and doughs and some frozen baked products are also available.

Standards

A high quality muffin is large for its weight. The crust is crisp, shiny, pebbly and golden brown. A smooth crust of low color can indicate toughness. The top should be well rounded and free from knobs. The interior crumb should be moist, light and tender with no tunneling. Plain muffins should have a creamy-white crumb with an even grain and a delicate, not bready or too sweet flavor. Loaf breads, quick coffee

Figure 15–19. Doughs may be placed into a refrigerator and retarded, or made-up and then frozen.

cakes and other variety breads are made from muffin-type batters and their standard may be much the same except for shape.

A high quality biscuit should be well shaped and regular, with straight, even sides and a level top and should have good volume. The crust should be tender but not crumbly and have a smooth, golden-brown color. The inside texture should be fine, even-grained and fluffy with a creamy-white color free from yellow or brown spots. The biscuit should break easily and the moist, soft crumb should pull away in thin flakes or layers. Dropped biscuits will vary somewhat from this standard, being shorter, less perfect in shape and have crust qualities similar to those of a muffin.

Figure 15–20. Service of quick breads such as shown here wins enthusiastic approval of patrons. (Courtesy General Foods)

Table 15–4. Approximate Ingredient Percentages in Quick Breads (*Based on flour at 100%*)

Ingredient	Biscuits %	Muffins %	Cornbread %	Griddle-cakes %	Waffles %	Popovers %	Eclair Paste %
Flour, bread	0 to 50						100
Flour pastry	50 to 100	100*	100**	100	100*	100	
Sugar	0 to 2	10 to 65	5 to 25	2 to 10	15 to 30		
Shortening	20 to 30	20 to 40	6 to 20	5 to 15	50 to 40		
Eggs	0 to 10	20 to 25	20 to 25	15 to 35	20 to 65	100	175
Liquid	60 to 70***	70 to 80	80 to 90	125 to 200	130 to 180	200	200
Milk, dry, non-fat	7	8	8	10 to 15	10 to 15	20	
Baking powder, double acting	6	6	8½	6 to 10	6 to 8		
Salt	1 to 2	1 to 2	1 to 2	1 to 2	1 to 2	1 to 2	1 to 2

*   For greater tenderness, cake flour may be used.

**   About 50% of the flour is cornmeal.

***For shortcakes reduce liquid to 50 to 60% and increase sugar to 15 to 20%.

(a)

(b)

(c)

Figure 15–21. (a) High quality in these popovers is indicated by their appearance. (Courtesy Wheat Flour Institute) (b) This muffin sells by its appearance. (Courtesy Processed Apples Institute) (c) The crumb on this cornbread indicates its excellence. (Courtesy General Foods)

A popover or eclair paste product should have a round, irregular top with a delicate tan and be large for its weight with good height. Low volume may indicate improper baking, excess moisture or a failure to mix properly. Too dark a color may indicate too high a baking temperature or too long baking. Popovers may be popped over on their sides at the top. They will not have as deep or even a color as eclair paste products. The interior should be hollow and large. Bottoms should be shiny and even with no holes. Crusts should be crisp, brittle and tender. The interior should be slightly moist but not pasty, damp or excessively dry.

A good pancake (griddlecake or hotcake) should have a clear, even brown color and a good round shape with no pitting on the top or bottom. The texture may be moist, slightly heavy and thin, which sometimes gives the cake the name of "flannel." Others may be less moist, firmer, drier, light, porous, open and about ¼-inch thick. All should be well cooked inside and tender with firm, slightly crisp exteriors. They should be hot. Flavor should be pleasing and only slightly bready.

Waffles should be a light, even, brown color with distinct grid markings and even shape without ragged edges. Crusts should be tender and crisp but crispness may vary according to the basic recipe and baking time. The interior should be open with a tender, cream-colored crumb. The flavor should be slightly sweet, nutty and pleasant.

Muffins

The thick and lean muffin batter gives good opportunity for gluten development in the mixing and handling. Overmixing gives a tough muffin. Increasing batter richness or using a weaker flour, such as cake flour, makes it possible to increase mixing. Mix at about 60° F to retard gluten development. Sift dry ingredients into the mixer bowl and dump the blended egg, liquid and liquid shortening into the middle. Use a mixer paddle and at slow speed mix 15 to 20 seconds. The flour should just disappear and the batter will be rough and lumpy, breaking easily when dropped from a spoon. The dry ingredients are sometimes mixed in a large batch, and then as required during service, a small part

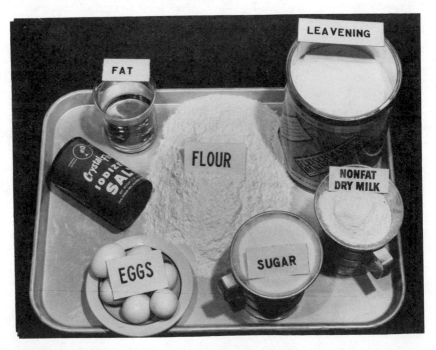

Figure 15–22.   The basic ingredients for a muffin batter. Similar to muffins are loaf breads, waffles, hot cakes and other products. Water would be included as an ingredient.

(a)　　　　　　　　　　　　　　　　　(b)

Figure 15–23. (a) Mix a muffin mixture until the dry ingredients barely disappear. It should appear rough and pebbly. (b) In removing batter, start at the outside and work out, reducing the tendency to toughen the batter.

is blended with the liquid ingredients and baked. Sometimes solid shortening is cut into the dry ingredients, as for biscuits, and then the liquid and eggs are added. Or, the shortening may be creamed with the sugar and the eggs and liquid added alternately with the sifted dry ingredients. If either of these two variations are used, more shortening is needed. Using fine sugar rather than coarser types speeds dissolving of the sugar.

Many variations are possible from one good basic muffin recipe. Portioning may be done with a No. 16 scoop or by hand dipping and squeezing portions into lightly greased pans. Take the batter from the inside edge out, thereby eliminating stirring and reducing toughness. Gingerbread, cornbread and other batters may be so thin that they may be poured. If the batter is too deep in the muffin pans or if the muffins are baked at too high a temperature, tunneling is encouraged.

Muffin pans should be conditioned and only lightly greased. Slight dusting with flour over the greased area helps reduce sticking. Pans should not be washed after use but thoroughly cleaned with a clean, soft absorbent cloth. Pan and bake muffins immediately after mixing; otherwise some quality is lost. After baking, to avoid a soggy or overmoist product, dump the muffins from the pans or set them on their sides in the muffin cups to allow steam to escape and the product to dry out somewhat.

Overmixing, mixing too slowly, too much flour or liquid, insufficient leavening or a low oven temperature results in heavy muffins. Overgreased pans or baking too long or in too hot an oven causes heavy crusts.

(a)   (b)

Figure 15–24. (a) A properly made muffin is shown on the left. Note the knob on the overmixed muffin on the right. (b) These two muffins cut. Note how tunnels inside the one on the top indicate toughness.

Normally about 6 to 7 pounds of flour or 14 to 16 pounds of batter gives 100 portions averaging 1½ muffins per portion. About 2½ ounces (a 3-inch square an inch thick) of coffee cake, Sally Lunn or cornbread is a portion. An 18 × 26-inch pan can be cut 5 × 10 or 6 × 8. A loaf from a 5½ × 10½ × 3-inch pan cuts into about 25 ⅜-inch slices (2 slices per portion); about 8 pounds of flour or 20 pounds of batter is needed for 100 portions.

Baking Powder Biscuits

Cut the shortening for baking powder biscuits into dry ingredients using a pastry blender or mixer paddle at low speed until it looks like loose, coarse cornmeal. Overmixing gives a fine bready texture while too little develops a coarse texture. Next, add the liquid using the paddle at low speed until a soft dough is formed. Overmixing or overkneading toughens biscuits. Then knead the dough on a lightly floured bench and fold lightly. Use the finger tips to lift the dough up and then press the dough down with the heel of the hand. Deft touch and light pressure are required. Give the dough a half turn after each kneading, about 20 in all, requiring about 30 seconds. At the end of kneading, the dough should be soft and springy but not sticky. If kneading is omitted, a shorter, crisper, lower-volume biscuit is obtained. Using slightly more shortening and cutting it in the size of a small pea, coupled with good kneading, gives a good flaky biscuit. Flakiness is achieved also by making a dough as slack or slightly more slack than for a dropped biscuit and then adding the remaining flour during kneading. To cut for baking,

Figure 15–25. The basic ingredients for a baking powder biscuit mixture. Water would be included.

roll the dough half the final height desired—for inch high biscuits roll a half inch thick — cut evenly and straight down, as twisting may give a poor shape. Roll out evenly and uniformly to give even biscuit size and baking. Many operations cut biscuits from the rolled dough in squares or triangles with a cutter or knife so that all the dough is used in one cutting. Additional reworking of cutting scraps may give tough, compact biscuits. Setting biscuits apart on baking sheets gives a more highly colored, crisper biscuit, especially if the cut biscuit is washed with or dipped into melted butter, margarine or shortening. The tops may be washed with a milk, evaporated milk or egg wash before baking to color them. Shortcakes are rich biscuit doughs containing extra sugar and shortening. Dumplings are variations of biscuit dough and may contain eggs.

A dropped biscuit is not kneaded. The dough is slightly more moist and leaner than regular biscuit dough. Dropped biscuits are dropped onto greased baking sheets from a spoon. The resultant product has less volume, a rougher appearance after baking, a crisper crust and a tenderer crumb than a regular biscuit. Bake all biscuit items at 425° F 15 to 20 minutes.

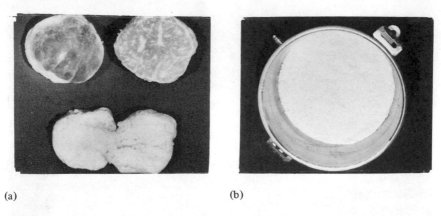

(a)   (b)

Figure 15–26. (a) The dry mixture for a baking powder biscuit should appear coarse as shown here. (b) The crumb shown here indicates a flaky, delicate texture.

Scones are made from rich biscuit dough containing egg. Raisins, nuts, currants and other items may be added. Mix, knead and roll as for biscuits, then pat out to cover the baking sheet. Cut next into rectangular shapes about an inch wide and two inches long. This cutting should be done with a scraper dipped into margarine or shortening to permit easy separation later after baking. The tops may be washed with

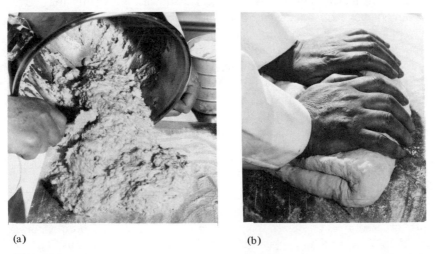

(a)   (b)

Figure 15–27. (a) After mixing the liquid into a baking powder biscuit mix, it should appear as shown. (b) Knead on a floured surface, using the palms of the hands to develop gluten.

(a)   (b)

Figure 15–28. (a) To save time and give a more consistent quality, cut biscuits into squares with a lightly oiled bench knife. (b) Scones being buttered after being cut as shown.

egg wash before baking. Sometimes scones may be cut on a board and panned apart. Many cut each scone in the center with a cutter dipped into margarine or butter so that a break appears at this spot after baking. (See Figure 15-28).

A beaten biscuit is a Southern quick bread which is not a typical biscuit since no leavening is used. The flour usually contains phosphates to assist in giving a lightened product. This soft dough is pounded with a stick "24 times for family and 48 times for company." During pounding, it is folded frequently to tenderize and to blend air into it.

Poor biscuit quality may result from one or more of the following:

Defect	*Causes*
Heavy or compact crumb	1) Overmixed or overkneaded dough, 2) insufficient baking powder or shortening, 3) too much liquid or flour or 4) oven not hot enough.
Pale crust	1) Oven not hot enough, 2) baked in too deep a pan or 3) too much flour.
Poor volume	1) Oven not hot enough or 2) insufficient baking powder.
Light but not flaky	1) Shortening cut too finely into flour or 2) insufficient kneading.
Poor shape	1) Too slack dough, 2) uneven rolling, 3) twisting the cutter or 4) careless cutting or panning.

Griddlecakes and Waffles

Waffle batter is between griddlecakes and muffins in batter density. Overmixing can toughen the waffle. As in muffins, richness or the use of cake flour permits more mixing. Griddlecakes having a thinner batter can receive more mixing because the liquid disperses the gluten, preventing it from forming a cohesive structure. Blending liquids into well-sifted dry ingredients is the usual mixing technique. Occasionally beaten egg whites are carefully folded into the batter at the end of mixing. This gives a lighter product and less baking powder may be required. If the ratio by weight of fat to liquid in a hotcake or waffle batter is 1:4, the griddle or waffle grid need not be greased. Swedish or French pancakes or blinis usually contain no leavening agent. They are thin batters high in egg content and are slightly less tender than the flannel cake.

Griddlecakes are baked on a lightly greased griddle at around 350° to 375° F. About two ounces are placed on the griddle for a small, and four ounces for a large, cake. For 100 portions of two large cakes, 17 pounds of flour or 50 pounds of batter (six gallons) are needed. As the heat strikes the batter, volume increases and bubbles rise to the top. When the edge shows a slight drying the cake should be deftly turned. Complete baking in one turn since additional turning lowers quality. The cake will rise slightly in the center after the turn. When this recedes and the top becomes even, the cake is done. An even griddle heat is necessary. Too low a temperature gives poor color and texture. If it is

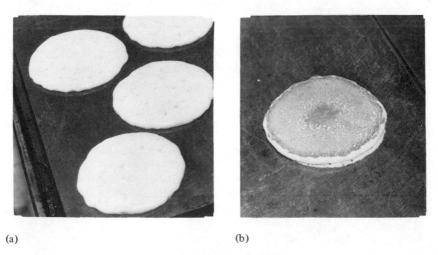

(a)   (b)

Figure 15–29. (a) These griddlecakes are ready to turn. Note the bubbles on the top and the puffy quality of the batter. (b) The griddlecake turned and ready to serve.

 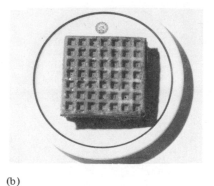

(a)   (b)

Figure 15–30. (a) This baker has been filled too full. It will overflow when the lid is lowered. (b) A well baked waffle.

too high, the color is dark and the cake is apt to undercook or be raw in the center. A pitted top after baking indicates too high a heat or too long a time lapse before turning.

Waffles should be baked in a well conditioned waffle baker. The batter should be placed in the center to about 1 to 1½ inches from the edge since baking spreads it out to the edge. About four ounces of batter is needed for a portion, 30 pounds per 100 waffles. Waffle batters contain usually more sugar, fat and eggs than griddle cake batter and some may be so rich that they are called cake waffles and can be served topped with ice cream and a sirup as a dessert. Increasing the baking time gives a crisper waffle. Crispness is also dependent upon batter richness.

Eclair (Choux) Pastes and Popovers

An eclair or choux paste is made by cooking flour, or shortening and water into a smooth paste. An insufficient amount of water or over-cooking may cause a broken emulsion, while an excess of water gives too soft a paste and a product with low volume. After cooking, the batter is cooled to about 150° F and eggs are added in about 4 or 5 additions. After each addition, the batter must be mixed well to obtain a smooth, velvety, shiny paste. Thickness of the batter should be suffi-cient to retain shape in panning. Frequently the batter is shaped with pastry tubes. A medium-size cream puff or eclair requires about two ounces of batter.

A popover batter is a *pour* batter like a hotcake batter. It should be beaten well to develop gluten strength and a firm structure. The batter

Table 15-5.   Scaling Weights and Baking Temperatures and Times for Breads

Product	Pan Size	Units Per Pan	Scaling Weight	Baking Temperature (° F)	Time (min)
Yeast Breads					
Rolls, small	8 in.*	12	1 to 1⅓ oz	400 to 425	15 to 20
	17 x 25 in.	72 to 100			
Rolls, medium	8 in.*	8 to 12	1½ to 1¾ oz	400 to 425	15 to 20
	17 x 25 in.	60 to 85			
Rolls, large	8 in.*	8	2 to 2⅓ oz	390 to 420	20 to 25
Cinnamon rolls	8 in.*	8 to 12	1 to 2 oz	375 to 385	25
	17 x 25 in.	72 to 100		375	30
Sweet rolls	17 x 25 in.	24	2 oz	380 to 400	25
Tea rings	8 in.*	1	10 to 12 oz each with 2 oz filling	375	30
Topped coffee cakes	8 in.*	1	10 to 12 oz each with 2 oz topping	375	30
Fancy coffee cakes	8 in.*	1	10 to 12 oz each with 2 oz filling	375	30
	17 x 25 in.	8			
Bread, white	1¼ lb	3 to 5	26½ oz	400	60
Bread, rye	1 lb	1	18 oz	400	45
Quick Breads					
Brown, steamed	4 x 9 x 4 in.	1	1½ lb	Steam	60 to 90
Biscuit, 2¼ in.	17 x 25 in.	88	1¼ oz	425	15 to 20
Dumpling	8 in.*	12	1½ oz	Steam	20 to 30
Cornbread	17 x 25 in.	1	6 lb	425	30
Griddle cakes			4 oz	350 to 375	3 to 5
Muffins, plain			1⅓ to 1½ oz	425	15 to 20
Muffins, bran			1½ oz	425	20 to 25
Breads, quick	7½ x 3½ x 2¼ in.	1	18 oz	350	60
Breads, date and nut	7½ x 3½ x 2¼ in.	1	22 oz	350	60
Breads, quick	4 x 9 x 4	1	1¾ lb	350	60 to 75
Cream puffs			1½ oz**	450	15
				15 min and then	
Eclairs or popovers			2 oz**	375	30 to 40

*round or square pan   **Fill cream puffs 2½ oz, eclairs 2 oz, using ¾ oz topping for eclairs.

Table 15–6. Yields from 30-lb Lots of Dry Mixes

Mix	Yield	Mix	Yield
Griddlecakes	725 (4 oz each)	Bran muffins	720 (1 oz)
Waffles	300	Corn bread	375 (2 x 3 in)
Biscuits	720 (2 in)	Corn bread	520 (sticks)
Plain muffins	800 (1 oz)	Coffee cake or	40 (8 in layer)
		Gingerbread	300 (2 x 3 in)

should be panned in deep, heavy muffin tins. If conditioned, the pans do not need greasing. Heavy iron preheated pans are desirable for quantity work and are filled to about half full and placed into a hot oven immediately after panning. A failure to achieve volume may be caused by improper mixing, insufficient eggs, excess liquid or too low heat.

The structure of a popover or eclair paste product is important to its quality. Leavening is by steam which forms rapidly inside the base of the batter early in baking. As the steam expands, it pushes upward, developing a large hole inside. Once full expansion is obtained, baking must then firm the structure to prevent the product from collapsing after the steam condenses. To achieve these results, the baking temperature should be 450° F for 15 minutes to develop steam, and then dropped to 375° F and baking continued for 30 to 40 minutes. During this last period, the structural walls are dried out. Browning is not always an indicator of doneness. A rapid cold shock upon oven removal may collapse these products. To avert this, pull to the front of the oven and allow to stand a few moments with the door open to reduce the heat gradually. About five minutes before the end of baking, the items may be lightly pricked at the top to allow steam to escape. Cream puffs, eclairs, French crullers (see doughnuts) and other choux pastes are made from eclair pastes. Yorkshire puddings are nothing but popover batters.

A recipe for a choux paste may call for $\frac{1}{4}$% baking ammonia to 100% flour. This helps give rapid expansion. Eggs may be reduced slightly when it is used. The ammonia quickly escapes as a gas through the thin walls. Ammonia is not used for popover batters since these are usually served hot and the ammonia flavor would still be present when eaten.

Crumpets and English Muffins

Crumpets and English muffins are yeast-leavened and their production is much the same as for yeast products. Their doughs are usually higher in liquid than regular yeast bread doughs. Crumpets leavened with

Figure 15–31.   (a) The basic ingredients for popovers: milk, flour, eggs and salt. (b) The basic ingredients for an eclair or cream puff batter: flour, butter or shortening, eggs, water and salt.

Figure 15–32. The baking of popovers and eclair (choux) paste products is a critical factor for quality. These products have been baked at too high a heat and taken from the oven too soon. Because they did not develop sufficiently strong walls, they collapsed when cool air struck them after oven removal.

baking powder are sometimes made but these do not have the chewy texture of the yeast-leavened ones. After fermentation, the crumpet batter is poured into greased rings ($2\frac{1}{2}$ to 3 inches in diameter and about $\frac{3}{4}$ to 1 inch thick) on a hot griddle. They are allowed to cook until bubbles on the top are firm. They are then turned and cooked on the other side like hotcakes. Most of the baking occurs before the turn and the top side is open, giving the crumpet a honeycomb or web-structured appearance. Its texture should be somewhat chewy.

English muffins are rich yeast doughs, soft to the point of being almost tacky. They are cut on the bench from the dough by a round cutter and are heavily proofed about 15 minutes. They are then carefully placed on a griddle, often in rings, and baked. When browned and partially done on one side, they are turned and baked on the other. The

Figure 15–33. Crumpets being baked in their metal shells (left) and English muffins being baked on the right.

temperature of the griddle should be about 350° F for both crumpets and English muffins.

Suggested exercises or laboratory experiences for Chapter 15:

1. Make a straight and a no-time dough into bread or rolls and keep track of the various step times. Use these doughs to make up various shaped rolls.
2. Make a sweet dough and use this for cinnamon rolls, coffee cakes, etc. Save a part and make a rolled-in dough from it. Shape this dough into butterhorns, bear claws and other products. Compare the products.
3. Make a plain muffin batter and then vary it making
   a. a small coffee cake topped with streussel topping.
   b. blueberry muffin by adding about a teaspoon of blueberries to the muffin cup after putting in about half the batter — if blueberries are not available make a different type.
   c. an upside-down pecan muffin by putting in a teaspoon of

butter, 2 t of brown sugar and 2 t of chopped pecans on the bottom of the muffin cup before adding the batter.
Overmix the last bit and bake, noting the product quality.

4. Make a basic baking powder biscuit recipe and use a part to make
    a. regular biscuits
    b. cinnamon rolls
    c. dumplings
    d. scones
5. Make a plain hotcake batter and a waffle batter. Compare the thickness of the two. Overmix a part of the hotcake batter and the waffle batter and compare product quality.

BIBLIOGRAPHY

Amendola, Joseph, *Baker's Manual,* 2nd ed., Ahrens Publishing, New York City, 1962.

Amendola, Joseph and Berring, J. M., *Practical Cooking and Baking,* Ahrens Publishing, New York City, 1971.

Casella, Delores, *The World of Baking,* D. While, New York City, 1968.

Jago, William, *Technology of Bread Making,* Baker's Helper, Chicago, 1971.

Lundberg, D. and Amendola, Joseph, *Understanding Baking,* Ahrens Publishing, New York City, 1970.

Proctor and Gamble Bakery Service, *Make-up Ideas for Sweet Doughs,* Cincinnati, Ohio, 1952.

Richards, Paul, *Breads, Rolls and Sweet Doughs,* Baker's Helper, Chicago, 1946.

Sullan, W. J., *Practical Baking,* Ahrens Publishing, New York City, 1965.

U. S. Department of Agriculture, *Bread, AIB,* No. 142, Washington, D. C., November 1955.

Wilfahrt, Julius E., *Treatise on Baking,* Standard Brands, Inc., New York City, 1950, (out of print.)

16

Cakes, Cookies and Decorations

CAKES

Cakes are not only a popular dessert, they are well suited to quantity food production. They are relatively low in cost, easy to prepare and have a good shelf life. The wide variety that can be made by varying slightly a few basic batters makes it unnecessary to carry a number of different ingredients and simplifies work. Variety is also achieved by using different shaped pans and different fillings and frostings. Years ago maximum skill was needed to overcome the limitations of ingredients in making *gateaux* (cakes) and *tortes*. At that time, cakes were leavened by air captured in egg foam (sponges), by creaming (pound cakes) or by gas developed by yeast (baba rhums), but today with chemical leavening agents, improved shortenings and high-stability cake flour, production is simplified. The introduction of cake mixes has further simplified cake and cookie making.

Quality ingredients, exact measurement and efficient equipment are needed to produce good cakes. Recipes should be tested and balanced to suit operational conditions. Layouts should allow work to flow smoothly and efficiently from scaling to mixing, to panning, to baking, to cooling and to makeup. Labor should be used efficiently. Insufficient or poor pans, mixers, scaling or holding space may increase labor costs. Labor-saving procedures should be established without sacrificing qual-

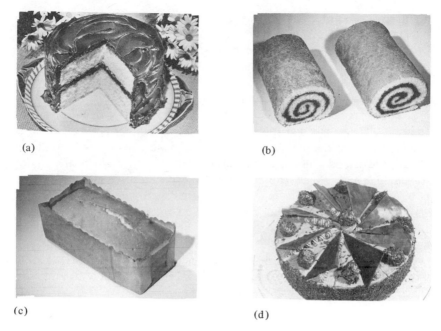

(a)

(b)

(c)

(d)

Figure 16–1. High standards are shown here for (a) a butter cake, (b) foam and (c) pound. Good standards for decoration are shown in (d).

ity. Cakes can be produced in quantity and variations introduced to obtain variety. As much time is needed to scale and mix a small batch as a large one. Fluctuating heat, poor temperature control, excessive vibration, warped or sagging oven shelves and uneven baking decks produce poor cakes. Reel ovens should be equipped with stabilized shelves. Severe vibration makes cakes separate in the center and have poor volume and crumb. Uneven heat gives low volume, dark and thick crusts, tunnels, uneven surface plus shrinkage and pulling away from pan sides. Even the best baker cannot overcome deficiencies in materials, equipment or operating conditions.

Types of Cakes

The ingredients or leavening agent used in cakes may serve to classify them. On this basis we can study production under butter, pound and foam cakes. Butter cakes are produced more widely than the others. The word "butter" may be a misnomer because hydrogenated shortening is usually used. Some claim butter makes a better flavored cake vehicle, others use butter coloring and flavoring to simulate it. The ingredients used in a butter cake are shortening, eggs, sugar, flour, salt, baking powder, liquid and flavoring. Pound cake batters are used for fruit cakes, nut cakes, steam puddings and so forth. Many pound cake recipes are modified toward a butter cake. For this, to maintain balance, shortening and eggs are decreased while sugar is increased; liquid in addition to eggs is added and some baking powder is required for leavening. The ingredients of a true pound cake are equal weights of sugar, shortening, eggs and flour plus a bit of salt and flavoring. Leavening is usually from air incorporated in creaming. Typical foam cakes are angel food, sponge and chiffon. Air incorporated by egg foam is the major leavening agent. Some chiffon and sponge cakes have some baking powder to assist in leavening. In chiffon cakes, oil is an ingredient. A sponge cake may have shortening but an angel food cake will not. Liquid is frequently used in a sponge or chiffon cake batter. The light, delicate quality of foam batters requires a high quality cake flour and eggs and fine grained sugar. Foam cakes are usually not prepared in more than 100 portions because their delicate structure may be destroyed by a heavier batch weight.

Standards

A good butter cake should be even on all sides, perfectly shaped and slightly rounded on the top. Rounding is less on large sheet cakes. The crust should be shiny, golden, tender, thin, daintily crisp and smooth, not blistered. It may have a slight puffy quality. The cut surface should show a fine, even grain that is soft, light, tender and velvety to the touch. This surface should show no dullness, cloudiness or streaks. The crumb is moist and tender. Color varies with the type of cake. Chocolate cake color varies, an alkaline batter having a rich, reddish brown not excessivly dark, while a non-alkaline one has a rich chocolate color. Butter cakes should have a mild, sweet, rich, delicate and buttery flavor. Chocolate cakes should have a similar flavor modified by the rich, smooth flavor of chocolate with no trace of bitterness or soapiness from excess alkalinity.

A pound cake should have an even shape, a slightly rounded top and a thin, soft, delicately browned crust slightly split in the middle. The crumb should be smooth and rich with no trace of oiliness, and the texture firm with fine, compact cells. The flavor should be sweet, delicately rich and substantial.

The grain of angel food cake should be even, fine, light, feathery and moist. It is more delicate and tender than a sponge or chiffon. The crumb should not be hard, brittle or excessively moist. Cell walls should

Figure 16–2. Good, accurate scales are needed to produce quality cakes.

be clear and white reflecting a delicate sheen. The sides should be even and the top slightly rounded. A delicately browned crust which is not moist or sticky is desirable. The cake should stand high for its weight. The texture of a sponge or chiffon cake should be delicate, springy and light. The crumb should be moist and soft with a delicate flavor and even grain, not coarse, excessively feathery or moist. The cells should be fine with a soft sheen; thin cell walls indicate lightness and delicacy. The cake's shape should be high and even, the crust lightly browned. Crumb color should be a light lemon-gold in a sponge and slightly lighter in a chiffon, unless other ingredients modify it.

Table 16-1.   Variations Possible from Three Basic Cake Batters

Cake	Icing	Filling	White	Gold	Chocolate
Almond Fudge	Almond Toffee	Almond Toffee			*
Almond Gold	Almond Toffee	Almond Toffee		*	
Banana	Banana	Banana	*	*	
Bittersweet Fudge	Bittersweet	Marshmallow		*	*
Butterscotch Walnut	Butterscotch Fondant and Walnuts	Butterscotch	*	*	*
Caramel Fudge	Caramel Fudge	Caramel Fudge	*	*	*
Cherry	Cherry Cream	Cherry Cream	*	*	*
Chocolate	Chocolate Fudge	Fudge	*	*	*
Chocolate Chip	Vanilla Fondant and Chocolate Shavings	Vanilla Fondant		*	*
Double Dip Caramel	Caramel Fudge and Marshmallow	Butterscotch	*	*	*
Double Dip Chocolate	Chocolate Fondant and Marshmallow	Marshmallow			
Double Fudge	Chocolate Fudge	Fudge	*		
Frosty Silver	Coconut Cream	Coconut Cream		*	
Golden Gate	Orange Cream	Orange	*		*
Lady Baltimore	Marshmallow or Nut and Fruit	Fruit and Nut Cream			
Lemonade	Lemon Fondant	Lemon Fondant	*	*	*
Malted Milk	Chocolate Malted Milk	Chocolate Malted Milk	*	*	*
Maple Cream and Nut	Maple Fondant, Walnuts	Maple Cream or Nut Cream	*	*	*
Maple Nut	Maple	Nut Cream	*	*	
Marshmallow Macaroon	Marshmallow topped with Macaroon Coconut	Chocolate Cream or Marshmallow	*	*	*
Marshmallow Pecan	Marshmallow topped with Pecans	Marshmallow			
Orange Coconut	Orange Fondant topped with Orange Coconut	Orange	*	*	
Pineapple Sundae	Pineapple Fondant	Pineapple Fondant	*	*	
Spumoni	Chocolate Fudge with Chopped Cherries	Fruit Cream	*	*	*
Strawberry Sundae	Strawberry Fondant	Strawberry Cream	*	*	

(Adapted from Procter & Gamble materials)

Cake Balance

Cakes are delicate products and a slight variation can make a great difference in their quality. Rules have been established by which balance can be judged and recipes corrected if adjustment is deemed needed.

A butter cake is considered in balance if 1) the weight of the sugar exceeds the weight of the flour, 2) the weight of the shortening does not exceed the weight of the eggs and 3) the weight of liquid (milk and eggs) is about $1\frac{1}{2}$ times the weight of the sugar. Whole eggs, whites and yolks are respectively around 65%, 75% and 50% moisture. If yolks replace whole eggs, the liquid is increased proportionately and if whites replace whole eggs, liquid is decreased proportionally. Before high-ratio shortenings and high-stability cake flours were developed, sugar could not exceed flour but now the sugar may go as high as 150%. Higher ratios of shortening and sugar are used in chocolate cakes, the starch of the cocoa or chocolate evidently allowing this. Blended cakes can contain more sugar than cakes made by other methods. A common rule in cake balancing is that as liquid is increased, eggs and shortening are reduced. (It is of interest to follow this change from a true pound cake, to a butter cake and then to a lean muffin cake formula.) The amount of liquid in a butter cake is governed more by the quantity of sugar than by the flour. Also, the quantity and type of shortening and sugar will control the sugar and liquid balance. If a sirup is used instead of sugar, the liquid in the sirup makes it necessary to reduce other liquids.

The balance of a pound cake can vary from a pound to pound ratio of flour, shortening, eggs and sugar to one that closely resembles a

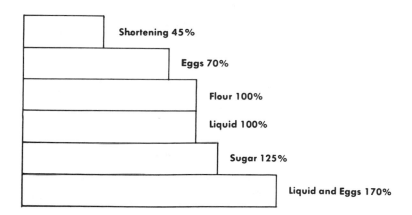

Figure 16–3. A graph of the ingredients for a balanced butter cake.

Figure 16–4. Cakes scored from first to last in order: liquid shortening-blended method (lower left), cake mix (lower right), typical blended method (upper right) and conventionally mixed cake (upper left).

butter cake. The rules followed are enumerated above in the discussion on butter cake balance.

An angel food cake is in balance if 1) the weight of the sugar exceeds the weight of the egg whites and 2) the weight of the flour is half to a third the weight of the sugar or egg whites. There are variations; for instance, a successful cake results from 13 ounces of flour (100%), 32 ounces of egg whites (245%) and 26 ounces (200%) of sugar. A sponge cake is in balance if 1) the weight of the sugar equals or slightly

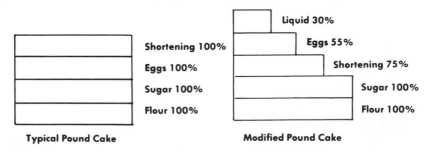

Typical Pound Cake   **Modified Pound Cake**

Figure 16–5. The balances for a typical pound cake and a modified pound cake are shown here. Leavening may be an added ingredient in the modified cake. Note that as the pound cake is modified, its balance tends more and more toward that of the balanced butter cake.

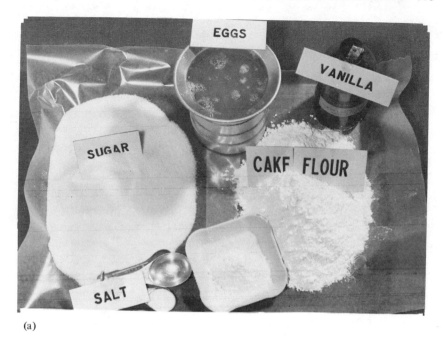

(a)

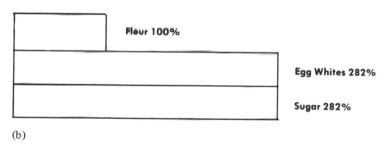

(b)

Figure 16–6. (a) Ingredients and (b) balance for an angel cake. (Cream of tartar, unlabeled is in the front dish.)

exceeds the weight of the eggs, 2) the combined weight of liquid and eggs is $1\frac{1}{4}$ times the sugar, 3) the weight of the whole eggs or sugar exceeds that of the flour and 4) the weight of the whole eggs and flour exceeds the combined weight of the sugar and liquid. A chiffon cake is considered in balance if 1) the weight of sugar is $1\frac{1}{4}$ to $1\frac{1}{2}$ that of the flour, 2) the weight of yolks is half that of the whites, 3) the weight of oil is half that of the flour, 4) the weight of the liquid is three-fourths that of the flour and 5) the combined weight of liquid and eggs is about equal to that of the sugar and flour.

Altitude Adjustment

Because the pressure of air is less at higher altitudes, cake formulas may have to be varied as elevation increases. This adjustment varies for different type cakes. Less change is needed in conventionally mixed butter cakes than those made by the blending method. A rich butter cake or one high in moisture such as an applesauce cake, requires different leavening adjustments from a common butter cake. At 3000 feet or over angel food cakes are reduced 10 to 12% in sugar and cream of tartar is doubled. Sponge cakes have lemon juice omitted and cream of tartar substituted and the eggs are beaten slightly less above 3000 feet. At 7000 feet sugar is also reduced in sponge cakes 10 to 12%. Flour and eggs may have to be increased in butter and pound cakes above 1000 feet to give a firmer structure. Above 5000 feet, shortening in these may need reduction to lessen its tenderizing effect. Butter cake pans may be greased more heavily since there is a greater tendency to stick at higher elevations. Above 4500 feet some increase oven temperatures 25° F while maintaining the same baking time. Oven dampers may be closed to reduce drying out during the last of the baking. See Tables 16-2 and 16-2a to ascertain the reduction recommended in leavening as altitude increases.

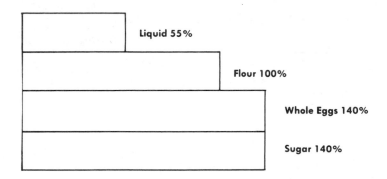

Liquid 55%

Flour 100%

Whole Eggs 140%

Sugar 140%

Figure 16–7. The rules for balancing a sponge cake: Rule 1 — the weight of the sugar is equal to or slightly exceeds the weight of the eggs. Rule 2 — the combined weight of liquid and eggs is 1¼ times that of the sugar. Rule 3 — the weight of the whole eggs or the sugar exceeds that of the flour. Rule 4 — the weight of the whole eggs and flour exceeds the combined weight of the sugar and liquids. This chart shows all four rules combined.

Table 16–2. Percentage Reduction in Leavening as Altitude Increases

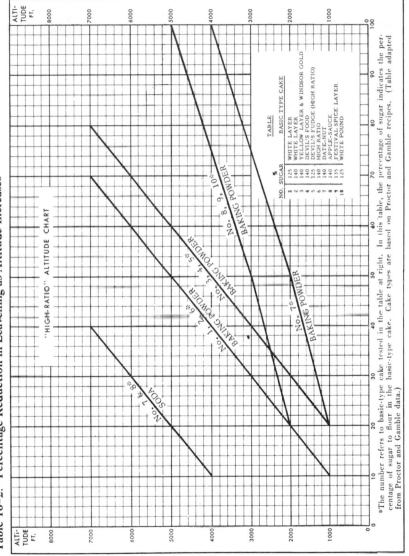

"HIGH-RATIO" ALTITUDE CHART

TABLE		
%		BASIC TYPE CAKE
NO.	SUGAR	
1	125	WHITE LAYER
2	140	WHITE LAYER
3	140	YELLOW LAYER & WINDSOR GOLD
4	140	DEVIL'S FOOD
5	125	DEVIL'S FUDGE (HIGH RATIO)
6	140	HIGH RATIO
7	140	DATE-NUT
8	140	APPLE-SAUCE
9	135	FESTIVAL SPICE LAYER
10	125	WHITE POUND

No. 8, 9, 10* BAKING POWDER

No. 3, 4, 5* BAKING POWDER

No. 1, 2, 6* BAKING POWDER

No. 7* BAKING POWDER

No. 7 & 8* SODA

*The number refers to basic-type cake tested in the table at right. In this table, the percentage of sugar indicates the percentage of sugar to flour in the basic-type cake. Cake types are based on Proctor and Gamble recipes. (Table adapted from Proctor and Gamble data.)

Table 16–2a.   Approximate Butter Cake Recipe Changes As Elevation Changes

Altitude	Reduction %		Increase %	Altitude	Reduction %		Increase %
	Baking Powder	Sugar	Moisture		Baking Powder	Sugar	Moisture
1500	5	0	0	6500	43.3	10.5	.056
2000	10	2	.01	7000	46.4	11.5	.06
2500	14.4	3	.015	7500	49	12.4	.067
3000	19.8	4	.02	8000	52.7	13.3	.072
3500	22.8	4.9	.025	8500	54.1	14.6	.077
4000	26.8	5.9	.03	9000	56.5	16	.083
4500	30.4	6.8	.035	9500	58.7	16.8	.088
5000	34	7.8	.04	10000	60.8	17.7	.093
5500	37.2	8.7	.045				
6000	40.5	9.6	.05				

Adapted from General Mills, Inc. materials

Cake Mixing Methods

Butter Cakes

The conventional (creaming) and the blending methods are usually used to mix butter cakes, the conventional sponge and muffin methods being used less often. Because blending gives a richer, sweeter cake with a better texture and shelf life and is simpler to use, it is favored over the creaming method. Cake quality is usually rated, from first to last, blended, cake mix, conventional (creaming) with conventional-sponge or muffin method mixed cakes coming last. In mixing butter cakes the mixing paddle should be used. The batter should be just above the mixing paddle when mixing is complete, and bowl adapters should be used to suit batch volume.

Table 16–3.   Butter Cake Production Scaling Weights by Variety

Size Cake	Variety Cake			
	Yellow	Chocolate	White	Wedding
4 in. layer	4 oz	4 oz	4 oz	7¼ oz
6 in. layer	7¼ oz	8 oz	8 oz	12 oz
7 in. layer	10 oz	12 oz	12 oz	1 lb
8 in. layer	13 oz	1 lb	1 lb	1 lb 4 oz
9 in. layer	1 lb 1 oz	1 lb 4 oz	1 lb 4 oz	1 lb 8 oz*
10 in. layer	1 lb 8 oz	1 lb 12 oz	1 lb 12 oz	2 lb*
12 in. layer	2 lb 8 oz	2 lb 12 oz	2 lb 12 oz	3 lb*
14 in. layer	3 lb 8 oz	3 lb 12 oz	3 lb 12 oz	4 lb*
16 in. layer	4 lb 12 oz	5 lb	5 lb	5 lb*
18 x 26 in. sheet	7 lb 8 oz	8 lb 8 oz	9 lb	

*Increase approximately 25% for square cakes; scale an 18-inch-square wedding cake 8 lb.

Note: Adjust all scaling weights to suit *your* batter weights; these are only guides.

The shortening is creamed first to a waxy stage in the conventional method and sugar is added with creaming continued until a light color and fluffy texture is obtained, assuring that maximum air incorporation has been achieved. Photomicrographs (see student's observations in Figure 16-8) show that the shortening is absorbed on the sugar crystal surface. Air bubbles are spread evenly throughout the mixture. During this and subsequent mixing, scrape down frequently, moving the ingredients from the bottom and sides into mixer action. (Mixing times do not include scraping down.) Add eggs in three equal parts, creaming well at medium speed after each addition. The mixture at the end of creaming should appear smooth and fluffy and the graininess from sugar should have disappeared because of some dissolving in egg moisture. If all the shortening, sugar and eggs are added together and the mixture creamed

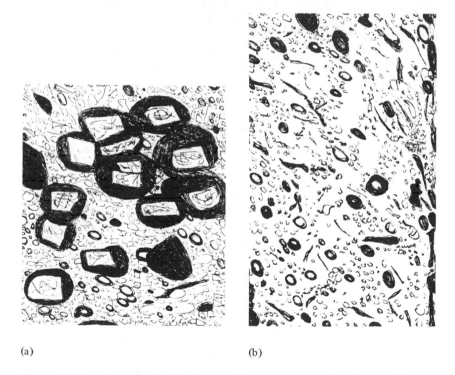

(a)   (b)

Figure 16–8. A student's drawings and comments on the change of sugar crystal size and fat adsorption in samples which he watched under a microscope as he made a conventional cake. (a) "The sugar crystals looked square and large pools of fat surrounded them. Dark areas represent fat." (b) "After the eggs were added and the mixture beaten for some time, the sugar and fat were more evenly dispersed. The fat globules were now smaller in size."

Figure 16–9. Well creamed shortening, sugar and eggs just before the addition of dry ingredients and milk in the making of a conventional cake.

at medium speed, time and labor are reduced but the cake quality will not be as good as when the method described here is used.

After creaming at low speed, add a fourth of the sifted dry ingredients and a third of the liquid. Usually there are four additions of dry ingredients and three of liquid. Overmixing after the addition of flour may give excessive gluten development and leavening loss, resulting in a heavy, compact cake with tunneling. Undermixing gives a coarse, poor crumb. The resulting batter is thick and smooth and must be spread in panning. Give several sharp raps after filling pans to free air bubbles caught in the batter.

In some conventional mixing, yolks only are added in creaming. Whites are beaten separately to a soft, glossy peak (stage three) or are made into a soft meringue with part of the sugar and carefully folded in just before panning. Use a whip, spoon or hand to fold using a down-and-under motion. Machine-blending, using care, may be done at low speed until all egg foam is incorporated. Underblending gives flecks of egg which rise to the surface and result in an uneven, blistered crust. Overbeating results in a loss of volume. If egg whites are added this way, less baking powder is required.

Ingredients mix best at 75° to 80° F. Shortening should be con-

(a)   (b)

Figure 16–10. (a) A conventional cake batter is so thick that it does not spread by itself in pans but must be spread with a spatula (b). Give a sharp rap after spreading to free air bubbles trapped in the batter.

ditioned at least 24 hours in advance. Use a waxy, workable shortening to incorporate air and give spread. Hard or excessively soft fats cream poorly. The temperature of the shortening may be adjusted somewhat to give desired consistency. Emulsifiers in shortening assist in giving improved creaming action.

Curdling may occur when eggs are added, especially if they are cold. Fine curds may be precursors of a fine cake texture but most prefer no curdling. Warm the eggs to reduce the tendency to curdle or add a bit of the flour during the latter stages of creaming. Dry eggs, if not added with the sifted ingredients, may be mixed with a part of the liquid needed to refresh them and the remaining liquid added later. This reduces curdling. Chocolate should be added during creaming and cocoa should be sifted in with the flour.

The blending method mixes flour and shortening together with a mixer paddle 3 to 5 minutes. This coats the flour with shortening, promoting tenderness and evenness of grain, and reduces moisture loss which extends keeping qualities. The batters also have a high tolerance to overmixing or undermixing. High-stability flour and emulsified shortening are best and ingredient temperatures should be around 75° F, although good tolerance is found from 60° to 80° F. The time and speed of mixing stated in the recipe should be followed. Undermixing gives a coarse grain and a lack of tenderness while overmixing toughens and gives a compact grain. The batter is thin and pours.

Scrape down frequently. (Add chocolate in melted form after blending the flour and shortening.) Sugar, salt, baking powder and dry milk solids are sifted and added with a third to a fourth of the liquid. Cocoa, spices and other dry ingredients may be sifted in at this time. Adding liquid in two stages gives a smooth batter without lumps. After mixing 3 to 5 minutes, eggs, remaining liquid and flavoring are added and mixed 3 to 5 minutes. Batter thinness is no indication of poor quality or low cake volume.

A variation of this method is to sift flour, salt, dry milk solids and sugar into the mixing bowl and add the shortening, mixing at medium or slow speed for two minutes, adding half to two-thirds the liquid early in this mixing. Scrape down frequently. Next, eggs, the remaining milk and the leavening agent are added and mixing continued another two minutes. Some vary times to three minutes for the first mixing and one for the second.

Another variation is the dump method. Flour, leavening agent, milk solids, salt and sugar are sifted into the mixer. Shortening, eggs and half the liquid are added and mixed a minute at low or medium speed. Next, remaining liquid is added and mixed for two minutes. Quality is lower unless emulsified liquid shortening is used, then it becomes excellent.

Cakes made by the muffin method stale quickly and should be served soon. It is used for non-rich cakes. The method mixes eggs, liquid and melted shortening or oil together. This mixture is poured into sifted dry ingredients and mixed together. Quality is not the best but adequate.

Use the conventional sponge method when soft shortenings must be used or high mixing temperatures are encountered. Add the shortening and cream half the sugar into it, then sift dry ingredients into this mixture and blend, followed by liquids. Beat warm eggs to a fluffy sponge with the remaining sugar and carefully fold into the batter. Another way is to dissolve the sugar into half to two thirds of the liquid, then add the soft shortening and sifted flour, leavening agent and mix 3 to 4 minutes. Add eggs, flavoring and remaining liquid and mix the entire batter one minute at medium speed.

Mixes

Most mixes contain all ingredients needed except water but some may require eggs. Cakes made from mixes at one time staled rather rapidly but some manufacturers have improved their products so that this is not as much of a problem. A wide variety of mixes are available and with relatively little skill, equipment or inventory of materials many different cakes can be offered on the menu. Manufacturers' directions must be followed carefully. Operations can prepare their own mixes by first blending flour, shortening, dry emulsifier and sugar together. The

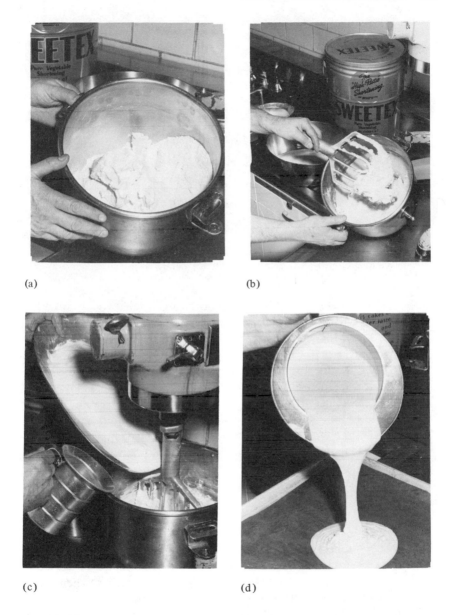

(a)   (b)

(c)   (d)

Figure 16–11. In making a blended cake, the shortening is placed on top of the flour, salt, and leavening, and the mixture is mixed at slow speed three to five minutes until it appears as shown at upper right. One-third of the liquid and the dry milk blended with the sugar are added, and the mixture is again mixed for three to five minutes, after which the eggs and remaining liquid are added. The resulting batter pours easily.

Figure 16–12. Typical shapes for pound cakes. Note the fine, tight grain and cracked top, both typical of this kind of cake.

emulsifier is usually ¾ to 1% of the total mix weight, or 3 to 6% of the shortening. If emulsified shortening is used, the quantity of emulsifer needed is less. Monoglycerides, diglycerides or polyoxethylenes or their derivatives are usually used as emulsifiers. After the first mixture is blended, non-fat dry milk solids, salt, sodium acid pyrophosphate baking powder and dried eggs are added. Use cocoa for chocolate cakes. Store the mixture and treat as a regular mix, using about a ratio of 40 — 60 of water to mix adding about two-thirds of the liquid and blending at low speed for a minute. Scrape down and mix four minutes at medium speed. Add remaining water and mix a minute at low speed, scraping down during and at the end of this mixing. Then mix four minutes at medium speed.

Pound Cakes

Cream the shortening and sugar thoroughly at around 75° F for pound cakes. Add the eggs and cream until the mixture is light and fluffy, adding some flour if necessary to prevent curdling. Then blend in the flour. Bread flour for half the total flour is frequently used to give structural strength. Use a flour with high absorptive power. Strong structure is needed for fruit cakes to carry the heavy weight of the fruit which may be 1 to 1½ times the weight of the batter. A variation in pound cake making is to beat warm eggs to a sponge with the sugar, fold in the flour and then blend in carefully the melted shortening, but quality is lower. If only egg whites are used, giving a higher liquid content, 3%

(a)

(b)

(c)

Figure 16–13. The making of an angel food cake. (a) Warm egg whites, salt, and cream of tartar are beaten to the upper second foam stage. The sugar is added and is just blended in until the mixture appears as shown in (b). (c) The remaining sugar, blended thoroughly with the sifted flour, is then carefully folded in by hand. Note the spread of the fingers to encourage more rapid incorporation of the flour-sugar mixture.

baking powder to flour is used. Use fine or berry sugar so that it will dissolve quickly. Pound cakes high in sugar and liquid have increased volume but the grain is more open and the top crust tends to break away from the cake more easily.

Foam Cakes

The use of eggs as foams should be reviewed in Chapter 10 for background in the making of foam cakes. The exact point at which an egg foam is stiff enough to hold the other ingredients for a foam cake and yet soft enough to allow blending in easily is a critical factor in its making. Knowing this point is a matter of experience and judgment.

Salt and cream of tartar make egg whites more extensible. The cake is also whitened because the cream of tartar, being acid, lightens the flour flavones. Cream of tartar is not a leavener. Beat the whites at 110° to 125° F until they reach a soft peak. These should bend over slightly at the top (stage two, upper level) in the foam. Overbeating or underbeating gives poor quality and low volume. Fold a third to half of the sugar into the beaten whites. The finer the sugar, the finer the cake grain. Some recipes use part powdered and part granulated sugar

for this reason or some roll the sugar with a rolling pin to break it
down. Then fold in flour sifted thoroughly with the remaining sugar
until it *just disappears*. This is a critical point. Too much mixing results
in a poor cake. Mixing part of the sugar with the flour makes the flour
easier to incorporate. Blending of whites and flour may be done by
machine at slow speed but most prefer to fold the flour in with a wire
whip, a spoon, spatula or by hand. Angel cake mixes are used frequently
in quantity production and they give excellent results. Frequently batch
sizes must be kept small to give higher quality, but because the dry eggs
are so much more stable in beating than fresh and the mix has so much
greater tolerance to over- or under-mixing, many operations prefer to
use the mix rather than make their own. Cost is about the same. A cake
mix is on the market to which one only need add water and beat the
blended flour, sugar and dried whites to produce an excellent, fine-
grained angel cake.

For sponge cakes, warm whole eggs or yolks are beaten to a stable
foam with salt, lemon juice or crystals or cream of tartar. Some sugar
added in the beating helps to give a more stable foam and one that
develops more rapidly. If desirable, beat over 150° F water. Eggs beat
best if from 120° to 125° F. Have the sugar slightly warm to achieve
this. Normally, beat at high speed until the eggs are a thick, lemon-
colored foam (about 10 to 15 minutes). Underbeating gives a tough
streak on the cake bottom and produces low volume and heavy and
compact grain. If egg yolks replace whole eggs, liquid such as hot water,
milk or lemon juice is added to give sufficient moisture. After beating
is completed, carefully fold in the sifted flour. This can be by machine
at slow speed. If baking powder or other dry ingredients are used, sift
in with the flour. Sponges may also be made by beating yolks separately
from the whites, using half the sugar. Add liquid and fold in the flour.
Make the whites, cream of tartar and salt into a soft meringue with
the remaining sugar and fold into the batter carefully. Overmixing at
this point results in a cake with a dry, heavy, close grain which has a
tough, rubbery texture. Undermixing gives a coarse texture and uneven
grain.

Delicate sponges may have hot milk and/or butter added after the
sifted dry ingredients are folded in. The butter should be melted or the
milk be at 140° F. Final batter temperature should be around 110° F.
Some recipes add hot milk alternately with the flour but this takes much
skill to do correctly without loss of foam. If the butter solidifies, the
cake collapses in the oven. Fat breaks down egg foam and so the melted
butter must be blended in skillfully, preferably by hand-mixing. In
place of warm milk or butter, hot water may be added to the beaten

Figure 16–14. Hot milk and melted butter being carefully folded into a sponge batter.

eggs just before the sifted dry ingredients are folded in to give a moist, soft, velvety sponge.

Chiffon cakes resemble sponges and are mixed very much the same. They are slightly more stable batters and are not so sensitive to over-mixing or undermixing. Eggs should be beaten while warm and all blending done carefully. Chiffon cakes have a better keeping quality than the other foam cakes.

Panning

Cake quality is affected by panning. Fill pans with butter or pound cake batter half or two-thirds full to allow for proper expansion. Overfilled pans spill over in baking with a loss of quality or even collapse. Sloping sides on the pans give less volume than straight-sided ones. Do not grease foam cake pans since they need to attach themselves to the sides to climb up in baking. Greased sides also reduce butter or pound cake volume. A greasing mixture may be made using seven pounds of short-ening, a pound of margarine, a pint of salad oil to four pounds of flour.

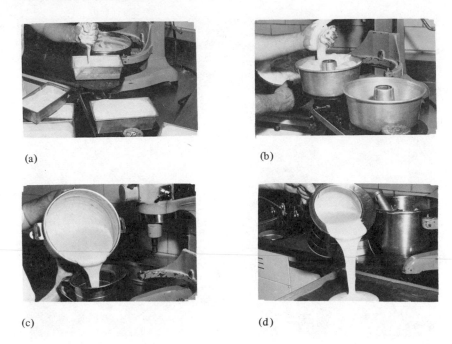

(a)   (b)

(c)   (d)

Figure 16–15. Pound and angel cakes are scaled as shown. Professional bakers scoop and dump rapidly using this hand method. Note how on the right balance, an empty pan is set to tare the other. A pound weight assures that a pound is added to the pan. Thin batters are poured into containers by weight. After weighing once, the container can be filled to the mark and poured without weighing.

A bit of butter flavoring and salt may be added. Butter is said to improve flavor when used as a greasing medium. Paper liners are desirable for lining pan bottoms. Remove these when the cake is cooled. Special silicon (teflon) coatings may eliminate the need for greasing. If bottom crusts dry out in baking, wet bottom paper liners, especially for jelly roll sponges. Cupcakes or muffins may be baked in paper cups. Moist products such as applesauce cupcakes may be removed from these after baking but drier products may be removed when eaten. Overbrowning and a turning-in of the rims at the edges of the cake indicate overgreasing of the pans.

Black pans give more volume and bake more rapidly because they absorb more heat. Use conditioned pans and handle pans with care; do not bang them around, drop them or handle them so that they lose shape. (See Chapter 6).

Protect thick cakes on the sides and bottoms from outside heat with half-inch thick wooden liners covered with fourth-inch asbestos mats. Baking temperatures for thick cakes are lower than for thinner ones. Ovens having well controlled heat may eliminate the need for these protective mats.

Observe panning weights. Machine depositing is used in large bakeshops. For butter cakes, use 0.2 ounces per square inch of pan. A round pan takes approximately 75% of this. Thus an 8-inch square pan takes 12¾ ounces of batter (8 × 8 × 0.2) and an 8-inch diameter round pan 9½ ounces of batter (8 × 8 × 0.2 × .75). Cakes with large surface areas should be panned thicker than those with smaller ones. Foam cake pans should be well filled with batter to build a structure in baking. (See also scaling weights in Table 16-5.) Standardizing scaling weights assures good portioning.

Baking

A cake's baking is critical to quality. It enters the oven a viscous, aerated, semi-fluid batter and comes out a solid, tender product. Batter movement occurs in baking. Warm portions rise while the cold batter sinks. Slip contributed by shortening and/or liquid is needed for such movement. Leavening makes the batter rise and firming takes place when the starch gelatinizes and the proteins coagulate. The result is a baked cake of stable volume.

A cake goes through four baking stages. The first is a rapid rise of a quite fluid batter. Rising continues in the second stage, the center rising higher than the sides. Bubbles and a slight surface tan appear and some batter firmness is evident on the sides. Rising is completed in the third stage. The structure sets, top browning increases and spreads over the surface. A slight aroma of baked cake is evident. In the fourth stage, browning is completed. The structure separates slightly from the pan and a full-baked aroma indicates that the cake is done. It is firm to the touch, springing back and leaving no imprint, although some rich butter

Table 16-4. Scaling Weights and Baking Temperatures and Times for Cookies

Product	Scaling Weight	Baking	
		Temperature (°F)	Time (min)
Brownies	7½ to 8 lb	350 to 360	20 to 45
Butter, tea	⅓ to ½ oz	375	8 to 10
Drop, medium	¾ oz*	350 to 400	8 to 15
Ice box, medium	1 oz	375	8 to 10
Rolled, small	½ oz	375	7 to 10
Rolled, large	1½ oz	375	9 to 12

*Use No. 40 scoop.

Table 16-5. Production Scaling Weights, Baking Temperatures and Times for Cakes

Type Cake	Scaling Weight	Baking Temperature (°F)	Time (min)
Layer			
Butter or Pound (1½ to 2 in. deep)			
6 in.*	6 to 8 oz	375	18
7 in.*	9 to 11 oz	375	20
8 in.*	12 to 14 oz	375	25
10 in.*	20 oz	360	35
12 in.*	1½ to 2 lb	360	
14 in.*	2¼ to 3 lb	360	
Foam cakes			
6 in.*	4 to 5 oz	375	20
8 in.*	9 to 10 oz	375	
10 in.*	16 to 18 oz	360	
12 in.*	1½ to 1¾ lb	360	
Loaf			
Pound, 3¼ x 3½ x 8 in.	1 lb	355	50
Pound, 3¼ x 6 x 11 in.	3 lb	325	100
Fruit, 3¼ x 3½ x 8 in.	1½ lb	315	90
Angel, 3¼ x 3½ x 8 in.	7 to 10 oz	365	
Angel, tube, small	8 to 10 oz		
Angel, tube, 10 in.	1½ to 2 lb	360	50
Sheet			
Butter, 1 x 18 x 26 in.	6 to 7 lb	360	35
Butter, 3 x 18 x 26 in.	8 to 10 lb	350	
Sponge, 1 x 18 x 26 in.	3 lb	360	25
Miscellaneous			
Ring, 6½ in.*	10 to 14 oz	375	
Oval loaf, 6¾ in.	8 oz	375	
Cupcakes, butter, per doz	14 to 16 oz	385	
Cupcakes, foam, per doz	7 to 8 oz	375	
Mary Ann Shells, butter, per doz	1⅛ to 2¼ lb	385	

*diameter

Note: Weights, times, and temperatures are average only; adjust for each cake. Butter cakes made by the blended method may be baked at slightly higher temperatures than those for conventionally made cakes; temperatures given here are for blended type.

and foam cakes may lack this spring. If a toothpick or wire tester is inserted, it comes out clean, indicating doneness.

Temperature is a critical factor in baking. Improved ovens and ingredients have made it possible to increase baking temperatures. Those mixed by the blending method are usually baked at higher temperatures than those mixed by the conventional method. Small cakes are baked at higher temperatures than large ones and thin ones at higher temperatures than thick ones. Too high a temperature retards flavor and volume development. Crusts become dark and the tops may split because inside areas are still rising after the outer area has set. Overbaking of a chocolate or cocoa cake impairs flavor.

Texture is improved if cakes are set into preheated ovens. Even heat distribution is essential and flash heat should be avoided. Pans

(a)   (b)

(c)   (d)

Figure 16–16. Stages in cake baking: (1) the batter is quite fluid and a rapid rise occurs; (2) rising continues, bubbles appear and a slight surface tan forms; (3) the rise is complete and the cake begins to set; (4) baking is complete, color is deep, a distinct aroma of baked cake and some separation from the sides of the pan are evident.

that touch in the oven reduce batter movement and proper cake development. Pans should not be placed against the oven sides where uneven heat occurs. Ovens should be level. Oven thermostats should give good oven control and oven heat should come mostly from the bottom and circulate around the cake except for jelly rolls and some others where more top heat is needed to give a soft bottom for rolling.

If the oven is too hot, the outside will be baked before the interior is and the cake may be tough and compact, have humps and show tunneling. Too cool an oven gives a crust that forms too late and cell walls that overexpand so that the cake is flat with a coarse, uneven grain and a pale, sticky crust. If underbaked or baked too slowly, the structure may not set sufficiently and the cake may suffer oven-collapse. A foam cake baked at too high a temperature becomes firm before complete expansion occurs resulting in a heavy, tough texture, poor cell

Figure 16–17.   Oven temperatures that were just right, too low and too high caused the effects shown here.

structure, low volume and a hard crust. If the temperature is low, the air cells overexpand giving a coarse-grained cake and a sticky-pale crust. Fruit cakes and other heavy cakes may be steamed instead of baked.

Cooling

After removal from the oven, cakes should be cooled for 15 minutes or longer, depending on size and shape, then freed from the pan sides and dumped onto racks. They may be turned right side up by reversing on another rack, if desired. Removing them from pans while still warm dissipates bottom moisture and avoids sogginess. Handle gently. Cool sponge cakes for jelly rolls to about 110° F, then roll into slightly moistened cloths to cool in this shape. Unroll, spread with jelly and reroll. (See also Figure 16-18).

Cooling too quickly causes shrinkage. Some thin cakes can be cooled in their pans, and while some moisture develops on the bottoms, this does not give a soggy cake. Butter cakes are usually loosened

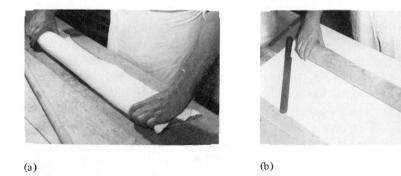

(a)   (b)

Figure 16–18.   Roll a warm cake into a cloth and let it cool; then unroll and fill.

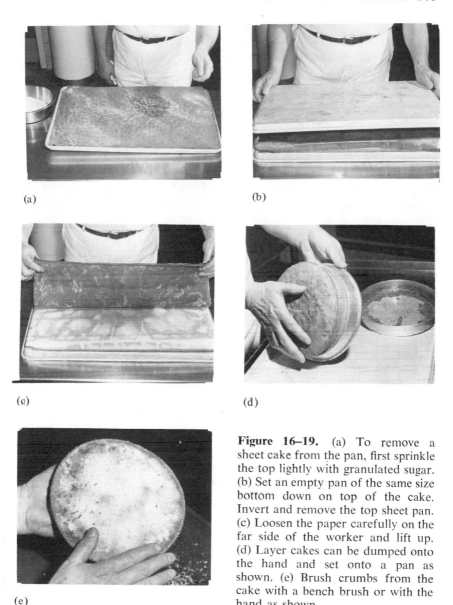

(a)

(b)

(c)

(d)

(e)

Figure 16–19. (a) To remove a sheet cake from the pan, first sprinkle the top lightly with granulated sugar. (b) Set an empty pan of the same size bottom down on top of the cake. Invert and remove the top sheet pan. (c) Loosen the paper carefully on the far side of the worker and lift up. (d) Layer cakes can be dumped onto the hand and set onto a pan as shown. (e) Brush crumbs from the cake with a bench brush or with the hand as shown.

around the pan sides and are inverted. Overcooling before removal may cause pan sticking, making removal difficult. Allow loaf or pound cakes to cool about 30 minutes. Then free edges and invert. Large bride or pound cakes should be removed from frames but not cut when warm. Invert foam cakes upon oven removal, resting sides on supports to prevent pressure on the cake. Remove them while slightly warm but cool enough to give firmness to the structure. Do not handle while warm. Loosen foam cakes from the sides and tube with a spatula or knife; tilt and draw out gently.

Storage

Store cakes in a clean, cool place where they do not dry out. Mold can be a problem especially in warm, humid climates. While staling is more rapid under refrigeration, they may have to be refrigerated to hold them. Many cakes develop mold where the cut surface was contaminated by a handler's fingers. By freezing in moisture-vapor-proof wraps, quality in cakes may be retained for a long time.

Makeup

The makeup is important to quality because appearance and flavor can be affected. Makeup includes final preparation for serving which may be cutting, shaping, filling, frosting and decorating.

Frostings and Icings

Many icings are used on cakes to enhance appearance and flavor and give moistness, although not all cakes require frosting. Some foam cakes may be served plain or merely filled but most others need some type of frosting and filling.

Table 16-6.   Variations Obtained from Plain Butter Cream Icing

Variation	To 10 lb Plain Butter Cream Icing Add:
Nut	Chopped Nuts, 1 lb
Raisin	Ground Raisins, 1 lb
Cherry	Candied Cherries. 1 lb
Candied Fruit	Candied Fruit, 1 lb
Jam or Marmalade	Jam or Marmalade, 1 lb
Almond*	Almond Paste, 1 lb and Almond Flavoring
Coconut	Macaroon Coconut Bits, 1 lb
Fondant	Plain Fondant, 5 lb
Chocolate (Cocoa)	Cocoa, 10 oz, and Water, 5 oz
Peppermint Candy	Peppermint Candy Bits, 8 oz
Lady Baltimore	Chopped Candied Cherries, Nuts, and Raisins, mixed, 1 lb
Fresh Fruit	Chopped Drained Fresh Fruit, 4 oz

*Thin the almond paste first with a bit of egg white so it goes into the butter cream without lumping.

Frostings may be classified as foam (meringue or marshmallow cream), as butter cream, or as fondant (fudge frosting). There are also plain water icings and glazes. High quality ingredients should be used and colors and flavors should be moderate because an excess of either detracts from, rather than adds to, quality. Fillings or frostings should be liberally spread onto cakes but not so freely as to give an over-sweetened, overmoist product. The filling or frosting should complement the cake. Warm temperatures or high humidity may make it necessary to use fondant or fudge frostings because they are more durable than some others. Stabilizers purchased from a bakery supply house can assist in problems of stickiness, lack of stability or a failure to set up, but agar-agar, gelatin, gums or cereals such as wheat, cornstarch or tapioca flour can also be used. Simple or corn sirup rather than water for moisture may curdle or separate some thin frostings

Use 1½ to 1¾ cups of fluffy frostings for a two-tier 8-inch layer cake (5 to 6 ounces) and 2 to 3 pints (10 to 15 ounces) for an 18 × 26-inch cake. Use 1¼ cups (10 ounces) and about 1¼ quarts (20 ounces) of filling respectively. To coat the sides of 8-, 9- and 10-inch layer cakes with chopped nuts, coconut or other coating, allow respectively 1½, 1¾ and 2⅛ ounces of material. See Table 16-7 for further amounts to use in frosting cakes.

Fondant

Fondant is a water-sugar mixture usually cooked to 240° F, cooled to 104° F and mixed until tiny crystals form. Cream of tartar or corn

Table 16-7. Quantities of Frosting to Use Per Cake

Cake Size	Type Frosting	Filling Weight	To Frost Sides and Tops
4 in. layer*	Butter cream		2 oz
6 in. layer	Butter cream		5 oz
7 in. layer	Butter cream	3 oz	6½ to 8 oz
8 in. layer	Butter cream	4 oz	8 to 8½ oz
9 in. layer	Butter cream		11½ oz
10 in. layer	Butter cream		1 lb
12 in. layer	Butter cream		1 lb 7 oz
14 in. layer	Butter cream		2 lb
16 in. layer	Butter cream		2 lb 9 oz
18 by 26 in. sheet	Butter cream		3 to 4 lb (top only)
Cupcakes, per doz	Butter cream		5 oz (tops only)
7 in. layer	Boiled type	2 oz	4 oz
8 in. layer	Boiled type	2¼ oz	5 oz
7 in. layer	Fudge or fondant	3½ oz	9 oz
8 in. layer	Fudge or fondant	4½ oz	10 oz

*All layer cakes are two layer.

(a)

(b)

Figure 16–20.   (a) A glaze from waxy maize starch is used to give gloss to fruit as seen in (b).

sirup is used to give invert sugar. Plain fondant is a simple, creamy, white smooth crystalline mass and usually purchased either in moist or dry form. Dry fondants, needing only water to make a good fondant, are now on the market. Fudge icings are rich, cooked fondant and the term may be applied to non-chocolate frostings such as penuche, maple and other creamy cooked mixtures. Fondant will make a butter cream icing but powdered sugar is more satisfactory. If fondant is used, eggs should not be added. To thin fondants, use simple sirup. Do not heat them above 100° F because this causes a loss of gloss.

Powdered Sugar Icings

Butter cream icing is a rich, smooth icing, mellow in flavor. Confectioners sugar (6X to 10X), butter or margarine or shortening, eggs, flavoring and other ingredients are used. Eggs, usually whites, give lightness, moisture and fluffiness. A high degree of creaming also gives lightness. The ratio of fat to sugar is usually 1:2 and eggs to sugar 1:10 by weight. Many variations can be made. A French butter cream can be made by folding carefully a fourth pound of softened butter or margarine into two quarts of boiled or marshmallow icing at about 70° F, with no stirring nor beating.

Simple or flat icings made from powdered sugar, called plain water icings, are mixtures of water or liquid milk, flavoring and confectioners sugar mixed to a smooth, thick paste. They are warmed to 100° F to coat Danish pastry and sweet breakfast rolls. They can also be used as a plain fondant for pouring over cakes and coating them as with a plain fondant icing. They usually do not contain fat.

Boiled or Cooked Icing

Boiled icings are made by boiling sugar, water and glucose or cream of tartar to a temperature of 240° to 250° F. This is poured over egg whites beaten to a soft but firm peak (upper stage two). As the hot sirup is added, beating is vigorous and is continued until a crystalline mass forms or the icing is almost stiff enough to spread. Stiffness depends upon the quantity of egg to sirup, the temperature to which the sirup is cooked and the temperature of the frosting. By adding some confectioners sugar and gelatin, a marshmallow frosting can be made. Commercial meringue preparations are used for making various kinds of boiled icings.

Glazes

A glaze is a heavy sirup made from sugar and water. It contains no eggs but may contain gelatin. It is brushed onto items or they may be dipped into it. It gives shine to products. A glaze also may be made from fruits such as apricot pulp or from a waxy maize starch.

Decorator's or Royal Icing

A stiff icing called royal or decorator's icing is used for ornamental work. It is made from egg whites, confectioners sugar, cornstarch, flavor-

Figure 16–21. Cakes covered with a fondant icing and decorated with decorator's icing.

ing and cream of tartar or lemon juice. The starch gives extra stiffness. Meringue powder with a bit of water can be used instead of egg whites. It makes stiff, hard decorations by rolling out thinly on wax paper so a design can be cut. This is then colored or decorated. A more plastic one can be molded with the hands or from a pastry tube. After drying, the decorations are placed onto the cake. Sometimes decorations are made directly on cakes. Store this icing in tightly covered containers in a refrigerator. If too stiff after storing, thin with simple sirup or a bit of egg white. A lighter decorator's icing is made with a tablespoon of water to a pound of confectioners sugar, beaten well. Decorate with this directly onto cakes because the air beaten into the mass makes the icing fragile so that after drying, items crumble in handling.

Procedures

Before icing, crusts may be removed from cakes. If a damp cloth is placed over a cake, the crust rolls away more easily. Trim ragged edges. Shape as required. Edges should be sharp. Do not attempt too intricate a design. Broad outlines are easier to do. Brush away all crumbs before icing.

Have the icing at a proper consistency, not too thin to be runny or too thick to pull away and break the cake. Select icings for stability, lack of bleeding or breakdown, absence of stickiness and a clear, glossy color. If too stiff, warm or add a bit of simple sirup. Use paste colors preferably. Blend any coloring with a small quantity of the icing first, obtaining an intense color, and use this to shade into the larger mass.

(a)

(b)

Figure 16–22. (a) To ice a layer cake with heavy frosting, frost the sides first and then the top. Finish by holding the spatula perpendicular as shown to give a smooth edge. (b) When the frosting is thin, frost by pouring on the top and working down the sides.

Good color sense is required as well as a knowledge of how to obtain various colors. The amateur is known by his excess of color as well as excess of flavor. Moderation is the sign of a craftsman.

For a layer cake, invert the first layer top down on a turntable or decorator's wheel. If there is a difference in layer thickness, place the thickest on the bottom. If no wheel is available, invert on wax paper. Spread fillings evenly over the first layer's bottom. Place the second layer right side up on this. Deposit a liberal supply of thin icing in the center of the top and work with a spatula to the sides guiding the icing down the sides using the spatula to spread over the sides. For very thin icings place the cake on an open rack and frost as for petits fours. (See Figure 16-22). If a thick frosting is used, start on the sides, spreading with a spatula from the bottom toward the top, turning as the side is frosted and holding the spatula in a nearly vertical position to give a smooth side. Next spread the top with a liberal portion, using a motion which pushes the frosting toward the edges. Make a smooth surface by dipping the spatula first into warm water and then smoothing out, or leave the surface irregular. An iced cake should give a feeling of height with the sides even and the top straight. Pile icing liberally on top to avoid a "tight, peeled" appearance. Dry iced cakes before decorating.

Free small cakes from crumbs after making them into proper

(a)

(b)

(c)

(d)

(e)

(f)

Figure 16–23.   Simple designs can be made as shown. The design made on the lower right is obtained by heavily dusting powdered sugar over the cake top covered by a grid, and then removing the grid, leaving the design. (Courtesy Standard Brands)

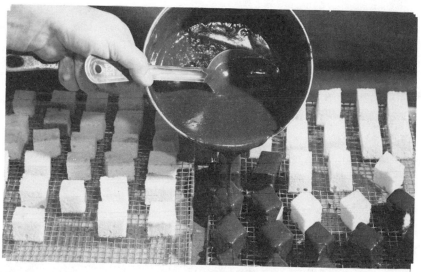

(a)

(b)

Figure 16–24. To frost small cakes, such as petits fours, cut into the desired shapes and then cover completely with fondant frosting as shown. Finish with decoration.

shapes. Pour a thin fondant or water icing over the tops as they set on a wire rack over a sheet pan, direct the icing to flow down the sides. Remove the rack and with a spatula pick up the surplus icing for reuse. Repeat if necessary to get a sufficiently thick coating on the cakes.

A pastry bag of canvas, rubber or plastic is used for decorating but many prefer to make their own from parchment paper which is simply made, easily discarded and as many can be made as the number of colors needed. Use heavy wax paper or brown wrapping paper if parchment paper is not available, although wax paper is more fragile and wrapping paper soaks up moisture, splitting easily.

If only writing is to be done, do not cut the cone tip and use no metal tip. Shape the tip to the writing size. Fill the bag or cone to about

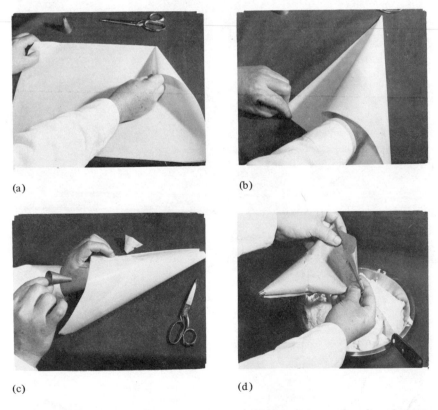

(a)

(b)

(c)

(d)

Figure 16–25. (a) To make a paper cone, cut the paper as shown and grasp it with two hands rolling with the right. (b) Finish the cone as shown, keeping the right hand inside to control the shape. (c) Cut about a half inch from the cone tip and insert the metal tip as shown. (d) After filling, using care to get the filling deep into the bag, fold with a double fold.

(a)

(b)

Figure 16–26. (a) Hold the cone at a 45° angle to decorate a cake top. When a large quantity of frosting is required, use the top hand, exerting pressure with the full hand. The bottom hand guides. (b) When decorating the sides, hold the cone tip at right angles. When light pressure is needed, force the frosting from the tip with light pressure from the right hand (top hand) finger tips as shown.

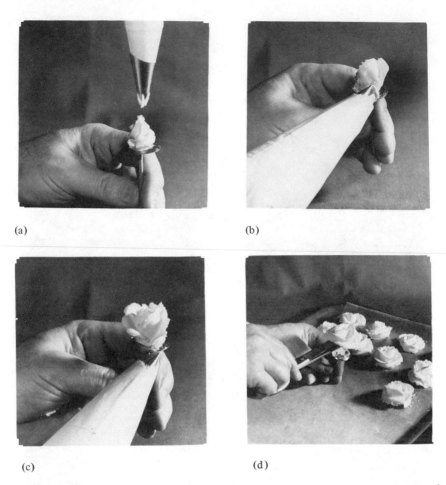

(a)

(b)

(c)

(d)

Figure 16–27. To make a rose: (a) using a star tube, set a rosette on top of a decorator's nail. (b) Now, with a petal tip, make petals around the rosette, continuing as shown in (c). (d) Remove the rose with scissors and place on wax paper to dry; then place into position on the cake.

half or three-fourths full. Deposit the icing down to the tip away from the sides and avoid capturing air which may ruin a decorating job by coming out with a burst during the work. Have the right consistency. For writing, the icing should flow or string out. If too thick, it breaks as the tip is moved over the surface. A medium consistency is needed for border work and stiffer for flowers, leaves or other objects to allow petals and other forms to stand up. After filling the cone or bag, fold

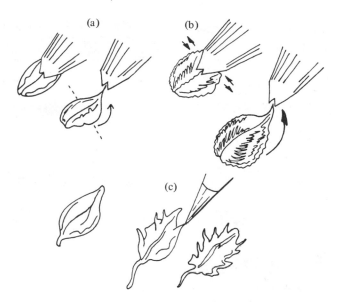

Figure 16–28. To make leaves, use a leaf tube. Force out a liberal supply of frosting and, at approximately the leaf center, release pressure lifting up to form the tip as shown in (a). To obtain a jagged edge, follow the same procedure but move the tip rapidly back and forth while the other motions are being made as indicated in (b). Or makes leaves as indicated in (a) and then with a fine tip, using the same color, add points as shown in (c).

over the top, making a double turn (apothecary's) to prevent the icing from coming from the top in decorating. Different tips are needed for making designs but about 10 do most of the usual decorating. Learn what tips do and use the right tip for the job.

Apply correct pressure and angle. Right-handed decorators apply pressure with the right hand using the left to guide or support the cone, or hold items while the right hand directs the tip and applies pressure; icing flowing from the top indicates left-hand pressure. Apply even pressure through the fingers and thumb for fine work and use the four fingers and palm for more gross work. Relaxing pressure in moving the tip causes a break in the icing. Exerting heavy pressure causes a blob to come suddenly from the tip. Hold the cone vertical (straight) for drop flowers or similar items, and at a 45° angle for writing, borders, leaves, flowers, stems or other objects on the tops of cakes. Hold the bag at a right angle when decorating a side. To set preformed decorations in place, put a bit of fresh icing at the spot and place the decoration on it.

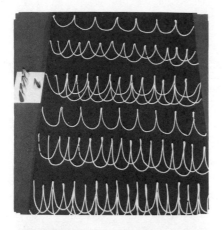

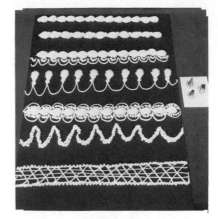

Figure 16–29. Some simple string designs. For this work, the frosting must be slightly thinner than that used for decorating objects. Many different borders are made using one tube. Types of borders may also be combined.

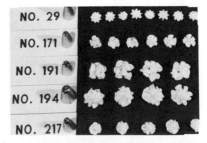

Figure 16–30. To make plain drop flowers, use the star tube. Hold the bag with the tube perpendicular above the object to be decorated or over wax paper where the flowers will be placed to dry. Force out the frosting, pushing down and breaking off abruptly with a pull up. A slight twist may be given to vary the shape slightly.

COOKIES

Ingredients for cookies are much the same as for cakes. Some cookies are made from batters that are nothing but cake batters. Most cookies, however, are made from doughs having a higher shortening and lower sugar and liquid content. The techniques of mixing are much the same as for cakes. Sugar, ice box and similar cookies are made by the conventional (creaming) method. Foam-types are made by methods similar to those used for foam cakes. Crisp cookies result from high ratios of fat and sugar to liquid, while soft cookies develop when the liquid is high and when hydroscopic sugars in them draw moisture. Chewy cookies are usually high in sugar and liquid and low in fat. Eggs give chewiness. The degree of baking affects crispness, soft cookies usually being baked a shorter time than crisp ones. Thickness and size are also factors affecting crispness and softness. Many cookies are tight-grained but some may be as open as cakes. Baking soda or ammonia is used to give spread. Ammonia is preferred in the amount of $\frac{1}{4}$ to $\frac{1}{2}$% of the flour because it leaves little aftertaste. Cookies high in sugar spread more than those made from a leaner dough. The coarser the sugar, the more the spread. Powdered sugar reduces spread. Large bakeshops usually deposit cookies onto pans by machine, using ammonia for spread. The use of ammonia is explained in Chapter 4. Products made with baking ammonia should be thin and not moist. The flavor of ammonia may be evident in thick, heavy or moist products.

Production

A sugar or ice box cookie is usually in balance if the flour is 100%, shortening 100%, sugar 50%, and eggs 10%. These are somewhat like a rich pie pastry, high in sugar. Most cookies of this type are made by the conventional method but a one-stage or dump method may be used, mixing all ingredients at one time at slow speed for about two minutes at 70° F. Basic doughs of sugar or ice box cookies may be made into many variations.

Some cookies are made by techniques and ingredients similar to those used in making foam cakes. Lady fingers, for instance, are from sponge cake batters and many other cookies are only modifications of other foam cake batters. In quantity work, macaroons are made from a base of almond paste, sugar, flour and unbeaten egg whites mixed at 85° F. Because of batter delicacy, only small batches of foam cookies are usually made. Meringue cookies are made from a hard meringue mixture. (The student should consult the discussions on meringue and egg foam in the chapter on egg cookery.) Kisses, meringue bars and macaroons can be rnade from egg whites beaten to a second stage foam. Underbeating gives a weak foam and a tough, gummy cookie. Over-beating extends air cells so that the product collapses in baking. Kisses are between soft and hard meringues in texture, taking less sugar than hard meringues. Flour and other ingredients are folded in carefully in the same manner as in foam cakes. Baking temperatures are usually 325° to 350° F. Adding glucose or invert sugar gives chewiness. If glucose, invert sugar or glycerine is added, the tendency of the sugar to crystallize is reduced. Weeping of egg foam can be reduced by sifting in at the end of beating a half ounce of cornstarch per pound of egg whites. Foam cookies may be glazed while hot with a sirup-gelatin glaze called a gelatin shine.

Chill stiff cookie doughs before cutting. If well wrapped in mois-ture-retarding wraps, they store well for several days. The time and labor involved makes it almost prohibitive to roll and cut cookies from doughs. If rolling and cutting *must* be done, use a canvas cloth for an underliner. Roll about ⅛-inch thick. Cut out as economically as possible so that as little dough as possible needs reworking, since this toughens the product.

Semi-soft batters are used for drop cookies. About 1 to 1½ ounces are dropped usually using a size 30 to 20 ice cream scoop respectively for these sizes. Scooping and depositing may be by spoon or pastry bag. Hand deposit by scooping a handful, using the side of the hand as a scoop, and then with a squeezing motion place the correct quantity on the baking sheet. Macaroons, kisses and meringues may also be de-posited in this manner. Deposit semi-soft batters approximately two inches apart. After depositing non-meringue type macaroons, allow them to stand 8 to 12 hours before baking. Holland or split macaroons are held refrigerated and in the morning are cut through the center with a sharp knife so that after baking a split appears. Kisses, meringues and paste macaroons may be placed onto greased paper, silicon-coated pans, greased and flour-dusted pans or thin sheets of rice paper. Remove while still warm with a wet spatula or pancake turner. If cold, hold the baking sheets a moment over heat. Rice paper can be broken away and left on the bottom since it is edible. Lady fingers may be deposited by making small fingers of sponge cake batter with a pastry tube about three inches long and a half inch wide. Allow at least an inch between these. Many foam-type or semi-soft batters are machine-deposited. Batters or doughs with nuts or chopped fruits, however, sometimes do not deposit well by machine, and must be hand-dropped.

Some semi-soft or soft batters, such as nut squares or brownies, may be spread evenly onto baking sheets about a half inch thick. After baking, while still warm, they are cut into desired shapes. If the cookies are frosted, cutting may have to be done when they are cold.

Quite stiff doughs are made into rolls for ice box cookies. For large cookies, scale off three pounds and make into 2-inch diameter rolls. Wrap in wax paper or plastic and refrigerate or partially freeze. Each roll makes approximately 50 cookies. Small roles — about $1\frac{1}{2}$ pounds each, $\frac{3}{4}$ to an inch in diameter — produce tea-size cookies. A sharp knife or a kitchen slicing machine may be used to cut the cookies about $\frac{1}{8}$ inch thick. Space on pans about an inch apart. If the dough contains ammonia, slice thicker and space on pans a greater distance apart. Remove while hot.

Some stiff doughs are made into long rolls about 1 to $1\frac{1}{2}$ inches in diameter and pieces about an ounce each are cut, using a pastry knife, and placed onto well greased pans about two inches apart. Flatten into thin discs and bake. Peanut butter cookies and others can be flattened with a fork or a small can may be put into a moistened cloth, the cloth-covered end dipped into granulated sugar and pressed down to flatten the dough into discs. The cloth is dipped again into sugar before another cooky is flattened. Fruit bars, hermits and other thick doughs are made into $1\frac{3}{4}$-pound rolls which are flattened into 3- to 4-inch wide strips on well greased 18 x 26 baking sheets about four to a pan. The strips are glazed with a wash. After baking, each strip is cut into $1\frac{3}{4}$-inch bars, about 12 to 13 bars per strip.

Use level, clean baking sheets. Some need not be greased. Others may need liberal greasing and dusting with flour. Have pans cool before cookies are placed onto them. Liberal greasing encourages spread. If dusting flour is used, spread is reduced. If pans are too lightly greased, cookies high in egg or sugar may be difficult to remove and may color too heavily at the edges in baking. Some cookies spread little while others double in diameter. A small cookie is about the size of a 50¢ piece after baking; a medium one is more the size of a silver dollar, and large cookies may be three inches in diameter. Bar or fruit cookies are usually scaled $\frac{3}{4}$ to an ounce each and sugar cookies a half ounce or less. A normal yield is 32 to 34 cookies per pound of dough. A dozen $3\frac{1}{2}$-inch diameter sugar cookies weigh between 11 and 12 ounces before baking and about 10 ounces after. Small cookies may be scaled 3 to 4 per ounce, and meringues or other foam-type cookies a half to two-thirds ounce each or 6 to 10 ounces per dozen. Post written scaling information so that it is used.

Baking

Cookies are normally baked at higher temperatures than cakes and must be watched carefully, for too much baking overcolors the cookies and ruins their flavor. Chocolate cookies, especially, burn easily. When cookies are done, they are of the proper color and spring back slightly to the touch. Too low an oven temperature gives tight-grained cookies with poor color. If temperatures are too high, the cookies lack spread and are overly dark. Closing the oven damper in the early stages of baking holds steam inside and assists in giving spread. Crisp cookies may be soft while still warm but crisp on cooling. After baking, protect cookies from drafts and too rapid cooling. Many cookies should be removed from the pans while still warm.

Storing

Most cookie batters or doughs freeze well except foam types. Stiff doughs should be thawed under refrigeration but softer mixes may be thawed at room temperature. Do not pack cookies while warm. Store into airtight containers or drawers. Frozen cookies thaw in opened packages in about 15 to 20 minutes. Sometimes a moist cut apple is stored with soft cookies to keep them moist. Do not stack soft cookies. Foam-types dry out easily, so make these in batches that are used quickly and store in airtight containers.

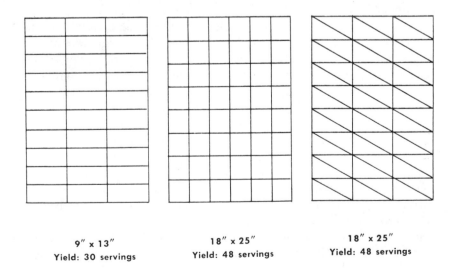

9″ x 13″
Yield: 30 servings

18″ x 25″
Yield: 48 servings

18″ x 25″
Yield: 48 servings

Figure 16–31.   Various ways to cut cakes.

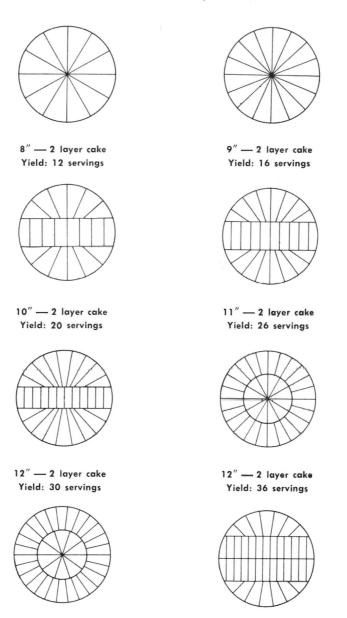

8″ — 2 layer cake
Yield: 12 servings

9″ — 2 layer cake
Yield: 16 servings

10″ — 2 layer cake
Yield: 20 servings

11″ — 2 layer cake
Yield: 26 servings

12″ — 2 layer cake
Yield: 30 servings

12″ — 2 layer cake
Yield: 36 servings

13″ — 2 layer cake
Yield: 36 servings

14″ — 2 layer cake
Yield: 40 servings

(Courtesy American Baking Institute)

Figure 16–31. Various ways to cut cakes (continued).

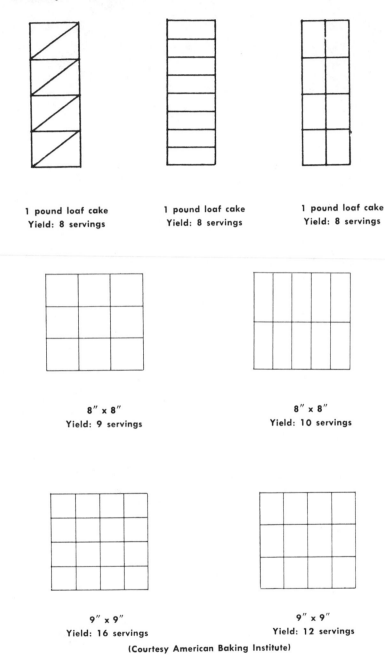

1 pound loaf cake
Yield: 8 servings

1 pound loaf cake
Yield: 8 servings

1 pound loaf cake
Yield: 8 servings

8″ x 8″
Yield: 9 servings

8″ x 8″
Yield: 10 servings

9″ x 9″
Yield: 16 servings

9″ x 9″
Yield: 12 servings

(Courtesy American Baking Institute)

Figure 16–31. Various ways to cut cakes (continued).

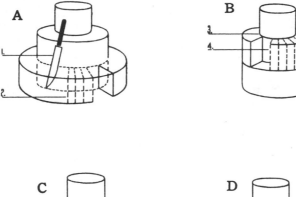

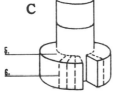

Figure 16–31. Various ways to cut cakes (continued).

Suggested laboratory exercises or work experiences for Chapter 16:

1. Take a cake or cookie recipe and check balance indicating how closely It conforms to the balance rules and where it varies.
2. Follow by chart or diagram the variation of shortening, egg, sugar and liquid from a pound cake to a butter cake to a muffin mixture showing how these vary as one moves to a leaner batter.
3. Prepare various cakes from a mix and compare them in quality, cost and time to prepare, with cakes made from scratch.
4. Prepare various types of cakes and cookies.
5. Using the text, practice making various types of decorations from different icings.

BIBLIOGRAPHY

Amendola, Joseph, *The Baker's Manual,* 2nd ed., revised, Ahrens Publishing Co., New York City, 1962.

Amendola, Joseph and Lundberg, D., *Understanding Baking,* Ahrens Publishing Co., New York City, 1970.

American Dry Milk Institute, *Cakes,* Bulletin No. 102, Chicago, 1953.

General Mills, *Quality Cakes and Icings,* revised ed., Minneapolis, Minn., 1959.

Lever Brothers, Consumer Service Dept., *Create a Finer Cake the New One Bowl Way,* Bakery Bulletin, New York City, n. d.

Pillsbury Company, *Cake and Frosting Mixes,* Minneapolis, Minn., 1963.

Standard Brands, *Cake Making,* New York City, 1950, (out of print).

Standard Brands, *The Basic Cake Formula,* New York City, 1965.

Wilton, McKinley and Wilton, Norman, *Cake Decorating,* 1st ed., Wilton Enterprises, Chicago, 1960.

Wilton, McKinley and Wilton, Norman, *Modern Cake Decorating,* 2nd ed., Wilton Enterprises, Inc., Chicago, 1954.

17

Pies and Pastry

Pies and pastries are popular products. They may take much labor, however, unless they are wisely selected, a convenient layout is set up for the work and good production techniques used. To achieve satisfactory costs, production standards should be established and these adhered to. In one operation an experienced baker hand-rolled 200 pie dough pieces in an hour. Assembly-line methods give increased production in quantity work. Three workers using pre-cut dough discs, a prepared pumpkin filling and a mechanical pie-rolling machine produced 160 pumpkin pies ready for baking in 171 worker minutes. The assembly line used is shown in Figure 17-2.

Pies may be single or double crust and filled with fruit, cream filling, egg custard, gelatin or other sweetened and thickened mixtures. Ice cream, mousse or other frozen desserts may be placed into baked pie sheets and served. Many pastries are closely related to pies, such as tarts and dumplings. In addition to variation in filling or shape, variety is obtained with different crusts such as puff paste, graham cracker, dark chocolate wafer, nut or meringue.

Standard

Regular pie crust is crisp and tender and has a short, easy break. It may be flaky, semi-flaky or mealy. The surface is golden or cream, darkening

(a) (b)

(c) (d)

Figure 17–1. High standards for pies are shown in (a) a milk chocolate cream pie, (b) apple pie, (c) glazed fried pies and (d) prune tarts. The latter are made from tart shells prefabricated and only filled.

to a golden brown at the edge. The appearance is rough and blistery on the surface rather than smooth, and this roughness varies with the crust flakiness. The crust should cut easily but not crumble. Test oiliness by rubbing between the fingers. The filling varies in consistency and type. A starch-thickened filling is delicate, smooth and soft, sagging only slightly at the cut edge. An egg custard filling should have a sharp edge, be firm with no flow and possess a good sheen at the cut surface. A fruit filling should ooze slightly at the edge. Each piece of fruit should be clear and distinct. The color should be clear and bright. Fillings should be neither gummy nor pasty. Flavor should be moderately sweet and pleasant, characteristic of the product. The flavor of custard fillings should be sweet and mellow, not eggy.

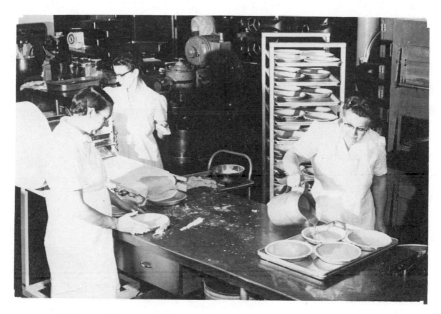

Figure 17–2. With assembly line methods, three workers can make 160 pumpkin pies in 171 worker minutes in contrast to 471 worker minutes when the three workers did the job separately.

Pie Doughs

Regular pie dough is made from flour, shortening, salt and water. The flour and liquid form a paste with the shortening serving as a lubricant, separating flour particles to give a tender product. Salt is added for flavor and since it strengthens gluten, is carefully controlled and added with the water. Milk powder or liquid milk may be used to improve color and flavor but the crust is less crisp. If dry milk is used, add it with the flour. To improve color and flavor, glucose or corn sirup in the ratio of 2% to flour is added with the water. Some specialty pie or tart doughs are almost as rich as cookie doughs. These may have eggs as an ingredient. Eggs improve color, raise cost and reduce crispness. More fat must also be used. Baking powder does not improve crust quality but vinegar or cream of tartar reduces water hardness, increases gluten tenderness and makes the dough whiter. The percentages of ingredients for different types of pie doughs are:

	Mealy	*Semi-flaky*	*Flaky*
Flour, pastry	100%	100%	100%
Shortening	50–60%	75%	100%
Salt	2–3%	2–3%	2–3%
Water	25–30%	30–35%	35–40%

Figure 17–3.   From left to right, a flaky, a semi-flaky and a mealy pie crust.

About 10% gluten pastry flour is most frequently used. This gives sufficient strength for a good pliable dough that holds up well in rolling and does not give a tough dough unless it is handled improperly. Bread flour is used for puff paste or flaky doughs. This flour makes a paste that spreads out into thin sheets between layers of shortening. Steam formed in baking between these sheets lifts them up developing flakiness after crisping.

Tenderness is an important quality factor. The amount of shortening and mixing plus the method of blending in the shortening are key factors in giving tenderness. A flour having a small amount of gluten or a weak gluten needs less shortening and can take more mixing than a stronger flour. To be tender, a strong bread flour may need a ratio of shortening as high as 80 to 100% by weight of the flour. Hard-wheat flour mixes less easily into shortening. Bread flour gives a chewy quality to the crust which may be desirable. Adding soy flour to a pie dough gives a shorter and mealier crust and also one having a creamier color. It reduces flakiness. Specialty crusts may be made from ground pecans, almonds, filberts or other products replacing 25% of the flour, and such replacement favors shortness and the development of a mealy crust. A graham cracker crust may be used. A formula by weight of 100% graham cracker crumbs, 30% sugar and 55% butter or margarine gives a good crust. Cinnamon, almond flour, powdered sugar and other ingredients may be added. Gingersnaps, vanilla wafers, chocolate wafers and other dried crumbs may be also used. About two ounces of the crumb mixture spread evenly and packed on the bottom and sides is sufficient for a 9-inch pie. Another pan is then firmly pressed onto the crumbs and the crust baked 10 minutes in a 350° F oven or left in a refrigerator overnight. Some of the crumb mixture may be saved for sprinkling over meringues or whipped cream toppings.

For proper tenderness, a shortening with good shortening power is needed. It should be sufficiently plastic to work well from 50° to 80° F, this shortening power and plasticity governing the quantity needed. Highly unsaturated or emulsified shortenings do not develop flaky doughs because they work too much into the flour. Lard is a good shortening for it gives good tenderness and flavor and has the correct plasticity. Butter or margarine is sometimes used for flavor but the amount of shortening is increased unless the curd and moisture are first removed by kneading and washing. Edible oils can be used but the dough may be oily and hard to handle. Oils permeate the flour so much that it is difficult to make flaky crusts with them. Hot-water pie crusts may be made using oil or shortening with ingredient proportions the same as those in a regular pie crust.

Only the water needed to give a soft, pliable dough should be used. Besides making the dough workable, water furnishes steam inside the dough layers, causing the crust to flake. If the crust is too dry, the steam is insufficient and a less flaky crust results. Excess water encourages toughness, possibly by allowing more complete hydration of the gluten. A sticky dough is difficult to roll and handle. Also, as the shortening increases, water is increased.

Production Methods

Precise scaling, good ingredients and skillful techniques are required to produce good pies. A horizontal-cylinder slow-speed mixer may be used to make large quantities of pie dough. Most operations use a vertical mixer at low speed. Many use a pie crust blade for cutting the shortening into the flour and a flat paddle to blend in the water. Others use only the flat paddle for both operations. Some prefer to hand-mix small quantities of dough because they can work the shortening into the flour better and feel the dough development more surely. Good rollers, pastry boards or canvas tops, cutters and other equipment are essential. Mechanical rollers reduce time and labor. A cool dough rolls and handles better than a warm one.

Mixing

The short and flaky qualities of a pie crust depend not only upon the types of ingredients and their quantity and quality but also on the method of mixing. Blending the shortening into the flour well gives a mealy crust.

A limited amount of mixing leaving the fat in large pieces gives a flaky or semi-flaky crust. The flakiness of such crust, puff pastes and strudels results from rolling and rerolling sheets of dough and shortening to make many finely separated layers of each.

The amount and vigor of mixing is critical to crust quality, especially after water is added to give gluten moisture for development. Excess speed or mixing time favors gluten development as does warmth so doughs should be kept cold. At 60° F the shortening blends well into the flour while still retaining firmness to give particles for flakiness. The friction of mixing and the absorption of water by the flour develop heat. Water at around 40° F or colder should be used. If the fat is too cold, the crust is toughened; if too soft, it is difficult to develop flakiness. Excess gluten development gives a dough which shrinks badly in baking. A 15-minute rest after mixing decreases baking shrink and makes the dough easier to roll. Some state that refrigerating 12 to 24 hours improves quality, but others claim that it makes no difference.

With an upright mixer, blending the flour and shortening takes from 15 to 90 seconds at slow speed, the time depending upon the size of the shortening particles desired. About 40 seconds at slow speed are sufficient for mixing in the water. Add all the water with the salt dissolved into it at one time, spreading it well over the blended shortening and flour. Mix only until the water is blended and the dough *just* leaves the sides of the bowl. In hand-mixing, the water may be sprinkled over the shortening and flour mixture.

A very short and tender crust — a mealy crust — is made by blending the shortening into the flour until the mixture looks like coarse cornmeal. Or, half the shortening may be blended well into the flour and the remainder mixed until the shortening is no longer sticky. A ratio of 50 to 60% shortening to flour is used. A mealy crust is short and quite tender and soaks less than flaky types. It bakes with low shrinkage and colors well. It is used for the undercrusts of double pies and for custard pies and others where soaking may be a problem. A batter method is used by some operations to make a mealy crust. Mixing is the same as for regular mealy crust but 20% of the flour is withheld and mixed with the water and blended in this way. Or about 50% of the flour can be creamed with the shortening until a smooth paste is formed and the rest of the flour added until it is blended in. Water with the salt is then added. The same ratios of ingredients can be used for a hot-water pie crust as for normal mealy crust dough. Boiling water is added to the shortening and beaten until the mixture is smooth and fluffy. The salt and flour are mixed only until all wet spots have disappeared. In all of these crusts, overmixing encourages toughening.

Semi-flaky dough has good tenderness and crispness and is considered best suited for all purposes. It colors well in baking. For a semi-flaky crust, a ratio of 60 to 75% shortening to flour is required. Good plasticity of the shortening is necessary for the shortening particles to flatten out well between sheets of the dough paste. The shortening is cut into the flour until it is large pea size, or a third to half of the shortening can be well blended into the flour and the remainder cut in until it is about the size of hazelnuts.

A flaky crust resembles puff paste in texture and to some extent in appearance. It makes excellent baked single crust shells but soaks quickly after fillings are added. Many add fillings just before service. It is good for top crusts of fruit pies and for tarts or tartlets, small pastry shells, tops for deep-dish pies, meat or poultry pies and so forth. It is seldom used for bottom crusts or custard-type pies because of its tendency to soak. The trimmings of semi-flaky or flaky doughs may be rerolled with mealy dough for bottom crusts of double crust pies. Reworking causes a loss of flakiness.

Pie doughs can be stored about a week under refrigeration. Some shape about six pounds of dough into 3-inch diameter cylinders from 15 to 18 inches long. These are rolled in moisture-vapor-proof wraps or in slightly moistened cloths. After chilling, a dough cutter is used to cut round pieces about an inch thick — 5 to 6 ounces each. These discs are then rolled for pie crusts. Pie dough mix may be left dry and kept stored for use as needed. Such storage should not be for more than 10 days as rancidity can develop quickly in such a mix.

Puff paste products are attractive because of their puffy, light quality. The French call puff paste *pâte de feuilletée* or "paste of many leaves." The specially manufactured waxy, plastic puff paste shortenings now on the market have simplified puff paste making. Also, in many localities frozen or chilled puff paste is available on the market ready to use. It needs only shaping and baking. If the old-fashioned method is used, with butter or regular margarine, the shortening should be well washed in cold water to remove moisture and curd, then kneaded until very plastic and chilled until waxy.

Puff pastes are made of bread flour. With flour as 100%, use 100% shortening, 1% salt and 35 to 50% water. Some recipes specify 3 to 12% eggs and 0.75% cream of tartar. Sift the cream of tartar with the flour. The cream of tartar tenderizes the gluten and gives a whiter dough, and the eggs contribute color, strength and nutritional value. Mix the flour, salt and water until the mass is smooth, soft and pliable. Sufficient strength of gluten is required for the dough to form a tenuous sheet or layer over and under the layer of shortening. Do not develop until stringy or ropy, however. Water and flour may be mixed together at 60% F for

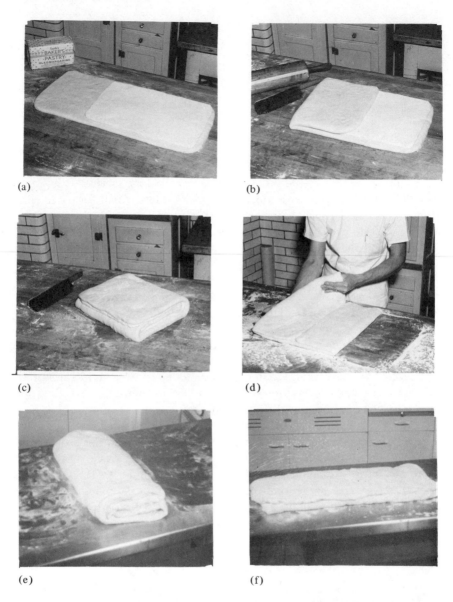

(a)

(b)

(c)

(d)

(e)

(f)

Figure 17–4. Making puff paste. (a) The dough paste is rolled out about three times longer than wide and about a half inch thick and covered with about a half-inch thick layer of puff paste shortening over two-thirds of the surface. (b) The uncovered third is folded over and then folded again as in (c) to completely seal the shortening between layers of dough. This is called a three-fold. Making a four-fold is shown in (d). (e) The dough has been given a four-fold. (f) After resting 15 to 20 minutes, it is given a turn and rolled out to its original shape. Note in making a turn, the dough is parallel to the worker and not perpendicular to him.

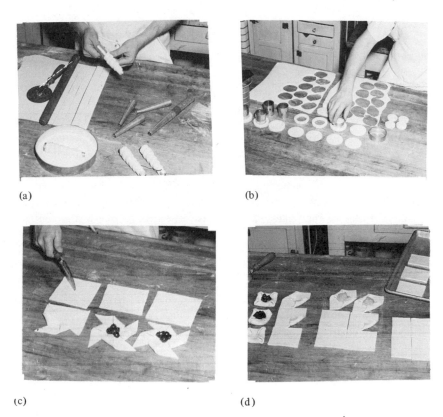

(a)   (b)

(c)   (d)

Figure 17–5. Some techniques for making items from puff paste. (a) Cream horns are made from strips of dough ⅛ inch thick, 1¼ inches wide, and about 15 inches long. Roll the completed horn in sugar and bake after a 30 minute rest. (b) Cut rounds with a plain cutter from dough 1/16 inch thick. Cut ⅜ inch thick dough with the same cutter, and cut out the centers with a smaller cutter. Wash first rounds with a bit of water around the edges with the pastry brush and place the rings upside down on top of the discs. (c) Cut ⅛ inch thick dough about 5 by 5 inches square and wash with water. Using a pastry wheel or scraper, cut into center as shown, leaving about one inch in the center uncut. Press every other corner into the center and fill with washed or glazed fruit. (d) Variations in shapes are shown. (Courtesy Swift & Company)

approximately two minutes using a pie blade and slow speed. Some add 15 to 20% of the shortening in this mixing. After mixing, allow the paste to rest for approximately 10 to 15 minutes, then roll into a half-inch thick rectangle twice as long as it is wide. Excess flour should always be brushed off in the rolling. Next spot the shortening evenly over two-thirds of the rectangle with a half-inch margin at the edges, and then fold the unspotted third over half the spotted portion. Fold the remaining third over this folded portion, giving a 3-fold dough. A 4-fold dough is sometimes made, a procedure in which the dough is marked into fourths with shortening dotted on the two inside fourths. Each outside fourth is folded over these. After being brushed free of flour, one of the tops of the fourths is dotted with shortening and another fold made, giving three layers of shortening and four of dough. After folding, allow the dough to rest for 20 to 25 minutes under refrigeration. Then give it a half turn so that the former length becomes the width, thus crisscrossing the folds of each turn. Roll the dough into a rectangle of the same dimensions as the original one. The maximum number of turns with three folds is six and with four folds, four. Smooth, even rolling is necessary to distribute evenly the layers of paste and shortening. The paste and shortening should be of the same consistency to distribute both more evenly and prevent rupture of the paste walls because of slippage of the shortening. The dough is now spotted again with these additional turns and rolling. After each turn, rolling and then folding, a 20 to 25 minute rest occurs under refrigeration. As the folding and rolling continue, thinner and thinner and more and more layers of paste and shortening are made. Each time a rolling occurs, a finger indentation is put into the dough to remind the worker the number of these that has been given, a one-finger indentation meaning one rolling and folding, a two-finger indentation meaning two rollings and foldings, etc. Excessive folding and rolling toughens the dough, giving too thin a paste sheet to give good flaking. Puff paste trimmings are usually pressed together, rolled out, given a 3-fold and used again but the quality of this reworked dough is usually not as good.

Puff paste can also be made with hard-wheat flour 100%, puff paste shortening 100%, water 35%, salt 1% and cream of tartar 0.75%. From 70 to 75% of the flour is mixed with 25% of the shortening and all of the water, salt and cream of tartar. This mixture is rested 30 minutes under refrigeration. The remaining flour and 75% of the flour are mixed together thoroughly and this is rested 20 minutes under refrigeration. Now, instead of the paste on the outside and shortening on the inside, the procedure is reversed and the paste is put over two-thirds of the shortening mixture. It is then given a 3-fold and the procedure followed for regular puff paste.

Rolling and Makeup

Regular pie crusts are usually rolled about ⅛ inch thick, although some crusts may be somewhat thicker. Bottoms should be cut about 6 ounces and tops 5 ounces for 9-inch pies. Crust thickness governs these amounts. Experienced bakers may require less since they have little or no waste in rolling. For machine-rolling, pieces for top and bottom are 8 ounces.

(a)

(b)   (c)

Figure 17–6. Making tartlets. (a) Puff paste or special tart shell dough is rolled out, cut into rounds, and placed into tartlet molds. Beans are placed in paper cups, which are placed in the tarts. Peas, rice, or rock salt may be used instead of beans. (b) On the upper top, the tartlet dough, shell, and rock salt used are shown. In the second row, the tartlet shell, thin round of cake, cream filling, and placement of the cake filling are shown. In the next row, fruits are placed in position, and in the bottom row the tart is shown glazed. (c) A franchipan batter is placed into a well greased tartlet shell and baked as shown on the row at the top. The second row shows shaping and the third the filling of the item. The bottom row shows the finished product. (Courtesy Culinary Institute)

To hand-roll, use a pin or roller approximately 1½ inches in diameter and 18 inches long, slightly tapered at either end. Have a smooth surface or board with only a little dusting flour on it. Dough is toughened by the addition of too much dusting flour. Keep the rolling pin and top of the dough only lightly dusted with flour. Rolling on a canvas requires less dusting flour. With quick, deft strokes starting from the center, roll

Figure 17–7.   A tray of finished puff pastries and tartlets. (Courtesy *Institutions*)

the dough into an oval shape, then turn it and make the circle. Lift and turn the dough as frequently as necessary. When this is done, check to see that dusting flour remains underneath. Dough should be cold but not overly stiff for rolling. When the crust is in the desired shape, fold once in the center and place into a pan without stretching. It can then be unfolded easily and shaped to the pan. Some bakers pick the dough up deftly with the rolling pin, lift to the pan and unfold into the pan with the pin. Docking, or making holes in the crust, is needed for single crust pie shells to prevent blistering in baking. If these crusts are double-panned — that is, baked between two pans — docking is not necessary. Some like to bake double-panned crusts upside down to reduce the tendency of the dough to shrink and fall down into the pan.

Time is saved if the excess dough from the bottom and top crusts is removed at the same time, removing excess by a quick, deft turning motion between the two hands. Edges can be made attractive by pinching the dough lightly with the thumb and index finger, pressing in with the index finger of the other hand. The use of a pie crimper, roller-docker, pastry cutter, bench brush and scraper facilitates rolling out. The bottom and top crusts of double crust pies should be carefully sealed around the

(a)

(b)

Figure 17–8. (a) Two identical pieces of pie dough baked except that the one on the left was stretched when it was rolled out and it shrank back when baked. (b) Single crust pie shells should be baked double-panned rather than as shown here. Note how the crust pulled back into the pan. When the crust is placed on the **outside** of the pan and another pan placed over it and this baked upside down (double-panning) a well-formed crust usually results.

edges to lessen the possibility of boil-out in the oven. If a hole is made in the center of the top and temperature is controlled, boil-out is usually not a problem. Moistening the edge of the bottom crust before putting on the top assists in giving a tighter seal. Washing the top with milk, cream, evaporated milk, eggs and milk, butter or margarine gives extra crust color. The type of wash governs the finished appearance of the crust. Usually, well made crusts need no wash. Butter and margarine are best for homemade appearing products.

Pastries

Pie doughs or puff pastes may be used for many pastries such as small pies, tarts, tartlets, turnovers, dumplings and others. To hold dough in place, beans or rice may be used to fill the insides of tart shells, etc. (See Figure 17-6 which shows how beans in paper cups are put into such shells.) Docking or double panning is not needed when this is done. The beans or rice are stored in jars and reused for this same purpose whenever needed. Baked pastry dumplings or turnovers may be filled with meat, fruit or other items. For these, the dough is usually rolled to a ⅛-inch thickness, a No. 12 scoop of filling is put in the center and the dough folded over. A special leaner dough is needed if the product is deep-fried such as fried pies. (See Chapter 12 on Deep-frying.) If tartlet tins are not available, muffin pans may be used. For this, rounds of dough are cut the proper size to fit over the outside, then

Figure 17–9.   A crust baked in too slow an oven, just right and too hot an oven.

docked and baked over these cups. Frequently a rich pastry dough resembling cookie dough is used for tartlets. Pastry rings or tin hoops may be placed on greased baking sheets and lined with dough for larger tarts. These are pinched to give a border at the edge, docked and baked. Small tart shells may be purchased already baked. Figures 17-5, 17-6 and 17-7 show some of the techniques for making pastries.

Baking Pie Crusts and Pastries

Single crusts and small pastry shells are baked from 425° to 450° F for about 15 minutes, and double crust pies and filled pastries at 425° to 450° F for 10 minutes dropping to 350° to 375° F for the remaining 35 to 50 minutes to complete baking. Many prefer no temperature change for these latter products but a temperature of 350° to 375° F for the full time. Too low a temperature toughens the crust while too much heat causes overbrowning and a poorly cooked filling. If the filling of a double crust pie is hot when it is placed into the oven, baking time is reduced. Brushing the bottom of a double crust pie with eggs or flour has not been shown to reduce the tendency to soak, although many bakers believe this is effective.

Fillings

Fillings should be made with the same care as the crust, for the filling gives identity to the item. A wide variety of fillings is used for single crust pies and tarts, blanc manges, cream puddings, bavarians, layers of cream pudding over which thickened layers of fruit filling are poured, marizpans, gelatin chiffons, frozen fillings and others. Toppings may be

(a)   (b)

Figure 17–10. (a) Roll crusts with a deft, light stroke, working the dough to all sides so that a good round about ⅛ inch thick is obtained. (b) Trim excess dough by rotating and cutting with the palms of the hands at the same time.

meringues, whipped cream, toasted coconut, crumbs or nuts. Unbaked single crusts may also be filled with custards, chiffons, soufflés or other uncooked fillings and baked. Double crust pies usually have fruit fillings. Lattice tops are sometimes used for these instead of solid crusts. A streussel-like topping, called "French" or "Dutch," may also be baked on top instead of a top crust.

About 1½ pints to a quart or 1¼ to two pounds of filling is needed for a 9-inch pie. When pies are topped with a meringue or whipped cream, the smaller quantity is used. Many fillings for single crust pies are similar to desserts and the methods for preparing these and soft meringues will be found either under the chapters on desserts or egg cookery.

The quality of the fruit filling is affected by the type of fruit, the thickening agent, the proportion of thickening agent, sweetening agents and other ingredients and the method of preparation. Low quality fruits should be avoided. The fruit may be broken, for appearance is not critical between the crusts. Fresh fruit should be kept under refrigeration and before being used, picked over, moldy or over-ripe fruit discarded and the fruit washed and drained. Sugar, thickeners and other ingredients are added and the fruit is allowed to stand for an hour or so. Canned fruits should be opened just before use as long standing causes a loss in their quality. Frozen fruits should be drained and the juice only thickened and then blended with the fruits. Instant or cold setting starches can be used to avoid cooking the juice thereby giving a much fresher flavor to the pie. The filling then gets only one heating which occurs in the baking of the pie. It is often best to allow thickened fillings to stand 1 to 2 hours after making them before using. Carry-over pie fillings should not be held for long periods but should be stored at 50° to 52° F. Some bakers add freshly made fillings to stored products and use immediately to obtain a fresher tasting product. Canned prepared pie fillings are available today and some are of high quality. Care should be taken, however, to see that not only is the flavor and color correct, but that an adequate amount of fruit to paste is in the filling. Fruit to liquid should be 2:1 to 3:1. It is also undesirable to extend a filling by adding excessive quantities of water to one's own fillings. The quantity of water must be governed by the type of fruit, and therefore it is difficult to establish exact ratios.

Cornstarch and flour are commonly used as thickeners. Fruit pie fillings are best thickened with a waxy maize starch because it gives clarity and brilliance to the fruit and gives a soft paste when cold. Waxy maize or converted starches are especially made for such fillings. They set up with the same consistency when hot as when cold. They have good tolerance in use and give a more standard thickened product than other types of thickeners. The following are the average quantities of thickeners used per gallon of liquid for fruit fillings:

Waxy maize starch or converted starch	10 to 10½ oz	(8% solution)
Cornstarch, arrowroot, tapioca, etc.	13 to 15½ oz	(10 to 12% solution)
Flour	20 to 30 oz	(16 to 20% solution)

Some bakers add gums such as carboxy-methyl-cellulose (CMC), gum tragacanth, locust bean gum or low-methyoxyl pectin to thicken these fillings and provide high clarity and brilliance to the fruit and juice. Bakery supply houses can be helpful in indicating new products which improve fillings.

Usually the thickener is mixed with the sugar and blended into the hot liquid. The thickener can also be blended with some of the liquid and added as a slurry. Cooking should continue until thickening is complete which for cornstarch and flour occurs at 203° F and for waxy maize and converted starch at 195° F. Rapid cooking and cooling are desirable to prevent the breakdown of the thickener by the fruit acid. To make a lemon cream pie filling, blend the cornstarch, grated lemon peel, sugar and salt together. Pour this into the water and thicken, giving good agitation. When thickening is complete, take a small quantity of the hot mixture and stir into lightly beaten egg yolks (stage one). Next blend this yolk mixture with good agitation into the hot thickened mixture. Cook for 3 to 5 minutes, stirring constantly. Add the lemon juice and butter to the hot mixture after removing from the heat. Cool rapidly.

If the quantity of sugar in fruit fillings is high, withhold some and add it after thickening. This prevents the excess sugar from retarding

Figure 17–11. The relative quantities of waxy maize starch (left), cornstarch (center) and flour (right) to give equal thickness to a pie filling. Note the softness of the waxy maize and the sheer firm qualities of the cornstarch compared with flour. Clarity also is a variable.

gelatinization of the starch. If a pound of starch is heated with seven pounds of sugar in 1¼ gallons of water, swelling or gelatinizing of the starch is prevented and a dull, thin, watery, unflavorful filling results. If the same starch is mixed with only 3 to 4 pounds of the sugar, good thickening occurs and the remaining sugar can be added later.

Custard and Chiffon Fillings

Custard pies are usually made with 2½ pounds of whole egg to a gallon of milk or liquid. If yolks are used, the eggs may be reduced and a finer custard results. The proportion of eggs should be higher than that used for dessert custards to give a firmer custard and keep the crust drier. Techniques for mixing and baking are much the same as discussed under egg cookery. Chiffon pies have fillings much like dessert soufflés but some are made of egg whites incorporated into starch-thickened or gelatin-thickened mixtures. These are not baked but are poured into baked pie shells and allowed to set.

    Gelatin desserts can be used to make chiffon pie fillings. These are actually snows or sponges, bavarians or whips discussed in the next chapter. Gelatin desserts may also be combined with fruits and used as pie fillings. A parfait pie filling is a gelatin mixture into which soft ice cream and fresh or frozen drained fruits have been folded just before the gelatin sets.

Figure 17–12. Waxy maize starch is not suitable for cream pie fillings. Note how it runs from the pie on the left compared with the cornstarch filling on the right.

Makeup and Service

In many operations, single crust cream pies are not filled until needed to avoid crust soaking. The filling is cold and of such consistency as can be spread and yet hold its shape when cut. Meringues and other toppings may also be added shortly before service. Use pie markers in cutting pies. Do not cut pies too far ahead of service. Many fruit pies are improved if they are slightly warm at service.

Suggested laboratory exercises or work experiences for Chapter 17:

1. Make a mealy, flaky and semi-flaky dough. Use each in pies and note the results. Use the mealy for a custard pie, the semi-flaky for a berry pie and the flaky for a single crust pie.
2. Prepare a puff paste and make up a number of items from it.
3. Make a pie crust using pastry flour and another with the same ingredients using bread flour. Bake a sample and check for quality and texture.
4. Roll a pie crust properly and roll a similar one but stretch it in rolling. Bake each on a baking sheet and note how the stretched crust loses shape. Also, bake a crust in a pan as shown in Figure 17-8 and double-pan and bake another and note the difference.

5. Make up a sample of paste from flour, cornstarch and waxy maize starch. Note the thickness of each compared to the amount of thickening used and also note clarity and softness of the paste.

BIBLIOGRAPHY

Bisno, Lou, "Pie Production," *Baker's Digest,* No. 102, Chicago, 1953.

Briant, Alice M., *et al.,* "Variations in Quality of Cream Pies," *Journal of the American Dietetic Association,* No. 7, July 1954, Chicago.

Corn Products Sales Co., *Snow Flake Milo Starch for Pie Fillings,* New York, 1957.

Fisher, Harry S., "Starch Helps Flavor," *Baker's Review,* August 1958.

Ford, Thomas W., "New Starch for Fruit Pies," *Baker's Weekly,* 1957.

Kite, Frances E., *et al.,* "Thick-boiling Starches," *Baker's Digest,* August, 1957.

Meister, John E., *Vest Pocket Pastry Book,* Hotel Monthly Press, Evanston, Ill., n. d.

National Starch Products, *Clearjel—a Fruit Pie Stabilizer,* New York City, n. d.

Proctor and Gamble, *Pie Formulas,* 1940 and *Quality Pies,* 1940, Research Department, Cincinnati, Ohio.

Richards, Paul, *Pastry for the Restaurant,* Hotel Monthly Press, Evanston, Ill., n. d.

18

Desserts

A dessert is a food, usually sweet, such as a cake, pastry, pie, pudding, frozen or gelatin dish or fruit, that completes a meal. Desserts should blend with and complement the meal they end. Just as first courses are used to sharpen the appetite, desserts should be selected to give final satiety and satisfaction in "topping off" a meal. They should be selected carefully for flavor, richness, color, variety, texture, form, appearance and quantity. For a light meal, a heavy dessert is in order. At a bridge dessert, a meringue filled with a delicate custard and topped with crushed ripe berries may be desired. A stuffed baked apple goes well after a pork roast dinner. Desserts provide opportunity to add decoration and color to a meal. An operation that pays attention to the desserts on its menu can do much to improve overall food acceptance.

Dessert preparation is changing. Many do not eat desserts or they by-pass rich ones for less rich ones. Many operations do not prepare desserts any longer but offer sherbets, ice cream or purchased bakery items. For other operations, the use of mixes has considerably changed production methods. Many highly acceptable desserts can be made from packaged mixes or purchased ready to use as frozen or canned preparations. For these reasons, some may think a discussion of desserts may be somewhat academic, but we must still know much about dessert production to purchase them prepared. Furthermore, there are many operations that still make their own desserts and gain a reputation from it. They also still need basic information.

Figure 18–1. High quality is indicated in this French apple dessert. (Courtesy Processed Apples Institute)

Standard

The standard for a good dessert varies with the dessert. In general, desserts should not be cloyingly sweet nor bitingly tart. Good form and attractive shape are essential. The texture should be crisp or soft depending upon the type, soft for some puddings, crisp for meringues and in between for frozen desserts. Untrue, insipid or overabundant flavor, pasty texture or excessive color is not the mark of a good dessert. Hot desserts should be served hot and cold ones cold. Form and shape should be correct for the particular dessert.

Fruit Desserts

Plain Fruits

One of the simplest and finest desserts is fruit. Fresh fruit should be tart, yet sweet and full of flavor, and should be served cold. Berries may be served plain, dipped in powdered sugar or with cream and sugar. At times, slightly sweetened crushed fruit may be served over custard, pudding or cake. Fresh berries may be cleaned by washing them a quart

Figure 18–2. On the left, fruit, cheese and crackers; lower center, a fresh fruit cup; upper center, canned pears and candied ginger; on the right, fresh fruit show four kinds of popular fruit desserts.

or two at a time either by running cold water over them, or placing them in a colander and dipping them into cold water, then sorting and examining. About three ounces or a half cup is a portion. Fresh fruit such as apples, apricots, bananas, cherries, oranges, peaches and pineapple may be served whole, halved or in pieces. Many are served plain but some may be served with cream and sugar. Grapefruit and oranges may be halved, seeds removed and the sections loosened for service or they may be peeled and thinly sliced. Grapefruit is excellent lightly broiled and served with a tablespoon of grenadine or *creme de menthe*. Oranges and grapefruit peel best when dropped into quite hot water for 3 to 5 minutes. The bitter white part should be completely removed. Fruits that tarnish can be dipped into a solution containing ascorbic acid, lemon juice, pineapple juice or a commercial antioxidant. Salt water is not as effective. Sugar added to some fruits retards discoloration. Using stainless steel, glass or silver knives avoids discoloration from iron salts.

Frozen fruits are best served with some ice still in them to help give them better texture. About 3 to 4 ounces (half cup) makes a portion. They usually come sweetened with sugar in the ratio of berries to sugar 4:1. A 5-pound carton at 0° F takes 2 to 3 hours at room temperature to thaw and 4 to 5 hours under refrigeration. For the best quality use soon after thawing.

Fruits cooked in light or medium sirup are called stewed fruit or sauce. If cooked in a heavy sirup, they are called compotes and if cooked in extremely heavy sirup, they are preserves. Table 18-1 gives formulas for these. Approximately 15 pounds EP of fruit cooked in 1½ gallons of light or medium sirup gives 100 half-cup portions. Four No. 10 cans

Table 18–1. Densities of Sirups for Cooking Fruit

Type of Sirup	To Make One Gallon of Sirup				Brix Reading
	Sugar		Water		
	(pounds)	(quarts)	(pounds)	(quarts)	(degrees)
Light	3	1¾	7½	3¾	11 to 13.9
Medium	4 to 5	2½ to 2¾	7 to 7¼	3½	14 to 19.9
Heavy	7 to 8	4 to 4½	6½ to 7	3	20 to 23.9

Figure 18–3. This Roman Beauty apple is baked to perfection.

of fruit usually serve 100 but the count of fruit per can is often a controlling factor. A 22 count per No. 10 peach is a large serving, a 35 to 45 count peach medium.

Dried fruits are stewed and the pulp used for desserts. Many can be prepared by first washing in cold water, draining and then covering with boiling water; after soaking 24 hours, they are ready to use without cooking. Normally, dried fruits are soaked and simmered until tender. Rapid cooking gives a tough fruit lacking plumpness. Approximately 100 half-cup portions are obtained from 10 pounds of dried apricots or figs or 12 pounds of peaches, pears or prunes. Some helpful conversions in calculating yields are: a pound of dried prunes yields 10 ounces (2 c) pitted prunes, 1¼ pounds (4 c) cooked prunes yields a pound (3 c) pitted prunes and 1¼ pounds pitted prunes equals a quart.

Low-moisture or vacuum dried fruits contain about 5% or less moisture. They take little storage space, give good quality products, are low in cost and do not require refrigerated storage to prevent insect infestation in warm climates. They are usually soaked and then cooked slowly or started in cold water, brought to a simmer and cooked until plump and tender. Sugar may be added at the start or after cooking, depending upon the fruit and firmness desired. The yield of a pound of low-moisture prunes is about 2¼ pounds, giving about 12 portions.

Table 18–2. Low-Moisture Fruit Equivalents

	Equivalent Per Pound of Low-Moisture Fruit			
	Fresh AP	Canned Regular Pack No. 10 Can	Canned Solid Pack No. 10 Can	Evaporated or Dried
Apple nuggets (sauce)	10 lb	3	1¼	3 lb
Apple nuggets (sauce)	10 lb	3		3 lb
Apple pie slices	10 lb	3	1¼	
Apricot slices			1	3 lb
Peach slices			1	2½ lb
Pitted prunes				2½ lb

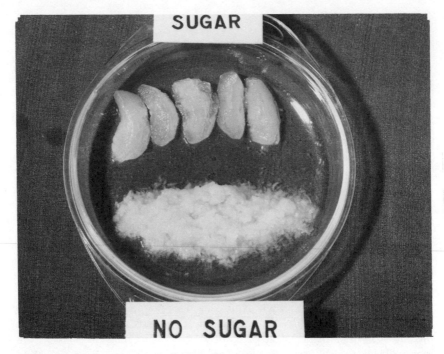

Figure 18–4.   The apple slices on the top were cooked gently in heavy sirup while the same number of slices from the same apple were boiled in water. This shows how sugar firms up cellulose in fruits and vegetables.

Crisps and Bettys

Crisps and bettys are best served warm with a light sweet-tart fruit sauce, whipped cream or hard sauce. Carry-over fruits or small quantities of odds and ends of fruit may be utilized for them. Crisps are fruit topped with a mixture of flour, sugar and fat and baked. The top is crisp with soft fruit underneath. Oatmeal rather than flour may be used. Bettys are made by spreading layers of cake crumbs between layers of fruit, butter and sugar. This is baked so that the interior and bottom are soft fruit and crumbs while the top is crisp.

Biscuit Fruit Desserts

Shortcakes are popular biscuit-type fruit desserts. They are made the same as baking powder biscuits except that the dough is richer and may contain eggs. The dough is baked in two layers with butter or margarine and served warm with crushed fruit between the layers and over the top with either whipped or unwhipped cream. The fruit is served

(a)

(b)

(c)

(d)

Figure 18–5. (a) A fruit crisp being made, the topping being placed over the fruit. After baking, the fruit is cooked while the top is a sweet, crisp crust. (b) Crumbs and sugar being put over a layer of fruit to make an apple betty. (c) Baked fruit roll in the form of hearts or elephant ears. (d) A rolypoly filled with fruit being rolled. After rolling it is baked and then the servings cut from it.

chilled. A Dutch cake is rich biscuit in which fruit such as peach or apple slices are heavily dotted. Sugar, spices and melted butter or margarine are sprinkled over the top and the item is baked. It is served hot with a warm, sweet-tart sauce over it. Cobblers are fruit topped with a layer of biscuit dough and baked and are usually served hot. Some cobblers are made with a pie crust topping.

Fruit rolls are made by placing fruit over biscuit dough and rolling as for a cinnamon roll. About inch-thick slices are cut and baked on a greased pan. A roly-poly is the whole roll baked with slices cut *after* baking. Fruit dumplings are rich biscuit dough about an $\frac{1}{8}$-inch thick filled with fruit, with the edges of the dough folded over to make a tight

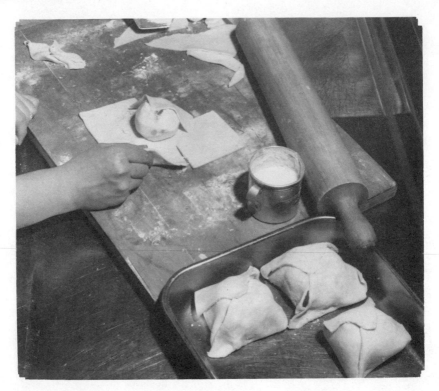

Figure 18–6. The procedure for making apple dumplings is shown. When the pan is filled a light sweet sirup is poured over the dumplings to about two-thirds full and the dumplings baked.

seal around the fruit. These are placed in pans, covered to about half with a fruit sauce, slightly sweetened water or plain water, and then baked or steamed. After baking, a thickened sauce surrounds the dumplings and is spooned over them when served. A greater quantity and thinner sauce results when they are steamed and this sauce may need some thickening. Steamed dumplings may be browned under a broiler to improve color, and some are deep-fried. Fruit rolls, roly-polies, dumplings and other fruit-biscuit desserts of this type are usually served warm with a fruit sauce, hard sauce, brandy or foamy sauce.

Puddings

Most puddings are easily made in quantity, are low in cost and require little labor. For this reason they may be served too frequently and lose appeal. There are many types of puddings and all are popular.

(a)   (b)

Figure 18–7. (a) Steaming a pudding in a cloth sack. (b) Various kinds of steamed puddings.

Some puddings are very much like cakes. A cottage pudding is this type. A date pudding or other cake-like products high in fruit may be served hot or cold with or without a hot or cold sauce. They are easy to make for large groups.

Steamed (Boiled) Puddings

Steamed or boiled puddings are served warm and usually with a sauce. They are usually made with suet as the shortening. Bread crumbs, strong flour and eggs act as binders for heavy ratios of fruits and nuts. Only a small quantity of moisture is added if the fruit is moist. The ratio of batter to fruit and nuts may vary from 1:1 to 1:2½. Many steamed puddings approximate pound cakes in proportions of flour, shortening and sugar. The leavening agent is usually soda which gives a porous texture and darkens the fruit, nuts, molasses and other ingredients if they are in the batter. Steamed puddings are heavier in texture than baked ones. The grain is usually tight and waxy but should not be pasty. Lighter puddings may be made which resemble rich muffin batters. These are apt to be open-grained and more delicate in texture.

Containers in which puddings are cooked may be large or individual. Grease and flour well and fill only two-thirds to allow for expansion in cooking. Provide covers or tops to keep out condensate. Steam for 2½ to 3 hours or bake about the same time in a 325° F oven in pans of shallow water. They can also be put into water, covered and boiled on the stove. To boil in a bag, dip a strong muslin cloth into cold water and wring it out. Turn it inside out and dip into flour. Turn this floured side in and drop in the batter. Tie loosely allowing for expansion in cooking, and lower into water that is just boiling. The bag can also be suspended in a steam bath. When cooked, remove, dip into cold water and free the cloth. Let the pudding cool under cover or in water so that it does not form a tough skin. Puddings may be stored in their containers and reheated in them or they may be removed, wrapped in foil and reheated in the foil wrap in steam or in a 325° F oven for about 45 minutes. Use very sharp or serrated knives for cutting. Heat individual puddings in a roll or bun warmer. Select a sauce that complements the flavor and texture of the pudding.

Starch-thickened Puddings

Blanc manges and cream puddings are the base for many desserts. Blanc mange is another name for cornstarch pudding made from hot milk, sugar, vanilla and a bit of salt with cornstarch, arrowroot or some other starch for a thickener. Cornstarch varies from 6 to 12 ounces per gallon of liquid depending upon the consistency desired. If the pudding is served molded, 12 ounces is used. If eggs are used, it is a *cream* pudding. The starch is reduced because of the thickening from the eggs. A chiffon or light, fluffy texture may be given a cream pudding by adding only the yolks, beating the whites into a meringue with part of the sugar and then folding them in while the mixture is hot. The hotter the mixture when blended with the meringue, the firmer the chiffon.

Make a blanc mange by heating the milk, reserving some for blending with the sugar and cornstarch or with only cornstarch. Add a bit of the hot milk to the cold milk and cornstarch mixture and blend well. With good agitation stir this into the hot milk and cook for about 10 minutes or until the temperature is over 200° F. An alternate method is to mix the sugar and cornstarch together and blend this with rapid stirring into the hot milk. Stir either while thickening.

For a cream pudding, blend the eggs or yolks well and add some of the hot thickened blanc mange to them, blending well. Return this blended egg mixture into the hot blanc mange giving good agitation so that the eggs blend before cooking. Keep stirring until the mixture is over 195° F. If either a blanc mange or cream pudding contains much sugar, withhold part until the starch and/or eggs are cooked and then add it. This prevents the sugar from interfering with the thickening of the starch and eggs.

Tapioca pudding is made by adding tapioca to sweetened milk or fruit juices and cooking to thicken. Either pearl or granular (quick-cooking) tapioca is used. Granular tapioca gives a less ropy pudding.

Figure 18–8. A cream pudding is a cornstarch pudding (blanc mange) with eggs added. To blend in the eggs, mix them well, add a bit of the hot pudding and blend well. Then, as shown, with good stirring, blend this egg mixture into the hot pudding mixture.

Pearl tapioca needs soaking before cooking. Overmixing causes ropiness and lowers quality. A tapioca cream contains eggs. The egg yolks are cooked with the tapioca and hot milk with part of the sugar, and flavoring is added. This hot, thickened mixture (above 190° F) is carefully folded in to give a chiffon texture. Sago, farina and cornmeal are also used in starch-thickened puddings. Indian pudding contains molasses and is thickened with cornmeal. Arrowroot gives a soft, delicate pudding and is used for high quality products. Serve half a cup of pudding for a portion; 3¼ gallons makes 100 portions.

Figure 18–9. A tapioca cream pudding is being prepared. The hot tapioca mixture is being folded into an egg white meringue. The hotter the pudding mixture when it is stirred into the meringue, the stiffer will be the final pudding.

Egg-thickened Desserts

The discussion in Chapter 10 on the properties of eggs should be consulted for technical information required to prepare good desserts from eggs, many of which are quite delicate products that can fail unless properly prepared.

Table 18-3.   Quantity of Starch and Eggs Required to Thicken One Gallon of Pudding

Type of Starch Thickener	Amount of Thickener*	Whole Eggs
Cornstarch	4 to 5 oz (1c)	1½ lb (1½ pt or 16 eggs)
Flour	8 oz (1 pt)	1½ lb (1½ pt or 16 eggs)
Rice, uncooked	9 to 14 oz (1 to 1½ pt)	
Rice, cooked	1 to 1½ gallon	
Tapioca, granular	6 to 9 oz (1½ to 2 c)	1½ lb (1½ pt or 16 eggs)
Tapicoa, pearl	12 oz (3 c)	1½ lb (1½ pt or 16 eggs)
Cake or bread crumbs	1 to 2 lb (1 to 2 qt)**	
Cornmeal, farina, or other	1 lb (1 qt)	

*Increase thickener if eggs are omitted.
**Quantity will depend upon moistness of crumbs.

Custards

Dry mixture, non-cooking custards or those that can be boiled are now on the market, considerably simplifying the preparation of custards. They are of such high quality that few operations today make their own custards from scratch.

A conventional baked custard is made with 1½ to 2 pounds of whole eggs per gallon of liquid. Use less if egg yolks are used or, if cereals such as bread, rice or cake crumbs are used, reduce eggs two ounces for every eight ounces of cereal. Some recipes may specify a small quantity of flour or other starch plus eggs. Low quality eggs make a weak custard. Baking temperatures are between 325° and 340° F. Too low a temperature develops a weak custard with a watery, open texture (syneresis) instead of a firm, smooth, solid clabber. The cut surface of a good custard is even

Figure 18–10. One of the best ways to test for doneness of a custard. The knife should come out clean.

and sharp, possessing a soft sheen tinted a slight creamy tan. The top should be delicately browned. The container containing the custard should be put into pans of water so that direct heat does not cause syneresis. Custards cook after they come from the oven. For this reason, they are usually removed before they are completely done. The time of removal must be judged carefully. A custard is completely cooked when the tip of a pointed knife comes out clean. An experienced baker tells doneness by moving the pan in the oven, noting the firmness. If desired, custards may be steamed. If steamed, they should be covered to keep condensate out.

For best results, have the milk hot and the final temperature of the custard at 140° F going into the oven. Add flavoring and eggs and blend well. Pour into pans or molds. To stop cooking after oven removal, set in a well aerated place or into a pan of cold water.

Stirred or soft custards are similar to baked ones in ingredients but are stirred instead of baked. When cool they have the consistency of thin to medium white sauce. Syneresis is a problem and constant stirring is required to prevent curdling. Coagulation is an endothermic action and 185° F is used as a guide to indicate when coagulation begins. As soon as the temperature is above 185° F, coagulation is completed. Disappearance of foam is also an indication of doneness. Soft custards can be made in 1 to 2 gallon batches in a trunnion kettle or over hot water, but good stirring is needed. If hand-stirred, quantities up to 2 to 3 quarts can be made. Again, preheating the milk so that the mixture is at 140° F gives better results. Soft custards are used over fruit or slices of cake. Floating island is a soft custard poured over soft meringues floated on top of the custard.

Soufflés

Some soufflé desserts are gelatin products in which beaten eggs may be used to give lightness. Their making is discussed under gelatin desserts. Baked soufflé is a dessert thickened and leavened by eggs. It is so delicate it is usually prepared to order. It is made by beating the yolks separately with sugar, blending in flavoring and then folding in stiffly beaten egg whites similar to the method used in making foamy omelets. It is then baked in a slow or moderate oven. Service must be immediate since it may collapse.

Meringues

A meringue is an emulsion of air cells dispersed in a heavy egg and sugar sirup. Hard meringues are often used as a base for desserts while soft ones are used for toppings for pies, puddings and other desserts.

Figure 18–11. A fruit soufflé. (Courtesy Poultry and Egg National Board)

Hard meringues may have an ounce of water added per pound of whites to aid in bringing sugar into solution. An ounce of vinegar or lemon juice or ¼-ounce of cream of tartar per pound of whites is used to tenderize them and give a stable foam. If vinegar or lemon juice is used, omit water. From 1¾ to 2½ pounds of sugar are used per pound of whites. Bake for 1½ hours at 275° F or for 50 minutes at 325° F. They should dry out rather than bake but not dry enough to shatter when handled. Heavy ovens may be preheated to 325° F, the heat turned off and the meringues placed into the oven and left overnight. Baking is on lightly greased pans, on ungreased paper or on nonresinous wooden boards an inch or more thick.

A 1:1 weight ratio is normal for sugar and egg whites for soft meringues but the ratio can go as high as 3:2 for a sweeter, more flavorful and tender product. Three-fourths teaspoon of cream of tartar is enough for one pound of egg white. A small quantity of salt adds flavor to both hard and soft meringues. Soft ones made from fresh eggs (dried or frozen egg whites, being pasteurized, are no problem) can be good cultures for bacteria and should therefore be baked well for 12 to 18 minutes at 350° F. Meringues from meringue mixes or processed whites can be baked five minutes at 475° F or six minutes at 425° F and can also be browned with a torch or a hot, flat, iron instrument. Scale meringue shells at 1¼ ounce each or 15 to 18 ounces per dozen.

(a)   (b)

(c)   (d)

Figure 18–12. (a) The ingredients and the making of a soft meringue for topping pies. (b) The ingredients for a hard meringue. (c) Putting hard meringue onto a baking sheet previous to baking. The center is usually filled with fruit, ice cream or pudding. (d) A small individual and a pie shell from hard meringue plus soft meringue on lemon pie.

For meringues, have the whites at 110° to 125° F. Use fine sugar to give a more rapid solution and prevent graininess. Whip to a good foam, third stage, adding salt and acid at the start of beating. Then add the sugar in small additions beating in well to blend and dissolve. A failure to whip enough gives a thin meringue lacking volume which may weep and have slippage. Do not overbeat before adding the sugar for this also can cause a meringue failure.

Meringues, especially soft ones, develop leakage, that is, moisture separating as tiny droplets or gathering under the meringues on a pie filling. This results from excess moisture, improper beating or placing an unbaked meringue on a cold filling before baking. A high sugar content may also encourage weeping. To avoid slippage put meringues on warm fillings. Or, use stabilizers such as locust bean gum, gum arabic, gum tragacanth, powdered carageenin gum or agar-agar. The two last stabilizers should be put into a small quantity of boiling water before adding. Some formulas call for a half ounce of cornstarch or tapioca flour per pound of whites. This is usually dusted over the meringue during the last stage of beating. Prepared stabilizers for meringues may be obtained from bakery supply houses. When spreading meringues on pies or other desserts attach the edges well to the crust or sides. From 3 to 5 ounces of meringue is a liberal topping for a 9-inch pie.

Two other meringues are used for topping desserts. One is Italian meringue, a boiled frosting with a ratio of sugar to egg whites of 1:1. The sugar is cooked in half its weight of water until 244° F and then beaten into the egg whites at a stage three foam (lower unit). The other is Swiss meringue made with a 1:1 up to a 2:3 egg-sugar ratio beaten over boiling water at medium or high speed until the meringue is quite stiff, using a fourth ounce of cream of tartar per pound of whites. A 7-minute frosting can also be used as a topping.

Manufacturers' directions for the use of meringue powders should be followed strictly. These are very fine stable products that are widely used today. Normally, a quart of lukewarm water to a pound of sugar is used to six ounces of powder.

Junket Desserts

A dessert resembling a custard can be prepared from unpasteurized milk and rennet, an enzyme that can set milk into a clabber. The milk and sugar is warmed to 98° F and flavoring and a junket tablet added. The mixture sets after pouring into containers and chilling. Jarring or stirring breaks the curd. Portions are a half to three-fourths cup. These are often used for diets.

Gelatin Desserts

Gelatin desserts are easily made, have a low labor and material cost and lend themselves to presentation and merchandising. They are well adapted to blend with fruits, foods or fruit juices carried over in production. They also store well and are not highly perishable. Information given in Chapter 7 on the use of gelatin mixtures should be consulted for background information.

Per gallon of liquid, 1½ pounds of gelatin dessert or 2½ ounces of pure gelatin is needed for a good jel. Sugar, flavoring and coloring are usually added to a pure gelatin mixture. After setting, these may be riced,

(a)   (b)

(c)   (d)

Figure 18–13.   (a) A plain gelatin mixture may be used for the preparation of many salads. (b) To chill a hot gelatin mixture quickly, add ice to equal the total liquid required. (c) Gelatin dessert cubes. (d) Riced gelatin may be served many ways. (Courtesy General Foods)

cubed and served this way or mixed with other items for service. They can also be beaten to a light foam. Gelatins poured over cake cubes or crumbs make attractive desserts. They should be at the sirupy stage to prevent soaking. Whipped egg whites, whipped cream, blanc manges, cream puddings or melted ice cream may be blended with gelatin mixtures to make many different desserts. A snow or sponge is made by chilling a gelatin mixture until sirupy and then whipping until volume doubles. Shredded pineapple or applesauce is used for a pineapple or apple snow. Beaten egg whites are often folded in to give a lighter texture. Apricot, prune, peach or other fruit sponges are also popular. Serve with a stirred custard.

(a) (b)

(c)

Figure 18–14. (a) To whip a gelatin dessert, have the gelatin mixture about this thick and (b) place in a mixer bowl in chipped ice. Beat at high speed. (c) Many types of desserts are made from whipped gelatin products.

A Bavarian is whipped cream folded into a sweetened gelatin mixture. The best bavarians contain milk instead of water as the liquid base. Cooked rice or cake crumbs, ground nuts or fruits may be added. Bavarians can also be made by blending a blanc mange or cream pudding into a gelatin mixture with stiffly beaten egg whites, whipped cream or a soft ice cream just before it sets. Some Bavarian mixtures may be whipped to a foam previous to the addition of other ingredients.

A Spanish cream is a thin, stirred custard to which gelatin or a flavored gelatin dessert is added in sufficient quantity to set it. Just before

(a)   (b)

Figure 18–15. (a) Beaten dry milk and gelatin being folded into a chocolate cream pudding mixture to make a low-calorie Bavarian cream. (b) An
orange marmalade Bavarian made from a General Foods recipe.

setting, whipped cream is folded in. Stiffly beaten egg whites may be
substituted for whipped cream but the product is not as rich. There are
many variations.

Frozen Desserts

Frozen desserts are popular and considerable variety on the menu can
be gained in their use not only by using different kinds but by changing
the way in which they are served. They are low in cost and, if purchased
prepared, take little production labor to have them available for service.

Types

Ice cream, sherbet and ices are mixtures frozen by mechanical
freezers which whip air into them as they freeze. Desserts such as mousse,
parfait, frozen pudding or frozen fruits are not whipped during freezing
but are whipped either before or not at all. Slushes or granites are only
partially frozen and are coarse and granular. There are many different
kinds of ice cream. Philadelphia ice cream is merely milk, cream, sugar
and flavoring and perhaps a stabilizer. If eggs are added, it is French
ice cream. Very frequently there is ground vanilla added which shows
as slight specks in the product. Ice cream is also combined variously with
fruits, nuts, cake crumbs, macaroons and other products. Vanilla ice
cream must be 10% or more milk fat to be called ice cream but if fruit,

(a)   (b)

Figure 18–16. Ice cream may be merchandised in many ways: (a) vanilla ice cream placed into individual pie shells and topped with shaved chocolate (Courtesy Armour & Co.), (b) rolling lemon sherbet balls into shredded coconut and serving over frozen strawberries. (Courtesy General Foods)

nuts, chocolate or other products are added — usually about 2% — the milk fat content can be no less than 8%. Mixtures used for milk shakes and malts may be lower in milk fat.

Ingredients

A good ice cream contains between 9 to $12\frac{1}{4}$% milk solids, 14% sugar, 10% or more milk fat and about $\frac{1}{2}$% stabilizer. Some may go as high as 22% milk fat and 18% sugar. Corn sirup may replace about 30% of the total sugar. A standard formula used by many operations which gives a mix of $14\frac{1}{2}$% sugar, 12% milk fat, 11% non-fat milk solids and $\frac{1}{2}$% gelatin is:

40% (heavy whipping) cream	20%	Vanilla	$\frac{1}{2}$%
4% milk	46%	Gelatin	$\frac{1}{2}$%
8% condensed milk	28%	Water gel	3%
Sugar	2%		

Some substitute non-fat milk solids and butter for cream. During pasteurization and homogenization, the melted butter is easily put back into stabile solution. It is not uncommon to use milk and cream that cannot be used as fresh products — a hotel, for instance, may send to the ice cream department carry-over milk or cream that cannot be used for cooking or service. If these are used, a neutralizer such as sodium bicarbonate or sodium carbonate and sodium hydroxide may be added to obtain a desirable pH. Mixes should be aged at least four hours at 30° to 40° F to increase viscosity of the mix and improve stability and

Figure 18–17.   Have ice cream from 8° to 12° F for best results in dishing. (The angle used in taking the picture distorts the reading which shows 8° F.)

colloidal properties. This aging gives better foam or overrun and body. Aging 24 hours is not unusual. Mixes made from dry milks are also improved in flavor if allowed to stand to allow the lactose to go into solution. Colorings or flavorings must be those approved by the federal government. Only the highest quality flavorings, spices, fruits and nuts should be used. Normally, only vanilla mix is made, it being the base for all other ice creams. Chocolate and a few other items may be added to it at the start of freezing but nuts, fruits, etc. are added just before the product is withdrawn from the freezer.

Milk fat tends to make a harder dessert while fillers such as non-fat milk solids and eggs counteract hardness. Excess milk fat may also cause graininess especially when rapid agitation churns the fat into small butter globules. Thus, an ice cream high in fat must not be overbeaten.

Equipment

To make its own mix, an operation needs mixing vats, pasteurizer, homogenizer, filter, cooler, freezer and hardening cabinet. If the volume frozen is small, a batch freezer is used but for large quantites a continuous freezer is more desirable. If an operation buys its liquid or dry mix, it will need only a freezer and hardening cabinets. The simplest procedure is to purchase frozen desserts ready to use. It is important that equipment be sized properly for the quantities made and no bottlenecks occur because some equipment is too small or unsuitable for the rest of the equipment. Smooth flow is extremely important. Hardening cabinets should be conveniently located so that a minimum time occurs between withdrawal from the freezer and entry into the cabinet. Sanitizing equipment, sinks, work tables, storage spaces and other accessories to the equipment should be placed so as to minimize labor requirements and speed work.

Production Procedures

Frozen dessert mixtures begin to freeze at about 27° to 28° F. Freezers usually do not go below 23° F since around 24° F the mixture hardens considerably and overburdens the motor. Freezing should occur in 5 to 8 minutes. Most desserts must be whipped as well as frozen and a dasher inside does this whipping in addition to removing the frozen portions from the sides during freezing and moving them into the center. During freezing the dasher moves slowly but, when the machine is put on whip, it moves at from 175 to 250 rpm. This develops a foam which increases volume, a process called *overrun*. Ice cream should have an overrun of 80 to 100%. If below 80%, the flavor is flat and the texture is compact, heavy and pasty. Excessive overrun (volume) gives a frothy and foamy product that also lacks flavor. Overrun for an ice containing no milk but some egg whites should be from 25 to 30% and for sherbet 20 to 50%. Thus, if one has 50 gallons of mix and gets 100% overrun, 100 gallons of ice cream are produced. A gallon of 100 and 80% overrun ice cream weighs respectively 4½ and 5 pounds. At these respective overruns, the weight of a pint of ice cream would be 9 and 10 ounces and a quart double these. This is without packaging materials, of course. Also, frozen ice cream cannot be scooped into a measure and then weighed to ascertain the overrun, since scooping packs it.

Mixtures with more than 18% sugar develop poor overrun. Gelatin increases it but also increases the time needed for whipping. Egg yolks speed overrun development and increase it. Citrates and phosphates increase it. Citrates and phosphates increase overrun while calcium salts decrease it. Butterfat decreases overrun while non-fat milk solids increase it. An item frozen too hard develops poor overrun.

When the dessert in the freezer is ribbony and appears slightly dry and dull, the proper amount of freezing and overrun has been obtained. It should now flow from the freezer slowly when it is operated at slow speed. Use prechilled cups or cans to catch the mixture as it comes from the machine.

Freezing should be rapid enough to develop fine crystals and the beating sufficiently hard to retain this fineness. Rapid hardening is also

(a)

(b)

Figure 18–18.   (a) The proper type and size of scoop is required to obtain best results in serving frozen desserts. (Courtesy Ice Cream Merchandising Institute) (b) The size scoop indicates the number of scoops that *should* be obtained per quart but never is. Shown here from left to right are: No. 40, No. 30, No. 24, No. 20, No. 16, No. 12 and No. 10. Normally, about half as many scoops are obtained per quart of frozen dessert as indicated on the scoop because of packing.

essential for fine, smooth texture development. The lowest temperature for most hardening cabinets is −25° F. Hardening should occur in 6 to 12 hours, as, if longer than this, the product may become coarse in texture. Stabilizers and emulsifiers help to retain fine crystal development in storage, as do milkfat, eggs and non-fat milk solids.

Sanitation

After pasteurizing, the bacterial count of a mix should not be more than 35,000 to 50,000 per gram or cubic centimeter. Nuts, spices, fruits and other products added later can add bacteria. Purchase these as sterilized or low bacterial count products and after opening use care to see that they remain uncontaminated. Moldy or spoiled fruit should not be used. The work area, storage spaces and equipment must be clean and sanitary. Use special solutions for sterilizing, or steam-clean or boil. Equipment is usually given a preliminary rinse and then dismantled, then given a thorough wash, rinse and sanitizing. Mechanical equipment is reassembled, filled to about half capacity with a sanitizing solution and the machine operated about a minute. The solution is then drawn off but the equipment is not rinsed but left open for free air circulation. Before using, this equipment is rinsed, sterilized and rinsed again. Only air-drying is recommended.

Quality Standards

Ice cream may be scored as follows: flavor 45, body and texture 30, appearance 15, color and packaging 5 and melting quality 5. The flavor should be pleasant and true with proper acidity and sweetness. Texture should be smooth with a fine grain or creaminess evident. Defective texture is described as fluffy, weak, crumbly, watery, icy, soggy or gummy. Body is associated with the "feel in the mouth." It should not be too heavy or pasty nor open or frothy. Some slight firmness is desirable. Appearance should be bright and smooth with a good bloom. Some

(a)   (b)

Figure 18–19. (a) Use a good sharp-edged scoop. See that it is in good working order. (b) To scoop, dip into cool water, drain for a moment on a pad and use.

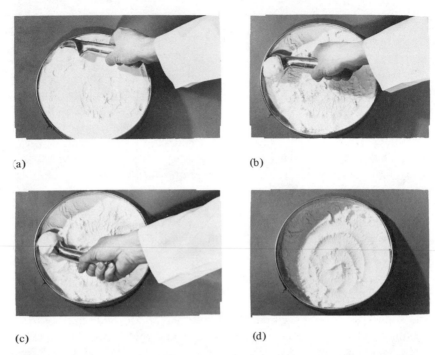

(a)

(b)

(c)

(d)

Figure 18–20. Scooping of frozen desserts with either the mechanical or non-mechanical scoop is much the same. Shown here is the use of the non-mechanical scoop. (a) Insert the scoop about a half inch deep into the frozen dessert, starting at the outer edge or where the last scoop left off. (b) Draw lightly and evenly across the surface, rolling the dessert into a ball. (c) When the scoop is filled, turn up with a twist of the wrist, breaking off the ice cream. (d) Keep the surface smooth, working evenly across the top as shown here.

brilliance is desirable in products low in milk. Some frozen desserts may contain excessive amounts of starch paste, gums or other fillers to build body and texture or otherwise mask inferior qualities. When the product is thawed, this shows up because the product still retains its frozen shape. Very little liquid appears. The best products thaw completely into a liquid.

*Service**

Store frozen desserts at 0° F or lower but for service have it from 8 to 15° F. Below or above these service temperatures a packed and less

* Much helpful information for serving frozen desserts can be obtained from the Ice Cream Merchandising Institute, Barr Building, Washington, D. C.

Figure 18–21. Standardize ice cream service. The standard sundae begins with about a ¼ ounce of sirup, two dippers of No. 24 scoop ice cream dropped *lightly*, topped with an ounce of sirup and topped with whipped cream, nuts and a cherry. (Courtesy Ice Cream Merchandising Institute)

flavorful product results. Avoid excess stocks. Obtain in sizes which are used quickly and rotate stocks as quickly as possible. Vanilla, strawberry and chocolate ice cream are usually stocked as standard items, as are orange and pineapple sherbets. Remove items from frozen storage to service cabinets at least 24 hours before serving to condition them.

Scooping incorrectly as well as having the dessert at the wrong tem-

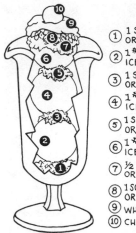

① 1 SODA SPOON SYRUP OR CRUSHED FRUIT

② 1 #30 DIPPER ICE CREAM

③ 1 SODA SPOON SYRUP OR CRUSHED FRUIT

④ 1 #30 DIPPER ICE CREAM

⑤ 1 SODA SPOON SYRUP OR CRUSHED FRUIT

⑥ 1 #30 DIPPER ICE CREAM

⑦ ½ SODA SPOON SYRUP OR CRUSHED FRUIT

⑧ 1 SODA SPOON OF NUTS OR NUTS IN SYRUP

⑨ WHIPPED CREAM

⑩ CHERRY

Figure 18–21A. The method for making the standard parfait. (Courtesy Ice Cream Merchandising Institute)

perature destroys texture. Normal scooping shrinkage is 40 to 45%. Five gallons of ice cream should give 100 No. 10 scoops or 130 No. 12 scoops. To estimate dipping efficiency, weigh six portions on a scale and calculate average weight. Divide this into the net weight of a full container. For instance if six dips weigh 18 ounces or average three ounces each, a 5-gallon container weighing 22 pounds six ounces or 358 ounces net, will give 119 scoops (358 ÷ 3 oz. = 119⅓). Usually 62, 51, 42, 35, 26 and 20 dips are obtained per gallon of dessert respectively from No. 30, 24, 20, 16, 12 and 10 scoops. If the dessert is too hard or soft this is not possible. Portioning and cupping frozen desserts as they are withdrawn from the freezer and then hardening so that they can be served without scooping avoids this packing loss as does freezing into bricks and slicing.

Many fountain operators recommend the following for portions:

Fountain Item	Size Scoop	Number of Scoops Per Portion
Banana Split	No. 30	3
Bowl of Ice Cream	No. 30	4
Parfait	No. 30	3
Ice Cream Soda, Malt, or Milk Shake	No. 24	2
Pie, Cake, or Pudding a la Mode	No. 20	1
Sundae	No. 20	2
Table d'hote, Plain	No. 16	1
Sundae, Meal Portion	No. 12	1
A la Carte Portion	No. 10	1

Have scoops clean and smooth, possessing a sharp edge without nicks. Dip into clear water before scooping. If the scoop is cold, the

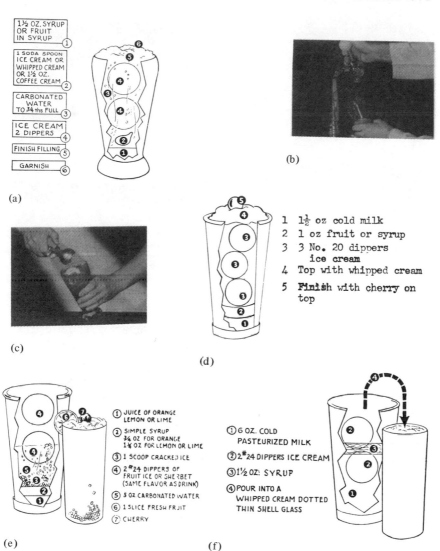

Figure 18–22. (a) To make a standard soda, add 1½ ounces of fruit in sirup, then a soda spoon of ice cream or whipped cream or 1½ ounces of coffee cream. (b) Tilt and add carbonated water to three-fourths full. (c) Drop gently two No. 30 scoops of vanilla. Finish filling with a fine stream. Garnish. (d) A frappe is made using 1½ ounces of cold milk, an ounce of fruit or sirup, three No. 20 dippers of ice cream and topped with whipped cream and a cherry. (e) Freezes and floats are shown. (f) The making of an old-fashioned milk shake is shown. By adding malt, a malted-milk is made. (Courtesy of Ice Cream Merchandising Institute)

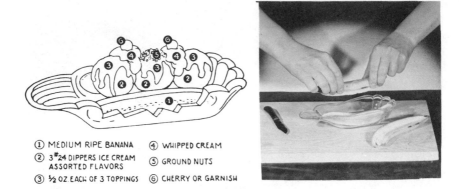

① MEDIUM RIPE BANANA   ④ WHIPPED CREAM

② 3#24 DIPPERS ICE CREAM   ⑤ GROUND NUTS
   ASSORTED FLAVORS

③ ½ OZ. EACH OF 3 TOPPINGS ⑥ CHERRY OR GARNISH

Figure 18–23.   (a) The method for making a standard banana split. (b) Drop the banana in gently as shown, even when not making it in front of customers. (Courtesy Ice Cream Merchandising Institute)

dessert sticks and packs. The procedure for scooping is illustrated in Figure 18-19.

Frozen desserts lend themselves to many different ways of service. Meringue shells filled with ice cream may be covered with fruit and topped with whipped cream. A baked Alaska, made by placing a No. 24 scoop of ice cream on a 2-inch square of sponge cake, covered completely with soft meringue and baked until the meringue is delicately browned has high appeal. Frozen log rolls, cupcakes, and eclairs filled with frozen desserts, bombes and coupes bring interesting variety to a menu without high cost. Combining flavors of ice cream, sherbets and ice, interesting accompaniments, and different and unusual toppings give menu interest, as do *a la modes,* frozen desserts in varied shapes and colors and combinations with other foods. Standard methods for preparing most common fountain items are illustrated in this chapter.

Fried Desserts

Fritters

Fritters are usually deep-fried but occasionally may be pan-fried in a liberal quantity of fat. Many are simply fruit dipped into a batter and fried. Others may be muffin mixtures containing leavening agents into which fruits are mixed. The batter is scooped with a No. 30 scoop and deep-fried. There are many variations and they are often served with a sirup.

Figure 18–24. Two types of fritters. The apple fritters on the left have been dipped in batter and fried. The ones on the right are banana fritters made by mixing diced bananas into a fairly stiff fritter batter and deep-frying.

Pancakes or Crêpes

Thin batters resembling plain omelet mixtures slightly thickened with flour are used instead of pancake batter to make dessert pancakes or crêpes. No leavening agent is used. The cakes are very thin. They are cooked by pouring only enough batter into a hot buttered pan to cover the bottom with a thin coating. Cooking should be fairly rapid. When the bottom is nicely browned turn and brown the other side. Since the second side never browns as well, it should be on the inside at service. Pancakes may be made ahead and rewarmed or frozen, thawed and rewarmed. When warm, they are placed on a clean surface, filled and folded and served. Small cakes, 4 to 5 inches in diameter, are served two to three to the portion while one large cake is usually a portion. The cakes are rolled after filling or folded in four as shown in Figure 18-25. Butter creams, applesauce, marmalades, red currant jelly, *bar-le-duc* jelly, sour cream or other fillings are used. The crêpes should be served quite warm. Many are flamed, while some are dusted with powdered sugar and some may be burned or scored as indicated for French omelets. A small quantity of granulated sugar over the top of the pancakes aids in drawing the liquor up for burning. The liquor also burns better if it is 100 proof or more and is warmed.

Figure 18–25. (a) Rolled crêpes or French pancakes. These are filled with strawberry preserves and dusted with powdered sugar. (b) Crêpes Suzette should be filled with an orange butter cream filling, folded in this manner and then flamed with rum or brandy or a mixture of liqueurs.

Figure 18–26. To make fried pies, use a dough about midway in richness between a baking powder biscuit and pie dough. Fill as shown.

Doughnuts

There are several kinds of doughnuts; cake, yeast and French. The first are made from a lean cake or rich muffin dough, the second from a sweet yeast dough and the French from a rich eclair paste (choux paste) and all are deep-fried. French doughnuts are also called crullers as are some twisted cake doughnuts. Cake doughnuts may be made into balls, fingers or other shapes and yeast doughnuts into bismarcks, longjohns and others. Quality depends upon recipe balance, ingredients, techniques of mixing and handling the dough, frying and subsequent handling after frying. Normally, a doughnut recipe is in balance if it is within these ratios:

Ingredient	Type Doughnut		
	Cake	Yeast	French(cruller)
Flour, bread*		65 to 100%	50 to 100%
Flour, pastry or cake*	100%	35 to 0%	0 to 50%
Sugar	10 to 50%	8 to 20%	
Eggs, whole	5 to 25%	3 to 15%	125 to 155%
Liquid (water)	50 to 60%	50 to 70%	155%
Shortening	2 to 8%	8 to 20%	30 to 65%
Baking powder, double-acting	2 to 4%		
Salt	½ to 1%	½ to 2%	1 to 2%
Mace, nutmeg, or other spice	¼ to ½%	¼ to ½%	
Vanilla, lemon, or other flavoring	¼ to ½%		
Milk, non-fat dry	5 to 11%	5 to 7%	0 to 3½%
Egg yolks	0 to 16%	2 to 8%	
Yeast		2 to 6%	
Baking ammonia**			0 to ½%**

*Pastry flour may be used in place of blends of bread and cake flour; overly tender cake doughnuts would result from 100% cake flour unless a quite lean dough is used.
**Best to omit baking ammonia since this breaks down the frying fat.

Variation in any of the major ingredients makes it necessary to adjust the others to obtain a desirable product. Do not store mixes over three months.

Only those operations making huge quantities of cake doughnuts make them from basic ingredients. Most operations today use the mix which is prepared from ingredients specifically designed to give a high quality product. Quality still can be lost, however, by improper measuring or poor mixing techniques. Follow the directions of the manufacturer of the mix carefully. Do not over- or under-mix. Keep the temperatures of ingredients around 50° to 60° to reduce the chance for gluten development and a toughening of the product. Doughnuts to be hand-cut and dropped should be slightly stiffer than those dropped by mechanical dropper. Scale cake doughnuts at an ounce each.

The sweet dough used for yeast doughnuts should be slightly more slack than for regular sweet dough products. A 4% yeast to 100% flour should receive its punch in 1¼ to 1½ hours and go to the bench 15 to 20 minutes later. Proof a maximum time — from 10 to 20 minutes. Six pounds of flour makes 13 pounds of dough, enough for about 10 dozen doughnuts. Scale at 1½ ounces each. Machine-cutting or hand-

Figure 18–27. Procter and Gamble show some types of doughnuts made from a cake doughnut recipe.

cutting may be used. Holes may be made also as shown in Figure 18-30. Handle carefully when adding to the fat.

French doughnuts are made from eclair (choux) paste as described in Chapter 15. The batter, preferably warm, is put into a large pastry bag fitted with a large star tube. About two-inch diameter circles, slightly under an ounce each, are made either on greased, heavy brown paper or on a light metal plate. The whole unit is then carefully slipped into hot fat and when the doughnuts free themselves, the paper or plate is removed. Usually four turns are required to cook the doughnut properly, since it must be crisped thoroughly before removal from the fat for the same reason that a cream puff, eclair or popover must be thoroughly baked before it is removed from the oven. The serrated edges left by the star tube on the top should appear after frying. French doughnuts may be machine-shaped if the quantities produced are larger.

When a doughnut, fritter or other product is dropped into hot fat and fried, it expands or develops. This development is frequently called a "break." Doughnuts need good break to reduce grease soaking, develop a good texture and good grain. The method of cutting and dropping, the temperature of the fat and the frying conditions all can affect break.

Figure 18–28. Cutting doughnuts from dough and then frying them was once the way they were made in quantity as shown. Now doughnuts are made by dropping the dough from an automatic dropper.

Fry cake doughnuts $1\frac{1}{2}$ to 2 minutes at 385° F, 390° F being considered best. Fry yeast doughnuts 2 to $2\frac{1}{4}$ minutes at 360° to 365° F and French doughnuts 2 to $2\frac{1}{4}$ minutes at 365° F. Temperatures must be adjusted so that the doughnut is completely cooked when the desired color is obtained. Excessive heat gives a dark doughnut with a raw interior, a tight, compact grain and low volume. The surface appearance will also be poor. Too low a temperature gives excessive expansion with a poor color, break and texture and a high fat absorption. Slide hand-cut doughnuts carefully into the fat. A mechanical dropper should be not more than two inches above the fat. The surface should not be crowded, allowing for expansion in cooking and turning of the doughnuts. Desirable fat absorption is about three ounces per dozen; four ounces or more is considered excessive.

(a)

(b)

(c)

Figure 18–29. The quality of a cake doughnut is affected by a number of factors including whether the dough is too rich or too lean (a), too slack or contains too much flour (b) or is poorly cut or dropped (c).

Figure 18–30. Cut raised yeast doughnuts out without a hole; give full proof and then when dropping the doughnut into the fat, make a hole *gently* as shown.

(a)   (b)

Figure 18–31. (a) To make French doughnuts, make a choux paste (eclair) and place on greased paper as shown. Instead of paper, metal plates may be used, sized to fit the fryer. The paper or metal plate is lowered into the fat. When the doughnuts begin to swell, they free themselves and rise to the top. At this time, the paper or metal plate is removed and the doughnuts fried as shown in (b).

Doughnuts may be dipped after drying into different coating materials. Cool to 80° F since, if dipped while warm, escaping steam will soak the coating. Greasy doughnuts also make the coating appear soaked. Good coatings may also be destroyed by improper storage. Powdered sugar coatings may be stabilized if from 5 to 10% starch or non-fat dry milk is added. A fondant or plain powdered sugar icing soaks less if some fat, 10 to 15% of the total icing weight, is creamed into it. Yeast doughnuts are best dipped into fine granulated sugar, sugar and cinnamon or are glazed. A glaze consists of 40% water, 10% glucose or 5% invert sugar, 1/10% cream of tartar or 3% glycerine brought to a boil with 100% 4 to 6 X sugar; 1% hydrated gelatin is stirred in after removal from the heat. The doughnuts are dipped into this glaze and then set on a wire rack over a pan to allow the excess to drip off into the pan. Have the glaze at about 110° F for dipping. Doughnuts may be iced or decorated. Yeast doughnuts, longjohns or bismarcks may be filled with jelly

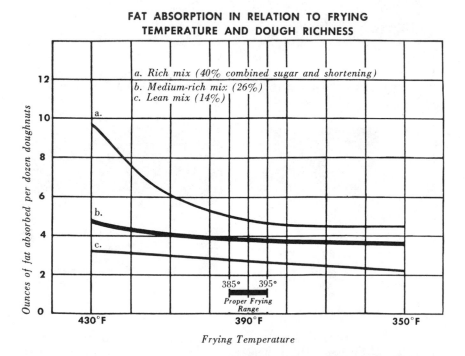

FAT ABSORPTION IN RELATION TO FRYING TEMPERATURE AND DOUGH RICHNESS

a. *Rich mix (40% combined sugar and shortening)*
b. *Medium-rich mix (26%)*
c. *Lean mix (14%)*

Ounces of fat absorbed per dozen doughnuts

385°   395°
Proper Frying Range

430°F   390°F   350°F

Frying Temperature

Figure 18–32.   Fat from 385° to 395° F fries a doughnut rapidly and seals the surface from fat penetration. Lower temperatures do not seal the surface as rapidly, and the doughnut absorbs more fat. Above 395° F absorption is less but the danger of scorching or breaking down the fat is increased.

Figure 18–33. Choux (eclair) paste can be given many shapes for various desserts. In the upper row, shapes are shown to make the body, head and neck of a swan. A basket handle may be made to use for a basket. Eclairs and cream puffs are also shown.

or jam, custard, marshmallow filling or butter cream and occasionally with whipped cream or a fruit filling. Consistency is important. If too soft, they will soak and, if too firm, they will not work well in filling and also have a pasty texture. Most doughnuts are filled with a cream puff filler or similar machine. Occasionally French doughnuts are filled but most often they are merely dusted with powdered sugar, or plain fondant or butter cream icing is brushed over them.

Suggested laboratory or work exercises for Chapter 18:

1. Prepare either a crisp or fruit betty.
2. Prepare a biscuit-type dessert such as a cobbler, shortcake, roly poly, fruit roll, etc.
3. Prepare various types of gelatin desserts including a bavarian.
4. Make a blanc mange and from this make a cream pudding.
5. Prepare a custard and a meringue.
6. Make a crêpe, fill it and flame it.
7. Prepare cake, yeast and choux paste doughnuts.
8. Be able to indicate the proper way to scoop ice cream and prepare various common frozen desserts from the fountain.

BIBLIOGRAPHY

Arbuckle, W. S., *Ice Cream,* American Publishing Co., Inc., Westport, Conn., 1966.

DeGouy, Louis P., *Soda Fountain and Luncheonette Drinks and Recipes,* Dahl Publishing Co., Stamford, Conn., 1940.

Ice Cream Merchandising Institute, Inc., Ice Cream Profit Maker, Nos. 1, 2, 3 and 4, Washington, D. C., 1956.

Fruit Dispatch Company, *Banana Recipes for Large Service,* New York, 1941.

Handy, Etta H., *Ice Cream for Small Plants,* Hotel Monthly Press, John Willy Co., Evanston, Ill., 1937.

Henderich, George W., *Let's Sell Ice Cream,* Ice Cream Merchandising Institute, Inc., Washington, D. C., 1952.

Meister, John E., *Vest Pocket Pastry Book,* Hotel Monthly Press, Evanston, Ill., n. d.

Appendix A

Table A-1. **Equivalents Between Fresh and Frozen Foods**

Food Item	Frozen	Fresh	% Waste Eliminated
(Fish and Sea Food)			
Cod and Haddock Fillets	5 lb	15 lb	67
Flounder Fillets	5 lb	20 lb	75
Halibut Fillets and Steaks	5 lb	10 lb	57
Lobster Meat	1 lb	32 lb	62
Mackerel Fillets	5 lb	9 lb	42
Red Perch Fillets	5 lb	25 lb	80
Swordfish Steaks	5 lb	6¼ lb	20
(Vegetables)			
Asparagus	2½ lb	5.4 lb	54
Broccoli	2½ lb	5.5 lb	55
Cauliflower	2½ lb	10.0 lb	75
Brussels Sprouts	2½ lb	7.0 lb	64
Corn, cut	2½ lb	2 doz ears	
Green Beans	2½ lb	4.0 lb	48
Wax Beans	2½ lb	4.0 lb	48
Beans; Limas, Fordhook, or Baby	2½ lb	7½ to 9 lb	63
Peas	2½ lb	7½ to 9 lb	67
Peas and Carrots	2½ lb	6 to 6¾ lb	63
Pumpkin	2½ lb	4.0 lb	48
Spinach	2½ lb	3.9 lb	63
Squash	2½ lb	6.9 lb	37
Succotash	2½ lb	4.0 lb	63
Mixed Vegetables	2½ lb	4.0 lb	63
(Poultry)			
Broilers, 12 to 24 oz	1 lb	1½ lb	33
Fryers, 1½ to 2½ lb	2 lb	3 lb	33
Fowl, 2 to 3½ lb	2½ lb	3¾ lb	33
Ducks, 3½ to 5 lb	4 lb	4¾ lb	30
Turkeys, 9 to 30 lb	22½ lb	30 lb	25
Geese	7 lb	10 lb	30
(Fruits) *			
Apples	30 lb (7:1)	35:4 lb	24
Apricots	30 lb (5:1)	26⅔:5 lb	6
Berries	30 lb (4:1)	25:6 lb	4
Cherries	30 lb (5:1)	27:5 lb	8
Canteloupe	30 lb (7:1)	52:4 lb	50
Peaches	30 lb (4:1)	31½:6 lb	24
Pineapple	30 lb (4:1)	47:6 lb	48
Rhubarb	30 lb (3:1)	25⅔:8 lb	14

*Most frozen fruit is packed in some sugar, and the ratio of fruit to sugar normally packed is shown in parenthesis after the 30 lb container size. In the next column for the fresh product, the quantity of fruit plus the sugar put in with it to equal the 30 lb is given. Waste is the excess over 30 pounds.

Table A–2.   Ounces and Their Decimal Equivalents of a Pound

When you use the FACTOR method for adjusting your recipe yields, you may find this table helpful if you prefer to work with pounds and decimal parts of a pound instead of multiplying pounds and ounces by the FACTOR. For example, ingredient A might appear in your recipe as 5 pounds 10 ounces. To change the ounces to decimal parts of a pound, read the value across from 10 ounces on the table. Your value is, thus, 5.625 pounds.

This table will also be useful in adjusting yield figures for operations which may have scales and recipes set up in decimal parts of a pound (tenths and hundredths).

Ounces	Decimal part of a pound	Ounces	Decimal part of a pound	Ounces	Decimal part of a pound	Ounces	Decimal part of a pound
¼	.016	4¼	.266	8¼	.516	12¼	.766
½	.031	4½	.281	8½	.531	12½	.781
¾	.047	4¾	.297	8¾	.547	12¾	.797
1	.063	5	.313	9	.563	13	.813
1¼	.078	5¼	.328	9¼	.578	13¼	.828
1½	.094	5½	.344	9½	.594	13½	.844
1¾	.109	5¾	.359	9¾	.609	13¾	.859
2	.125	6	.375	10	.625	14	.875
2¼	.141	6¼	.391	10¼	.641	14¼	.891
2½	.156	6½	.406	10½	.656	14½	.906
2¾	.172	6¾	.422	10¾	.672	14¾	.922
3	.188	7	.438	11	.688	15	.938
3¼	.203	7¼	.453	11¼	.703	15¼	.953
3½	.219	7½	.469	11½	.719	15½	.969
3¾	.234	7¾	.484	11¾	.734	15¾	.984
4	.250	8	.500	12	.750	16	1.000

Source: *Standardizing Recipes for Institutional Use*, Circular 233, Agr. Ex. Station, Michigan State University.

Table A–3. Approximate Substitution Equivalents in Quantity Food Production

Ingredient	Substitute	Measure	Weight
Flour (2 c, 8 oz)	Cornstarch	1 c	
Cake flour (1 qt, 1 lb)	Hard or all purpose flour	3¾ c and ¼ c cornstarch	13½ oz and 2½ oz cornstarch
Sirups, honey, etc. (1 pt, 1 lb 6 oz)	Sugar	2½ c sugar, ½ c water, ⅛ t cream of tartar	1¼ lb sugar, 4 oz water, ⅛ t cream of tartar
Chocolate, bitter (2 c, 1 lb)	Cocoa	3½ c, ¾ c shortening	12½ oz, 3½ oz shortening
Milk, whole (1 qt, 2 lb)	Dry milk, whole*	⅞ c, 3⅞ c water	3¾ oz, 1⅞ lb water
Milk, whole (1 qt, 2 lb)	Dry milk, non-fat*	¾ c, 3½ c water, 2 T shortening	3½ oz, 1¾ lb water, 1 oz shortening
Milk, non-fat (1 qt, 2 lb)	Dry milk, non-fat*	¾ c, 3⅞ c water	3½ oz, 1⅞ lb water
Milk, whole (1 qt, 2 lb)	Evaporated milk	No. 1 tall can plus water to equal qt	14½ oz plus water to equal 1 qt
Eggs, whole (1 pt, 1 lb)	Dried whole eggs	1¼ c, 1¾ c water	5 oz, 12½ oz water
Eggs, whites (1 pt, 1 lb)	Dried whites	1⅛ c, 1¾ c water	3 oz, 14 oz water
Eggs, yolks (1 pt, 1 lb)	Dried yolks	1⅛ c, 1¾ c water	6 oz, 11 oz water
Eggs, whole (1 pt, 1 lb)	Frozen whole	1 pt (10 eggs)	1 lb
Eggs, whites (1 pt, 1 lb)	Frozen whites	1 pt (18 whites)	1 lb
Eggs, yolks (1 pt, 1 lb)	Frozen yolks	1 pt (24 yolks)	1 lb
Butter (1 pt, 1 lb)	Margarine	1 pt	1 lb
Butter or margarine (1 pt, 1 lb)	Fat or oil	1⅞ c plus ½ t salt, 2 T water	14 oz, ½ t salt, 1 oz water
Cream, coffee, 18% (1 qt, 2 lb)	Milk, non-fat and butter	3½ c milk, ¾ c butter	26 oz milk, 6 oz butter
Cream, whipping, 40% (1 qt, 2 lb)	Butter	Butter	40% of cream weight
	Milk, non-fat and butter	3 c milk, 1⅓ c butter	20 oz milk, 12½ oz butter
Leavening agents			
Tartrate baking powder (¾ c, 4 oz)	phosphate SAS/baking powder	⅜ c	2 oz
Tartrate baking powder (¾ c, 4 oz)	Soda and cream of tartar	3 T and ⅔ c	1 oz and 3 oz
SAS Phosphate baking powder (⅜ c, 2 oz)	Phosphate baking powder	½ c plus 1 T	3 oz
SAS Phosphate baking powder (⅜ c, 2 oz)	Soda plus liquid	3 T plus 1 c sour milk or 1 c buttermilk or 1 c milk, 1 T vinegar or lemon juice or ½ to 1 c molasses	

*Measure equivalent is for regular dry milk; for instant use 1⅓ c for every ¾ of regular.

Table A–4. Food Equivalents, Weights and Measures

Food	Weight	Approximate Measure
Beverages		
Cocoa	1 lb	4½ c
Coffee, urn grind	1 lb	4½ c
Coffee, instant	1 oz	½ c
Tea	1 lb	1½ qt
Cereals and Cereal Products		
Barley, pearl	1 lb	2½ c
Bran, all-bran	1 lb	2 qt
Bran flakes	1 lb	3 qt
Bread, crumbs, dry	1 lb	1¼ qt
Bread, crumbs, fresh	1 lb	2½ qt
Bread, crumbs, dry sifted	1 lb	1 qt
Bread, soft, broken, ¾ in. cubes	1 lb	2¼ qt (packed 2 qt)
Bread, slices, ⅝ in.	1 lb	16 slices
Cake crumbs, soft	1 lb	1¼ qt
Crackers, crumbled	1 lb	2 to 2½ qt
Crackers, crumbs	1 lb	1¼ qt
Crackers, graham	1 lb	40 crackers
Crackers, small, square saltines	1 lb	108 crackers
Crackers, large, soda	1 lb	56 crackers
Cracked wheat	1 lb	3½ c (5 to 6 c cooked)
Cornflakes	1 lb	1¼ gal
Cornmeal	1 lb	3½ c (3 qt cooked)
Cornstarch, stirred	1 lb	3½ c (1 c = 4¾ oz, 1 oz 3½ T)
Farina	1 lb	2⅔ c
Flour, graham or whole wheat	1 lb	3½ c
Flour, cake, unsifted	1 lb	3¾ c
Flour, cake, sifted	1 lb	1 qt
Flour, rye, straight grade, sifted	1 lb	1¼ qt
Flour, white, bread, sifted	1 lb	1 qt
Flour, white, bread, unsifted	1 lb	3¾ c
Farina	1 lb	2⅔ c
Hominy grits	1 lb	2½ to 3 c (6½ lb or 3¼ qt cooked)

Macaroni, 1 in. pieces	1 lb	3½ to 4 c (3¾ lb or 2½ qt cooked)
Noodles	1 lb	6 to 8½ c (3¾ lb or 2¼ qt cooked)
Oats, rolled	1 lb	4¾ c (2¼ qt cooked)
Rice	1 lb	2⅛ c (2½ lb or 2½ qt cooked)
Spaghetti, 2 in. pieces	1 lb	1¼ qt (4 lb or 2½ qt cooked)
Soya flour	1 lb	1¼ to 1½ qt
Tapioca, quick cooking	1 lb	2⅔ c (7½ c cooked)
Tapioca, pearl	1 lb	2¾ c (soaked and cooked 7½ c)
Wheat cereals	1 lb	2⅞ c (cooked 6 c)
Wheat, shredded	1 lb	20 small biscuits
Dairy Products		
Butter or Margarine (see also fats)	1 lb	2 c
Cheese, grated or ground	1 lb	2¼ c light pack, 3¾ c loose pack
Cheese, cubed	1 lb 1 oz	1 qt
Cheese, cottage	1 lb	2¼ c
Cheese, Philadelphia cream	1 lb 9 oz	3 c
Cream, 18%	8¾ oz	1 c
Cream, 30 to 40%, whipping	1 lb	1 pt (doubles volume in whipping)
Milk, condensed, sweetened	11 oz	1 c
Milk, dry, instant	1 lb	5¾ c
Milk, dry, non-fat, regular	1 lb	1 qt
Milk, dry, whole, regular	1 lb	3¾ c
Milk, evaporated	1 lb	1⅞ c
Milk, fresh, liquid	8½ oz	1 c
*Eggs, large**		
Eggs in shell	1½ lb	1 doz
Eggs, whole	1 lb	1 pt (9 to 11)
Eggs, whites	1 lb	1 pt (17 to 20)
Eggs, yolks	1 lb	1 pt (19 to 23)
Eggs, hardcooked, chopped	1 lb	2½ c (1 doz = 3½ c)
Eggs, dry, whole, packed	1 oz	¼ c
Eggs, whole dry	1 lb	1¼ qt (1½ c (6oz) and 1⅞ c water= 1 doz eggs)
Eggs, whites, dry	1 lb	2 qt (¾ c (2 doz) and 1½ c water= 1 doz whites)
Eggs, yolks, dry	1 lb	4¼ c (1⅛ c (4 doz) and ⅝ c water= 1 doz yolks)
Meringue	6 oz	1 c

*Eggs lose approximately 11 to 12% weight in shelling. Medium eggs are about 10% less in weight than large.

(continued)

Table A–4 (cont.) Food Equivalents, Weights and Measures

Food	Weight	Approximate Measure
Fats and Oils		
Bacon fat	15 oz	1 lb (1 lb = 2⅛ c)
Butter or margarine	14 oz	1 pt
Creamed fat	1 lb	2½ c
Hydrogenated shortening	14½ oz	1 pt
Oil	1 lb	2¼ c
Suet, chopped	1 lb	3¾ c
Fruits		
Apples	1 lb	3 size 113 (3 c pared, diced or sliced)
Apples, sliced	1 lb	4 to 4½ c
Apples, diced half inch	1 lb	1 qt
Applesauce	1 lb	1⅞ c
Apples, canned, solid pack	1 lb	1 pt
Apple nuggets	1 lb	6⅔ c
Apricots, dried	1 lb	3¼ c (1¾ lb or 5 c cooked)
Apricots, canned, heavy pack	1 lb	1 pt
Apricots, canned, halves, no juice	1 lb	1 pt (21 halves)
Apricots, fresh	1 lb	8 medium
Avocados, Calavos, medium size	1 lb	2 to 3
Bananas, AP, medium size	1 lb	3 (peeled 10 oz)
Bananas, peeled	1 lb	2½ c diced, 1 medium banana = 30 ⅛ in. slices or ¾ c or ⅓ to ½ c mashed
Blackberries, fresh	1 lb	1 qt
Blackberries, water pack, drained	1 lb	3 c
Blueberries, fresh	1 lb	3 c
Cantelope	1 lb	1 melon 4 in. in diameter
Cherries, red, heavy pack, drained	1 lb	3 c
Cherries, Royal Anne, drained	1 lb	3 c
Cherries, candied	1 qt	3 c or 120 cherries
Cherries, Maraschino	1 lb	60 to 70 cherries
Citron, chopped	1 lb	2½ c
Cranberries, fresh	1 lb	1 qt (1 lb AP = 3¼ c sauce)
Cranberries, dehydrated	1 lb	8½ c

Food	Amount	Measure
Cranberries, whole	2½ lb raw	1 qt cooked
Currants	1 lb	3½ c (1 c = 4½ oz)
Dates, pitted	1 lb	2¾ c (1 c = 6 oz, 1 c = 8¼ oz if packed)
Dates, unpitted	1 lb	2½ c (1¾ c pitted)
Figs, dry	1 lb	3 c (1 c = 5 oz)
Grapefruit, 32's	1 lb	12 sections, 1¼ c juice
Grapes, whole, stemmed	1 lb	1 qt
Grapes, cut	1 lb	2⅔ c
Oranges, 88's, diced with juice	1 lb	2¼ c (1 orange = ½ c diced or ⅓ c juice)
Oranges, 88's, Florida	1 doz	1 qt juice
Oranges, rind, grated (also lemon)	1⅔ oz	¼ c (1 t = ⅛ oz)
Oranges, rind, grated (also lemon)	6½ oz	1 c
Peaches, canned, sliced with juice	1 lb	⅞ c
Peaches, fresh	1 lb	3 to 5 peaches
Peaches, dry, loose pack	1 lb	1 qt
Pears, canned, drained, diced	1 lb	2½ c
Pineapple, slices	1 lb	8 to 12 slices (2½ c)
Prunes, dried, size 30 to 40, uncooked	1 lb	3 c (2½ lb or 5 to 6 c cooked)
Prunes, cooked, pitted, with juice	1 lb	2¼ c
Pumpkin	1 lb	2½ c
Raspberries	1 lb	3½ c (2¼ c cooked)
Raisins	1 lb	3 c (1 c = 5¼ oz, 1 lb cooked = 1 lb 9½ oz or 1 qt)
Rhubarb, raw, 1 in. pieces	1 lb	3¼ c
Strawberries, fresh	1 lb	1 qt (cooked 1⅜ lb or 2½ c)
Meats		
Bacon, diced, packed	1 lb	2¼ c
Bacon, raw, sliced	1 lb	15 to 25 slices
Bacon, cooked	1 lb	85 to 95 slices
Beef, dried, solid pack	1 lb	1 qt, scant
Beef, ground, raw	1 lb	1 pt
Beef, cooked, diced	1 lb	3 c
Chicken, ready-to-cook	5 lb	5 c cooked, diced meat (40% yield)
Chicken, cooked, cubed	1 lb	2½ c
Crabmeat, flaked	1 lb	3 c
Ham, cooked, diced	1 lb	3¼ c
Ham, cooked, ground, packed	1 lb	1 pt
Ham, raw, AP	1 lb	1 c fine diced cooked

(continued)

Table A-4 (cont.) Food Equivalents, Weights and Measures

Food	Weight	Approximate Measure
Meats, chopped, cooked, moist, packed	1 lb	1 pt (loose pack = 1 qt)
Oysters, 1 qt, Eastern	2 lb	40 large, 60 small
Salmon, canned	1 lb	1 pt
Sardines, canned	1 lb	48, 3 in. long
Sausage, link	1 lb	16
Sausage meat	1 lb	1 pt
Shrimp, 2 lb AP	1 lb EP	3¼ c (5 lb in shell = gal)
Tuna Fish	1 lb	1 pt
Turkey, ready-to-cook	30 lb	15 lb clear meat
Weiners	1 lb	10 (frankfurters 6 to 7)
Miscellaneous		
Chocolate, see spices		
Compressed yeast	½ oz	1 cake
Compressed yeast	8½ oz	1 c
Dry active yeast	1 lb	2½ lb compressed
Gelatin, granulated, unflavored	1 lb	3½ c (1 oz = 3½ T)
Gelatin, prepared, flavored	1 lb	2⅓ c (1 oz = ¼ c)
Marshmallows (1¼ in.)	1 lb	80
Nuts		
Almonds, shelled	1 lb	3½ c (¼ lb shelled)
Almonds, blanched	1 lb	3 c
Coconut, shredded	1 lb	4½ c to 7 c depending on type shred and tightness of pack
Coconut, ground or fine shred	2⅜ oz	1 c
Coconut, shredded, medium	1 oz	7 T
Filberts	1 lb	3⅓ c (½ lb shelled)
Peanut butter	1 lb	1⅞ c
Peanuts, chopped	1 lb	1 qt (⅔ lb shelled)
Pecans	1 lb	4¼ c (⅓ lb shelled)
Walnut meats	1 lb	4¾ c (½ lb shelled)
Walnut meats, chopped	1 lb	1 qt
Nut meats, ground	4¼ oz	1 c

Salad Dressings and Condiments

Catsup or Chili Sauce	9 oz	1 c
Cooked Salad Dressing	1 lb	1 pt
French Dressing	1 lb	2⅛ c
Horseradish, ground	1 lb	2¼ c
Mayonnaise	1 lb	2⅛ c
Olives, small	1 lb	3½ c or 135 olives, 1 No. 10 = 4½ lb drained weight or 350 large olives
Pickles, chopped	1 lb	2½ c
Pickles, small	1 gal	80 (about 225 gherkins or 25 large per gal)

Spices, Seasonings, Leavenings

Allspice, ground	1 lb	4½ c (1 oz — 4½ T)
Baking Powder	1 lb	2½ c (1 T = 7/16 oz, 1 oz = 2½ T)
Celery Seed	1 lb	1 qt (1 oz = ¼ c)
Chili or Curry Powder	1 oz	3 T
Chocolate, grated	1 lb	1 qt (1 lb = 16 squares)
Chocolate, grated	1 oz	5 T (1 c = 3¾ oz)
Chocolate, melted	1 lb	1⅞ c (1 oz = 2 T)
Cinnamon, ground	1 lb	1 qt (1 oz = ¼ c)
Cloves, ground	1 lb	3¾ c (1 oz = 3¾ T)
Cloves, whole	1 oz	5 T
Cream of Tartar	1 lb	3 c (1 oz = 3 T)
Flavoring Extracts	⅜ oz	1 T (⅛ oz = 1 t)
Ginger, ground	1 lb	4¾ c (1 oz = 4¾ T)
Mustard, ground	1 lb	5 c (1 oz = 5 T)
Nutmeg, ground	1 lb	3½ oz (1 oz = 3½ T)
Paprika	3¼ oz	1 c (1T = ⅜ doz)
Pepper	1 oz	¼ c
Sage, ground	1 oz	½ c
Salt	1 lb	1⅔ c (1 oz = 1 T, 2 t)
Soda	1 lb	2½ c (1 oz = 2 T, 6½ t = 1 oz)
Vinegar	1 lb	2 c (1 oz = 2 T)
Worcestershire Sauce	9½ oz	1 c

Sugars and Sirups

Corn sirup	11 oz	1 c
Honey	12 oz	1 c
Jam or jelly	1½ lb	1 pt

(continued)

Table A–4 (cont.) Food Equivalents, Weights and Measures

Food	Weight	Approximate Measure
Sugar, cocktail cube	1 cublet	½ t (small cube = 1 t, tablet = 1½ t, 96 cubes, medium, per lb)
Sugar, granulated	1 lb	2¼ c (superfine 2 c)
Sugar, confectioners, stirred	1 lb	3½ c
Sugar, confectioners, 4 X, sifted	1 lb	4½ c unsifted 2¾ c)
Sugar, brown	1 lb	3 c (packed 2¼ c)
Molasses	11 oz	1 c
Vegetables		
Asparagus, fresh	1 lb	20 stalks
Asparagus, canned tips, drained	1 lb	19 stalks
Asparagus, canned, cuts, drained	1 lb	2½ c
Beans, baked	1 lb	1⅞ c
Beans, dried, lima, small, AP	1 lb	2⅓ c (2½ lb or 1½ qt cooked)
Beans, lima, fresh, unshelled	1 lb	⅔ c shelled
Beans, lima, fresh, shelled	1 lb	2¼ c (1½ lb = 1 qt)
Beans, lima, drained, cooked fresh or canned	1 lb	2⅔ c (1½ lb = 1 qt)
Beans, kidney, dry, AP	1 lb	2⅓ c (2¼ lb or 1½ qt cooked)
Beans, string, cut, uncooked, EP	12 oz	1 qt
Beans, navy, dry, AP	1 lb	2⅓ c (2½ lb or 1¾ c cooked)
Bean Sprouts	1 lb	1 qt
Beets, cooked, diced, drained	1 lb	2¼ c (3 to 4 medium whole)
Beets, cooked, sliced, drained	1½ lb	1 qt (1 lb = 2¾ c)
Brussels Sprouts, AP	1 lb	1 qt
Cabbage, shredded, EP	12 oz	1 qt (1 lb = 5½ c or 1 lb = 7 c loose pack)
Cabbage, AP, shredded, cooked, drained	1 lb	3½ c
Carrots, half inch cube, raw	1 lb	3¼ c
Carrots, diced, cooked, drained	1 lb	2½ to 3 c
Carrots, ground, raw, EP	1 lb	3¼ c
Carrots, AP	1 lb	4 medium, 6 small
Cauliflower, 1 crate	12½ lb, net, EP	10 qt
Cauliflower, head, medium	12 oz	4 to 5 portions
Celery, diced, EP	1¼ lb	1 qt (1 lb = 3¼ c)
Celery, dehydrated	1 lb	9½ c

Food	Amount	Yield
Corn, cream style	1 lb	1⅞ c
Corn, whole kernel, drained	1 lb	2⅓ c
Cucumbers, diced	1 lb	2½ c
Eggplant, diced half inch cubes	1 lb	4½ c
Eggplant, sliced, 4 in. diameter, half inch thick	1 lb	8 slices
Garlic, crushed	1 oz	6 to 9 cloves
Lettuce, average head	1 lb	10 to 12 leaf cups
Lettuce, shredded	1 lb	8 c (packed 5 c)
Lettuce, leaf	1 lb	30 salad garnishes
Onions, AP	1 lb	4 to 5 medium
Onions, chopped	1 lb	2½ to 3 c
Onions, grated or minced	5 oz	1 c
Onions, dehydrated	1 lb	9½ c
Mushrooms, fresh	1 lb AP	1⅓ c cooked (6 c chopped)
Parsley	1 lb	3 bunches (6 c chopped)
Parsnips, AP	1 lb	3 to 4 medium
Parsnips, diced, raw	1 lb	2½ to 3 c
Parsnips, diced cooked	1 lb	2½ c
Parsnips, mashed	1 lb	1 pt
Peas, fresh, 2½ lb AP	1 lb EP	1 pt scant, 5 portions
Peas, canned, dried	1 lb	2¼ c
Peas, dried, split	1 lb	2⅓ c (2½ lb or 5½ c cooked)
Peppers, green	1 lb	5 to 6 medium
Peppers, green, chopped	1 lb	3½ c
Pimientos, chopped	8 oz	1 c
Potatoes, white, medium, AP	1 lb	3 to 4 (¾ lb pared, 1 pt mashed)
Potatoes, dehydrated cube	1 lb	4¾ c
Potatoes, dehydrated, flake	3½ oz	1 c
Potatoes, granule, dehydrated	7 oz	1 c
Potatoes, cooked, diced half inch cube	1 lb	3 c
Potatoes, sweet	1 lb	3 medium
Potato chips	1 lb	5 qt (20 1 c portions ¾ oz)
Pumpkin, cooked	1 lb	1 pt
Radishes, whole, topped and cleaned	1 lb	1 qt
Rutabagas, cubed, cooked	1 lb	3 c
Rutabagas, raw, cubed, EP	1 lb	3⅓ c
Sauerkraut, uncooked	1 lb	3 c
Spinach, raw	1 lb	5 qt, loose pack

(continued)

Table A-4 (cont.) Food Equivalents, Weights and Measures

Food	Weight	Approximate Measure
Spinach, 1 lb raw, AP, cooked	13 oz (EP)	1½ c cooked, 3 portions
Spinach, canned, drained	1 lb	1 pt
Squash, summer, AP	1½ lb	1 3 in. diameter
Squash, Hubbard, cooked, mashed	1 lb	2⅞ c
Tomatoes, canned	1 lb	1 pt
Tomatoes, dried	1 lb	3½ c
Tomatoes, fresh	1 lb	3 to 4 medium
Tomatoes, fresh, diced	1 lb	2¼ to 2¾ c
Turnips, AP	1 lb	4 to 5 medium
Turnips, raw, diced	1 lb	3½ c
Watercress	1 lb	5 bunches

Table A-5. Standard Portions

Food	Portion and Serving Method
Meats	
American chop suey	4 oz ladle, rounded
with corn soya	2 T, No. 32 scoop
with rice	No. 16 scoop
Baked hash, beef or	
corned beef	No. 10 scoop or heaped serving spoon, 5 to 6 oz
Beef or other meat and	No. 8 scoop rounded or 6 oz ladle rounded, about 7
noodles	oz (¾ c)
Beef patty	No. 8 scoop before cooking, use tongs
Beef or other meat stew	6 oz, (¾ c), ladle
Chili con carne	6 oz ladle rounded to give 8 oz
Corned beef and cabbage	3 or 4 oz sliced beef, tongs; 3 to 4 oz cabbage, spoon
Cold cuts	3 oz, tongs or spatula
Cabbage rolls	2 rolls, 3 oz each (use 2 oz meat filling), use spoon
Creamed meats	½ c, 4 oz ladle; use 8 to 10 lb cooked meat per 100; serve over toast, biscuits or No. 16 scoop rice
Croquettes	No. 10 or 12 scoop for 1; No. 20 scoop for 2; 1½ oz sauce
Frankfurters, 6 to 7 lb	2, tongs
with sauerkraut	1 rounded serving spoon, 3 oz
Fritters	2, tongs; portion with No. 20 scoop; 2 strips bacon
Ham a la king	4 oz ladle rounded
Ham, baked, boned	5 to 6 oz before cooking, tongs
Ham, baked, slices	3 to 4 oz after cooking, tongs
Ham, fried	6 oz before cooking, tongs
Hamburgers	2, portion with No. 20 dipper, tongs
Liver, braised	3 to 4 oz before cooking, 2 strips bacon, tongs
Meat balls and spaghetti	No. 20 scoop, 2 balls, 2 serving spoons spaghetti and sauce
Meat sandwich, hot	2 oz meat, 1 or 2 slices bread, tongs; 2 oz ladle gravy
Meat loaf	4 to 5 oz cooked, slice and use spatula or tongs
Meat pie	2 serving spoons, rounded, 8 oz
with pie crust	Cut 17 x 25 baking pans 5 x 9, 45 portions
with biscuit	2½ in diameter, serve 1 with 6 oz stew
Meat turnover	2 oz meat, No. 16 scoop; serve with 2 oz gravy, ladle
Mock drum sticks	5 oz before cooking, serve 1
New England boiled dinner	6 oz before cooking, 3 to 4 oz after, tongs, 5 oz vegetables and 5 oz potatoes
Pork chop	3 to lb before cooking, serve 1; 6 to lb serve 2
with dressing	2 to 3 oz; use serving spoon or No. 16 scoop
Pork chop with pocket	3 to lb, 1½ oz stuffing; tongs
Roasts, meat or poultry	3 oz cooked, tongs
with dressing	2 to 3 oz meat cooked; 4 oz (½ c), No. 10 scoop rounded of dressing
Sausage, bulk	3 oz before cooking, tongs
Sausages, link, 14 to 16 per lb.	2, tongs
Spareribs	8 to 12 oz before cooking, tongs
Steak, braised, Swiss, etc.	6 to 7 oz raw, 4 to 5 oz cooked, spoon
Steak, dinner, dry heat type	8 oz AP, no bone, tongs; size may vary with institution
Steak, ground	3 to pound, No. 8 scoop rounded; 4 oz cooked, tongs
Steak, stuffed	5 to 6 oz before cooking; 1½ oz dressing, tongs
Stew	No. 8 scoop rounded or 6 oz ladle rounded (¾ c)
Veal birds	5 oz before cooking; 1½ oz dressing; spoon
Veal cutlet	4 oz before breading; 5 oz breaded
Veal chop	5 oz
Weiners, 10 to lb	2, tongs

(continued)

Table A-5 (cont.)   Standard Portions

Food	Portion and Serving Method
Fish	
Fillet, baked or fried	3 to pound before cooking; 4 oz if breaded
Steak	3 to pound unless wasty in eating, then 6 oz
Creamed fish dishes	4 oz ladle rounded; 1 slice toast, 1 biscuit or No. 16 scoop of rice
Shrimp wiggle	4 oz ladle rounded; slice of toast or biscuit or No. 16 scoop of rice
Shrimp, deep fried. fantail	4 to 5, tongs
Strips, breaded and deep fried	1 oz each, serve three, tongs; about 35% breading
Croquettes	No. 10 scoop for 1; No. 20 scoop for two; 1½ oz sauce
Loaf	4 oz slice; in 17 x 25 pan, cut 5 by 9, in 12 by 20 pan, cut 4 by 6; bake in these 1 in. deep
Scalloped salmon, tuna, etc.	1 4 oz ladle rounded, 5 to 6 oz; if thick, rounded serving spoon
Fish and noodles	Serving spoon rounded, 5 to 6 oz
Tuna fish, potato chip dish	Serving spoon rounded, 5 to 6 oz
Souffle	Cut 17 x 25 pan, 5 by 9, 12 by 20 pan 4 by 6
Poultry	
Chicken fricassee. unboned	12 oz raw meat, spoon
Chicken, creamed	6 oz (¾ c); about 2 oz cooked chicken meat per portion
Chicken, fried	2 pieces or half (12 oz before cooking)
Chicken or turkey, roast	2 to 3 oz with dressing, 4 oz without, 2 oz gravy
Duck or geese	12 oz to 1 lb before cooking
*Luncheon Entrees**	
American noodles	5 oz, serving spoon well rounded
Baked beans	6 oz ladle or two serving spoons or one heaped
Baked lima beans	6 oz, serving spoon heaped
Baked eggs, creole	4 oz ladle, rounded
Beef biscuit roll	1, 4 in. diameter, 2 oz ladle gravy
Buttered apples with sausage	3 apple halves, 2 sausages
Cheeseburgers	1 No. 16 scoop, 2 each, slice cheese ¾ to 1 oz each
Cheese fondue	4 oz, 1 oz sauce; cut 12 by 20 pan 4 by 6, spoon and ladle
Rice and cheese baked	5 oz (⅔ c), well rounded serving spoon
Creole spaghetti	1 serving spoon well rounded (6 oz)
Eggs a la king or creamed eggs	2 halves egg on half slice of toast; 2 oz sauce
Omelet	4 oz, spoon; if cut, use spatula
Goulash	6 oz ladle
Italian delight	4 oz ladle
Italian spaghetti	1 heaped serving spoon spaghetti, 4 oz ladle sauce
Macaroni and cheese	1 heaped serving spoon. 5 to 6 oz
Macaroni hoe	1 heaped serving spoon, 5 to 6 oz
Meat souffle	1 heaped serving spoon, 1½ oz sauce
Pizza Pie	Cut 18 x 20 in baking sheet 4 by 5, use spatula
Scalloped ham and potatoes	1 heaped serving spoon, 5 to 6 oz
Scalloped meat dishes	1 heaped serving spoon, 5 to 6 oz
Scrapple	4 oz, 2 slices
Spanish rice	1 well rounded serving spoon, 5 oz
Stuffed cabbage	1 or two

*A 12 by 20 in. baking pan 4 in. deep with food (16 to 18 lb of food) may be cut 5 by 8 to give 40 6 to 7 oz portions. (Use 6 in. deep pan)

Table A-5 (cont.)   Standard Portions

Food	Portion and Serving Method
Swedish meat balls	2 2 oz each after cooking; portion with rounded No. 20 scoop
Tamale pie	1 heaped serving spoon, 5 to 6 oz
Welsh Rarebit	½ c, 4 oz ladle, on toast, biscuit or No. 16 scoop rice

Vegetables

Food	Portion and Serving Method
Most canned vegetables	3 oz (½ c), 1 rounded serving spoon
Apples, buttered	½ c, 3 to 4 pieces, serving spoon
Asparagus tips	3 to 5 canned, 4 to 6 fresh
Beans, navy, lima or other	4 to 5 oz, serving spoon
Beets, Harvard	½ c, serving spoon rounded
Beet greens, other greens	3 oz (½ c), tongs or serving spoon
Broccoli, buttered	2 to 3 pieces, 3 to 4 oz, tongs
Cabbage, steamed, fried, etc.	3 oz (½ c), serving spoon
Onions, creamed	2 to 3 small onions, serving spoon
Potato puff	5 oz, ⅔ c, spoon
Potato, browned, steamed, etc.	5 oz, serving spoon
Potato, au gratin, creamed, etc.	4 to 5 oz, serving spoon
Potato, baked	5 to 6 oz, tongs
Potato, hash brown, etc.	4 to 5 oz, serving spoon
Potato, mashed	1 No. 10 scoop or serving spoon, 4 oz
Potato, French fried	4 oz, 8 to 10 pieces, tongs or spoon
Potato cakes	4 oz, serving spoon
Rice, steamed	No. 10 scoop rounded (⅔ c)
Squash, acorn, baked or steamed	⅓ or ½ squash
Squash, hubbard	6 to 7 oz piece before baking
Squash, mashed	4 oz, rounded serving spoon
Sweet potatoes, baked	5 to 6 oz, tongs
Sweet potatoes, candied or glazed	2 slices, 4 oz
Scalloped sweet potatoes and apples	4 oz, serving spoon
Tomatoes, escalloped or stewed	4 oz ladle
Vegetable pie	5 oz, well rounded serving spoon
Vegetables, creamed	3 to 4 oz

Salads

Food	Portion and Serving Method
Cole slaw	3 oz, serving spoon
Cottage cheese	No. 20 scoop
Deviled egg	2 halves
Gelatin	12 by 20 pan, 1 in. deep, cut 5 by 10, 50 portions
Mixed fruit	1 rounded serving spoon, No. 12 scoop
Mixed vegetable	1 rounded serving spoon
Sliced tomato	2 large or 3 medium slices
Head lettuce, 1 lb average	⅛ head, 2 oz serving
Potato, cold or hot	1 No. 10 or No. 12 scoop (4 to 5 oz)
Waldorf	1 rounded serving spoon, 3 oz
Fish or meat salad, entree type	5 to 6 oz, 1 c
Brown bean	4 to 5 oz

(continued)

Table A–5 (cont.)   Standard Portions

Food	Portion and Serving Method
Dressings and Sauces	
Mayonnaise, boiled, etc.	1 to 2 T; portion depends upon salad size
French or other liquid	1 to 2 T; portion depends upon salad size
Cranberry sauce, applesauce, etc.	2 to 2½ oz, scant serving spoon or No. 16 scoop
	1 to 2 T
Soup	
Cup	6 oz, ¾ c
Bowl	8 oz, 1 c
Tureen	10 to 12 oz, 1¼ to 1½ c
Breads	
Biscuits	2 to 3 1 oz each**
Bran rolls	2 1 oz each
Cinnamon rolls	2 1½ oz each
Cornbread, coffee cake, etc.	1 piece 2 oz, cut 18 x 26 in. baking sheet 6 by 8
Muffins	2 2½ oz each
Griddle cakes	3 3 to 4 oz each
Potato doughnuts	2 2 oz each
Hot rolls	2 1 oz each
Sweet dough items, breakfast	1 3 oz each
White or other bread, sliced	1 to 2 slices, 1 oz each

Desserts	*Pan Size*	*Portion*
Cakes, butter		
Sheet, 1 layer	18 x 26 in.	Cut 6 by 8, 48 portions
	13½ x 22⅞ in.	Cut 5 by 9 or 6 by 8, 45 or 48 portions
	12¾ x 23 in.	Cut 5 by 9 or 6 by 8, 45 or 48 portions
Sheet, 2 layer	18 x 26 in.	Cut 12 by 5, 60 portions
	13½ x 22⅞ in.	Cut 3 by 20, 60 portions
	12¾ x 23 in.	Cut 3 by 20, 60 portions
Square, 1 layer	9½ x 9½ in.	Cut 3 by 4, 12 portions
Square, 2 layer	9½ x 9½ in.	Cut 3 by 7, 21 portions
Round, 2 layer	8 in. diameter	Cut 12

Eight 8 in. round layer cakes will serve 96
Six 9 x 13 in. sheets will serve 96
One 9 x 13 in. sheet, two layer, will serve 30
Four 12 in. round layer cakes will serve 120   (See also portioning information
Three 14 in. layer cakes (round) will serve 120   in chapter on cakes and cookies)

Angel food	16 oz	Cut 16
Chocolate roll, jelly, ect	18 x 26 in. rolled	34 to 36 portions
Cup cakes	1 No. 16 scoop	1 each
Doughnuts, cake	1 oz	2
Cookies		
Brownies, date bars, etc	18 x 26 in.	Cut 54, serve one
	13½ x 22⅞ in.	Cut 5 by 9, 45 portions

**weight is calculated from raw weight before baking

Table A–5 (cont.) Standard Portions

Desserts	Pan Size	Portion
Pies		
One or two crust	10 in.	Cut 8
(use marker)	9 in.	Cut 7
	8 in.	Cut 6
Crust, double	9 in.	12 oz
Crust, single	9 in.	6½ oz
Filling, cream	9 in.	1½ to 2 pt (1½ to 2 lb)
Filling, custard type	9 in.	1½ pt (1½ lb)
Filling, fruit	9 in.	1½ pt (1½ lb)
Puddings		
Apple crisp, brown		4 oz
betty, etc		
Apricot whip		¾ c
Bread Pudding	13½ x 22⅞ in.	½ c, cut 5 x 9
Cobblers, etc	13½ x 22⅞ in.	½ c, cut 5 x 9
	12 x 20 in.	½ c, cut 6 x 8
Cream, rice, tapioca, etc		½ c, No. 10 scoop
Cream puff or eclair batter		1 oz (small), 2 oz (large)
Cream puff or eclair filling		1½ oz, No. 20 scoop
Ice box cake	12¾ x 23 in.	Cut 5 x 10
Ice box pudding		No. 20 scoop
Jello	12¾ x 23 in.	Cut 5 by 9
	12 x 20 in.	Cut 6 by 8
Whipped cream topping		2 T, 2 qt whipped tops
		100 portions
Ice Cream, etc		
Brick	**quart**	Cut 8
Bulk		No. 12 scoop
Sundae		No. 16, 2 oz sauce
(See also portioning information in frozen desserts)		
Miscellaneous		
Graham craker roll, etc	Loaf 9⅝ x 5½ x 3¼ in.	Cut 16
Pineapple delicious		½ c, No. 10 scoop rounded
Shortcake		2½ in. diameter biscuit,
		⅓ c fruit, 2 T whipped
		cream
Steamed pudding	1 qt mold	Cut into 12 (3½ oz);
		2 oz sauce
	12 x 20 in.	Cut 6 by 10
Meringues		⅓ c, 2 oz ladle sirup or
		sauce, 2 T whipped cream
Sauces for topping		3 T, vary with richness

Table A–6. Canned Foods: Servings Per Can or Jar

PRODUCT	Content — Can or Jar (Approx.)		Servings	Size of Each Serving (Approx.)
	Net Weight or Volume	Cups or Pieces		
FRUITS				
Apples; Applesauce; Berries; Cherries; Grapes; Grapefruit and Orange Sections; Fruit Cocktail; Fruits for Salad; Sliced Peaches; Pears; Pineapple Chunks, Crushed, Tidbits	8½ to 8¾ oz	1 c	2	½ c
	16 to 17 oz	1¾ to 2 c	4	½ c
	1 lb 4 oz	2¼ to 2½ c	5	½ c
	1 lb 13 oz	3¼ to 3½ c	7	½ c
	6 lb 2 oz to	12 to 13 c	25	½ c
Apricots, Whole (Medium Size)	6 lb 12 oz	8 to 14	4	2 to 3 apricots
	16 to 17 oz	15 to 18	7	2 to 3 apricots
	6 lb 10 oz	50 to 60	25	2 to 3 apricots
Apricots, Halves (Medium Size)	8¾ oz	6 to 12	2	3 to 5 halves
	16 to 17 oz	12 to 20	4	3 to 5 halves
	1 lb 13 oz	26 to 35	7	3 to 5 halves
	6 lb 10 oz	95 to 130	25	3 to 5 halves
Peaches, Halves or Pears, Halves	16 to 17 oz	6 to 10	3	2 medium halves
	1 lb 13 oz	7 to 12	7	1 large half
	6 lb 10 oz	45 to 65	25	2 medium halves
Pineapple, Sliced	9 oz	4	2·	2 slices
	1 lb 4 oz	10	5	2 slices
	1 lb 14 oz	8	8	1 large slice
	6 lb 12 oz	28 to 50	25	1 large slice or 2 small slices
Plums; Prunes	8¾ oz	7 to 9	2	2 to 3 plums
	16 to 17 oz	10 to 14	4	2 to 3 plums
	1 lb 14 oz	12 to 20	7	2 to 3 plums
	6 lb 10 oz	40 to 60	25	2 to 3 plums
Figs	8 to 9 oz	6 to 12	2	3 to 4 figs
	16 to 17 oz	12 to 20	4	3 to 4 figs
	1 lb 14 oz	18 to 24	7	3 to 4 figs
	7 lb	70 to 90	25	3 to 4 figs

Item				
Cranberry Sauce	6 to 8 oz	¾ to 1 c	4	¼ c
	1 lb	2 c	8	¼ c
	7 lb 5 oz	12 to 13 c	50	¼ c
*Olives, Ripe	4½ oz	—	—	3 olives
	9 oz	—	—	3 olives
	1 lb 2 oz	—	—	3 olives
	4 lb 2 oz	—	—	3 olives

VEGETABLES

Item				
Asparagus Cuts; Beans, Green and Wax, Kidney, Lima; Beets; Carrots; Corn; Hominy; Okra; Onions; Peas; Peas and Carrots; Black-Eyed Peas; Pumpkin; Sauerkraut; Spinach and Other Greens; Squash; Succotash; **Sweet Potatoes; Tomatoes; Mixed Vegetables; Potatoes, White, Cut, Sliced	8 to 8½ oz	1 c	2	½ c
	12 oz	1½ to ¾ c	4	½ c
	16 to 17 oz	2 c	4	½ c
	1 lb 4 oz	2¼ to 2½ c	5	½ c
	1 lb 13 oz	3¼ to 3½ c	7	½ c
	6 lb 2 oz to 6 lb 12 oz	12 to 13 c	25	½ c
Asparagus Spears (Medium Size) (Count in spears)	10½ oz	9 to 12	2	4 to 6 spears
	14½ to 16 oz	16 to 28	3	4 to 6 spears
	1 lb 3 oz	20 to 30	5	4 to 6 spears
	4 lb 4 oz	115 to 145	25	4 to 6 spears
Potatoes, White, Peeled, Whole, Small	16 to 17oz	8 to 12	4	2 to 3 potatoes
	6 lb 6 oz	55 to 65	25	2 to 3 potatoes
Beans; Baked; with Pork; in Sauce	8¾ oz	1 c	1 to 2	½ to ¾ c
	1 lb	1¾ c	3 to 4	½ to ¾ c
	1 lb 10 oz	3 c	4 to 6	½ to ¾ c
	6 lb 14 oz	12 to 13 c	16 to 25	½ to ¾ c
Mushrooms	2 oz	⅓ c	1	⅓ c
	4 oz	⅔ c	2	⅓ c
	8 oz	1½ c	4	⅓ c
	6 lb 7 oz	12 to 13 c	36	⅓ c
Pimientos; Peppers, Red, Sweet	2 oz	¼ c	—	—
	4 oz	½ c	—	—
	7 oz	1 c	—	—
	6 lb 13 oz	12 to 13 c	—	—

(continued)

Table A-6 (cont.) Canned Foods: Servings Per Can or Jar

PRODUCT	Net Weight or Volume	Cups or Pieces	Servings	Size of Each Serving (Approx.)
JUICES				
Apple; Cherry; Cranberry; Grape; Grapefruit; Grapefruit-Orange; Loganberry; Nectars; Orange; Pineapple; Prune; Tangerine; Carrot; Sauerkraut; Tomato; Vegetable Cocktail; Vegetable	6 to 8 oz	3/4 to 1 c	1 to 2	4 to 6 oz
	12 fl oz	1½ c	3	4 oz
			2	6 oz
	1 pint	2 c	4	4 oz
			3	6 oz
	1 pt 2 fl oz	2¼ to 2½ c	5	4 oz
			3	6 oz
	1 pt 7 fl oz	3 c	6	4 oz
			4	6 oz
	1 quart	4 c	8	4 oz
			5	6 oz
	1 qt 14 fl oz	5¾ c	12	4 oz
			8	6 oz
	3 quarts	12 c	24	4 oz
			16	6 oz
Lemon; Lime	5½ to 6 oz	3/4 c	—	—
SOUPS				
Condensed	10½ to 12 oz	1¼ c (2½ c prepared soup)	3	3/4 c
	3 lb 2 oz	5¾ c (11½ c prepared soup)	12 to 16	3/4 c
Ready-to-serve	8 fl oz indv	1 c	1	1 c
	12 fl oz	1½ c	2	3/4 c
	15 fl oz	2 c	3	3/4 c
	1 pt 5 fl oz	2½ to 3 c	4	3/4 c
	1 pt 9 fl oz to 3 qt	12 c	20	3/4 c

MEATS & POULTRY

Chili Con Carne; Chili Con Carne with Beans	15 to 16 oz	2 c	3 to 4	½ to ⅔ c
	1½ lb	3 c	4 to 5	½ to ⅔ c
	6 lb 12 oz	12 to 13 c	18 to 24	½ to ⅔ c
Corned Beef	12 oz	—	4	3 oz
	6 lb		30	3 oz
Corned Beef Hash	8 oz	1 c	1 to 2	½ to ⅔ c
	1 lb	2 c	3 to 4	½ to ⅔ c
	1½ lb	3 c	5 to 6	½ to ⅔ c
	5 lb 8 oz to 5 lb 14 oz	12 to 13 c	18 to 24	½ to ⅔ c
Deviled Ham	2¼ to 3 oz	⅓ c	3 to 4	1½ T
	4½ oz	½ c	5 to 6	1½ T
Deviled Meat; Potted Meat; Meat Spreads	2 to 3¼ oz	⅓ c	3 to 4	1½ T
	5½ oz	¾ c	8	1½ T
Luncheon Meat	12 oz	—	4	2 slices (3½" x 1¾" x ⅜")
	6 lb		32	3 oz
Tongue: Beef; Lamb; Pork	6 oz		2	3 oz
	12 oz		4	3 oz
	1 to 2 lb		5 to 10	3 oz
Hams, Whole (Small)	1½ to 4 lb		3 to 4 per pound	2 slices (4" x 3" x ⅛")
(Medium)	6 to 8 lb			
(Large)	9 to 14 lb			
Poultry, Boned: Chicken; Turkey	5 to 6 oz		2	3 oz
	12 oz		4	3 oz
	1 lb 14 oz		10	3 oz
	2 lb 3 oz		12	3 oz
Sausage, Pork; Frankfurters	8 oz	11 to 12	3 to 4	3 sausages
	12 oz	8 to 9 large	4	2 sausages
Stew: Beef, Lamb	1 lb	2 c	2	¾ c
	1 lb 4 oz	2½ c	3	¾ c
	1½ lb	3 c	4	¾ c
Vienna Sausage	4 oz	8 to 10	2	4 to 5 sausages
	9 oz	16 to 20	4	4 to 5 sausages

(continued)

Table A–6 (cont.)   Canned Foods: Servings Per Can or Jar

PRODUCT	Content — Can or Jar (Approx.)			Size of Each Serving (Approx.)
	Net Weight or Volume	Cups or Pieces	Servings	
FISH AND SEAFOOD				
Clams	7½ oz	1 c	2	½ c
Crab Meat	5½ to 7½ oz	¾ to 1 c	2 to 3	⅓ to ½ c
Mackerel	1 lb	2 c	4	½ c
Oysters	8 oz	1 c	2	½ c
Salmon	7¾ oz	1 c	2	½ c
	1 lb	2 c	4	½ c
Sardines	3¼ to 4 oz	6 to 10	1½	5 to 7 sardines
Sardines, Pilchards	15 oz	6 to 7 large	4	1½ sardines
*Shrimp	4½ to 6½ oz	25 to 35	3 to 4	10 to 12 medium size
				6 to 8 jumbo size
Tuna in Oil	6 to 7 oz	1 c	2	½ c
	13 oz	1¾ c	4	½ c
INFANT FOODS				
VEGETABLES AND FRUITS				
Infant: Strained; Homogenized	4¾ oz	½ c	—	—
Junior: Chopped	6½ oz	¾ c	—	—
	8 oz	⅞ c	—	—
MEATS				
Infant: Strained	3½ oz	7 T	—	—
Junior: Chopped	3½ oz	7 T	—	—

SOUPS

Infant	4¾ oz	½ c
Junior	8 oz	⅞ c

*Declared as drained weight. (The number of olives per container varies as to size of the olives.)

**Sweet potatoes also come in 1 lb 2 oz to 1 lb 7 oz cans.

NOTE: The net weight of various foods in the same size can or glass jar will vary with the density of the food. For the most part only minimum weights are shown in the table.

Cups or pieces and servings in the table have been given in approximates; and sizes of servings are given in rounded numbers in order to furnish a practical guide.

Table A-7.   Can Sizes

Size Can	Approximate Quantity		Products Contained
	Net Weight	Cups	
8 oz	8 oz	1	
Picnic	10½ to 12 oz	1¼	Fruits, vegetables, specialties
12 oz (vacuum)	12 oz	1½	Soups, fruits, vegetables, meat and fish specialties
No. 300	14 to 16 oz	1¾	Pork and beans, baked beans, meat products, cranberry sauce, blueberries, specialties
No. 303	16 to 17 oz	2	Fruits, vegetables, meats, ready-to-serve soups, specialties
No. 2	1 lb 4 oz or 1 pt 2 fl oz	2½	Juices, ready to serve soups, fruits and vegetables, specialties.
No. 2½	1 lb 13 oz	3½	Fruits, vegetables such as pumpkin, sauerkraut, pork and beans, greens, tomatoes
No. 3 cylinder or 46 oz	3 lb 3 oz or 1 qt 14 fl oz	5¾	Fruit and vegetable juices, pork and beans, condensed soup and some vegetables
No. 10	6½ lb to 7 lb 5 oz*	12 to 13	Fruits and vegtables for institutional use

*Jellies and jams and other heavy items will weight more than this.

Table A-8.   Can Substitutions for No. 10 Size

Net Weight of No. 10	Number Cans to Substitute	Net Weight Substituted
6 lb 10 oz	7 No. 303's	7 lb
6 lb 10 oz	5 No. 2's	6 lb 2 oz
6 lb 10 oz	4 No. 2½'s	7 lb 2 oz
6 lb 10 oz	2 No. 46 oz or 2 No. 3 cylinder	5 lb 12 oz to 6 lb 4 oz

Table A–9 through A–11

Tables A–9 through A–11 were originally developed by the Nutrition Services Division of the New York State Department of Mental Health under Mrs. Kathryn Flack and adapted by Pearl J. Aldrich and Grace A. Miller in *Standardizing Recipes for Institutional Use,* Circular Bulletin 233, Agr. Experiment Station, Michigan State University, 1963.

Instructions for Using Table A–9

1. Locate column which corresponds to the original yield of the recipe you wish to adjust. For example, let us assume your original recipe for meat loaf yields 100 portions. Locate the **100** column.

2. Run your finger **down** this column until you come to the amount of the ingredient required (or closest to this figure) in the recipe you wish to adjust. Say that your original recipe for 100 portions of meat loaf requires 21 pounds of ground beef. Run your finger down the column headed 100 until you come to **21 pounds**.

3. Next, run your finger **across** the page, in line with that amount, until you come to the column which is headed to correspond with **the yield you desire.** Suppose you want to make 75 portions of meat loaf. Starting with your finger under the 21 lb. (in the 100 column), slide it across to the column headed 75 and read the figure. You see you need 15 lb. 12 oz. ground beef to make 75 portions with your recipe.

4. Record this figure as the amount of the ingredient required for the new yield of your recipe. Repeat Steps 1, 2, 3 for each ingredient in your original recipe to obtain the adjusted ingredient weight needed of each for your new yield. You can increase or decrease yield in this manner.

5. If you need to combine two columns to obtain your desired yield, follow the above procedure and **add together** the amounts given in the two columns to get the amount required for your adjusted yield. For example, to find the amount of ground beef for 225 portions of meat loaf (using the same basic recipe for 100 we used above) locate the figures in columns headed 200 and 25 and add them. In this case they would be: 42 lb. + 5 lb. 4 oz., and the required total would be 47 lb. 4 oz.

6. The figures in Table 1 are given in **exact** weights including fractional ounces. After you have made yield adjustments for every ingredient, refer to Table 4 for "rounding-off" fractional amounts which are not of sufficient proportion to change product quality. No "rounding-off" is required for amounts needed for adjusted ingredients in the examples we have used here.

Table A-9. **Direct-reading table for adjusting yield of recipes with ingredient amounts. (This table is primarily for adjusting recipes with original and desired portion yields which can be divided by 25. It may be used along with Table A-10, which is similarly constructed for measures.)**

ABBREVIATIONS IN TABLE:
oz. = ounce
# = pound

BASIC INFORMATION:
1 pound = 16 ounces

25	50	75	100	200	300	400	500	600	700	800	900	1000
(a)	(a)	(a)	¼ oz.	½ oz.	¾ oz.	1 oz.	1¼ oz.	1½ oz.	1¾ oz.	2 oz.	2¼ oz.	2½ oz.
(a)	(a)	(a)	½ oz.	1 oz.	1½ oz.	2 oz.	2½ oz.	3 oz.	3½ oz.	4 oz.	4½ oz.	5 oz.
(a)	(a)	(a)	¾ oz.	1½ oz.	2¼ oz.	3 oz.	3¾ oz.	4½ oz.	5¼ oz.	6 oz.	6¾ oz.	7½ oz.
¼ oz.	½ oz.	¾ oz.	1 oz.	2 oz.	3 oz.	4 oz.	5 oz.	6 oz.	7 oz.	8 oz.	9 oz.	10 oz.
(a)	(a)	(a)	1¼ oz.	2½ oz.	3¾ oz.	5 oz.	6¼ oz.	7½ oz.	8¾ oz.	10 oz.	11¼ oz.	12½ oz.
(a)	¾ oz.	(a)	1½ oz.	3 oz.	4½ oz.	6 oz.	7½ oz.	9 oz.	10½ oz.	12 oz.	13½ oz.	15 oz.
(a)	(a)	(a)	1¾ oz.	3½ oz.	5¼ oz.	7 oz.	8¾ oz.	10½ oz.	12¼ oz.	14 oz.	15¾ oz.	1# 1½ oz.
½ oz.	1 oz.	1½ oz.	2 oz.	4 oz.	6 oz.	8 oz.	10 oz.	12 oz.	14 oz.	1#	1# 2 oz.	1# 4 oz.
(a)	(a)	1¾ oz.	2¼ oz.	4½ oz.	6¾ oz.	9 oz.	11¼ oz.	13½ oz.	15¾ oz.	1# 2 oz.	1# 4¼ oz.	1# 6½ oz.
(a)	1¼ oz.	2 oz.	2½ oz.	5 oz.	7½ oz.	10 oz.	12½ oz.	15 oz.	1# 1½ oz.	1# 4 oz.	1# 6½ oz.	1# 9 oz.
(a)	(a)	2 oz.	2¾ oz.	5½ oz.	8¼ oz.	11 oz.	13¾ oz.	1# ½ oz.	1# 3¼ oz.	1# 6 oz.	1# 8¾ oz.	1# 11½ oz.
¾ oz.	1½ oz.	2¼ oz.	3 oz.	6 oz.	9 oz.	12 oz.	15 oz.	1# 2 oz.	1# 5 oz.	1# 8 oz.	1# 11 oz.	1# 14 oz.
(a)	(a)	2½ oz.	3¼ oz.	6½ oz.	9¾ oz.	13 oz.	1# ¼ oz.	1# 3½ oz.	1# 6¾ oz.	1# 10 oz.	1# 13¼ oz.	2# ½ oz.
(a)	1¾ oz.	2¾ oz.	3½ oz.	7 oz.	10½ oz.	14 oz.	1# 1½ oz.	1# 5 oz.	1# 8½ oz.	1# 12 oz.	1# 15½ oz.	2# 3 oz.
1 oz.	2 oz.	2¾ oz.	3¾ oz.	7½ oz.	11¼ oz.	15 oz.	1# 2¾ oz.	1# 6½ oz.	1# 10¼ oz.	1# 14 oz.	2# 1¾ oz.	2# 5½ oz.
1 oz.	2 oz.	3 oz.	4 oz.	8 oz.	12 oz.	1#	1# 4 oz.	1# 8 oz.	1# 12 oz.	2#	2# 4 oz.	2# 8 oz.
1 oz.	2¼ oz.	3¼ oz.	4¼ oz.	8½ oz.	12¾ oz.	1# 1 oz.	1# 5¼ oz.	1# 9½ oz.	1# 13¾ oz.	2# 2 oz.	2# 6¼ oz.	2# 10½ oz.
(a)	2½ oz.	3½ oz.	4½ oz.	9 oz.	13½ oz.	1# 2 oz.	1# 6½ oz.	1# 11 oz.	1# 15½ oz.	2# 4 oz.	2# 8½ oz.	2# 13 oz.
(a)	2½ oz.	3½ oz.	4¾ oz.	9½ oz.	14¼ oz.	1# 3 oz.	1# 7¾ oz.	1# 12½ oz.	2# 1¼ oz.	2# 6 oz.	2# 10¾ oz.	2# 15½ oz.
1¼ oz.	2½ oz.	3¾ oz.	5 oz.	10 oz.	15 oz.	1# 4 oz.	1# 9 oz.	1# 14 oz.	2# 3 oz.	2# 8 oz.	2# 13 oz.	3# 2 oz.
(a)	2¾ oz.	4¼ oz.	5½ oz.	11 oz.	1# ½ oz.	1# 6 oz.	1# 11½ oz.	2# 1 oz.	2# 6½ oz.	2# 12 oz.	3# 1½ oz.	3# 7 oz.
1½ oz.	3 oz.	4½ oz.	6 oz.	12 oz.	1# 2 oz.	1# 8 oz.	1# 14 oz.	2# 4 oz.	2# 10 oz.	3#	3# 6 oz.	3# 12 oz.
(a)	3¼ oz.	4¾ oz.	6½ oz.	13 oz.	1# 3½ oz.	1# 10 oz.	2# ½ oz.	2# 7 oz.	2# 13½ oz.	3# 4 oz.	3# 10½ oz.	4# 1 oz.
1¾ oz.	3½ oz.	5¼ oz.	7 oz.	14 oz.	1# 5 oz.	1# 12 oz.	2# 3 oz.	2# 10 oz.	3# 1 oz.	3# 8 oz.	3# 15 oz.	4# 6 oz.
2 oz.	3¾ oz.	5¾ oz.	7½ oz.	15 oz.	1# 6½ oz.	1# 14 oz.	2# 5½ oz.	2# 13 oz.	3# 4½ oz.	3# 12 oz.	4# 3½ oz.	4# 11 oz.
2 oz.	4 oz.	6 oz.	8 oz.	1#	1# 8 oz.	2#	2# 8 oz.	3#	3# 8 oz.	4#	4# 8 oz.	5#
2¼ oz.	4¼ oz.	6½ oz.	8½ oz.	1# 1 oz.	1# 9½ oz.	2# 2 oz.	2# 10½ oz.	3# 3 oz.	3# 11½ oz.	4# 4 oz.	4# 12½ oz.	5# 5 oz.
2¼ oz.	4½ oz.	6¾ oz.	9 oz.	1# 2 oz.	1# 11 oz.	2# 4 oz.	2# 13 oz.	3# 6 oz.	3# 15 oz.	4# 8 oz.	5# 1 oz.	5# 10 oz.
2½ oz.	4¾ oz.	7¼ oz.	9½ oz.	1# 3 oz.	1# 12½ oz.	2# 6 oz.	2# 15½ oz.	3# 9 oz.	4# 2½ oz.	4# 12 oz.	5# 5½ oz.	5# 15 oz.
2½ oz.	5 oz.	7½ oz.	10 oz.	1# 4 oz.	1# 14 oz.	2# 8 oz.	3# 2 oz.	3# 12 oz.	4# 6 oz.	5#	5# 10 oz.	6# 4 oz.
2¾ oz.	5½ oz.	8¼ oz.	11 oz.	1# 6 oz.	2# 1 oz.	2# 12 oz.	3# 7 oz.	4# 2 oz.	4# 13 oz.	5# 8 oz.	6# 3 oz.	6# 14 oz.
3 oz.	6 oz.	9 oz.	12 oz.	1# 8 oz.	2# 4 oz.	3#	3# 12 oz.	4# 8 oz.	5# 4 oz.	6#	6# 12 oz.	7# 8 oz.
3¼ oz.	6½ oz.	9¾ oz.	13 oz.	1# 10 oz.	2# 7 oz.	3# 4 oz.	4# 1 oz.	4# 14 oz.	5# 11 oz.	6# 8 oz.	7# 5 oz.	8# 2 oz.
3½ oz.	7 oz.	10½ oz.	14 oz.	1# 12 oz.	2# 10 oz.	3# 8 oz.	4# 6 oz.	5# 4 oz.	6# 2 oz.	7#	7# 14 oz.	8# 12 oz.
3¾ oz.	7½ oz.	11¼ oz.	15 oz.	1# 14 oz.	2# 13 oz.	3# 12 oz.	4# 11 oz.	5# 10 oz.	6# 9 oz.	7# 8 oz.	8# 7 oz.	[illegible]# 6 oz.
4 oz.	8 oz.	12 oz.	1#	2#	3#	4#	5#	6#	7#	8#	9#	10#
4½ oz.	9 oz.	13½ oz.	1# 2 oz.	2# 4 oz.	3# 6 oz.	4# 8 oz.	5# 10 oz.	6# 12 oz.	7# 14 oz.	9#	10# 2 oz.	11# 4 oz.

(a) The amounts cannot be weighed accurately without introducing errors. Change to measurement by using conversion table.

Table A-9—Concluded

25	50	75	100	200	300	400	500	600	700	800	900	1000
5 oz.	10 oz.	15 oz.	1# 4 oz.	2# 8 oz.	3# 12 oz.	5#	6# 4 oz.	7# 8 oz.	8# 12 oz.	10#	11# 4 oz.	12# 8 oz.
5½ oz.	11 oz.	1# ½ oz.	1# 6 oz.	2# 12 oz.	4# 2 oz.	5# 8 oz.	6# 14 oz.	8# 4 oz.	9# 10 oz.	11#	12# 6 oz.	13# 12 oz.
6 oz.	12 oz.	1# 2 oz.	1# 8 oz.	3#	4# 8 oz.	6#	7# 8 oz.	9#	10# 8 oz.	12#	13# 8 oz.	15#
6½ oz.	13 oz.	1# 3½ oz.	1# 10 oz.	3# 4 oz.	4# 14 oz.	6# 8 oz.	8# 2 oz.	9# 12 oz.	11# 6 oz.	13#	14# 6 oz.	16# 4 oz.
7 oz.	14 oz.	1# 5 oz.	1# 12 oz.	3# 8 oz.	5# 4 oz.	7#	8# 12 oz.	10# 8 oz.	12# 4 oz.	14#	15# 12 oz.	17# 8 oz.
7½ oz.	15 oz.	1# 6½ oz.	1# 14 oz.	3# 12 oz.	5# 10 oz.	7# 8 oz.	9# 6 oz.	11# 4 oz.	13# 2 oz.	15#	16# 14 oz.	18# 12 oz.
8 oz.	1#	1# 8 oz.	2#	4#	6#	8#	10#	12#	14#	16#	18#	20#
8½ oz.	1# 1 oz.	1# 9½ oz.	2# 2 oz.	4# 4 oz.	6# 6 oz.	8# 8 oz.	10# 10 oz.	12# 12 oz.	14# 14 oz.	17#	19# 2 oz.	21# 4 oz.
9 oz.	1# 2 oz.	1# 11 oz.	2# 4 oz.	4# 8 oz.	6# 12 oz.	9#	11# 4 oz.	13# 8 oz.	15# 12 oz.	18#	20# 4 oz.	22# 8 oz.
9½ oz.	1# 3 oz.	1# 12½ oz.	2# 6 oz.	4# 12 oz.	7# 2 oz.	9# 8 oz.	11# 14 oz.	14# 4 oz.	16# 10 oz.	19#	21# 6 oz.	23# 12 oz.
10 oz.	1# 4 oz.	1# 14 oz.	2# 8 oz.	5#	7# 8 oz.	10#	12# 8 oz.	15#	17# 8 oz.	20#	22# 8 oz.	25#
11 oz.	1# 6 oz.	2# 1 oz.	2# 12 oz.	5# 8 oz.	8# 4 oz.	11#	13# 12 oz.	16# 8 oz.	19# 4 oz.	22#	24# 12 oz.	27# 8 oz.
12 oz.	1# 8 oz.	2# 4 oz.	3#	6#	9#	12#	15#	18#	21#	24#	27#	30#
13 oz.	1# 10 oz.	2# 7 oz.	3# 4 oz.	6# 8 oz.	9# 12 oz.	13#	16# 4 oz.	19# 8 oz.	22# 12 oz.	26#	29# 4 oz.	32# 8 oz.
14 oz.	1# 12 oz.	2# 10 oz.	3# 8 oz.	7#	10# 8 oz.	14#	17# 8 oz.	21#	24# 8 oz.	28#	31# 8 oz.	35#
15 oz.	1# 14 oz.	2# 13 oz.	3# 12 oz.	7# 8 oz.	11# 4 oz.	15#	18# 12 oz.	22# 8 oz.	26# 4 oz.	30#	33# 12 oz.	37# 8 oz.
1#	2#	3#	4#	8#	12#	16#	20#	24#	28#	32#	36#	40#
1# 1 oz.	2# 2 oz.	3# 3 oz.	4# 4 oz.	8# 8 oz.	12# 12 oz.	17#	21# 4 oz.	25# 8 oz.	29# 12 oz.	34#	38# 4 oz.	42# 8 oz.
1# 2 oz.	2# 4 oz.	3# 6 oz.	4# 8 oz.	9#	13# 8 oz.	18#	22# 8 oz.	27#	31# 8 oz.	36#	40# 8 oz.	45#
1# 3 oz.	2# 6 oz.	3# 9 oz.	4# 12 oz.	9# 8 oz.	14# 4 oz.	19#	23# 12 oz.	28# 8 oz.	33# 4 oz.	38#	42# 12 oz.	47# 8 oz.
1# 4 oz.	2# 8 oz.	3# 12 oz.	5#	10#	15#	20#	25#	30#	35#	40#	45#	50#
1# 5 oz.	2# 10 oz.	3# 15 oz.	5# 4 oz.	10# 8 oz.	15# 12 oz.	21#	26# 4 oz.	31# 8 oz.	36# 12 oz.	42#	47# 4 oz.	52# 8 oz.
1# 6 oz.	2# 12 oz.	4# 2 oz.	5# 8 oz.	11#	16# 8 oz.	22#	27# 8 oz.	33#	38# 8 oz.	44#	49# 8 oz.	55#
1# 7 oz.	2# 14 oz.	4# 5 oz.	5# 12 oz.	11# 8 oz.	17# 4 oz.	23#	28# 12 oz.	34# 8 oz.	40# 4 oz.	46#	51# 12 oz.	57# 8 oz.
1# 8 oz.	3#	4# 8 oz.	6#	12#	18#	24#	30#	36#	42#	48#	54#	60#
1# 10 oz.	3# 4 oz.	4# 14 oz.	6# 8 oz.	13#	19# 8 oz.	26#	32# 8 oz.	39#	45# 8 oz.	52#	58# 8 oz.	65#
1# 12 oz.	3# 8 oz.	5# 4 oz.	7#	14#	21#	28#	35#	42#	49#	56#	63#	70#
1# 14 oz.	3# 12 oz.	5# 10 oz.	7# 8 oz.	15#	22# 8 oz.	30#	37# 8 oz.	45#	52# 8 oz.	60#	67# 8 oz.	75#
2#	4#	6#	8#	16#	24#	32#	40#	48#	56#	64#	72#	80#
2# 2 oz.	4# 4 oz.	6# 6 oz.	8# 8 oz.	17#	25# 8 oz.	34#	42# 8 oz.	51#	59# 8 oz.	68#	76# 8 oz.	85#
2# 4 oz.	4# 8 oz.	6# 12 oz.	9#	18#	27#	36#	45#	54#	63#	72#	81#	90#
2# 6 oz.	4# 12 oz.	7# 2 oz.	9# 8 oz.	19#	28# 8 oz.	38#	47# 8 oz.	57#	66# 8 oz.	76#	85# 8 oz.	95#
2# 8 oz.	5#	7# 8 oz.	10#	20#	30#	40#	50#	60#	70#	80#	90#	100#
2# 12 oz.	5# 8 oz.	8# 4 oz.	11#	22#	33#	44#	55#	66#	77#	88#	99#	110#

3#	6#	9#	12#	24#	36#	48#	60#	72#	84#	96#	108#	120#
3# 4 oz.	6# 8 oz.	9# 12 oz.	13#	26#	39#	52#	65#	78#	91#	104#	117#	130#
3# 8 oz.	7#	10# 8 oz.	14#	28#	42#	56#	70#	84#	98#	112#	126#	140#
3# 12 oz.	7# 8 oz.	11# 4 oz.	15#	30#	45#	60#	75#	90#	105#	120#	135#	150#
4#	8#	12#	16#	32#	48#	64#	80#	96#	112#	128#	144#	160#
4# 4 oz.	8# 8 oz.	12# 12 oz.	17#	34#	51#	68#	85#	102#	119#	136#	153#	170#
4# 8 oz.	9#	13# 8 oz.	18#	36#	54#	72#	90#	108#	126#	144#	162#	180#
4# 12 oz.	9# 8 oz.	14# 4 oz.	19#	38#	57#	76#	95#	114#	133#	152#	171#	190#
5#	10#	15#	20#	40#	60#	80#	100#	120#	140#	160#	180#	200#
5# 4 oz.	10# 8 oz.	15# 12 oz.	21#	42#	63#	84#	105#	126#	147#	168#	189#	210#
5# 8 oz.	11#	16# 8 oz.	22#	44#	66#	88#	110#	132#	154#	176#	198#	220#
5# 12 oz.	11# 8 oz.	17# 4 oz.	23#	46#	69#	92#	115#	138#	161#	184#	207#	230#
6#	12#	18#	24#	48#	72#	96#	120#	144#	168#	192#	216#	240#
6# 4 oz.	12# 8 oz.	18# 12 oz.	25#	50#	75#	100#	125#	150#	175#	200#	225#	250#
7# 8 oz.	15#	22# 8 oz.	30#	60#	90#	120#	150#	180#	210#	240#	270#	300#
8# 12 oz.	17# 8 oz.	26# 4 oz.	35#	70#	105#	140#	175#	210#	245#	280#	315#	350#
10#	20#	30#	40#	80#	120#	160#	200#	240#	280#	320#	360#	400#
11# 4 oz.	22# 8 oz.	33# 12 oz.	45#	90#	135#	180#	225#	270#	315#	360#	405#	450#
12# 8 oz.	25#	37# 8 oz.	50#	100#	150#	200#	250#	300#	350#	400#	450#	500#

Instructions for Using Table A-10

1. Locate column which corresponds to the original yield of the recipe you wish to adjust. For example, let us assume your original sour cream cookie recipe yields 300 cookies. Locate the **300 column.**

2. Run your finger **down** this column until you come to the amount of the ingredient required (or closest to this figure) in the recipe you wish to adjust. Say that your original recipe for 300 cookies required 2¼ c. fat. Run your finger down the column **headed 300** until you come to 2¼ c.

3. Next, run your finger **across** the page, in line with that amount, until you come to the column which is headed to correspond with **the yield you desire.** Suppose you want to make 75 cookies. Starting with your finger under the 2¼ c. (in the 300 column), slide it across to the column headed 75 and read the figure. You see you need ½ c. + 1 T. fat to make 75 cookies from your recipe.

4. Record this figure as the amount of the ingredient required for the new yield of your recipe. Repeat Steps 1, 2, 3 for each ingredient in your original recipe to obtain the adjusted measure needed of each for your new yield. You can increase or decrease yield in this manner.

5. If you need to combine two columns to obtain your desired yield, follow the above procedure and **add** together the amounts given in the two columns to get the amount required for your adjusted yield. For example, to find the amount of fat needed to make 550 cookies (using the same basic recipe as above) locate the figures in columns headed 500 and 50 and add them. In this case they would be 3¾ c. + 6 T. and the required total would be 1 qt. + 2 T. fat.

6. The figures in Table 2 are given in measurements which provide absolute accuracy. After you have made yield adjustments for each ingredient, refer to Table 4 for "rounding-off" odd fractions and complicated measurements. You can safely "round-off" to 1 qt. as shown in Table 4, for the amount of fat needed in the recipe for 550 cookies.

Table A-10. Direct-reading table for adjusting yield of recipes with ingredient amounts given in measurement. (This table is primarily for adjusting recipes with original and desired portion yields which can be divided by 25. It is intended for use along with Table A-9, which is similarly constructed for adjusting weights.)

ABBREVIATIONS IN TABLE:

t. = teaspoon
T. = Tablespoon
c. = cup
qt. = quart
gal. = gallon
(r) = slightly rounded
(s) = scant

BASIC INFORMATION:

Measuring spoons
1 T.
1 t.
½ t.
¼ t.
for ¾ t. combine ½ t. + ¼ t.
for ⅛ t. use half of the ¼ t.

Equivalents
3 t. = 1 T.
4 T. = ¼ c.
5 T. + 1 t. = ⅓ c.
8 T. = ½ c.
10 T. + 2 t. = ⅔ c.
12 T. = ¾ c.
16 T. = 1 c.
4 c. = 1 qt.
4 qt. = 1 gal.

Measurement needed for number of portions indicated below.

25	50	75	100	200	300	400	500	600	700	800	900	1000
¼ t.	½ t.	¾ t.	1 t.	2 t.	1 T.	1 T. + 1 t.	1 T. + 2 t.	2 T.	2 T. + 1 t.	2 T. + 2 t.	3 T.	3 T. + 1 t.
¼ t. (r)	½ t. (r)	1 t. (s)	1¼ t.	2½ t.	1 T. + ¾ t.	1 T. + 2 t.	2 T. + ¼ t.	2½ T.	2 T. + 2¾ t.	3 T. + 1 t.	3 T. + 2¼ t.	4 T. + ½ t.
¼ t. + ⅛ t.	¾ t.	1 t. + ⅛ t.	1½ t.	1 T.	1½ T.	2 T.	2½ T.	3 T.	3½ T.	4 T.	4 T. + 1½ t.	5 T.
½ t. (s)	¾ t. (r)	1¼ t. (r)	1¾ t.	1 T. + ½ t.	1 T. + 2¼ t.	2 T. + 1 t.	2 T. + 2¾ t.	3½ T.	4 T. + ¼ t.	4 T. + 2 t.	5 T. + ¾ t.	5 T. + 2½ t.
½ t.	1 t.	1½ t.	2 t.	1 T. + 1 t.	2 T.	2 T. + 2 t.	3 T. + 1 t.	4 T.	4 T. + 2 t.	5 T. + 1 t.	6 T.	6 T. + 2 t.
½ t. (r)	1 t + ⅛ t	1¾ t. (s)	2¼ t.	1½ T.	2 T. + ¾ t.	3 T.	3 T. + 2¼ t.	4½ T.	5 T. + ¾ t.	6 T.	6 T. + 2¼ t.	7½ T.
½ t. + ⅛ t.	1¼ t.	2 t. (s)	2½ t.	1 T. + 2 t.	2½ T.	3 T. + 1 t.	4 T. + ½ t.	5 T.	5½ T.	6 T. + 2 t.	7½ T.	8 T. + 1 t.
¾ t. (s)	1¼ t. + ⅛ t.	2 t. (r)	2¾ t.	1 T. + 2½ t.	2 T. + 2¼ t.	3 T. + 2 t.	4 T. + 1¾ t.	5½ T.	6 T. + 1¼ t.	7 T. + 1 t.	8 T. + ¾ t.	9 T. + ½ t.
¾ t.	1½ t.	2¼ t.	1 T.	2 T.	3 T.	¼ c.	5 T.	6 T.	7 T.	½ c.	½ c. + 1 T.	½ c. + 2 T.
1 t. + ⅛ t.	2¼ t.	1 T. + ¼ t. + ⅛ t.	1½ T.	3 T.	¼ c. + 1½ t.	⅓ c. + 2 t.	¼ c. + 3½ T.	½ c. + 1 T.	½ c. + 2½ T.	¾ c.	¾ c. + 1½ T.	¾ c. + 3 T.
1½ t.	1 T.	1½ T.	2 T.	¼ c.	¼ c. + 2 T.	½ c.	½ c. + 2 T.	¾ c.	¾ c. + 2 T.	1 c.	1 c. + 2 T.	1¼ c.
1¾ t. + ⅛ t.	1 T. + ¾ t.	1 T. + 2½ t. + ⅛ t.	2½ T.	¼ c. + 1 T.	¼ c. + 3½ T.	½ c. + 2 T.	¾ c. + ½ t.	¾ c. + 3 T.	1 c + 1½ T.	1¼ c.	1¼ c. + 2½ T.	1½c. + 1 T.
2¼ t.	1½ T.	2 T. + ¾ t.	3 T.	⅓ c. + 2 t.	½ c. + 1 T.	¾ c.	¾ c. + 3 T.	1 c. + 2 T.	1¼ c. + 1 T.	1½ c.	1½ c. + 3 T.	1¾ c. + 2 T.
2¼ t. + ⅛ t.	1 T. + 2¼ t.	2 T. + 1½ t. + ⅛ t.	3½ T.	¼ c. + 3 T.	½ c. + 2½T.	¾ c. + 2 T.	1 c. + 1½ T.	1¼ c. + 1 T.	1½ c. + ½ T.	1¾ c.	1¾ c. + 3½ T.	2 c. + 3 T.
1 T.	2 T.	3 T.	¼ c.	½ c.	¾ c.	1 c.	1¼ c.	1½ c.	1¾ c.	2 c.	2¼ c.	2½ c.
1 T. + 1 t.	2 T. + 2 t.	¼ c.	⅓ c.	⅔ c.	1 c.	1⅓ c.	1⅔ c.	2 c.	2⅓ c.	2⅔ c.	3 c.	3⅓ c.
2 T.	¼ c.	¼ c. + 2 T.	½ c.	1 c.	1½ c.	2 c.	2½ c.	3 c.	3½ c.	1 qt.	1 qt. + ½ c.	1¼ qt.
2 T. + 2 t.	⅓ c.	½ c.	⅔ c.	1⅓ c.	2 c.	2⅔ c.	3⅓ c.	1 qt.	1 qt. + ⅔ c.	1¼ qt. + ⅓ c.	1½ qt.	1½ qt. + ⅔ c.
3 T.	6 T.	½ c. + 1 T.	¾ c.	1½ c.	2¼ c.	3 c.	3¾ c.	1 qt. + ½ c.	1¼ qt. + ¼ c.	1½ qt.	1½ qt. + ¾ c.	1¾ qt. + ½ c.
¼ c.	½ c.	¾ c.	1 c.	2 c.	3 c.	1 qt.	1¼ qt.	1½ qt.	1¾ qt.	2 qt.	2¼ qt.	2½ qt.
¼ c. + 1 T.	½ c. + 2 T.	¾ c. + 3 T.	1¼ c.	2½ c.	3¾ c.	1¼ qt.	1½ qt. + ¼ c.	1¾ qt. + ½ c.	2 qt. + ¾ c.	2½ qt.	2¾ qt. + ¼ c.	3 qt. + ½ c.
⅓ c.	⅔ c.	1 c.	1⅓ c.	2⅔ c.	1 qt.	1¼ qt. + ⅓ c.	1½ qt. + ⅔ c.	2 qt.	2¼ qt. + ⅓ c.	2½ qt. + ⅔ c.	3 qt.	3¼ qt. + ⅓ c.
⅓ c. + 2 t.	¾ c.	1 c. + 2 T.	1½ c.	3 c.	1 qt. + ½ c.	1½ qt.	1¾ qt. + ½ c.	2¼ qt.	2½ qt. + ½ c.	3 qt.	3¼ qt. + ½ c.	3¾ qt.

Table A-10—Concluded

25	50	75	100	200	300	400	500	600	700	800	900	1000
6 T. +2 t.	¾ c. +4 t.	1¼ c.	1⅔ c.	3⅓ c.	1¼ qt.	1½ qt. +⅔ c.	2 qt. +⅓ c.	2½ qt.	2¾ qt. +⅔ c.	3¼ qt. +⅓ c.	3¾ qt.	1 gal. +⅔ c.
¼ c. +3 T.	¾ c. +2 T.	1¼ c. +1 T.	1¾ c.	3½ c.	1¼ qt. +¼ c.	1¾ qt.	2 qt. +¾ c.	2½ qt. +½ c.	3 qt. +¼ c.	3½ qt.	3¾ qt. +¾ c.	1 gal. +1½ c.
½ c.	1 c.	1½ c.	2 c.	1 qt.	1½ qt.	2 qt.	2½ qt.	3 qt.	3½ qt.	1 gal.	1 gal. +2 c.	1 gal. +1 qt.
½ c. +1 T.	1 c. +2 T.	1½ c. + 3 T.	2¼ c.	1 qt. +½ c.	1½ qt. +¾ c.	2¼ qt.	2¾ qt. +¼ c.	3¼ qt. +½ c.	3¾ qt. +¾ c.	1 gal. +2 c.	1¼ gal. +¼ c.	1¼ gal. +2½ c.
½ c. +4 t.	1 c. +2 T. +2 t.	1¾ c.	2⅓ c.	1 qt. +⅔ c.	1¾ qt.	2¼ qt. +⅓ c.	2¾ qt. +⅔ c.	3½ qt.	1 gal. +⅓ c.	1 gal. +2⅔ c.	1¼ gal. +1 c.	1¼ gal. +3⅓ c.
½ c. +2 T.	1¼ c.	1¾ c. +2 T.	2½ c.	1¼ qt.	1¾ qt. +½ c.	2½ qt.	3 qt. +½ c.	3¾ qt.	1 gal. +1½ c.	1¼ gal.	1¼ gal. +2½ c.	1½ gal. +1 c.
⅔ c.	1⅓ c.	2 c.	2⅔ c.	1¼ qt. +⅓ c.	2 qt.	2½ qt. +⅔ c.	3 qt. +1⅓ c.	1 gal.	1 gal. +2⅔ c.	1¼ gal. +1⅓ c.	1½ gal.	1½ gal. +2⅔ c.
½ c. +3 T.	1¼ c. +2 T.	2 c. +1 T.	2¾ c.	1¼ qt. +½ c.	2 qt. +¼ c.	2¾ qt.	3¼ qt. +¾ c.	1 gal. +½ c.	1 gal. +3¼ c.	1¼ gal. +2 c.	1½ gal. +¾ c.	1½ gal. +3½ c.
¾ c.	1½ c.	2¼ c.	3 c.	1½ qt.	2¼ qt.	3 qt.	3¾ qt.	1 gal. +2 c.	1¼ gal. +1 c.	1½ gal.	1½ gal. +3 c.	1¾ gal. +2 c.
¾ c. +1 T.	1½ c. +2 T.	2¼ c. +3 T.	3¼ c.	1½ qt. +½ c.	2¼ qt. +¾ c.	3¼ qt.	1 gal. +¼ c.	1 gal. +3½ c.	1¼ gal. +2¾ c.	1½ gal. +2 c.	1¾ gal. +1¼ c.	2 gal. +½ c.
3 c. +4 t.	1⅔ c.	2½ c.	3⅓ c.	1½ qt. +⅔ c.	2½ qt.	3¼ qt. +⅓ c.	1 gal. +⅔ c.	1¼ gal.	1¼ gal. +3⅓ c.	1½ gal. +2⅔ c.	1¾ gal. +2 c.	2 gal. +1⅓ c.
¾ c. +2 T.	1¾ c.	2½ c. +2 T.	3½ c.	1¾ qt.	2½ qt. +½ c.	3½ qt.	1 gal. +1½ c.	1¼ gal. +1 c.	1½ gal. +½ c.	1¾ gal.	1¾ gal. +3½ c.	2 gal. +2½ c.
¾ c. +2 T. +2½ t.	1¾ c. +4 t.	2¾ c. +½ t.	3⅔ c.	1¾ qt. +⅓ c.	2¾ qt.	3½ qt. +⅔ c.	1 gal. +1⅔ c.	1¼ gal. +1⅓ c.	1½ gal. +2 c.	1¾ gal. +1⅔ c.	2 gal. +1⅓ c.	2¼ gal. +1 c.
¾ c. +3 T.	1¾ c. +2 T.	2¾ c. +1 T.	3¾ c.	1¾ qt. +½ c.	2½ qt. +¼ c.	3 qt. +3 c.	1 gal. +2¾ c.	1¼ gal. +2½ c.	1½ gal. +2¼ c.	1¾ gal. +2 c.	2 gal. +1¾ c.	2¼ gal. +1½ c.
1 c.	2 c.	3 c.	1 qt.	2 qt.	3 qt.	1 gal.	1¼ gal.	1½ gal.	1¾ gal.	2 gal.	2¼ gal.	2½ gal.
1¼ c.	2½ c.	3¾ c.	1¼ qt.	2½ qt.	3¾ qt.	1¼ gal.	1½ gal. +1 c.	1¾ gal. +2 c.	2 gal. +3 c.	2½ gal.	2¾ gal. +1 c.	3 gal. +2 c.
1½ c.	3 c.	1 qt. +½ c.	1½ qt.	3 qt.	1 gal. +2 c.	1½ gal.	1¾ gal. +2 c.	2¼ gal.	2½ gal. +2 c.	3 gal.	3¼ gal. +2 c.	3¾ gal.
1¾ c.	3½ c.	1¼ qt. +¼ c.	1¾ qt.	3½ qt.	1¼ gal. +1 c.	1¾ gal.	2 gal. +3 c.	2½ gal. +2 c.	3 gal. +1 c.	3½ gal.	3¾ gal. +3 c.	4¼ gal. +2 c.
2 c.	1 qt.	1½ qt.	2 qt.	1 gal.	1½ gal.	2 gal.	2½ gal.	3 gal.	3½ gal.	4 gal.	4½ gal.	5 gal.
2¼ c.	1 qt. +½ c.	1½ qt. +¾ c.	2¼ qt.	1 gal. +2 c.	1½ gal. +3 c.	2¼ gal.	2¾ gal. +1 c.	3¼ gal. +2 c.	3¾ gal. +3 c.	4½ gal.	5 gal. +1 c.	5½ gal. +2 c.
2½ c.	1¼ qt.	1¾ qt. +½ c.	2½ qt.	1¼ gal.	1¾ gal. +2 c.	2½ gal.	3 gal. +2 c.	3¾ gal.	4¼ gal. +2 c.	5 gal.	5½ gal. +2 c.	6¼ gal.
2¾ c.	1¼ qt. +½ c.	2 qt. +¼ c.	2¾ qt.	1¼ gal. +2 c.	2 gal. +1 c.	2¾ gal.	3¼ gal. +3 c.	4 gal. +2 c.	4¾ gal. +1 c.	5½ gal.	6 gal. +3 c.	6¾ gal. +2 c.
3 c.	1½ qt.	2¼ qt.	3 qt.	1½ gal.	2¼ gal.	3 gal.	3¾ gal.	4½ gal.	5¼ gal.	6 gal.	6¾ gal.	7½ gal.
3¼ c.	1½ qt. +½ c.	2¼ qt. +¾ c.	3¼ qt.	1½ gal. +2 c.	2¼ gal. +3 c.	3¼ gal.	4 gal. +1 c.	4¾ gal. +2 c.	5½ gal. +3 c.	6½ gal.	7¼ gal. +1 c.	8 gal. +2 c.
3½ c.	1¾ qt.	2½ qt. +½ c.	3½ qt.	1¾ gal.	2½ gal. +2 c.	3½ gal.	4¼ gal. +2 c.	5¼ gal.	6 gal. +2 c.	7 gal.	7¾ gal. +2 c.	8¾ gal.

3¾ c.	1¾ qt. +½ c.	2¾ qt. +¼ c.	3¾ qt.	1¾ gal. +2 c.	2¾ gal. +1 c.	3¾ gal.	4½ gal. +3 c.	5½ gal. +2 c.	6½ gal. +1 c.	7½ gal.	8¼ gal. +3 c.	9¼ gal. +2 c.
1 qt.	2 qt.	3 qt.	1 gal.	2 gal.	3 gal.	4 gal.	5 gal.	6 gal.	7 gal.	8 gal.	9 gal.	10 gal.
1¼ qt.	2½ qt.	3¾ qt.	1¼ gal.	2½ gal.	3¾ gal.	5 gal.	6¼ gal.	7½ gal.	8¾ gal.	10 gal.	11¼ gal.	12½ gal.
1½ qt.	3 qt.	1 gal. +2 c.	1½ gal.	3 gal.	4½ gal.	6 gal.	7½ gal.	9 gal.	10½ gal.	12 gal.	13½ gal.	15 gal.
1¾ qt.	3½ qt.	1¼ gal. +1 c.	1¾ gal.	3½ gal.	5¼ gal.	7 gal.	8¾ gal.	10½ gal.	12¼ gal.	14 gal.	15¾ gal.	17½ gal.
2 qt.	1 gal.	1½ gal.	2 gal.	4 gal.	6 gal.	8 gal.	10 gal.	12 gal.	14 gal.	16 gal.	18 gal.	20 gal.
2¼ qt.	1 gal. +2 c.	1½ gal. +3 c.	2¼ gal.	4½ gal.	6¾ gal.	9 gal.	11¼ gal.	13½ gal.	15¾ gal.	18 gal.	20¼ gal.	22½ gal.
2½ qt.	1¼ gal.	1¾ gal. +2 c.	2½ gal.	5 gal.	7½ gal.	10 gal.	12½ gal.	15 gal.	17½ gal.	20 gal.	22½ gal.	25 gal.
2¾ qt.	1¼ gal. +2 c.	2 gal. +1 c.	2¾ gal.	5½ gal.	8¼ gal.	11 gal.	13¾ gal.	16½ gal.	19¼ gal.	22 gal.	24¾ gal.	27½ gal.
3 qt.	1½ gal.	2¼ gal.	3 gal.	6 gal.	9 gal.	12 gal.	15 gal.	18 gal.	21 gal.	24 gal.	27 gal.	30 gal.
3 qt. +1 c.	1½ gal. +2 c.	2¼ gal. +3 c.	3¼ gal.	6½ gal.	9¾ gal.	13 gal.	16¼ gal.	19½ gal.	22¾ gal.	26 gal.	29¼ gal.	32½ gal.
3½ qt.	1¾ gal.	2½ gal. +2 c.	3½ gal.	7 gal.	10½ gal.	14 gal.	17½ gal.	21½ gal.	24½ gal.	28 gal.	31½ gal.	35 gal.
3½ qt. +1 c.	1¾ gal. +2 c.	2¾ gal. +1 c.	3¾ gal.	7½ gal.	11¼ gal.	15 gal.	18¾ gal.	22½ gal.	26¼ gal.	30 gal.	33¾ gal.	37½ gal.
1 gal.	2 gal.	3 gal.	4 gal.	8 gal.	12 gal.	16 gal.	20 gal.	24 gal.	28 gal.	32 gal.	36 gal.	40 gal.
1 gal. +1 c.	2 gal. +2 c.	3 gal. +3 c.	4¼ gal.	8½ gal.	12¾ gal.	17 gal.	21¼ gal.	25½ gal.	29¾ gal.	34 gal.	38¼ gal.	42½ gal.
1 gal. +2 c.	2¼ gal.	3¼ gal. +2 c.	4½ gal.	9 gal.	13½ gal.	18 gal.	22½ gal.	27 gal.	31½ gal.	36 gal.	40½ gal.	45 gal.
1 gal. +3 c.	2¼ gal. +2 c.	3½ gal. +1 c.	4¾ gal.	9½ gal.	14¼ gal.	19 gal.	23¾ gal.	28½ gal.	33¼ gal.	38 gal.	42¾ gal.	47½ gal.
1¼ gal.	2½ gal.	3¾ gal.	5 gal.	10 gal.	15 gal.	20 gal.	25 gal.	30 gal.	35 gal.	40 gal.	45 gal.	50 gal.
1¼ gal. +1 c.	2½ gal. +2 c.	3¾ gal. +3 c.	5¼ gal.	10½ gal.	15¾ gal.	21 gal.	26¼ gal.	31½ gal.	36¾ gal.	42 gal.	47½ gal.	52½ gal.
1¼ gal. +2 c.	2¾ gal.	4 gal. +2 c.	5½ gal.	11 gal.	16½ gal.	22 gal.	27½ gal.	33 gal.	38½ gal.	44 gal.	49½ gal.	55 gal.
1¼ gal. +3 c.	2¾ gal. +2 c.	4¼ gal. +1 c.	5¾ gal.	11½ gal.	17¼ gal.	23 gal.	28¾ gal.	34½ gal.	40¼ gal.	46 gal.	51¾ gal.	57½ gal.
1½ gal.	3 gal.	4½ gal.	6 gal.	12 gal.	18 gal.	24 gal.	30 gal.	36 gal.	42 gal.	48 gal.	54 gal.	60 gal.
1½ gal. +1 c.	3 gal. +2 c.	4½ gal. +3 c.	6¼ gal.	12½ gal.	18¾ gal.	25 gal.	31¼ gal.	37¼ gal.	43¾ gal.	50 gal.	56¼ gal.	62½ gal.
1½ gal. +2 c.	3¼ gal.	4¾ gal. +2 c.	6½ gal.	13 gal.	19½ gal.	26 gal.	32½ gal.	39 gal.	45½ gal.	52 gal.	58½ gal.	65 gal.
1½ gal. +3 c.	3¼ gal. +2 c.	5 gal. +1 c.	6¾ gal.	13½ gal.	20¼ gal.	27 gal.	33¾ gal.	40½ gal.	47¼ gal.	54 gal.	60¾ gal.	67½ gal.
1¾ gal.	3½ gal.	5¼ gal.	7 gal.	14 gal.	21 gal.	28 gal.	35 gal.	42 gal.	49 gal.	56 gal.	63 gal.	70 gal.

Instructions for Using Table A-11

1. Locate column which corresponds to the original yield of the recipe you wish to adjust. For example, let us assume your original custard sauce recipe yields 24 portions. Locate the **24 column.**

2. Run your finger down this column until you come to the amount of the ingredient required (or closest to this figure) in the recipe you wish to adjust. Say that your original recipe for 24 portions requires 1½ T. cornstarch and 1¼ qt. milk. Run your finger down the column **headed 24** until you come to 1½ T. (for cornstarch) and then 1¼ **qt.** (for milk), etc.

3. Next, run your finger **across** the page, in line with that amount, until you come to the column which is headed to correspond with **the yield you desire.** Suppose you want to make 64 portions. Starting with your finger under the 1½ T. (in the 24 column), slide it across to the column headed 64 and read the figure. You need ¼ c. cornstarch for 64 portions. Repeat the procedure starting with 1¼ qt. in the 24 column; tracing across to the 64 column, you find you need 3¼ qt. + ⅓ c. milk.

4. Read this figure as the amount of the ingredient required for the new yield of your recipe. Repeat Steps 1, 2, 3 for each ingredient in your original recipe to obtain the adjusted measure needed of each for your new yield. You can increase or decrease yield in this manner.

5. If you need to combine two columns to obtain your desired yield, follow the above procedure and **add together** the amounts given in the two columns to get the amount required for your adjusted yield. For example, to find the amount of cornstarch needed for 124 portions of pudding (using the same basic recipe as above) locate the figures in colufns 60 and 64 and add them. In this case you would add 3 T. + 2¼ t. and ¼ c.

6. The figures in Table A-9 are in measurements which give absolute accuracy. After making yield adjustments for all ingredients, go to Table A-10 for "rounding-off" awkward fractions and complicated measurements. In our example (increasing from 24 to 64 portions) you can "round" the adjusted amount of milk to 3¼ qt. without upsetting proportions. The total amount of cornstarch in our example need not be "rounded-off" since it can be measured easily (¼ c.).

Table A-11. Direct-reading table for adjusting yield of recipes with ingredient amounts given in measurement. (This table is primarily for use with recipes with original or desired yields which can be divided by 8; yields of 20 and 60 portions are also included.)

ABBREVIATIONS IN TABLE:

t. = teaspoon
T. = tablespoon
c. = cup
qt. = quart
gal. = gallon
(r) = slightly rounded
(s) = scant

(a) = too small for accurate measure; use caution

BASIC INFORMATION

Measuring Spoons
1 T.
1 t.
½ t.
¼ t.
for ¾ t. combine ½ t. + ¼ t.
for ⅛ t. use half of the ¼ t.

Equivalents
3 t. = 1 T.
4 T. = ¼ c.
5 T. + 1 t. = ⅓ c.
8 T. = ½ c.
10 T. + 2 t. = ⅔ c.
12 T. = ¾ c.
16 T. = 1 c.
4 c. = 1 qt.
4 qt. = 1 gal.

8	16	20	24	32	40	48	56	60	64	72	80	88	96
(a)	(a)	⅛ t.(s)	⅛ t.	⅛ t.(r)	¼ t.(s)	¼ t.	¼ t.(r)	¼ t.(r)	¼ t.(r)	¼ t. + ⅛ t.	½ t.(s)	½ t.(s)	½ t.
(a)	⅛ t.(r)	¼ t.(s)	¼ t.	¼ t.(r)	½ t.(r)	½ t.	½ t.(r)	½ t.(r)	¾ t.(s)	¾ t.	¾ t.(r)	1 t.(r)	1 t.
¼ t.(s)	¼ t.(r)	½ t.(s)	½ t.	¾ t.(s)	¾ t.(r)	1 t.	1¼ t.(s)	1¼ t.	1¼ t.(r)	1½ t.	1¾ t.(s)	1¾ t.(r)	2 t.
¼ t.	½ t.	½ t.(r)	¾ t.	1 t.	1¼ t.	1½ t.	1¾ t.	1¾ t.(r)	2 t.	2¼ t.	2½ t.	2¾ t.	1 T.
¼ t.(r)	¾ t.(s)	¾ t.(r)	1 t.	1¼ t.(r)	1¾ t.(s)	2 t.	2¼ t.(r)	2½ t.	2¾ t.(s)	1 T.	1 T. + ¼ t.	1 T. + ¾ t.	1 T. + 1 t.
½ t.(s)	¾ t.(r)	1 t.	1¼ t.	1¾ t.(s)	2 t.	2½ t.	1 T.(s)	1 T. + ⅛ t.	1 T. + ¼ t.	1 T. + ¾ t.	1 T. + 1¼ t.	1½ T.	1 T. + 2 t.
½ t.	1 t.	1¼ t.	1½ t.	2 t.	2½ t.	1 T.	1 T. + ½ t.	1 T. + ¾ t.	1 T. + 1 t.	1½ T.	1 T. + 2 t.	1 T. + 2½ t.	2 T.
½ t.(r)	1¼ t.(s)	1½ t.	1¾ t.	2¼ t.(r)	1 T.(s)	1 T. + ½ t.	1 T. + 1 t.	1 T. + 1¼ t. + ⅛ t.	1 T. + 1¾ t.	1 T. + 2¼ t.	1 T. + 2¾ t.	2 T. + ½ t.	2 T. + 1 t.
¾ t.(s)	1¼ t.(r)	1¾ t.(s)	2 t.	2¾ t.(r)	1 T. + ¼ t.	1 T. + 1 t.	1 T. + 1¾ t.	1 T. + 2 t.	1 T. + 2¼ t.	2 T.	2 T. + ¾ t.	2 T. + 1¼ t.	2 T. + 2 t.
¾ t.	1½ t.	1¾ t.(r)	2¼ t.	1 T.	1 T. + ¾ t.	1 T. + 1½ t.	1 T. + 2¼ t.	1 T. + 2½ t.	2 T.	2 T. + ¾ t.	2½ T.	2 T. + 2¼ t.	3 T.
¾ t.(r)	1¾ t.(s)	2 t.	2½ t.	1 T. + ¼ t. (r)	1 T. + 1¼ t.	1 T. + 2 t.	1 T. + 2¾ t. (r)	2 T. + ¼ t.	2 T. + ¾ t.	2 T. + 1½ t.	2 T. + 2¼ t.	3 T.	3 T. + 1 t.
1 t.(s)	1¾ t.(r)	2¼ t.(r)	2¾ t.	1 T. + ¾ t. (s)	1 T. + 1½ t.	1 T. + 2½ t.	2 T. + ½ t.	2 T. + ¾ t.	2 T. + 1¼ t.	2 T. + 2¼ t.	3 T.	3 T. + 1 t.	3 T. + 2 t.
1 t.	2 t.	2½ t.	1 T.	1 T. + 1 t.	1 T. + 2 t.	2 T.	2 T. + 1 t.	2½ T.	2 T. + 2 t.	3 T.	3 T. + 1 t.	3 T. + 2 t.	¼ c.
1½ t.	1 T.	1 T. + ¾ t.	1½ T.	2 T.	2½ T.	3 T.	3½ T.	3 T. + 2¼ t.	¼ c.	¼ c. + 1½ t.	¼ c. + 1 T.	⅓ c. + ½ t.	⅓ c. + 2 t.
2 t.	1 T. + 1 t.	1 T. + 2 t.	2 T.	2 T. + 2 t.	3 T. + 1 t.	¼ c.	¼ c. + 2 t.	¼ c. + 1 T.	⅓ c.	⅓ c. + 2 t.	⅓ c. + 4 t.	⅓ c. + 2 T.	½ c.
2½ t.	1 T. + 2 t.	2 T. + ¼ t.	2½ T.	3 T. + 1 t.	¼ c. + ½ t.	¼ c. + 1 T.	⅓ c. + ½ T.	⅓ c. + 2¾ t.	⅓ c. + 4 t.	¼ c. + 3½ T.	½ c. + 1 t.	½ c. + 3½ t.	½ c. + 2 T.
1 T.	2 T.	2½ T.	3 T.	¼ c.	¼ c. + 1 T.	⅓ c. + 2 t.	¼ c. + 3 T.	¼ c. + 3½ T.	½ c.	½ c. + 1 T.	½ c. + 2 T.	½ c. + 3 T.	¾ c.
1 T. + ½ t.	2 T. + 1 t.	2 T. + 2¾ t.	3½ T.	¼ c. + 2 t.	⅓ c. + ½ T.	¼ c. + 3 T.	½ c. + ½ t.	½ c. + 2¼ t.	½ c. + 4 t.	½ c. + 2½ T.	⅔ c. + 1 T.	¾ c. + 2½ t.	¾ c. + 2 T.
1 T. + 1 t.	2 T. + 2 t.	3 T. + 1 t.	¼ c.	⅓ c.	⅓ c. + 4 t.	½ c.	½ c. + 4 t.	½ c. + 2 T.	⅔ c.	¾ c.	¾ c. + 4 t.	¾ c. + 2½ T.	1 c.

Table A-11—Concluded

8	16	20	24	32	40	48	56	60	64	72	80	88	96
1 T. +2¼ t.	3 T. +2¾ t.	¼ c. +1¼ t.	⅓ c.	¼ c. + 3 T.	½ c. +2½ t.	⅔ c.	¾ c. +½ T.	¾ c. +4 t.	¾ c. +2 T.	1 c.	1 c. +5 t.	1 c. +3½ T.	1⅓ c.
2 T. +2 t.	⅓ c.	⅓ c. +2 T.	½ c.	⅔ c.	¾ c. +4 t.	1 c.	1 c. +2½ T.	1¼ c.	1⅓ c.	1½ c.	1⅔ c.	1¾ c. +4 t.	2 c.
3 T. +1¾ t.	⅓ c. +5 t.	½ c. +2¾ t.	⅔ c.	¾ c. +2 T.	1 c. +5½ t.	1⅓ c.	1½ c. +1 T.	1⅔ c.	1¾ c.	2 c.	2 c. +3½ T.	2¼ c. +3 T.	2⅔ c.
¼ c.	½ c.	½ c. +2 T.	¾ c.	1 c.	1¼ c.	1½ c.	1¾ c.	1¾ c. +2 T.	2 c.	2¼ c.	2½ c.	2¾ c.	3 c.
⅓ c.	⅔ c.	¾ c. +2 t.	1 c.	1⅓ c.	1⅔ c.	2 c.	2⅓ c.	2½ c.	2⅔ c.	3 c.	3⅓ c.	3⅔ c.	1 qt.
⅓ c. +4 t.	¾ c. +4 t.	1 c. +2 t.	1¼ c.	1⅔ c.	2 c. +4 t.	2½ c.	2¾ c. +2½ T.	3 c. +2 T.	3⅓ c.	3¾ c.	1 qt. +2½ T.	4½ c. +4 t.	1¼ qt.
⅓ c. +5¼ t.	⅔ c. +3½ T.	1 c. +5¼ t.	1⅓ c.	1¾ c. +1¼ t.	2 c. +3½ T.	2⅔ c.	3 c. +2 T.	3⅓ c.	3½ c. +2½ t.	1 qt.	4¼ c. +3 T.	4¾ c. +2 T. +1 t.	1¼ qt. +⅓ c.
½ c.	1 c.	1¼ c.	1½ c.	2 c.	2½ c.	3 c.	3½ c.	3¾ c.	1 qt.	1 qt. +½ c.	1¼ qt.	1¼ qt. +½ c.	1½ qt.
½ c. +2¼ t.	1 c. +5¼ t.	1⅓ c.	1⅔ c.	2 c. +3½ T.	2⅔ c.	3⅓ c.	3¾ c. +2 T.	1 qt. +2½ T.	4¼ c. +3 T.	1¼ qt.	1¼ qt. +⅓ c.	1½ qt. +5 t.	1½ qt. +⅔ c.
½ c. +4 t.	1 c. +3 T.	1⅓ c. +2 T.	1¾ c.	2⅓ c.	2¾ c. +1½ T.	3½ c.	1 qt. +4 t.	1 qt. + ¼ c. +2 T.	1 qt. +⅔ c.	1¼ qt. +¼ c.	5½ c. +3 T.	1½ qt. + ¼ c. +2½T.	1¾ qt.
⅔ c.	1⅓ c.	1⅔ c.	2 c.	2⅔ c.	3⅓ c.	1 qt.	1 qt. +⅔c.	1¼ qt.	1¼ qt. +⅓ c.	1½ qt.	1½ qt. +⅔ c.	1¾ qt. +⅓ c.	2 qt.
¾ c.	1½ c.	1¾ c. +2 T.	2¼ c.	3 c.	3¾ c.	1 qt. +½ c.	1¼ qt. +¼ c.	1¼ qt. +⅔ c.	1½ qt.	1½ qt. +¾ c.	1¾ qt. +½ c.	2 qt. +¼ c.	2¼ qt.
¾ c. +1¼ t.	1½ c. +2¾ t.	1¾ c. +3 T.	2⅓ c.	3 c. +2 T.	3¾ c. +2 T.	1 qt. +⅔ c.	5¼ c. +3 T.	5¾ c. +1½ T.	1½ qt. +¼ c.	1¾ qt.	1¾ qt. +¾ c.	2 qt. + ½ c. +1 T.	2¼ qt. +⅓ c.
¾ c. +4 t.	1⅔ c.	2 c. +4 t.	2½ c.	3⅓ c.	1 qt. +2½ T.	1¼ qt.	5¾ c. +1 T.	1½ qt. +¼ c.	1½ qt. +⅔ c.	1¾ qt. +½ c.	2 qt. +5 T.	2¼ qt. +3 T.	2½ qt.
⅔ c. +3½ T.	1¾ c. +1¼ t.	2 c. +3½ T.	2⅔ c.	3½ c. +1 T.	4¼ c. +3 T.	1¼ qt. +⅓ c.	1½ qt. +¼ c.	1½ qt. +⅔ c.	1¾ qt. +2 T.	2 qt.	2 qt. + ¾ c. +2 T.	2¼ qt. + ¾ c. +½ T.	2½ qt. +⅔ c.
⅔ c. +¼ c.	1¾ c. +4 t.	2¼ c. +2 t.	2¾ c.	3⅔ c.	4¼ c. +4 t.	1¼ qt. +½ c.	1½ qt. + ¼ c. +3 T.	1½ qt. + ¾ c. +2 T.	1¾ qt. +⅓ c.	2 qt. +¼ c.	2¼ qt. +2½ T.	2½ qt. +1½ T.	2¾ qt.
1 c.	2 c.	2½ c.	3 c.	1 qt.	1¼ qt.	1½ qt.	1¾ qt.	1¾ qt. +½ c.	2 qt.	2¼ qt.	2½ qt.	2¾ qt.	3 qt.
1 c. +4 t.	2 c. +2½ T.	2⅔ c. +2 t.	3¼ c.	1 qt. +⅓ c.	5⅓ c. +4 t.	1½ qt. +½ c.	1¾ qt. + ⅓ c. +¼ c.	2 qt. +2 T.	2 qt. +⅔ c.	2¼ qt. +¾ c.	2½ qt. + ¾ c. +1½ T.	2¾ qt. + ¾ c. +3 T.	3¼ qt.
1 c. +5¼ t.	2 c. +3½ T.	2¾ c. +½ T.	3⅓ c.	4¼ c. +3 T.	5½ c. +1 T.	1½ qt. +⅔ c.	1¾ qt. +¾ c.	2 qt. +⅓ c.	2 qt. + ¾ c. +2 T.	2½ qt.	2¾ qt. +2 T.	3 qt. +¼ c.	3¼ qt. +⅓ c.
1 c. + 2 T. +2 t.	2¼ c. +4 t.	2¾ c. +2½ T.	3½ c.	1 qt. +⅔ c.	5¾ c. +1 T.	1¾ qt.	2 qt. +3 T.	2 qt. +¾ c.	2¼ qt. +⅓ c.	2½ qt. +½ c.	2¾ qt. + ½ c. +2 T.	3 qt. + ¾ c. +1½T.	3½ qt.

1 c. +3½ T.	2¼ c. +3 T.	3 c. +1 T.	3⅔ c.	4¾ c. +2 T.	1½ qt. +2 T.	1¾ qt. +⅓ c.	2 qt. + ½ c. +1 T.	2¼ qt. +2½ T.	2¼ qt. +¾ c.	2¾ qt.	3 qt. +¼ c.	3¼ qt. + ¼ c. +3 T.	3 qt. 2⅔ c.
1¼ c.	2½ c.	3 c. +2 T.	3¾ c.	1¼ qt.	1½ qt. +¼ c.	1¾ qt. +½ c.	2 qt. +¾ c.	2¼ qt. + ¼ c. +2 T.	2½ qt.	2¾ qt. +¼ c.	3 qt. +½ c.	3 qt. +1¾ c.	3 qt. +3 c.
1⅓ c.	2⅔ c.	3⅓ c.	1 qt.	1¼ qt. +⅓ c.	1½ qt. +⅔ c.	2 qt.	2 qt. +1⅓ c.	2½ qt.	2¾ qt. +⅓ c.	3 qt.	3 qt. +1⅓ c.	3 qt. +2⅔ c.	1 gal.
1⅔ c.	3⅓ c.	1 qt. +2½ T.	1¼ qt.	1½ qt. +⅔ c.	2 qt. + ¼ c. +1 T.	2½ qt.	2¾ qt. +⅔ c.	3 qt. +½ c.	3¼ qt. +⅓ c.	3¾ qt.	1 gal. +⅔ c.	1 gal. +2⅓ c.	1¼ gal.
2 c.	1 qt.	1¼ qt.	1½ qt.	2 qt.	2½ qt.	3 qt.	3½ qt.	3¾ qt.	1 gal.	1 gal. +2 c.	1¼ gal.	1¼ gal. +2 c.	1½ gal.
2⅓ c.	1 qt. +⅔ c.	5¾ c. +1½ T.	1¾ qt.	2¼ qt. +⅓ c.	2¾ qt. +⅔ c.	3½ qt.	1 gal. +⅓ c.	1 gal. +1½ c.	1 gal. +2⅔ c.	1¼ gal. +1 c.	1¼ gal. +3⅓ c.	1½ gal. +1⅔ c.	1¾ gal.
2⅔ c.	1¼ qt. +⅓ c.	1½ qt. +⅔ c.	2 qt.	2½ qt. +⅔ c.	3¼ qt. +⅓ c.	1 gal.	1 gal. +2⅔ c.	1¼ gal.	1¼ gal. +1⅓ c.	1½ gal.	1½ gal. +2⅔ c.	1¾ gal. +1⅓ c.	2 gal.
3 c.	1½ qt.	1¾ qt. +½ c.	2¼ qt.	3 qt.	3¾ qt.	1 gal. +2 c.	1¼ gal. +1 c.	1¼ gal. +2½ c.	1½ gal.	1½ gal. +3 c.	1¾ gal. +2 c.	2 gal. +1 c.	2¼ gal.
3⅓ c.	1½ qt. +⅔ c.	2 qt. +⅓ c.	2½ qt.	3¼ qt. +⅓ c.	1 gal. +⅔ c.	1¼ gal.	1¼ gal. +3⅓ c.	1½ gal. +1 c.	1½ gal. +2⅔ c.	1¾ gal. +2 c.	2 gal. +1⅓ c.	2¼ gal. +⅔ c.	2½ gal.
3⅔ c.	1¾ qt. +⅓ c.	2¼ qt. +2½ T.	2¾ qt.	3½ qt. +⅔ c.	1 gal. +2⅓ c.	1¼ gal. +2 c.	1½ gal. +1⅔ c.	1½ gal. +3½ c.	1¾ gal. +1⅓ c.	2 gal. +1 c.	2¼ gal. +⅔ c.	2½ gal. +⅓ c.	2¾ gal.
1 qt.	2 qt.	2½ qt.	3 qt.	1 gal.	1¼ gal.	1½ gal.	1¾ gal.	1¾ gal. +2 c.	2 gal.	2¼ gal.	2½ gal.	2¾ gal.	3 gal.
1 qt. +⅓ c.	2 qt. +⅔ c.	2½ qt. + ¾ c. +1½ T.	3¼ qt.	1 gal. +1⅓ c.	1¼ gal. +1⅔ c.	1½ gal. +2 c.	1¾ gal. +2⅓ c.	2 gal. +½ c.	2 gal. +2⅔ c.	2¼ gal. +3 c.	2½ gal. +3⅓ c.	2¾ gal. +3⅔ c.	3¼ gal.
1 qt. +⅔ c.	2¼ qt. +⅓ c.	2¾ qt. +⅔ c.	3½ qt.	1 gal. +2⅔ c.	1¼ gal. +3⅓ c.	1¾ gal.	2 gal. +⅔ c.	2 gal. +3 c.	2¼ gal. +1⅓ c.	2½ gal. +2 c.	2¾ gal. +2⅔ c.	3 gal. +3⅓ c.	3½ gal.
1¼ qt.	2½ qt.	3 qt. +½ c.	3¾ qt.	1¼ gal.	1½ gal. +1 c.	1¾ gal. +2 c.	2 gal. +3 c.	2¼ gal. +1⅙ c.	2½ gal.	2¾ gal. +1 c.	3 gal. +2 c.	3¼ gal. +3 c.	3¾ gal.
1¼ qt. +⅓ c.	2½ qt. +⅔ c.	3 qt. +1⅓ c.	1 gal.	1¼ gal. +1⅓ c.	1½ gal. +2⅔ c.	2 gal.	2¼ gal. +1⅓ c.	2½ gal.	2½ gal. +2⅔ c.	3 gal.	3¼ gal. +1⅓ c.	3½ gal. +2⅔ c.	4 gal.
1½ qt. +⅔ c.	3¼ qt. +⅓ c.	1 gal. +⅔ c.	1¼ gal.	1 ½gal. +2⅔ c.	2 gal. +1⅓ c.	2½ gal.	2¾ gal. +2⅔ c.	3 gal. +2 c.	3¼ gal. +1⅓ c.	3¾ gal.	4 gal. +2⅔ c.	4½ gal. +1⅓ c.	5 gal.
2 qt.	1 gal.	1¼ gal.	1½ gal.	2 gal.	2½ gal.	3 gal.	3½ gal.	3¾ gal.	4 gal.	4½ gal.	5 gal.	5½ gal.	6 gal.

Table A–12. Guide for Rounding-off Weights and Measures

These values for rounding have been calculated to be within the limits of error normally introduced in the handling of ingredients in preparing foods. They are intended to aid in "rounding" fractions and complex measurements and weights into amounts which are as simple as possible to weigh or measure while maintaining the accuracy needed for quality control in products.

Scan your adjusted recipe yields for measurements or weights which would be difficult to handle with the equipment you have. Check the table to see how to "round" these amounts safely without changing the quality of the product.

WEIGHTS

Item	If the total amount of an ingredient is	Round it to
	less than 2 oz.	$^1/_4$, $^1/_2$, $^3/_4$ oz. amounts oz. amounts
Various Miscellaneous Ingredients	2 oz. to 10 oz.	closest $^1/_4$ oz.
	more than 10 oz, but less than 2 lb. 8 oz.	closest ½ oz.
	2 lb. 8 oz. to 5 lb.	closest full oz.
	more than 5 lb.	closest ¼ lb.

MEASURES

Item	If the total amount of an ingredient is	Round it to
	less than 1 tbsp.	closest = ⅛ tsp.
Primarily spices seasonings flavorings condiments leavenings and similar items	{more than 1 tbsp. but less than 3 tabsp.	closest ¼ tsp.
	3 tbsp. to ½ cup	closest ½ tsp. or convert to weight
	{more than ½ cup but less than ¾ cup	closest full tsp. or convert to weight
	{more than ¾ cup but less than 2 cups	closest full tbsp. or convert to weight
	2 cups to 2 qt.	nearest ¼ cup
Primarily milk water eggs juice oil syrup molasses etc.	{more than 2 qt. but less than 4 qt.	nearest ½ cup
	1 to 2 gal.	nearest full cup or ¼ qt.
	{more than 2 gal. but less than 10 gal.	nearest full qt.
	{more than 10 gal. but less than 20 gal.	closest ½ gal.
	over 20 gal.	closest full gal.

Source: *Standardizing Recipes for Institutional Use;* Circular 233, Agr. Ex. Station, Michigan State University.

Appendix B
Converting to the
Metric System

The metric system originated with the French right after the Revolution. For a long time they had operated on a cumbersome system and, in the drastic overhaul they were making of many systems in France, the French decided to introduce a new system of weights and measures based on the decimal units. They also wanted as much as possible to make the translation of weights into measures or vice versa as simple as possible.

The basic unit they selected for weight was a gram, which was also a cubic millimeter of water at 20°C., so 1,000 millimeters of water was equal to a kilogram or 1000 grams. Various terms were taken from the Greek language to indicate values. Some of the most common were:

Liter:	Basic unit of measure is 1,000 milliliters and equal to 1,000 grams of water; slightly more than our quart.
Gram:	Basic unit of mass; 1,000 grams is equal to a liter of water, equivalent of about 2.2 pounds.
Meter:	Basic unit of length; slightly longer than our yard.
Deca-:	Means 10 times; thus a decameter is 10 meters.
Hecto-:	Means 100 times; thus a hectoliter is 100 liters.
Kilo-:	Means 1,000 times; thus a kilogram is 1,000 grams.
Mega-:	Means 1,000,000 times; thus a megacycle is a million cycles.
Giga-:	Means a billion times; thus a gigameter is a billion meters.
Tera-:	Means a trillion times; thus a teragram is a trillion grams.
Deci-:	Means 1/10 of; such as a decimeter.
Centi-:	Means 1/100 of; such as a centigram.
Milli-:	Means 1/1,000 of; such as a milliliter.
Micro-:	Means a millionth of; such as a micrometer.
Nano-:	Means a billionth of; such as a nanoliter.
Pico-:	Means a trillionth of; such as a picometer.

Thus, a hectometer is 100 meters; if used to indicate square meters, the term may be hectare instead of hectometer, which is 2.5 acres.

To translate one of our units of weight or measure to metric, we need to know how much or how many units we have and then we can multiply this value by the value given in Table 5-2 on page 116. For instance, if we have six feet and wish to change this to meters, the table indicates that we multiply the number of feet by 30 to get centimeters, which would give a value of 180 and since centimeters are 100 to the meter, we find we have 1.8 meters. Or if we wish to move from metric to our own system, this table also lists a factor which we use to multiply the metric value. For instance, if one had a value of 700 grams and wanted to know how many ounces they equalled, the table on page 116 indicates the metric value is multiplied by the factor of 0.035, which would give 24½ ounces.

There are other ways to translate metric to our values or our values into metric. For instance, there are slightly over 28 grams in an ounce or 454 in a pound. Thus, if one had 10 ounces and wanted to change this to grams, one would have about 280 (283 to be exact) grams. Or if one had 1½ pounds in a recipe, the translation would be 1½ × 454 = 681 grams. The text gives a number of these equal values between our system and the metric; these are in Tables 6-4 through 6-8 found on pages 138 and 139. Using these values will give slightly more accurate values than Table 5-2 (page 116). However, Table 5-2 is much more simple to use to translate values.

Table 5-2 is suitable for translating all Canadian and English values except for Imperial or British liquid volume. This is because the Imperial gallon (used in these countries) is 277.42 cubic inches while ours is only 231 cubic inches. This makes all British units 1.20 times larger than the American. Thus, a British pint, quart and other standard liquid units based on the gallon would be 1.2 times larger than ours and, if we wish to translate American units into British, we would multiply by 1.2 and to translate British units back into American, multiply by 0.833. Table 6-5 on page 138 gives many units between these two already worked out. Thus, we see in this table that an Imperial pint equals 0.15 American gallons, 0.6 American quarts, 1.2 American pints and 4.8 American gills. The metric measure and weight values are also given for the Imperial units.

The difference in the fluid ounce, however, between the American and British ounces is not the same as the other fluid measures. In the United States a fluid ounce is 1/16 of a pint or 29.6 cc (cubic centimeters) or 455.1 grains.* The British ounce is 1/20 of their pint, which is therefore 28.4 cc or 437.5 grains. (The British pint is 568 cc or 568 grams). The following table gives a multiplying factor similar to Table 5-2 and converts the British liquid volume into metric values and vice versa.

---

*A grain was set long ago as the weight of a grain of wheat.

British Imperial Fluid Measure Conversion to Metric Values

Liquid volume	When you know	You can find	If you multiply by
	Ounces	Milliliters	28.400
	Pints	Liters	0.568
	Quarts	Liters	1.136
	Gallons	Liters	4.544
	Milliliters	Ounces	0.035
	Liters	Pints	1.760
	Liters	Quarts	0.883
	Liters	Gallons	0.220

Our American cup used in measuring ingredients is about a fourth liter, but not quite if one wishes to be exact, for it contains in fluid measure 236 milliliters. There are 16 tablespoons in a cup which makes a tablespoon in our measure 15 milliliters. There are three teaspoons in a tablespoon so a teaspoon would hold 5 milliliters. (In British values this would make a cup 284 ml (milliliters), a tablespoon 18 ml, and a teaspoon 6 ml.) One can easily translate these values into grams as follows:

	American	British
Cup	236 grams	284 grams
Tablespoon	15 grams	18 grams
Teaspoon	5 grams	6 grams

However, an American cup of molasses or honey which is heavier than water would weigh about 300 grams and a British cup of this heavier material about 360 grams. But an American cup of flour is about 110 grams (British about 132 grams). It is much wiser, though, in working with most foods not to measure but to weigh — and recipes should call for weights rather than measures whenever possible because this gives far more accuracy and more standard products.

Using such equivalents as given here, the recipe for Bechamel Sauce on page 28 would translate into metric values as follows:

1. A gallon is 3.8 liters and $2 \times 3.8 = 7.6$ liters is the total yield.
2. A ¼ c portion is calculated as $236 \times .25 = 60$ ml.
3. The 1½ gal of white stock would be $1½ \times 3.8 = 5.7$ liters.
4. 2 oz of sliced onions or ¼ cup would be respectively 55 grams or 60 ml.
5. The carrots would be 225 grams or about 350 ml.
6. Since the bay leaves are by count, there is no change in values.
7. A pound of butter is 450 grams or 2 c or about 470 ml.
8. A pound of flour is 450 grams or 4 c or about 940 ml, about a liter.
9. A gallon of milk is 3.8 liters.
10. A ½ oz of salt is about 15 grams or 1 T equals 15 ml.

11. A t of pepper equals 5 ml.
12. In the first instruction under Method, the 4 qt of liquid would be changed to 3.8 liters.

Undoubtedly as we move into the metric system, many recipes will be retested and perhaps some slightly different amounts may be specified to round off values in metric units, such differences not causing an appreciable difference in the product.

Many of the tables we use will also have to be revised. For instance, Table A-3, page 586, could easily be revised to read:

Beverages

Cocoa	100 g	235 ml (1 c)*
Coffee, urn grind	100 g	235 ml (1 c)
Coffee, instant	25 g	120 ml (1/2 c)
Tea	100 g	330 ml (1-1/3 c)

Cereals and Cereal Products

Barley, pearl	100 g	130 ml (.55 c)
Etc.		

*Measures are American and not British.

We will also change our kitchen measures. Our 2-oz ladle used to portion gravy will become a 60 ml measure, but the size of the portion will be about the same. Similarly, a No. 12 ice cream scoop used as a tool to dish a rounded portion of about three ounces will be called perhaps a 90-ml scoop. A basting spoon holding a rounded three ounces might also be called a 90-ml spoon. Since potatoes are usually portioned at five ounces, the standard portion will become perhaps 150 grams, but the same dishing tool will be used.

Gradually, however, the names and labeling will change to the metric terms and, while there may be some slight confusion in making the change, once started and some familiarity is gained using it, there will be much less difficulty than expected. It will be much the same as changing a country over from driving on the lefthand side of the road to driving on the righthand side. When this was done in Sweden, a day for the change was selected when traffic was light. The driving speed was also drastically reduced. Within a few days drivers became accustomed to the change and soon developed driving habits and reactions based on the new system. The same will be true of the metric system. We might have a bit of difficulty at first, but soon we will become accustomed to the change and see that it is much more simple and easy to use. We are working today with a terribly complex and cumbersome system and it is high time we got rid of it.

(Author's note: Since the translation of Fahrenheit to Celsius or Centigrade values and vice versa is covered on page 114, it is not covered here.)

Glossary[1]

A la, a le (au, aux)   *To the, with, at* or *in;* in the mode of style; *a la Colbert* with Colbert sauce; *au jus,* with natural juice; *a la moutarde,* in mustard.

Abaisse   Thin bottom or under crust.

Abalone   Tenderized, thin muscle of a large sea snail; the portion looks much like a veal cutlet in shape and is like a scallop in texture, flavor, and color.

Abatis   Giblets; *abatis,* heads, liver, kidneys, giblets, and so forth.

Absinthe   A liqueur having a licorice-like flavor.

Acids   Acidulated liquids used in cooking, such as plain or seasoned vinegar, lemon juice, tomato juice, and other tart liquids.

Agar Agar   Seaweed product with gelatinous properties used to make permanent emulsions.

Aide   Kitchen or dining room helper.

Aiguilettes   Small strips of cooked meat; stuffed puff pastes served as hors d'oeuvres.

Ail   Garlic; *aillade* or *aioli,* mayonnaise garlic sauce that may also contain mustard.

A la king   With cream or bechamel sauce containing mushrooms, green peppers, and pimientos.

A la mode   In the usual fashion; *boeuf a la mode,* braised larded beef; *cake* or *pie a la mode,* topped with ice cream.

Alimentary Pastes   Macaroni products, rice, and so forth.

Allemande   Velouté sauce thickened with egg yolks, *a l'allemande,* German style.

Almond   *Amande* (Fr.); *a l'amande,* slivered almonds sautéed lightly in butter and served over fish; *amandine,* served with almonds.

Almond Paste   Ground almonds, sugar, and egg whites; also called marzipan.

Ambrosia   A mixture of fruit and coconut used as a dessert; *ambrasin* (Fr).

Amontillado   A semi-dry sherry.

---

[1] Diacritical markings to indicate pronounciation in many foreign words are omitted in this text. The author has taken the viewpoint that these words are now so commonly used in the food service field that in a text of this type such markings are not necessary. Many of these words may now be considered to be Anglicized. For instance, there is no longer a need to write *purée* when we no longer write *fricassee* with the accent. To avoid mispronunciation, the author has at times used the markings. This should be taken, not as a lack of consistency, but as a necessary guide to those not acquainted with such terms.

Anchovy   A small salted fish used for appetizers and seasoning; *anchois* (Fr.)

Andalouse   Spanish style; mayonnaise mixed with heavy red tomato puree and perhaps chopped peppers and pimentos; not to be confused with our Spanish sauce made of whole tomatoes, onion, peppers, and garlic, which is more heavily seasoned.

Angel Food   A white cake leavened with egg whites.

Angels on Horseback   Oysters broiled with strips of bacon around them and served on toast.

Anisette   A cordial heavily flavored with anise seed, giving it a licorice flavor.

Annatto   A yellow food coloring frequently used to color cheese and butter.

Antipasto   Italian hors d'oeuvres, relishes, and other foods used as a first course or as snacks.

Arroz con Pollo   A Spanish dish of chicken and rice; the sauce usually has tomatoes in it.

Artichoke   *Artichaut* (Fr); bud of a plant belonging to the thistle family and usually called Globe or French artichoke in contrast to the Jerusalem or Girasole artichoke, which is a tuber resembling a potato.

Aspic   Gelatin-set mixture; may be clear or seasoned with meat stock, spices, tomato puree, or other foods; may be used as a glaze or as a body in which to set other foods.

Attereaux   Skewers; to alternate pieces of food on a skewer and then bake or broil or cook.

Au Beurre   Cooked in butter.

Au Bleu   Live fish stunned with a sharp blow on the head, cleaned quickly, and plunged into a boiling, acidulated liquid or court bouillon; the flesh turns slightly blue.

Au Four   Baked in an oven; *petits fours,* small cakes; *paté de petit four,* pastry of the little oven; *four* is French for oven.

Au Gras   See *gras (au).*

Au Gratin   Escalloped and covered with cheese; food covered with a sauce (usually cream or bechamel), sprinkled with crumbs and cheese, and baked; cheese may be omitted.

Au Lait   With milk.

Au Jus   With natural gravy.

Au Maigre   With no meat; a Lenten dish.

Au Naturel   According to nature; cooked simply, or uncooked.

Baba   A light yeast raised cake or rich sweetened bread; usually served soaked with rum and called baba rum (see *brioche*).

Bagels   Crisp hard rolls in the shape of a ring, frequently served with lox (salmon) during the Jewish holidays.

Bagration   Fish-base soup, made from a thin velouté, cooked macaroni, sole, fish quenelles, crayfish, and so forth; the macaroni and velouté base are the characteristic features.

Bain-Marie A hot-water bath for holding foods for service; a double boiler in which foods are cooked.

Bake To cook by dry heat; now usually done in an oven, but occasionally in ashes, under coals, or on heated stones or metals; when applied to meats it is called roasting.

Baked Alaska Ice cream on cake covered with meringue and baked in a quick oven.

Banbury A small tart filled with spiced citrus peels and raisins; also a small round English cheese.

Bannock Scotch cake made usually of oatmeal or ground barley.

Barbecue To roast slowly on a gridiron or spit, or over coals, or on hot stones in a covered pit or trench; while cooking, the food is usually basted with a highly seasoned sauce, or it may be cooked in the sauce, which is made of tomato catsup or puree, chili sauce, mustard, vinegar, spices, chopped vegetables, and perhaps some sweetening.

Barde Bacon or salt pork slices used to cover poultry or fish in roasting.

Bar-le-Duc A preserve of white currants, but also may be red currant jelly, gooseberry, strawberry, or other fruit preserve; seeds should be removed.

Baron Double sirloin of beef; saddle and leg of lamb or mutton.

Barquettes Small pastry shells for filling for hors d'oeuvres or desserts.

Baste To moisten food while cooking for added flavor or to prevent drying out; the liquid is usually melted fat, meat drippings, stock, water, water and fat, or a sauce.

Batter-dip To dip into a batter consisting of egg, milk, flour, salt, leavening, and perhaps sugar; used for deep-frying.

Bavarian A fruit gelatin mixture into which whipped cream has been folded before setting; called also bavarian cream; Fr. *bavarois.*

Bearnaise Hollandaise sauce seasoned with tarragon; *a la bearnaise,* Swiss style; means from Berne, Switzerland.

Beat To mix vigorously to incorporate air.

Beaten Biscuit A Southern unleavened bread made light by pounding and folding; phosphates have usually been added to the flour.

Bechamel One of the basic sauces; made of chicken or veal stock, thickened with *roux,* and finished with rich milk or cream.

Beef Steak Pie A meat pie, two-thirds beef and one-third kidneys, with vegetables in a gravy; baked with a biscuit crust.

Beignets Fritters.

Bel Paese A soft, rich Italian cheese.

Benedictine Orange-flavored liqueur originated by Benedictine monks.

Bercy A sauce of white wine or lemon juice, onions, meat marrow, demi-glaze, and melted butter; a fish sauce.

Beurre See *butter.*

Bifsteck A steak cut from the butt or large end of the beef tenderloin, weighing about 5 to 6 ounces.

Bigarrade Brown sauce seasoned with orange peel and juice; may be slightly sweet and used with roast duck; the sour and bitter Seville orange is best to use, if available.

Bill of Fare   The menu.

Biscuit   A small roll, either yeast or quick bread; a rusk, toast, and so forth; in French *biscotte* usually means a rusk.

Bisque   A thick cream soup made of shellfish; also indicates a frozen dessert, ice cream with finely chopped nuts added.

Blanc   White; white sauce.

Blanch   To precook or cook in boiling water or steam (1) to inactivate enzymes and shrink food for canning, freezing, or drying (vegetables are blanched in boiling water or steam, fruits in boiling fruit juice, sirup, water, or steam); or (2) to aid in removal of skins from nuts and fruits; many items after blanching are then dipped into cold water.

Blanc Mange   Cold pudding made of cornstarch, milk, sugar, and flavoring; usually molded.

Blanquette   Stew or ragoût in white cream or velouté sauce; the meat is white, such as veal or chicken breast; a light fricassee.

Blend   To mix thoroughly two or more ingredients; a creaming paddle, wire whip, or pastry cutter may be used on a mechanical mixer; see *beat, cut, knead,* and *mix.*

Blue Points   Small oysters, usually from Chesapeake Bay.

Boil   To cook in water or a liquid largely water at a boiling temperature (212° F at sea level).

Boitelle, a la   Cooked with mushrooms.

Bombe   Molded dessert of two or more ice creams; may also be called *bombe glacé.*

Bon Bons   Candies or sweets.

Bonne Femme   Term used for soups, stews, and so forth; simple home-style.

Bordelaise   Brown sauce seasoned with red wine, garlic, shallots, and diced or sliced poached marrow; onions are reduced in white wine and added to a velouté sauce and finished with butter, after which tarragon is added for a white *bordelaise* or a *bonnefoy sauce.*

Border   (Fr) *bordure* (*en*); to surround with a border, such as a planked item circled with duchess potatoes.

Borscht   Russian or Polish soup containing beets and cabbage and garnished with sour cream.

Boston Cream Pie   Two layers of cake filled between with cream pudding custard sauce and topped with powdered sugar or whipped cream.

Bouchee   Small cake or small patty shell or choux paste with cream filling; literally, "mouthful"; may also be small hors d'oeuvre made from puff paste.

Boucher   Butcher.

Bouillabaisse   Thick fish soup or stew; served in large soup plates or dishes with toast; may be seasoned with saffron, and should contain five or six different fish, among which should be mussels, clams, and lobsters; also called *soupe marseillaise.*

Bouillon Soup; stock is richer than a broth and usually comes from beef; (Fr) *bouilli,* boiled beef.

Boulanger Baker.

Boulettes Forcemeat balls.

Bouquet Garni Parsley, bay leaves, thyme, onions, and other herbs finely chopped; usually tied in a small cloth and cooked with the food but removed when proper seasoning is attained; also called *sachet* or *fagot.*

Bourgeois Natural; plain, family style; *a la bourgeoise,* to serve with vegetables; sometimes confused with *Bourguignonne.*

Bourguignonne A Brown sauce for fish, meat, and eggs, reduced with red wine and small cooked onions, with mussels added; for snails, a basic butter seasoned with chopped thyme, tarragon, garlic, chervil, marjoram, parsley, and lemon juice; cleaned, drained snails are returned to the shells and baked with this sauce.

Braise To brown meat or vegetables in a small amount of fat, then cook slowly in a covered utensil in small quantity of liquid; the liquid may be juices from meat, water, milk, cream, stock, tomato juice, and so on.

Bread (1) To coat with bread crumbs alone; (2) to coat with egg or liquid and then crumbs; or (3) to coat with flour, egg, and/or liquid and then crumbs; "to egg" usually means to bread.

Bread Sauce Milk flavored with onions, bay leaf, and cloves, thickened with fresh white bread crumbs.

Brie A soft, rich French cheese.

Bretonne Brown sauce with tomatoes, chopped onions, and garlic; or cold tart sauce with mustard and horseradish slightly sweetened.

Brioche Baked yeast bread, frequently sweetened and almost rich enough to be called a cake; may be somewhat like sweet dough products.

Brochet A skewer; *en brochette,* meat and food roasted or broiled on a skewer; *a la broche* is also used.

Broil To cook by radiant or direct heat.

Brouillé Scrambled.

Brown Betty Rich cake or bread crumb pudding, heavy with apples or other fruit.

Brown Bread Steamed bread served with baked beans; the bread usually is distinguished by the ingredients of white and rye flour, cornmeal, molasses, and raisins.

Brown Sauce One of the four basic sauces; see *espagnole.*

Brunoise Vegetables or meat diced in ⅛ inch squares.

Brunswick Stew Southern dish of chicken or rabbit or ground meat with corn, onions, okra, salt pork, tomatoes, and lima beans; the true stew is made of squirrel meat.

Brush To clean with a stiff brush; to brush on ingredients such as butter and fondant frosting.

Bubble and Squeak Corned beef and cabbage.

Buffet A large table displaying foods that are served from it; see *Russe.*

Burn To burn sugar on top of food with a hot poker, as for an omelet.

Butter   (Fr) *Beurre; au maitre d'hotel*, with soft butter spread over or with butter melted until it froths; *au meuniere*, with browned butter; *au beurre noir*, with black butter; each is butter with a bit of lemon juice, a bit of cayenne, and parsley added. *Beurre fondu*, melted butter; *beurre d'anchois*, softened butter seasoned with anchovy paste. Many basic butters are used as spreads for canapes or in cooking as seasonings.

Café   Coffee; *café noir*, black coffee; *café au lait*, coffee with milk; also used to indicate coffee house or restaurant.

Camembert   A rich, soft, French cheese.

Canapé   A small open-faced sandwich used for an appetizer; may be on a fried or toasted piece of bread or crisp cereal product; the spread is tangy.

Canard   Duck; *canardeau* or *caneton*, young or female duck, respectively.

Candy   (1) When applied to fruit, fruit peel, or ginger, it means to cook in a heavy sirup until plump and transparent, then drained and dried; can also be called crystallize. (2) When applied to sweet potatoes and carrots, it means to cook in sugar or sirup.

Canneloni   Thin strips of Italian paste stuffed with meat and cooked.

Capers   Small pickled buds used for garnish or seasoning; (Fr) *cappone*.

Capon   Desexed male chicken weighing usually from five to six lbs.

Caramel   Sugar heavily browned; to caramelize is to heat sugar or foods containing sugar until a brown color and a characteristic flavor develops.

Carne   Spanish for with meat; *chili con carne*, beans with meat.

Carré   Back and shoulders; the rack.

Casserole   A hollow mold of rice or potatoes or other products; a dish in which foods are braised or baked; a *cassolette* is an individual casserole.

Caviar   Salted roe of the sturgeon; see *roe*.

Cepe   A wild mushroom.

Cervelat   A smoked bologna sausage.

Chablis   A white, good-bodied wine; sometimes called white Burgundy.

Champignon   Mushroom.

Chantilly   Sweetened and flavored whipped cream.

Chapon   Capon (Fr); a crust of bread boiled or soaked in the soup; a crust of bread rubbed with garlic and placed in a salad for flavoring.

Charlotte Russe   A mold lined with bread, cake, lady fingers, or sponge cake and filled with a Bavarian; may also be bread or cake soaked with fruit sauce and served cold with whipped cream.

Chartreuse   A famous liqueur; a dish consisting of only vegetables and no meat, after the custom of the monks who founded this order.

Chasseur   A sauce consisting of equal parts of brown and tomato sauce with chopped onions or shallots, parsley, and a bit of lemon juice; oftentimes, on American menus, called *hunter sauce*.

Chateau, au   Specialty of the house; see *maison*.

Chateaubriand   A steak weighing about 12 oz or more cut from the center of a beef tenderloin; may be cooked variously; also the name given to a cold or hot sauce served with this steak.

Chaud Hot.

Chaud-froid Cooked meat prepared for service cold; frequently highly decorated; a sauce used to cover cold decorated meats; called *mayonnaise collée* if from mayonnaise, *chaud-froid brun* if from brown sauce, and *chaud-froid blanc* if from velouté sauce.

Chausson Fruit jam in a pastry puff; a covered tart.

Chef de Cuisine Head chef; *chef de nuit,* night chef; *sous chef,* assistant chef.

Chef's Salad Tossed greens and chopped vegetables garnished with strips of tongue, ham, cheese, or chicken and served with French dressing.

Chemise (en) Cooked with the skins on (usually potatoes); *chemiser* (Fr), to line or coat a mold.

Chenoise China cup; a strainer.

Cherries Jubilee Dark cherries in sirup slightly thickened with starch, covered with kirsch, and ignited, and perhaps served with a garnish of ice cream or whipped cream.

Chevalier Food dipped in batter, fried, and served with cream sauce.

Chicken Cacciatore Chicken sautéed in olive oil, then braised with diced onions, green peppers, whole tomatoes, and a bit of consomme and white wine, until tender. Mushrooms may be added.

Chiffonade Shredded or minced vegetables; shredded or minced onions, beets, parsley, green peppers, and chopped egg in French dressing.

Chili con Carne Beans with meat.

Chipolata Brown sauce with onions, mushrooms, little veal sausages, bacon, and carrots, seasoned with madeira or sherry wine; can also be tiny sausages served as hors d'oeuvres.

Chitterling Fried or pickled sausages made from hog intestines.

Chop To cut into small pieces with a knife or other sharp tool.

Chop Suey Chinese mixed vegetables seasoned with meat and soy sauce and served with rice.

Choux Cabbage.

Choux Paste An eclair or cream puff batter.

Chowder A thick soup containing diced potatoes and sautéed onions and bacon or salt pork.

Chow Mein Chicken or pork Chinese vegetable dish, with fried noodles and soy sauce.

Chutney A sweet East Indian relish made of mangoes and other ingredients; the usual accompaniment for curry.

Civet Rabbit stew or ragoût; see *jugged.*

Clairet Claret wine.

Clam Bake Roasting ears of corn, lobster, fish and clams, and potatoes, rolled with wet seaweed, then in wet cloths, and baked in a barbecue pit or 350° F oven; typical procedure is to bake on hot stones in a pit dug in the sand.

Cloche Glass bell used for covering a dish; *sous cloche,* under cover or bell.

Cochon Pig; *cochon de lait,* suckling pig.

Cockie-leekie or Cocky-leeky A Scotch soup; chicken broth with celery and leeks; cooked prunes may be served separately, and many recipes call for the stock from a rooster or cock.

Coddled Egg   Boiling water is poured over an egg; as it stands in the water, the egg is allowed to cook to desired firmness; in quantity cookery, placing eggs in cold water, bringing to a boil, and removing from heat to cook until done.

Colbert   Brown sauce seasoned with onions previously reduced in white wine; sauce is finished with maitre d'hotel butter; consommé with spring vegetables and poached egg.

Coleslaw   Shredded cabbage with boiled dressing or mayonnaise; hot slaw served after heating in a hot dressing.

Collops   Cutlets; may also be called *escalopes*.

Compote   Stewed fruit; occasionally poultry stew.

Confit   Preserve or jam; may also be called *confiture*.

Conserve   A preserve; fruit or vegetables in heavy sirup.

Consommé   A strong, clear, clarified soup made of two or three kinds of meat.

Coq-au-vin-rouge   Chicken sautéed in red wine and brown sauce with mushrooms and onions.

Coquille   Shell of shellfish used for *au gratin* fish dishes; coral of lobster.

Corned Beef   Pickled beef.

Côte   Rib, cutlet, or chop; *côtes de boeuf,* ribs of beef.

Cotellette   Cutlet or cutlet-shaped.

Cottage Potatoes   Thinly sliced raw potatoes sautéed in shallow fat.

Cottage Pudding   Warm cake served with hot fruit sauce over it; baked pudding served with a warm dessert sauce.

Coulis   Rich meat juice; frequently jellied strained gravy.

Country Style   Served with salt pork or fat bacon.

Coupe   Cup, goblet, or bowl; diced fruit served in a coupe glass topped with a frozen dessert or whipped cream.

Court Bouillon   Water, vinegar or wine, herbs, and seasonings in which fish is cooked or over which it is steamed; fish bones and trimmings may be used to enrich the stock.

Couvert   Setting; cover; place setting.

Cover Charge   Fixed charge added to a meal or food prices for entertainment.

Cream   To work one or more foods to a soft and creamy mass using a spoon, mixer, or other tool; applied to thorough mixing of fat and sugar to incorporate a large quantity of air, which gives a light, fluffy mixture; on mechanical mixer, creaming paddle is used.

Cream Sauce   A white sauce to which cream or rich milk has been added; a term sometimes incorrectly applied to bechamel sauce.

Crecy   With carrots.

Creme de Menthe   A liqueur flavored with mint; there are white and green varieties.

Creole   Louisiana-type cookery, using green peppers, rice, *filé* seasoning, okra, saffron, and so forth, in dishes.

Crêpe Pancake; *crêpes suzette,* thin pancakes rolled with orange butter, with cream center, covered with warm brandy or rum, and served flaming; the Russians call crepes *blinis* or *piroshki,* depending upon the type of filling used.

Crevette Shrimp; *crevette rose,* prawn about 1½ to 2 inches long.

Crimp To make deep gashes on salmon, cod, haddock, or skate as it leaves the water; soak in cold water for an hour or so, and then boil in salted water, and cook only to doneness.

Crisp To moisten and refrigerate until crisp; to cook until the outer surface is crisp.

Croissant Crescent-shaped rolls or croutons; also crescent-shaped confectionery.

Croquette Chopped meat, cone-shaped, breaded and deep-fried; binder of meat is usually heavy white sauce; sometimes applied to sweet deep-fried pastries.

Croustade Hollow, fried bread square into which food in a sauce is placed; may also be any starch product shaped to contain other foods.

Croute (en) Placed under crust.

Crouton Toasted or fried bread; frequently used as a soup garnish; *croutes* (Fr).

Cuisinier A cook.

Cuisson Meats braised or cooked in their own juices.

Cullis A puree soup made of pulped flesh of game, meat, poultry, or fish.

Cumberland A sauce made of currant jelly, lemon juice, port wine, lemon and orange rind, mustard, onions, and ginger; may be hot or cold.

Curaçoa An orange-flavored liqueur.

Curry East Indian stew containing curry seasoning; frequently, cooked meat added to a bechamel sauce which has been seasoned with curry; served with chopped nuts, shredded coconut, chutney, and other dishes.

Cut (1) To chop. (2) To incorporate fat into dry ingredients with the least amount of blending; on a mechanical mixer the pastry blender paddle is used.

Dagout Drippings; see *fond.*

Danish Pastry Yeast, sweet dough, and shortening rolled out similar to puff paste to give a flaky soft bread; used for breakfast rolls and other rich rolls.

Dariole A mold lined with thin paste, filled with custard, and topped with whipped cream.

Daube To braise in wine.

Dauphenoise Braised dish in sauce topped with buttered crumbs.

Decouper To cut up.

Degust To cook; to reduce or get rid of.

Dejeuner Breakfast; *dejeuner a la fourchette,* luncheon.

Delayer To soak; see *soak.*

Delicatessen Place where cold buffet foods are sold.

Dente (al)   Means *to the tooth;* a slight firmness remaining in foods after cooking, as in vegetables or macaroni products, giving some chew.

Denver Sandwich   Filling of chopped cooked ham added to lightly beaten egg; frequently served on toasted bread.

Devil   (Fr) *Diable;* usually tangy sauce with meat-stock base, seasoned with mustard, cayenne, and onions, reduced in white wine; pimientos, green peppers, and other minced items may be added; sometimes a tangy tomato sauce; deviled crab or deviled eggs are tangy preparations.

Devonshire Cream   Cream clotted by scalding it and removing clots as they form on the surface; served chilled.

Dice   To cut into cubes around ½ to ¼ inch in size.

Dinde   Female turkey; *dindon,* male turkey; *dindonneau,* young turkey.

Diplomate   Normandy sauce seasoned with lobster.

Dobos Cake   Thin layers of sponge cake filled with rich chocolate cream.

Dock   To pierce, prick, gash, or cut.

Dolma   Turkish forcemeat; ground meat mixture cooked in cabbage leaves.

Dredge   To coat lightly; see *flour.*

Dresser   To garnish.

Duchesse   Usually applied to mashed potatoes that contain egg yolk; the mixture is frequently used for potato puff; used also as a topping for baked meat pies; can be forced from a pastry tube into forms, piped around planked items, or used otherwise and baked.

Dugléré   With tomatoes.

Du jour   Food ready to be served; *du jour* means "of the day."

Eau   Water.

Eau de Vie   Brandy; literally, "water of life."

Eclair   Finger-like choux filled with cream or pastry cream; frequently chocolate-frosted.

Ecarlate   Any sauce containing red food, such as lobster coral, beets, and red tongue.

Ecrevisse   Crayfish.

Egg   See *bread.*

Emince   Finely minced; mincemeat; sometimes used to indicate thin slices.

Empanades   See *pasty.*

En Bellevue   In aspic; literally, "in good sight."

Enchiladas   Mexican tortillas filled with a chicken, cheese, tomato mixture, grated cheese on top; usually some raw chopped lettuce is added at the last minute.

En Cocotte   In small individual casserole.

En Coquille   In shell.

English Monkey   See *monkey.*

English Muffin   Round yeast bread baked on griddle.

En Papillote   To cook in paper bag.

Entrecote   Literally, "between the ribs"; frequently used to indicate a steak.

Entrée   Main dish.

Entremets Desserts served either cold (*froid*) or hot (*chaud*); *entremets de danseur,* desserts served at the end of a course meal; may also be applied to buttered vegetables or large salads.

Epaul de Mouton Shoulder of mutton.

Epigramme Small cutlet of tender meat.

Espagnole Brown sauce; one of the basic sauces made from brown stock and browned roux; a small quantity of tomatoes may be added.

Essence Rich stock of meat or vegetable flavors; an extract of meat flavors; finely divided or pulped foods used to give predominant flavor to a food; dessert flavorings may also be called this.

Estouffade (Etuver or Etouffer) Smothered and braised; frequently a term used to indicate chicken cooked in this manner.

Etuvee Type of stew.

Fagot Celery, bay leaf, pepper corn, thyme, and garlic wrapped together and used as a *bouquet garni.*

Faisan Cock pheasant; *faisans,* hen pheasant; *faisandeau,* young pheasant.

Fanchonette Small pie or tart topped with meringue.

Farce Forcement stuffing; *farci,* stuffed, filled with forcemeat.

Farina (Fr) *farine;* coarsely ground endosperm of wheat; French are apt to call all finely ground flours *farine.*

Fariner To dredge with flour; see *flour.*

Fausse Tortue Mock turtle; usually a soup made of green peas in imitation of real turtle soup; seasoned with sherry or madeira wine; stock is usually rich veal, and diced meat from cooked calves' head may be added.

Fermlere "Farmer's wife" style; baked in earthen dish with minced green onions, chives, parsley, butter, and a bit of white wine.

Feuilletée (pâte) Puff paste; means "many leaves;" reworked scraps are called demi-feuilletée.

Filet Boneless piece of meat, usually the tenderloin; *fillet,* boneless piece of fish.

Financière "Banker's style"; brown sauce containing diced ham, usually seasoned with mushrooms, truffles, and white or madeira wine.

Fines Herbes Finely cut green herbs used for seasoning or garnish.

Finnan Haddie Lightly smoked salted haddock.

Flamande Velouté sauce seasoned with rich fish stock, mustard, lemon juice, and chopped parsley; carrots, pickles, and grated horseradish may sometimes be added.

Flamed (Fr) *Flambé;* set afire with brandy, liqueur, or other product, usually served flaming.

Flan Custard; open tart.

Florentine With spinach; frequently means an item served over creamed spinach; Florentine soup is cream of spinach soup.

Flour To coat with flour; to dredge in flour; usually salt, pepper, and other seasonings are added to the flour, and paprika may be added for color.

Foie Liver; *foie de veau,* calf's liver; *foie gras,* goose liver.

Fold   To combine by using two motions, cutting vertically through the mixture and turning over and over by sliding the implement across the bottom of the mixing bowl with each turn; usually done with a spatula or whip; can be done with care with whip in mixer; with very delicate products, such as a butter sponge, the hands should be used.

Fond   Drippings in a pan; *fond brun,* brown drippings; also a rich stock of meat and vegetables.

Fondue   Melted or blended; a light custard-like entree that resembles a soufflé; hot melted cheese entree; *Swiss fondue,* melted Swiss cheese in white wine seasoned delicately with kirsch and dipped up with French bread; custard of eggs and milk poured over bread and diced meat or fish added, and product baked.

Forcemeat   Pulped meat bound together with soft crumbs and egg yolks and poached in tiny balls or pieces; used as a garnish.

Four   Oven.

Fourré   Coated with sugar, cream, or other preparations.

Franconia   Browned; potatoes browned with the roast.

Frappé   Partly frozen; coarsely frozen.

French Dressing   Oil and vinegar or lemon in the ratio of 2:1; a variety of seasonings may be added to give many variations.

French Ice Cream   Rich ice cream containing eggs; may also be seasoned with ground vanilla bean.

French Onion Soup   A bouillon soup thick with sautéed, thinly sliced onions and served in a *petite marmite* dish, topped with a slice of French bread covered with grated parmesan cheese, the whole dish richly toasted under a broiler before serving.

French Toast   Bread dipped in egg and sautéed.

Friandines   Small patties or croquettes.

Fricandeau   Larded and braised leg of veal; can also be large larded slice from the rump.

Fricassee   To cook by braising; usually applied to fowl, rabbit, or veal; for white fricassee, no browning occurs.

Fricot   Stew or ragoût.

Frit   Fried.

Froid   Cold.

Fromage   Cheese; *fromage glacé,* ice cream molded in shape of cheese.

Fruit   Fruit; *fruit divers,* mixed fruit; *fruit glacé,* candied fruit; *fruit secs,* dried fruit.

Fry   To cook in fat; (1) cooking in a small amount of fat and also called sautéing or pan-frying; (2) cooking in deep fat, called deep-fat frying.

Fumet   Stock from fish, game, or meats, reduced with wine and slightly more concentrated than an essence; a rich stock over which foods are steamed.

Galantine   Decorated boneless meat, game, or poultry piece; frequently has a crust around meat with decoration in the meat; boned meat or poultry cooked in a casing and served cold.

Garbure   Baked stew or thick soup containing much cabbage and salt pork.

Garde Manger   Cold meat cook.

Garnish   An edible food used to decorate another; (Fr) *Garniture.*

Gateau   Cake; *gateaux assortis,* assorted cakes.

Gaufre   Waffle; a crisp ice cream wafer.

Gelee   Jelly; any type of jel.

Genevoise   Rich fish essence reduced with red wine; sauce contains no meat; Geneva style, not Genoa style.

Genoise   Genoa style; rich in butter and eggs.

Glacé   Iced, frosted, frozen, glassy, glazed, candied, crystallized; some desserts are said to be *glacé* when covered with a thick sauce; a glaze; to coat with a thin sirup cooked to the crack stage, or to cover with a starch- or pectin-thickened gel; in the latter, pies, tarts, and bread may be glazed with apricot or strawberry glaze, a jam or jelly, and so forth; *glacé de viande,* meat glaze; *glacé de boeuf,* beef glaze; *glacé de veau,* veal glaze.

Glacé Royale   An icing; a sauce made of mousseline sauce and mornay sauce or cream sauce blended in equal amounts.

Glaze   A rich stock reduced one-fourth in volume used to heighten flavor in stocks, sauces, or meat dishes; a demi-glaze is rich stock reduced one-half; to coat meat, poultry, or fish with a meat essence containing a high amount of gelatin; to give a glossy, shiny coat; to place vegetables in a mixture of butter or margarine and sugar or sirup and coat with a glaze by sautéing or ovenizing.

Gnocchi   Italian pastry or cracker seasoned with parmesan cheese; Italian dumpling.

Godiveau   Forcemeat made of veal kidney.

Golden Buck   Welsh rarebit over poached egg.

Gorgonzola   Italian cheese resembling Roquefort cheese.

Goulash   Hungarian stew heavily seasoned with paprika.

Gras (au)   *Gras* is French for fat; cooked in fat, or covered with a rich meat gravy.

Gras-double   Tripe.

Gratin (au)   Browned; a food covered with sauce, sprinkled with crumbs and perhaps grated cheese, and browned.

Greek   (Fr) *Greque;* Greek style; usually seasoned with olive oil and garlic.

Grid   The part of a broiler on which foods are placed for broiling.

Grill   To fry on a griddle; sauté or toast; (Fr) *grille,* broiler; the term is no longer used in indicate broiling.

Grind   To reduce to small particles by cutting, crushing, or grinding.

Grits   Coarsely ground hominy cooked as a porridge and served for breakfast; (Fr) *gruau,* oatmeal, grits, groats, gruel.

Groseille   Gooseberry; *groseille rouge,* red currant; *groseille noire,* black currant.

Gruyere   Cheese resembling Swiss cheese.

Guava   An apple-like fruit that makes a tart, deep pink (almost red) jelly.

Gumbo   Also indicated by the term "okra"; a Creole-type dish; usually contains okra, tomatoes, and rice.

Hachis   Hash; minced meat, sometimes spelled *hachée*.

Haggis   Scotch sausage cooked in sheep's stomach.

Ham   Cured, smoked leg of pork. *Smithfield*, Virginia ham from pigs eating a heavy diet of peanuts; a drier, more heavily cured ham.   Westphalia, Prague, Polish, and Bayonne hams are similar to the Smithfield and require slow and extended cooking to tenderize.

Hard Sauce   Creamed butter and powdered sugar, flavored variously; used as a dessert sauce.

Haricot   Kidney or navy bean; stewed meat with turnips; *haricot vert*, green bean; *haricot d'Espagne*, red bean.

Harlequin   See *Neapolitane*.

Hasenpfeffer   Rabbit stew cooked with tart wine; may be finished with sour cream.

Hash Browned Potatoes   Boiled potatoes, sliced, chopped, or diced, and sautéed until they have a crisp outer crust.

Hashed Potatoes in Cream   Boiled, sliced, or diced potatoes in rich bechamel or cream sauce.

Hatelet   Small skewer; silver skewer.

High Tea   A formal tea more elaborate than an ordinary tea.

Hodgepodge (hotchpotch)   A mixture; a stew; *hoche pot* is a mixture of meat and vegetables served with broth in a soup dish.

Hollandaise   Sauce made of egg yolks, butter, lemon juice or vinegar, and seasonings.

Homard   Lobster.

Hors d'oeuvre   Appetizer; side dish after the soup in a very formal meal; means dishes served outside of the ordinary dishes.

Huitre   Oyster.

Hungarian Goulash   See *goulash*.

Hush Puppies.   Cornmeal paste deep-fried; a Southern dish, and very delicious.

Ice   Sweetened fruit juice and water; frozen.

Imperatrice   Rich supreme sauce; also name of a consommé.

Indian Pudding   A New England dessert of baked cornmeal, milk, brown sugar, eggs, raisins, and flavoring.

Indienne   Generally used to indicate dishes flavored with curry.

Irish Stew   A stew made of lamb or mutton with dumplings.

Italienne   Dishes distinguished by the use of Italian pastes and grated parmesan cheese; may also be used to indicate use of tomato sauce; ground meat sauce with vegetables and oregano used with spaghetti.

Jackson (a la)   A cream of potato soup; vegetables and macaroni may be added.

Jambalaya   Creole rice dish containing tomatoes, onions, saffron and other seasonings, and fish, shellfish, poultry, or meat.

Jambe   Leg; *jambon*, ham.

Jardinière   Mixed garden vegetables with carrots and turnips usually included; usually cut in strips ⅛ inch thick by 1 inch long, or diced.

Jolie Fille   Dishes fair to look upon; usually decorated pieces.

Jugged   Braised, and usually served in a casserole, as in "jugged hare."

Julienne   Vegetables or meats cut into matchlike strips; used for garnishing and seasoning.

Junket   A dessert of sweetened and flavored milk set to a clabber with rennet.

Jus   Juice of fruit, vegetable, or meat; see *au jus*.

Kebabs or Kebobs   Marinated pieces of lamb or mutton cooked on skewers; may also have vegetables or other foods between pieces of meat.

Kiev   Stuffed with seasoned butter.

King   See *a la king*.

Kippered   Lightly salted and smoked fish; *kippers*, smoked herring.

Kirschwasser   Liqueur made from cherries.

Kisses   Meringue-type dessert.

Knead   To work a thick product with a pressing motion by folding and stretching; to knead with a mechanical mixer is to use the dough hook.

Knöpfll   Tiny Swiss dumplings; made much like *spaetzle* except that dough is thicker; *klösse* (Ger).

Kosher   Food handled according to Jewish religious customs.

Kuchen   German cakes, not necessarily sweet; see *lebkuchen* below.

Kummel   Caraway; liqueur seasoned with caraway seed.

Lachs   Smoked salmon; *lox* or *locks*, a Jewish dish of thinly sliced smoked salmon served with bagels.

Lait   Milk.

Langouste   Spiny-back lobsters with no claws; only tails used.

Langues de Chat   Small cakes called "cat's tongues."

Lard   Bacon, salt pork, pig's fat; *to lard* is to pull strips of salt pork, bacon, or fat through meat previous to cooking it; *lardoon*, larding needle; *lardon*, strips of fat used for larding.

Lasagne   Broad, ribbon-like Italian noodle.

Lebkuchen   German cakes which are quite sweet; usually honey is a part of the sweetener used.

Legumes   Group of vegetables composed of beans, peas, and lentils.

Liaison   Thickening agent such as starch, yolk of eggs, and so forth.

Limburger   A soft, strongly flavored German cheese aged similar to the manner in which camembert is aged.

Limpa   A Swedish bread.

Locks   See *lachs*.

Loin   Area from last rib to rump, except on pork, which is from shoulder blade tip to rump; *longe* (Fr); *longe de porc*, loin of pork; *shortloin*, area from last rib to edge of hip bone.

London   *London mixed grille* is an English (double or two sides of loin) chop with kidney, bacon, small sausage, and mushrooms; a London broil is tender flank steak cooked rare and sliced thin.

Lox   See *lachs*.

Lucullus   Rich brown sauce garnished with truffles, cocks' combs, quenelles, foie-gras, chicken kidneys, and mushrooms; seasoned with sherry; applied to costly dishes.

Lyonnaise   Heavily seasoned with onions and perhaps some parsley.

Macaroon   Small cake or cookie made of beaten egg whites and sugar and almond paste or fine coconut.

Macedoine   Mixture of vegetables, either raw or cooked, for salad or vegetable; can also refer to a mixed fruit sauce or mixture of fruit.

Madeira   A wine much like sherry; brown sauce reduced with madeira wine; some make a madeira sauce with half brown sauce and half tomato sauce, and season with madeira wine or sherry; *Madere* (Fr).

Maggi   A flavoring essence, largely monosodium glutamate (MSG), used to add flavor to stocks, sauces, and gravies.

Maigre (au)   Without meat; food other than meat; used to indicate Lenten dishes.

Mais   Corn; sometimes used to refer to wheat or other cereals.

Maison (a la)   Specialty of the house.

Maitre d'Hotel   Person in charge of dining room; head waiter; see *butter*.

Manhattan   A cocktail made from bourbon whiskey and sweet (French) vermouth.

Marasquin   A liqueur made of maraschino cherries.

Marengo   Chicken fried in oil and braised in white wine and mushrooms; garlic and tomatoes are frequently added.

Marinade (also Marinate)   To soak in oil and vinegar or wine to give added flavor in the case of meats, also to tenderize; sometimes the marinade may be a pickling or brine solution.

Marmite   Small soup dish in shape of pot (see *petite marmite*); *grande marmite*, soup in which large pieces of meat cooked in the soup are sliced and served with the soup.

Marseillaise   Chopped onions, fine herbs, garlic fried in oil, reduced in red wine and chopped anchovies added to tomato sauce; *soupe a la Marseillaise* is a bouillabaise.

Martini   A cocktail made of gin and dry (Italian) vermouth.

Maryland   Meat or poultry dredged with flour, egg, and crumbs and fried; served with cream gravy and corn fritter.

Marzipan   Almond, egg white, and sugar paste confections in shape and color of fruit or vegetables; see *almond paste*.

Mask   To cover completely; usually applied to a cover of mayonnaise or other thick sauce, but may refer to a cover with forcemeat or jelly.

Matelote   Sailor fashion; onions and mushrooms sautéed, then reduced in red wine, with rich essence of fish added, and brown sauce; a dish of different sorts of fish (eel, carp, perch, and so forth) braised with vegetables and red or white wine.

Matignon   Minced raw or cooked mashed vegetables used for seasoning foods.

Mayonnaise   Oil, eggs, and vinegar or lemon juice in emulsified form for use as a salad dressing or preparation of other sauces; *mayonnaise collee* (see *chaud-froid*).

Meat Loaf   Ground meat with diced or minced vegetables shaped into loaf form and baked; loaf may be made of ground beef, ground veal, ground ham, or mixed ground meats or fish mixtures.

Meat Pie   Diced meat with vegetables in gravy, usually cooked under a biscuit or pastry crust; see also *pasty, pirog, piroshki, ruff, shortcake, tourtiere, turnover*.

Medaillon   A cake shaped like a large medal; beef tenderloin tips or small pieces of *foie gras* or other items.

Melba   Usually a dessert consisting of a half peach on ice cream, covered with Melba sauce (pureed raspberries or strawberries seasoned with Curaçao).

Mêlé   Mixed.

Melt   To liquefy.

Mere Poularde   A flat, unfolded plain or French omelet.

Meringue   Egg whites beaten stiff with sugar, used to top pies or desserts; adding more sugar makes a stiff meringue used as a base for many desserts.

Meuniere   Dredged with flour and sautéed in butter; see *butter*.

Mexican   Usually a dish containing *frijole* beans, onions, tomatoes, hot chili peppers, mild peppers, and kernel corn.

Mignon   A delicate morsel; filet mignon, the butt of the tenderloin cut as a steak and frequently wrapped in bacon; the French use the small end of the tenderloin for the *filet mignon*.

Milanaise   A dish with tomato sauce combined with *allemande* or *bechamel* sauce with some Italian pastes; some add parmesan cheese.

Mince   *Emince* (Fr); to cut or chop into small pieces.

Minestrone   Thick Italian vegetable soup distingushed by a leafy vegetable, red kidney beans, and an Italian paste among other products; usually served with parmesan cheese; there are at least four distinct types of minestrone soup originating in various districts of Italy.

Mint   *Menthe* (Fr.); *crème de menthe*, a mint-flavored after-dinner liqueur; *menthe poivree*, peppermint; a mint sauce may be served hot or cold and is made of mint, vinegar, water, and sugar combined with the drippings of meat (usually lamb or mutton); some chefs add a bit of orange marmalade.

Minute Steak   Steak (usually sirloin) ½ inch thick cooked only a short time.

Mirabeau A velouté sauce from rich chicken stock with crushed garlic added; may also be applied to an egg, steak, or garnish varying considerably in ingredients used.

Mirepoix Diced vegetables used for imparting flavor to dishes.

Miroton Cold meats warmed up.

Mix To combine ingredients so as to blend them together.

Mixed Grill A Frenched chop, kidney, bacon, sausage, broiled or grilled tomato, and mushroom.

Mock Turtle Soup See *fausse tortue.*

Mold To obtain a desired form by placing in a mold or device (see *shape*).

Monkey Very similar to rarebit (rabbit), except thickening agent will be soft bread crumbs soaked in milk, instead of flour or other starch thickener; normally served over toasted English muffins; usually called English monkey; burned sugar dissolved in water to give a brown color to foods.

Montmorency Dark or pie cherries used in a product; a sweet-sour cherry sauce sometimes served over baked ham.

Mornay A bechamel, white, or cream sauce seasoned with grated parmesan cheese.

Mousse A froth or foam; used to describe a delicate, aerated, smooth mixture; a frozen dessert made from a base of whipped cream.

Mousseline A custard-like forcemeat made of egg whites and cream; a very smooth mixture; *mousseline sauce,* one part whipped cream to two parts mayonnaise or hollandaise sauce; see *glacé royal.*

Mulligatawny Chicken broth, rice, corn, raw apples, and curry combined to make a soup; vegetables, meats, and chutney may be added.

Muscat The large muscat raisin; *muscatel,* a sweet (dessert) wine.

Nantaise Normandy sauce with shrimp, chervil, and tarragon added; also called *Nantira sauce.*

Napoleon Puff paste pastry consisting of sheets of puff paste filled with custard filling, frosted, and cut into finger shapes.

Natural *Au naturel* (Fr); in the natural form.

Neapolitane (Napolitaine) A dish containing spaghetti; a brown sauce containing some currant jelly, diced ham, nutmeg, thyme, and a bit of malaga wine; some chefs add a bit of horseradish; name also indicates two or more layers of ice cream, ice, or sherbet in brick form; also indicates gelatin layers in different colors; *harlequin* is used synonymously; see *panache.*

Neutral Sauces Sauces that contain no meat stock, such as hollandaise, mayonnaise, and bread sauce.

Newburg (Newberg or Newburgh) Bechamel or cream sauce flavored with sherry; may be thickened by a liaison of egg yolks.

New England Boiled Dinner Boiled beef or ham or both with boiled cabbage, carrots, rutabagas, turnips, onions, parsnips, and potatoes.

New Orleans Same as *Creole.*

Nivernaise Shredded vegetables in poulette sauce; glazed carrots.

Noisette Nuts, hazel nuts; the kernel or eye of the main loin muscle (*longissimus dorsi*) or fish fillets; pieces from small end of beef tender-loin (see *tournedos*) about 1½ in. in diameter and usually two or three served as a portion; a *noisette* of lamb may be a piece from the loin; *noisette sauce,* a hollandaise or supreme sauce to which a small amount of hazelnut butter or paste is added just before service and served with salmon, trout, or other boiled fish.

Noix Nut or walnut; *noix de coco,* coconut; *noix de pistache,* pistachio nut; *noix de veau,* veal cutlet taken from the muscle called the kernel on the leg.

Normandy Rich fish velouté and cream reduced; a bit of cayenne may be added; for desserts, *a la Normandy,* means a delicate, smooth mixture often containing whipped cream.

Nougat Almond cake; an amorphous confectionery containing chopped or whole almonds.

Nouilles Noodles or shredded egg paste; see *knöpfli, spaetzles,* and so forth.

O'Brien Chopped green pepper, onion, and pimiento added; usually applied to cooked potatoes diced and sautéed with these items added.

Oeuf Egg: *ôeufs brouillés,* scrambled eggs.

Oka A cheese; see *port salut.*

Onion Soup See *French onion soup.*

Orly A dough using beer for a liquid.

Ovenize To place in an oven to sauté or fry; to oven roast.

Pailles Straws; *pailles au fromage,* cheese straws; *pailles pommes de terre,* shoestring potatoes.

Pain Bread.

Pain de Boeuf Meat loaf.

Panache Two or more kinds of one item in a dish; panache ice cream may also be called *neapolitan* or *harlequin* ice cream.

Panade Bread soaked and squeezed dry and used for stuffings, dressings, or forcemeats; *empanades,* a pasty.

Panard Thick white sauce used as binding for croquettes.

Pan-Broil To cook on a hot frying pan or grill without added fat or liquid; fat is poured off as it accumulates.

Paner To cover with bread crumbs; also called at times *panure.*

Pan-Fry Sauté or cook in small quantity of fat in a sauté pan.

Panier Basket.

Papillote (en) In paper; to bake in paper; *cotellette en papillote,* cutlet baked in paper; term is also used to indicate paper frills on chops and other items.

Parboil To partially cook by boiling.

Pare To trim or cut off outside covering; see *peel.*

Parfait Vari-colored foods; a frozen dessert served in a parfait glass with layers of ice cream separated by layers of fruit or sirup and topped with whipped cream; a smooth mousse-like frozen dessert.

Parfumer   To flavor or season.

Parisienne   Paris style; cut into small, round ball shapes; *parisienne potatoes,* small round potato balls, deep-fried.

Parker House Rolls   A rich yeast dinner roll folded in half like a pocket book and baked.

Parmentier   Name of man who introduced potatoes into French cookery; *a la Parmentier,* with potatoes.

Parmesan   A hard Italian cheese, usually grated and used as a seasoning with macaroni products.

Passer   To strain.

Pastrami   A highly spiced corned beef brisket.

Pastry   Made of pie or puff paste dough, such as pies or tarts; *pâtisserie* (Fr).

Pasty   Flaky pie dough filled with diced meat and potatoes in gravy and baked; *empanades* (Fr).

Pâté or Paste   May mean fine paste mixture, a pie, or thick dough; a patty which may be a shell of puff paste, a small, round, flat cake, or a hamburger, potato, or vegetable patty.

Paupiette   Thin slices of meat spread with forcemeat, rolled, dipped in batter, and fried; a *roulade* or *rouleau.*

Paysanne   In peasant style; usually a dish served with shredded or diced cooked vegetables; the name given a fairly thick country type soup; a diced product.

Peel   To remove outside skin or rind by mechanical means or heat; *pelure* (Fr).

Pêle-mêle   Mixed up; tossed.

Pepper Pot   Soup popularized in Philadelphia; salt pork, onions, green peppers, potatoes, and other vegetables diced with sliced julienne tripe in a rich stock, usually beef.

Perigeux   Truffles; Perigord is a district in France known for its fine truffles.

Persillade   With parsley; *persillées,* new potatoes boiled, buttered, and dusted with chopped parsley.

Petit   Small, little, tiny, dainty.

Petit Dejeuner   Breakfast.

Petite Marmite   A vegetable or *pot au feu* soup containing sliced beef or chicken, served in a small individual pot and topped with a cheese-toasted crouton; see *marmite.*

Petits Fours   See *au four.*

Petit Lait   Buttermilk.

Petits Pois   Green peas.

Pfeffernüsse   Hard German cookies that contain a small amount of ground black pepper; literally, pepper nuts.

Philadelphia Ice Cream   Simplest type of ice cream, consisting of thin cream, sugar, and flavoring.

Pièce de Resistance   Main dish, the most important dish.

Pièce Montée   A display piece.

Pilaff   Turkish rice dish; *pilau* (Fr).

Pipe To place a border around an item; see *border*.

Piquant *Piquante* (Fr); tangy sauce containing vinegar, white wine, and sautéed onions with chopped capers and fine herbs added; some chefs add brown sauce; served with hot or cold pork, mutton, or fatty meats.

Piqué Larded with strips of salt pork or bacon.

Pirog Minced or finely diced meat baked in yeast, pastry, or biscuit dough; *calzoni* (It).

Piroshki Baked biscuit dough filled with meat, cheese, vegetable, or fish mixture; sometimes means pancakes rolled with a filling of this type.

Pizza Italian pie with crisp yeast bottom baked with a seasoned tomato mixture, cheese, and other items on top.

Plank To broil fish or meat on a plank, surrounded with vegetables and a border of duchess potatoes, and serve.

Plat Plate or platter; *plateau,* tray.

Plombiere A mixture of candied fruits with ice cream.

Pluck Lights, heart, liver.

Poach To simmer in a small quantity of water that barely covers the item; *pôcher* (Fr).

Poëler To brown in a saucepan in butter and then cover and braise; the cooking is fast and excess moisture is avoided in braising; a process between braising and roasting; sometimes a white mirepoix is called a *poële*.

Pois Peas.

Poisson Fish; *poissonier,* fish cook.

Poivrade A tangy, tart brown sauce used on game meats, especially venison; a part of the marinade in which meat is soaked.

Polenta Dish made of cornmeal or farina; grated parmesan cheese is usually sprinkled over it.

Pollo Chicken (It or Sp).

Polonaise Polish style; velouté sauce made slightly tart with lemon juice and a bit of horseradish; may also mean with beet, horseradish, and cabbage with sour cream.

Pomme Apple; *pomme de terre,* potato; *pomme d'amour,* tomato.

Pompano A fine fish caught in Florida or Caribbean waters.

Popover A bread made of a mixture of flour, milk, and eggs and leavened by steam.

Port (du) Salut A soft, richly flavored cheese also called *oka* or *trappist* after the Trappist monks, who originated it.

Potage Soup, usually thick; *potagier,* soup cook.

Potato Chips Thinly sliced rounds of potato cooked to a crisp stage in deep fat.

Pot-au-feu Literally, "pot on the fire"; a soup made from rich stock of somewhat nondescript character because the ingredients are waste items obtained in other food production; usually a flavorful vegetable soup; may also refer to a stock pot cooking on a range or in a steam-jacketed kettle.

Poulet Young fowl; poularde, a fat pullet; *poulette sauce,* egg yolks added to supreme sauce for thickening; may contain chopped mushrooms; normally a chicken stock is used for the basic velouté sauce, but some poulette sauces used for fish are made from a fish stock.

Praline   A confection made of brown or maple sugar and pecans; mixed broken pecans caramelized; brown sugar or maple sugar nougat; sometimes refers to burnt almond flavoring.

Prawn   A large shrimp.

Printaniere   Spring vegetables cut in small dice with peas and asparagus; the name of a consommé containing these vegetables.

Profiterolles   Tiny choux (eclair) pastes filled with vegetables, meats, or tangy fillings; sometimes used as a garnish for soup; may also be filled with sweetened mixtures and used as a dessert.

Prosciutto   An Italian ham, usually thinly sliced.

Provençale   Brown sauce heavily diluted with tomato puree and seasoned with garlic; the true sauce is made by cooking tomatoes with minced garlic and a few onions, salt and pepper, and a bit of oil and then sieving.

Provolone   A smoked Italian cheese with a rich, mellow flavor.

Puff Paste   Mixture of strong flour and water layered with shortening between folds and rolled out many times until thin sheets of dough and shortening are in thin layers; baked and used as a pie dough.

Pumpernickel   Bread made from whole rye flour.

Puree   Foods rubbed through a sieve; slightly coarser than pulped foods; a soup made from pureed food.

Quadrillé   Checkered by layering.

Quenelles   Oval or other fancy-shaped forcemeats.

Quiche Lorraine   A pie dough overlaid with bacon and Swiss cheese in a custard and baked; nutmeg may be sprinkled on top; used as an hors d'oeuvre.

Rabbit   See *rarebit*.

Ragoût   A stew of meats and vegetables, usually quite thick and savory; a thick concentrate of an item, such as tomato puree, often called tomato ragoût.

Ramekin   Small individual baking dish or pastry shell, or item baked in it; small cheese cake served as an hors d'oeuvre.

Rare   Underdone.

Rarebit   Also called *rabbit* or *Welsh rarebit;* melted cheese dish made with white sauce or stale beer or ale thickened with an egg yolk liaison; seasoned rather heavily; see also *fondue, golden buck, monkey,* and *Yorkshire buck;* when seasoned with anchovy and served with oysters, the dish is called *Capetown Rarebit.*

Rasping   Crumbs; grated cereal particles; *râpé* (Fr).

Ratafia   Name of a liqueur.

Ravigote   Cold sauce, quite tart, with chopped eggs and fine herbs and capers; usually made of oil and vinegar but sometimes with mayonnaise;

also may be a tart sauce with fine herbs served hot; means to give appetite or vigor.

Ravioli   Small Italian pastes filled with meat, cheese, or vegetables, served in a rich tomato sauce and sprinkled over with parmesan cheese.

Réchauffé   Warmed over.

Recherché   The best; the most refined.

Reduce   To evaporate part of a liquid by simmering or boiling. The recipe should state the amount of reduction.

Reforme   Dishes named after the famous Reform Club of London; a poivrade sauce made quite tart with gherkins, capers, cooked white of egg, and tongue, all cut julienne.

Refroisir   To cool or chill.

Regency (Regence)   Allemande sauce with mushrooms and truffles diluted with rich stock from the item it is to accompany.

Reine (Regina)   Chicken soup; creamed, or sweetbreads in patty shell; means also young or fat chicken.

Releves (Removes)   Roasts and boiled meats on the menu; entrees but in larger quantity than just a serving; *relever,* to improve.

Remoulade   Mayonnaise seasoned with mustard, chopped dill pickles, anchovy, capers, and fine herbs, usually highly seasoned with ground pepper; may mean in cookery to reduce to a paste or grind.

Render   To free fat from a connective tissue by means of heat.

Rhin   Rhine; *Rhin du vin,* Rhine wine.

Riblette   Thin slices; a rasher.

Riced   Put through a ricer, as is frequently done with hot boiled potatoes.

Richelieu   Sauce, usually over a tenderloin steak, consisting of brown sauce seasoned with madeira sauce and tomato paste; also a consommé or a garnish.

Ris   Sweetbread; *ris de veau,* veal sweetbreads.

Risotto (Rizotto)   A rice dish.

Rissolé   Browned or seared; with a brown or toasted coat; oven-browned potato.

Roast   To bake; applied to certain foods, such as meats and chestnuts; see *bake.*

Robert   Rich brown sauce with minced onions, mustard, and white wine.

Rockefeller   Creamed spinach and fine herbs; usually spread over raw oysters topped with bread crumbs and parmesan cheese and baked; worcestershire, tabasco, anchovy paste, and absinthe or anisette may be added to the mixture for seasoning.

Rocks   Semi-hard dropped cookies or cakes containing raisins and nuts.

Roe   Fish eggs; beluga caviar is best quality; pressed sturgeon caviar widely used for spreads, pastes, and so forth; codfish and whitefish roe (both hard and frequently colored gray or black) and herring and salmon (both soft, the latter tinted red) and other roe are used as substitutes for caviar.

Roly-Poly Pudding   Rolled pastry or biscuit dough covered with fruit paste or jam and steamed or baked; served with a hot sauce.

Roquefort Famous French bleu cheese; *Roquefort dressing,* about 5 oz Roquefort cheese to quart of French dressing; chopped chives may be added.

Rothschild See *Angels on Horseback.*

Rouennaise A dish featuring duck; made famous in the city of Rouen, France.

Rôtir To roast; *rôti or rôt,* a roast; *rosbif,* roast beef; *rôtisseur,* roast cook; *rôtisserie,* equipment for roasting before an open fire, usually on a spit.

Roulade Roll; rolled meat; term *rouleau* is used synonymously.

Roux A mixture of equal parts of flour and fat used to thicken sauces and other foods.

Royale In the royal style; a custard plain or combined with other foods used as a soup garnish.

Ruff A meat pie or fried meat turnover.

Rusk A crisp twice-baked bread.

Russe Russian style; *Russian buffet,* foods on a buffet distinguished by caviar and Russian fish in a large glass or ice bowl on a stand.

Sachet See *bouquet garni.*

St. Florentin Deep-fried mashed potato croquettes containing diced ham.

St. Germain A split pea soup; a dish containing puree of peas.

St. Hubert Hunter style.

Salamander A small broiler used for browning dishes in the cook's section.

Salisbury A steak made of ground beef, milk, bread crumbs, and seasonings.

Sally Lunn A breakfast coffee cake about the richness of a muffin.

Salmagundi An old English dish of fresh and salted meats, fish, onions, and various seasonings.

Salmis Also *salmi;* a stew of roasted game or meat in a rich brown sauce.

Salpiçon Finely diced or chopped meat and vegetables (sometimes mushrooms and truffles are included) for flavoring sauces and other dishes; a mixture used for croquettes.

Saratoga Indicates fried potato chips; also a shoulder or neck lamb chop.

Sauce A concentrated, flavored accompaniment to food, usually liquid; *saucer,* to cover with sauce; *saucier,* sauce cook; *sauciere,* sauceboat; *sauce vin blanc,* a velouté made of rich fish stock.

Saucisse Sausage.

Sauerbraten Pot roast (German) marinated in wine or water, vinegar, and seasonings; *sauer,* sour; *sauerkraut,* soured or pickled cabbage.

Sauté To fry quickly with just enough fat or butter to prevent sticking; see *fry* and *pan-fry; sautoir,* a frying pan.

Scald To heat liquid to just below boiling point or to dip an item into very hot or boiling water so that removal of an outer surface is facilitated or for other reasons; see *blanch.*

Scallop Also *escalope;* to bake food, usually cut in pieces, in a sauce or other liquid; top is usually covered with crumbs; food and sauce may be mixed together or placed in alternate layers; *au gratin* may be used synonymously; to cut food on a bias.

Scallopine Veal cutlet sautéed; *scallopine Bolognese,* ham and potatoes served with cutlet or minced veal with sauce, seasoned with parmesan cheese.

Scallops Meat or muscle of the sea or bay scallop, a shellfish.

Schnitzel Breaded and sautéed; see *wiener schnitzel.*

Scone A rich biscuit dough baked usually in triangular form; a Scotch tea cake made from wheat, rye, or barley flour.

Score To cut lightly across an item; to mark lightly, as scoring an omelet by burning.

Scotch Broth Soup made from mutton stock containing cooked barley and vegetables; often called Scotch mutton broth.

Scotch Woodcock Half of hard-cooked or chopped creamed eggs seasoned with anchovy paste.

Scrape To remove in thin layers with a sharp or blunt instrument.

Scrapple Diced or ground pork cooked in cornmeal and seasoned.

Scrod Cod or haddock about 2½ pounds in size.

Sear To brown the surface by a short application of heavy heat; used to develop flavor and color.

Sec Dry; *sauté sec,* braise in dry white wine.

Semolina Paste Macaroni products; semolina is the endosperm of durum wheat, which makes a high quality macaroni product.

Shake To toss vigorously up and down in a container.

Shape To form into desired pattern either with hands or with molds.

Shepherd's Pie A meat pie covered with mashed potatoes and baked.

Sherbet A frozen dessert consisting of fruit juices, milk, sugar, stabilizer, and coloring; *sorbet* (Fr).

Shir To bake.

Shore Dinner Combined seafoods and shellfish served with French fried, shoestring, or baked potatoes and cole slaw.

Shortbread A rich Scotch cookie.

Shortcake A rich biscuit dough slightly sweet, split, with fruit in between and on top, and served with whipped cream or plain cream over; shortcake biscuit covered with meat in gravy.

Shred To tear or cut into small pieces.

Simmer To cook in a liquid at a temperature around 185° F with bubbles forming slowly and breaking at the surface.

Simple A menu term meaning coffee or tea or other light food served without another food.

Singe To remove hair or feathers by fire.

Skewer A wood or metal pin for securing meat or on which to place meat for roasting or barbecuing; also used as a verb, as to *skewer* a roast; see *attereaux* and *hatelet.*

Slice To cut with a knife or mechanical slicer into thin pieces in fairly substantial sizes; not cut or chopped; to carve.

Smorgasbord   A buffet of light foods acting as appetizers in which herring, butter, and rye bread are a part.

Smothered   Covered; *calf's liver smothered,* grilled calf's liver covered with fried or sautéed onions.

Soak   To immerse for an extended period of time in a liquid to rehydrate, to prevent from drying out, to keep from tarnishing in the air, or as a preliminary step in cleaning.

Soubis   A sauce made from cooked pureed onions added to a bechamel sauce.

Soufflé   Puffed: a dish made light, usually by folding in beaten egg whites and baking; a puffed-up French fried potato, either Irish or sweet.

Sous chef   Assistant to head chef.

Sous cloche   See *cloche.*

Southern Fried Chicken   Dredged in flour and deep-fried; see *Maryland.*

Spaetzle   Austrian noodle made by running heavy noodle batter through colander into boiling stock; used with braised meats; *spätzle* (Austrian).

Spanish   A tomato sauce with chopped ham or bacon, celery, carrot, and onion sautéed in bacon or ham fat, with added brown or tomato sauce; *Spanish omelet,* filled with tomatoes, peppers, onions, mushrooms, olives, celery, parsley, and spices; *Spanish cream,* a custard mixture firmed with gelatin and with whipped cream usually folded in just before the mixture sets.

Spareribs   Rib sections of pork behind the area from which the bacon is taken; would be the bone section behind the plate and brisket in beef.

Spit   A skewer on which meat is turned before open heat.

Sponge   A cake made light with beaten eggs; a soft bread batter considered the first stage in bread production, with the second addition of flour occurring after fermentation has proceeded to a certain point; a soft, light, aerated mixture.

Spoonbread   A Southern soft bread made of cornmeal paste, eggs, and milk; actually a soufflé.

Springerle   A cookie pressed with a mold before baking.

Spumone   A rich Italian ice cream; sometimes spelled *spomoni.*

Squab   A young pigeon that has not left the nest.

Squid   A seafood related to the octopus; usually deep-fried after batter-dipping for hors d'oeuvres, or cooked with tomato or other sauces.

Steak and Kidney Pie   See *beef steak pie.*

Steam   To cook in steam with or without pressure; the steam may be applied directly to the food, as in a steamer or pressure cooker.

Steep   To allow a substance to stand in liquid below the boiling point for the purpose of extracting flavor, color, or other qualities.

Stew   To simmer or boil in a small bit of liquid; for meat, temperature is around 185° F; a meat and vegetable dish in gravy.

Steward   Person in charge of purchasing and ordering, who may plan menus with chef; is largely responsible for food cost.

Stilton   An English bleu-type cheese with a brown outer crust.

Stir To mix foods with a circular motion in order to blend or obtain a uniform consistency.

Stock A liquid seasoned by meat or vegetable essence.

Stollen A German yeast-leavened cake containing milk, eggs, butter, sugar, fruits, and nuts in addition to basic bread ingredients.

Stroganoff Sautéed beef in sauce of sour cream, mushrooms, and onions.

Strudel Viennese dessert consisting of thin sheets of cooked paste, fruits, cheese, honey, and other items.

Succotash A vegetable mixture of fresh corn and lima beans; tomatoes may sometimes be added.

Suèdoise Swedish, a whipped cream sauce containing horseradish and applesauce.

Suki Yaki A Japanese dish of mixed vegetables sautéed in a light oil seasoned with beef or other meat and a bit of sugar.

Supreme Of finest quality; velouté sauce to which heavy cream is added.

Sweetbreads Thymus glands of animals.

Sweetdough A yeast-leavened dough rich with sugar and eggs.

Sweetmeats Candies.

Swiss Fondue See *fondue.*

Swiss Steak A braised steak.

Tamale Meat in cornmeal roll flavored with chili and baked or boiled in corn husks.

Tartar Sauce Chopped onions, dill pickles, celery, shallots, chives, and parsley in mayonnaise with capers; most chefs specify *no sweet pickles.*

Tarte Small pie or pastry-filled item; *tartelette,* small tart.

Tasse Small cup.

Tea A beverage; tea served with dessert items such as tarts, cookies, small cakes, sandwiches, or other foods; *high tea,* elaborate service with quite fancy foods; see *simple; thé* (Fr).

Terrine A stew or ragoût; an earthenware pot resembling a casserole.

Thermidor Cream sauce seasoned with wine and herbs; cream added to *sauce vin blanc.*

Thicken To add eggs, flour, or other products to foods and cook them until more firm; gelatin, rennet, and other products may be added to foods to thicken when cold.

Thousand Island Dressing Mayonnaise and chili sauce with chopped eggs, green peppers, chives, and other items.

Timbale A chopped or pureed meat, vegetable, or other food bound with eggs and baked in a mold or pan; may also be a crust or case in which foods are served.

Toad-in-the-Hole Sausages or meat baked or fried in batter.

Tomato Sauce Fine herbs sautéed, usually in salt pork, seasoned with bay leaf, thyme and other seasonings; next cooked with tomato puree or paste and white or brown stock; then thickened with roux. This sauce is considered one of the basic sauces; may contain no meat stock.

Torte   Pie or cake; may be rich, cake-like product.

Tortillas   Mexican flat pancake-type items containing cornmeal, flour, eggs, and seasonings into which seasoned meat or other items are rolled.

Tortoni   A frozen dessert containing tortoni biscuit (ground dried macaroons and chopped blanched almonds); usually a very rich ice cream is the base.

Toss   To mix lightly.

Tournedos   Small steak cut from the narrow part of beef tenderloin about 1½ inch thick. They resemble kernels or noisettes, which are the eye of the meat taken from lamb loins, pork loins, or other animals; weight is about 2½ oz each; cooked much like filets, Chateaubriands, or other tenderloin steaks.

Tourner   To cut or shape vegetables; an expression used to indicate curdling.

Tourtiere   Canadian meat pie containing salt pork.

Tranche   Slice of meat or bread; *tranche de saumon,* slice of salmon; *trancher,* to slice or carve; see *slice.*

Trifle   Sponge cake soaked in wine and served with sauce or whipped cream.

Tripe   Stomach of cattle.

Truffle   *Truffle* (Fr); fungi grown in France in clusters below ground under oaks; pigs are trained to root them out; they resemble mushrooms, are black in color, and are used for flavor and garnish of meat dishes; see *Perigeux.*

Turbot   A delicately flavored, white-fleshed fish.

Turn   To carve or trim in some manner; a *turned olive* is a pitted olive, and a *turned mushroom* is a mushroom carved or decorated on the top, which also may be called a *mushroom crown.*

Turnover   A baked or fried food encased in pie or puff paste.

Turtle   Reptile used largely to make soup; tenderest parts may be used for steaks.

Tutti-frutti   A mixture of fruits.

Veal Cutlet   Slice of meat from the leg; *veal cutlet Holstein,* breaded cutlet sautéed in butter and served with fried egg, anchovy, and potatoes; see *wiener schnitzel; cotelette du veau* (Fr); *veal birds,* dressing or forcemeat rolled in thin slices of veal cutlet and braised.

Velouté   A basic sauce of white stock thickened with *roux;* means "velvet" or "smooth"; may also be used to indicate a white stock. There is also a fish velouté, which is a white stock or sauce made from lean white fish flesh and bones; the sauce is seasoned with white wine and may be called *sauce vin blanc.*

Venison   Flesh of all antlered members of the deer family: deer, antelope, elk, moose, and so forth.

Verjuice   Juice of unripe fruit; usually tart juice of grapes or apple; *verjus* (Fr).

Vichy   Famous springs in France; vegetables cooked in the water had excellent flavor; now a term used to indicate boiled and buttered vegetables, usually sprinkled with parsley; usually applied to carrots.

Vichysoisse   Hot or cold cream of potato soup; when cold, served with garnish of chopped chives on top.

Villeroi   Allemande sauce seasoned with the article which it accompanies; may be seasoned with mushroom and ham stock or with onions or tomatoes.

Vin   Wine; *vin de Xérès,* sherry or madeira-type wine.

Vinaigrette   Tart sauce; see *ravigote.*

Vin Blanc Sauce   See *velouté.*

Vol-au-vent   Puff paste shells to be filled with sauce mixtures, such as creamed chicken, braised lamb kidneys and mushrooms, and crab Newburg.

Waldorf   Term used to indicate an apple salad containing celery and walnuts with a boiled or mayonnaise dressing.

Welsh Rarebit   See *rarebit.*

Western Sandwich   Chopped ham, green peppers, onions, and beaten egg, fried and served as a sandwich.

White Sauce   Seasoned milk thickened with a starch paste; one of the basic neutral sauces; if cream is added, it is called a cream sauce.

Wiener Schnitzel   Breaded veal cutlet braised until tender and served with slice of lemon and anchovy filet; some bake cutlet in sour cream or tomato sauce.

Woodcock   Small game bird; see *Scotch woodcock*

Yankee Pot Roast   Braised pot roast with vegetables; frequently accompanied by dumplings or corn fritters.

Yorkshire Buck   Welsh rarebit on poached egg on toast; *Yorkshire rabbit,* bacon instead of egg is used.

Yorkshire Pudding   Popover batter poured into roast beef drippings and baked; served with roast beef with some *au jus* spooned over it.

Zeste   The colored part of the peel of citrus fruit.

Zwieback   Hard, crisp bread toasted and then baked again until thoroughly dry; a rusk.

Index